D0398659

GHOST
FLAMES

GHOST FLAMES

LIFE AND DEATH IN A HIDDEN WAR,

KOREA 1950–1953

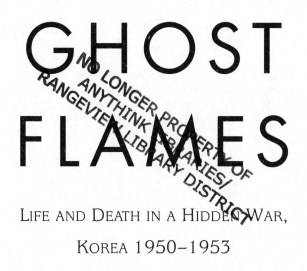

CHARLES J. HANLEY

PUBLICAFFAIRS

NEW YORK

Epigraphs taken from *Brother Enemy: Poems of the Korean War* used by permission of White Pine Press.

The maps in *Ghost Flames* are the work of Jenni Sohn.

PublicAffairs
Hachette Book Group
1290 Avenue of the Americas, New York, NY 10104
www.publicaffairsbooks.com
@Public_Affairs

Printed in the United States of America
First Edition: May 2020

Published by PublicAffairs, an imprint of Perseus Books, LLC, a subsidiary of Hachette Book Group, Inc. The PublicAffairs name and logo is a trademark of the Hachette Book Group.

The Hachette Speakers Bureau provides a wide range of authors for speaking events. To find out more, go to www.hachettespeakersbureau.com or call (866) 376-6591.

The publisher is not responsible for websites (or their content) that are not owned by the publisher.

Print book interior design by Linda Mark.

Library of Congress Cataloging-in-Publication Data
Names: Hanley, Charles J., author.
Title: Ghost flames : life and death in a hidden war, Korea 1950–1953 / Charles J. Hanley.
Other titles: Life and death in a hidden war, Korea 1950–1953
Description: First edition. | New York : PublicAffairs, 2020. | Includes bibliographical references and index.
Identifiers: LCCN 2019036790 | ISBN 9781541768178 (hardcover) |
  ISBN 9781541768154 (ebook)
Subjects: LCSH: Korean War, 1950–1953—Biography. | Korean War, 1950–1953—Social aspects.
Classification: LCC DS918.A553 H37 2020 | DDC 951.904/20922—dc23
LC record available at https://lccn.loc.gov/2019036790

ISBNs: 978-1-5417-6817-8 (hardcover), 978-1-5417-6815-4 (ebook)

LSC-C

10 9 8 7 6 5 4 3 2 1

"My dead brother . . . he keeps on showing up. The people he killed, too, have been appearing before me. They speak to me."

"Me, too."

"You mean you see these phantoms, too?"

"At first they simply showed themselves, but then, at twilight, as I walked the cow home from the fields, I would see lines of the dead walking along the levee across the way. Sometimes when the weather was bad, I would see spirit fires. . . . They speak to me. . . . I suppose the time is ripe for them now, for the people who were there. They're ready now, I think. So they appear before us as part of their redemption."

—**Hwang Sok-yong**, *The Guest* (2001)

CONTENTS

TO THE READER

On August 31, 2002, a typhoon designated "Rusa," the most powerful to strike South Korea in four decades, slammed ashore along the southern coast and raged northward up the peninsula. It caused billions of dollars in damage, flooded huge swaths of farmland, and left scores of people dead. Rusa also did something else: it tore a hole in time.

Near the southern village of Yongyang, on a small pepper farm, the torrential rains and wind washed away a layer of earth that for a half century had concealed a mass grave, hiding from history the evidence of atrocity, the skeletal remains of 140 people—men, women, and children. A storm's fury had opened a window on one small corner of a dark past, a time when the southern government summarily executed tens of thousands of political prisoners, potential northern collaborators, in the first weeks of the Korean War.

The war that ravaged the Korean peninsula for three years in the mid–twentieth century was a watershed of modern history. It was the first major clash of arms of the Cold War and remains the last armed conflict between great powers. It was America's first undeclared war. It turned the United States into a permanently militarized nation and made China a global player. It planted the seeds of a nuclear crisis that confronts the world today. And it's a war not truly ended, a war on hold, under a truce and not a peace treaty.

Despite its pivotal role in recent history, the Korean War became known as the "forgotten war," an indecisive conflict in a far-off place, overshadowed by the triumphant "good war" that ended five years before.

Even more than forgotten, however, much of what happened in Korea in those years has simply never been known, beyond the buried memories of survivors, the whispered conversations in traumatized villages, the yellowing pages of telltale documents secreted away in classified archives.

The Yongyang discovery, the happenstance of a typhoon, offered an early clue. Through the 2000s, more emerged. The perseverance of survivors, historical researchers, journalists, and others uncovered more mass graves, gave voice to witnesses, reported on shocking events of wholesale killing of noncombatants. In the period 2005–2010, the Truth and Reconciliation Commission of the South Korean government investigated scores of incidents of mass political executions in 1950–1951 and mass killings of refugees and other South Korean civilians, both by southern and U.S. military forces and by the northern invaders and southern leftists. The declassification of U.S. military archives, documenting indiscriminate air and ground attacks on unarmed civilians, attested further to the war's savagery.

The U.S. order to "bomb every village," the stunning scale of political executions, the Americans' decision to machine-gun refugees—these and similar discoveries of recent years are essential to understanding what happened in the years 1950–1953.

Conventional histories of the Korean War have too often ignored its greatest impact, on the ordinary people of Korea, focusing instead on leading personalities and grand strategy, troop movements and headline battles. This book is unconventional, telling the story of the Korean War on a human scale, through the wartime experiences of twenty people who lived through it, people from all sides, soldiers and civilians, male and female, young and old, witnesses both to atrocity and to heroism.

They include soldiers from both Koreas and from America and China, a Korean refugee girl, an American nun, Korean and British journalists, a displaced Korean mother, a Seoul socialite, a Chinese interpreter at the truce talks.

The characters' experiences—in cities destroyed by U.S. aircraft, as a witness to prisoners driven off to slaughter, as a bystander at a "people's court" summary execution—provide the context for expanding on the war's long-buried truths. The reader will see the real war through their eyes. Meanwhile, the broader story of the war's progress will unfold month by month in the characters' interwoven episodes.

The narratives are drawn from many sources—memoirs, biographies, diaries, letters, personal interviews conducted in South Korea and the United States, declassified archival documents, and other materials. The Truth and Reconciliation Commission's reports provided additional crucial information.

It was important to enlist characters of diverse backgrounds, to offer the reader a wide array of perspectives on a war whose causes and conduct remain controversial today. But they were chosen, too, for the power and eloquence of their stories—late-in-life reflections of soldiers still burning with resentment or regret over the insanity of their war, the lifelong nightmares of aging women retold in tears, the unadorned accounts by journalists of unimaginable events. "Millions of people killed," one young soldier concludes, "but nothing has changed except for the destruction of human lives and their dreams."

A "Primary Sources" bibliography notes the basis for each character's story. Because human memory can err, particularly in memoirs written or interviews conducted years or decades afterward, the accounts in this book have been checked as much as possible against the known facts and documentation of events described.

Casualty tolls from the Korean War have never been definitive, but it is estimated that at least 3 million lives were lost, most of them Korean civilians. Many of the dead were dumped anonymously into common graves. Many were left to decompose on the slopes and in the valleys of a mountainous peninsula. People in the countryside soon told of seeing *hon bul*, "ghost flames," or "spirit fires," flickering in the night over the killing fields. This may have been phosphorous from bones, kicked up by wind and rain, shimmering in the moonlight. But Korean lore also holds the deeply rooted notion that a ball of light, *hon bul*, leaves the body upon death. For many, the ghost flames of Korea became associated with the restless dead of the war.

This book is dedicated to the memory of those restless dead of a hidden war and to helping in a small way, perhaps, to ease their uneasy spirits.

Charles J. Hanley
New York, May 2019

A NOTE ON LANGUAGE

In transliterating from Korean and Chinese to roman letters, this book generally uses the systems that were current during the Korean War—that is, McCune-Reischauer for Korean and Wade-Giles for Chinese. In both cases, regarding personal names, the family name generally comes first, followed by the given name, which is hyphenated. It is customary for Korean and Chinese wives to retain their birth surname after marriage.

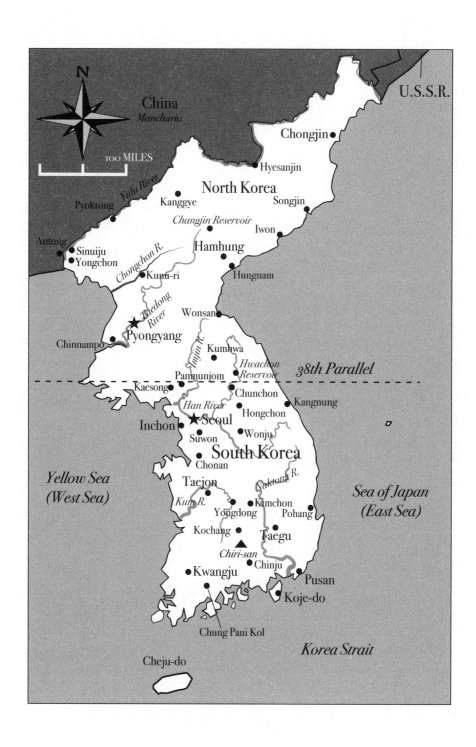

N

China
Manchuria

100 MILES

U.S.S.R.

Chongjin

Hyesanjin

Pyoktong

Yalu River

Kanggye

North Korea

Songjin

Changjin Reservoir

Iwon

Antung

Sinuiju
Yongchon

Chongchon R.

Hamhung

Kunu-ri

Hungnam

Taedong River

Wonsan

Chinnampo

★Pyongyang

Imjin R.

Kumhwa

Hwachon Reservoir

38th Parallel

Panmunjom

Kaesong

Chunchon

Kangnung

Han River

Hongchon

Inchon

★Seoul

Suwon

Wonju

South Korea

Chonan

Yellow Sea
(West Sea)

Taejon

Naktong R.

Kum R.

Kimchon

Yongdong

Pohang

Sea of Japan
(East Sea)

Kochang

Taegu

Chiri-san

Chinju

Kwangju

Pusan

Koje-do

Chung Paui Kol

Korea Strait

Cheju-do

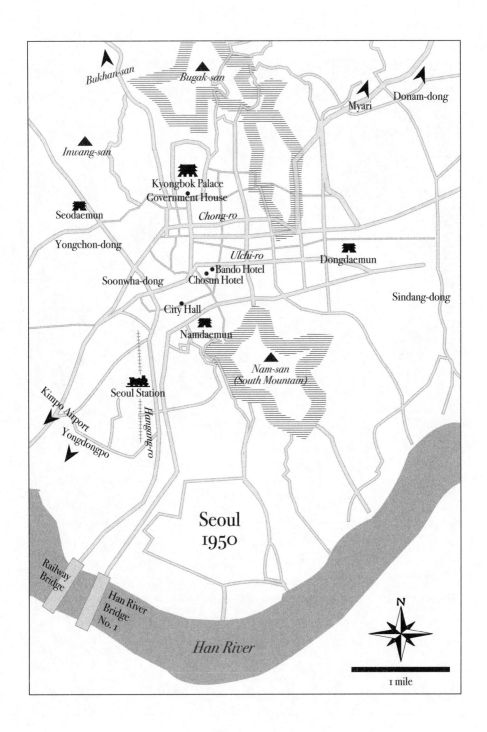

KOREAN WAR CHRONOLOGY

1950

June 25	The North Korean army invades South Korea.
June 28	Seoul falls to the invaders.
Early July	Beginning of mass political executions by South Korean authorities; "people's court" executions by North Korean occupiers.
July 20	U.S. Army units sent to help the retreating South Koreans are driven from the strategic central city of Taejon.
July 26–29	U.S. military's massacre of refugees at Nogun-ri.
August 4	U.S.–South Korean forces establish the Pusan Perimeter defense line in the southeast. They hold off repeated attacks.
September 15	A U.S. amphibious landing at Inchon turns the tide of war.
September 16–22	U.S.–South Korean forces drive north from the Pusan Perimeter; summary executions by retreating North Koreans.
September 26–28	Seoul falls to the U.S.-led U.N. forces, who push on into North Korea.
October–December	Widespread South Korean executions of alleged northern collaborators.
October 19	U.S. troops seize Pyongyang; Chinese troops enter North Korea.
November 1	At Unsan, North Korea, Chinese clash with U.S. troops for the first time.
November 10–26	U.N. forces advance toward the Yalu River, the Chinese border.
November 25–27	The Chinese counterattack U.N. forces.
December 8–24	U.N. forces retreat below the 38th Parallel.
December 31	The Chinese launch an offensive to recapture Seoul.

1951

January 4	Communist troops recapture Seoul; U.N. forces retreat to the 37th Parallel.
January 25	U.N. counteroffensives are launched, the first against the Chinese.
March 14	U.N. forces retake Seoul.
April 10	President Truman relieves General MacArthur; General Ridgway succeeds him as Far East commander.
April 22	The Chinese open a major offensive, their fifth, driving U.N. forces back as much as twenty miles.
May 16–22	U.S. forces finally halt the Chinese and launch a counteroffensive.
July 10	Truce talks open in Kaesong.
October 25	Truce talks are transferred to Panmunjom.
November 12	Ridgway ends U.N. offensive action in favor of "active defense."

1952

January 2	U.S. negotiators propose voluntary repatriation of prisoners of war.
February 18	To block such defections, North Korean POWs battle U.S. troops in the Koje-do camp; 78 prisoners die in one of several bloody POW riots.
April 19	U.S. negotiators tell the communists only 70,000 of 132,000 POWs want to return to North Korea or China.
May 2	The communists reject the idea of voluntary repatriation.
May 7	North Korean prisoners kidnap, and then release, the U.S. Koje-do camp commander; in the coming weeks, U.S. troops crush resisters, with dozens dead.
June–October	Hill battles rage, but the battlefront remains in stalemate.
July 10	On the talks' first anniversary, all issues are tentatively resolved except exchange of prisoners.
July–August	Heavy American air strikes practically obliterate Pyongyang.
October 6–24	The Chinese are repulsed in their biggest ground attack in a year.
December 2–5	President-elect Eisenhower tours Korea.

1953

March 5	Stalin, an obstacle to a Korea truce, dies.
March 23–July 7	Battle of Pork Chop Hill.
April 20–May 3	Operation Little Switch exchanges sick and wounded POWs.
June 4	The communists effectively agree to all U.N. truce proposals, with a compromise on voluntary repatriation.
June 18–19	President Rhee unilaterally frees 27,000 North Korean POWs wishing to stay in the South, endangering the truce.
July 12	Under U.S. pressure, Rhee agrees not to obstruct the armistice.
July 13	The communists launch an offensive against the South Koreans, their biggest in two years. Lines stabilize by July 18.
July 19	Delegates reach final agreement at Panmunjom.
July 27	The Korean armistice is signed.
August–December	Operation Big Switch exchanges all POWs willing to be repatriated.

THE CHARACTERS

In order of appearance, with their occupations and ages on June 25, 1950.

Chang Sang—Refugee girl from North Korea, ten (*on the right*)

Ri In-mo—North Korean communist party functionary, thirty-two (with bride Kim Sun-im)

Park Sun-yong—South Korean mother, wife of a law student, twenty-three (here at age seventeen)

Yu Song-chol—North Korean People's Army general, thirty-three (here in later years)

Matthew B. Ridgway—U.S. Army
deputy chief of staff, fifty-five

No Kum-sok—North Korean Naval
Academy cadet, eighteen

Clarence C. Adams—American
infantryman, twenty-one

Sister Mary Mercy—American Maryknoll nun and physician, forty-seven

Chung Dong-kyu—North Korean
medical student, eighteen

Leonard (Buddy) Wenzel—
American infantryman, nineteen
(here in later years)

Bill Shinn—South Korean journalist,
thirty

Alan Winnington—British journalist in Peking, forty (here with future
wife Esther Cheo Ying)

Hurh Won-moo—Seoul high school senior, seventeen

Shin Hyung-kyu—High school student from Kochang, South Korea, sixteen (photo unavailable)

Ahn Kyong-hee—Seoul university student, newspaper editor's daughter, twenty (here in later years with husband Han Muk)

Chi Chao-chu—Chinese student at Harvard University, twenty (here in later years)

Paul N. (Pete) McCloskey—U.S. Marine
Reserve lieutenant, twenty-two (*on the right*)

Gil Isham—American infantryman,
eighteen

Peng Teh-huai—Chinese People's
Liberation Army general, fifty-one

Chen Hsing-chiu—Chinese army medic,
sixteen

PART I
1950

Should the United States and the Soviet Union continue to reinforce the military strength in their zones of former occupation, the resultant Korean fighting may launch the final conflict of the world.

> —**Cornelius Osgood**, author, *The Koreans and
> Their Culture*, writing in 1949

I light a cigarette, pretending calm.
I knew this was bound to happen.
And it has come at last.

> —**Cho Chi-hun,** "Journal of Despair (June 25, 1950),"
> from *Brother Enemy: Poems of the Korean War*

A KOREAN ADAGE HAS IT THAT "SHRIMP GET BROKEN backs in a whale fight."

In 1945 the Korean people celebrated liberation from thirty-five years of Japanese colonial rule and looked forward to the promise of independence, of Korea as a sovereign nation again. But those hopes were crushed in the Cold War rivalry of the Soviet Union and the United States, the two great powers occupying and sponsoring rival Koreas, a communist North and a capitalist South. The Americans and Soviets failed to meet a commitment to reunite Korea's halves. Now, by the summer of 1950, border skirmishes between two Korean armies have brought the peninsula to the brink of war.

In the drizzly predawn of June 25, following a plan drawn up by Soviet military advisers, seven North Korean divisions invade South Korea. For the first time in a millennium, Korean armies will fight each other.

The southern capital of Seoul falls quickly, and the United States rushes in troops to bolster the retreating South Korean army. The decision by President Harry S. Truman to use military force to oppose the spread of communism is swift and unprecedented, done without approval of Congress.

The Americans, too, are driven back by the tank-led North Koreans, finally forming a defensive quadrant in the peninsula's southeast corner.

From the very first days, the fighting unleashes the murderous impulses of an ideological civil war. South Korean authorities carry out mass executions of tens of thousands of suspected southern leftists. In their occupied territory, the North Koreans execute many southern rightists after summary "people's court" trials.

At the same time, in their desperate retreat, American troops and warplanes open fire on columns of South Korean civilians fleeing the fighting. Rumors have spread that disguised northern infiltrators lurk among the refugees.

In late summer, overall U.S. commander General Douglas A. MacArthur strikes back, landing a large amphibious force west of Seoul, behind North Korean lines. American and

South Korean forces then advance north from their southeast perimeter. In disarray, the northern army retreats and perpetrates a new round of atrocities against suspect southerners. When the South Koreans return to Seoul, they again stage executions, this time of alleged collaborators with the northern occupation.

The momentum of MacArthur's counteroffensive takes his forces deep into North Korea, all the way to the Chinese border, setting the stage for an even greater war, the Cold War's first armed collision of communist and capitalist powers.

JUNE

SUNDAY, JUNE 25, 1950

In Seoul, ten-year-old Chang Sang awakens to war

"Sang-*iyah*. Wake up." The urgent whispers stir Sang from sleep. "Sang-*iyah*. Something is happening."

Rubbing her eyes open, she sees the white beard and the handsome tanned face of Grandfather Kim. The Bible says God made man in his own image. This is how God looks, the girl likes to think.

This morning the old man seems worried. An uprooted farmer lost in the teeming city, Grandfather Kim knows this clever grandchild can discover what's behind the commotion in the streets outside. At age ten, Chang Sang is the oldest and brightest of a half-dozen cousins, refugee children from the North, crammed into a little house in old Seoul.

Obedient, curious, she quickly dons her white cotton top and skirt. She hurries out into the gray morning, trailed by a couple of little cousins, leaving a roomful of others asleep. It's barely past dawn, the summer sun rising pale beyond low clouds. The feel of approaching rain is in the air. For so early on a Sunday, the streets are strangely active, people rushing here and there, or standing talking in pairs or small groups. The girl, tall for her age, and confident, darts from group to group, listening, picking up the news. She hurries back home, where the adults are returning from church, and announces to Grandfather and any who will hear:

North Korea is attacking South Korea. North Korean soldiers are coming to Myari, coming to Seoul.

The child's words send a chill through the Kim household of northern-born Christians, one extended family among tens of thousands of people who have poured south in recent years, a human tide driven by social upheaval, fleeing the rise of communism in the northern half of a poor, backward land.

Someone turns on Uncle's radio. All sounds normal until, at 7:00 a.m., Korean Broadcasting breaks in to report the attack.

"There is little cause for concern," it reassures listeners. "The 100,000-strong Republic of Korea armed forces are sound and intact."[1]

But beyond Seoul's sprawl of mud-walled houses and tile roofs, of squat office buildings and antique temples, somewhere north of the two-thousand-foot-high mountains ringing the centuries-old capital, the South Korean army is falling to pieces in the thunder and lightning of artillery and heavy tanks pushing south, in drizzle and fog, through the valleys that point toward Seoul.

As the city's 1.5 million people awaken, almost one-third of them refugee northerners, word of the sudden attack is alarming, but hardly a surprise.[2] In the five years since World War II's end, when the U.S. and Soviet victors divided this former Japanese colony into separate occupation zones, the two halves have followed divergent paths, communist and capitalist, under their Russian and American mentors, each forming a government claiming sovereignty over the entire five-hundred-mile Korean peninsula. And their newly organized armies have clashed repeatedly at latitude 38 North, the dividing line, especially since American occupation troops left Korea a year ago, a few months after the Soviet army withdrew from bases in the North.

On this Sunday, as news and rumors mount hour by hour about the fighting at the 38th Parallel, just fifty miles to the north, the people of Seoul hope this, too, is another border skirmish, soon to end.

———

*In North Korea, revolutionary Ri In-mo wonders,
"Has the time finally come?"*

"In-mo! In-mo!" His mother's voice startles the exhausted Ri In-mo awake. "Listen to the news. It's war!"

The young man collapsed in sleep just before dawn this Sunday morning. He now looks up from his mat. Beside his mother stands his young wife, arms wrapped tightly around their slumbering two-year-old girl. All fall silent and listen. The radio announcer repeats the news: the southern Syngman Rhee puppet clique, tool of American imperialists, has attacked North Korea from across the 38th Parallel.

Ri sits, shaking off his deep sleep, collecting his thoughts.

As propaganda chief for the communist Korean Workers' Party in Hungnam, a port city on North Korea's east coast, he spent the previous day in meetings at the local KWP headquarters. He is studying the new three-year economic plan promulgated from Pyongyang, the capital, in order to develop ways to promote it to the people.

Returning past midnight to their home in nearby Honam-dong, he found his mother, Kye-sun, and wife, Sun-im, waiting up for him. They talked into the small hours, Ri patiently explaining the visionary ideas of the great General Kim Il-sung, North Korea's leader, a vision of a better future for poor Koreans like them. Their daughter, Hyun-ok, would be five years old at the end of the three-year plan, his wife remarked.

"Then we should buy a tricycle for her," said the grandmother.

Her lighthearted words struck Ri, remembering how she regretted always that she could never buy her boy the playthings other children had. Their poverty deepened in 1917 when his father died from a mysterious disease, unable to pay for a doctor, seven months before In-mo was born, leaving her both a widow and a new mother at eighteen. In their hometown of Phungsan, in Korea's mountainous far north, she scratched out a bare living farming rocky soil and weaving hemp clothing at night. Finally, in desperation, she had to entrust the boy to her schoolteacher brother and his wife, a childless couple, to be brought up as their own.

At age thirteen, running an errand, In-mo witnessed Korean nationalist guerrillas assassinate the hated local Japanese police chief. One gunman beckoned to the boy and told him Koreans could be free and prosper only when they rid themselves of such colonial oppressors. In-mo thought of his mother's struggles and of the plight of so many others, reduced to eating pine bark in the spring when stored food ran out. In-mo and school friends began visiting a well-known local political agitator, a man who told them about "capitalism, socialism, Marx, Engels, Lenin and Stalin," he recalls.

In-mo became a boy revolutionary, breaking police station windows, collecting firewood for the needy, reading leftist anti-Japanese tracts to younger children in a secretive "Red Reading Society." By age sixteen, he was in jail. After his release, the young Ri spent the coming years as a student and worker on the surface and as an activist underground seeking to subvert Japan's colonial regime. In August 1945 he was in hiding in the mountains when jubilant friends came and told him Japan had surrendered and Korea was liberated.

He and local comrades formed Phungsan's first cell of the Communist Party, soon renamed the Korean Workers' Party. As the party's postcolonial focus shifted to purging landlords and pro-Japan collaborators, he rose in the ranks. The tall, handsome In-mo *Tongmu* (Comrade In-mo) also attracted the attention of young party enthusiast Sun-im, ten years his junior. She pursued him, and they fell in love. During their courtship, his gifts to her included a bound history of the Soviet Communist Party.

By 1947 the growing Cold War hostility between the Americans and Soviets doomed to failure the two powers' vague plans to reunify Korea. In 1948 both North and South declared themselves independent states, as the Democratic People's Republic of Korea (DPRK) in Pyongyang and the Republic of Korea (ROK) in Seoul.[3] In that year, Ri was sent to join the Hungnam party committee, riding the eighty miles in the back of an open truck with his mother and his bride-to-be.

He now has put in two years of hard work with the Hungnam party, while the two Koreas have been locked in an increasingly explosive stand-off, each threatening to take the other by force. On this Sunday morning, he wonders, "Has the time finally come?"

Young mother Park Sun-yong goes to church in Seoul

Park Sun-yong is dressing her two small children for church this Sunday morning. She has brought four-year-old Koo-pil and his two-year-old sister, Koo-hee, to Seoul to visit their father, taking the train up from a village in central South Korea, where they're staying with her in-laws. He is studying law in the capital, and the little family fills his rented student's room near the south bank of the broad Han River, across from central Seoul.

As she fusses over the children, she and husband Chung Eun-yong catch the sound of people shouting outside. They hear a siren. What's happening? He finds neighbors gathered around a radio. A nervous announcer is reporting the news of a North Korean attack, adding the reassuring words, "All the nation's people are urged to remain calm and carry on business as usual."

The young couple are at a loss, like almost everyone in Seoul, uncertain of the seriousness of what they're hearing. They have seen so much. Like most of their countrymen, the twenty-three-year-old mother, quiet and modest, and her husband, twenty-six, have lived through years of turmoil in the new Korea, where liberation in 1945 meant the collapse of institutions and of the colonial agricultural economy, the deeper impoverishment of millions in the countryside, the rise of political violence, and a rural guerrilla war inspired by the communist North.

A year ago in Shimchon, Sun-yong's hometown, a small country village where her father is a government fiscal officer, guerrillas attacked a neighbor landlord with picks and sickles, killing him in broad daylight, stealing his grain, and burning down his house.

Her husband's experience is more direct. Eun-yong joined the national police force in the final year of Japanese rule, and four years later, in 1948, he was sent to the southern island of Cheju to join the bloody suppression of a leftist revolt.

Cheju islanders, jealous of their autonomy and opposed to the breakup of Korea into two separate states, had staged demonstrations denouncing President Syngman Rhee's policies, protests that were crushed by a new right-wing governor and militias sent south by Seoul. Islanders replied with vicious attacks on police. The government campaign that followed left Cheju villages in smoldering ruins and at least one-tenth of the island population dead—at least thirty thousand people, a bloodbath largely hidden from the outside world.[4]

Demoralized by what he had to do and see, and disgusted by police corruption, Eun-yong resigned from the force in 1949 and entered Seoul's Chung Ang College.

It was during her husband's time on Cheju, away from the young couple's home in the central city of Taejon, that the worried Sun-yong was persuaded by a local pastor to begin attending services at his Presbyterian church. Christians remained a small minority, but the troubling times were driving more Koreans toward religion. The convert Sun-yong soon was there every Sunday, praying for her husband's safety.

Now, on this Sunday, she gathers up little Koo-hee, takes Koo-pil by the hand, and walks to church once more. Sound trucks roll down the streets, dispatched by the army to order soldiers on leave to report for duty. Vehicles carrying troops roar toward the nearby Han River Bridge No. 1, heading into Seoul and beyond.

What will happen? Settling into her pew, her children at her side, Park Sun-yong is soon comforted by the familiar words of scripture. Then, in this cool and peaceful sanctuary as the day grows warmer, the pastor asks the congregation to join him in prayer, to call on their God to protect the men of the South Korean military.

— ⊶ —

In their command cave, Yu Song-chol and other northern generals let out a cheer

Yu Song-chol knows the claim that South Korea attacked first this Sunday morning is a colossal lie, one preceded by an even more elaborate lie: that North Korean troop movements along the 38th Parallel the past two weeks, the preparation for invasion, were actually a training exercise.

That ruse was embellished with uncoded messages describing maneuver plans, praising some units' work, chiding others, communications the northern commanders knew would be monitored by the South Koreans. Chinese master Sun Tzu counseled Asian warriors long ago: deception is your first weapon.

Yu, the thirty-three-year-old army operations chief, newly promoted to major general, has been awake for hours, and on edge. He has joined other young generals of the Korean People's Army (KPA) and Soviet military advisers in a cave outside Pyongyang, at a place called Seopo, where they have set up their makeshift command post (CP) for the southern liberation campaign.

Junior officers are delivering reports on the battle situation, and in late morning one confirms that Kaesong, the ancient Korean capital and first city on the road to Seoul, has fallen to the KPA. Cheers echo off the cavern walls. The officers, including Kang Kon, KPA chief of staff, hug and slap each other's backs in congratulation. The southern army is collapsing even more easily than expected, Yu concludes. The meticulous planning is paying off.

The planning was the work of those Soviet advisers, hardened World War II veterans, but Yu had a central role. As a Soviet Korean, grandson of Korean emigrants in Russia's Pacific Far East, it fell to him, with others, to translate the strategists' operational orders from Russian to Korean and to revise as necessary.

In early June the complex plan was passed up to Kim Il-sung. The North Korean leader scribbled a simple "concur" on the document. The fate of millions of Koreans was sealed. It will be many months before Yu Song-chol learns the background to his onetime guerrilla comrade's decision to go to war.

It was a decision not universally applauded. The invasion should have been led by defense chief Choe Yong-gon, another Kim Il-sung comrade from their days fighting the Japanese in Manchuria. But Yu learned that Choe was passed over because he'd told the "Great Leader" he opposed all-out war, fearing intervention by the United States, a risk Kim deemed unlikely. Instead, command fell to the tall, imposing Kang Kon, at thirty-two even younger than Yu, but admired by colleagues for his aggressiveness and tactical know-how.

Yu and Kang worked together closely on the attack plan. Timing was crucial: a Sunday in late June, when many southern troops would be on weekend passes or on longer leaves to help with weeding in the rice paddies at home.[5] The timing proved luckier than expected, since many frontline commanders of the Republic of Korea Army traveled to Seoul last evening for the grand opening of a new officers' club. In fact, Major General Chae Byung-duk (Fat Chae), Kang's southern counterpart, didn't lay his famously rotund body down to sleep until about two this morning.[6]

Just two hours later, around four, massed North Korean artillery opened fire along the 38th Parallel. Over the next hour, at five major points, seven northern infantry divisions, more than seventy thousand troops, struck across the border, their mustard-drab columns marching south or rumbling down the rough roads in Soviet-made trucks, through darkness and rain.

The predawn barrages shook sleeping defenders awake, from the Ongjin peninsula in the west to the remote east coast, 180 miles away across the Taebaek Mountains. A mere four regiments of the ROK Army, perhaps ten thousand men, manned defensive positions at the parallel.[7]

General Kang's invasion force isn't totally modern. Oxcarts are transporting some supplies.[8] But about one-third of the troops are tough war veterans, having fought with Mao Tse-tung's victorious communist army in the civil war that ended in China just months ago.[9] And the Soviets have endowed the KPA with 150 tanks, the T-34s of World War II fame, fast thirty-two-ton machines equipped with powerful 85-millimeter guns.[10] More than 40 of these giants are leading the infantry push down Route 43 toward the crossroads town of Uijongbu.[11]

The South Koreans have nothing to stop them, no tanks of their own, no antitank guns potent enough to crack their armor.[12] Directly fired 105-millimeter howitzers are striking them but not stopping them. Within hours the outnumbered, outgunned southern troops are too terrified to confront the armor-led columns and are pulling back, or dying, or scattering into the hills.

In Honam-dong, Ri In-mo dresses quickly and hurries back down to Hungnam, to the Korean Workers' Party headquarters he left just a few hours earlier. There he finds people crowded around loudspeakers, comrades nodding silent greetings to comrades as they arrive. Pyongyang Radio reads the announcement blaming the South for the hostilities: "Early on the morning of 25 June 1950, troops of the so-called 'army of national defense' of the puppet government of South Korea began a surprise attack on the territory of North Korea along the entire 38th Parallel. . . . At the present moment, the security forces of the Republic are stubbornly resisting the enemy." It warns the southerners of "serious consequences."[13]

Listening to the tinny speakers announce this over and over, Ri In-mo, onetime boy revolutionary, tells himself this is the longed-for opportunity to bring the socialist revolution to all of Korea.

"It's war, at last."

In the streets of Seoul, dampened now by rain showers as early summer temperatures edge toward ninety degrees Fahrenheit, jeeps and army trucks speed urgently northward.[14]

Radios blare from open windows with the army's emergency broadcasts. Strange planes buzz the city.

Inside their crowded home, the Kims sink deeper into uncertainty. What should they do?

The rest of the world is savoring peace five years after the greatest war mankind has ever seen. The political rivalries and border flare-ups of

Korea are forgettable events in a distant corner of Asia. But to people like the girl Chang Sang and her family, they're events that are shaking lives and shaping futures.

Sang is haunted by nightmares of the terrifying crossing of the 38th Parallel made with her mother under the guns of North Korean soldiers three years ago, when she was seven. She remembers, too, the earlier time when she witnessed a band of landless peasants waving scythes and hoes descend on Grandfather Kim's small farm in North Pyongan Province, in Korea's far northwest, declaring they were confiscating his land. First they sent Sang and other visiting children home, and then they chased Kim and his wife away with just some meager belongings.

Around the same time, in the early months after the 1945 liberation from Japan, the North's newly emboldened tenant farmers and farmhands seized a much bigger prize, the large landholdings of Sang's late Grandfather Chang, her father's father. Decades earlier, he was an official in the court of the dying Yi dynasty, the monarchs who last ruled an independent Korea. He then became the highest-ranking Korean in North Pyongan after Japan annexed the peninsula as a colony in 1910.

Again, an angry throng arrived at the door of the fine Chang home and in the name of "the people" drove his widow away, off the family's ancestral domain.

Chang's widow was known as the first Christian in their town of Yongchon. The Christianity that missionaries brought, particularly to northern Korea, was viewed as something of a Western counterweight to Japanese colonialism, becoming associated with education and with the independence movement. But in a secular, communist North after 1945, the matriarch's descendants found themselves ostracized as members of a Christian elite, as were the Kims, Sang's mother's family. Children like the precocious Sang learned that their lives could be blown in unexpected directions by forces outside their families, beyond their villages.

Kims and Changs, the purged grandparents among them, then filtered south in ones and twos, at first relatively easily through an open 38th Parallel, in later years more perilously as the communists closed the crossings.

Sang's sister, Chang Ran, ten years older, came south early to study and found work in Seoul as a teacher. Mother's younger brother, Kim Kap-hyun, also arrived early, by boat with his dispossessed parents, and landed a good job with the Seoul electric company, thanks to his education at

Tokyo's prestigious Waseda University. He speaks not only Japanese but workable English as well. His company has even sent him to the United States on business.

It is in Uncle Kap-hyun's Seoul home that Sang, her forty-six-year-old mother, Kim Bong-hyun, a widow since Sang was a baby, and other Kims have crowded in recent months for temporary shelter. Now their hope for a new life seems suddenly under threat.

Amid the clatter of Pentagon teleprinters, Matt Ridgway ponders World War III

What might this mean? What are the Russians up to? What's happening in Europe?

Matt Ridgway and other top American generals stand watch over teleprinters at the Pentagon.[15] They are headline names from World War II, men who have seen the worst of war in places like Kasserine Pass and Omaha Beach. On this Sunday, a June morning growing unusually steamy along the Potomac, they've been summoned to deal with a new emergency, in a place few of them know.

Lieutenant General Matthew B. Ridgway, army deputy chief of staff, the man who on D-Day six years ago parachuted into Normandy with his 82nd Airborne Division troops, is worried about America's unreadiness for another war so soon after the last. As the army's hands-on "chief executive officer," Ridgway knows its ranks lack manpower, training, and equipment, especially in the Far East.

He's standing alongside General Omar Bradley, chairman of the Joint Chiefs of Staff, as operations and intelligence officers of the army, navy, and air force read the dialogue tapping out on the teleprinters with General Douglas A. Macarthur's Far East headquarters in Tokyo.

When Tokyo is told it is authorized to use U.S. air and naval power to evacuate Americans from Seoul, Ridgway turns to Bradley to ask whether this means American ground troops won't be used in this Korea emergency.

"Yes," the chairman replies. Ridgway is relieved. After all, the chief U.S. military adviser in South Korea has previously reported to Washington that southern forces could handle any northern ground attack.[16]

In Seoul an order to evacuate women and children caps a confused, fearful day for the seventeen hundred Americans in the Korean capital.

By six in the morning, senior officers of the Korea Military Advisory Group, the five hundred trainers left behind when the U.S. occupation army pulled out a year ago, knew the fighting represented a major North Korean attack.[17]

Still, early messages weren't dire.

"No evidence of panic among South Korean troops," the U.S. Embassy's military attaché telegraphed MacArthur's headquarters. At midday the U.S. ambassador in Seoul, John J. Muccio, went on the local U.S. armed forces radio, assuring listeners, "There is no reason for alarm."[18]

Around the same time, however, four North Korean Yak fighters appeared over Seoul and strafed the railroad station, an armory, and other targets, killing a handful of civilians.[19] Yaks also dropped down on Seoul's Kimpo Airport, destroying a U.S. Air Force C-54 transport and seven South Korean trainer planes.[20] By late afternoon, U.S. Embassy staff who ventured to the roof of Seoul's seven-story Bando Hotel, which houses the mission, could hear the rumble of artillery to the north.[21] The nervousness grew. Embassy communications staff wheeled out cartloads of documents and set them ablaze, the bonfire lighting up the night sky in central Seoul.[22]

Learning that North Korean tanks are at Uijongbu, just twenty miles from Seoul, Muccio has ordered the evacuation tomorrow morning of dependent American women and children, aboard two freighters docked in nearby Inchon Harbor.[23]

In Washington, where clocks are a half day behind Seoul time, first word of the North Korean attack arrived late Saturday. Secretary of State Dean Acheson, aroused at his Maryland farm retreat, immediately telephoned President Harry S. Truman, on a weekend visit home to Independence, Missouri.[24] Then the late-night duty officers of the U.S. bureaucracy began tracking down the "must calls" on their crisis lists, high among them Matt Ridgway.

The big, balding, craggy-faced fifty-five-year-old general was on a getaway, a "busman's holiday," with Penny, his attractive thirty-two-year-old third wife, reviewing an Army National Guard unit in the Pennsylvania countryside. Awakened by the predawn call from the Pentagon, Ridgway told Penny after putting down the phone, "There goes our quiet, happy weekend." They began the two-hour drive back to Washington.

The thirty-seven-year army veteran, who grew into a staunch anticommunist as the Cold War took hold, couldn't help worrying that a new world war might be breaking out. Moscow has now developed its own atom bomb to match America's. No one would want to see these two great powers clash. "Armageddon," he thought. This could well be the beginning.

As the Ridgways sped down U.S. 15 under a rising sun, the night was clearing and a half-moon rising over Seoul, where Americans stuck close to their radios and the U.S. armed forces station for news.[25] At one point, the record-spinning host played a new hit from Guy Lombardo and His Royal Canadians. "Enjoy yourself," Lombardo's voices sang, "it's later than you think."[26]

No Kum-sok comes down from a mountain and finds war

My schoolmate was right, he tells himself. I never should have applied for the Naval Academy. War was inevitable. What I did was suicidal.

North Korean naval cadet No Kum-sok, age eighteen, had a privileged upbringing in Hungnam. As a boy, an only child, he had his own room and desk, a small library, and a phonograph with dozens of Korean and Japanese records. Under the Japanese, his father was a railroad executive in northern Korea, making a comfortable living, with a home to match, one heated by electricity, not by the poor man's traditional *ondol* system of underfloor flues warmed by the kitchen oven.

Growing up, the boy was pulled this way and that by contending influences. His father was an admirer of America who played amateur baseball and greeted his son at breakfast with an English "Good morning!" As a young teenager, Kum-sok hung a pinup photo of a pretty American blonde on his wall. But the indoctrination in Japanese colonial schools shaped him as well. At age thirteen, one day at home late in World War II, he announced that he wanted to enlist as a Japanese air cadet and become a kamikaze pilot, sacrificing his life to help destroy the American fleet. His father was furious.

When Soviet occupation troops marched into northern Korea at war's end, the entire populace grew furious. The undisciplined, often drunk Russian soldiers robbed, assaulted, and raped Koreans with near impunity. For his father, the outrages reinforced his businessman's antipathy to communism, a disdain passed on to the son. The teenaged Kum-sok thought constantly, if unrealistically, of making his way to southern Korea, or even America. But he could be inspired as well in the new, liberated Korea.

At a grand assembly of workers and students in 1948, in a cavernous factory building in Hungnam, Kim Il-sung himself appeared, visiting from Pyongyang. Kim's speechmaking and commanding presence, tall and brawny for a Korean, impressed the young man. The thirty-five-year-old communist chief had begun calling himself *suryong*, Great Leader. His portraits were appearing everywhere.[27] Kum-sok could see how the former guerrilla commander, with his talk of a workers' paradise, might stir the hopes of ordinary Koreans.

The seventeen-year-old Kum-sok's own hopes were dashed a year later when his father died of stomach cancer. The grieving son and mother suddenly were without income, except for her part-time trade in buying and reselling food items. And the 38th Parallel had become perilously near impossible to cross.

His late father's ambitions for his son demanded Kum-sok get a university education, but it now was beyond financial reach. Then in mid-1949 he saw a posting for applicants for the new North Korean navy's academy for officers, a free three-year university-level education. His application was accepted, and in late July 1949 No Kum-sok entered the Naval Academy, soon to move to a site outside the port of Chongjin, in the far northeast.

He quickly came to detest the place. Cadets had no days off, no vacations, no visitors. They endured harsh discipline, grinding work details and guard duty, with insufficient sleep, short rations, cold water, and poorly heated barracks.

In Kum-sok's mind it became a "penitentiary" more than an education. But he was careful: he earned top marks in the communist history course, staying in good stead with political instructors.

On this Sunday, Kum-sok's twenty-five-man unit spent the day crawling on their bellies up a mountainside, with heavy rifle and backpack, in grueling infantry-style training. They have now marched back to base for the evening meal, coated with grime and soaked with sweat. But first a somber political officer stands before them outside the dining hall and announces that war has begun, that the treacherous South Koreans invaded this morning and advanced more than a mile before the People's Army counterattacked and struck up to twenty miles into the south.

War. Filing in to their meager meal of rice and soup, the cadets are lost in thought, subdued. No Kum-sok remembers a year earlier over-hearing one schoolmate warning another who was considering applying to the Naval Academy: "Are you crazy? War may start any day. You'd become a pawn and die."

Now it has started, and No Kum-sok feels he has lost control of his life.

———

The battle plan that Yu Song-chol helped develop calls for a double envelopment of Seoul. A main force in the west is to take Uijongbu, which commands a wide valley pointing to the capital, while a sec-ondary force is to capture Chunchon, farther east, and then turn west toward Seoul.[28]

Beleaguered South Korean units are running out of ammunition. Communications are breaking down.[29] Reinforcements are slow to or-ganize and head north to the battle.[30] As evening falls this fateful Sun-day, the Korean People's Army is pressing the defenders of Uijongbu from three sides. Northern artillery shells have set the town ablaze.[31] The plan calls for the capture of Seoul within four days. As General Yu scans his situation reports in the shadowy Seopo cave, ninety miles from the gun smoke and fire of Uijongbu, he thinks they may beat that schedule. And then, he tells himself, this lightning war will be over.

———

Clarence Adams, black soldier in a segregated army, hears the news

In three years in the U.S. Army, on occupation duty in South Korea and Japan, Clarence Adams has shown he is a born boxer.

He's only 140 pounds, five-foot-six, but he punches with a fury that can dominate even heavier opponents. After going unbeaten in army boxing matches, he has been promised a professional tryout by a San Francisco promoter after his discharge. On this Sunday, back from Japan and counting the days at Fort Lewis, Washington, that's what he's work-ing on, his army separation papers. His enlistment is nearing its end.

For a black teenager growing up in Memphis, Tennessee, son of a single mother, the army was literally an escape.

On the morning of September 11, 1947, eighteen-year-old Clarence Cecil Adams bolted out the back door of his family's house as two Memphis police officers stood out front asking for him, billy clubs at the ready. He ran straight to an army recruiting station on Front Street, enlisted, and was on a train to an army transit camp in Biloxi, Mississippi, that afternoon. He never learned which offense brought the police to his front door: stabbing a black neighborhood bully in a fight or beating a white hobo with his street gang.

Running from the white police was a childhood sport for black boys in Memphis. Clarence was chased if he took out his box to shine shoes for a nickel on "white" Main Street. He was chased if he stepped into a "white" park. Segregation was total in the American South of the 1940s. Black teachers taught only black students. Black doctors treated only black patients. Black mailmen carried mail only for black neighborhoods. Southern blacks were among the most impoverished Americans. Clarence grew up in worn secondhand clothes, eating discarded chicken feet and soup made from castoff neck bones, scavenging for lumps of coal in a railyard. While white kids rode new store-bought bicycles, he had to scour junkyards for parts and build his own.

Working in the white world was risky and humiliating. Sixteen-year-old Clarence landed a summer job washing dishes in a white bar and grill, hidden away in the kitchen, but was fired after talking to a white waitress.

"You know, nigger, you're not allowed to talk to that white girl," he remembers being told by the owner. Like many black Americans, he grew ever more bitter.

He found the racial divide in the army little better. Blacks and whites were trained separately and served in black or white units. Ten months after Adams enlisted, President Truman issued his Executive Order 9981, mandating racial integration in the armed forces, but a reluctant army was slow to carry it out, especially in General MacArthur's Far East Command.[32]

Adams's first assignment took him to South Korea and a black military police (MP) unit, part of the post–World War II U.S. occupation army on the newly divided peninsula. In October 1948 he was transferred to the 24th Infantry in Japan, an all-black regiment.

Now on this Sunday in June, back in the States after two and a half years away, Clarence Adams, a high school dropout with no occupational skills, hopes he's on the verge of a career as a professional welterweight.

In the transient barracks, full of other young black Americans headed somewhere new, the public-address system suddenly comes to life, announcing that all units are put on alert, that war has broken out in Korea.

What does this mean for them? Rumors spread through the streets and mess halls of Fort Lewis in the coming hours and days. Finally, the army announces all soldiers' enlistments will be extended by one year. The "Truman year," they'll call it. The boxing ring and Clarence Adams's new life will have to wait.

Sister Mary Mercy is desperate to get to Korea, "my first love"

Sunday looms hot and humid in New York City. Thousands head for the ocean breezes of Coney Island. Others will find relief in the air-cooled movie houses, taking in *Annie Get Your Gun* or *The Asphalt Jungle*.

Two dozen miles up the Hudson, in a hilltop Maryknoll Sisters convent overlooking the river, Sister Mary Mercy spends the day within earshot of the radio. The news from Korea grows more dire as the day goes on.

In reports this morning, American military advisers are quoted as saying the invaders took Kaesong, Ingu, and Pochon, and are pressing Uijongbu. Later, just after dawn Monday in Seoul, Yak warplanes flew in again from North Korea, one dropping three bombs on the city.[33]

The news is heartbreaking to Mary Mercy. A month ago, at her medical mission in Bolivia, she was notified that her superiors were at last going to send her back to Korea to open a clinic, ten years after she left temporarily, only to be barred from returning with the outbreak of World War II.

"I'm Korea-bound," she wrote John and Rosemary, her brother and sister-in-law. "I'm deeply grateful to be returning, though it is not going to be easy to leave Bolivia. Korea is my first love—and I'll be able to give myself whole-heartedly to souls. . . . 'Tis a wonderful feeling."

Now, at the Maryknoll motherhouse outside Ossining, New York, where she has returned to prepare for the Far East, her feeling is more despondent than wonderful, especially for "all the suffering Korean people." She writes her other brother, Herb, and his wife, Myrtle.

"I presume you are talking much about Korea—as we are. There are many extra prayers being offered here," she tells them. She tries to strike an upbeat note: "I'll keep myself busy at Maryknoll for a while!" But for this devout, hardworking forty-seven-year-old nun—otherwise known as Elizabeth Hirschboeck, M.D.—even the busiest days to come are to feel almost wasted until she is back among the Korean people.

MONDAY, JUNE 26, 1950
Ten-year-old Chang Sang senses their lives, once more, will be upended

Seoul has spent a restless night listening to the engine roar and grinding gears of military convoys rolling through a blacked-out city, headed north with men and ammunition. In the predawn gloom on this second day of war, sleepless people toss over in their minds the questions: What should we do? Are we in danger? As the sun rises on a clear, warm day, they again hear the drone of approaching planes and then exploding bombs. Perhaps they've bombed Seoul Station again.[34]

Two miles from the rail terminal, beyond the eight-hundred-foot-high hill called Nam-san, South Mountain, in a one-story home with a heavy wooden door in Sindang-dong, a district of narrow streets and alleyways, the Kim household is making decisions. For ten-year-old Chang Sang, the hurried conversations, the packing of bags, the troubled look on Mother's face all signal that their lives will again be altered.

Ever since they came south three years ago, with little more than a Bible, a hymn book, and the clothing they wore, mother and daughter have had to struggle. They first settled in a shantytown of northern refugees called Haebangchon, "Freedom Village," spreading over empty fields on the western side of Nam-san, near Seoul Station.

They survived there in a hovel made of flattened tin cans. Mother worked at odd jobs, and their only real meal each day came from an American missionary kitchen. The bright little girl helped out, collecting scraps of wood for the fire, beating the slum boys at *jegichagi*, a street game whose winner takes the losers' paper shuttlecocks, perfect kindling.

At first, there was no school for Sang, but her mother, a self-taught woman, was able to instruct her in doing sums and in reading, both in Hangul, the Korean alphabet, and in Chinese characters, before Sang was accepted into the American mission school.

By 1949 they had moved to a village north of Seoul where Sang's older sister had a new teaching job. But when Sister grew ill and needed treatment, the little family moved back to crowded, noisy Seoul and into Uncle's house. Now the Kims and Changs, refugees of the 1940s, must ponder becoming refugees again in 1950.

The government radio confuses the population.

This morning Shin Sung-mo, the defense minister, has gone on air, heralded by martial music, to claim the northern enemy is retreating before a ROK Army counteroffensive.

"Soon they will advance all the way to the Yalu River"—North Korea's northern border—"and realize our people's dream of national reunification."[35]

Shin and General Chae, chief of staff, repeat this claim in meetings at the Defense Ministry and with National Assembly members.[36] Skeptical generals urge that the army instead establish defensible positions on the southern banks of the Han, across the river from Seoul. Shin and Chae declare they'll never abandon the capital.

But the counteroffensive planned for dawn, launched from Uijongbu, has in fact collapsed. Southern army units are too few, too scattered, too disorganized. By early afternoon, Uijongbu falls to the North Koreans.[37]

Panicked civilians, some leading oxcarts loaded with possessions, are streaming into Seoul from towns to the north, and city residents, bundles of bedding on their heads, belongings strapped to wooden back frames, or *jige*, have begun to flee the city, converging on Seoul Station or Han River Bridge No. 1.[38]

At the same time, army reinforcements in trucks or commandeered buses, young men in tan fatigues singing patriotic songs and waving South Korea's white-red-and-blue flag, still roll northward, cheered by bystanders shouting Koreans' traditional "*Mansei!*" (Long live!).[39]

Around four in the afternoon, the acting chief of the American military advisers, Colonel William H. S. Wright, radios MacArthur's Tokyo headquarters that the invaders are now six miles south of Uijongbu, barely a dozen miles from Seoul. The defense, he says, is in "rapid decline."[40]

In the Kim house in Sindang-dong, they remember the arrests they witnessed in the North, of Westernized Koreans, of landlords, of Christian clergy. If the invaders arrive in Seoul, they'll be harshest on "traitors" like them who fled the North.

Kap-hyun and two other of Sang's uncles, unmarried men, decide they must leave. Young men surely will be at particular risk, and they're confident the northerners wouldn't harm women, children, and old people. Before they go, however, amid the tears and reassurances of parting, they take one precaution, collecting Kap-hyun's English-language books and magazines, clues to a family's "capitalist" ties. They don't destroy them but bury them in the back courtyard. All of this, many believe, might be over soon enough.

Medical student Chung Dong-kyu learns belatedly
his North Korea is at war

In Chongjin, the hilly port city in Korea's far northeast, Chung Dong-kyu and the two hundred other students of Chongjin Medical School have been ordered to assemble on the soccer field to hear a message from "our hero," Kim Il-sung.

With no radios in their dormitory, eighteen-year-old Chung and the others spent their Sunday day of rest—and study—unaware of what was happening 250 miles to their south, below the 38th Parallel. Now, a little after 9:30, more than twenty-four hours since their country went to war, they're led in patriotic song for a few minutes, until the signal comes for silence. The loudspeakers erupt with a scratchy but urgent voice.

"Dear brothers and sisters!" It's the North Korean leader, broadcasting from Pyongyang. Kim speaks of the war that has begun with "the Syngman Rhee clique" and of the need to liberate the South.

"The war we are forced to wage is a just war for the unification and independence of the motherland, and for freedom and democracy!"

At first confused, the medical students soon grow excited. When the loudspeakers fall silent, they shout with anger, punch their fists into the air. More patriotic songs follow. Chung Dong-kyu feels a muddle of emotions—shock at the news, a sudden swelling pride in his country, but also a kind of sadness, and foreboding. What will this mean for him?

It has been a difficult five years for his family since the worldwide war ended in 1945. Dong-kyu, his mother, and three sisters had to flee from their longtime home among the Korean emigrant community in Harbin, Manchuria, back to their ancestral area in Korea, Chu Ul, near the coast twenty miles south of Chongjin. Dong-kyu's father, an unreliable, usually absentee parent, had worked for the Japanese occupiers of Chinese Manchuria. Reprisals were in store for such collaborators and their families. The father left Harbin earlier, hoping to find work in Seoul.

What the boy Dong-kyu hoped to find was an education as a doctor.

Ever since a Japanese surgeon saved his life as a thirteen-year-old, by removing a ruptured appendix, Dong-kyu dreamed of becoming a physician. Through sheer ambition and native intelligence, he won a place in 1946 at a new vocational high school in Chongjin specializing in health care. Two years later, he was promoted to the new professional medical school opening nearby. He was only sixteen, and looking younger at a diminutive five-foot-four.

His forty-seven-year-old mother, a woman who never learned to read and write and who makes a bare living in Chu Ul selling used clothing, takes immense pride in her only son. When he takes the one-hour train trip home on weekends, she tells him she knows he will become a *keun saram*, a "great man." He thinks of her as his "anchor," his "compass."

But now, on this clear, hot Monday morning, Chung and his classmates suddenly face war. He should have seen this coming. First, last September, the authorities imposed pointless military training, every day, on these future doctors. Then, in early spring, Chung began seeing Korean soldiers passing through Chongjin, headed from Manchuria to the south. They were Korean veterans of China's communist army, the shock troops of this new war, a war whose bloody reality is to confront Chung Dong-kyu in the days and weeks to come.

<hr />

"KOREA AT WAR": Buddy Wenzel, 1st Cavalry trooper,
has barely heard of the place

In these first hours of the North Korean invasion, General MacArthur at his Tokyo headquarters seems uncertain of the severity of what is happening across the Sea of Japan.

The official U.S. position has been that the North Koreans posed no serious threat to a tough, U.S.-trained southern army.[41] Meeting with a visitor today, the seventy-year-old MacArthur, World War I hero and victorious World War II strategist, expresses his disdain for the invaders.

If he sends over his own prized 1st Cavalry Division to take them on, the Far East commander tells Truman envoy John Foster Dulles, "why, heavens, you'd see these fellows scuttle up to the Manchurian border so quick, you would see no more of them."[42]

But across town, in that division's comfortable brick barracks beside Tokyo Harbor, Buddy Wenzel and his fellow troopers are far from ready for war. His 7th Cavalry Regiment has been put through only limited maneuver training at company level and none at battalion and regimental level. In post–World War II cutbacks, army regiments have been reduced to two battalions from three and lost some artillery and armor support. Eighth Army, the regional command, now plans to take seven hundred sergeants from the 1st Cavalry Division to transfer them to the 24th Infantry Division, given higher priority in contingency planning.[43]

Private Leonard B. Wenzel first learned about the invasion on Sunday from an "extra" edition of the military's *Stars & Stripes* newspaper. "KOREA AT WAR," declared the huge headline. Wenzel and friends had barely heard of Korea. But they sensed something important was happening when 7th Cavalry jeep patrols began circulating in Tokyo's back streets rousting men from the small homes, "hooches," many shared with Japanese girlfriends.

The U.S. occupation army in Japan has performed more as a police force and parade army than as a combat-ready formation. Five years after Japan's defeat, the soldiers' life is easy and enjoyable—with cheap goods, liquor, and entertainment.

The curly-haired, pug-nosed Buddy Wenzel, nineteen, who sometimes joins in the partying around Tokyo's Ginza, has had minor disciplinary problems, keeping him from promotion. He was bounced from a bugler's job when he couldn't master the somber notes of "Retreat." But he's a quiet recruit who seems to like best sitting atop his bunk writing letters to pen pals, mostly the sisters of barracks mates.

He's counting the days—413 as of this morning—until his discharge. He enlisted at age seventeen as an "out" from a broken household in South River, New Jersey, where he dropped out of high school to care for two younger sisters after his mother walked out on the family. When his father died and she moved back into the house with her boyfriend, the teenager rebelled and joined friends in signing up, his mother gladly supplying the parental signature required for an underage army recruit.

Young Wenzel didn't sign up for war. But as rumors spread that they're Korea bound, some 2nd Battalion buddies sound eager, swaggering, buying long knives, getting menacing "Mohawk" haircuts, disguising any trepidation with bravado. One of Wenzel's best friends, James Hodges, a farm boy from Florida whose sister is a Wenzel pen pal, isn't disguising his fears. He writes home that "I'm in a dangerous position," and he is increasing his soldier's insurance to $10,000. "If I do get bumped off, the family will be sitting purty."

TUESDAY, JUNE 27, 1950

Ri In-mo is inspired by the party's call for wartime solidarity

At the Korean Workers' Party office in Hungnam, on this third day of war, local propaganda official Ri In-mo sees a newly arrived message from the party Central Committee in Pyongyang. It's reassuring. "The war for national independence and sovereignty against the reactionary forces will enjoy the warm support of the anti-imperialist democratic camp of the world including the great Soviet Union," reads the letter to all party members across North Korea. It calls for putting party organizations "on a war footing."[44]

The thirty-two-year-old Ri has seen membership in the communist organization explode since liberation. From fewer than 5,000 party members across northern Korea in late 1945, it approached 1 million members by early 1948, in a population of 9 million.

The key moment came in March 1946 when the Pyongyang leadership, with guidance from the Soviet occupation authorities, ordered redistribution of land to the landless peasantry.[45]

Korean agriculture was almost feudal in nature. In the 1930s, 3 percent of the agricultural families—Japanese and Korean—owned two-thirds of the cultivated land. Millions of peasants toiled as tenants, turning over much of their production as rent. Forced exports to Japan and periodic crop failures often pushed the rural population to near starvation.[46]

In just twenty-five days in 1946, the "Land to the Tiller" program redistributed 2.4 million acres of farmland to 710,000 peasant households. The wildly popular program boosted farm production in some provinces by as much as 50 percent. It also boosted KWP membership, along with such other popular measures as eight-hour workdays, equal rights for women, and the nationalization of industries, often Japanese owned.[47]

Ri In-mo, junior party official, grew more committed and worked harder for the KWP as time went on. Now unification of the entire peninsula, under the KWP, is at hand. An enthusiastic Ri tells his boss, the Hungnam party committee chairman, he wants to volunteer for the war front. The chairman rejects the idea. He's needed in the rear, just as the Central Committee message says. But the chairman doesn't have the last word.

Bill Shinn must get his wife and son out of Seoul

The scene in Seoul since Sunday has been a confusing montage of conflicting claims, of defiance and defeatism, of government troops both retreating south and deploying north. Bill Shinn is trying to unravel it all. As the local Korean reporter for the U.S.-based Associated Press (AP) news agency, Shinn has been helping the lead correspondent, O. H. P. (Okey) King, get news of this sudden war out to the world.

The news this Tuesday morning is that advance units of the North's Korean People's Army are probing the outskirts of Seoul,[48] and the seventy-five-year-old President Rhee, his Austrian-born wife, Francesca, and the presidential cabinet have abandoned the city, headed for Suwon, twenty miles south.[49]

Many who hear of their flight fall into a deeper panic, and the streets teem with people laden with their belongings, converging on the Han River Bridge No. 1, on Yongdongpo on the opposite bank, and then onto the road south. With ROK Army reinforcements still rolling in from the south on trains, trucks, and buses, the streets around the bridge and Seoul Station are tied up in chaotic knots of humanity.[50] North Korean planes, meanwhile, are dropping leaflets demanding surrender.[51]

These are the last reports King files from Seoul. The Tokyo-based American journalist, without sleep for more than two days, is near collapse. At the same time, international communications from Seoul are breaking down.

King is to catch a ride with the U.S. Embassy staff evacuating southward. First, driving an abandoned embassy jeep, the correspondent finds the AP's bank open and empties the office accounts, in U.S. dollars and Korean *won*. Spotting his assistant Shinn in the street, he stops and hands him a bundle of Korean currency.

"You're on your own, Bill," he tells him, and then drives off, only to find the embassy convoy gone, leaving him to make his way to Kimpo Airport, where U.S. Air Force planes are flying Americans to Japan and safety.[52]

Unable to file news reports to Tokyo, Shinn must think of his family first, his pregnant wife, Sally Kim, and their three-year-old son, Johnny. And he has the means of escape, his 1929 Model A Ford. The blue sedan is rolling evidence of the resourcefulness of this young reporter, whose journey since 1945 has taken him from his northern Korea home, to Seoul, to an education in America, and back to South Korea and an enviable job, with his own American automobile in his ship's cargo hold.

Shinn and Sally must head south. First he stops by the AP office to gather files and notebooks, then drives to their home in northern Seoul.

Meanwhile, in late morning, in another live teleprinter conference with the Pentagon, General MacArthur reports from Tokyo that Colonel Wright, the chief U.S. adviser in Seoul, believes the North Koreans can take the city within twenty-four hours.

"Our estimate is that complete collapse is possible," MacArthur says.[53]

The Pentagon chiefs advise their Far East commander that President Truman has authorized the U.S. Air Force to go on the attack against the North Korean force below the 38th Parallel. MacArthur quickly relays word of this to the advisory group, saying, "Be of good cheer. Momentous events are pending."[54]

The glib wording leads to near disaster. The remaining U.S. advisers in Seoul have evacuated south across the Han earlier this day, following the South Korean general staff, but after MacArthur's assurances Wright now orders three dozen of them to return with him to their posts in the capital. As they recross Han River Bridge No. 1, they see mounds of explosives under rice-straw matting, set to blow and bring down the steel-and-concrete span.[55]

A heavy rain falls on the city. The sounds of battle to the north grow more intense. Unknown hands are firing tracer bullets over downtown buildings.[56] The radio speaks of help coming from U.S. warplanes and from a new combat command MacArthur is dispatching from Tokyo.[57] American fighter planes flying in from Japan do shoot down six North Korean aircraft over Seoul, but B-26 bombers arriving overhead find the cloud cover too thick for them to locate the tank columns they're told to target.[58]

On Seoul's northern edge, windows and floors shake with the thunder of artillery and tank fire. Around eight in the evening, just as Bill Shinn is finishing his first meal at home in three days, a huge blast rattles the dishes, seemingly from the nearby Myari Pass, a northeastern gateway to Seoul.

"We had to flee at once," he later writes. "We hastily packed our essential belongings and fled in the old Ford." His younger brother and sister join them.

Headlights off, horn honking, hearing the sounds of war fade behind them, they speed through city streets toward Bridge No. 1, the lone pedestrian-vehicle span over the Han.

All the desperation of Seoul is funneling into the Hangang-ro approach to the bridge. The broad avenue is blanketed end to end by a sea of people clad in traditional Korean white, families fleeing on foot, people pulling carts, pushing loaded wheelbarrows, pedaling bicycles, riding in oxcarts, a lucky few in automobiles or trucks, engines revving as they edge through the jostling crowds.

Shinn drives slowly toward the span, only to reach a checkpoint where military police, trying to control the crush of humanity, turn him back at gunpoint. Reluctantly, Shinn heads the car east, upriver three miles to the Kwangnaru ferry crossing. There they find the throngs of civilians and wounded soldiers impossible to penetrate.

Turning back again and reaching the bridge once more, as the rain pours down, they're met by a military policeman who threatens to shoot if they don't stop. As Sally cowers in the corner of her seat with Johnny, Shinn shouts back that he's a journalist.

"Shoot if you will!" he says as he steps on the gas. Minutes later, they're safely across the half-mile-long bridge.

It is 11:45 p.m. Tuesday. They drive a few miles south to a small village, Shinwon-ri, and the house of a friend, where they fall into a deep sleep. They don't hear a midnight signoff by government radio, a hoarse voice lamenting, "My country, my compatriots, my land!"[59]

Not long after, Shinn is awakened by massive explosions. It's Han River Bridge No. 1, blown up while crammed with fleeing civilians and retreating soldiers.

WEDNESDAY, JUNE 28, 1950

Park Sun-yong, her husband, and their children begin a trek south

Like so many in Seoul, Park Sun-yong's two small children cannot sleep. When the deafening roar shakes the floor of their rented room, Koo-pil and Koo-hee are wide awake. The burst of bluish light illuminates their small, frightened faces in the dark.

It is a little after two in the morning. Torrents of rain still fall, and few here on the Han's south bank are venturing outside. Sun-yong and husband Chung Eun-yong have little idea what is happening across the river in central Seoul, where it has been a momentous and deadly night.

After the U.S. advisers withdrew from Seoul at midday yesterday, and then returned in the evening because of General MacArthur's reassuring words, the sounds of battle on the city's northern outskirts indicated the invaders were near. Past midnight, the Americans learned that General Chae, the ROK Army chief of staff, had ordered Han River Bridge No. 1—along with railroad bridges—to be blown up at two in the morning. Angry American officers rushed to army headquarters to demand a delay to allow evacuation of retreating Korean troops. Frontline commanders, whose units would be stranded with their backs to the river, made their own urgent appeals, and operations officers finally dispatched a colonel with orders to delay. His jeep, jammed in traffic, could not reach the demolition team in time.

Shortly after two, as masses of refugees and soldiers on foot and in vehicles slowly passed over the bridge, the explosives were detonated in a cataclysmic blast, dropping a huge span of Bridge No. 1 into the Han and sending hundreds of people plummeting seventy-five feet into the fast-flowing river. Panicked people pressing from behind pushed countless more into the newly opened gap and to their deaths.

Through the rest of this morning, as North Korean troops approach central Seoul, thousands of civilians and southern soldiers, and the American advisers, manage to cross the Han on a motley flotilla of ferries, small boats, and even makeshift rafts.[60] Now, when Chung Eun-yong emerges from his building, the rain having stopped and the sun breaking through, he sees a river of white filling the road south from the Han.

On a neighbor's radio, he hears a pleading message: "Citizens! Please stay at your jobs. Let's defend Seoul." But he knows it's time to go, that he, Sun-yong, and the children should head to Chugok-ri, his home village one hundred miles to the south.

They pack up whatever they can carry and head down to join the white-clad multitudes. All around they find disheartening scenes, of fearful people shuffling along in rice-straw sandals, *komu-sin* flat rubber shoes, or barefoot, men hefting overloaded *jige* back frames, one man carrying his frail, elderly mother on his. Women in clumsy, long *hanbok* skirts try to keep children in line or in their arms. Some soldiers straggle along as well, dried blood on the bandaged wounds of many, few carrying weapons.

After walking all day, in hot but thankfully dry weather, the exhausted family reaches Suwon, where they find shelter at a school, sleeping atop classroom desks. Like millions of other Koreans at this moment, Sunyong and Eun-yong trust the emergency will end in days or weeks, when they can resume their lives.

In China, Alan Winnington follows the war
from afar, for the moment

In the heat of a summer evening in Peking, hurrying through the Chinese capital's swarms of bicycles, horse carts, and rickshaws, a British journalist heads to the main telegraph office to cable the news to London.

"Seoul, the capital of Korea, was completely liberated at 11:30 this morning, Korean time," Alan Winnington reports. "The majority of the puppet troops in the city were annihilated owing to the speed and power of the People's Army attack. Their fleeing remnants were pursued." He cites a North Korean communiqué from 3:00 p.m. today, Wednesday.

Winnington's newspaper, the *Daily Worker*, organ of the British Communist Party, beats others with the news. "Seoul is taken," reads its front-page headline. Once more, the party's decision to send Winnington to China in 1948 looks inspired. His reporting has been a rare Western window into Mao Tse-tung's victorious communist revolution.

Seventeen months ago, the urbane, handsome Englishman rode into Peking with the People's Liberation Army as it seized the city from Chiang Kai-shek's defeated Nationalist troops without a fight. He earlier stormed the strategic town of Fengtai with commandos of the PLA's 42nd Army. He has breakfasted on dried meal with troops in the field and lunched on finer fare with Mao himself.

Well educated to a point, widely read beyond that—"the Depression was my university," he says—Winnington gravitated to the British communists in the mid-1930s. The twenty-four-year-old with the posh accent became a hero to the proletarian party in 1934 when he pulled off a daring stunt that ended with hidden protest banners unfurling down the facade of a leading London hotel. Here in China, where Winnington serves as a representative of the British party as well as the *Daily Worker* correspondent, PLA overall commander Marshal Chu Teh has playfully adapted the brawny Briton's first name to the Chinese, addressing him as "Ah Lan," translatable as "Little Orchid."

Just a week ago, Winnington dined with army chief Chu, along with Mao and his top deputy Chou En-lai in the Chung Nan Hai, the government compound next door to the emperors' sprawling old Forbidden City.

It was a "jolly" evening, he recalls, since things are going well in the new China. Inflation is dropping and plans are under way to demobilize much of the huge communist army left over from the civil war, while keeping an efficient and large-enough force to retake the island of Taiwan, where Nationalist remnants retreated last December. The People's Consultative Assembly approved the military drawdown last Saturday.[61]

Then on Sunday, Mao was startled by the news of war in Korea.[62] North Korea's Kim Il-sung had visited Peking on May 13 and advised Mao he would move on South Korea at some point. But he didn't indicate a date. This sudden new war strikes Mao as premature.[63]

He is even more surprised by news that President Truman decided to commit U.S. air and naval forces to defend South Korea and the U.S. Seventh Fleet to blockade the Taiwan Strait, in effect reentering the Chinese civil war on the Nationalists' side, as was done in the late 1940s.[64]

In a statement yesterday, Truman declared, "Communism has passed beyond the use of subversion to conquer independent nations and will now use armed invasion and war. . . . Accordingly, I have ordered the Seventh Fleet to prevent any attack on Formosa (Taiwan)."[65]

Speaking to his Central Government Council in Peking today, Mao denounces the United States for "tearing to shreds" agreements on nonintervention in China's internal affairs. China's new leaders cannot forget that Japan's attempt in recent decades to conquer China began with its colonization of Korea early in the century. America's anticommunist fervor may lead it on a similar path.[66]

The United Nations Security Council also infuriated communists yesterday by calling on the world's nations to aid South Korea "to repel the armed attack."[67]

Winnington's *Daily Worker*, echoing Moscow's view, describes this as an "illegal" act, since the U.N. council adopted the resolution while the Soviet delegate, who could have vetoed it, was boycotting council sessions to protest its failure to award the China seat to the victorious communists.

The daily surprises are changing the "jolly" mood among Peking's leadership. In the coming days they postpone plans to invade Taiwan.[68]

In Washington, in a weekly report, the Central Intelligence Agency (CIA) concludes China is "not expected to play a major role in the Korean invasion."[69]

At least one man in Peking does hope to play a role. Alan Winnington, busy at the moment conveying war communiqués to his British readers, is determined to get to the war himself.

THURSDAY, JUNE 29, 1950

A victorious Yu Song-chol sets foot in Seoul for the first time

As he rides over the hilltop in Myari in his Soviet-built jeep, Major General Yu Song-chol, more a son of Russia than of Korea, is impressed with his first view of Seoul. From the ridgeline he sees the fabled, centuries-old city of palaces and grand ceremonial gates spreading out toward the Han River. Descending toward the center of the capital, he also sees it's a more prosperous city than he imagined. And the Korean People's Army operations chief sees that Seoul has been little damaged by the four-day-old war.

The KPA's 3rd and 4th Divisions, infantrymen led by the 105th Tank Brigade, took this same route into Seoul yesterday from Uijongbu, as ROK Army units collapsed before the assault of heavy armor.[70] Some outgunned southern soldiers did put up a heroic resistance, slowing the advance. One company-size group held out for hours on Nam-san, the South Mountain dominating central Seoul, until all lay dead.

Disorganized ROK Army survivors then fled as best they could across the Han, leaving artillery, vehicles, and other heavy equipment behind. But thousands were trapped and were killed or captured. The invaders, meanwhile, paid their own price on the fifty-mile route from the 38th Parallel to Seoul. The 10,000-strong 4th Division alone lost more than 1,000 men killed, wounded, or missing.[71]

Today the city's streets are filled with thousands of northern soldiers. Big T-34 tanks sit triumphantly at intersections. Red flags already flutter here and there. The conquerors were greeted yesterday by young southern leftists who emerged from hiding wearing red armbands, supporters who tried to rally neighbors to celebrate and who today are busy plastering walls with posters of Kim Il-sung and Soviet leader Josef Stalin. But most citizens remain behind closed doors, uncertain, fearful. Only 100,000 of the city's population of 1.5 million were able to flee south before the main bridge was blown, trapping the remainder on the north side of the river.[72]

Yesterday's news of Seoul's capture thrilled General Yu and his staff at the command post outside Pyongyang. "The war has ended," the young operations commander thought to himself.

Seizing the enemy's capital has always signified the ultimate victory. But now, today, realities are sinking in. The Syngman Rhee government has not capitulated, and a promised uprising of the left in South Korea isn't happening.

The southern communist leader Pak Hon-yong, serving in Pyongyang as vice premier and foreign minister, had guaranteed that 200,000 of his followers in the South, underground members of the South Korean Workers' Party, would mount a powerful guerrilla campaign simultaneous with the invasion, swiftly winning over the rest of the South to the communist cause. But Pak apparently underestimated the impact of Rhee's bloody crackdown on the left in the late 1940s, which has badly weakened the movement.

"Our war scenario was flawed from its basic conception," General Yu comes to realize. Since the KPA's invasion plans focused on seizing Seoul, the strategy beyond these first four days must now be improvised.

The improvisation begins immediately, as Yu and a KPA engineer commander hurry down to the Han River to survey crossing sites. Two railroad bridges remain serviceable, only partly damaged by the retreating army's explosives. Engineers soon set about laying flooring over the rails for tanks and other vehicles to cross. Ferries and other watercraft, meanwhile, are being collected for troop crossings. Reconnaissance teams soon reach midriver islands.[73]

For Yu Song-chol and his commanders, the greatest obstacles loom in the skies and in their worst fears: the U.S. airpower suddenly deployed against them and the possibility that U.S. troops will enter the war. As Yu settles into a command post in the basement of Government House, the national capitol building, American B-29s for the first time bomb targets in Seoul, hitting the railroad station and Kimpo Airport and wrecking one of the remaining railroad bridges.[74]

Later, twenty-seven of the big bombers raid the northern capital of Pyongyang for the first time, dropping three hundred bombs, causing major damage and terrorizing the population.[75] The war is taking a daunting new turn for the confident KPA leadership. Pyongyang Radio gives voice to those fears: "Aggressive American imperialists . . . take your bloody hands off our Fatherland immediately!"[76]

FRIDAY, JUNE 30, 1950
Park Sun-yong and family reach the shelter of Chugok-ri

The exhausted little family is finally home. Park Sun-yong, husband Chung Eun-yong, and their two small children have arrived at Chugok-ri. His parents are overjoyed as they spot the four coming through the front gate of their house.

The journey from Seoul has been wearing. After spending a night at the Suwon school, they struck out again on the road. A few hours later, reaching Osan, Eun-yong and Sun-yong saw what they hoped for, a train about to leave. It was overloaded with desperate people, inside and atop the cars.

Former police lieutenant Eun-yong, a slightly built but self-assured young man, managed to make room for his family on one car's roof. As they clattered along on the main line south, darkening monsoon skies opened up and a heavy rain soaked the wretched refugees. Sun-yong and her husband pulled the children closer, huddling low against the pelting, chill headwind.

Finally, they reached Taejon and made their way to the shelter of Eun-yong's older brother's house. This morning they found a place aboard another refugee-crammed train, getting off at the Yongdong station and walking the last four miles to Eun-yong's ancestral village.

The *ri*, or village, of Chugok is not just a refuge from war. It's a return to the embrace of traditional life, the Korean way enshrined in twenty-nine thousand villages spread through the valleys of the mountainous peninsula.

The dirt lanes of Chugok-ri, a place of five hundred inhabitants, have been patted down by the feet of many generations of the same families. The homes of earthen walls and roofs of yellow-gray thatch, renewed and rebuilt from time to time, have stood on their plots for centuries. And the annual rhythm of the rice cycle has forever governed village life. That cycle now has residents out in the paddies weeding, as the young rice plants mature from the light green of spring toward the deep green of summer.

Sun-yong first came to Chugok-ri at age eighteen, in December 1944, the day after her wedding to Eun-yong, then twenty-one. As is the custom, the bride departed Shimchon, her home village on the other side of Yongdong, leaving her parents, two younger sisters, and younger brother behind, to move in with her husband's family. As is also the custom, the marriage was arranged, by go-betweens who found the two families of compatible status and the two young people highly eligible.

The Chung clan, extended families of brothers, uncles, cousins bearing the same name, dominate Chugok-ri, as clan networks typically dominate villages across Korea. These blood ties are the social support system allowing these tiny farming communities to carry on almost independent of the world around them.

Sun-yong retreated to the Chung household late last summer, with year-old Koo-hee and three-year-old Koo-pil, when Eun-yong resigned from the police, they left their home in Taejon, and he began his law studies in Seoul. Now all four are back together in familiar surroundings, amid scenes of children at play along the village stream, of ancestral gravesites on the hillsides, of the nearby railroad's familiar steam whistles.

Other Chung cousins, along with refugees of the Suh and Yang families, have been filtering in from the north, crowding into other Chugok-ri homes. They bring more hands for the backbreaking work of slogging through the paddies, pulling up and burying the weeds in the mud.

In quiet Chugok-ri, this sudden war can seem a million miles away. On this early summer evening, however, the first North Korean army units are crossing the Han River.[77]

—⬥—

For all the lightning success in seizing Seoul, progress is slower on the central front. The North Korean divisions tasked with striking south and then heading west, to trap southern forces retreating from the capital, have been stalled by a determined ROK 6th Division.

That division's commander didn't fall for the North Korean ruse of "military exercises" in the days leading up to Sunday's invasion. He correctly interpreted troop movements as preparations for an attack. He canceled leaves and maneuvered his artillery and infantry into strong defensive positions covering the narrow valleys leading south into Chunchon and to Hongchon beyond.

For days the 6th Division's batteries and infantry ambushes inflicted heavy casualties on the northern units that struck across the 38th Parallel, destroying many T-34 tanks. The ROK division pulled back only slowly, finally abandoning Chunchon on Wednesday.[78]

Yu Song-chol has now rushed the forty miles from Seoul to inspect the lines before Hongchon. The KPA operations chief finds troops of his badly bloodied 7th Division sprawled, asleep, at the foot of a hill. The lead division is depleted and exhausted. He orders another, the 12th, up from the rear to pick up the attack.

The 12th Division's commander, Senior Colonel Choe Chun-guk, is an old friend and comrade from the days of the Soviet-trained 88th Separate Rifle Brigade, the partisan unit in which they served with Kim Il-sung in the anti-Japanese guerrilla war of the early 1940s in Manchuria. Kim, five years Yu's senior, had risen to battalion commander and came to rely on Yu as his Russian interpreter. In fact, Yu accompanied Kim on their return to northern Korea after World War II's end, when the group lived above a noodle shop in the port of Wonsan, awaiting word on what the Soviets had in mind for them.

Yu was not alone in his surprise when General Terenti Shtykov, the occupation commander, chose the thirty-three-year-old Kim, highly ambitious but hardly qualified, to lead the emerging North Korean communist state. By 1948, when Kim declared the new Democratic People's Republic of Korea, Yu and the others were taking leading roles in a new Korean People's Army. And now Yu Song-chol, Choe Chun-guk, and their comrades are facing the challenge of their young lives.

Colonel Choe has joined General Yu as they oversee the exchange of divisions, riding along behind the front lines in Choe's jeep, when they suddenly come under a South Korean barrage. A hilltop forward observer clearly has spotted their group and called in mortar fire.

The driver swerves off the road as they jump out to seek cover. But one shell lands directly on the vehicle as Choe stands, shredding his legs, mortally wounding him.

The officers abruptly become an ambulance team, commandeering another vehicle, loading the dying Choe aboard, and speeding north toward medical help. Yu hears his friend, in his final minutes, muttering a woman's name, his wife's. Riding along, distraught, Yu cannot help but wonder why the shell found Choe and not him. "In war," he thinks, "what significance does one individual really carry?" He wonders how many individuals' lives are now being snuffed out across a wide swath of Korea.

As KPA ground units cross the Han River at Seoul, followed by the first of the deadly T-34 tanks, rolling over a repaired railroad bridge, the fresh 12th Division punches through Hongchon and reaches the outskirts of Wonju, twenty-five miles farther south.[79]

The northern juggernaut is rolling south again. But the worry about the Americans is deepening.

The Soviet ambassador in Pyongyang is preparing a coded telegram to Stalin in Moscow, saying the North Koreans are indirectly sounding him out about a possible Soviet entry into the war, because of "the difficulties of conducting a war against the Americans."[80]

The ambassador is the same General Shtykov who handed northern Korea over to an aggressive young Kim Il-sung five years ago, the same Kim who, Yu Song-chol knows, dismissed the risk of U.S. intervention in his war.

—⁂—

Before dawn this Friday in Washington, Matt Ridgway, deputy chief of staff, leaves Penny behind in their Fort Myer quarters with their sleeping Matty Jr., fourteen months old, and drives through the darkness the short distance to the Pentagon. He joins his boss, General J. Lawton (Joe) Collins, army chief of staff, and other officers in reviewing a long message from General MacArthur, who is back in Tokyo after a lightning visit to Korea and the Han River war front yesterday.

MacArthur's tone is urgent. "The only assurance for the holding of the present line, and the ability to regain later lost ground, is through the introduction of U.S. ground combat forces into the Korean battle area," the Far East commander tells his superiors in Washington.

He says the ROK Army is "in confusion," lacks leadership, and has no more than twenty-five thousand effective troops, out of a prewar total of ninety-eight thousand. (In the coming days, as straggling units reappear, the South Koreans muster fifty-four thousand troops.)

The MacArthur cable goes on to a sketchy plan to deploy an army regimental combat team—perhaps five thousand men—to stop the North Korean advance south of Seoul, followed by two American divisions, twenty to thirty thousand troops, to mount a counterattack.

In the darkened conference room, the Pentagon generals now raise MacArthur and his staff on the teleprinter. The dialogue taps out on a projection screen for all to read. Collins reminds MacArthur his request would require presidential approval, taking "several hours."

"A clear-cut decision without delay is imperative," Macarthur replies.

MacArthur, sixteen years Collins's senior, one of only three five-star generals in the army and a national hero from his World War II exploits, is much honored, if much disliked, among top ranks. The Joint Chiefs of Staff, chaired by General Bradley, have seemed skeptical of ground intervention in Korea, but now Collins, in the absence of the other chiefs, quickly accommodates MacArthur.

He telephones the army secretary, Frank Pace, who in turn calls Truman, already risen at five in the morning. The president, heavily influenced on Korea this week by a hawkish Secretary of State Acheson, immediately agrees to sending a regimental combat team into the war zone.

Pace relays approval to Collins, who advises MacArthur on the still-open teleconference.[81] Within two hours, the Far East commander orders Lieutenant General Walton H. Walker, in command of the four-division Eighth Army, the U.S. occupation force in Japan, to ship his 24th Infantry Division to the port of Pusan, in Korea's far south. First a vanguard "stopping force" should be sent by air, MacArthur says.[82]

As the morning hours pass, military and civilian leaders in Washington are astonished to learn about the speed of this move to all-out war, without the seeming constitutional requirement of congressional approval.[83] But Matt Ridgway knows the shift toward decisive action probably began two days earlier, with the visit of another "five star," Dwight D. Eisenhower.

The supreme European commander in World War II, now leading the year-old North Atlantic Treaty Organization (NATO), Eisenhower was in Washington for a routine physical exam and met with Collins, Ridgway, and others at the Pentagon.

As army chief three years earlier, Eisenhower signed off on a Joint Chiefs memo dismissing Korea as of "little strategic interest." But now he chastised his former wartime subordinates for indecisiveness, "in most vigorous language," Ridgway noted in his diary. Eisenhower urged them to mobilize the U.S. armed forces and take the strictures off MacArthur in Korea.

After that lecture, Collins seemed simply to be waiting for MacArthur's report from the war front.

This afternoon, after a series of meetings, Truman's White House is-sues a terse statement reporting matter-of-factly that "General MacArthur has been authorized to use certain supporting ground units." Despite the low-key language, the significance of the news isn't missed. "U.S. SENDS GROUND TROOPS INTO KOREA," the *Washington Evening Star* announces in an afternoon headline.[84]

Matt Ridgway has worried about an "Armageddon," a clash of the atomic bomb–wielding capitalist and communist superpowers, ever since he was awakened last Sunday with news of the invasion. In its classified daily summary on Korea, the CIA dismisses the likelihood of Soviet in-volvement in Korea.[85] But it cannot know that Ambassador Shtykov in Pyongyang is preparing his "extremely urgent" cable to Moscow raising just that possibility.

The shadow of Armageddon remains. In his Wednesday diary entry, Ridgway also noted that Eisenhower told his former lieutenants "even to consider the use of one or two atomic bombs" in Korea.[86]

As rapid-fire decisions are made in Washington, some two hundred Americans in Suwon, South Korea, are preparing to evacuate farther south, to Taejon, seventy miles away, down muddy nighttime roads through driving rains. Along with the U.S. military advisory group and U.S. Embassy staff, they include the dozen officers of ADCOM, an ad-hoc Advanced Command sent from Tokyo late Tuesday under Brigadier General John H. Church.[87]

South Korean commanders remain with a few U.S. advisers in Su-won, a town that now becomes the site of one of the war's earliest mass atrocities, a bloodbath perpetrated by the South Korean national police.

Associated Press correspondent Okey King, who quickly returned to Korea after Tuesday's evacuation to Japan, reports being told by a police chief that sixty jail inmates, South Koreans suspected as "leftists," have been summarily shot and dumped into mass graves in Suwon.[88] But his report is only a glimpse of the carnage.

An American adviser left behind in Suwon, Major Donald Nichols, an air force intelligence officer, eventually discloses he has witnessed "the unforgettable massacre of approximately 1,800 at Suwon."[89]

South Korea has begun exterminating its own people, in a paroxysm of bloody ideological fervor, revenge, and the wartime fear that freed political prisoners will aid the advancing enemy.[90]

JULY

SATURDAY, JULY 1, 1950

Bill Shinn slips out of North Korean hands, only to face South Korean guns

Where have they gone?

Through the morning rain Bill Shinn sees the thatched-roof homes of Shinwon-ri looking abandoned. He finds his old Ford sitting outside the friend's house where he left Sally and the others yesterday. But the house is empty—no sign of them, no note.

Then his eye catches movement in the distance: three men on a hill beyond the village. They seem to be keeping watch. They're in uniform. Could they be North Koreans? Then, far across the rice paddies, along the main road from Seoul, he sees other soldiers filtering southward. He freezes. He has stumbled onto the enemy.

How could he have been so foolish? Why did he think his family would be safe if he took a day in Suwon to reconnect with his employer?

At first, anyway, he thought they'd be safe, when he set out yesterday to walk with long lines of refugees the fifteen miles south to Suwon, fearing that driving his Model A would draw too much attention. At the makeshift Suwon command post, he found his Associated Press boss, Okey King, and briefed him on details of his final hours in Seoul, enough for the American to write a dramatic story on the city's fall.

But Shinn grew more nervous as the day went on, as he heard the dire reports from the war front. Deeply worried, he left after dusk to trek back north and rescue his family, a small bag of clothing and essentials on his back. Fatigue finally forced him off the road to sleep in a barn through the small hours. And now he has arrived back in Shinwon-ri, too late.

Driving the Ford would be even more conspicuous now. He abandons it, tossing away his wallet full of incriminating items, such as his AP identification card, keeping only his South Korean driver's license, and walks to the main road. He finds northern soldiers everywhere and lines of refugees being turned back to Seoul under escort. He has no choice but to join them.

As the afternoon wanes, they reach a ferry crossing on the Han River's south bank. Frantic not to get trapped back in the city, he slips repeatedly to the rear of the waiting throng. Finally, he concocts a tale, telling a guard officer his weary, pregnant wife is resting among nearby houses and he must go find her. The soldier orders him sternly to return within twenty minutes. Shinn cautiously walks into the village as dusk descends.

Out of sight, finding a humble home on a back lane, he pounds on the wooden gate. An elderly white-haired woman opens it.

"I'm a refugee. Please let me stay the night," he pleads.

She considers. "All right, just for one night," she says. She explains that the rest of her family fled during a battle yesterday, but "even the communists will tolerate an old woman like me." She fixes him a meal of rice, barley, and kimchi, Korean fermented vegetable, and Shinn soon falls asleep.

Awaking Sunday morning, he is at a loss. He hopes Sally and the others somehow reached South Korean–held territory with other refugees on Friday. But how can he elude the northerners? All he can do is hunker down, wait for nightfall, and try to walk overland.

By midafternoon, the din of a full-scale battle has erupted around the village. Troops of the KPA 3rd Division who crossed the Han yesterday are clashing with rearguard units of the South Korean 2nd Division.[1] American warplanes streak overhead, hunting northern tanks and supply vehicles.

Shinn is now alone. Sometime during the day the old woman left the house and hasn't returned. The stutter of machine guns and the roar of explosions send him crouching into a corner. Then he hears soldiers in the small front yard. Suddenly, they're in the house. "Hands up!" a North Korean officer shouts, leveling his submachine gun at him.

The lieutenant hurriedly interrogates Shinn, studies the photo on his driver's license, angrily dismisses his stammered story of trying to return to Seoul.

"Where are you from?" he demands, detecting Shinn's accent, sign of a "traitor" from the North. He lies, saying he was born in the North but brought to Seoul as a child.

"Don't lie!" the officer yells.

Just then, urgent shouts call the soldiers back outside. The enemy is closing in.

Shinn collapses with relief. But a firefight now rages directly outside. Bullets pierce the earthen walls. Facedown, hands over his ears, he presses his body against the floor. He's resigned to die in this house.

The shooting lasts long minutes, and finally he hears, "Hurry! Hurry!" He dares to peer out through a hole in a paper window and sees northerners retreating toward the river, carrying wounded on their backs.

He hears a new shout, "Anyone in this house, come out! Or be ready to die!"

He looks: it's South Korean soldiers. Shinn emerges, his bag on his back, holding up his driver's license. The soldiers are nervous, wary.

"Show us a *taegukki*!" one demands—a South Korean flag. "I don't have a *taegukki*," he replies, and begins to tell them, rapid fire, about his work as a South Korean reporter for an American news agency.

"If he doesn't have a *taegukki*, shoot him!" another soldier shouts.

Shinn shouts back still louder about his importance in getting news to America and military help from America.

"Take me captive and take me to your commanders in Suwon!" he tells them. Impulsively, he jumps onto an army truck, deciding this is his safest way south.

He finds two trembling North Korean captives already in the truck bed. He quickly pulls a notebook and pencil from his bag and begins interviewing them. The mood changes instantly. The guards on the truck seem to accept that this brazen fellow must, indeed, be a reporter.

They drive through the night to Suwon, where Shinn talks his way into a jeep ride farther south from that threatened city, reaching Taejon around midnight. On Monday morning, he reunites with King and other journalists. He has yet another story to tell, but he has no word on the fate of his family.

A DAY IN EARLY JULY 1950

High school student Hurh Won-moo stumbles across a "people's court"

In the shadow of the fifteenth-century Namdaemun, Seoul's castle-like South Gate, three dozen people are gathered. A man, apparently a local communist, points to a terrified-looking policeman and denounces him as corrupt, a cruel exploiter of the poor. A North Korean army officer looks on approvingly. Seventeen-year-old Hurh Won-moo, passing by, stops. "What is this?" he wonders.

Someone in the crowd shouts, "Death to the accused!" Won-moo senses what's happening. The North Korean turns to the crowd.

"What is your verdict?" he asks. A startled silence follows, then some speak up. "Guilty." "Guilty!" Others begin to drift away.

Won-moo turns and hurries down the street. A shot rings out. The policeman has been summarily executed. Won-moo breaks into a run, headed for his family's small house in central Seoul, two blocks away.

He and his mother, a young widow, and his nineteen-year-old sister, sharing the three-bedroom home with two younger sisters and little brother, have been uncertain about what to do since the North Koreans seized Seoul last week.

They've heard that these "people's courts" have been playing out on city streets in recent days. Bills are being slapped up on walls across Seoul bearing Kim Il-sung's demand to "ruthlessly prosecute and liquidate reactionaries." The targets are ROK Army officers, judges, and prosecutors, who "shall unconditionally be put to death." Town, village, and neighborhood chiefs "are to be tried in the people's court."[2]

The Hurhs were never political, never connected with the government, not big landlords. But they have been relatively well-to-do businesspeople. Will they ultimately be targets? At the very least, since they hear the northerners are setting up conscription points around Seoul, they fear Won-moo may be forced into the northern army.

Both the Hurhs and the Eums, Won-moo's mother's family, long operated successful rice-milling businesses in farm country south of Seoul. But the world depression of the 1930s hit the Hurh family wealth hard, particularly because of Grandfather Hurh's speculative investments.

They moved to Seoul, where the boy's father, who studied two years at a Tokyo university, opened a store selling Japanese-made farm equipment, and the retired patriarch now made an avocation of educating his sweet-faced, first-born grandson.

Won-moo was a prize pupil. By age five, remarkably for one so young, the boy had learned to read a thousand Chinese characters, still important in Korean life. Grandfather Hurh also taught him the brush strokes of Chinese calligraphy. When he entered school, it was time to learn Japanese. He took to it immediately and began devouring Japanese novels and Western books in Japanese, novels by Mark Twain, Daniel Defoe, on up to Tolstoy and Goethe.

He was always "class leader," the boy with the highest grades, who would command classmates to rise and bow to entering teachers. He was the fifth grader who won a calligraphy contest at a Shinto shrine in the midst of World War II. The prescribed slogan he wrote large on rice paper: "Annihilate America and Britain!"

When his grandfather heard this, he frowned and shook his head. Like most Koreans, the Hurhs chafed under Japanese domination and cheered in August 1945 when they learned their country would be freed. But for young Won-moo, it was a time of tragedy and disillusionment, if also ultimately of success.

His father died of tuberculosis not long after the war, after which his uncle partnered with Mother at the store. Like the adults, the thirteen-year-old Won-moo could see that the division of his country by the Americans and Soviets was a blow to the hopes of all Koreans. At the same time, however, he achieved his father's dream for him, being admitted to Seoul's Kyonggi High School, Korea's finest. "I was one of the chosen few!"

He and his classmates were at the hilltop high school on June 26 when they heard explosions and saw black smoke rising from nearby government buildings being bombed by North Korean Yak aircraft. School was dismissed and students rushed home.

Now the North Korean–run Seoul Radio has announced that Kyonggi High School is reopening.

Won-moo, an industrious student beginning his final year in the six-year program, aspires to study at Seoul National University's law school. He wants to return to the classroom. But he is skeptical. He fears a trap and stays home and later learns that those who did report for class were immediately sent north for military training.

He feels no political allegiance to either side in Korea, but a deep resentment is building inside seventeen-year-old Hurh Won-moo for the North Korean invaders who have upset his life plans.

TUESDAY, JULY 4, 1950

Bill Shinn assures readers North Korea "will suffer defeat very soon"

General MacArthur's "stopping force," four hundred soldiers sent ahead from Japan by the 24th Infantry Division, landed in Korea on Saturday.

Today this battalion-size vanguard, dubbed Task Force Smith after its commander, Lieutenant Colonel Charles B. Smith, is headed toward a blocking position south of Suwon, to await the North Koreans.[3]

Back in Taejon, headquarters for the newborn U.S. command, Bill Shinn is putting together a personal report on the South Korean view of events for the Associated Press news wire, just days after his own close encounter with the invaders.[4]

The Korean journalist writes that his countrymen believe, "now that U.S. troops are in the field," the "North Korean army will suffer defeat very soon."

But when he recounts his own loss—his separation from his pregnant wife and little son, trapped behind North Korean lines—he betrays disappointment that this powerful ally had not better shielded South Korea. He had hoped "true friends" among Koreans "would be protected better by the Americans," he writes. He raises a common Korean complaint, that "Uncle Sam was a little slow-motioned" in supplying Syngman Rhee's army with heavy weapons. He's referring to Washington's decision in the late 1940s to deny the bellicose, threatening Rhee the means to start a war to reunify Korea's two halves.

At a moment when their country's survival rests in American hands, knowledgeable Koreans like Shinn remain ambivalent about the U.S. role in their recent history. They remember what Shinn considers American "duplicity," under President Theodore Roosevelt in 1905, in supporting Japan's takeover of Korea at the end of the Russo-Japanese War.

Shinn grew up under that harsh colonial rule, born Shin Wha-bong, a poor country boy with ambitions.

In his village near the Changjin reservoir in Korea's mountainous northeast, his father refused to allow him to go beyond primary school, but the determined teenager forged his father's signature and won a scholarship to a Presbyterian mission high school in the northern city of Hamhung. A top student, he went on to four years at Tokyo's Chuo University.

Back in Korea, he left the North for Seoul within days of Japan's World War II surrender. There his good English quickly won him favor with commanders of the U.S. occupation army, who made him assistant manager of Seoul's grand Chosun Hotel, their quarters. In that position, the poised young Korean, handsome and smiling, got to know rising Korean politicians as well.

With American officers' financial help and his Presbyterian connections, twenty-eight-year-old Bill Shinn was sent off in 1947 for graduate studies at church-affiliated Hastings College in Nebraska. Upon his return to Seoul, he landed the job with the U.S. news agency AP.

Shinn abhorred what he saw briefly of the communist ascendancy in Korea's North in 1945. But even more, like all Koreans, he resented the action of Washington and Moscow in dividing the peninsula without even consulting the Korean nation and then in failing to fulfill a commitment to reunify Korea by 1950.

Instead, year by year, he saw them fall into superpower bickering, the Soviets rejecting a role for Rhee and his rightists in a reunited Korea, the Americans banning the left in the South.

Now in this American Independence Day article, the troubled Korean journalist tries to sound an upbeat note, but finally observes bitterly, "It is really an unspeakable disaster—that brother should kill brother—but that's what we Koreans are doing now."

WEDNESDAY, JULY 5, 1950

MacArthur's "stopping force" is routed, as Mary Mercy
follows Korea's ordeal

It's pouring rain outside the Maryknoll convent north of New York City where Sister Mary Mercy sits, listening for the latest news from Korea and hoping for a go-ahead from her superiors to return.

"Everything is in abeyance," she writes brother Herb. Meantime, she tells him, she's organizing medicines for the planned clinic and will begin refreshing her Korean-language skills. After all, it has been a decade since she worked as a doctor among the poor people of Sinuiju, on the Yalu River in Korea's far north.

This middle-aged nun feels a strong attachment to a country so little known to other Americans. "Poor Korea is being crushed under this ordeal," she writes, as the news grows worse by the hour.

Tonight's *New York Times* says of Task Force Smith, the "stopping force" General MacArthur ordered to Korea from Japan, that it has been "isolated" by the invaders.[5] In reality, the 540-man task force has been routed by the North Koreans rolling southward down the road from Suwon. The Americans' 2.36-inch bazooka rockets bounced harmlessly off the armor of the T-34 tanks. The attackers inflicted heavy casualties on the Americans—some 180 dead and wounded—before Smith ordered a withdrawal. The defenders fell back in disarray, many abandoning their weapons.

On Friday in New York, against this background of bleak reports from Korea, the U.N. Security Council authorizes formation of an allied military force under U.S. command and the blue U.N. flag "to assist the Republic of Korea in defending itself." President Truman names General MacArthur commander.[6]

MONDAY, JULY 10, 1950

Shin Hyung-kyu comes home to find his father facing execution

After a two-day trek through the sweltering summer hills of southern-most Korea, Shin Hyung-kyu is home at last in Kochang. His mother needs him.

Police have thrown local men and women into a makeshift jail, and his father is among them. People say the prisoners will be executed as leftist sympathizers who might otherwise collaborate with the oncoming North Korean army.

His father taken away, his older brother, a college student, facing an unknown fate in Seoul, sixteen-year-old Hyung-kyu is suddenly the man of the house, with five younger brothers and sisters. The shocks and dis-locations of war have reached even into this family far from the fighting front.

Just a month earlier, Hyung-kyu saw a dream fulfilled, starting high school in Chinju, thirty-five miles to the south. He scored second in all South Kyongsang Province on the entrance exam.

In middle school, the precocious teenager devoured every high school science and math book he could find. His father, a tax office clerk, sold their rice and barley farm, in the family for generations, to pay for this second son's out-of-town education and boarding. Hyung-kyu envi-sioned a future as a scientist.

Then suddenly, leaving his boardinghouse in Chinju to begin the school week on Monday, June 26, he found students gathered around newspapers pasted up at street corners. His nation was at war. Mother soon got word to him that his father had been taken into custody. Now he has made it home, in the midst of a terrible family crisis.

Father once told Hyung-kyu of his flirtation with leftist politics, when he attended political meetings in December 1945, just months after U.S. Army occupation forces landed in southern Korea.

"People's Committees" had cropped up and asserted control in counties and towns across the newly liberated country, committees sometimes dominated by leftists seeking land redistribution, but sometimes also including landlords or Korean officials from the Japanese colonial regime. Workers' committees, meanwhile, took over some factories.

Of southern Korea's nine provinces, these committees were strongest in South Kyongsang.[7] In early 1946, peasants even blocked trucks of the U.S. military government from carting off rice routinely collected as a tax.[8] By then, Hyung-kyu's father had abandoned political activism, and by late 1946 the U.S. occupation authorities had disbanded the "communist" committees.

The collapse of the farm economy in the aftermath of World War II led to sporadic peasant uprisings, put down by police gunfire, sometimes with the help of U.S. occupation troops.[9]

In April 1948, the protests began on Cheju Island, followed by the authorities' ferocious crackdown there. On the mainland, in South Kyongsang's neighboring province of South Cholla, two regiments of the fledgling South Korean army mutinied rather than join the Cheju campaign. Their rebellion, during which they murdered police and local officials, was crushed by loyalist troops directed by U.S. military advisers. Surviving guerrillas then carried on sputtering hit-run operations in the far south.

After one guerrilla attack in Kochang, the boy Hyung-kyu witnessed an outdoor scene in which young right-wingers pointed out poor peasants to police as supposed leftist sympathizers, men and women who were then viciously beaten with rifle butts and clubs and taken away, never to be seen again.

Through all this turmoil, President Rhee's government, the post-occupation authority, packed tens of thousands of political prisoners into its jails. Many more suspected sympathizers were forced to join a new National Guidance League, supposedly a "reeducation" organization, but one whose membership rolls—more than three hundred thousand people by 1950—have now given the wartime government a target list for rounding up those it deems unreliable, such as Hyung-kyu's father. Those rolls include uneducated peasants duped into joining on the promise of rice rations, made by police chiefs needing to fill membership quotas.[10]

The young student, his distraught mother, and an uncle go to the "jailhouse," a collection of tents heavily guarded by police on the grounds of a government building in Kochang, a riverside town ringed by piney mountains.

The streets around the detention center teem with family members hoping for a glimpse or a word with men abruptly torn from their homes. In the heat of the afternoon, Hyung-kyu finally spots his father peering out from a tent. They shout to each other, unintelligibly. His mother weeps. The son has never seen this strong-willed woman shed tears this way.

Later, two truckloads of detainees are driven away. Someone shouts, "Police are taking them somewhere to be executed!" Wailing relatives run after the speeding trucks, one old woman collapsing in grief in the street.

Hyung-kyu, who just two weeks ago saw calculus class as his greatest challenge, feels helpless to save his thirty-eight-year-old father, a poor but respected local civil servant whose only "crime" was to sit in on some meetings long ago. The boy and his mother can do nothing but stand by, day after day, in the hope at least he'll see them there.

Meantime, the war moves closer. Leftist guerrillas are newly active, and the North Korean 4th Division is just seventy-five miles to the north, pushing toward a fateful clash with the newly arrived U.S. 24th Infantry Division at Taejon, after which the northerners are to take aim at the Kochang-Chinju area.[11]

SUNDAY, JULY 16, 1950

The girl Chang Sang hears the roar of B-29 bombers and cheers

There it is again. *Crump-crump-crump.*

The distant pounding can be heard across Seoul. From ten thousand feet up, forty-seven B-29 bombers of the U.S. Air Force, flown eight hundred miles from an air base in Okinawa, are unloading showers of five-hundred-pound bombs onto Seoul's main railyard, destroying rail-cars and the military supplies they hold, tearing up tracks, setting repair shops ablaze.[12]

The U.S. command, desperate to relieve the pressure on the 24th Division at Taejon, ninety miles to the south, is trying to cut off the streams of ammunition and other matériel feeding the advancing North Korean divisions.

The explosions can be heard in the house in Seoul's Sindang-dong district, where ten-year-old Chang Sang, her mother, Bong-hyun, and the rest of the extended Kim family huddle behind drawn curtains, as they have since the North Koreans marched into the southern capital eighteen days ago.

The U.S. bombing raids, steadily taking more and more civilian lives, are one reason to remain indoors. But Sang and her young cousins are told that the northern army the Kims fear so much can be defeated only with American help. In their hidden back courtyard, the children cheer when they hear the bombers overhead.

The northern soldiers are the other reason to venture only carefully into Sindang-dong's narrow lanes. Mother has warned Sang that when they must go outside, to buy food or for other pressing reasons, they must never speak. Their telltale northern accents would betray them. As northern Christian refugees, deserters from the cause of the "new Korea," they're vulnerable, and nervous.

By yesterday, July 15, people with bourgeois backgrounds were to have reported to the nearest police station to "confess."[13] Official Seoul Radio implies such "traitors" will face less harsh treatment than if discovered later. The radio is among the institutions now staffed by some of the thousands of communist functionaries who came south behind the Korean People's Army, in a meticulously planned takeover of power in conquered territory.

By now everyone has heard about the outdoor "people's courts" dispensing instant justice, executions of police, government officials, and other "reactionaries," death verdicts ordained by simple shouts from onlooking crowds of communist sympathizers, even children. Near the East Gate police station, not far from the Kims' home, some have seen the bodies of soldiers and police stacked up under rice-straw sacks.[14]

The occupiers seem to have put up posters of Kim Il-sung and Josef Stalin at every street corner, ordered every truck to fly the red-starred North Korean flag, and filled every workplace with a new regimen of lectures, even sessions learning songs of the new Korea, especially "The Song of General Kim Il-sung."[15]

The communists have quickly set up a ruling city People's Committee, headed by North Korea's justice minister, Lee Sun-yup, with subcommittees down to the block level. They promise Korea will be a nation of eight-hour workdays, of farmland taken from big landlords and given to peasant families, of equality for women.[16] The two occupation newspapers devote their front pages to speeches and messages from Kim and other communist leaders. On Seoul Radio the political talk never ends. Ordinary farmers and laborers are interviewed and extol the rosy future they foresee.[17]

Many Seoul residents who remain, resentful of being abandoned by Syngman Rhee's government and army, are cooperating with the new regime, hoping life will improve.[18] In fact, surveys in the late 1940s had found southerners overwhelmingly favorable toward socialism, a result of generations of subservience to Japanese colonialists and a landed Korean elite.[19]

In the giant, ramshackle Dongdaemun (East Gate) market, as elsewhere in Seoul, food is growing scarcer because of the upheaval of war. The price of rice is multiplying severalfold. Those working for the new regime have rations, but others are left on their own, to try to sell whatever they can—watches, clothing, household items—to buy rice, or at least some barley.[20]

The Kims have been left with enough Korean *won* to get by, but for how long?

As the bombs fall this mid-July Sunday, the North Koreans are preparing a decree ordering nearby provinces to assess how their food reserves might help city residents. The decree includes another, more ominous, provision: instructing Seoul occupation authorities to organize "the evacuation of 500,000 people from the city to rural locations and to industrial enterprises of North Korea"—a forced migration, to alleviate population pressure in Seoul and help man the wartime industries of the north.[21]

The communists are already pressuring doctors, nurses, engineers, and other skilled South Koreans to head north to help the war effort. Eventually, the entire staff of Seoul's electric company is forced to trek to Pyongyang, a fate Sang's uncle, company manager Kim Kap-hyun, escaped by fleeing Seoul within hours of the June 25 invasion.[22]

As she sits and ponders on the tatami mats of their crowded rooms, in the darkness of blacked-out Seoul, as American bombers hit more and more neighborhoods, as food becomes a daily concern and the northerners hunt down "traitors," Bong-hyun begins to think she and daughter Sang must find a safer place to wait out this war.

A DAY IN LATE JULY 1950

University student Ahn Kyong-hee and family find refuge in the southwest

Ahn Kyong-hee doesn't recognize the old man—she has never met him—but she and her mother, and younger brother and sister, are overjoyed at the sight of him. He's an uncle from Mother's side of the family, and their final day's difficult trek has brought them to his home in an isolated, wooded area of Korea's southwestern corner.

Twenty-year-old Kyong-hee and her family have been on the refugee road for almost a month. They're on the verge of collapse. In this village in the countryside of South Cholla Province, called Chung Paui Kol, Uncle's family opens their home to them, with first a filling meal and then a place and time to rest. The uncle also tries to lift their sunken spirits.

"Take heart," he says. "Nothing is really so bad as it seems." He recounts for them an old Korean fable about a villager whose fortunes swing continually between good and bad, and he relates it to their situation.

"Your father enjoyed a reputation under the Republic of Korea. For that reason, he's a marked man by the North Koreans. Your good fortune was but the beginning of a bad one. Now your bad fortune is but the beginning of a good one."

Kyong-hee can only hope so. Uncle knows the Ahns lived well in Seoul, where Kyong-hee's father was a well-known newspaper editor, the family owned a fine home, and Kyong-hee was a highly regarded student at Ewha, the women's university, one of the most prestigious in Korea.

The June 25 invasion changed that life overnight.

At first Kyong-hee, an attractive young woman who couldn't have been happier with her place in life, found it impossible to believe all could suddenly be taken away. But then it was decided the entire newspaper staff, including her father, must evacuate to Pusan, with no room to take their families. Then the four of them—without the elder of her two brothers, a ROK Army lieutenant—set out from Seoul to stay with Mother's relatives in South Cholla, more than two hundred miles away.

With ample money for food, shelter, and occasional transportation, they were luckier than many on the southbound roads, but their weeks of travel still proved harrowing. They stopped first at one home of relatives in South Cholla, but found it was unbearably overcrowded. Besides, word from travelers, that the North Korean army was drawing nearer, frightened them into leaving for the refuge farther south.

The North Korean force is the 6th Division. It split off on July 11 from the main northern attack down the peninsula's central corridor, and has been pushing down the west coast road network against essentially no resistance, except for lightly armed South Korean police. It seized the port of Kunsan in North Cholla Province and has now taken aim at Chonju, that province's capital.

Peasants from the rice-growing Chollas rallied to leftist causes before the war, and pro-northern guerrillas have now begun emerging to further harass the overwhelmed police. The violence is driving still more refugees before it. One guerrilla's diary entry, later captured, details the kind of terror taking hold these days in the southwest: "Apprehended 12 men; National Assembly members, police sergeants, and township leaders. Killed four of them at the scene, and the remaining eight were shot after investigation by the people's court."[23]

To Kyong-hee, this new refuge of theirs, Chung Paui Kol, among thickly forested hills thirty miles from the south coast, seems so remote that they surely will be safe. She's confident the war will pass them by.

SATURDAY, JULY 22, 1950

Buddy Wenzel and fellow 7th Cavalrymen land in Korea

As evening falls, Private Buddy Wenzel and the rest of the 2nd Battalion, 7th U.S. Cavalry Regiment, sit jammed side by side, M-1 rifles upright between the knees of their olive-drab fatigues, as they ride two-and-a-half-ton trucks to their overnight bivouac area outside the port of Pohang.

First the oppressive heat of southeastern Korea hit them, then the maddening insects. And now the stink of human excrement, mixed with ash to fertilize the rice paddies, greets them in the countryside.

"Many realized Japan was clean in comparison to this so called Korea," a junior officer primly notes in the regiment's official diary.

The young soldiers are happy at least to be on solid ground, after a sickening five-day crossing from Japan through a typhoon. The need for

1st Cavalry Division troops in Korea was so urgent that the Tokyo command's planners couldn't wait for smoother seas. Disasters are occurring daily. Two days ago, the North Koreans routed the U.S. 24th Infantry Division from Taejon.

The 25th Infantry Division was sent from Japan last week to bolster the faltering U.S.–South Korean lines. The 7th Cavalry, known as the "Garryowens," is now the last of the 1st Cavalry Division's three regiments to arrive. After anchoring off Pohang this afternoon, they were quickly ferried in from their troopship in small Higgins boats.

Wenzel, the nineteen-year-old who collects female pen pals from as many U.S. states as possible, is eager to see Korea, an entire new country. Besides, he tells himself, the brass say we're here for just a couple of weeks, to clean up a mess and then go home—to their easy occupation duty in Tokyo.

Beyond the hills to the west, however, American troops who preceded the 7th Cavalry from Japan to "clean up the mess" are in desperate fights for their lives.

A company from the 25th Infantry Division, almost surrounded by attacking North Koreans, have their backs against a swollen stream, and frantic young Americans are drowning in their panic to get across.[24] Southwest of there, North Korean tanks are attacking freshly dug-in troops of the 8th Cavalry, the Garryowens' sister regiment. It's the 1st Cavalry Division's baptism of fire in Korea, on the outskirts of the old crossroads town of Yongdong.[25]

After a night in bivouac, fighting off mosquitoes in their tents, Wenzel and his H Company comrades spend the morning readying themselves for movement to the front, rechecking and cleaning their weapons, stocking up on eight-round ammunition clips for their cartridge belts, water for the canteens, C rations.

But some rations are old, leftovers from the last war, and much else is obsolete or missing. The regiment is short on bazookas, mortar rounds, even binoculars and Korea maps. One other sign the division is unprepared: it has landed in Korea without fingerprint sets, personal-effects bags and mattress covers, the gear of a graves registration unit. It is unequipped to handle its own dead.

Later in the day, the 2nd Battalion's five companies load onto a train for a slow ride to the front, through a countryside of rice paddies steaming in the sun, of low earthen huts capped with thatch, and of silent, sullen people working their fields or pushing south, loaded down with belongings, along roads paralleling the tracks.

The 7th Cavalrymen are "curious and dubious as to what lay before them," the regimental diarist writes. Wenzel's buddy James Hodges spoke for many in his last letter home from Japan, telling his sister, "As for myself, I hate to go over there," adding, "I don't imagine I will be home on time."

Aboard the train, Wenzel's company commander, the crewcut Captain Mel Chandler, briefs his men, telling them, among other things, that disguised enemy soldiers may lurk among the Korean refugees.

The U.S. Air Force in early July reinforced its bomber units for the air campaign against North Korea. Dozens of giant B-29s of the Strategic Air Command island-hopped across the Pacific from the United States to Japan. On July 13, they bombed North Korea's eastern port city of Wonsan, targeting railyards and an oil refinery. The rapid deployment showed a "high degree of esprit, mobility and technical competence," boasted the air force chief of staff, General Hoyt Vandenberg.[26]

Alan Winnington has now come to Wonsan. Entering the city's north end, the British journalist, his driver, and his Chinese-speaking Korean escort are stunned at what they find.

In their bulky Russian sedan, at the end of a 120-mile journey across the peninsula from Pyongyang, they drive down streets lined with collapsed and burned houses and past desperate residents collecting what they can from the ruins.

In his first dispatch from Korea back to London's communist *Daily Worker*, the correspondent reports he is told more than a thousand homes and other buildings have been destroyed in Wonsan and 1,249 people killed, mostly women and children.

"The largest girls' school, the centre of the working-class district, and the primary school on the seashore were hit," he writes.

He speaks with a man named Wan whose wife and children were killed while he was at work. He tells Winnington life is no longer worth living, except "I would give my last drop of blood to get revenge and drive those murdering dogs from our country."[27]

The *Daily Worker* reporter reached Pyongyang a week ago after a three-day trip from his base in Peking, arriving on what he believes was the last daylight train from the Chinese border. He found a North Korean capital still carrying on, despite U.S. air raids that began June 29, attacks the northern government has condemned as "inhuman" in a protest letter to the United Nations.[28]

One bomb-damaged hotel remained operating, one that Winnington found less than commodious. A nearby bomb blast blew in his window's blackout blanket, forcing him to turn off his lights, leaving this journalist unable to type in the dark. Bedbugs and the heat then drove the lanky Englishman to sleep, naked and sweating, atop a sheet on the floor, surrounded by a ring of insecticide.

From Wonsan, Winnington returns to Pyongyang and sets out immediately for the South, to catch up with the advancing Korean People's Army and report from the front lines. Not far south of Pyongyang, he meets the war head-on.

He and his companions have hidden their car beneath roadside trees to eat a lunch of cold rice, when a U.S. P-51 Mustang fighter-bomber suddenly swoops in and opens fire along the road, crowded with foot-bound peasants. Winnington throws himself on the ground, deafened by the noise of the low-flying plane.

It's gone just as abruptly, leaving behind "screams, moans, babies' cries, calls for help, death, tears, blood, bereavement and life disfigurement," Winnington reports.

The next day brings a kind of revenge. Their sedan has the road to itself just after dawn, approaching the 38th Parallel, when up ahead another Mustang streaks in. As they brake, tumbling from the car and into a rice paddy, they hear a huge explosion. The pilot has lost control and slammed into a hillside.

After waiting for the plane's ordnance to stop exploding, they approach and find the American's body hurled from the cockpit. Papers from his pockets are strewn about. Winnington finds photographs of a woman with two small children and a letter from his wife, urging him not to take risks, to think of them.

Ri In-mo has arrived in Pyongyang after an overnight truck ride from Hungnam on the east coast. He cannot get his bearings. Too many landmarks have vanished in the repeated U.S. bombing.

Sirens suddenly sound. Ri follows others running to a basement shelter. After some minutes, they hear the blasts and feel the tremors from a new American attack. Some explosions seem frighteningly close.

When the all-clear sounds and they climb back into the daylight, Ri sees through the smoke and dust that bombs have leveled buildings on a nearby street. Fire and rescue teams rush here and there, but people otherwise simply resume going about their business.

He has been summoned to the North Korean capital by the party's Central Committee, told to report to the army's cultural department. It seems they have a wartime assignment in mind.

For the past month, Ri continued his work as propaganda chief for the Workers' Party branch in Hungnam. It was a difficult time for the seaport city, important for its chemical and other industries. It was struck repeatedly by U.S. Air Force bombers and by attack planes flying off the U.S. aircraft carrier *Valley Forge* and the British carrier *Triumph*, cruising offshore.[29]

Ri's mother wept on hearing of the deaths of Hungnam civilians in destroyed homes. "They are not human beings," she said to her son, speaking of the Americans.

When the time came yesterday for Ri to leave for Pyongyang, his mother stood stoically in the doorway watching him go, fighting back tears.

His wife was not so controlled. She promised the night before not to cry when he left, but as he sat in the entrance hall putting on his shoes, she couldn't help herself. She stood there sobbing, clutching their two-year-old girl in her arms.

At the outer gate, he turned to her. "If I don't return, you mustn't remain a widow," he told her. "You must marry some kind-hearted man." He was thinking of his mother's hard life from age eighteen, when she became a widow and a new mother in the same year.

Now he has reached the offices of the People's Army cultural department, in charge of party propaganda in the military ranks. He learns that an old party comrade has recommended him for a job, as a frontline correspondent for North Korea's Central News Agency, assigned to the 6th Division, advancing down South Korea's west coast.

SUNDAY, JULY 23, 1950

Americans order Park Sun-yong's family and other
villagers to evacuate

White cumulus clouds tower above the mountains of central South Korea, threatening thunderstorms later today. But the villagers of Chugok-ri already hear distant rumbling, to the northwest beyond Yongdong town. The North Koreans' 3rd Division, having driven the Americans from Taejon on Thursday, have begun their artillery and tank attack on U.S. 1st Cavalry Division troops defending Yongdong.[30]

At midday a jeep drives up to Chugok-ri, two hundred yards off the main Seoul-Pusan road. A U.S. Army officer jumps out and through an interpreter tells villagers they must evacuate. They'll soon be in the midst of battle.

A near panic takes hold. Parents shout for their children, villagers collect squealing pigs and chickens and tie them to their oxcarts, families gather up what they might need: bags of barley and rice, extra clothing, sleeping quilts, cooking utensils.

Park Sun-yong's husband, Eun-yong, places keepsakes in a leather box and buries it beneath a shed at the Chung family home. The trove includes a prized photograph of their firstborn, Koo-pil, in a traditional gaily colored costume for his first-birthday party three years ago.

Some five hundred people trek to the readiest refuge, the village of Imke, lying a mile deeper into their side valley. Once there, they find shelter where they can, the Chungs claiming space in a shed housing a small millstone.

As rain falls and they try to sleep, Sun-yong tells her husband she thinks the family should head farther south. They have heard frightening stories from refugees of brutality by the northerners, including against policemen, Eun-yong's old job.

In the morning, Eun-yong raises this possibility with his father, who objects that the children shouldn't undertake such an arduous journey in the July heat. He tells Eun-yong he alone should go, that the North Koreans won't harm women, children, and old people.

The twenty-six-year-old law student is torn, but when Sun-yong tells him she agrees with her father-in-law, Eun-yong decides he must go. His mother quickly prepares a small backpack of food and clothing, and he soon strides off toward the main road.

The displaced Chugok-ri villagers and their Imke-ri neighbors pass another day and sleepless night listening to the approaching sounds of war. Sun-yong sees crisscrossing red streaks in the northwest sky and worries. Her home village, Shimchon, lies in that direction.

Around dusk on Tuesday, a U.S. Army truck bumps up the rough track to Imke-ri, and a dozen soldiers jump down. They shout that everyone should assemble, to be led "to a more secure area."

Park Sun-yong is relieved. She sees the Americans as saviors. She and her in-laws gather up their bags and cooking gear. She will lead four-year-old Koo-pil by the hand. Her mother-in-law will wrap two-year-old Koo-hee to her back.

Some Imke-ri villagers, in particular, are reluctant to leave for the unknown. The Americans grow angry, dragging people from their homes, pushing them along, as a column of several hundred descends the valley back toward the main road.

Nearing Chugok-ri, they first smell smoke. Then they see the flames. Soldiers are setting the thatch-roofed homes ablaze with their cigarette lighters. Across the war front, the Americans have adopted "scorched-earth" tactics as they retreat, trying to deny the enemy any shelter or material support.

At the sight of their homes in flames, shocked villagers halt or stumble in their steps. Some begin wailing in despair. Most fall into a stunned silence. So this is war? The soldiers, growing harsher in their commands, push them on.

Southbound on the main road, which turns east at this point, they walk through the moonlit night for a mile, until the Americans bring them to a halt and start ordering and pushing them off the road. They're told to spend the night on a dry gravel streambed. Families begin unrolling bedding to try to sleep—it's after midnight—but it's impossible. The night is filled with explosions and gunfire, with trucks speeding down the packed-earth road, churning up dust. Sun-yong, holding Koo-hee and Koo-pil close, is terrified.

The North Koreans have taken Yongdong, five miles to the west of the refugee villagers, and 1st Cavalry Division troops are in retreat.[31]

American commanders, meanwhile, are sowing dangerous confusion over handling civilians at the front. Orders have been issued to evacuate civilians southward, but leaflets also have been dropped telling people to head north, away from the Americans. Other instructions insist people stay put. These newly arrived commanders are wary, hearing rumors that North Korean soldiers are infiltrating U.S. lines disguised as refugees. Eighth Army, overall U.S. command, is preparing an order to stop all refugee movements.[32]

But just two days earlier, 24th Infantry Division troops reported searching almost all refugees crossing their lines and finding no signs of infiltrators.[33]

—∞—

In the darkness barely a mile east of the frightened villagers, Buddy Wenzel and the rest of the 2nd Battalion are in disarray and fumbling their way toward the rear.

After arriving by train from Pohang, the 7th Cavalry Regiment troops took up a hillside position overlooking the main road east of Yongdong, covering the retreat of the 8th and 5th Cavalry Regiments from that town. Now an order to pull back, to readjust defense lines, has somehow been misinterpreted by inexperienced officers as an indication the North Koreans have broken through on their right flank. The rumor has spread, and fearful men are streaming down the pitch-black hillside, losing sight of their sergeants and officers, stumbling, losing weapons, sometimes throwing them away.

In fact, the North Koreans are not attacking. Instead, they have taken up positions on the eastern edge of Yongdong, expecting an American counterattack.[34] Occasional gunfire exchanges the men hear are "friendly fire."

On the roadway, H Company's Captain Chandler begins organizing men and sending them up onto the parallel railroad tracks. He leads some three hundred rearward toward new positions, on ridges on both sides of the main road and tracks and overlooking a concrete railroad trestle near the tiny village of Nogun-ri.

Meanwhile, far to the rear in the southern city of Taegu, Eighth Army staff officers have met with U.S. Embassy and South Korean officials to discuss the problem of refugee columns interfering with military traffic and the perceived threat of enemy infiltrators among the white-clad civilians.

An Eighth Army order goes out to all units saying, "No repeat no refugees will be permitted to cross battle lines at any time." It goes on to describe a tightly controlled, ultimately unworkable process for permitted civilian evacuation.

John Muccio, the U.S. ambassador, writes confidentially to the State Department in Washington that Eighth Army has also decided to fire on refugee groups that approach U.S. lines despite warning shots. He is alerting the department to this, he says, "in view of the possibility of repercussions in the United States from the effectuation of these decisions."[35]

WEDNESDAY, JULY 26, 1950

Fleeing war, Park Sun-yong meets unimaginable terror and tragedy

After a sleepless, nerve-racking night, as the sun rises at 6:30 a.m., the stranded refugees of Chugok-ri and Imke-ri begin slowly to get to their feet.

Looking around, they find their American guards have vanished. The roadway is quiet, empty of trucks. The frightening sounds of combat have subsided. Then, one by one, they discover victims of a violent, chaotic overnight—seven of their number shot dead by the Americans, apparently when they wandered off in the darkness to relieve themselves. Two are children.[36] Their families collapse, screaming in disbelief.

Faced with these horrors, a buzz of talk builds among the hundreds of uprooted villagers. Some announce they're returning to their homes. But most decide they'll be safer farther south. Family by family, they climb back to the road and resume the trek. The early-morning heat points to a grueling day, with ninety-degree temperatures.

The Chung family group numbers a dozen, half of them children. Park Sun-yong's mother-in-law still carries two-year-old Koo-hee on her back. Sun-yong takes four-year-old Koo-pil by the hand.

They push on eastward, toward where the road will turn south again. Two miles farther along, the column is stopped by American soldiers, who tell the refugees to clear the road and move up an embankment to the parallel railroad tracks.

On the tracks, soldiers wade in among them, ordering all bags emptied. They confiscate kitchen knives, scythes, all sharp implements. The villagers' pleas to keep these essentials are ignored.

They see many other soldiers in their green uniforms popping in and out of holes on the surrounding hills. As families settle down atop the tracks for lunch, they see a light plane circling overhead. Some see a nearby soldier with a handset, talking on a radio. Not long after, they're alarmed at the piercing sound of soldiers' whistles. What does it mean?

Suddenly, a whine from over the southern horizon grows to a roar. They look up. American planes are dropping toward them.

In the flash of a moment, their world is ripped apart. Deafening explosions rock the ground beneath them. They're enveloped in a darkness of falling earth and rock, dust and gravel and smoke, and of bits of bushes, of bags, of white clothing, and of people and parts of people. Again and again, bombs are dropped or rockets fired into the midst of the shrieking refugees strung out along the railroad embankment. Whole families are being blown to pieces. Frenzied people run, crawl, not knowing where to turn, as the planes wheel about and drop more bombs. Children scream for their mothers. One young man, hugging the ground, feels something heavy fall on his back—the head of a baby. Through the smoke, survivors see hellish scenes, of the tracks strewn with dead and dying people. And now bullets are raining down on them from the hillsides. Dug-in troops of the 7th U.S. Cavalry Regiment have opened fire.

Amid the thunder and terror, Park Sun-yong, mad with fear and desperation, looks around for the others. She sees the family cow, its head gone, a geyser of blood spurting from its neck. But she can't see her family through the smoke and her tears.

She sees people running, some staggering, back down toward the road. Some are falling, struck by bullets. She follows.

Stunned villagers are heading for what looks like a shelter, one of two cavernous twin underpasses beneath a concrete railroad bridge. A small stream flows slowly through the other underpass. The largely dry streambed in the first serves as a pathway from the main road to the village of Nogun-ri, three hundred yards away.

Sun-yong sees quickly this is no shelter. Its entrance is littered with bodies of people killed in fusillades from the hillsides. Tripping over the dead, she enters a bedlam beneath the bridge. The young mother's horror, for a brief moment, gives way to relief: her two children are safe inside, unharmed, with her in-laws.

The sights and sounds are infernal beneath the forty-foot-high archway. Infants cling to unconscious or dead mothers. Frantic parents cry out their lost children's names. Family groups push and shove atop the sandy floor to get to the safest spots, away from the road.

"I couldn't get my senses back. You couldn't even raise your head," Sun-yong is to recall.

Why are the Americans killing us? the terrified villagers ask themselves. What have we done? We're not communists.

In her confusion in those first minutes, Sun-yong thought the planes were dropping bombs to destroy the railroad. But just yesterday a colonel at the U.S. Air Force command center in Taegu reported to his commander that American warplanes, at the U.S. Army's request, were attacking refugee groups approaching U.S. front lines, for fear of North Korean infiltrators. In that memo, classified "Secret," the colonel, Turner Rogers, recommended the practice be halted, to avoid "embarrassment to the U.S. Air Force and the U.S. government." But indiscriminate attacks on refugees go on.[37]

The right side of Sun-yong's *hanbok* top is soaked red with blood. A piece of shrapnel tore into her arm on the railroad embankment. Now, during a lull in the firing, the trapped refugees are stunned to see two American medics approach and start bandaging some wounded, including Sun-yong. When other soldiers appear just outside the tunnel, a Chung cousin who knows some English, a university student, speaks with them and then returns, saying they've told him they're under orders to shoot.

"Now we're all dead," the young man says. Those who hear are paralyzed with fear.

Periodic gunfire erupts through the afternoon. Tracer bullets from machine guns ricochet red through the tunnels. Explosions, apparently mortar rounds, rock the bridge. The gunfire is coming from both ends of the underpasses, sending the terror-stricken Koreans rushing from one side to the other, crawling over bodies. Each time, fewer and fewer move.

Hours pass. It's suffocatingly hot inside, and their thirst is overwhelming. Little Koo-hee cannot stop crying from hunger and thirst, her face turning red. Her grandmother suddenly picks up the two-year-old and, inexplicably, walks outside.

Gunfire rings out. The grandmother staggers back in, splattered with blood. She crumples to the tunnel floor, wounded in the shoulder and buttocks. She tells them a bullet pierced Koo-hee's neck and she had to leave the child outside, dead. Sun-yong reels in crazed, sobbing grief.

In their foxholes on the barren hillsides, men of the 2nd Battalion, 7th Cavalry, are in disbelief at what they are doing. Their field training in Japan, the Hollywood war movies, the recruiting sergeants never prepared them for this.

"Word came through the line, open fire on them," Buddy Wenzel later recalls. "They were running toward us and we opened fire." Over in G Company, rifleman Joe Jackman hears his company commander behind the trench line shouting, "Kill 'em all!" Jackman opens fire. He also hears the screams from the Koreans at the concrete trestle below.

"Jesus Christ, what the hell are we into?" he asks himself.

Not everybody fires.

Delos Flint of F Company was too far forward and was caught in the initial air attack. With refugee families seeking safety, he fled to a low, narrow culvert under the tracks. Escaping from there during a lull and returning to his position, he's told by his sergeant to fire on the Koreans. He refuses. "It was civilians just trying to hide" is how he'll remember them.

The officers have received Eighth Army's order of today that "movement of all Koreans in groups will cease immediately." And Ambassador Muccio is informing the State Department this means the army will shoot refugee groups approaching its lines.

The laws and customs of war make targeting noncombatants a war crime, but this lethal attitude toward ordinary Koreans has been building for days in the hard-pressed U.S. command. On Monday, 1st Cavalry Division headquarters, through a liaison officer, instructed the 8th Cavalry Regiment that "no refugees to cross the front line. Fire everyone trying to cross lines."[38] Later today, troops of the 25th Infantry Division, deployed east of the 7th Cavalry Regiment, are told by the division command that civilians in the war zone "will be considered as unfriendly and shot."[39]

Fast-spreading rumors of infiltrators among refugees have taken charge, as has racism.

Journalists with U.S. units tell of the troops' growing hatred for the "gooks."[40] In one directive to his staff, Major General Hobart R. Gay, commander of the 1st Cavalry Division, refers to South Korean refugees as "trash" that "clutter up the roads."[41] He has dismissively ordered Korean national police out of his operations area.[42] Today he tells reporters at his Kimchon headquarters, fifteen miles to the rear, that he believes most of the white-clad people on the roads are North Korean guerrillas.[43]

Wenzel, the high school dropout who had to care for two sisters at home in New Jersey, never saw himself as a killer. But when he spotted in his M-1 sights a little girl running down the tracks, "I think I shot her."

THURSDAY, JULY 27, 1950

In his own little convoy, Alan Winnington heads for the war front

For a morning in wartime, it's peaceful as the three-jeep convoy crosses the Han River and drives south away from Seoul. Village women are out early along the streams, slapping laundry on the smooth rocks. Peasants by the roadside wave and then gape at the surprising sight of a tall Englishman rolling by.

Alan Winnington has experienced enough already to know it's unwise to drive in daylight in Korea, especially in three closely bunched vehicles kicking up a dust storm. But on this very first day, he couldn't argue with his Korean escorts, who are treating the southern excursion as a lark.

Two days ago, at the North Korean army headquarters in Seoul, officers dragooned an English-speaking man named Choi Tai-ryong to deal with the newly arrived British journalist. They knew Winnington was important, the man who could get to the front and get out the real story of the KPA's victories to the Western world.

Choi, a southern communist and longtime political prisoner, had been told he would be put in charge of southern industry under the occupation. But "Comrade Choi really has no industry to manage at present," one of the officers pointed out. He became the Englishman's translator.

Choi then recruited an old cellmate, Pak Bong-min, as an organizer for their little group. They were given the three vehicles, rations, and an army captain and eight soldiers as escorts.

Now they've reached a point a few miles south of the capital. Someone is singing "Arirang," the Korean folk song. "Many stars in the clear sky . . . many dreams in our heart."

Suddenly, they see women ahead dropping their bundles, running. They look up. An American P-51 has materialized from somewhere. They slam on their brakes and roll out of their jeeps, crawling for cover. The Mustang opens fire, roars past, and is gone.

Climbing back to the road, they survey the damage: one jeep wrecked by the big .50-caliber bullets and one terrified soldier who broke his leg and will have to be escorted back to Seoul by a comrade. They're down to two vehicles and seven KPA men and a consensus decision to travel henceforth only after the sun goes down.

FRIDAY, JULY 28, 1950

Park Sun-yong tries to escape with her boy from the hell of Nogun-ri

Horrific scenes of suffering have unfolded minute by minute through the long hours since the slaughter began at midday Wednesday under the Nogun-ri railroad bridge.

Machine-gun fire ricocheting around the concrete walls, potshots from M-1 rifles when the Americans hear noise or spot movement among the trapped refugees, a return of strafing warplanes attacking them—all have left more and more of the Koreans, mostly women, children, and old men, dead or dying.

Some of the dwindling number still alive are losing their senses, muttering a loved one's name endlessly over and over, mumbling gibberish. One pregnant woman, tortured with multiple wounds, begged her nine-year-old daughter to strangle her with her cloth belt, but in the end simply faded away.

Those with the strength have piled up bodies at the tunnel entrances as a shield against the gunfire. Children burrow beneath the dead to hide from the bullets. The heat, hunger, and thirst are overwhelming. A trickle of stream water flowing through the underpass has grown viscous with blood. Their throats parched, some drink from it anyway.

Park Sun-yong is no longer among them. It's past midnight, and the twenty-three-year-old mother is in the darkness and undergrowth hundreds of yards from the bridge, trying to escape and save her surviving child.

Last evening in the underpass, she prayed for guidance. She has clung to her Bible throughout. "Though I walk through the valley of the shadow of death, I will fear no evil, for thou art with me." The words of the psalm echoed in her mind.

Poor little Koo-hee is dead, but I must save Koo-pil, she decided. Her wounded, hobbled mother-in-law told her, "Go, go!"

Sun-yong awakened the Chung family's houseboy, a fifteen-year-old named Hong-ki, and told him to accompany her, to carry four-year-old

Koo-pil on his back. They slipped out the Nogun-ri side of the tunnel and slowly, laboriously crept away from the bridge, seeking the thickest vegetation, freezing when searchlights swept the area. It took them hours to move just a few hundred yards in the direction of Hwanggan, the next town on the way south.

Now they've reached a point where she feels they can risk walking through concealing brush. They carefully push on in the darkness, now up a slope with Sun-yong in the lead, in her clumsy *hanbok* skirt.

Suddenly, machine-gun fire erupts, the gun's barrel flashing from a nearby rise. They hear the hiss of bullets around them, over their heads. They drop to the ground. "*Umma! Umma!*" Koo-pil cries out.

She sees the houseboy running back down the hill. Then she looks more closely at the abandoned Koo-pil. His right leg has been torn by a bullet. He's crying in pain. Distraught, she wraps him in her arms to try to comfort him. Then, with her teeth, she rips off a strip of cloth from the hem of her skirt and ties it around the wound. Feeling utterly helpless, she looks to the heavens. "What have we done to deserve this?" she silently asks.

As they lie on the hillside, the skies begin to lighten. The boy cries that he's hungry. He cries for his "*Appa*," Eun-yong. She tells him that's where they're going, to see his father, and she starts up the slope again, with Koo-pil on her back.

Almost immediately, in the dim light of dawn, she spots through the mist the form of an American soldier, standing under a pine tree. He raises his rifle in their direction. She's petrified, speechless. She finally screams, "*Jebal! Ssoji ma! Jebal!*" (Please! Don't shoot! Please!)

She feels like she's hit with a sledgehammer, just as she hears the crack of his M-1. She's on the ground, with an unbearable, burning pain in her side, barely conscious. She looks around: Koo-pil is on his back, motionless, blood spreading from his chest. The bullet that passed through her side struck him in the heart as she carried him.

"Koo-pil, my little boy! Oh, please, wake up!" she pleads. "My little boy!"

She leans back to lie beside him on the grass, to die. She closes her eyes and begins to recite the Lord's Prayer, as the blood pours from her wounded torso.

Then she hears someone approaching. She opens her eyes. Two soldiers stand over her. One leans down, checks the boy's eyes, his pulse. He's dead. But they see she's still breathing. The other soldier pulls out a first-aid kit and applies antiseptic and bandaging to her wounds, in her right arm and side. She hears other soldiers arrive, and then she hears shoveling. They've wrapped the boy's body in a white cloth. They place him in a shallow grave, shoveling the dirt back over him.

Soldiers arrive with a stretcher. They carry Sun-yong to the nearby road and load the stretcher onto a jeep. It drives off. As she's borne toward the unknown, the now-childless mother prays to her Lord to take her, too.

In the torrid, rainy Korean summer, the northern invasion force remains disjointed, with poor coordination and communications and with simple orders for each division to push south as best it can. Despite these handicaps, the 3rd and 4th Divisions of the Korean People's Army took Taejon from the Americans. Major General Yu Song-chol, chief of operations, has moved with the KPA headquarters to a secluded Buddhist temple near that strategically situated city.

The weeklong battle proved relatively easy for the North Koreans.[44] After two disastrous weeks of war in Korea, the ill-prepared U.S. 24th Infantry Division was bloodied, depleted, and demoralized. Barely four thousand of its eleven thousand troops could be mustered for Taejon's defense.

The KPA exploited gaps in the thin U.S. lines, crossing the moatlike barrier of the Kum River and flanking the city and its defenders from the southwest. As the Americans retreated southward from the hopeless situation on July 20, they often met North Korean roadblocks to their rear, where more were killed, captured, or scattered.

Of the two fresh U.S. divisions in Korea, the 25th Infantry is deployed in the east, reinforcing South Korean units struggling to hold back the North Koreans moving down the coast and eastern valleys, and the 1st Cavalry is in the center, along the main Pusan-to-Seoul road and railroad. After resting and reprovisioning, the KPA's 3rd Division on Tuesday routed the 1st Cavalry's 8th Cavalry Regiment from Yongdong, twenty-five miles southeast of Taejon.

As other North Korean units sweep unopposed down the western corridor of the peninsula, American intelligence reports strike an alarming note. "The invaders are massing all available manpower and equipment along the entire front in what may be their supreme effort to drive the UN forces into the sea before US reinforcements can arrive," warns a daily CIA report.[45] An expanded North Korean force now has nine divisions in the offensive, against four ROK and three U.S. divisions.[46]

On this night, Yu Song-chol is inspecting one of those KPA reinforcement operations, in a party led by Kang Kon, the army chief of staff. The thirty-two-year-old Kang, a head taller than other officers, a young general whose self-importance sometimes grates on older colleagues, is nonetheless respected for his professional, hands-on approach to directing the campaign.

Traveling in the darkness to avoid American warplanes, they've inspected one unit and its plans for crossing the Kum River to join the battle farther south. Their jeep convoy is driving along the riverside to another unit. Yu's mind wanders as he gazes at the peaceful waters of the Kum, in a place where men were fighting and dying only days ago.

Suddenly, an explosion shatters the calm, and Yu sees Kang's jeep, just ahead, flung upward and to the roadside. It has hit an enemy land mine laid before the Taejon retreat. Yu and others leap from their jeeps to help but find Chief of Staff Kang has been killed instantly.

A grim General Yu accompanies the body back to headquarters. He must quickly subdue his shock and consider what must be done. News of the overall commander's death would demoralize the army right down to the lowest ranks. It would encourage the enemy. He decides to report what happened only secretly to Pyongyang, after committing the witnesses to silence.

Kang Kon's death won't be announced for weeks. Meanwhile, Kim Il-sung quietly promotes Yu Song-chol to lieutenant general and names him acting chief of staff, as the victorious KPA takes aim at liberating the major southern cities of Taegu and Pusan, driving the enemy "into the sea."

But the thirty-three-year-old Yu has grown uneasy at the prospect of battling the world's mightiest military, with its countless warplanes, artillery pieces, warships, and industrial might.

On the day Taejon fell, the American president went on U.S. radio and television to rally the American people behind the looming fight. "This challenge has been presented squarely. We must meet it squarely," Harry Truman declared.[47]

For the moment, however, the U.S. Army is falling back before the onslaught, and the retreating army is venting its frustrations, fears, and hate in a deadly way, on any and all Koreans, an estimated 380,000 of whom—South Korean refugees—have been moving south with the American and South Korean troops.[48]

Some journalists hint at the extent of atrocity. "Troops do not know who are their friends and enemies, and increasingly regard all as enemies. Some innocent people inevitably get killed," *The Times* of London reports. "Every mile of road behind the front gives evidence of this human tragedy."[49]

The North Korean radio is more graphic: "The human slaughterers have been perpetrating atrocity murders of patriotic people—tearing them to death, cutting out the breasts of innocent girls, dragging patriots to death." It likens American actions to the crimes of Hitler. And it ascribes them to racism, "following in the footsteps of the Ku Klux Klan."[50]

SATURDAY, JULY 29, 1950

Leaving behind Nogun-ri's carnage, Buddy Wenzel's
7th Cavalrymen face their own

Sporadic North Korean artillery and mortar fire breaks the early-morning stillness. But all is quiet at the Nogun-ri bridge, among the mounds of bodies. At three thirty the order comes: The 7th Cavalry Regiment must pull back. The American retreat is resuming.

Some 2nd Battalion men climb up and over the railroad embankment, getting their first close look in the darkness at the white-clad victims strewn over the tracks and stacked at the tunnel entrances. A few soldiers stop and fire off a final clip of their M-1s into the underpass. They then move on, to encounters with a real enemy. Whatever their officers note in the record about the massacre is to be lost to history, when the 7th Cavalry log vanishes, inexplicably, from military archives.[51]

Later in the day, the first North Korean troops approach Nogun-ri on the road from Yongdong. Amid the shocking carnage at the bridge, the human remains of two villages, they find a handful of survivors, mostly children hiding among the heaps of bodies. A North Korean journalist traveling with the KPA's 3rd Division views the "indescribably gruesome scenes."

"Shrubs and weeds in the area and a creek running through the tunnels were drenched in blood, and the area was covered with two or three layers of bodies. About 400 bodies of old and young people and children covered the scene, so that it was difficult to walk around without stepping on corpses," journalist Chun Wook reports to his newspaper, *Cho Sun In Min Bo*.[52]

The 7th Cavalry's two battalions withdraw eastward, through a narrow valley of terraced rice paddies swollen from recent rains. Red, white, and green flares illuminate the predawn. Buddy Wenzel is sure the North Koreans are tracking them. After sunrise, the regiment digs in to a new defensive line east of Hwanggan, under increasingly accurate enemy artillery and mortar fire, beginning to inflict casualties.

Around four in the morning Sunday, North Korean tanks appear and attack. The entire 1st Cavalry Division front line is under fire, in an hours-long standoff that ends only when clearing weather allows U.S. jets to find and strike the advancing North Korean columns, knocking out T-34 tanks, forcing the attackers to withdraw.[53]

The 7th Cavalrymen have begun to accept the bloodshed around them, but Buddy Wenzel is still shocked at the paralyzing sight of a medic's head blown off by a heavy round as he rushes to help wounded men. Less than two weeks from their easy life as parade-ground soldiers in Tokyo, these crewcut teenagers are seeing their barracks buddies carried off on bloody stretchers. Wenzel's turn is coming.

Just after midnight, the regiment withdraws again, three miles farther east to where the road turns south again. Then, before dawn, heavy mortar fire suddenly falls on the 2nd Battalion's hastily dug positions. One round detonates within feet of Wenzel, slamming him to the ground. Dizzy and disoriented as he slowly regains consciousness, he feels excruciating pain in his right hand. He looks. It's swollen "as big as a football." Shrapnel has torn into it. Another piece has ripped a gash right across his helmet. Without his two-pound steel "hard hat," he would be dead.

He finds a medic who treats and bandages the hand and tags him for transport back to the division field hospital, a jeep ride over Autumn Wind Pass, where the entire regiment is soon to retreat.

On Sunday, General Walker, Eighth Army commander, visited the front and declared that "everyone must fight to the death without any thought of withdrawal."[54] His bold "stand or die" declaration quickly gives way to reality, however, as American forces are soon withdrawn across the

Naktong River to establish a final defense line, the "Pusan Perimeter," in the peninsula's southeast quadrant. Elements of desperately needed U.S. reinforcements—from the 2nd Infantry Division, the 1st Marine Division and the 5th Regimental Combat Team—are already landing in Korea.[55]

As the 7th Cavalry Regiment troops departed Nogun-ri, Park Sun-yong lay in a military field hospital eighteen miles to the southeast, at the 1st Cavalry Division's rear headquarters in the small city of Kimchon.

She is still there, drifting in and out of consciousness. At one point she sees a U.S. Army doctor standing over her, checking her heavily bandaged wounds. The American bullet tore away much flesh, but damaged no major organs. The wounds in her right arm and side, sewn closed by the doctors, aren't life-threatening, but remain painful.

She is confused and lost. She has a horrible dream of the mass death around the trestle. Are her children truly dead? Why? Where is her husband?

Her husband, the intense law student Eun-yong, has been closer than she can imagine.

When she was brought to the hospital on Friday, Eun-yong had been in Kimchon for three days, having paused there on his trek south, staying in a relative's house, in hopes of spotting his family among the refugees pouring through the city. He spent hours, day and night, scanning the faces along the main road and at the railroad station, all in vain.

His desperation turned to dread two days ago after a boy shouted from the crowd on the road, "Uncle!" It was a nephew, looking filthy and frightened, traveling not with his family but with other boys.

The boy told him a confusing story about having escaped from a mass killing of "the people of the village" by the Americans.

Eun-yong was stunned. "They came to save us, but they're killing us?" he asked himself in disbelief. "Why?"

He then pressed the stammering boy about Sun-yong and the children. "Are they okay?"

"Yes . . . safe," the tearful nephew replied.

That night Eun-yong couldn't sleep. And then on Friday, from dawn until evening, he frantically, futilely checked every group of passing refugees.

The refugee columns were thinning. At the railroad station it was announced the last train was leaving. He knew he had no choice but to go, to find his brother, now in Taegu. Otherwise, as a captive of the North Koreans, or a victim of their executioners, he could never help his family.

He left, but it was not the last train. The Americans will not withdraw from Kimchon for four more days. Beforehand, they load their hospital patients onto another train. Sun-yong is taken beyond Taegu, to Pusan. And as they pull out, the 1st Cavalry Division troops set Kimchon ablaze, as they had Chugok-ri and other South Korean towns and villages on their retreat.[56]

A LATE JULY MORNING, 1950

No Kum-sok and Chung Dong-kyu witness the bombing of Chongjin

Just past dawn, cadet No Kum-sok is on sentry duty on a mountaintop, just uphill from the cave that now houses his second-year class of North Korea's Naval Academy. The cadets moved there, on the northern outskirts of Chongjin, after an American air attack destroyed the academy buildings in the port city.

Around six thirty he spots the silvery glints flying low up the coast, wave after wave of U.S. Air Force B-29 SuperFortresses. They begin at the city's southern edge, dropping five-hundred-pound bombs methodically in a line, "carpet bombing," destroying everything below. Then the next wave sweeps in, stitching bombs along the next line farther north.

From his lofty perch, No watches in horror, hears the whistles of the diving bombs, sees the flash and smoke, hears the endless explosions. The ground beneath him trembles, and the eighteen-year-old cadet is shaking uncontrollably, terrified.

The bombers move closer, and he drops his rifle and tumbles into a foxhole. At the last minute, they turn away from his seemingly empty mountain, to strike targets now farther and farther away. Soon, it ends.

The teenager who told his father as a boy he wanted to be a Japanese kamikaze pilot has never before witnessed the ferocity of American airpower. He has watched much of a city disintegrate under a rain of American bombs and realizes what horror the people of Tokyo and Berlin must have endured in the last war. And what of all those poor people down below, he wonders, staring at the smoldering remnants of Chongjin.

Chung Dong-kyu is down below, headed for the smoke and flames of central Chongjin. He and other students of the Chongjin Medical School bounce down the main road in a convoy of open trucks, hastily organized as a first-aid corps responding to the devastating bombing.

They drive as far as they can into the city. Rubble blocks the roads. The young men and women, given first-aid kits of bandages, antiseptics, injectable morphine, and other items, are divided into teams of four or five and sent in every direction, wearing Red Cross armbands. The need must be great, Chung thinks, if the authorities are calling on untested medical students. He quickly sees the need is overwhelming.

He first comes across a young woman crushed between two concrete slabs, her left arm neatly severed, her mouth agape, her dead eyes wide open, cast upward, with a look of shock and surprise. The young student freezes at the sight of his first war casualty. His heart sinks. "I hope she died instantly," he tells himself.

Fanning out, the students see through the dust and smoke that hundreds of civilians lie dead or grievously wounded across the landscape of ruins. Many are legless or armless. Disemboweled intestines or shredded chunks of flesh lie beside bodies. Dust-covered heads or limbs protrude from among piles of brick and plaster and wood.

In a kind of daze, Chung and the others rush to wherever they hear screaming or sobbing. Other victims are found sitting silently in shock. They help some by cleaning, sterilizing, and bandaging wounds. But in many cases, all they can do is administer a morphine shot to trapped victims, while impromptu groups of local rescuers try to dig them out.

For hours the students dispense first aid as best they can, using rudimentary knowledge and skills learned in the classroom and clinics. At sunset city officials suspend the effort for the night.

As the students are driven back to the school, Chung can see that in this city of one hundred thousand people, the extent of the destruction means countless injured will surely die before being pulled from the rubble. He has come face-to-face with the stunning cruelty of war. He feels a hatred building inside him for those who make it.

Half a world away, the U.S. Joint Chiefs of Staff inform General MacArthur in Tokyo they are sending him two more medium-bomber groups, almost two hundred planes. It is "highly desirable to undertake mass air operations against North Korea," the Pentagon chiefs say. It is the beginning of a U.S. Air Force campaign that, in the months and years to come, levels cities and towns throughout the northern half of the peninsula.[57]

As a major port and iron and steel center, Chongjin offered obvious industrial targets for this day's bombardiers. But the carpet bombing of this, the Americans' northernmost target city, has obliterated residential areas, schools, markets, and other nonmilitary targets. Other raids follow, and the air force eventually estimates two-thirds of Chongjin is destroyed.[58]

The Joint Chiefs also send another, even more ominous, message to MacArthur. It informs the Far East commander that the air force will fly nonnuclear components for atomic bombs to the Pacific island of Guam for storage. They add, "Shipment of nuclear components, requiring 72 hours, plus Presidential decision authorizing use would be necessary before atomic bombs could be employed."[59] MacArthur has proposed to the Pentagon chiefs that nuclear weapons be dropped on North Korea.[60]

<hr />

The people around Chung Paui Kol village heard it from refugees trickling past: the North Koreans are coming. Now the KPA has arrived in their area of the far south, and Ahn Kyong-hee, privileged daughter of a prominent South Korean, is worried.

The soldiers in mustard-colored uniforms, passing through in small groups, are elements of the northerners' 6th Division, which has pushed down the peninsula in a looping maneuver along the west coast, advancing some twenty miles a day, largely unhindered and undetected by U.S. military intelligence.

The division will soon strike eastward, taking aim at the southernmost forces among the retreating Americans and South Koreans and then, beyond, the port of Pusan. Its commander tells his troops this "means the final battle to cut off the windpipe of the enemy."

But the 6th Division, like the rest of the KPA, is ill-prepared for a decisive battle. It is short on ammunition, food, and other essentials. Its supply lines are open to U.S. air attack on the long journey from North Korea. Rations have been cut in half.[61] Passing troops are "requisitioning" food from local people in Chung Paui Kol.

Some soldiers left behind to occupy and secure the area begin to lecture villagers, delivering rote recitations on the benefits of the coming socialist state, promises to "liberate you from the yoke of capitalism," predictions that the entire South will be liberated within days.

The refugee Kyong-hee, twenty-year-old university student, member of a well-to-do family from Seoul, is inwardly dismissive of the northerners' claims. But she knows the best thing for her to do, with her mother and younger brother and sister, is to avoid the soldiers and blend in with Uncle's family, which is sheltering them. That includes wearing the long *hanbok* skirt and short jacket of village women and working in the rice paddies and soybean fields.

One hot afternoon, Kyong-hee leaves the house to join Mother and a neighbor woman tending to a nearby bean field. Making her way through some brush, she's suddenly startled and gasps at the sight of a gaunt face, an American face, staring up at her from the undergrowth. Then she realizes three American soldiers are lying hidden among the shrubs, looking skeletal, starved, in ragged uniforms. They have somehow become separated from their unit, are lost, and must be moving only at night. They have no weapons, except for a large stick one carries.

At first they seem frightened at being discovered. But one quickly holds out a canteen. "Water," he mutters in a weak voice. Kyong-hee, with barely a thought, hurries back to the house. She returns with a bowl of water and a plate of boiled sweet potatoes.

The ravenous soldiers devour the potatoes and pour the water into their canteens. "Thank you, thank you," they keep repeating. One then asks, pointing off to the east, "Taegu? Taegu?" To their amazement, this young woman in peasant dress—in reality a well-educated city girl—replies in English, describing the best path east and warning them about northern soldiers in the area. The young Americans set off quickly, one turning back to look at her in seeming disbelief, waving good-bye.

Before they've gone far, a shriek breaks the silence. Mother and the neighbor woman have come upon the scene and spotted two North Korean soldiers rushing up a path toward the Americans. They're upon them instantly, gesturing with their rifles for them to raise their hands.

Seeing how angry and tense the northerners seem, Kyong-hee is sure they're about to shoot their captives. But when one stalks away to investigate a sound in the bushes—a small animal, Kyong-hee thinks—the

American with the heavy stick swings it down in a flash, clubbing the other Korean in the head. He goes down, and the Americans sprint away, disappearing into the thick bush.

The first soldier, back on the path, summons help, but a belated search for the Americans proves fruitless. The soldier on the ground remains motionless throughout. He's dead. He is carried off on a stretcher. By now a crowd of villagers has gathered, Kyong-hee has retreated to Uncle's house, and whispers spread that the young refugee woman from Seoul was somehow involved.

A DAY IN LATE JULY 1950

Alan Winnington discovers the mass killing of thousands and signs of a U.S. role

Alan Winnington has walked into the midst of a nightmarish vision. He proceeds slowly down a slender solid path between long pits of loose earth. Waxy, putrefying hands, legs, skulls protrude through the surface. A stench of death sinks deep into his throat.

After their harrowing trip south from Seoul, dodging American pilots' bullets, the British journalist and his Korean escorts have arrived in the area of Taejon, a city in smoky ruins and still under daily U.S. bombardment as a crossroads for North Korean supply lines.

He has heard reports of "a very big slaughter" outside the city. Now he has been taken to the valley of Sannae and the village of Rang Wul, five miles southeast of Taejon.

Villagers there tell him South Korean police made them dig the pits in the first days of July and again in mid-July before the North Koreans captured Taejon. The police brought prisoners to the site by the truckload, laid them down along the edge of the trenches, and shot them in the head, then tipping the bodies over into the mass graves.

The villagers, who were then ordered to cover the dead and dying with the thin layers of soil, estimate seven thousand men and women were killed—South Korean leftists, supposed sympathizers, some simply hapless minor criminals.

The executioners used U.S.-supplied M-1 rifles and carbines and U.S. ammunition. American officers, riding up in jeeps, stood by during the carnage, the villagers say. They say the trucks were American and sometimes driven by American soldiers.

As he walks the narrow path down the valley, Winnington peers into fissures in the rain-washed earth, seeing unidentifiable messes of rotting flesh, heads blown open by bullets, wrists bound with wire. He paces out the six pits, which measure from thirty yards to two hundred yards in length. He takes photographs. He collects U.S. cartridge cases. He picks up empty cigarette packs, Lucky Strikes, where he's told the Americans stood.

The group finally retreats, wordless and stunned. Winnington sees his escort Pak Bong-min sitting with a local woman whose son's remains lie somewhere in the valley. Both are weeping. Comrade Choi then informs Winnington that Pak's wife was among the political prisoners in the Taejon prison, and now—he nods toward the mass graves.

Winnington files a report back to the communist *Daily Worker* in London, via Seoul, Pyongyang, and Peking. It runs in the August 9 edition under a banner headline: "U.S. BELSON IN KOREA." "Americans drove women to pits of death."

He writes that the thousands of political prisoners were "horribly butchered" by South Korean police "under the supervision of American officers." He likens the scene to the Nazi death camps of Belsen and Buchenwald in the war ended five years ago.[62]

The U.S. Embassy in London quickly denounces Winnington's published report as an "atrocity fabrication."[63] In Washington Secretary of State Acheson cables U.S. Ambassador Muccio in Korea, asking for a "categorical denial if possible," something Muccio draws out of the Rhee government.[64] But U.S. officers know Winnington's report is true.

An American major at the scene of the mass slaughter took a series of eighteen macabre photographs of the killing process, photos that Lieutenant Colonel Bob Edwards, army attaché with the U.S. Embassy in Korea, sends on to the Eighth Army and Tokyo commands and to army intelligence at the Pentagon. There they are classified "Secret" and hidden away.

In an accompanying memo, Edwards writes he believes "thousands of political prisoners were executed within few weeks after fall of Seoul to prevent their possible release by advancing enemy troops." He concludes that "orders for execution undoubtedly came from top level as they were not confined to towns in front line areas."

As long ago as early July, the CIA and U.S. Army intelligence in Washington circulated classified memos tersely mentioning reports of mass political executions in Taejon and Suwon, though saying nothing about the U.S. presence or about U.S. oversight. A captured North Korean army document, translated and distributed within the U.S. command in mid-August, tells of more than eleven thousand prisoners killed by the southerners in twelve cities.[65]

That vastly undercounts the toll. In his *Daily Worker* article, Winnington writes confidently that between two and four hundred thousand have been killed. Official investigators eventually estimate the number executed by the Rhee government in the war's early weeks at one to three hundred thousand.[66]

As soon as the war began, "orders were given for the systematic physical annihilation of all political prisoners then in Syngman Rhee's jails," Winnington writes. The prewar prisoner ranks were expanded after the war broke out with the roundup of members of the National Guidance League, the "reeducation" organization designed to keep track of supposed leftist sympathizers in the South. The extent of the American role and responsibility for the mass executions is to remain unclear.

On this muggy, hot day in central South Korea, having collected his notes, photos, and evidence of the U.S. presence at Rang Wul, Winnington and his escorts return to a large abandoned house two miles from bombed-out Taejon, the home of a rich landlord who has fled south. Camouflaging and hiding their two jeeps, they hope this rural refuge will keep them safe from marauding aircraft. The sweet scent of peaches and nectarines wafts from the absentee owner's orchard. But it's the reek of death that Alan Winnington tastes in his mouth for days to come.

AUGUST

TUESDAY, AUGUST 1, 1950

Teenager Shin Hyung-kyu flees across the countryside

Every time they hear the roar of American planes, sixteen-year-old Shin Hyung-kyu and his uncle throw themselves into the nearest brush, with the terrified hope it will hide their white clothing. So far, they have survived. Many have not.

Four days ago, when he tearfully separated from his mother outside Kochang, as his father languished in detention, the boy told her to make sure she and his younger brothers and sisters wear traditional white, so the pilots can see they're civilians, not North Korean soldiers.

How naive, Hyung-kyu now thinks. The planes strafe everybody. He has seen the victims along the route he and Uncle have traveled in southernmost Korea, trying to stay ahead of the invading army.

As Colonel Rogers reported in his July 25 memo, the U.S. Army asked that American pilots attack refugee columns headed south.[1] Some pilots, in classified after-mission reports, say their airborne controllers are telling them to attack "people in white."[2] Just today, sixty villagers have been killed in a U.S. air attack on hundreds sheltering on a riverbank to escape fighting at Jojang-ri, near Chinju, the city where high schooler Hyung-kyu began his trek home to Kochang last month.[3]

At least Mother and his five younger brothers and sisters are safer in their shelter south of Kochang than on the roads, Hyung-kyu thinks.

For his mother, the decision to leave Kochang and her imprisoned, seemingly doomed husband was wrenching. Husband and wife, in the Korean way, never showed affection in front of their children, but the boy knew they were devoted to each other, having struggled to bring up their large brood—nine children—through almost twenty difficult years of marriage.

She was from a well-to-do family and was married to this poor young man, Hyung-kyu's father, when a matchmaker's words misled her parents to equate a distinguished family background with money. The best he would manage was the low-paying local government post he still holds. Her vegetable garden and ingenuity helped put food on the table when money or their small farm's rice and barley harvests fell short.

The children grew up adoring her, her good humor, her storytelling. Hyung-kyu became especially attached, always thinking of her as a small woman walking a mile to their farm with a load balanced on her head, meals for the harvest crew, and a baby on her back.

Four days ago, the day came when war broke up the family.

Every day, the mother and teenaged son had stood vigil outside the temporary detention camp where the police had crammed Kochang's supposed "leftists," including her husband, awaiting inevitable execution. They hoped, futilely, to at least speak with him. But now the war had come to Kochang's doorstep.

They could hear machine-gun fire outside town. The North Korean 4th Division, after helping rout the U.S. 24th Division from Taejon, sped unimpeded down into South Kyongsang Province, where the American division's battered 34th Infantry Regiment hastily put up a ragged defense.[4]

Now Hyung-kyu's heartbroken mother finally gave up, for the sake of the children's safety, including the one on the way. She was seven months pregnant. They must flee.

They packed all they could carry, including food, and joined the southbound lines of refugees. Older children carried younger siblings on their backs. Father's brother, Hyung-kyu's uncle, accompanied them.

Mother led them to an abandoned mine she knew, a seemingly safe haven. But Uncle told her Hyung-kyu must get farther away, because the North Koreans were impressing teenagers into their army. Uncle would take him to his home, twenty miles farther south.

After a long, anxious discussion, she relented. The survival of an elder son guarantees the future of a Korean family, and the fate of her eldest, the Seoul college student, remained unknown.

Uncle and nephew set out around two that afternoon, after tearful farewells. His mother stood by the roadside, waving both hands, watching Hyung-kyu disappear around a curve, as the boy walked backward, stumbling, to make his final look last.

Now, four days later, Hyung-kyu and his uncle face a more perilous journey than they imagined.

By the second day on the refugee route, they learned from others that Kochang had fallen to the northerners. Then uncle and nephew were turned back by South Korean military police on the road to Sanchong, Uncle's hometown. The North Koreans had overrun that town, too, they were told.

Hyung-kyu and his uncle could only turn east toward Pusan, eighty miles away, the far southern port city that has become an overcrowded magnet to masses of refugees.

At times the advancing invasion army overtakes the pair, its tanks pushing down the roads as they and other refugees hide on the hillsides and trek overland along rice-paddy dikes, over country trails, seeking out grassy, protected spots to spend the night.

American jets streak in regularly, strafing and bombing. Hyung-kyu sees the bodies or freshly dug graves along the roadsides, not only of strafing victims, but also of the elderly and infirm who don't survive the punishing journey, in ninety-degree heat, often short on food.

Death comes not only from the air. Many miles to the north of Hyung-kyu and his uncle, along the Naktong River, the natural barrier behind which the Americans are laying their Pusan Perimeter defenses, U.S. Army engineers blow up two large bridges as throngs of refugees cross. Hundreds perish, mostly women and children, deaths that go unrecorded in U.S. military reports.[5] Other uprooted Koreans try wading across the shallow stream, but an army colonel orders, "Shoot all refugees coming across river."[6] Dug-in machine gunners comply. Countless bodies are seen floating downriver.

It will take two more wretched weeks of flight across the peninsula to reach Pusan, where the boy and his uncle have relatives, somewhere in a city made teeming, nervous, and chaotic from war.

WEDNESDAY, AUGUST 2, 1950

Sailing for Korea, Clarence Adams assures his mother,
"Don't be concerned"

On a sparkling cool day in Puget Sound, the troopship USS *General Mitchell* sails from Tacoma Harbor, carrying hundreds of tank crewmen, military police, signal corpsmen, and other support troops of the 2nd Infantry Division, bound for Korea.[7]

Down in the stacks of berths, in the quarters for "colored" troops, Clarence Adams is settling in for the trans-Pacific voyage to war.

In a final call home to Memphis from Fort Lewis, the twenty-one-year-old private first class was reassuring. "Momma, I'm going to Korea to fight the North Koreans, but don't be concerned about me," he said. If anyone survives, "that'll be me," he told his mother.

A transient soldier headed for discharge, he was caught in the Korean emergency, his enlistment extended for a year. His status now is that of an unassigned replacement, awaiting a job within the 2nd Division. After almost three years serving in the army's segregated black units, he'll remain in uniform, bossed by white officers, barred from white mess halls, viewed as a second-class soldier, and kept from his dream of making it as a professional boxer. Meantime, he's going to war.

Adams and the rest of the men aboard the *General Mitchell* will be among the last in the division to steam into Pusan Harbor. The advance infantry battalions began arriving in mid-July and are now headed for the front line to reinforce the 24th, 25th, and 1st Cavalry Divisions, the hard-pressed troops falling back into the Pusan Perimeter.

The Americans hold the western front of that defense line, stretching eighty-five miles north to south, mostly along the Naktong River. South Korean divisions hold the northern front, running sixty miles east to the Sea of Japan.

The defenders badly need reinforcement. Since the war began, the Americans have suffered six thousand casualties, almost two thousand of them dead, and the South Koreans an appalling seventy thousand dead, wounded, or missing. But the North Koreans are estimated to have sustained similar losses and have lost all but about 40 of their 150 T-34 tanks, crucial spearheads of the invasion.[8] The battles to come will be decisive.

SATURDAY, AUGUST 5, 1950

At the Naktong front, Alan Winnington tells of American "blunders," but harbors doubts

The Korean People's Army's 4th Division, the victors of Taejon, are digging in on the west bank of the Naktong River, preparing for final battles to push the Americans into the sea. "This giant is hollow," one confident commander tells the comrade from Britain.

Alan Winnington, with his interpreter Choi and KPA escorts, has made his way to the front lines, driving at night through the stultifying heat of the Korean midsummer, avoiding the daylight American air attacks. In a dispatch back to London, he tells his *Daily Worker* readers why the Americans and South Koreans "are losing."

For one thing, they're opposed by "the whole of the people of Korea," Winnington writes. And they've committed "grave military blunders."

He quotes one ranking officer saying the Americans' "helpless reliance on machines, plus their fear of the people, keeps them on or near the highways." That enabled the attackers to encircle them repeatedly, and then "they can do nothing but hold up their hands and surrender."[9]

Winnington spends several overnight hours on a hillside observing, under the moonlight, the KPA supply chain at work. He sees an oxcart loaded with mortar shells being guided by four civilian men over rough spots along a path and then a procession of white-clad people carrying food supplies southward. They're both northerners and southerners. He quotes one as saying the KPA's advances protect the peasants' own advances under land reform. "From the moment that dusk falls until the sun drives the shadows off the road, the whole countryside starts to move North and South," he reports.[10]

For all the upbeat reporting, however, Winnington senses that the North Koreans have overextended themselves.

He and his entourage are put up in a comfortable abandoned house in the rear, listening to the rumble of artillery on the Taegu front. Choi looks forward to the city's imminent fall. Winnington, for the moment, confides to himself his worries that the thin, long, vulnerable line of supplies and reinforcements cannot sustain this offensive much longer.

American intelligence determines the vaunted 4th Division has been depleted to seven thousand men, from eleven thousand, and its three dozen artillery pieces have dwindled to six.[11] Meanwhile, more American troops are landing, building the defenses.

⚬⚬⚬

The incident of the lost American soldiers who got away has made the village of Chung Paui Kol a target of suspicion. North Korean troops go out of their way to visit the isolated place, to confiscate food and other goods, to deliver political lectures and warnings against failing to cooperate with the occupation authorities.

One young village man named To-ri, uneducated but full of self-importance, has made Ahn Kyong-hee a special target. He has allied himself with "the Cause" of the northerners, joining their Democratic Youth League, the *Minchong*; advising them on the backgrounds of various villagers; and idling much of the time around the refugee Ahn family's haven, the home of Kyong-hee's mother's relatives.

To-ri clearly wants to gain favor with this pretty young woman. But one day he tries a harsher approach, shouting from the front gate for the "female comrade." When Kyong-hee appears, he startles her. "I hear that you gave food and water to some American soldiers the other day," he says. "Is that true?"

Kyong-hee tries to remain composed. "Yes," she says. "Is there anything wrong in giving starving men something to eat?"

To-ri raises his voice, accuses her of a crime deserving of a "people's trial." He says her fate now rests in his hands. Then he softens, saying he'll give her a chance, he'll help her, he'll file a harmless report on her. He leaves with a smile.

More visits follow, when To-ri makes "inspections" of the house, at times walking away with some small thing the Ahns brought on their trek south. Sometimes he is accompanied by one or another of two other men, a stern northern army officer named Nam Ki-tae and a younger man named Han Muk, a civilian who Kyong-hee assumes is a member of a northern security service.

They question her and her mother about their background, getting vague answers disguising the fact that Kyong-hee's father is a leading South Korean editor now taking refuge in Pusan, that Kyong-hee is a university student, and that the family was socially prominent in Seoul. The men seem just as interested, however, in simply spending time, in the midst of war, with an attractive, mysterious young woman.

Han Muk, in particular, begins stopping by alone on seeming social visits, to chat, winning over Kyong-hee's mother with his easy charm and helpfulness on living with the occupation. The daughter warns her not to be too trusting. After all, she says, he's a communist.

MONDAY, AUGUST 7, 1950

Ri In-mo encounters the American "morons"

After long nights traveling the roads to the south, Ri In-mo finally reached his assigned KPA 6th Division at the Chinju front, fifty miles west of Pusan. The newly appointed war correspondent is making it a priority to report on the "new society" forming in the rear.

Among burned villages, rotting animal carcasses, and bomb craters, South Korea's peasants still labor in the rice paddies of the far south, weeding and fertilizing in wet green fields under the baking summer sun.

In his reports back to North Korea's Central News Agency, Ri says longtime tenant farmers are grateful for the acreage they've been given as their own, seized from landlords under the occupiers' land reform. It's "the most important undertaking carried out in the liberated area," Ri writes.

But the northerners are taking a cautious initial approach here in the peninsula's agricultural heartland. For one thing, landlords are not being expropriated unless they hold more than twenty *chongbo* (fifty acres) of land, as opposed to a five-*chongbo* ceiling under the 1946 land reform in North Korea.[12]

Ri's upbeat reports are what's expected of a Workers' Party loyalist. But others are more frank in their assessments.

The Soviet ambassador in Pyongyang, Terenti Shtykov, reports in a cable to Moscow that food shortages have become "the most burning issue" in occupied areas. "There turned out to be no food reserves in the south," he notes.

Meanwhile, American air raids on northern cities are having "a serious effect on the morale of the Korea people," Shtykov reports, and many Koreans fear they cannot hold out against the Americans "without the armed assistance of the Soviet Union and China."[13]

In the South, the North Koreans call American pilots *mojori*, "morons," for their propensity to attack civilians and to miss well-camouflaged KPA units.[14] But in a ground operation that kicks off on this day, the war's first major U.S. counterattack, American airpower makes the difference.

In the morning fog, a joint U.S. Army–Marine task force—troops of the 25th Infantry Division and the newly arrived 5th Regimental Combat Team and 5th Marine Regiment—move out from the Pusan Perimeter against Ri's 6th Division, which by chance is launching its own offensive, an effort to puncture a hole in the perimeter.

The two forces collide among the thousand-foot hills east of Chinju, just inland from Korea's south coast, touching off days of fighting. Hilltop positions are lost, regained, then lost again. In hundred-degree-plus temperatures, heat prostration fells as many combatants as does enemy fire.

The North Koreans are stopped repeatedly by Marine Corsair fighter-bombers, strafing and rocketing the KPA ranks as they try to drive U.S. defenders from their hilltops. The battle ends in stalemate, but the Americans have blunted a dangerous North Korean thrust toward Pusan.[15]

Ri In-mo, meanwhile, encounters the enemy airpower himself one day as he leaves 6th Division headquarters. As he walks toward a bridge over the Nam River, a formation of planes sweeps in, targeting the span. He sprints into a field where he finds a discarded iron cauldron, big enough for the tall, lanky Ri to pull over him as a shield.

Earth-shaking blasts destroy the bridge, and the planes fly off. Ri tips back his iron shelter, to find he has been blackened, head to toe, by soot shaken loose by the reverberations.

Sitting by the riverside, washing himself and his clothes, and seeing nearby homes aflame from the attack, Ri In-mo is seized with a sudden deep hatred for the Yankees, the *mojori*.

TUESDAY, AUGUST 8, 1950
The "brilliant" General MacArthur wins over
Matt Ridgway on his bold plan

Matt Ridgway hasn't seen his old boss for many years, and he's impressed.

Three decades ago, young Captain Ridgway was posted to the U.S. Military Academy faculty under Brigadier General Douglas A. MacArthur, the World War I hero who was then West Point superintendent. There above the Hudson River the junior officer learned to appreciate MacArthur's intelligence and military acumen and to endure his outsize ego and haughtiness.[16]

The Joint Chiefs have sent Ridgway to Tokyo with a fellow lieutenant general, the air force's Lauris A. Norstad, to assess the Korea situation, the Far East commander's needs, and his bold plan for winning the war—by striking behind enemy lines with an amphibious landing, just as his forces did many times on the way to victory in the Pacific five years ago.[17]

The two are now settled in MacArthur's wood-paneled office, spacious but spare, on the sixth floor of his headquarters, former home of the Dai-Ichi insurance company, a squat modern building facing the imposing moats and outer walls of Emperor Hirohito's Imperial Palace.

From a green-upholstered swivel chair, over two and a half hours, MacArthur lays out the strategic situation, his requirements, his ambitious plans.[18]

He tells his visitors the North Koreans have fielded as tough an army as he has ever faced, but they must soon reach their limits in manpower, equipment, and supplies. He says a decisive blow must be struck before the brutal Korean winter sets in and before the Chinese or Soviets intervene on the northerners' side. He describes the elaborate blueprint for a landing at Inchon, west of Seoul, to trap the northern forces in a pincer between a U.S. amphibious corps and Eighth Army forces breaking out of the Pusan Perimeter to the south.

Ridgway finds it a "brilliant exposition." But he has another reason to be receptive to swift action. He spent Monday in Korea, inspecting Eighth Army operations, and has grown increasingly worried.

Even with the arrival last week of the 2nd Infantry Division and Marines from the U.S. West Coast, and the 5th Regimental Combat Team from Hawaii, the U.S.–South Korean defense line can be only thinly held, with units covering fronts extending three or four times wider than normal. Most of the defense consists of scattered hilltop outposts along the Naktong River, with reserve units in the rear to rush to any emergency.[19]

Just hours before Ridgway, Norstad, and their staffs landed in Taegu, and just thirty miles southwest of that Eighth Army headquarters city, the North Koreans made their first major crossing of the Naktong, penetrating a two-mile gap between dug-in companies of the 24th Infantry Division. It set off bloody battles that are to rage on, up and down the perimeter, for weeks to come.

Now, back in MacArthur's hushed office in Tokyo, Ridgway is impressed with the eloquent old warrior's persuasive arguments.

Like many at the Pentagon, Ridgway has been troubled by the Far East commander's demands for ever more troops, from an army vastly diminished from its World War II size and stretched to cope with missions at home and in Europe, in the midst of the tense Cold War face-off with the Soviet Union. Moreover, the Pentagon generals and admirals believe MacArthur's plan for an Inchon landing may be overly risky. The navy, in particular, is concerned, because the tidal dynamics around Inchon are treacherous. Suddenly falling tides might ground assault vessels on vast mud flats.

But the powerful case laid out by MacArthur for the urgent need and feasibility of the Inchon plan wins over his visitors. "My own doubts were largely dissolved," Ridgway later writes. On the flight home, he and Norstad agree they will advocate on MacArthur's behalf for his requested reinforcements and for the Inchon plan.[20]

Two days after Ridgway's delegation departs for Washington, South Korean military police truck two to three hundred prisoners, including women and a girl twelve to thirteen years old, to the lip of a mountain canyon north of Taegu, line them up in groups, and shoot them in the head, their bodies falling into the ravine. The mass slaughter of suspected leftists is continuing across South Korea.

Passing American MPs happen upon the scene and file a detailed report up the chain of command. It says the Korean soldiers showed "extreme cruelty" toward the prisoners before killing them. Because of poor aim, some did not die immediately. "At about three hours after the executions were completed, some of the condemned persons were still alive and moaning. The cries could be heard coming from somewhere in the mass of bodies piled in the canyon," the MPs say.

The report finds its way to Eighth Army commander Walker in Taegu, who informs MacArthur. Since early July, MacArthur has had formal command of the South Korean military, but he now avoids dealing with this matter, instead instructing Walker to pass it along to U.S. diplomats in Korea. The killings go on.[21]

A MID-AUGUST EVENING, 1950

Learning Ahn Kyong-hee's identity, a KPA officer
tries to take advantage

The occupation authorities in the South—a mix of newly arrived northerners and local leftists—are moving swiftly to remake the captured territory in the image of North Korea. Besides the redistribution of land to tenant farmers, elections also are under way, ultimately of more than a hundred thousand southerners as members of People's Committees at the county, town, and village level.[22] But the new regime also has a murderous side.

On the hilly green island of Chindo, in Korea's southwestern corner, the North Korean occupation army and southern leftist sympathizers have begun executing scores of "reactionaries," including officials of the old local government.[23]

It's a turn in a bloody cycle: last month, some five hundred supposed leftists were murdered in Chindo County at the hands of South Korean police, in the nationwide massacres of National Guidance League members.[24]

Vague reports about a new round of political killings have reached the small hamlet of Chung Paui Kol, fifty miles from Chindo. There, Ahn Kyong-hee's worries are growing, that she and her mother and younger brother and sister, sheltering with relatives in Chung Paui Kol, might be identified as reactionaries, as members of an important Seoul family.

Kyong-hee is afraid clues around their temporary home might betray them, especially a thick family photo album they brought with them in their flight from the capital.

On this evening, she pulls the album from its hiding place, beneath other items at the bottom of a large box. She has decided she must destroy the more incriminating pictures, those that make their home in Seoul look too rich or show her father, the well-known editor, at a civic event, or in his grand office at the newspaper, before he fled to Pusan ahead of the invading northerners.

As she spreads photos across the floor of a small room, poring over them by candlelight, Kyong-hee gets lost in recollections of their good life in the city, her childhood days, her happy times as a pretty and popular student at Ewha University.

Homesickness, melancholy overcome her. She cannot destroy these memories. Instead, she must find a better hiding place for them.

As the young woman's mind lingers over scenes from the past, the door opens. In the dim light, she sees Nam Ki-tae standing in the doorway, the officer from the KPA occupation who has badgered her in recent days with questions about her background and allegiances. He steps in, sees the photos, and scoops some up. They confirm rumors he's heard or suspicions he's held.

"So this is your father," he says, brandishing one picture. "Rather a prominent man under the Syngman Rhee regime, I understand."

She's horrified. The rest of the household, intimidated by Nam, have retreated to far corners of the house.

Nam steps closer, lifts her chin up with his finger, and asks, "Why are you so aloof from me?" He tells her he's "probably the only man who could protect you."

She can only stare. Suddenly, he grabs her around the waist and tries to kiss her. Stunned, she struggles to break free, and they both fall to the floor. He pulls away her *hanbok* top and grasps a breast. His other hand gropes up her leg under her skirt. She screams.

In a moment, a flashlight shines from the doorway. Nam, startled, looks up, shouting, "Who's that?"

"Comrade Nam, will you come out?" a man answers. She recognizes the voice. It's Han Muk, the northern secret policeman who has befriended her and Mother.

Nam goes outside. She gets up, straightens her clothes. She hears harsh whispers and through a half-opened door sees Han seemingly reproaching his comrade for what he's done.

Nam stalks off, and Kyong-hee impulsively rushes out to Han, leans into his chest, and sobs. He tries to console her, and she blurts out to him that Nam has left with potentially damaging photos. Coming outside, her mother, upset over what has happened, is further distressed to learn about the photos. Wanting to believe in Han's basic decency, she asks him to help them.

"I understand," Han says.

⸺∞∞⸺

The loud crack startles them. Their hearts stop. It's a gunshot, and it's next door.

Hurh Won-moo dashes into the living room to lift the floorboards. Before he drops into his hiding place, they hear someone shout, "Where is your son?"

North Korean soldiers have raided the house next door, looking for the young man who lives there, to draft him into their army. He's gone into hiding somewhere, just as seventeen-year-old Won-moo has done, in his case right in the center of their small city home in Seoul's Soonwha-dong district.

Won-moo can hear more shouting, muffled now that he's underground. They may come for him next. Mother, his three sisters, and little brother can only wait, while he huddles in the darkness, clinging to his homemade knife. Urgent thoughts race through his mind. Will he resist? Surrender? Commit suicide?

An hour passes. Nothing happens. Won-moo climbs back up to rejoin the family.

In the weeks since the Korean People's Army entered Seoul, and since Hurh Won-moo escaped the mass conscription of his high school class, young men all across the nervous city have hidden from the draft in attics and crawl spaces, in relatives' houses, in country homes. The northerners nonetheless have rounded up tens of thousands throughout the South to fill their bleeding ranks, with little or no training.

Won-moo and a friend first tried hiding in an outlying village where the friend had relatives. They set out from Seoul disguised as farm boys in straw hats, a suddenly popular look in the communist-occupied city, where men hid away their Western-style jackets and young women were going without makeup.[25]

The trek took them along a trail of horrors, of unburied bodies of soldiers and civilians—even children—on riverbanks and piled under bridges. They saw the true human waste of war. The stench sickened them.

Then, once the boys settled in the village, the relatives grew nervous about sheltering draft dodgers, and the pair had to risk the trek back to Seoul.

There, Won-moo's shopkeeper mother spread a story in the neighborhood that her elder son had fled south. Meanwhile, he began digging his hideout under the floor, eventually a five-by-six-foot hole, four feet deep, more than enough for the compact Won-moo. Every dawn, his mother and sisters carried the excavated dirt away in small bags.

Now, any knock on the door sends Won-moo rushing to the hideout, while his mother or nineteen-year-old sister slowly respond.

Won-moo, the studious high school senior, passes his time behind locked doors listening to South Korean broadcasts on a crystal radio of his own making. He reads novels in Japanese. As an eleven-year-old, this perennial "class leader" pored over the twenty-five volumes of the Hurh family genealogy, printed in Chinese characters on rice paper and found in the attic of the family's main residence in a Seoul suburb. He proudly learned he's descended from a long-ago king. He is determined to preserve a future for himself. No peasant sergeant will get this Hurh killed in some war.

His hideout serves another purpose as well, as a family shelter when U.S. bombers appear over Seoul.

The air raids are incessant, and they have scored an important success, finally collapsing the western railway bridge over the Han River, a key link in the KPA's supply chain to the south. But the Americans then discover the North Koreans have spanned the river with a pontoon bridge, which is disassembled and concealed during the day, defying the bombers.[26]

SUNDAY, AUGUST 20, 1950

Buddy Wenzel and other wounded are shuttled back
into threatened U.S. lines

After the 7th Cavalry chaplain holds a Sunday service for men of G Company on the Naktong River front line, James Hodges pulls out some paper, smudged with a bit of red Naktong mud, and writes sister Juanita in Florida.

"Everything is quiet here today," he tells her. He'll be on outpost duty tonight, he says, "and that means no sleep." The nineteen-year-old "BAR man" (Browning automatic rifle), Buddy Wenzel's harmonica-playing barracks mate in Tokyo, wraps up his letter with thanks to Juanita for asking the family minister, at Turkey Creek Baptist, to dedicate prayers to the soldiers of "George."

"You can tell the preacher I said thanks for the prayer and to keep praying for we can really use God's help over here."

Something helped them on August 12, when one thousand troops of the North Korean 10th Division crossed the shallow river and attacked 7th Cavalry companies from behind before dawn, igniting three days of vicious, often hand-to-hand combat. Overwhelming American fire-power—artillery barrages and air attacks—finally crushed the offensive, which had threatened Taegu, ten miles to the rear.

Afterward, vultures and clouds of huge black flies descended on the Naktong bottomlands, strewn with corpses. Squads of 7th Cavalrymen went down there as well, sent by their officers to find wounded and stranded North Koreans and kill them.

The Americans suffered casualties in far lesser numbers, but every loss further weakens defense lines already overstretched. George Company alone lost seven men killed and twenty-seven wounded over the three days.[27]

Strapped for fighters, Eighth Army is shuttling wounded back from the rear as soon as they're barely capable. Wenzel is now among them, returning this time to Hodges's G Company, his original home before he was seconded to a needy H Company when the regiment landed in Korea.

After three weeks at an army hospital in Japan for treatment of his hand wound, Wenzel finds the scene at the front unreal, frightening. He jumps at every sound. He dreads every night assigned to an outlying listening post on the river's reedy edge. Learning of friends killed or badly wounded, he grows despondent, questioning. "What the hell are we here for? Police action?" he asks himself, using a term President Truman adopted to explain the U.S. intervention in Korea.

Soldiering has become misery, the temperatures at times hitting one hundred degrees Fahrenheit, thick dust clogging weapons and coating bodies, or rains soaking men through. The army's food pipeline regularly fails them, leaving them dependent on sometimes outdated C rations. Men grow hungrier, skinnier. Patrolling, climbing hills, they've learned to keep it light—fatigue shirt and pants, steel helmet, combat boots, weapon and web belt with canteen, first-aid packet, bayonet, entrenching tool and ammunition clips attached.

On quiet days they daydream—of fried chicken, clean sheets, women. Some have torn out a photo of "Miss Morale" from the military's *Stars & Stripes* newspaper, an unknown starlet named Marilyn Monroe. Some have also saved another photo to keep in their helmets, of twenty-six dead GIs found with hands bound and shot in the back by their North Korean captors on a hill designated "303."[28]

Deadly hate for the "gooks" grows daily. It extends even to desperate South Korean civilians trying to cross to their side of the river, fleeing North Korean retribution, U.S. bombing, hunger, or all of these. A month after Wenzel and his comrades killed the refugees at Nogun-ri, General Gay, 1st Cavalry Division commander, issues an order that "all refugees to be fired on."[29]

AN AFTERNOON IN LATE AUGUST 1950

Ahn Kyong-hee does the unthinkable to protect her family

The war along the Naktong—the dawn surprise attacks, the nighttime ambushes, the cries of the wounded and dying—seems a world away from a quiet glade many miles to the west, in South Cholla Province, where three people enjoy a basket lunch and cool drinks beside a waterfall.

The picnickers are Ahn Kyong-hee, her protector Han Muk, and—improbably—the KPA occupation officer Nam Ki-tae, enjoying the company of the young woman he sexually assaulted just days ago.

The outing was arranged by Han, knowing how desperate Kyong-hee was to retrieve the family photographs Nam seized, telltale photos that could condemn her and her loved ones to persecution as wealthy enemies of the people.

Han asked Kyong-hee to trust him and join in the "reconciliation" excursion. She doesn't know that her tormentor Nam has been led to believe she's willing to submit to him in exchange for the photos.

It was a two-hour hike from the village of Chung Paui Kol, past the terraced hillsides, up through the forest to the secluded spot. While Kyong-hee sips cider, the two men drink beer, then *soju*, Koreans' potent rice liquor. Han pours round after round. As the two men banter, she notices Han is spilling his drinks out of Nam's sight.

Before long, the North Korean soldier, inebriated, sidles over to Kyong-hee and puts his arm around her. She recoils, but Han gestures to her, winks, and remarks, "Let's enjoy ourselves!" She senses there's a purpose, still trusting this young civilian she and Mother believe is a member of the northern secret police.

She allows Nam to hold her, but gently turns away his attempts at kisses. In minutes, he grows limp and nearly senseless. He releases her, crawls away, and passes out, lying in the shade of a tree.

Han eventually walks over to the unconscious man and shakes him violently. He doesn't awaken. "The medicine seems to have worked," he quietly tells a confused Kyong-hee. He explains that he has slipped sleeping powder into Nam's drinks.

What Han tells her next shocks her: they must throw the oblivious Nam over the nearby cliff, to the rocks at the base of the waterfall.

She's dumbstruck. Why would this man, a member of the communist secret police, kill a North Korean comrade? Is some kind of murderous jealousy, over her, behind this?

"You know, there are things that have to be done whether we like it or not," Han says. He reminds her that Nam has her photos. Pulling them from the officer's pocket, he tells her Nam expected to trade them for sex.

They have no other choice now, he says. He speaks of "the cause we're fighting for," further confusing Kyong-hee. He reminds her that Nam has been ruthless in his dealings with helpless villagers. Finally, he tells her, "Yes, you may have guessed it by now. I'm not a communist."

Ahn Kyong-hee is even more at a loss, unsure who this Han Muk really is. She's repelled by the unthinkable idea of throwing a drugged man to his death. Yet she finds Han's conclusion inescapable. She knows that if Nam Ki-tae lives, she and her family will be his next victims.

She relents.

Han tells her to grab the prone man's hands. Han takes his feet. They half-drag him to the cliff edge, lift him up, swing him out, and let the inert body plummet through the cool spray of the cascade, to the rocks far below.

She nearly faints, swaying atop the cliff. Han pulls her back. She covers her face with her hands, wanting to banish from her mind what they've done. "Let's go!" she cries out. "Let's forget it all!"

Miles to the east on this day, in the hellish heat of the Pusan Perimeter, many more North Korean officers and men are dying in the daily slaughterhouse of the two-month-old war. The commanders of a badly depleted KPA invasion force know they can muster only one final thrust to achieve the victory that once seemed so close.

FRIDAY, AUGUST 25, 1950

Shin Hyung-kyu escapes refugee misery to become a "boy soldier"

In the August heat, Pusan seethes with humanity.

A tide of homeless from the north has flooded the old port city in Korea's southeastern corner, an estimated 275,000 refugees seeking shelter wherever they can find it.

Squatter settlements blanket Pusan's hillsides with *hakobang*, "box homes" made of packing cases, flattened tin cans, corrugated metal sheets. Refugees desperate to sell possessions or services throng the Kukje Market. Telephone poles are plastered with scribbled notes—people trying to find lost parents, separated children. Ragged, filthy children roam the streets, begging, selling fruit, amid the flow of bicycles, rickshaws, oxcarts, and the honking horns of U.S. military trucks rushing men and supplies from the Pusan wharves to the war front, thirty miles away.[30]

For sixteen-year-old Shin Hyung-kyu, the city that was the salvation sought at the end of a two-week flight from Kochang is now an ordeal. He and his uncle found the home of their Pusan relatives, but it was already overrun by two hundred refugees, many from Kochang. Food was desperately short, drinking water a problem, the only sleeping space the bare earth.

The miserable boy thinks constantly of his mother and father and brothers and sisters trapped in North Korean–occupied territory. He has grown anxious, too, about his own predicament. He can't survive long in Pusan. Should he join the army?

Yesterday, he told Uncle that's what he wanted to do. He's too young—the army's minimum age is eighteen—but he'll lie about his age. Uncle objected strongly, but finally relented when Hyung-kyu assured him that as a high school student, an educated youth, he can find a unit safely in the rear. He hears that Pusan's school for military police is recruiting, and MPs don't have frontline duties.

First, he hurries to a provincial education office to obtain a high school attendance certificate. Then, in the wilting midafternoon heat, he doubles back across the hilly city to the elementary school the army has taken over for military police training. He sees young men there being driven up in official cars by important-looking people. That confirms it for Hyung-kyu: this is the place to be.

The "entrance test" turns out to be only a physical exam. When ordered, Hyung-kyu strips off his old shirt, his tattered hemp pants and underpants, and stands naked, a scrawny, ill-fed five-foot-three boy, before army doctors seated at a long desk.

"What's this?" the surprised doctor in front of him exclaims. Hyung-kyu decides not to lie, but to tell him he'll turn seventeen next month.

"You're sixteen. . . . Go home, boy," the doctor says. Hyung-kyu must do something.

"No, sir!" he shouts. "I will do my duty to defend our motherland. . . . I have no place to go. I am a refugee from Chinju High School, sir."

"You're from Chinju?" asks another doctor. "I'm from Chinju, too."

The examiners consult, and the first doctor abruptly declares, "Okay, you passed," stamps his application, and Hyung-kyu is shuttled to a supply room where he's issued a fatigue uniform.

It's too big, hanging off his skinny frame. When he emerges, other recruits break into laughter. "Hey, scarecrow!" says one. But Shin Hyung-kyu, the would-be scientist turned would-be soldier, doesn't care. "I'm in the army!" he tells himself, looking forward to his first army meal.

Fifty miles northwest of Pusan on this day, across the Naktong River, an additional North Korean division, the 9th, is maneuvering into position to join a planned all-out attack on the Pusan Perimeter by a force of ninety-eight thousand. The U.S. 2nd Infantry Division has moved into that line, taking over from the exhausted 24th Division. And in distant Hong Kong, as pipers play "Auld Lang Syne," two battalions of British troops set sail for Pusan, to join their American allies in the last-ditch defense of South Korea, under the U.N. command established by the Security Council in early July.[31]

At the Pusan city line, police are stopping the flow of refugees and turning them back. The city cannot hold any more people. But one young man in a broad-brimmed straw hat must get through. Husband and father Chung Eun-yong must find his wife and children.

Eun-yong learned only a week ago that his missing wife, Park Sun-yong, was in Pusan, hospitalized with wounds from the horrible events at Nogun-ri. She managed to get a telephone call through to Eun-yong's brother at the Taegu prison, where he is working as a guard and where Eun-yong was staying. The brother, Kwan-yong, told him how to find Sun-yong, but he didn't disclose what else he learned from her—that their two small children were dead.

Eun-yong set out immediately from Taegu with two cousins, the brothers Kim Bok-jong and Kim Bok-hee, who had reached the city soon after Eun-yong and also bedded down at the prison. Bok-hee, who had been briefly trapped at the Nogun-ri bridge, told Eun-yong his family was alive when he last saw them there.

It was a punishing weeklong journey from Taegu, seventy miles in oppressive heat. They made their way only in the cooler early morning and evening. Running out of food, they begged in villages along the way. They grew weaker, leaned on walking sticks. When Bok-jong spotted a recruiting table in a town fifteen miles from Pusan, he left them for the army, as other young men were doing for the promise of food rations.

Now finally at Pusan's gates with sixteen-year-old Bok-hee, Eun-yong won't turn back at the police checkpoint. The law student and former policeman spots a senior police officer and tells him his story of separation, of a wounded wife in Pusan. The sympathetic officer lets them through.

They go straight to where Sun-yong was said to be recovering, a central Pusan school converted to a military hospital. But they're told she was taken five days ago to a refugee settlement on Yong-do, a Pusan Harbor island.

Eun-yong and Bok-hee hurry over a harbor bridge to Yong-do and on to Hedong College, now Refugee Camp No. 19002, according to the sign outside.

Children at play swarm over the dusty grounds, and Eun-yong's eyes search in vain for his boy and girl among them.

He must find his wife. He spots women doing laundry at a well. One has her right arm bandaged and in a sling. It's Sun-yong. He calls out to her. She turns, straightens up, and runs to him, sobbing. He wraps his arms around her. She buries her face in his chest, her back heaving with her cries, her shoulders trembling. She says nothing.

"Where are the children?" Eun-yong asks. She can only sob. "Where are the children?" he repeats. He knows instantly. They're dead. He's stunned, crushed. "I'll never have another happy day in my life," he tells himself.

Eun-yong joins Sun-yong in the miserable life of the camp, where people cook church-donated food over outdoor fires, sleep in cramped spaces in the school buildings among snoring men and filthy baggage, and wait for some change in the fortunes of war, something that will allow them to go home.

The young couple see their children's faces in the boys and girls dashing around the camp. They reach out for the missing children in their sleep. Sun-yong's feelings of guilt overwhelm her.

"It was me that led them toward death," she tells Eun-yong. "It's me."

Guilt weighs even more heavily on Eun-yong, the father who abandoned his family to the mercies of the Americans. He doesn't even know where his children are buried. He vows to find the truth, to find who was responsible for this massacre of innocents.

Meantime, he spends what money he has on a private doctor to mend Sun-yong's crooked arm. He finds work laboring on Pusan's wharves, unloading American cargo.

As for Bok-hee, who stays with them at the camp, he goes out one day to look for work and doesn't return. The teenager has been drafted off Pusan's streets to help refill the depleted ranks of the South Korean army.

Clarence Adams, Memphis street fighter and army boxer, arrived in Korea full of bravado. After all, they were told they'd be fighting a primitive, ill-equipped North Korean army. "Bring on that big bad enemy," he told himself.

But since landing at Pusan with other 2nd Infantry Division troops and heading to the front, the reality of Korea has chastened him—the unpredictable incoming enemy shelling, the fear of snipers and infiltrators in their rear, the constant threat of an all-out attack.

On his second day ashore from the troopship USS *General Mitchell*, Adams finally got his assignment: the 503rd Field Artillery Battalion, an all-black unit attached to the 2nd Division.

He is now an ammunition bearer in the battalion's A Battery, a 120-man company fielding six 155mm howitzers. A machine gunner when he was with U.S. occupation troops in Japan, Adams hasn't been trained for artillery. But he knows that's "the army way."

Korea's reality hits home hardest for the men of the 503rd when they see the bodies of fellow black soldiers hauled past them in the backs of trucks. They're casualties from the 24th Infantry, an all-black regiment of the 25th Infantry Division locked in vicious fighting with the North Korean 6th Division over "Battle Mountain," at the south end of the Pusan Perimeter.

Adams may know some of the dead. The 24th, one of the first units sent into the Korea conflict, was his outfit in Japan.

Deploying in the 2nd Division sector along the Naktong River, the artillerymen must also adjust to the reality of the daily wretchedness of life at war in the Korean summer, in the stifling afternoons of buzzing insects, on overnight watch fighting off mosquitoes and on edge, alert to a stealthy enemy.

A LATE SUMMER DAY, 1950

In their "safe" haven, the child Chang Sang is caught
in an American bombing

Bong-hyun and ten-year-old daughter Sang have moved from Seoul to the familiar village of Yonchon, among green rice paddies and scrubby hills just north of the city. They spent time there last year with Sang's sister, the teacher, who has since married and is staying in the capital. Her husband, a university student, is hiding from the leftist bands seizing young men for the Korean People's Army.

Bong-hyun feels safer now, away from the American bombs and the North Korean soldiers who might question the background of people like them, refugees from the North. But life is austere for mother and child in the simple thatched-roof house they have secured.

When they left the crowded Kim household in Seoul, Bong-hyun took along a sack of rice that she tells Sang must last thirty days. The clever girl first separated the grain into thirty portions and now is scavenging daily in the fields for abandoned plots of grain, wild fruits, and vegetables to supplement their meals.

On this day, they're walking to a deserted vineyard beyond the village, to pick grapes for selling in Yonchon. Others come and go along the country road as the morning sun pushes temperatures toward ninety degrees.

Suddenly, a barely heard drone grows louder. Someone shouts, and people drop to the dirt and gravel. Sang hears another shout: "Don't look up!" Then, a deafening blast shakes the ground and darkens the sky with smoke and dust.

The Americans have bombed them. Why? People pick themselves up, and young Sang sees a sight that horrifies her, two bloody bodies, the first dead of her war.

Two men, peasants unknown to others at the scene, they're quickly "buried" beneath piles of sand scooped from the banks of a nearby stream. Everyone moves on. Bong-hyun, frightened, grabs Sang and heads quickly back to the village.

Such civilian dead are accumulating by the hundreds across South Korea, both in northern-occupied areas and even in villages and refugee encampments behind U.S.–South Korean lines, as the U.S. command pursues its policies of targeting "people in white" to guard against enemy infiltrators and of "scorched earth" in occupied areas to deny the invaders the shelter and resources of southern communities.

The tactics outrage southerners and trouble some Americans. In the war's earliest days, White House adviser Clark M. Clifford expressed concern to President Truman that "in bombing towns and cities in South Korea, we are bombing friendly people and friendly areas."[32]

On August 3, American warplanes bombed a docked ship loaded with refugees at Yeosu on the south coast, killing hundreds.[33] On August 11, American warplanes and ground troops killed eighty-two people seeking refuge in a village shrine at Kokan-ri, near the fighting front in the far south.[34] Three days later, U.S. pilots left seventy refugees dead when they strafed and bombed an encampment behind U.S. lines near Kyongju, as the white-clad civilians waved a South Korean flag.[35] Through the rest of August, hundreds more "people in white" have been killed in U.S. air strikes on villages and refugee camps in the South, in such places as Hyunggok-dong, Kumjon-dong, Booksong, and Haman.[36]

The navy destroyer USS *De Haven*, under army instructions, shelled a shoreline refugee encampment near Pohang, behind U.S.–South Korean lines, obliterating whole families in a barrage from five-inch naval guns, scattering panicked refugees, some to be hit by shrapnel in the surf of the Sea of Japan. Up to two hundred men, women, and children were killed. "They told us to evacuate. So we did and we all died at once . . . like dogs," says a woman survivor. "Arms . . . necks . . . legs blown apart. Organs poured out. And the sea was all red."[37]

The intent is clear in classified U.S. military documents. In mid-August, the Tokyo air command ordered "carpet bombing" of twenty-seven square miles of North Korean–held territory across the Naktong River from the Pusan Perimeter defenses, a swath of South Korea dotted with villages and refugee gatherings. Almost a hundred U.S. Air Force B-29 SuperFortresses turned hillsides and valleys into lakes of fire, dropping bombs filled with napalm, a gasoline gel that sticks and burns through the skin.[38]

On August 15, the Pentagon messaged Tokyo that its communiqués should cease reporting that warplanes have destroyed villages and instead call them "military targets."[39] On August 29, one month after his troops killed the refugees at Nogun-ri, Major General Hobart R. Gay told his artillery units that refugees are "fair game."[40]

Ordinary Koreans, like those caught with Sang and her mother in the sudden attack outside Yonchon this day, are unaware of the sweeping nature of the U.S. policies behind such tragedies. But they know the Americans, with their jet planes and big bombers, can end this terrible war.

SEPTEMBER

FRIDAY, SEPTEMBER 1, 1950

At Harvard, Chi Chao-chu feels the tug of his homeland

Among the grassy quadrangles of Harvard University, the worries of this new academic year include fear of the draft. Some spring graduates were ordered to report to Boston-area reception stations for duty during the Korean emergency.

Students and professors are debating the wisdom of the U.S. intervention in that distant land. Asian experts on the faculty mostly favor the American war. But today's *Harvard Crimson* newspaper quotes China scholar John K. Fairbank as warning that the Chinese might intervene militarily in support of North Korea. "War with Red China, he said, would be a bleeding conflict in which 'we could not beat them or they us,'" the newspaper reports.[1]

Universities are embroiled as well in a new domestic anticommunist campaign stoked by Joseph McCarthy, the fiery Republican senator from Wisconsin who has even accused World War II hero General George C. Marshall of being soft on communism, of "losing China" while serving as special China envoy and secretary of state.[2] Demands for "loyalty oaths" are rising on campuses.[3]

At Harvard, Chi Chao-chu, class of '52, and his Chinese classmates hear rumors they're under U.S. government surveillance.

It's not surprising. These Chinese-born students have met regularly in a communist reading club, discreet but hardly secret gatherings at which they discuss the writings of Mao Tse-tung, Marx, Lenin, and others. Since the communist victory in China last October, they've talked more earnestly about their own plans for returning home to help build the new China.

Twenty-one-year-old Chi feels as committed as any to the revolutionary cause. It runs in the family. But he also feels a familial duty to complete his American studies, ultimately with a doctorate in chemistry, as he promised his father.

The Chi family seem unlikely communists. Chao-chu's grandfather was a rich landlord in the northern province of Shanhsi. His father is a Japan-educated lawyer, professor, and former Shanhsi education commissioner. But it's Chao-chu's much older half-brother, Chao-ting, who is the link to the victorious revolutionaries.

In the 1920s, as young men and new members of the Chinese Communist Party, Chao-ting and Chou En-lai became good friends. The fast-rising Chou and other party leaders would later sponsor the brilliant Chi Chao-ting in his studies in America, where he earned a Ph.D. in economics at Columbia University and engaged in clandestine party activities. He eventually became a "mole" in China, taking up high-level finance positions under Chiang Kai-shek's Nationalist government while quietly working to advance the cause of Chiang's civil war enemy.

In 1939, as the Chi family fled before China's Japanese invaders, Chou En-lai arranged for father Chi Kung-chian and his wife and younger children to relocate to America so the two younger sons also could obtain a first-class education.

Chao-chu's father, no partisan communist but a leftist sympathizer, started a Chinese-language newspaper, *China Daily News*, in New York. Meanwhile, nine-year-old Chao-chu, small for his age, was registered as a seven-year-old for school, so he'd adapt better to English starting in lower grades. The boy flourished, advancing through elite private schools in New York and on to Harvard, all on scholarships.

After eleven years, now grown tall for a Chinese, the young scholar Chao-chu feels almost American. But his native patriotism hasn't faded.

A map of China hangs on his dormitory room wall, filled with pushpins marking the Red Army's wartime advances. In their reading club last October, Chao-chu wept upon hearing the words of Mao's declaration of the People's Republic. And when war broke out in Korea in June, he grew concerned, sensing it might inevitably involve his homeland.

Chao-chu feels the tug of family as well. Older brother Chao-ting is now a high official in the communists' Finance Ministry in Peking. His father returned to China in early 1946 to become dean of Peking University's law school. In fact, father and brother helped negotiate the bloodless surrender of Peking's Nationalist garrison last year, a climactic event in the civil war.

Chi Chao-chu, incoming junior at America's greatest university, promising scholar, future scientist, feels a mounting urge to return home, to go China and join the army. All he needs is a push.

One moonlit early September evening, as he walks through Harvard Yard with friends, he hears from an open window the pulsing chords of Beethoven's *Emperor Concerto*. It stirs something urgent in him. "Gotta run!" he suddenly shouts to his companions. He dashes to his room, packs a bag, and heads for South Station and an overnight train to New York, where he breaks the news to his mother that he's going home. "There's going to be trouble between America and China," he tells her. "I want to be in China when it comes."

───※───

The trouble has already begun. American warplanes have attacked a Chinese air base at Antung in Manchuria, across the Yalu River from Sinuiju, North Korea. Alan Winnington is there. "Two U.S. fighters suddenly appeared above the airfield and dived, letting go their guns when they came down to about 200 yards from the ground," Winnington reports in a *Daily Worker* dispatch. He says three airfield workers were killed and nineteen wounded.

On the same day, Winnington reports, locomotives and rail coaches were damaged in an air attack on two train stations at the Chinese town of Linjiang, farther up the Yalu. And two days later, in two separate attacks, five more Chinese were killed along the Yalu, including three fishermen in their boats.

Foreign Minister Chou En-lai filed a protest to the U.N. Security Council, saying the events "clearly expose and testify to the intention of the United States Government to violate world peace."[4]

The U.S. Far East Command acknowledges only the Antung incident, describing it as an "error."

The Americans are clearly concerned about a potential Chinese intervention in Korea. Their intelligence reports note the buildup of Chinese ground forces in Manchuria and of aircraft sent to bases at Antung and elsewhere.[5]

Winnington is making his way back to his home base in Peking after five eventful weeks covering the Korean conflict, a wearing experience during which the solidly built Englishman has lost twenty pounds on a haphazard diet of boiled millet, kimchi, and an occasional sweet potato. In Peking this "foreign friend" of the Chinese Communist Party returns to a comfortable home provided near central Peihai Park, equipped with cook, houseboy, and driver.[6]

Brief as Winnington's initial stay was in Korea, it drew the attention of the British cabinet in London, which considers filing treason charges against the forty-year-old communist journalist.

A secret cabinet meeting is told Winnington's reporting of the Taejon mass executions and of indiscriminate U.S. air attacks was treasonous in that it "made grave allegations . . . and attacked the United Kingdom government for their support of United Nations action in Korea," thereby bringing "aid and comfort to the King's enemies."

In the end, the cabinet takes no action, apparently sensing that any trial would show that Alan Winnington was reporting the truth.[7]

———

The sun is setting, and it's time for Han Muk to go, after a brief visit to Ahn Kyong-hee and her mother at the house in Chung Paui Kol. The talk has been about the lingering summer heat, the coming autumn, and, as always, the latest rumors about the war. But the women both know the subject of most interest to the North Korean security agent is Kyong-hee herself.

Just then there's a commotion at the front gate and a shout of "Don't move!" Three KPA soldiers rush into the *madang*, the front yard, pointing their rifles at Han. He's stunned and can only stare at their fixed bayonets. But he quickly recovers and calmly asks, "What can I do for you, comrades?"

"Don't move!" one shouts back. "Silence. Put your hands up!"

Kyong-hee is terrified. Have they discovered the truth behind Nam Ki-tae's disappearance? Do they know she and Han threw him to his death at the waterfall?

One soldier pulls out a short rope and binds Han's hands. All the while Han is loudly demanding an explanation, to know what this is about. Finally, the sergeant in charge tells him angrily, "We know what you've been doing. We know all about your firing off rockets. We have a witness."

"I shot rockets?" Han asks, his voice now trailing off.

Everyone in the village knows of the mysterious rockets that can be seen on some nights fired into the skies from places nearby. The rumor is that a spy is tipping off U.S. pilots to KPA locations and movements.

As they lead Han away, a shocked and tearful Kyong-hee turns back into the house, torn with emotions. She knows she'll never again see this intriguing man she has grown close to, reliant on. Will he be shot? Will they next come for her, for her family? Will they torture Han and in that way learn about the gruesome fate of Nam Ki-tae?

SUNDAY, SEPTEMBER 10, 1950

Yu Song-chol's KPA launches a desperate final offensive

The rhythmic boom of big guns can be heard in Taegu, seven miles south of the front. The South Korean government and U.S. Eighth Army headquarters have moved farther south, to Pusan. City residents and refugees who haven't fled south have been living in dread of a collapse of the Pusan Perimeter. North Korea's divisions have pushed closer than ever to breaking the back of the U.S.–South Korean defenses.[8]

But at the KPA's frontline headquarters in the ruins of Kimchon, west of the Naktong River, Yu Song-chol, acting chief of staff, knows his troops have reached their limit.

In the tropical heat of southernmost Korea, in more than a month of seesaw battles along the looping, 150-mile defense line, the KPA repeatedly made near breakthroughs only to be beaten back. Yu's troops are exhausted, short on ammunition and food, and now outnumbered.

He has lost more and more men killed, wounded, captured, or missing. His army's disintegrating medical care means one in three wounded soldiers is dying. The ranks are being refilled with South Korean conscripts with scant training and poor motivation.[9]

The KPA is "fighting under the worst conditions since the outbreak of the war," Lieutenant General Yu later recalls. He has seen American airpower not only devastate the supply lines for his invasion force, but also leave his troops traumatized with "aircraft fright."[10]

Yu and his officers were in a race against time with the Americans, struggling to score decisive victories, to liberate Taegu, and then Pusan, before the U.N. force could be expanded to an unbeatable strength.

He lost that race by late August, after additional U.S. Army and Marine forces and British troops arrived to help plug gaps in the perimeter, reinforcing the U.N. command consisting of the original three U.S. divisions and six ROK divisions.

These were fresh, full-strength units, compared with Yu Song-chol's drained divisions. For the first time in the two-and-a-half-month-old conflict, the KPA was badly outnumbered, 179,300 to an estimated 98,000. It's also outgunned. The enemy now fields five times as many tanks as the North Koreans and vastly more artillery.[11]

All that Yu Song-chol and his planners could try was a last-ditch blow, the "Great Naktong Offensive."

It opened on the night of August 31 with barrages from those depleted northern artillery batteries. The KPA divisions attacked simultaneously at multiple points along the Pusan Perimeter, down the north-south valleys inland from the east coast, across the Naktong to attack the western defense line, and against the southernmost defenders in front of the city of Masan.

Furious days of back-and-forth fighting followed, as the din and smoke of battle covered the hillsides and rice paddies from north of Pohang in the northeast to the valleys of the south coast.

On that southernmost front, two of Yu's divisions took aim at Pusan via the coastal route and managed at one point to surround a U.S. 25th Infantry Division battalion, but were finally driven back with tremendous losses.

In the middle, where the Naktong River loops and creates a bulge on its east bank, the American line was thinly held. Two more North Korean divisions struck across the river there, split the U.S. 2nd Infantry Division in two, and might have had a clear field to Pusan. But the U.S. command threw the 5th Marine Regiment into that fight, and the North Koreans were devastated, losing thousands more troops and retreating back across the Naktong by September 5.

The attacks fared better to the north of Taegu and farther east toward the coast, but again the U.S. command had the strength of reserves to hold off the attackers well short of their objectives. As of today, under relentless air and artillery bombardment, Yu's shattered, spent forces are themselves now clinging to defensive positions.[12]

"All we did was lose tens of thousands of troops as the situation deteriorated day by day," the general later reflects. He and his subordinates are sharply aware of another fact: their rear area, from the Naktong battlefront back to Seoul and beyond, is largely wide open to an enemy flanking attack.

WEDNESDAY, SEPTEMBER 13, 1950

In San Francisco, young Marine officer Pete McCloskey answers the call

The late summer day is cool. A brisk Pacific breeze washes over San Francisco. Stepping in from the busy city streets, into a cavernous room in an old post office, Pete McCloskey is momentarily startled at the sight before him: perhaps three hundred young men stripping themselves naked. He joins them.

McCloskey, twenty-two, had been expecting this day since Sunday, June 25, when he heard the news of the North Korean invasion. Two weeks earlier, he had received a letter from the Marine Corps commandant congratulating him on being commissioned a second lieutenant in the U.S. Marine Reserves. He sensed the sudden new war might involve him.

Not that he'd necessarily mind. Ever since his boyhood in Southern California, Paul N. McCloskey Jr., known as Pete, had been fascinated by stories of men in battle. At age eleven, he devoured the book *Fix Bayonets!* from his father's library, an account of the 5th Marine Regiment's heroics at the 1918 Battle of Belleau Wood. He went on to read biographies of the Duke of Wellington and other military legends and developed a teenager's expertise on the American Civil War.

With parental permission when he turned seventeen, he joined the navy as World War II entered its final two months. Leaving the service in December 1946, he enrolled at Stanford University with the help of the GI Bill's tuition payments. Like his father before him, young Pete played Stanford baseball and planned for a career in law, taking summer classes at Stanford Law School.

Late for the last war, feeling a debt to his country for the GI Bill's largesse, McCloskey at Stanford joined the Marines' Platoon Leaders Class

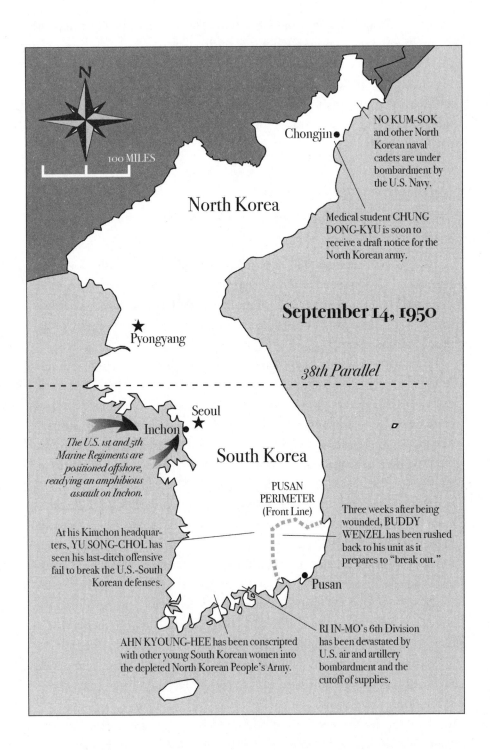

N

100 MILES

North Korea

Chongjin

NO KUM-SOK and other North Korean naval cadets are under bombardment by the U.S. Navy.

Medical student CHUNG DONG-KYU is soon to receive a draft notice for the North Korean army.

September 14, 1950

★ Pyongyang

38th Parallel

Seoul ★

Inchon

The U.S. 1st and 5th Marine Regiments are positioned offshore, readying an amphibious assault on Inchon.

South Korea

PUSAN PERIMETER (Front Line)

At his Kimchon headquarters, YU SONG-CHOL has seen his last-ditch offensive fail to break the U.S.-South Korean defenses.

Three weeks after being wounded, BUDDY WENZEL has been rushed back to his unit as it prepares to "break out."

Pusan

AHN KYOUNG-HEE has been conscripted with other young South Korean women into the depleted North Korean People's Army.

RI IN-MO's 6th Division has been devastated by U.S. air and artillery bombardment and the cutoff of supplies.

program, which turned former enlisted servicemen into reserve junior officers through six weeks of summer training at the Marine base in Quantico, Virginia.

Having earned his bachelor's degree in June, McCloskey embarked on more summer law courses. Then his Marine call-up message arrived, to report on this day for a physical examination.

Dropping his clothes in a pile beside him, he waits for the medical team to work their way down the motley line of naked young men. He looks the part of a Marine—a sturdy five-foot-eleven and 165 pounds—but he's in the wrong place.

"You're an officer! Put on your shorts!" says a surprised navy corpsman, who sends the new second lieutenant to an officer clearance area. There Pete McCloskey the war buff gets his wish, being activated as a wartime platoon leader, volunteering for the Marine infantry, and being told to report to Quantico on September 28 for additional training.

Meantime, all is not well at home. Caroline, McCloskey's college sweetheart and wife of one year, is four months pregnant. She knows this could have given her husband an exemption from overseas duty, an "out" that he has declined. The pull of adventure and the push of patriotic obligation outweigh a young wife's wishes.

Across the Pacific from downtown San Francisco, things also have not gone well. The North Korean threat to Taegu, just six miles from the Pusan Perimeter front line, remains dangerous, despite the failure of the latest communist offensive.[13]

"Our lines will hold," Eighth Army commander Walker declared last week.[14] And they have, thanks in part to the storied 5th Marine Regiment, which arrived from Camp Pendleton, California, in early August with the rest of a provisional Marine brigade to help hold those lines.[15] But just yesterday those Marines left, steaming away from Pusan aboard troopships bound for a destination known only to those with a need to know.[16]

"**Welcome to the** Volunteers' Army of the People's Army!"

To Ahn Kyong-hee, it's a chilling welcome, this banner atop the training center, a former school building. She winces, shivering for an instant at what lies ahead.

The note from the occupation authorities arrived at the house in Chung Paui Kol a few days ago, advising her to "volunteer" for the North Koreans' adjunct southern force. It amounted to an order.

In the end, the KPA's southern reinforcements—not just young men but also women—will total four hundred thousand, half true volunteers and sympathizers, half coerced conscripts. In South Cholla, they're forming what's called the "Kwangju Brigade," after the province's major city.[17] Kyong-hee had already watched To-ri, the young villager who embraced "the Cause," proudly march off to join the invading army.

She knew she'd be labeled a reactionary if she evaded the northern draft, endangering her family. But complying would quickly put her in the front lines for the coming "final battles." It was common knowledge the KPA command was sacrificing poorly trained southerners in order to spare their best troops.

Mother was distraught over their dilemma. They wished they still had the sympathetic Han Muk to consult, to somehow protect them. But he was under arrest.

As Kyong-hee stalled, word came from the local communists that they might draft her sixteen-year-old brother in her place. That decided her. At least joining the KPA will place her farther away from any investigation of the disappearance of the murdered Nam Ki-tae.

Now she has reported for the paltry ten days' training the northerners devote to these conscripts. She's given a uniform and a patch bearing her serial number. Ahn Kyong-hee, the twenty-year-old university student and Seoul socialite, is now Soldier 218 in the Kwangju Brigade.

FRIDAY, SEPTEMBER 15, 1950

Bill Shinn is first to tell the world of a turning point in the war

The compactly built young Korean squeezes through the locked door's overhead transom and lowers himself to the office floor. There's what he's looking for—a U.S. Army telephone.

Bill Shinn calls the local Pusan military switchboard and is forwarded to a number in Tokyo, the Associated Press regional headquarters. An editor picking up hears the Korean's voice over the scratchy connection. "Bill! Are you still alive?" he jests.

"I've got an urgent story!" the nervous Shinn shoots back, and proceeds to lay out what he has learned of the biggest story since the North Korean invasion itself, a story he alone has.

Some seven hours earlier, at 6:30 a.m., a battalion of the U.S. Marines' 5th Regiment landed on the North Korean–held island of Wolmi, facing the port city of Inchon, west of Seoul. The Marines have quickly taken the island, killing or capturing its four hundred defenders. Now that the tide has risen again, landing craft are putting other battalions ashore at Inchon itself, where they scale its seawalls against light resistance.

It's the decisive amphibious blow General MacArthur has planned since early in the war, striking far north and well behind the enemy's front lines at the Pusan Perimeter, to cut off their supply routes to the south, to recapture Seoul, and to drive the invaders back to North Korea.

The operation is daring, the planning fraught, particularly because of the treacherous Yellow Sea tides at Inchon, with a thirty-two-foot difference in depth between high and low. But meticulous preparation and coordination between navy and ground forces is paying off on this D-Day.

The operation began days ago when South Korean units seized strategically situated islands farther offshore. Last Sunday, forty-three U.S. warplanes swept in over Wolmi Island, dropping napalm bombs and strafing a wide area, killing dozens of civilians.[18] In the following days, every building on Wolmi was destroyed.[19] Now the navy's massed warships of the invasion fleet of 261 vessels are shelling Inchon itself, inflicting untold civilian as well as North Korean military casualties.

In the rainy late afternoon and early evening, it's the 1st Marine Regiment and the remainder of the 5th Marines mounting the assault on Inchon. Pushing inland, they're to link up by daylight Saturday, encircling the city. The 7th Marines and the Army's 7th Infantry Division are to land in the coming days, reinforcing the newly created X Corps to more than 50,000 American and South Korean troops advancing toward Seoul.[20]

In today's fighting, the Marines lose only 21 killed or missing and 174 wounded, while the North Koreans' 2,000-man garrison has been largely annihilated in the air and sea bombardments and ground fire.[21] The number of trapped civilians killed is unknown.

That this mighty amphibious attack was imminent was an open secret within the Japan and Korea press corps. But the details—including just where and when—were unconfirmed, and any premature reporting would be punished as a grave breach of security.

Though a novice at news, the energetic, gregarious Bill Shinn has quickly accumulated a stable of well-placed Korean military sources. He was determined to get the story.

This morning he circulated among those sources in Pusan and learned of the Wolmi landing. But he needed to attribute the report to an authority by name. At Pusan army headquarters, he approached the new South Korean chief of staff through an aide, explaining that since the operation was under way it was no longer secret and appealing to General Chung Il-kwon's Korean pride, saying his people should be informed immediately of the great news. The general approved, and Shinn's report now could rest on a Chung announcement.

Next Shinn needed a way to get the news out. The most reliable connection was the U.S. military telephone in the office of South Korea's navy chief. Rushing there, he found the office locked. It was then he saw the way in, via the transom.

The novice newsman has beaten the official U.S. announcement of the landing by nine hours and eclipsed the reports of the veteran war correspondents afloat with the fleet off Inchon.[22]

A displeased American command briefly bans Shinn from further use of U.S. military phones. But he's little ruffled, basking in his colleagues' new nickname for their "native" reporter—"Scoop." He's elated for a more personal reason, too. Douglas MacArthur's bold stroke should now bring a guilt-ridden Bill Shinn closer to finding and reuniting with Sally and Johnny, the wife and child he foolishly separated from in the war's first days.

MONDAY, SEPTEMBER 18, 1950

The 7th Cavalry "breaks out," and Buddy Wenzel loses a friend

The KPA remnants in the South are a spent force, and Eighth Army has now gone on the offensive, to close the second half of General Mac-Arthur's trap.

While the Marines advance toward Seoul from Inchon—joined this day by the U.S. 7th Infantry Division—the 1st Cavalry Division and other U.S., South Korean, and British units two hundred miles to the south are breaking out of the defensive perimeter, crossing the Naktong River, and clashing with the North Koreans to the west and north, to pin them down, kill or capture them, and keep them from reinforcing Seoul's defenders.[23]

For the 2nd Battalion, 7th Cavalry Regiment, the first objective is Hill 300, a 975-foot-high promontory three miles east of the Naktong. Its North Korean defenders have a controlling view over the road from Taegu to Waegwan and the river, blocking the 1st Cavalry Division's advance to the Naktong and beyond, eventually to link up with the Inchon beachhead troops.

The riflemen and machine gunners of Buddy Wenzel's G Company kicked off the assault yesterday, crossing rice paddies and open terrain under enemy fire, then slowly moving up the slope of Hill 300, only to be forced back, with a heavy toll of American dead, including company commander Captain Fred DePalma.[24]

Now this morning, as three companies prepare to resume the assault, South Korean scouts reconnoiter the lower reaches of Hill 300. They return to Wenzel's position and report spotting a GI's unrecovered body. Wenzel and a medic scramble up the slope. They see a tree splintered by a mortar round and then the dead soldier in a ditch, his bloody back gouged open by the giant splinters. Wenzel sees the blond hair and knows instantly. It's James Hodges. Another friend, a close buddy, lost.

The medic double-checks Hodges's dog-tag identification and takes his billfold, his wristwatch, and his harmonica, beginning the process of getting the body into the hands of the division graves registration unit.

A shaken Wenzel can only return to the foxholes, where the 7th Cavalrymen soon renew the attack. It takes two more days of stop-and-go advances uphill, and a U.S. air strike, before the surviving defenders flee and Hill 300 is taken, allowing the division's "breakout" to proceed.

In August, in a last letter home, James Hodges told sister Juanita, "As for me, I am alive." After signing off, he added a P.S., "Ask the preacher for a prayer for all George Company for we are about the move into bloody territory."

A reply from Juanita pleaded with her brother to write. "It has been about three weeks since I heard from you," she said. "I am so worried about you I don't know what to do." The war might be over soon, she wrote. "I do hope it is and you can come back home to see us all. You just don't know what a happy time that will be for all of us."

That letter is sent back to Florida. Besides "Return to Sender," the envelope bears another stamp, from an adjutant general's office: "Verified Missing in Action."

Buddy Wenzel has decided to wait before writing Hodges's sister Dorothy, one of Wenzel's pen pals, to allow time for army channels to notify the family of his death. He cannot know that somehow James Hodges has not, on paper, officially died in the "bloody territory" of Korea.

On this day a report from Korea on communist China's English-language news wire tells of earlier "barbarous" U.S. actions near Yongdong. "In one railway tunnel more than 200 corpses of old men, women and children were discovered," it says.[25]

The advancing Garryowens have mapped out a northbound route more easterly than their line of retreat in July, which had them dug in for three days at Nogun-ri. But as 7th Cavalry buddies fall one by one, those who fight on can't erase the memory of what they did there, in a tunnel east of Yongdong.

—⊶⊷—

The tide has turned. Disaster looms. Yu Song-chol orders his thirteen beleaguered infantry divisions to withdraw northward from the Naktong.[26] As he receives the distressing reports and shouts out retreat orders at the KPA command post in Kimchon, the young acting chief of staff grows emotional. He must hide his tears.

Everyone knew the rear area leading back to Seoul was wide open, dangerously vulnerable. But word of the American landing at Inchon still came as a shock. Lieutenant General Yu received an immediate appeal for help from the overwhelmed units at Seoul, but he could offer nothing.

The collapse of the KPA's victorious forces of July has been swift in the past month under the punishing air and artillery attacks and the strangling of overstretched North Korean supply routes. An inventory in one battalion may be typical, showing it at one-quarter strength—151 men, including only six officers, with a mere eighty-two rifles and pistols and ninety-two grenades among them and fewer than three hundred rounds of ammunition for its remaining six light machine guns.[27]

Yu looks at his maps and decides they must establish a new defensive line along the Kum River, scene two months ago of the triumphant crossing by northern troops on their way to taking Taejon. But coordinating such defenses is impossible. Communications are unraveling below division level.

In the coming days, regiments, battalions, even individual squads find they are on their own. Some 100,000 troops must make their way north, or melt into the countryside as stragglers or guerrillas, or simply head for home in the case of many unwilling South Korean conscripts.[28]

Meanwhile, two hundred miles to the north, U.S. Marines reach the south bank of the Han River as they close in on Seoul.[29]

SATURDAY, SEPTEMBER 23, 1950

Retreating with the 6th Division, Ri In-mo makes a fateful decision

Under cover of darkness, the rear guard of the KPA 6th Division abandons its blocking position in the narrow Chinju Pass and pulls back five miles across the Nam River in Korea's far south. The division's main body, defeated, demoralized, is already retreating northward, as the U.S.-led breakout from the Pusan Perimeter presses hard on North Korean forces.[30]

At the war's outset, the 6th was the northern army's most formidable division, consisting mostly of Korean veterans of China's communist revolutionary army of the late 1940s. But it has been ground down by weeks of fighting and casualties and of dwindling food, water, and ammunition.

From eleven thousand men, it shrunk to some three to four thousand before the KPA began reinforcing it in August with poor-quality South Korean conscripts, raising the division's numbers but hardly its strength.[31]

On this cool autumn night, Ri In-mo plods northward with a division headquarters unit. He senses all is collapsing around him. After two months of writing upbeat Central News Agency dispatches, the Workers' Party loyalist and propagandist realizes he faces a difficult choice.

Many committed soldiers, especially southern leftists who volunteered for the KPA, are splitting off to join the southern guerrillas, to climb into the Chiri-san, the "Mountains of Exquisite Wisdom," a forested cluster of peaks dominated by six-thousand-foot Mount Chiri, 35 miles inland from the central south coast.

A region of isolated villages and centuries-old Buddhist shrines, the Chiri-san has harbored leftist guerrillas since the uprisings against the Rhee government in 1948. Its role as a haven for irregular forces dates back centuries, to the resistance against Japanese warlord Hideyoshi's army in the sixteenth century and to the struggle against the new Japanese colonialists in the early twentieth century, by "righteous armies" striking from within the mountainous redoubt.[32]

Ri is torn. He is pulled northward by homesickness, by his feelings for his wife and mother. He feels guilt as well.

Sun-im's mother had warned her against marrying an older man so devoted to the party. He knows his mother-in-law was right, that he neglected Sun-im and their two-year-old daughter while working too hard for the revolution at home and then by leaving them behind in his enthusiasm to go to war.

But the idea that the Americans, these foreign imperialists, would keep his countrymen from reunification infuriates him. As a Korean patriot, he feels he has no choice. "Now I must take up the rifle instead of the pen," he tells himself.

When his retreating 6th Division group reaches Hamyang, thirty miles northwest of Chinju, he breaks away. He is directed to a nearby village and guerrilla recruiters of the Workers' Party provincial committee.

An examining officer looks skeptically at the gangly thirty-three-year-old and his thick eyeglasses. Guerrilla combat is "out of the question for an unhealthy man," he tells him.

Ri remains determined. He learns fighters also are being recruited near the ruins of Taewonsa, an ancient Buddhist temple in Mount Chiri's foothills, burned down by government forces in the 1948 antiguerrilla campaign. Survivors among those leftist rebels of 1948, after a brief return to the lowlands under the northern occupation, are now back in the mountains.

Ri sets out on a solitary twelve-mile trek, hiking through forests of maple and soaring diamond pine, over a thousand-foot-high mountain pass, and sleeping overnight in an abandoned farmhouse.

When he finally locates the organizers, local Workers' Party members, they also are doubtful about this pale, unarmed older man. They assign him to tending some cows they had appropriated, a lowly job Ri finds insulting. Within days, however, a representative of the provincial party tracks him down and apologizes for their "mistake" in rejecting him. They have learned about Ri's background as a propagandist in the North. They have a job for him in the Chiri-san guerrilla ranks.

By now an estimated fifteen thousand unorganized North Korean soldiers have joined the core of southern insurgents in highlands stretching from the Chiri-san northeastward 150 miles to Mount Odae. They are raiding enemy supply convoys, looting food storehouses, cutting communications lines, and attacking police posts.[33]

One group is harassing the vital east-west road that skirts the northern edge of the Chiri-san and links Korea's southwest to the southeast. That is the group Ri In-mo joins.

MONDAY, SEPTEMBER 25, 1950

Eighteen-year-old Gil Isham, U.S. infantryman,
finds his war and is sickened

It has been ten days since the Marines landed in Inchon.

The harbor and the nearby waters of the Yellow Sea are filled with the gray hulls of U.S. Navy ships and with low-riding cargo vessels backed up for unloading. The beaches are lined with crates of ammunition, food, and equipment, with newly delivered trucks and jeeps, and with men, reinforcements awaiting their marching orders in the final push for Seoul.

Private Gil Isham is focused not on the scene around him but on a single immediate task, of cautiously negotiating his way down a cargo net hanging from the deck of his troopship and into a landing craft.

Unlike the ill-prepared U.S. troops of July, the 7th Infantry Division, including Isham's Easy Company, 17th Infantry Regiment, has had time in Japan to better train its men in such skills as the proper way to descend the tricky nets for an amphibious landing.

But 7th Division officers and sergeants, many of them World War II veterans, could never fully prepare the eighteen-year-old Milwaukee high school dropout Isham ("EYE-shum," he tells people) for what he would face in Korea.

Big navy guns still fire at distant targets onshore, the sound reverberating through the ship's hull as Isham makes it down the side and into the landing craft. He takes up his assigned position as the boat heads for shore through gentle swells. It grounds at Blue Beach, designation for one of the Marine landing points of September 15, and the men of the 2nd Platoon disembark, lay makeshift ladders against a sixteen-foot seawall, and climb up, one by one, into their war.

The Marines have steadily but cautiously advanced on Seoul, twenty-five miles northeast of Inchon. Only yesterday did a Marine battalion finally cross the Han River, in the open-hatched amphibious trucks called DUKWs, and attack and capture a North Korean–held ridgeline overlooking the city from the southwest. The fighting was extremely costly. In taking one hill, a Marine company suffered 178 dead and wounded out of 206 men.[34]

Now thousands of North Korean troops await the Americans in the capital, behind street barricades, on rooftops, hidden in courtyards. It's the job of Isham's 7th Infantry Division to swing farther east, south of the Han, and then attack the city from the southeast. Two of the division's three infantry regiments have preceded the 17th Infantry into action.[35]

Easy Company now forms up and marches off along the eastbound road in two ragged columns. Gil Isham, a wiry five-foot-six, is loaded for war—his M-1 rifle, two bandoliers of ammunition over his shoulders, six grenades, first-aid packet, cartridge belt, canteen, bayonet, shovel.

On this balmy September day, the sights, sounds, and smells of war are everywhere: a whiff of charred wood and of putrefying bodies, the sight of burned-out North Korean tanks and their crewmen's corpses nearby, and off in the distance the boom of artillery. Isham and his buddies are struck, too, like all newly arrived Americans, by the powerful odor of human excrement—fertilizer—hanging over the rice paddies.

Some Koreans work in the green terraced fields as though oblivious to the war. But villages show the ravages of combat, in crumpled thatched-roof homes, dead animals, abandoned fields.

As Isham's 17th Infantry deploys on this day, a sister 7th Division regiment, the 32nd, together with a South Korean regiment, crosses the Han River and strikes at the heart of Seoul from the southeast, taking the commanding heights of Nam-san, South Mountain.[36]

Isham's Easy Company, meanwhile, advances steadily eastward, south of the river, colliding with scattered KPA units. The regiment eventually comes up against two strategically vital hills south of Seoul and fights an intense half-day battle against dug-in KPA troops.[37] The overwhelming American firepower—of tanks, artillery, and fighter-bombers—leaves the area strewn with enemy dead.

Isham watches, amazed, as a Marine tank, with bulldozer blade, simply pushes the bodies together and then "buries" them by dumping loads of earth atop the pile of lifeless young Koreans.

The grisly realities of war are sinking in.

Not long after the hill fight, Isham's squad takes a North Korean prisoner. Because the Easy Company riflemen must leave the area, they turn the prisoner, lightly wounded in the leg, over to a Marine lieutenant.

The Marine, in front of Isham's group and his own men, immediately pulls out his .45-caliber pistol, aims it at the Korean's head, and shoots him. "He's all taken care of. Prisoner secure," the lieutenant announces.

Young Gil Isham, in his first days of combat, is sickened. But it's happening elsewhere as well. In his own Easy Company, a division document reports a GI joined South Korean Marines in killing five POWs atop a hill south of Seoul. "Shoot 'em! Shoot 'em!" other Easy Company men shouted as the doomed Koreans were led past.[38]

It's past midnight. Soldier 218 lies awake on her mat quietly weeping—from homesickness, from dread, from the hardships of the concentrated training preparing this roomful of young South Korean women for joining the North Koreans' war.

It has been several days since Ahn Kyong-hee and the other women conscripts reported to the makeshift training center. Some quickly escaped, to find their way home down South Cholla's familiar routes. The KPA trainers tightened the guard. Then some of those remaining developed dysentery in the unsanitary conditions of the crude facility and began dropping out of the daily training. Along with the short rations that leave them all hungry and weak, chronic anemia is further weakening Kyong-hee.

As thoughts and scenes of what she has lost and what lies ahead flash through her mind, she sees a glow through a window. She hears a crackling sound, something burning. The KPA officers are destroying documents, she later learns.

Finally, she falls into a deep sleep, until an explosion startles her awake, then a minute or so of gunfire somewhere in the darkness. The trainees are so exhausted that only one tries to rise to investigate, only to fall back to her mat.

Kyong-hee is next awakened by the noise of vehicles and shouting outside. She struggles up and goes to a window. Soldiers are moving about in the schoolyard. Squinting into the sunlight, she sees they're wearing tan fatigues. She looks up. They've raised a *taegukki* on the flagpole, the

South Korean flag. The North Koreans have fled. A murmur among the trainees rises to a loud buzz of excitement.

They step outside and suddenly are facing the South Koreans' guns. They shout to the women to raise their hands. Of course, Kyong-hee thinks, we're wearing northern uniforms.

Within minutes, word spreads that the soldiers are saying they'll be taken to a prisoner-of-war camp. In shock and disbelief, some young women burst into tears. They plead with the soldiers to understand they're southerners forced into the KPA, not volunteers. But they're ignored.

Kyong-hee then approaches a young officer and explains their situation. He tells her he's acting "according to orders from above." She won't relent, tearfully asking him to reconsider. He puts his hands gently on her shoulders and says he understands, since his own brother was taken as a "volunteer" and is now in a POW camp. She knows it's useless.

"It's only a matter of days and you'll be released," he assures her. "The army is simply checking for communists."

A column of trucks pulls up, and the women, with their meager belongings, are ordered aboard. They hear they're bound for the Pusan area.

The convoy sets out in swirls of dust and down the poor roads of Korea's far south. Leaning back in her cramped space, Kyong-hee thinks about all she has been through since the June 25 invasion, sees the worried face of her mother, wonders how her father is faring in Pusan, prays that her brother the ROK Army lieutenant is safe. After some time, she falls asleep.

When she awakens, it's dark and the trucks are moving slowly. She senses they're nearing their destination. In the headlights she sees a fence of triple strands of barbed wire and, beyond, the barracks of a prison camp. Her heart sinks.

She is just one in a deluge of prisoners captured in the North Korean rout. The number of POWs is surging from fewer than 1,000 in August to more than 130,000, presenting the U.S. command with a sudden challenge in housing and controlling them.[39]

———

The U.S. 2nd Infantry Division has pushed swiftly westward across Korea's southern tier in the breakout from the Pusan Perimeter. In quick succession, its 38th Regiment, driving seventy-three miles in one ten-hour span, took Chogye, then Kochang, and now Chonju, capital of North Cholla Province.[40]

The gun crews of the 503rd Field Artillery Battalion must scramble to keep up, their tractors towing howitzers over the muddy, cratered roads.

For ammo bearer Clarence Adams, these first weeks at war have been fearsome, as the division reeled and then rebounded against determined North Korean attacks across the Naktong, and he lugged and fed heavy 155mm shells into their guns and watched battery mates fall to enemy fire. One day a sudden rain of mortar shells blew a soldier to pieces before his eyes, and another was killed by a sniper's bullet to the head as Adams spoke to him.

Like many GIs by now, men in the 503rd question why they were sent halfway around the world to fight in someone else's war. But these black Americans have an added layer to their doubts: How can white America ask us to fight hard overseas, they ask themselves, when we're treated so badly at home?

At least we're helping the Korean people, Adams assured himself at first. But as they now push north, more and more he sees towns and villages leveled by American firepower and dead civilians by the roadsides, including women and children, some even crushed beneath American tanks. "What kind of war is this where such things happen?" he wonders. "Should we really be here killing innocent civilians?"

WEDNESDAY, SEPTEMBER 27, 1950

The battle for Seoul unfolds outside Hurh Won-moo's window

From his bedroom window, Hurh Won-moo watches as the Americans fight to drive the Korean People's Army from Seoul. His mother, sisters, and little brother have crammed into his hideout hole beneath the living room floor. But despite Mother's pleas, the spellbound Hurh can't tear himself away from the battle raging before him.

To the north, he can see machine-gun tracer bullets streaming toward North Korean positions on Inwang-san—Hill 338 to the Americans—an 1,100-foot promontory on Seoul's western edge. Jets appear overhead, unleashing rockets. The thud of artillery reverberates in the background. A bomb lands in their Soonwha-dong neighborhood, its shrapnel showering down into their backyard.

The young man, just turned eighteen, knows his own liberation is at hand, after two months of hiding out from the KPA squads rounding up southerners for their army.

Soon after the September 15 landing, he heard on his crystal radio about General MacArthur's Inchon operation. But he couldn't know how imminent the recapture of the city was until the Hurhs began hearing explosions and gunfire drawing closer.

The Americans' capture of Nam-san, the landmark South Mountain whose ridgeline points northwest into the heart of Seoul, took place under cover of a morning fog Monday, as troops of the U.S. 32nd Infantry Regiment crossed the Han River aboard amphibious tractors and advanced up the slopes. They easily drove outnumbered North Korean defenders off the 860-foot summit. Before dawn yesterday, the North Koreans counterattacked and were repelled, but only after hours of furious fighting. The slopes were strewn with northern dead.

Meanwhile, the U.S. Marines who landed at Inchon finally entered Seoul proper from the west, having taken ten days to advance twenty miles from the coast against determined opposition. To the east, the South Koreans' 17th Regiment, having crossed the Han, seized strongpoints commanding the main eastbound highway from Seoul.

The "battle of the barricades" still raged this morning, as Marines who seized Seoul Station began to push north deeper into central Seoul. At one intersection after another, they faced KPA rear guards firing machine guns and antitank guns from behind chest-high barricades of earth-filled rice bags.

These block-by-block fights fell into a routine, inevitably fatal for the defenders. Marine or navy aircraft were called in to strafe and rocket the barricades. Tanks rolled up and blasted them with their guns or, at times, with flamethrowers, leaving behind incinerated KPA soldiers and barricades.

In midafternoon, as Hurh Won-moo watches from afar the hourslong battle to take Hill 338, Marines are raising the American flag over the U.S. Embassy, the old Bando Hotel. Others take Government House, a prime objective. By seven o'clock, the Marines complete the capture of Hill 338. The night skies are aglow from fires raging across central Seoul.

On Thursday the last of the KPA rear guard straggles northward toward Uijongbu, key crossroads in their lightning assault on Seoul three months ago, and toward North Korea beyond.[41]

The U.N. command eventually estimates fourteen thousand North Korean defenders were killed in the two weeks of fighting to take Seoul. American and South Korean dead and missing are put at more than five hundred, with some three thousand wounded.[42]

Not all are killed in the heat of battle. In one instance, a group of North Korean prisoners are found stripped and dead, dumped into a large, empty Japanese-style bath in the basement of a Seoul hotel, shot by the advancing Marines.[43]

Hurh and other residents venturing into Seoul's streets find a smoldering city in ruins. Twisted, bloody bodies of northern soldiers and of hapless civilians caught in crossfires lie about.

They also see American soldiers looting, taking things of seeming value, food, simple consumer goods catching their eye, and they see columns of captured KPA soldiers trudge by in their underwear.[44] Hurh Won-moo feels enormous relief at not having been discovered and forced into their ranks. His hiding days are over. But now he must confront decisions about the ROK draft and defending his southern homeland.

—⊗⊗⊗—

One moment the *madang* is empty, and in the next Chang Sang sees them standing there on the front yard's tamped-down dirt, two young soldiers, their filthy uniforms in tatters, faces gaunt, eyes pleading. Can they just have something to eat?

Northern soldiers have passed through Yonchon since ten-year-old Sang and mother Bong-hyun found shelter in the village north of Seoul. But none has ever stopped at their house. Things are different now.

The village's lone radio brought the news: the Americans—"the United Nations forces"—have arrived in Seoul. They have heard the stepped-up tempo of air strikes and artillery beyond Bukhan-san mountain.

The northern army is retreating in disarray, from Seoul and from positions farther south. Its food and ammunition were cut off days ago. Its communications have broken down. Across South Korea, bands of stragglers, heading north overland or on back roads, are begging or simply seizing food from farmers and village families.

Suddenly faced with two of them, Sang's mother hesitates. Then she hears their accent. Yes, they tell her, they're from North Pyongan, the far northern province Bong-hyun and Sang left behind more than three years ago. She hesitates no longer. She invites them inside to share her precious rice.

Watching them, Sang is amazed. These soldiers are just boys, skinny, innocent-looking boys with guns, caught up in the North's need to conscript as many males as possible to carry out its plan, now collapsing, to conquer the entire peninsula.

The beaten young soldiers gratefully devour the rice and then quietly rest. When it grows dark, they leave.

Sang is amazed, too, at her mother, doing the "Christian" thing, made easier knowing these were hometown boys. The girl remembers how, when she was six years old, Japanese women came to the young widow Bong-hyun's front door in North Pyongan, begging for food, and how her mother helped them. It was 1945, a terrible time for the Japanese colonial families in Korea. After thirty-five years of their harsh rule over the Koreans, the tables had turned and the defeated Japanese were being driven out of Korea, in a chaos of family separation and sometimes violent retribution from Koreans.

Japanese wives and mothers, stranded and penniless, seemed to know that Kim Bong-hyun, daughter-in-law of the prominent Chang family, would help.

Now the people here in Yonchon also know that the widow woman with the little girl is kind and generous. Sang fears someone might report what her mother has done, might accuse her of being a communist sympathizer. But in the end the cruelty, hatreds, bloody recriminations, and summary executions of this war don't reach Yonchon. No harm comes to Bong-hyun and her child.

FRIDAY, SEPTEMBER 29, 1950

Kim Il-sung needs an air force; naval cadet
No Kum-sok wants to be part of it

The Soviet ambassador in Pyongyang is blunt in his encrypted telegram back to Moscow and Josef Stalin, reporting on a meeting with a "nervous" Kim Il-sung. "In the present difficult situation one can feel some confusion and hopelessness," Ambassador Shtykov writes. The ex-general tells of the "dramatically worsening" military situation for the North Koreans.

In a separate telegram to Stalin, Kim Il-sung recounts the ways in which the enemy's unchallenged airpower has brought about the current "extremely grave situation." "After taking over Seoul completely, the enemy is likely to launch a further offensive into North Korea," Kim writes the Kremlin chief.[45]

He needs an air force. Through the summer, U.S. air attacks reduced North Korea's air arm from 132 to 18 or fewer combat planes.[46] "But we do not possess well-trained pilots. . . . Therefore, dear Iosif Vissarionovich, we cannot help asking You to provide us with special assistance."[47]

Three hundred miles from the nervous capital, in a disused rail tunnel in Korea's far northeast, naval cadet No Kum-sok observes a strange exercise. Fellow cadets are being seated, one by one, on a swivel chair that is spun around for twenty revolutions. Then they are told to put their finger to the ground and circle around that axis twenty times. When they then try walking a straight line, many fall down from dizziness.

They haven't been told the reason for the test, but No Kum-sok is sure he knows. What else could it be but a way to find young men suitable for flight training?

The cadets were marched sixty miles north to this tunnel, the Naval Academy's latest home, after the American bombing in late July that devastated Chongjin, where they were housed in a mountainside cave.

Soon after they settled into their damp new quarters, training outdoors at night and listening to mostly political lectures during the day, the mountainous area came under daily shelling from U.S. Navy ships offshore. The naval pounding went on for two weeks, the Americans seemingly trying, and failing, to pinpoint their location.

They're training in infantry subjects. Like the North Koreans' tiny air force, their navy, consisting of some forty-five small craft, including a few sixty-foot, Russian-built torpedo boats, was largely destroyed in the war's first days.[48] The naval trainees are needed much more in the ground war than at sea.

As he watches the "spinning" cadets, No Kum-sok quickly calculates that this test might get him into pilot training, which would last many months, keeping him out of ground combat. By then, judging from the latest they hear about the North Korean rout, the war should be over.

He asks to be tested. The solidly built five-foot-eight cadet passes without a stumble. He goes on to be cleared through other physical exams, and eighteen-year-old No Kum-sok is soon to be sent off to flight school in China.

On Sunday in Pyongyang, meanwhile, Kim Il-sung entrusts another, crucial, message to deputy Pak Hon-yong, a letter to be delivered personally to Mao Tse-tung in Peking, "urgently soliciting that the Chinese People's Liberation Army directly enter the war to support us."[49]

OCTOBER

MONDAY, OCTOBER 2, 1950

Park Sun-yong and husband return home to count the family dead

It's already evening when the Korean jeep driver lets them off on the main road beside Chugok-ri. As they approach the village, their hearts sink as they see the Chung family home was among those burned down by the Americans when they "scorched" Chugok-ri in late July.

For Park Sun-yong, husband Chung Eun-yong, and his brother Kwan-yong, the two-day trip home from the south, including a night at an inn along the Naktong River, has been a journey through a landscape of butchery and ruin.

In one sense they were lucky: first a U.S. Army truck driver and then the South Korean soldier, an acquaintance of Kwan-yong's, picked them up along the road and took them most of the distance. Although Sun-yong shrank back in fear from the American, Eun-yong coaxed her aboard his truck.

All along the route they saw roadside bodies, the blackened hulls of villages, the carcasses of destroyed tanks and vehicles. At one point, they saw villagers pulling North Korean soldiers' decomposing bodies from a hut—men apparently wounded and left to die when the KPA retreated. In the final miles, in the darkness, they also passed by the bridge at Nogun-ri.

Now, two months after the massacre there, and after two months as refugees, they're making a fearful homecoming.

They learn that the remnants of the Chung family have crowded into a relative's surviving house in Chugok-ri. Rushing there, Eun-yong and

Kwan-yong reunite with their parents. They survived, their mother with the scars of wounds from Nogun-ri. Then the tragic accounting begins.

Kwan-yong's wife, Young-ok, was killed under the bridge. Their baby son and one of three daughters later died of wounds.

Like Sun-yong and her children, Young-ok and her four were left behind when Kwan-yong, a Taejon prison guard fearing execution by the northerners, fled farther south in July, to Taegu. When the Americans opened fire on the refugees, this family of five hid in acacia bushes away from the bridge. But at one point Young-ok, for some reason, went to the underpass with the baby. She later was found there shot dead, with the wounded infant sucking at her breast.

Kwan-yong collapses in grief into his tearful mother's arms. The entire family begins to sob. A heavy toll was inflicted on these Chungs: four children, including Sun-yong's, and one mother of four.

In Chugok-ri's other surviving homes, and in Imke-ri up the valley, similar scenes have played out over the weeks since the massacre. One family of nine is now four. One sixteen-year-old girl has been orphaned and lives alone, with only herself to save the family harvest. One young wife who lost a newborn under the bridge is now losing her mind. One widowed father weeps all day, his little daughter in his lap. In some families, no one survived.

At the bridge itself, Nogun-ri villagers returning from the south have covered unclaimed bodies with piles of dirt, awaiting later burial in mass graves.

Haunted by what happened within sight of their homes, these villagers soon report seeing *hon bul*, "ghost flames," under the bridge. Such a nighttime glow or lights may have natural causes, but Korean tradition associates the phenomenon with the souls of the dead, seeking release, possessing a place until the *han*, an injustice, is set aright. For some, the "flames" in Korea's hills and valleys represent the war's restless dead.

The newly returned Chungs see that months of rebuilding lie ahead for Chugok-ri. But at least the golden yellow of the paddies shows the harvest has been bountiful and has been saved. The North Koreans retreated so hurriedly they were unable to confiscate much of the rice crop, as they had planned.

During the brief occupation, villagers were forced to work for the North Koreans. Others hid in the hills during the day, out of sight of prowling American pilots. Nine young villagers were conscripted into the northern army, six never to be seen again.

Consequently, the midsummer rice paddies were neglected. But in this Year of the White Tiger, the most propitious in the Korean zodiac, perfect weather rescued the harvest.

The villagers find, too, that the North Korean retreat is hardly complete, that the leapfrogging American offensive northward bypassed thousands of northern soldiers. These stragglers, often armed, pass through area villages in the night, trying to make their way north, as residents huddle behind closed doors. Sometimes they stop and ask for food. One young woman soldier asks whether Chugok-ri villagers can arrange a local marriage for her, to save her from this terrible war.

As Eun-yong ventures farther afield, more of the war's cost can be seen.

The nearby town of Yongdong has been flattened by U.S. bombs. An American reporter flying overhead likened it to atom-bombed Nagasaki. When Eun-yong travels to the even bigger city of Taejon, their home until a year ago, he sees that only a few buildings are left standing.

Relatives there tell him the North Koreans, before retreating, took southern policemen, soldiers, government officials, and other "rightist" prisoners from their Taejon detention places, carted them to a nearby valley, forced them to dig a long ditch and to line up along it, and then shot each in the head, to tumble into the mass grave.

American troops who retook Taejon found those hundreds executed by the North Koreans, including forty American prisoners. But the U.S. Army went on to suggest that the victims may total six thousand, attributing all Taejon's dead and suspected mass graves to the northerners. The truth—that thousands were summarily executed by the South Koreans in early July—lies only in U.S. military reports stamped "Secret" and in Alan Winnington's *Daily Worker* reporting, labeled a fabrication by the Americans.[1]

TUESDAY, OCTOBER 3, 1950

Chang Sang returns with her mother to Seoul
and a sad, fearful reunion

It's Chang Sang's eleventh birthday, but there's little to celebrate.

Now that the northerners have been driven out, she and her mother have trekked from Yonchon village on Seoul's outskirts back down to the

Kim family house in the Sindang-dong district. In a city devastated by months of bombing and the days-long final battle, it's one house that has survived unscathed. All the adults and children are unharmed. But the reunion is bleak.

They learn the communists finally found and seized Bong-hyun's son-in-law, the newlywed student husband of Sang's sister, Ran, apparently taking him north to induct him into the Korean People's Army.

Son-in-law Kang Ki-suk is just one of thousands of people abducted by the retreating North Koreans, not only conscripts soon to face the American firepower they thought would save them, but also professors, engineers, technicians, and others forced to go north to enrich the talent pool there for the war and the future.

Others fled north willingly, out of sympathy with the communist cause, or simply out of fear of retribution by the Rhee regime for having cooperated during the occupation.[2] The dying days of Seoul's summer were days of tears and separation for many families.

"We must pray for Ki-suk," her mother tells Sang.

Sang and her cousins are also told they must stay away from their church, the Central Church of Sindang-dong. It is filled with bodies. The pastor is among the dead.

Clumps of bodies are being discovered all across Seoul, some of the thousands of civilians slain by the KPA and leftist militias in the South Korean provinces they ruled for three months, a slaughter that built into a frenzy in the final days of North Korea's brief occupation.

The victims are police and military men, government officials, former Japanese collaborators, landlords, "reactionaries"—and their families, even children. The grim reports are filtering in now, in the aftermath of Seoul's recapture.

U.S. Eighth Army intelligence officers are told more than 1,000 civilians were killed just two days ago before KPA troops retreated from Wonju, fifty-five miles southeast of Seoul. Earlier, at Yangpyong, thirty-six miles east of the capital, some 700 civilians in a prison camp were shot, stabbed, or burned to death by KPA officers and a leftist youth group, the army tells American war correspondents.[3]

Beyond their front door, young Sang and her cousins find a city half destroyed. Heaps of bricks and plaster are what's left of many buildings. Everywhere lie broken beams and shattered glass, splintered trees, toppled telephone poles, wrecked vehicles blocking streets.

Decomposing bodies lie scattered about, and the smell of ash and smoke, and death, lingers over streets where torn, smudged posters of Kim Il-sung and Stalin still survey the scene. Local authorities are to estimate at least 4,250 of Seoul's civilians have been killed in U.S. air bombardment since the war began.[4] Countless more died in the recent battle. "Few people can have suffered so terrible a liberation," correspondent Reginald Thompson cables back to London's *Daily Telegraph*.[5]

The sickly odor of unburied dead hung over the shell-pocked Government House building four days ago when General MacArthur, flying in from Tokyo, joined President Rhee in a ceremony celebrating the recovery of the capital.[6] "By the grace of a merciful Providence our forces fighting under the standard of that greatest hope and inspiration of mankind, the United Nations, have liberated this ancient capital city of Korea," the Far East commander declared before an audience of Korean and American officers and officials in the National Assembly chamber. Rhee, in his remarks, said he expected a North Korean surrender.

In far-off New York, the U.N. General Assembly is pondering just such a future for Korea, discussing a resolution, to be adopted later this week, effectively authorizing a military advance into the North, with the goal of unification.[7]

But from the crowded Kim household, hopeful for better times, to MacArthur's Tokyo headquarters and to the U.N. halls in New York, all are unaware that others on this day, in China, are conceiving a different future in Korea.

Meanwhile, new fears are rising in Seoul—of reprisal against those who cooperated with the northern occupiers.

The fears are well founded. Just days ago, the U.S. Embassy military attaché shipped to Washington the classified photographs of the Rhee regime's mass executions of political prisoners at Taejon in July, with the accompanying note saying the order "undoubtedly came from top level."

In his remarks at the capitol building, Rhee sounded reassuring. "There will be no witch hunt," the South Korean president said.[8] But the killings have already begun.

In the dim light of a candle, flickering beneath the small home's rice-straw roof, they at first don't recognize the man stepping from the shadows.

But when Bill Shinn calls out his wife's name, she lets out a cry and bursts into tears.

Three-year-old Johnny, meanwhile, simply stares, uncomprehending. The three-month separation has been too long.

Journalist Shinn arrived in recaptured Seoul earlier this day from Pusan. He was moving into a billet for correspondents when his Associated Press colleague Okey King tracked him down and passed on the news: someone saw a woman and child who looked like Sally and Johnny near Seodaemun, Seoul's West Gate.

After so much time gripped with fear over what might have befallen them, Shinn was overjoyed. He hugged his friend King. It made sense. She must be staying with her parents in Yongchon-dong, in the Seodaemun district. He commandeered a U.S. Army jeep and, despite a curfew, sped through the night to the Kim house.

He last saw his little family on June 30 when he left them, with his brother and sister, in the village of Shinwon-ri, ten miles south of Seoul, as he continued on to Suwon to reconnect briefly with King. When he returned to Shinwon-ri the next morning, they were gone. He himself then only narrowly escaped capture by the fast-moving North Koreans.

Now they've been reunited, and Sally tells her husband of her summerlong ordeal.

When KPA troops approached Shinwon-ri, she and Shinn's siblings first moved to a more remote village. But food was short and life too hard, especially for Sally, six months pregnant, and they made their way back to Seoul.

The food situation at her parents' was no better. They had to sell their possessions, Sally's wristwatch being the last to go, a treasured gift from Bill. For weeks they survived on dumplings in soy soup.

But the worst was the U.S. air bombardment of the North Korean–occupied city. It finally forced them to move to a World War II–era air-raid shelter built into the hillside above Yongchon-dong. There they crowded into a twenty-by-twenty-foot space with two dozen other people, with a small common toilet outside.

"While bringing meals from my parents' home, I saw gruesome corpses scattered around," she wrote in a diary. Some were too slow and feeble to save themselves. "Many old women died from bomb shrapnel."

WEDNESDAY, OCTOBER 4, 1950

Peng Teh-huai, trusted commander, is urgently called to Peking

The silvery, Soviet-made Ilyushin speeds northeastward over the peaks of China's Luliang Mountains, carrying a perplexed passenger, General Peng Teh-huai, to Peking. The men sent to escort him to the Chinese capital couldn't explain the reason for the summons from Mao Tse-tung, only that it was urgent. The general quickly left Hsian, where he governs China's Northwest, accompanied only by his secretary and a bodyguard.

At age fifty-one, Peng Teh-huai stands in the top leadership ranks in his nation of 600 million people, after a long journey from a peasant childhood that at one point forced him to beg in the streets of his village.

As he looks out the window of the plane, those days lie beyond the southern horizon, in Hunan Province, where the boy Teh-huai labored in a coal mine and as a teenaged soldier for a local warlord, eventually to be trained at a Hunan officers' academy. The injustices of a feudal society, the famines, the cruelties led him more and more to see the grain merchants and landlords and mandarins as his enemies, to assembling his own small fighting force, and to joining up with the communists led by Mao, the tall, bookish revolutionary who emerged from the same Hunan county, Hsiangtan, as Peng.

Peng's soldiers went on to lead the way on the Long March that took the communists to their northern safe haven in 1934–1935, a fighting retreat on which the comradeship between Peng and Mao—*Ta Ko* (Elder Brother) to Peng—was cemented.

While leading armies in civil-war victories, the poorly educated Peng immersed himself in Marxist and Maoist readings and grew into a committed communist. In the end, when Mao stood atop Peking's Tien An Men Gate a year ago and proclaimed the founding of the People's Republic of China, the shaven-headed, bulldog-faced Peng stood with him.

Now, landing in Peking as the sun drops toward the Western Hills, Peng is driven to Chung Nan Hai, the Communist Party compound in central Peking. Inside the Hall of Longevity, he finds China's dozen top communists, the Politburo of the party Central Committee, in deep discussion. They all rise to greet Peng, a Politburo member himself, but one who is rarely in Peking.

"Old Peng!" Mao welcomes him. "You've come at the right time."

The subject is Korea, the party chairman tells him, and whether China should send troops to help the North Koreans. Everyone is expressing their opinion, and they'll want to hear yours, Mao says.

Peng is taken aback. Unprepared, he can only sit and listen as one after another Politburo member raises worrying questions about such an intervention. The Chinese are weary of war, the People's Liberation Army's equipment is old and worn, and finances are weak.

Only one member speaks in favor, but it's the most important one, Mao Tse-tung, who ends the meeting sounding conciliatory but unconvinced. "All you have said is not without basis," he tells the skeptics. "But when other people are in crisis, how can we stand aside with our arms folded? This will make me grieve."

The Korea question may be new to Peng Teh-huai, but the leaders in Peking have pondered it since midsummer. They have already taken contingency steps, ordering one People's Liberation Army unit after another to redeploy to Manchuria in the Northeast, across the border from North Korea.

Spending the night at the Peking Hotel, Peng cannot sleep. The old soldier blames the soft bed and moves to the floor, but remains wide awake, thoughts flashing through his mind about the Korean conflict and what it means for China.

Two South Korean divisions have now crossed the 38th Parallel into North Korea, and American troops seem poised to do the same. If they take all of Korea, they will be sitting just across the Yalu River, threatening China's Northeast. Peng summons an old saying: "The tiger wants to eat people, and will do so when he's hungry."

In the morning, he meets again with Mao in his personal office at Chung Nan Hai. The chairman asks for his thoughts.

"I had almost no sleep last night," the general begins. He acknowledges the difficulties raised by others, but says focusing on the problems risks missing the potential disastrous consequences of America's march toward the Yalu. He has given it careful consideration, he says, and "I favor the decision to send troops to Korea."

"Good! Good!" Mao responds.

They discuss the challenges further, and then Mao turns to a practical matter: Who should lead the Chinese army in Korea?

Peng suggests Lin Piao, celebrated commander in the civil war's final decisive victories. Mao tells Peng that Lin already has pleaded ill health—actually he opposes the intervention—and that Mao and his closest advisers believe Peng should take on the job.

"What do you think?" Mao asks.

Peng, again unprepared, is silent at first. But since the top leadership has made the decision, he finally replies, "I will obey it."

"You, Old Peng, are a fine man!" Mao exclaims. "You, Old Peng, are a fine man!"

Later, at the reconvened Politburo meeting, the indecisive discussion continues. Then Peng speaks for the first time, warning that the conquest of all Korea by an America on an anticommunist crusade would directly threaten China. "It is better to strike them early rather than later," he says.

Seizing on this respected commander's "convincing" words, Mao drives home his own views: "The Americans are now forcing us to enter the battle."

Decisiveness begins taking charge. The meeting's mood shifts inexorably toward intervention. Mao gets unanimous approval to appoint Peng commander of the Chinese expeditionary force.

Later, at dinner, Mao and Peng discuss organization and timing. A demanding Mao hopes to have troops entering North Korea by mid-October. But one great uncertainty remains: the extent of Soviet help in weapons, vehicles, and especially airpower. Mao tells Peng that Chou En-lai, who fills two roles as Chinese premier and foreign minister, will go to Moscow to meet with Soviet leader Stalin and secure an aid package.

As the late-night talks end, Mao raises a personal note, telling Peng he will assign his eldest son, PLA officer Mao An-ying, to Peng's staff.

Peng is uneasy. His wartime headquarters will be a dangerous place. But he must acquiesce to Mao's wishes.

Back at the hotel, Peng sinks into his sofa, smoking a cigarette, deep in thought. There's so much to do. His Hsian staff must be given instructions for carrying on. He must organize his new command. And he must send word to his wife of this new assignment, the latest of many to separate them since 1938, when he, at forty, married the beautiful Pu An-hsiu, twenty-six, a university-educated party bureaucrat, in Ya'nan, the communists' civil war refuge in Northwest China.[9]

It was a match typical among commanders in those days, men whose wives had perished on the Long March or were lost in some distant province and whose eyes then fell on pretty young intellectuals flocking to the party's cause.

In Peng's case, it meant abandoning another part of his peasant past, a long-ago arranged marriage in his home village to a friend's twelve-year-old sister. She grew into lonely womanhood while he fought somewhere beyond her imagining. Nationalist agents began hunting for this communist commander's wife. In desperation, she remarried to throw them off her trail. But they did find Peng's two brothers and executed them.

Remembering those brothers, Peng calls in his secretary to give him one last instruction for the night: summon Peng's fatherless niece and nephew from their school in the provinces. He must supply them with some clothing and other provisions before he heads off to his latest war.

On Sunday in Pyongyang, China's ambassador delivers a cable from Mao to Kim Il-sung. "In view of the current situation, we have decided to send volunteers to Korea to help you fight against the aggressors," it says.

The North Korean leader claps his hands, overjoyed. "Well done! Excellent!" he shouts.[10]

A MID-OCTOBER DAY, 1950

Chung Dong-kyu, in hiding, watches U.S. jets strafe farmers

Medical student Chung Dong-kyu has seen repeated tragic bombings since July, when U.S. B-29s first turned Chongjin, the North Korean port city, into a smoking ruin of rubble and broken bodies. But what he's witnessing on this day particularly shocks him.

Watching from his hideout in a mountain village, Chung sees American F-80 Starfighters, reviled by local people as the "swallow-planes," swoop in without warning and strafe farmers in their oxcarts. "What do they think they're hauling in their carts?" the outraged eighteen-year-old asks himself.

He and other North Koreans cannot know that General MacArthur in Tokyo is soon to issue a classified order instructing his air arm to "destroy every means of communication and every installation, factory, city, and village" in North Korea.[11] The devastation will only spread.

Like peasants all across North Korea, the farmers of Chu Ul village learn to work their fields only at night.

In some cases those fields were "given" to them by the schoolboy Chung Dong-kyu. In the great agricultural reforms of 1946, when farmlands were redistributed from big landlords to landless peasants, the communist authorities recruited help from Dong-kyu and other eighth graders adept at math, a skill many North Koreans lacked. Partnering with a middle-aged farmer, Dong-kyu spent long days measuring land and applying redistribution formulas in and around Chu Ul, the ancestral village where he lived.

Now, four years later, he has returned to Chu Ul and gone into hiding from those same authorities.

Soon after he was promoted last month to the third year at Chongjin's four-year medical college, the school was shut down. Wartime needs had grown too demanding, and the half-trained students were sent to help out at hospitals in the region. Fortunately for Chung, he was assigned to the small facility in Chu Ul, south of Chongjin.

A week after joining the hospital staff, however, he received a notice from the medical school that his entire junior class was being inducted into the Korean People's Army. His world was abruptly crashing around him. Lacking a doctor's qualifications, he knew at best he'd be assigned as a medic in the deadly front lines.

That same day he took part in his first surgical operation, carried out by a Dr. Kim from the medical school, a kindly man much admired by the students. Young Chung told Kim about the draft notice and his fears. The doctor whispered into his ear that the South Koreans had crossed the 38th Parallel and were advancing rapidly northward. "You might well be killed just getting to your assigned post," the doctor warned him.

That evening after dinner, Chung told his mother about the notice and what Kim had said. Almost without a word—"quick to hear and slow to speak" is how he thinks of her—she packed up some things and said they would trek that very night the four miles up to her mother's house, in a more elevated, more remote spot.

She cared nothing about the politics or meaning of the war. She wanted simply to protect her only son, in a Korean family the foremost treasure. After all, before Dong-kyu's birth, after two daughters, she had climbed a nearby mountainside every morning to pray to Buddha for a baby boy. When he was born a sickly infant, this uneducated woman consulted with shamans for mystical cures and nursed him watchfully through boyhood in Manchuria. When he almost died from a burst appendix—to be saved in

Harbin by a Japanese surgeon—she grew still more protective of the son she knows will become a "great man."

At his grandmother's, Chung spends tedious days in the barn, hiding from the view of any passersby. His grandmother keeps a lookout for military or police who might be hunting draft dodgers, sometimes having the diminutive teenager hide in a giant clay pot.

As the autumn days pass into weeks, a cold front moves in from the north, and a thin coat of white drapes the nearby two-thousand-foot mountains. Chung hears the distant sound of artillery to the south.

WEDNESDAY, OCTOBER 18, 1950

A troubled Matt Ridgway watches as MacArthur plunges into North Korea

Within the ring corridors of the Pentagon, the army's deputy chief of staff for operations is studying the battle reports crossing his desk on a daily, even hourly, basis. The reports are good, but Matt Ridgway, the seasoned field commander, is troubled. He doesn't like the look of the strategic map.

Since the success of the Inchon landing and the recapture of Seoul, the U.S. and South Korean forces have rolled on, retaking all of occupied South Korea from the invaders of June and driving on beyond the 38th Parallel. The ROK Army's 3rd Division crossed the line in the east on October 1. A week later, the U.S. 1st Cavalry Division drove into North Korea from Kaesong, north of Seoul, followed by the 24th Infantry Division and the 27th British Commonwealth Brigade, which joined the breakout from the Pusan Perimeter after Inchon.[12]

The plunge into the North was based on cautious, at times ambiguous, authorizations from the U.N. General Assembly and the U.S. Joint Chiefs of Staff, directives that foresaw an offensive that would reunite Korea by force. But the Joint Chiefs wanted MacArthur to take care not to provoke the Chinese or Soviets. It instructed him on September 27 to send only Korean troops into the northern third of North Korea, the provinces bordering China and the Soviet Union.[13]

At this critical point, President Truman decided he should meet his Far East commander face-to-face, and for the first time.

The president and General MacArthur convened with their entourages on Sunday, four days ago, at a "halfway" point, remote Wake Island in the mid-Pacific. It was an exceedingly brief and superficial meeting that left many questions unexplored. One question Truman did pose: What are the chances of Chinese or Soviet intervention? "Very little," MacArthur replied.[14]

Through all of this, the Pentagon leadership seems to have developed what Matt Ridgway later describes as an "almost superstitious regard for General MacArthur's infallibility." But this Pentagon deputy, whose support for the Inchon plan proved crucial in allaying Washington nervousness over that bold operation, is himself developing serious concerns about MacArthur's next plan, about what he sees unfolding on the map.

The problem is that the Far East commander has conceived a final blow that is really two unrelated blows, by Eighth Army up North Korea's western corridor, and by X Corps, repositioned after the Inchon operation, up the eastern corridor.

Matt Ridgway can look back for lessons to the climactic Battle of the Bulge in 1944, when the Germans attacked massively in Belgium, against the Allied northern flank. Ridgway, who had fought from Sicily through Normandy and risen from a forty-six-year-old lieutenant colonel to a forty-seven-year-old major general, was able straightaway to lead his XVIII Airborne Corps into the battle and to help turn the tide against the Germans.

Now, in Korea, separated by a forbidding mountain range, under separate commands, unable to support and closely coordinate with each other, and as the harsh Korean winter approaches, each thrust by the U.N. command will become more vulnerable. Ridgway believes the next step instead should be a linkup creating a solid front across the peninsula, offering flank support on all sides.

For now, MacArthur's troops push on forward.

On this day, the South Koreans seize the Hamhung-Hungnam industrial port complex in North Korea's east. In the west, combined Korean and American forces are taking aim at Pyongyang. And the U.S. leadership is telling itself, with MacArthur, that there's little chance the Chinese will become involved. Repeated CIA assessments reassure them on that.

China's Chou En-lai has warned the Americans otherwise. Through back channels, he has signaled the Chinese would, indeed, step in if U.S. forces crossed the 38th Parallel. But Secretary of State Acheson dismisses that warning as "bluff."[15]

THURSDAY, OCTOBER 19, 1950

Peng Teh-huai crosses the Yalu, and a die is cast

The Yalu River first spills from a lake atop snowcapped Mount Paektu in Korea's northeastern corner and then winds five hundred miles south-westward, where its shallow gray-green waters flow between two cities, Antung in China and Sinuiju, North Korea, before it empties into the Yellow Sea. A pair of sturdy steel bridges built by the Japanese in colonial days, three-quarters of a mile long, link the two cities.

In the deepening darkness this evening, General Peng Teh-huai stands on the Antung riverside and watches as a long, shadowy stream of figures crosses one of those bridges in near silence, the armed manpower of China pouring south into Korea.

An advance guard of the People's Liberation Army's 40th Army led the way at five thirty, as the sun set, taken by train over the railroad bridge. Thousands of other troops are following, in vehicles and on foot, joined by oxcarts, pack ponies, and thousands of Manchurian laborers impressed into service as bearers of ammunition and other supplies.

Every soldier has stripped the red star from his cap and other PLA insignia from his green cotton uniform. They're now the "Chinese People's Volunteer Force," a charade devised by the leadership to pretend the communist Chinese government, which seeks U.N. membership, is not going to war against the United Nations in Korea.[16]

"Volunteers, indeed!" Peng later jokes. "I'm no volunteer. My chief sent me here!"[17]

It's growing colder by the hour, and the time comes for the commander to join his troops.

Peng climbs into an automobile with his Chinese-speaking North Korean liaison. His secretary, bodyguards, and a Korean interpreter fill out the small party in the car and a trailing radio truck, as it rolls south over the Yalu, toward the war.

This scene, this full-scale Chinese intervention in the Korean conflict, almost didn't happen.

At eight o'clock on Wednesday night just a week ago, General Peng, at his Manchurian headquarters in Shenyang, received an urgent coded telegram from Mao Tse-tung in Peking ordering him to stand down, freezing Mao's orders to launch the secretive operation.

Chou En-lai, negotiating with Josef Stalin at the Kremlin leader's Black Sea villa, had alerted Mao that Stalin was reneging on what was thought a commitment to supply Soviet air cover for the Chinese army's ground operations in Korea. Stalin plainly feared an all-out war with the Americans.

The entire operation might be called off. Peng rushed to Peking for an emergency session of the Communist Party Politburo. There he put on a display of his notorious short temper, angrily railing against the Russians, threatening to resign from his new command.

Mao then took charge, calming the discussion. He said the Soviets had pledged substantial military equipment for the war and would provide an air umbrella over Chinese cities exposed to possible U.S. Air Force retaliation.

With or without Soviet air cover in Korea, failing to keep the Americans away from China's borders would still be a direct threat to our revolution, Mao told them. As usual, the chairman prevailed. The meeting ended with a consensus that China must act. But the uncertainty didn't end there.

Mao kept Peng in Peking another day to discuss strategy. It was decided Peng would adopt a defensive posture for some months, digging in on a line between the Yalu and Pyongyang to deter further American advances. If the U.N. command doesn't attack, Peng will have time to prepare an offensive.[18]

Returning to Manchuria, Peng convened a meeting in Antung of his generals. He knew they'd grown uneasy over the rushed mobilization and the firepower of the Americans. In his gruff Hunanese peasant's accent, he tried to reassure them, as soldiers and as Communist Party loyalists.

The Americans' morale is poor, and they're dispersing their forces vulnerably in North Korea, he said. Tactically, "we are better than the enemy." Our troops will seek to close with the Americans, with bayonets, with hand grenades, he said. "The enemy is afraid of such operations."

He told them "a handful of big U.S. capitalists" were behind the war. "How pathetic for the world revolution if we stood by with folded arms and did not actively help a neighboring nation struggle against aggression."

That night, Monday, a regiment of the 42nd Army, a vanguard unit, crossed the Yalu via a railroad bridge at Manpojin, 130 miles upriver from Antung.

But the concerns were not eased. The next day, after returning to his Shenyang headquarters, 130 miles north of the Yalu, Peng received a telegram from several of his top commanders urging a delay in deployment until next spring. Without air support, and with too little antiaircraft artillery, the Chinese forces will be cut up by American airpower, artillery, and armor, they said. "We have not been fully prepared," they wrote.

This admission of halfheartedness disturbed Peng. He advised Mao, who once more summoned him to Peking. By now Chou En-lai had returned from Moscow with reassuring words: the Soviets will supply all the weapons, ammunition, and other matériel we need; they will defend Chinese territory from the air; and their air force might still, later, enter the Korea conflict itself.

Mao was adamant. The decision cannot be changed "no matter how many difficulties," he told his inner circle. They scheduled the initial major crossing for this evening.[19]

Peng's two-vehicle convoy has now reached the Korean side of the Yalu and is met by Pak Hon-yong, North Korea's vice premier and foreign minister. They set off together to locate the latest temporary headquarters of the retreating North Korean government. General Peng is to meet with Kim Il-sung.[20]

The Chinese plan is to move their divisions across the Yalu as quickly as possible, crossing at three locations, before the Americans spot the operation and bomb the bridges.

Advance parties are posting Chinese signs on Korean roads and establishing field kitchens and supply points. Troops will move at night, covering twenty to thirty miles before each dawn, concealing themselves during the day in villages or in woods, in camouflaged tents. Along with darkness, the low cloud cover and mists of late October in northern Korea will help keep this huge army undetected. By early November, three hundred thousand Chinese troops are to be in Korea.[21]

Earlier this day, as Peng waited for night to fall, South Korean and American troops took Pyongyang, abandoned by the North Korean army. On Friday, a confident General MacArthur flies into the conquered northern capital, telling reporters the conflict is "definitely" in its final stage.[22]

Peng Teh-huai comments to an aide, "The more arrogant MacArthur is, the better for us."[23]

SATURDAY, OCTOBER 21, 1950

Buddy Wenzel and the 7th Cavalry enter Pyongyang

The 7th Cavalry Regiment has rolled more than 250 miles north since breaking out of the Pusan Perimeter a month ago.

Once across the 38th Parallel and into northern territory, the regiment and the rest of the 1st Cavalry Division inflicted ever-greater damage on the enemy and whatever else lay in its path, summoning artillery and airpower or applying Zippo cigarette lighters to thatched-roof homes, destroying entire villages along the way. "Every enemy shot released a deluge of destruction," writes London *Daily Telegraph* correspondent Reginald Thompson, accompanying 7th Cavalry and 8th Cavalry troops. "Civilians died in the rubble and ashes of their homes."[24]

Buddy Wenzel and his 7th Cavalry comrades view it as self-protection. "In combat you either become an animal and live, or stay timid and die," automatic rifleman Tom Boyd is to recall. "I personally killed anything in front of me when we moved up."

North Korean rear guards still slowed the advance, wounding and killing Americans, turning young soldiers like Wenzel even more bitter over being caught in this war between Koreans. "We had a lot of hate," he is to recall. When checking village homes, "instead of sticking your head in the door, you take a hand grenade and throw it in there. You didn't care if anybody was in there or not. Sometimes you hear a scream. But you weren't going to take any chances."[25]

Now, in weather turned unseasonably wintry, the 7th Cavalry has entered Pyongyang, seventy-five miles north of the 38th Parallel. Two days ago, other lead units of the 1st Cavalry Division and ROK Army were the first to move into the northern capital, hastily abandoned by the KPA and the North Korean government.

The 7th Cavalrymen find a hilly, half-deserted city of bombed-out buildings, broad boulevards, and nervous people. Walls are plastered with large propaganda posters denouncing the "evil and cruel" Americans and with giant portraits of Kim Il-sung and Stalin. The earlier U.S. troops have been busy looting government offices and private homes. The South Korean military has been seen summarily executing some KPA prisoners.[26]

Within hours of entering Pyongyang, the regiment is ordered to move on, to occupy the port of Chinnampo, thirty-five miles to the southwest. In the early-morning darkness on Sunday, after pushing aside light resistance, they take the town, and in the coming days they settle in. For the first time in three months at war, Wenzel and his buddies enjoy the comfort of sleeping under roofs and for more than two hours at a stretch, along with hot food and hot baths. Some even get to return to Pyongyang to see comedian Bob Hope, who brings his USO show to the newly captured city.[27]

Back home in the States, another entertainer, country signer Jimmie Osborne, is on the airwaves with a new single, "Thank God for Victory in Korea."[28] The men in Korea tell each other they should be home by Christmas. First Cavalry Division officers even make plans for a victory parade back in Tokyo. Buddy Wenzel hopes the "Truman year" extension will be canceled and he can reunite sooner than expected with "Green Eyes," his girl Dot.

Then, barely a week into their soft occupation duty, the 7th Cavalry Regiment is ordered to move north, to join in what General MacArthur believes will be the final rout of the communist enemy.[29]

SUNDAY, OCTOBER 29, 1950

Chi Chao-chu returns to China, lamenting his
"two beloved nations" are at war

The driver turns down the street that borders the eastern moat of Peking's Forbidden City. Up ahead Chi Chao-chu sees Father waiting, standing in front of his house in a traditional long robe, a bald man with a stringy gray beard.

The car pulls up. Chao-chu jumps out.

"*Wah*, you have come back!" Father says with a broad smile.

"Yes, *Ba*, I am back." They grasp hands and gaze at one another for a long moment.

It has been more than four years since Father left the family in the United States to return to China as dean of Peking University's law school. And it has been little more than a month since twenty-one-year-old Chao-chu announced to his mother in New York that he was abandoning his studies at Harvard to return home in China's time of need.

Four days ago, he debarked from the SS *President Cleveland* in Hong Kong Harbor. When he reached the Chinese mainland, he knelt and kissed the ground. A long train ride later, he is in the capital, where he can see much has changed since he left China as a nine-year-old in 1939.

Every building and utility pole seems to fly a red flag. Walls adorned with revolutionary slogans exhort the people to ever-greater efforts. Driving past Tien An Men Gate, the Gate of Heavenly Peace, he sees a giant, two-story portrait of Mao Tse-tung hanging over the entrance to the Forbidden City. The look is mirrored in the streets, where the people of Peking have adopted the blue tunic uniform, with turned-down collars and soft caps, associated with Mao and his communists.

What has also changed, Chi Chao-chu finds in his short time back in China, is his ability to speak his native tongue. After a dozen formative years in America, his English is better than his Chinese.

Luckily, Father is fluent in both, and they talk into the evening in his comfortable living room, sipping green tea, catching up on family news.

Mother was upset when he told her he was leaving, Chao-chu says, and she's unsure whether she, too, will return to China. Chagrined to hear this, his father says it may soon be difficult to come to China from America. "China is in the war, and who can say where it will end."

Chao-chu then tells him he wants to join the "People's Volunteers" headed for Korea. Father scoffs that he'd make "a poor soldier with those eyeglasses." "And what will happen if you don't understand Chinese and someone shouts, 'Duck!'?" he asks his son.

No, he tells him, you must enroll in university and relearn Chinese as soon as possible. He explains that Chao-chu's older half-brother, Chao-ting, the well-connected communist loyalist who is now deputy director of the People's Bank, has left a recommendation letter that will win Chao-chu admission to Peking's prestigious Tsinghua University.

In the morning, he sets out by bicycle to the campus in northwestern Peking, pedaling ten miles through the bustling city streets, past scenes and smells so different from America and feeling conspicuous as an unusually tall Chinese in a Western suit. He must get a "Mao" outfit as soon as possible.

Relieved to find many of the university staff speak English, he is quickly enrolled and within days moves into a cramped, barracks-like dormitory, confronts the spartan student diet of sorghum, millet, and the like, and embarks on intensive studies in chemistry, as his father has always intended, and in Chinese.

Of his new circumstances, harsh in comparison with Harvard, Chi Chao-chu tells himself he's serving an "apprenticeship as a revolutionary." He fancies that someday he'll help China build an atomic bomb, to stand up to the imperialists. But he also laments that "my two beloved nations" are now at war.

Peking government radio has been calling the "aggressors" in North Korea a threat to Manchuria and is summoning all Chinese to "be on the same front as the Korean people—opposed to American imperialism."[30] It has also announced the huge Chinese army, legacy of revolution, is advancing in the west as well, invading Tibet to absorb that independent land into China.[31]

———❈———

Temperatures are already dipping below freezing along the northeast coast as troops of the 17th Infantry Regiment, aboard seven LSTs (landing ship, tanks), approach the beaches flanking Iwon, North Korea, 160 miles above the 38th Parallel.[32]

For Private Gil Isham, in Korea for barely a month, it's the second amphibious landing of his war. The regiment and the rest of the 7th Infantry Division were to make a fighting assault on Iwon, but then they learned South Korea's Capital Division, racing up the coast, had driven North Korean forces from the town days ago.

The same happened more than 100 miles to the south, when the 1st Marine Division landed at Wonsan. Delayed by the navy's minesweeping of the harbor, the Marines, set to storm ashore, instead found a port city so pacified by fast-moving South Korean troops that a U.S. headquarters unit, a Marine air wing, and Bob Hope's USO show were already in Wonsan to greet them.[33]

The Marines, Isham's 7th Division and allied Korean units— comprising X Corps—are the strike force in General MacArthur's plan for seizing the eastern corridor of North Korea. MacArthur has issued a directive brushing aside instructions from Washington, fearing a wider war, that only South Korean troops—and no Americans—should enter the northern provinces bordering China and the Soviet Union.[34]

Instead, MacArthur and the X Corps commander, Major General Edward M. Almond, ordered the two American divisions to attack northward until they reach the Manchurian border. In Washington, learning of this, the Joint Chiefs queried MacArthur about the seeming policy violation. He dismissively told them it was a "matter of military necessity." He wasn't countermanded.

Isham and the 17th Infantry have had scant rest since landing at Inchon on September 25, to back up the Marines in the recapture of Seoul.

The eighteen-year-old recruit and his fellow infantrymen got their baptism of fire in clashes south of the Han River with retreating North Korean troops in the last days of September. The regiment was then ordered 220 miles south to Pusan, by truck and tank, to embark on this new seaborne operation.

Now the landing ships have opened their great bow doors and deposited the men of the 17th Infantry on the soft sands of Iwon's beaches, after a journey through rough seas and debilitating seasickness. No other American unit has advanced this far north.

As they regroup and acclimate to the frigid weather, they're issued down-filled winter sleeping bags to replace the summer variety, and they give up their suede-leather combat boots for something new called "shoepacs," boots whose lower part is rubber and upper half is leather. They're told this footwear is better suited to winter fighting.

They're also told that only demoralized, scattered North Korean army units stand in the way of their mission, to join in the conquest of all North Korea. The 17th Infantry's objective is the town of Hyesanjin, over difficult mountain roads 90 air miles north of Iwon, on the Yalu River across from Chinese Manchuria.

MONDAY, OCTOBER 30, 1950

Bill Shinn joins Syngman Rhee on a visit to the enemy capital

The news spreads through the streets of the city: Syngman Rhee has come to Pyongyang, barely a week after its capture. Thousands stream toward the city hall plaza, where the white-haired South Korean president is holding forth from a balcony.

"I was last here in 1911," Rhee, born nearby seventy-five years ago, tells the gathering crowd. "I am able to come again because the United Nations have driven out the communists. I'll come again any time you want me to. . . . No one, ever again, can divide our people."[35]

It's a moment, with its promise of reunification, that the old Korean nationalist has hungered for ever since the Americans flew him into Seoul in 1945 to lead the southern half of the divided peninsula. But that dream, of leading all Korea, may still elude him.

Standing nearby, Bill Shinn listens to Rhee expound emotionally on "this beautiful land of ours"; about the mythical founder of the Korean nation, Tangoon; and about the Koreans as a "homogeneous race for more than four thousand years."

The enterprising reporter Shinn managed to insert himself as the only journalist aboard the plane that carried Rhee on this unannounced visit to the northern capital, where they're greeted by fluttering *taegukki*, South Korean flags, that city residents have produced from somewhere.

The journalist accompanies Rhee on a sentimental detour to the tiny Pubyong Pavilion, the fifteen-hundred-year-old "Floating Pavilion" that offers romantic views of the Taedong River, a scene marred by the wreckage of bridges destroyed in U.S. bombing.[36]

Along the riverside, they stumble across a disturbing sight—the bodies of two bound American soldiers, prisoners coldly shot as Pyongyang's defenders melted away in mid-October. Most prisoners are said to have been taken farther north, but a week ago the world learned of the chilling massacre of sixty-eight Americans by the retreating North Koreans, outside a railroad tunnel thirty-five miles north of Pyongyang.[37]

Flying back to Seoul, Shinn asks Rhee his feelings after his brief time in the enemy capital.

"I've never been happier," he says. "Our victory is at hand. Not an inch of our territory should be in communist hands."

As he speaks, however, U.S. and other representatives at the United Nations in New York are preparing to foil Rhee's hopes of governing all Korea, instead envisioning a U.N.-overseen or U.S. military regime in the North. Rhee has even been told some in Washington want to remove him as South Korean president.

In October 1945, when he was flown on General MacArthur's personal plane from Tokyo to Seoul, Rhee was the choice of U.S. intelligence and military officials to lead South Korea. The U.S.-educated, English-speaking Christian was viewed as a reliable anticommunist protégé, despite objections from a State Department that had dealt with the egotistical, troublesome Rhee for decades as he agitated in U.S. exile for Korean independence.[38]

After taking power, Rhee's ruthlessness and unpredictability, and his reliance on former Japanese collaborators, alienated both Americans and

Koreans. Five months ago, when the opposition gained greater leverage in National Assembly elections, it was on the verge of stripping the president of much of his power. Then the North Korean invasion intervened.[39]

Meanwhile, another force also seeks to frustrate Syngman Rhee's plans—the huge, unseen "volunteer" Chinese army that has just clashed with South Korean units for the first time, forty miles south of the Yalu.

TUESDAY, OCTOBER 31, 1950

Shin Hyung-kyu journeys into the "insane" realm of war

Badly in need of a wash, the teenaged military policeman wanders down a street along the south bank of the Taedong River, across from central Pyongyang, and knocks on a door.

An old woman finally opens it and is startled at the sight of a soldier, a gun, a strange uniform, filthy and dust covered. Shin Hyung-kyu tells her he'd simply like some hot water to wash away days of grime. She smiles. "A South Korean soldier is here!" she shouts inside. Shortly, two haggard young men, her sons, climb out of an underground shelter. They have been hiding from the northern army's draft since the war began— four months buried in the dark.

As she heats up water and Shin washes, he realizes again that, whatever his misfortunes, he's more fortunate than many in this dreadful time, especially those in the bombed-out North Korean capital. As he leaves, he thanks them for their hospitality and hands them some of his ration biscuits.

Shin's ROK Army unit, B Company, 3rd Military Police Battalion, has arrived early this morning in the Sunkyo-ri district on the Taedong's south bank, after days traveling in a convoy up from Seoul. In the past month, since graduating from the MP academy in Pusan, the "boy soldier" from Kochang in the deep south has seen more of his homeland than in all his seventeen years, and more of the evil of war than he ever could have imagined.

He and his MP comrades patrol Sunkyo-ri and the nearby Pyongyang airport, teaming up in the coming days with American MPs. His middle school English helps the smart, hardworking young Korean mesh well with the Americans.

The ROK soldiers feel grateful to the foreigners who have come to their country's aid. But at the same time, they're repelled by the racism they see and hear every day—"Goddamn gooks!"—and by worse. Many of these young Americans are on the prowl for sex, pressing Korean soldiers or local men to guide them to prostitutes or to women in such distress they'll sell themselves. Shin also becomes aware of cases of outright rape.

After days of relative calm, his B Company is next transferred to help guard Pyongyang's main prison, now a temporary lockup for prisoners of war before they're sent to POW camps in the South. The scene is shocking.

Prisoners are jammed by the dozens into lightless cells where a man can't lie down without half-lying on his neighbor—one hundred men in a place the size of one of Shin Hyung-kyu's school classrooms. Men suffer from wounds and disease. The stench from open-bucket latrines overwhelms even the sickening smell of the men themselves. Many prisoners are hapless "volunteer soldiers," southerners conscripted by the KPA after it invaded the South.

Most horribly of all, two major fires break out during his time at the prison, burning to death trapped POWs. The fires are fed by piles of cotton wadding stored in makeshift cells that were workrooms where civilian prisoners in the past made padded-quilt winter clothing for the North Korean army.

Its horrors aside, the prison turns out to be an improbable boon for Shin and his secret avocation as a would-be scientist. He finds chemistry and physics books in an office, no doubt belonging to a North Korean officer. They add to a textbook collection he began building from abandoned libraries on his unit's trek north. In hidden moments, with a flashlight in his sleeping bag, he devours these introductions to modern science. He won't abandon the idea of returning to school, even in this war's worst days.

One of those days occurs after the prison is closed and B Company is assigned to patrol Pyongyang's streets. Word comes that the falling water level in the prison's reservoir has exposed decomposing bodies stacked at the bottom, believed to be South Korean civilians kidnapped and taken north last summer, and then shot, with hands tied behind their backs, when the northern army fled Pyongyang.

The news sickens Shin in a visceral, personal way: he and his comrades drank that water daily.

Repeatedly on their journey up from the South, the MPs saw the aftermath of northern atrocities—mass graves, clumps of bodies, wailing relatives of the dead, usually local southern officials, policemen, land-owners, and their families. Over three days in mid-October, retreating North Korean troops summarily executed some two thousand people abducted from South Korea, burying them in mass graves at a place called Kiam-ri, north of Pyongyang.

Shin and his comrades also saw signs of the bloody retribution exacted by ROK Army units and others—a rampage of terror in captured northern territory carried out by vengeful southern police and soldiers and by right-wing youth groups transported above the 38th Parallel to hunt down real or imagined political enemies.

In a single county, Sinchon, fifty miles south of Pyongyang, northern civilians are being murdered en masse, many of them women and children, many meeting death in barbaric ways, through torture, burning, being buried alive. It eventually emerges that right-wing Korean militant groups, both locals and returning refugees, many Christian, are responsible, in violence that broke out between leftists and rightists as northern troops retreated.[40] American knowledge of these events is clear. On November 16, a U.S. Eighth Army colonel reports "communist hunting activity by ROK troops in North Korea."[41] The Sinchon death toll reaches into the thousands.

The escalating brutality, even among his fellow MPs, horrifies Shin. "Have we gone insane?" the teenager wonders. "What has become of our human compassion?"

In the cold nights, as the north wind slices through the ruins of the office building that's become their "barracks," he summons up images of his mother, disappearing behind the bend in the road last July when he left her, and of his father, helpless, awaiting his fate in a detainee tent in Kochang. When would he be able to rejoin his family?

The ROK and U.S. Armies are pressing their advance toward the Yalu River. Perhaps the war—and the insanity—will end soon.

NOVEMBER

WEDNESDAY, NOVEMBER 1, 1950

Peng Teh-huai's troops stumble upon their first Americans
at a place called Unsan

An early winter is descending on northernmost Korea as General Peng Teh-huai deploys his forces across one of the peninsula's most rugged regions.

He has established his headquarters in an abandoned gold mine in Taeyu-dong, a town deep in the Chogyruyong, the Red Ghost Mountains, ninety miles north of Pyongyang. It's where the Chinese commander first found Kim Il-sung and his retreating government and where he learned from the North Koreans that the enemy was advancing more rapidly up the peninsula than he thought. Peng would have to abandon his plan for a cautious defense and go on the attack. While tens of thousands of Chinese troops march down North Korea's eastern valleys, he is concentrating nine divisions in the west, against the advancing and now outnumbered ROK 6th and 8th Divisions.

A week ago, Peng's troops ambushed and destroyed a ROK battalion marching north near Pukchin, just twelve miles southeast of his command post. Within two hours, 325 ROK soldiers were killed and 161 captured.[1] Then the Chinese took aim at South Koreans holding a strongpoint at Unsan, a mining town fifteen miles farther south, fifty miles from the Yalu and China. They found Americans instead.

Peng's huge Chinese People's Volunteer Force has skillfully maintained the secrecy of its move into North Korea, marching only at night, camouflaging itself expertly during the day. On the approach to Unsan, troops of the 116th Division set forest fires to further block aerial surveillance.[2]

They launched their attack after dark yesterday, swarming over hills north of Unsan, meeting little resistance. Finally, before dawn, they ran up against heavy artillery and machine-gun fire from one well-defended height. They were cut down in great numbers, and word spread: they're Americans, the first Peng's troops have encountered. When Chinese reinforcements arrived, the defenders pulled back toward Unsan.[3]

The 8th Cavalry, one of three infantry regiments of the 1st Cavalry Division, had been sent forward from Pyongyang to relieve the South Koreans at Unsan. Two of its three battalions took up positions at the northern and western edges of the town. Its 3rd Battalion dug in to the southwest.

As dusk falls on this evening, thousands of Chinese troops have closed in on Unsan from the north and west and are looping around to the south. As whistles and bugles blare in the dark, they strike the 1st and 2nd Battalions, finding a gap between the two and soon engaging in hand-to-hand combat with the Americans. As midnight approaches, low on ammunition, the defenders pull back down the only road open to the south. Many vehicles make it through, but at about two-thirty in the morning a Chinese force overruns and blocks the road, slaughtering trapped Americans, sending survivors scattering overland.

The 3rd Battalion area, bordered on the south by the meandering Nammyon River, has remained quiet. Then, around three, a small column of soldiers crosses a bridge over the shallow stream. American sentries take them for South Koreans. They're Chinese commandos wearing captured ROK uniforms.

When they approach the battalion command post, one blows a bugle and his comrades hurl satchel charges and grenades, a signal for other 116th Division troops to storm across the Nammyon. Third Battalion troopers sleeping in their foxholes awaken to the sight of enemy soldiers rushing them with bayonets fixed. In the light of burning trucks, Americans and Chinese lock in close combat. Men on the outer perimeter retreat from ground littered with wounded and dead. Survivors gather in a tight perimeter around three tanks and the command bunker, holding out until daylight.

The morning brings U.S. air strikes that keep the attackers at bay. Meanwhile, a rescue column from the sister 5th Cavalry Regiment tries but fails to break through a Chinese roadblock south of the 3rd Battalion area, suffering heavy casualties. By nightfall, U.S. higher headquarters pulls back the rescue force and orders the entire 1st Cavalry Division to withdraw to more defensible positions on the south side of the Chongchon, a shallow, broad river closer to Pyongyang.

The abandoned men of the 3rd Battalion, 8th Cavalry Regiment, fight on, beating back a half-dozen attacks Thursday night. The ground around their two-hundred-yard-wide perimeter is covered with hundreds of enemy bodies. American casualties mount, from enemy mortar as well as machine-gun and sniper fire. Finally, on Saturday, after more than forty-eight hours under siege, 200 able-bodied survivors infiltrate eastward from the perimeter, leaving behind 250 wounded to be taken prisoner. Many heading south do not make it alive to friendly lines. Of the battalion's 800 men, about 600 are dead or captive.[4]

Thirty miles north of Unsan, in his mineshaft command post, General Peng welcomes news of the unexpected American rout. But he doesn't order pursuit of the withdrawing forces. His marching foot soldiers can't keep up with the highly mechanized enemy, and he's wary about so quickly engaging the powerful American main force.

The Chinese commander lays out his current thinking in a coded telegraph to Mao Tse-tung in Peking. He proposes allowing the enemy to advance northward toward the Yalu, far into North Korea, and then striking, trapping him. Mao approves.

Peng is still reinforcing his troops. Within weeks, his strength will rise to 450,000 men from 300,000.[5] But MacArthur and the Americans are still oblivious to what they face. Although a few Chinese prisoners have been taken, and frontline officers have sounded alarms, the Tokyo command chooses to interpret the Chinese presence as token. In Washington, the CIA concludes in an intelligence memo that "between 15,000 and 20,000" Chinese troops are in North Korea.[6]

—⁂—

He's free. It's a miracle.

Kang Ki-suk, young Chang Sang's brother-in-law, the newlywed husband of older sister Ran, seized by the North Koreans from his hiding place during the occupation of Seoul, simply reappeared one day at the Kims' front door, filthy, weary, and telling the story of his escape.

It was in late summer, when the communists were marching off skilled southerners northward and drafting others into their army or labor gangs. Ki-suk's contingent of fearful conscripts was being led toward the 38th Parallel through hilly Gangwon Province, northeast of Seoul, when he and two friends saw an opportunity and eluded their guards.

They found a cave and hid there for some time, living on food from sympathetic local people, until they learned in October the North Korean army had withdrawn and South Korean divisions had rolled up behind them, retaking Gangwon. The three escapees then slowly made their way back to Seoul.

After weeks of prayer for his safety and return, Sang's sister and mother are overjoyed.

MONDAY, NOVEMBER 6, 1950

Bill Shinn witnesses a mass execution; "Father in Heaven, please help me!" a doomed girl cries

Bill Shinn has yet another reason to smile. Just a month after they were reunited, after her ordeal under the North Korean occupation, wife Sally has given birth to their second child, another healthy boy.

But on this crisp fall day, under clear blue skies, the young reporter's mind is on the grim job before him, less on new life, more on death.

He's riding in a small convoy that stops at the foot of a hill four miles west of Seoul. A half-dozen South Korean military policemen order twenty civilians—sixteen men and four women—off the back of a truck. Hands bound behind their backs, heads bowed, the prisoners are ordered to walk up the hill.

Shinn is there to witness a mass execution of collaborators, Seoul residents said to have been convicted on charges of cooperating with the North Korean occupation forces in violation of South Korea's National Defense Law. He is the only correspondent invited to report on the event by General Chung Il-kwon, army chief of staff.

When they left Seoul's Seodaemun (West Gate) Prison, Shinn sensed these doomed people were unaware of what was about to happen. One older man told the guards he worried because he left his blanket in his cell.

But as they come off the truck and begin trudging up the hill, the guards' rifles in their backs, sobs break out among them.

One white-clad woman, thirty years old, turns to Shinn and says through her tears, "I know my last moment has come." Please, she asks, tell her three children, "my eight-year-old daughter, my six-year-old son, my six-month-old son," that she loves them.

Shinn later learns she was convicted for organizing women to sew underwear for the North Korean military.

One man appeals to the guards and their officers for "just one more day" to prove his innocence. Others shout and cry, and Shinn can no longer make out what they're saying.

They've reached a seven-foot-square hole, three feet deep. They're forced down into it, crouching, jammed together. Shinn hears an eighteen-year-old girl, the youngest prisoner, loudly praying, "Oh, our Father in Heaven, please help me!"

The soldiers' carbines are aimed at the huddled mass of people. The mother of three is pleading for mercy when the rifles ring out, over and over. Shinn sees burst heads, blood spurting, backs soaked red. Some are dead instantly. Others writhe in pain, as the soldiers deliver final shots.

"Then they filled over the shallow grave," Shinn concludes his report, written when he returns to the Associated Press office in Seoul's Ulchi-ro business district.

In death, their walks in life are meticulously noted by the journalist: "a telephone operator, a maid, two students, a farmer, two day laborers, four merchants, a bookkeeper, a clerk, a carpenter, a bank officer, an iron-smith, an actor, a printing compositor and two unemployed."

Shinn's story says the day's executions bring to ninety-one the number of convicted collaborators killed by order of a military court in Seoul since the return of the South Korean army in early October. He earlier reported more than six hundred people have been condemned to death throughout South Korea and more than six thousand face trial for alleged wartime offenses.[7]

But the number of victims clearly reaches into the tens of thousands, stretching back to the National Guidance League massacres of the war's first weeks, mass executions without trial.

As long ago as mid-August, Brigadier General Francis W. Farrell, the new chief U.S. adviser to the ROK Army, called for an investigation into the South Koreans' mass killings.[8] As recently as late October, the International Red Cross delegate in Seoul, Fred Bieri, complained to a South Korean vice minister that people were being summarily executed merely as communist "sympathizers."[9] Dean Rusk, assistant secretary of state, told a protesting British diplomat in Washington that U.S. commanders are doing "everything they can to curb such atrocities."[10] But the killings go on.

One thing that is done after Bill Shinn's "Execution Hill" story stirs public revulsion in the United States: the South Korean command bans correspondents from attending future executions.

SUNDAY, NOVEMBER 12, 1950

News of missionary killings stuns the Maryknolls,
but doesn't deter Mary Mercy

"I hope there will be no further delays. There is so much to be done there."

Sister Mary Mercy is writing to family once more from the Maryknoll motherhouse on the Hudson. This time she's hopeful she'll finally get to Korea, to open a much-needed clinic. She has a South Korean visa and a new passport with a ban on Korea travel removed. Now she needs travel orders from her superiors and, most important, clearance from General MacArthur.

The latest news from Korea stuns the Maryknolls. Members of the order who followed U.S. and South Korean troops into Pyongyang report that an estimated sixty-eight priests and nuns, mostly Korean, are believed to have been killed by the North Koreans. Among the unaccounted for is an American bishop, Patrick Byrne, sixty-two, known to have been seized by the invaders in Seoul last July and then taken north.[11]

Byrne founded the first Maryknoll mission in Korea in 1923. It was ten years later that Milwaukee native Elizabeth Hirschboeck arrived in the Japanese colony as Sister Mary Mercy, five years after graduating from Marquette University's medical school and joining the Maryknolls.

She opened a one-room clinic beneath the steps of the Catholic church in Sinuiju. There, and in a later larger clinic, she tended to thousands of poor Koreans, coping with everything from malaria and dysentery to floods and famine, and overcoming deeply rooted superstition and useless folk cures. Along the way, she grew devoted to the stoic, long-suffering Korean people.

Now, whatever the bleak war news, she grows impatient to return. "I'll let you know when I go," she writes her brother and sister-in-law.

A MID-NOVEMBER EVENING, 1950

Shin Hyung-kyu rescues a child from her nightmare

The jeep's headlights fall on a little girl sitting by the roadside in the twilight, amid the smoldering ruins of a North Korean mountain hamlet.

"What is she doing there?" the young MP corporal shouts. His driver slams on the brakes. Shin Hyung-kyu knows he has to help.

They're speeding back from delivering orders to frontline units north of Pyongyang and are anxious to return to their base in the northern capital. The war that just days earlier Shin hoped might soon end is entering a risky new phase. Somewhere in these mountains, a Chinese army is massing.

The teenaged military policeman jumps out of his jeep. He sees no one else among the blackened, flattened homes, just this frail, frightened child. He asks what happened, but she simply stares, seemingly in shock. He lifts her into the jeep and wraps his jacket around her shivering body as they resume the drive to Pyongyang.

Once there, Shin takes her to the MPs' mess hall for something to eat. The warm food calms her, although her hands still tremble, not from cold, but apparently from the memory of what she has been through.

Finally, she speaks, telling him a terrible battle engulfed their homes two days earlier, and her parents were killed. When she and other relatives tried to escape, more bombs fell, she says, and she became separated from the others, including her little brother.

"Oh, maybe he's dead . . . ," she says, crying.

She tells him her name is Lee Hy-sun; she's nine years old, in third grade. She coughs constantly. Two days of exposure to the elements have taken a toll. In the mess hall's candlelight, she closes her eyes at last and puts her head down.

The little she has spoken tells Shin she is intelligent and poised beyond her years. Later in the evening, he takes her to a nearby Pyongyang family he has gotten to know. They take her in for the night. Her seventeen-year-old rescuer says he will bring some food and clothes tomorrow.

TUESDAY, NOVEMBER 21, 1950

*In arctic cold, Gil Isham and the 17th Infantry reach
the Yalu and gaze at China*

Forty miles downstream from its source on Mount Paektu, the Yalu is a
narrow, fast-flowing river beneath a thick layer of ice. On this day, under
a clear blue sky, Gil Isham and his buddies line the southern riverbank,
urinating.

The 17th Infantry Regiment has ended its drive to the Manchurian
border at Hyesanjin, a mountain-ringed lumber town now almost completely destroyed by U.S. bombing.[12]

The GIs want to leave their mark as the first Americans to reach
the Korea-China border, to boast that they "yellowed the Yalu." For the
eighteen-year-old Isham, as far from Milwaukee and home as he can
imagine, the bawdy little ritual means taking part in history.

In Tokyo, General MacArthur marks the event in a more dignified
way, messaging his "heartiest congratulations" to the commanders. "The
7th Division hit the jackpot," a delighted MacArthur tells them.[13]

The three-week advance north from their amphibious landing point
at Iwon has been arduous, along winding, primitive roads—"cow trails,"
they call some of them—among six-thousand-foot mountains, engaging
in occasional firefights with stubborn North Korean army elements, shivering in cold that dips well below zero Fahrenheit.[14]

Catching up with the 17th Infantry column as it approached Hye-
sanjin and the Yalu, the 7th Division commander, Major General David
G. Barr, told an accompanying journalist, "It makes you proud to be an
American, to see our people perform like this."[15]

These Americans have grown exhausted, grimy, and chilled to the
bone as they push on into the Siberian wind, eating frozen C rations,
scrambling for nighttime shelter, by either blowing foxholes into the frozen ground with grenades, assembling lean-tos from tree branches, or, if
lucky, finding abandoned peasants' huts.[16]

Isham and the rest of Easy Company use their new winter sleeping bags at every opportunity, pulling them out at halts and wrapping
themselves in the down warmth, while stomping their feet to ward off
frostbite. After eighteen men were crippled with severe exposure when
ordered to wade across a waist-deep river, the regiment got an emergency

delivery of 250 squad tents and 500 oil-burning stoves to create "warming tents" for the troops.[17]

Officers report the communist resistance appears to be disintegrating. Other 7th Division units to the southwest, where the 1st Marine Division is deploying around the Changjin Reservoir, report clashing with small numbers of Chinese soldiers. But the Tokyo command is still dismissive of the possibility of a large Chinese presence in North Korea.[18] MacArthur's intelligence chiefs estimate the Chinese may number 34,500, in small task forces.[19] In truth, some 400,000 Chinese troops have infiltrated into Korea.[20]

Two months into his war, Private Gil Isham, standing by the riverside relieving himself as he gazes at China across the ice, is finally confident he can handle it. "At Hyesanjin we were starting to get used to being soldiers. We didn't have a lot of heavy fighting, and we didn't have a lot of casualties, but at least we knew what it was all about. Or we thought we did."

On this numbingly cold afternoon seventy-five miles to the east, draft evader Chung Dong-kyu is huddled in his hiding place, his grandmother's barn, when his mother rushes in, fear in her face, and tells him to look out over the fields.

There he sees North Korean soldiers in a ragged column plodding over the icy ground, headed toward the mountains to the north. Some are limping; some have bandages over their heads or their arms or legs. They're beaten young men, pushing on in silence with what strength they have left.

Not an hour later, against the sound of scattered gunfire, Mother rushes in again. "Look out there," she tells her son. "Different soldiers."

The ROK 18th Infantry Regiment has reached the village of Chu Ul, as the parent Capital Division advances toward North Korea's northeast corner.

THURSDAY, NOVEMBER 23, 1950

Turkey and fixin's: Buddy Wenzel enjoys a Thanksgiving dinner

Within the old walls of historic Yongbyon, now mostly a town of war ruins, Buddy Wenzel and the other men of the 7th Cavalry Regiment sit down at tables draped in white cloths for their Thanksgiving dinner. In wartime, the U.S. Army makes a special effort for this American holiday: turkey, pots of cranberry sauce, mince, and pumpkin pies.[21]

On the nearby roads, slow processions of refugees flow southward. In this area sixty miles north of Pyongyang, the enemy has been elusive, the combat fitful and small-scale. But the people sense they must get out of the way.

—⊗⊗⊗—

Fifteen miles to the east, in hill country across the Chongchon River, Clarence Adams and his howitzer crewmates have heard rumors of white tablecloths for the white troops this Thanksgiving—even candlelight.

No such niceties are laid out for the men of the 503rd Field Artillery, but it doesn't matter, as long as they have a warm turkey meal and the expectation they'll be going home soon. They're also finally getting some winter clothing, having faced a brutal early winter for too long in summer fatigues.

After the 503rd and the rest of the 2nd Infantry Division "broke out" from the Pusan Perimeter in September, they advanced northward and eventually took on security duties in the rear area stretching from Seoul to Pyongyang. Then, in early November, the division was reassigned to the northern front, in preparation for General MacArthur's planned advance to take all North Korea.

Along the way, the crew chief for their 155mm gun was killed in an enemy encounter, and Private First Class Adams was promoted by the A Battery commander from ammo bearer to gunner and to corporal. The captain knew this high school dropout had scored well on his army math aptitude tests. Adams is proving adept at the quick calculations demanded in his new job.

The battery of six guns is attached to the division's 38th Infantry Regiment, taking positions along the Eighth Army front line sixty-five miles northeast of Pyongyang and an equal distance from the Yalu River and China. Since the American rout at Unsan in early November, whatever Chinese troops were in North Korea seem to have pulled back, perhaps even to China, the Tokyo command believes.

After Thursday evening's American-style feasts, General MacArthur flies into Sinanju, on the Chongchon River, on a bright, freezing morning, to witness the jump-off of the new operation with Eighth Army's General Walker.

In a press statement, the supreme commander calls this the "decisive effort" that "should for all practical purposes end the war."[22]

Farther upstream on the Chongchon, 38th Regiment troops move out cautiously, meeting light or no resistance, as they launch this new offensive. But escaped prisoners who reach friendly lines tell of a large enemy force massing just miles to the north. Aerial observers issue similar warnings.[23]

SATURDAY, NOVEMBER 25, 1950

Peng Teh-huai sees the son of "Elder Brother"
incinerated by American napalm

American warplanes have repeatedly bombed the area around Peng Teh-huai's headquarters, but a stubborn General Peng this morning is refusing to join his top lieutenants for a strategy meeting in a "command cavern" dug out by Chinese army engineers on a Taeyu-dong hillside.

The commander in chief wants to meet in his own wooden cabin. "I'm not afraid of American airplanes. I don't want to hide in the shelter," he tells Hong Hsue-chi, his deputy for logistics in the Chinese People's Volunteer Force and the man in charge of headquarters arrangements.

When they first arrived at Taeyu-dong, thirty miles from the Yalu River and China, conditions were primitive for Peng and his staff. Since then they have moved into sleeping and office cabins, the food has improved, humming generators supply light and power, and bomb shelters have been gouged out of the sandstone. Telephone operators, clerks, doctors, nurses, and Korean interpreters have been added to the headquarters. General Peng has veteran generals from the civil war as top deputies: Teng Hua as first deputy commander, Hong as second deputy, and Tu Ping as political director, a key job in a communist army.

He also has a personal staff of officers, including Mao An-ying, Mao Tse-tung's twenty-eight-year-old son.

An-ying's childhood ordeal is a well-known story in China. In 1930, while his father was away at the communists' wartime refuge in Ya'nan, his mother, Yang Kai-hui, Mao Tse-tung's second wife, was tortured and executed by Mao's Chinese Nationalist enemies. The eight-year-old boy and his younger brothers ended up begging in the streets of Shanghai. Rescued by the communists, An-ying was sent to be educated in Moscow and served as a Soviet army officer in World War II. In Taeyu-dong,

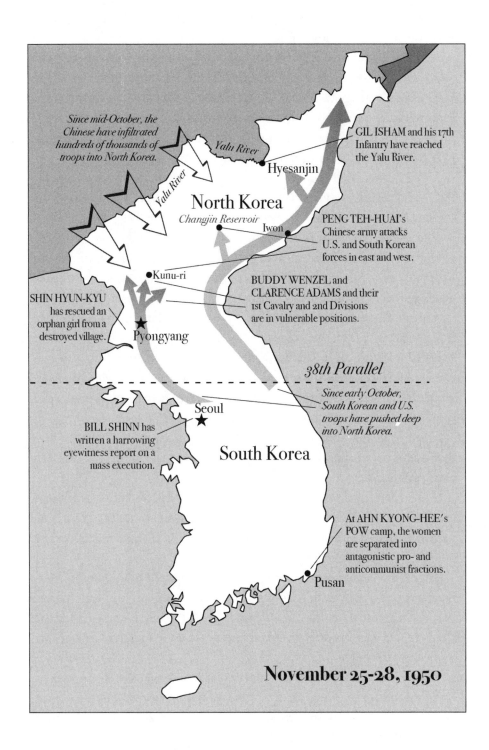

Since mid-October, the Chinese have infiltrated hundreds of thousands of troops into North Korea.

Yalu River

Yalu River

GIL ISHAM and his 17th Infantry have reached the Yalu River.

Hyesanjin

North Korea

Changjin Reservoir

Iwon

PENG TEH-HUAI's Chinese army attacks U.S. and South Korean forces in east and west.

Kunu-ri

BUDDY WENZEL and CLARENCE ADAMS and their 1st Cavalry and 2nd Divisions are in vulnerable positions.

SHIN HYUN-KYU has rescued an orphan girl from a destroyed village.

Pyongyang

38th Parallel

Seoul

Since early October, South Korean and U.S. troops have pushed deep into North Korea.

BILL SHINN has written a harrowing eyewitness report on a mass execution.

South Korea

At AHN KYONG-HEE's POW camp, the women are separated into antagonistic pro- and anticommunist fractions.

Pusan

November 25-28, 1950

he works as Peng's secretary and as Russian translator for dealings with North Korea's Soviet advisers.

Yesterday, four U.S. planes made two bombing runs against the town, destroying an electrical substation. Then, late in the day, a single U.S. P-51 Mustang made a circling reconnaissance flight over the area, leading Hong to fear a further attack this morning.

Now the others have sent him from the shelter to persuade Peng to join them. He finds an angry commander in his cabin.

"Big Hong, where did you hide my planning map?" Peng demands. Hong had stealthily moved Peng's large, annotated operations map to the shelter. "Your map is already there in the cave," he replies. "Everybody is waiting for you to chair the meeting."

After more angry and pleading words, Peng finally allows himself to be led uphill to the cavern. But the meeting has barely begun when they hear approaching aircraft and then the sound of explosions. From the cavern mouth they see huge billowing pillars of flame rise from below, from napalm bombs. As the planes fly off, Peng and the others rush to the scene. Peng's cabin has been incinerated in mere minutes, and two officers, trapped inside, have been burned to death. One is Mao An-ying. He had been with the senior officers in the cave shelter but then inexplicably returned to the cabin at the last minute.

Peng Teh-huai slips into shock. He climbs back to the shelter, where he sits in silence for hours. It's Hong again who must approach him. Peng grasps his hands.

"Big Hong, I think you are a good person," he tells him. "You saved the old man's life today." He falls back into deep thought. What will he tell An-ying's father, his old comrade? "Why did An-ying have to be killed?" he wonders aloud.[24]

After the Peking dinner when Mao Tse-tung told him he was assigning his son to Peng's staff, Mao suggested Peng maintain his headquarters on the Chinese side of the Yalu. Peng insisted it would be necessary to be closer to the war, inside Korea. But was Mao, consciously or not, trying to protect An-ying?[25]

The Chinese have no reason to believe the Americans have pinpointed Peng's headquarters. They are simply bombing everywhere, not just military targets and supply and transport systems, but also population centers in North Korea.[26]

Under General MacArthur's "destroy everything" instruction of early November, pilots are told that "all buildings capable of affording shelter" are legitimate targets. Seventy bombers attacked Sinuiju, the city on the Yalu, dropping more than five hundred tons of incendiaries and destroying 60 percent of the city.[27] An investigation by an international women's socialist federation finds that sixty-eight hundred of eleven thousand dwellings in Sinuiju were destroyed and more than five thousand inhabitants killed, four thousand of them women and children.[28] Similar devastating attacks are being mounted every day across the northern half of North Korea. MacArthur last week privately told the U.S. ambassador to Seoul, John J. Muccio, "Unfortunately, this area will be left a desert."[29]

On the radio, the Chinese have heard MacArthur's boast that his new offensive will bring U.S. troops home by Christmas. It means he is still unaware of the might of the Chinese army they will confront.

On this night, at the end of a day on which the Americans killed Mao Tse-tung's eldest son, the forces amassed by Peng Teh-huai spring their long-planned trap, as MacArthur's two widely separated armies push northward, deeper into a vicious early northern winter. Four Chinese armies, some 120,000 men in twelve divisions, attack the unsuspecting U.S., South Korean, and British units in the western corridor. In the east, the blow comes two days later, on Monday, as Chinese divisions ambush U.S. Marine and Army units around the Changjin Reservoir.[30]

THURSDAY, NOVEMBER 30, 1950

Clarence Adams tries to escape a Chinese trap, and fails

For five days the men of A Battery, 503rd Field Artillery, have pulled back in confusion and fear, step by step, inching away from an often-hidden Chinese enemy, with little sleep, little time to eat, firing off rounds from their 155mm howitzers into the unknown, then getting orders to mount up and drive off to another frozen rice paddy, to take another short-lived stand.

Clarence Adams and his fellow gunners now have run out of ammunition, and the battered 2nd Infantry Division has run out of options. All it can do, as overwhelming numbers of Chinese troops close in, is to make a run for it down the road from Kunu-ri to Sunchon.

The Chinese first struck last Saturday night as the 2nd Division's 38th Infantry Regiment, with A Battery firing in support, was advancing cautiously near the Chongchon River, halfway between Pyongyang and the Yalu, in the first stage of MacArthur's planned final offensive. All across the western front, from the Yellow Sea to the central mountains, twelve of General Peng's People's Liberation Army divisions fell on six U.S. and South Korean divisions in an all-out assault.[31]

Behind the chilling din of bugles, whistles, and loudspeakers blaring threats in crude English, the Chinese isolated and cut apart companies of the 38th Infantry. The regiment repeatedly pulled back one thousand yards, then two thousand yards, and regrouped, only to be hit again from a new direction.

Infantry companies of 150 or more men were reduced to 40 or 50 within two or three days. Some wounded left behind froze to death. Battle areas were strewn with even more Chinese dead. Meanwhile, South Korean units on the 38th's right flank withdrew still more rapidly, passing through the regiment's lines to the area of Kunu-ri, just south of the Chongchon.[32]

Adams's A Battery could only reposition itself as ordered and fire off its dwindling rounds into ever-shifting target areas. Now the final retreat has been ordered, down the only road south.

Infantry battalions, other artillery units, military police, and headquarters companies are rolling southward first, in a miles-long convoy. They find the road has become a deadly gauntlet of Chinese machine gunners and mortarmen dug into the surrounding hillsides. Along a six-mile stretch, trucks are hit with mortar rounds and set ablaze. Screams and moans of wounded and dying soldiers are heard amid the explosions and gunfire. Men desperately push disabled vehicles to the roadside, along with American dead and wounded.

At the convoy's northern end, the black American soldiers of A Battery watch fearfully, realizing they may be among the last out. As dusk darkens into night, and the temperature falls further below zero Fahrenheit, they finally join the retreating column, their tractors slowly pulling six howitzers.

They, too, come under heavy fire where the road narrows. Corporal Adams, originally trained as a machine gunner, is manning a mounted .50-caliber gun atop the second tractor, firing away at the nearby slopes as they push south.

The convoy suddenly halts. The battery's lead vehicle has been disabled, then the rear tractor as well. They're trapped. Adams jumps down, grabbing a .30-caliber machine gun, and climbs beneath the vehicle, firing again into the hills.

Closest by, up ahead, a Chinese machine gunner has them pinned down from behind a roadblock. As Adams looks on, a fellow corporal crawls forward and hurls grenades at the gun. They explode, the firing stops, and the corporal rises. The gun abruptly comes back to life and cuts the American almost in two.

Adams must get away. He abandons the machine gun and picks up a carbine rifle.

A rice paddy lies alongside the road, and he sees a cut in the hills beyond. But the scene is lighted like day from the fires of burning vehicles. Small groups of men trying to run across the paddy are being felled by hails of machine-gun bullets.

When another group starts out, he waits ten seconds and then dashes off alone at a different angle. The machine guns focus on the group, and Adams makes it to the far edge of the field.

He doesn't stop running, as fast as the boy Clarence ever did from Memphis police. He fears bullets in his back at any moment. None come. He finds a trail through the snow-covered hills and hopes it will take him south. Then, at a bend in the path, he almost collides with someone running the other way. It's a Chinese soldier who raises his submachine gun, fires, but misses. Adams raises his carbine, fires off rounds, also misses, and they both quickly turn and dash away in opposite directions.

He goes on aimlessly through the early-morning darkness. Finally, exhausted, he collapses into the snow and passes out.

Daylight awakens him, feeling frozen to the bone, especially his feet. He hobbles away and eventually happens upon some dead Americans. Despairing, knowing he cannot roam around in daytime, he lies down with these corpses, to play dead until nightfall.

Then he hears American voices. A dozen soldiers, both white and black, are passing by. Overjoyed, he pulls himself up and joins them. But about an hour into their wandering, first in one direction and then another, gunfire suddenly erupts, and half of them are hit and fall.

Adams and another black soldier run off, find a ditch, and tumble in. But in a flash a Chinese soldier is up above, pointing his rifle down at them. The two still have their weapons, but the second soldier, an older sergeant, tells Adams he has five children and will take his chances surrendering. He throws his rifle and pistol out of the ditch. Adams follows suit with his carbine.

They climb up, look around, and see four other Chinese standing by. The enemy soldiers stare back at these two black Americans. Then one walks up to Adams and, to his amazement, wraps his arms around him, hugging him. He does the same with the second American.

He gestures for them to sit down and pours each of them a handful of grain from the stocking-like grain pack all Chinese soldiers wear around their necks. The starved and disbelieving Americans gobble it down. Now the Chinese, a mortar crew, lead them away, making them carry the tube and heavy base plate for their weapon. They may not shoot us after all, Clarence Adams thinks.

Miles to the south, regrouping at Sunchon, the 2nd Infantry Division is counting its losses. About one-third of its 15,000 men have been killed, wounded, or listed as missing since mid-November.[33] In A Battery, about half the 120 men are dead or missing. The fatal retreat from Kunu-ri is one of the worst disasters in U.S. military history. At Sunchon, Colonel George B. Peploe, 38th Infantry Regiment commander, is seen weeping.[34]

DECEMBER

FRIDAY, DECEMBER 1, 1950

Chi Chao-chu is stunned by news of an American nuclear threat

In Peking the *People's Daily* newspaper trumpets the Chinese successes against "the imperialist tiger" in Korea, reporting that the "People's Volunteers" have wiped out thousands of Syngman Rhee's "puppet soldiers" and sent the Americans into headlong retreat.

For weeks, the walls of schools and other public places have been plastered with recruiting posters urging young Chinese to volunteer to "resist Americans," "assist Korea," "safeguard our nation." At Tsinghua University, Chi Chao-chu finds that some fellow students are suddenly packing up and leaving without explanation, presumably off to military training.

Chi himself still feels a patriotic urge to volunteer for the Korea fight, but the university provost and his father both insist the Harvard dropout would help the new China more by completing his studies in Peking. Meantime, he despairs over what he sees as a clash between Chinese communist dogmatism and American aggressiveness, undoing a history of goodwill between his two nations. The daily news headlines deepen his despair.

On this night, he and others crowding around a shortwave radio in their dormitory are stunned to hear that President Truman has warned of possible use of atomic bombs in the Korea conflict.

At a Washington news conference on Thursday, the U.S. chief executive denounced the Chinese intervention in the war and said, "We are fighting in Korea for our own national security and survival," and the United States would "take whatever steps are necessary to meet the military situation."

"Will that include the atomic bomb?" a reporter asked.

"That includes every weapon that we have," Truman replied.[1]

The statement stirred immediate nervousness worldwide. Prime Minister Clement Atlee of Britain plans to visit the White House this weekend to discuss his concerns, saying such a grave decision must involve allies fighting alongside America under a U.N. flag.[2]

In the Peking dormitory, the news astonishes Chi and the other students. How can the Americans think we are a threat to them? they ask their U.S.-educated classmate. Chi can only shrug. It makes no sense.

To him it should be obvious that it's China, in view of its history of foreign domination, that feels threatened by the U.S. forces approaching Manchuria. The Americans are the aggressors in a war that China did not start, he tells himself. It's China that's surrounded, not America.

TUESDAY, DECEMBER 5, 1950

Amid a chaotic retreat, Shin Hyung-kyu seeks out the orphan Hy-sun

It's a clear night in Pyongyang, the temperature dropping into the teens Fahrenheit. Artillery can be heard to the north. The Chinese are approaching.

Corporal Shin Hyung-kyu cannot sleep. Past midnight, his mind racing, he jumps from his bedding at the military police command post and heads out into darkness, rushing to the house of the family that has cared for nine-year-old Hy-sun since he rescued the orphan from her burning village. His MP company will be withdrawing from Pyongyang in the morning, along with other rearguard units. He wants to help the family and girl escape to the South.

Since November 25–26, when the Chinese army smashed into unready U.S. and South Korean divisions advancing toward the Yalu, the mood has swung from elation that final victory seemed near to the sudden prospect of defeat. Demoralized, often disorganized American and South Korean troops, beaten back from the Chongchon River line forty miles to the north, are streaming south through the northern capital, in snowy gales and the shortening days of an early winter.

One recent day, Shin's company commander called his MPs together and told them the time was nearing when they might have to give their lives for their country. He ordered each to cut off a lock of hair and pieces of fingernail—final remains—and place them in envelopes addressed to their families. It sent a chill through seventeen-year-old Corporal Shin.

Yesterday, his B Company took on the mission of evacuating ROK Army wounded from a Pyongyang field hospital, crossing the U.S. Army–built pontoon bridge over the Taedong River, to trains waiting at the rail station. Utter confusion reigned as retreating U.S. military vehicles jammed the floating span and ammunition stores exploded in the background, where the Americans were setting supply dumps ablaze.

Up and down the riverside, civilians desperate to reach the south bank piled into small boats, or makeshift rafts, dangerously overloading them. The iron bridge across the Taedong had been heavily damaged by American bombing, but hundreds of frantic civilians, including women and children, crawled across and up and down the twisted girders to reach the other side.

Shin's company next was dispatched to set up roadblocks on the city's northern fringe, to intercept South Korean army stragglers and deserters, a sometimes dangerous job as panicked, wild-eyed soldiers, having just fled scenes of wholesale death to the north, resisted the MPs, even opening fire on them.

Now, in this morning's first hours, Shin has that final mission: to save a little girl for whom he has taken responsibility. Reaching the Pyongyang couple's house with jeep and driver, he tells them to gather up Lee Hy-sun and pack some things. Then the "boy soldier," the girl orphan, still with a bone-shaking cough, and her protectors speed through the predawn, crossing the pontoon bridge and reaching the railroad station in an hour's time.

A final southbound train sits by the platform, bursting with refugees. Shin helps push his charges aboard a boxcar and steps back as the train pulls away. In a half year of war he has never seen such a wretched sight—of pathetic people clinging to the roofs and sides of the moving cars, women with babies on their backs crying to be pulled inside, others left behind beside the tracks, including children separated from their families, crying "*Umma! Umma!*"

He has told Lee Hy-sun and the Pyongyang couple he will look for them at the station in Kaesong, ninety miles to the south. The couple may wonder if he can manage it, but he's sure Hy-sun, at least, believes this "big brother" will save her again.

—∞∞—

Buddy Wenzel and other 7th Cavalrymen huddle atop a tank rumbling south through Pyongyang, hunkering down against the cold, leaving behind a city in flames. The U.S. command labels the huge bumper-to-bumper withdrawal in the face of the Chinese offensive a "retrograde movement." The men have begun giving it another name, "the Big Bugout."

Army engineers are setting key installations in the North Korean capital ablaze. They're destroying American equipment, ammunition, and other supplies that can't be transported south, burning thirty thousand gallons of gasoline supplies, even setting fire to a store of fruitcake, whiskey, and other rations for the "victorious" army's Christmas feast.

At one halt, Private Wenzel and his buddies find quartermaster troops offering anything soldiers can carry from the depots—tobacco, alcohol, rations. Wenzel spots a favorite treat, fruit cocktail, a case of it in large cans. He clings to the heavy box as they resume their retreat.

It has been a demoralizing week since the regiment was first hit hard by the Chinese.

That chaotic clash came with little warning to either side as Chinese troops marched down a nighttime road into the positions of the 7th Cavalry's two battalions, forty miles northeast of Pyongyang at a place called Sinchang-ri, on the Eighth Army's right flank.

The first Chinese to attack pushed the center of the American line back and reached the 2nd Battalion command post in the town, where machine gunners finally cut them down. Then, through the predawn hours, the enemy threw waves of attackers against the dug-in 7th Cavalrymen. Regimental officers called in barrage after barrage of artillery fire, and the wall of high explosives and machine-gun fire drove the Chinese back. In the light of day, the Americans saw hundreds of enemy bodies strewn about within their own perimeter and beyond.

Thirty-eight cavalrymen also were killed and many more were wounded or missing, and the U.S. command was finally grasping that it faced a formidable new enemy. It ordered a step-by-step pullback that has now developed into a headlong retreat.

Earlier that day at Sinchang-ri, the 2nd Battalion's E Company lost its commanding lieutenant in a terrible episode harking back to last summer and the fear of infiltrators that so often proved fatal to refugees.

As retreating South Korean troops and northern refugees passed through an E Company roadblock, the Americans were told enemy soldiers were among the civilian-clad throng. When First Lieutenant John E. Sheehan stepped forward to inspect one group of men, they pulled out weapons and fired, killing him and wounding some of his men. Other soldiers immediately opened fire on the refugee column, felling women, children, old people.[3]

Ordinary northerners are desperate to get away from this new collision of two giant armies. But flight has become perilous, too. After the E Company incident, Lieutenant Colonel "Billy" Harris, 7th Cavalry commander, issued an order instructing his troops, "All refugees attempting to enter our lines will be repelled by fire if necessary. Mortar and artillery."[4]

Now the regiment itself, along with tens of thousands of other men of Eighth Army and its allies, is in flight from North Korea. They're dispirited soldiers, blank faces behind frozen beards, on overloaded trucks or tanks, some with frostbitten toes or fingertips, noses or ears. And they're taking revenge. Eighth Army once more is "scorching the earth" on retreat, burning houses, destroying livestock and food, wrecking machinery. Looking back, 7th Cavalry rifleman Ralph Bernotas is to liken it to the German army of recent memory in Ukraine: "We burned everything. Food, whatever the hell. They left nothing."[5]

WEDNESDAY, DECEMBER 6, 1950

Trapped Marines perish, and Gil Isham's regiment withdraws
as MacArthur's plan collapses

Engineers of the 17th Infantry Regiment are bringing up miles of barbed wire. Clerks and cooks are forming provisional platoons to help hold the line. The regiment is digging into frozen ground, building defensive positions, laying mines along a perimeter north of Hamhung and its port, Hungnam, to await the oncoming Chinese.

It has been a week since Private Gil Isham's 17th Infantry, in Korea's far northeast, began pulling back from the Yalu River border with China. General MacArthur's "final offensive" to take all of North Korea has fallen apart in the face of the Chinese intervention.

Over some two hundred miles of icy mountain trails, by truck, by foot, and a final stretch by railroad, the 17th Infantry wound its way south after X Corps ordered withdrawals by all units of the 7th Infantry Division and 1st Marine Division, troops that had been spread across too wide a landscape of few roads and a hidden enemy in eastern North Korea.

On the way south, the 17th Infantry had little enemy contact, but men still were disabled in the freezing temperatures and biting wind.[6]

Gil Isham was one of many suffering frostbite. Their new "shoepacs" were to blame. When they halted, feet soaked with sweat from marching in the rubber footwear would freeze. Isham was kept overnight at the 2nd Battalion aid station while his two frostbitten feet were slowly warmed. "What the medics were worried about was if my feet were going to turn black. Then I would have been in trouble. But they didn't. They just hurt like hell." He was soon sent back to Easy Company.

For all their misery, the men of Easy are fortunate. Sixty miles to the southwest, in the desolate heart of North Korea's mountain country, two regiments of Marines fell into a fatal Chinese trap and are in desperate retreat.

Like the 17th Infantry in mid-November, the 5th and 7th Marine Regiments found little sign of the enemy as they pushed north from their landing zone at Wonsan and up narrow roads onto the four-thousand-foot-high Kaema plateau, toward the giant Changjin Reservoir, on their way toward the Yalu River.

But the enemy was there. Strung out along the scant road network, the two regiments of the 1st Marine Division were walking into an ambush by seven Chinese divisions.[7]

On Thanksgiving Day, November 23, from a base at the remote town of Hagaru-ri at the southern tip of the eleven-mile-long reservoir (called the Chosin Reservoir by the Japanese), the Marines struck out northward on the reservoir's western shore. They bivouacked at a village called Yudam-ri, with perimeter outposts atop surrounding ridges. Just before midnight on November 27, in an explosion of green tracer bullets, mortar barrages, and blaring bugles, the Chinese attacked in overwhelming numbers.

They drove the unsuspecting Marines back from their ridgeline positions, overrunning command posts, killing and wounding many, some caught in their sleeping bags. The reserve companies below struggled up the ice-slick, boulder-strewn mountainsides to help their fellow Marines and ran into sweeping enemy automatic-weapons fire and showers of grenades and into wounded men stumbling downhill. Somehow, Marine reinforcements finally made it to the top and shot, clubbed, and bayoneted the Chinese they found in American foxholes, driving survivors down the rear slope. For the next three days, the Marines at Yudam-ri clung to defensive positions, resisting repeated Chinese nighttime attacks and suffering mounting casualties.

On the reservoir's eastern shore, 7th Infantry Division units, from sister regiments of the 17th Infantry, were also ambushed by the Chinese. Hundreds were killed on both sides. And a combined Marine-army task force dispatched to help the Yudam-ri Marines was blocked and cut up by this suddenly appearing enemy.

When the X Corps order came for a withdrawal across the entire eastern front, the Marines at Yudam-ri began a final ordeal by road, in heavy snowfall, retracing their northward march southward.

Their wounded and dead, bodies frozen in grotesque positions, were loaded onto trucks. Some wounded were strapped to hoods, fenders, and the roofs of truck cabs. As the strung-out convoys slowly rolled south through the valleys, with Yudam-ri set ablaze behind them by Marine engineers, the decimated rifle companies had to fight to secure the parallel ridgelines on either side, while the pursuing Chinese maneuvered to cut them off with roadblocks.

During the day, when weather allowed, American fighter-bombers flew in to beat back Chinese formations with bombs and napalm. But snipers still picked off Marines from the hills, and well-placed machine guns raked the lines of trucks. At night on that lone road out, as the Marines manned perimeters around the halted convoys, the Chinese mounted massed charges to try to break through, to be stopped by Marine machine-gun and mortar fire. Hundreds of enemy bodies could be counted after each dawn.

The cold inflicted casualties as much as the Chinese. The mercury dipped to twenty-five below overnight, and the north wind reached forty miles an hour. Frostbite made fingers useless for pulling a trigger. The navy corpsmen who served as Marine medics, rushing to inject the wounded with morphine, took to carrying the syrettes in their mouths, to keep them from freezing.[8]

Pushing down the steep passes with their casualties, the 5th and 7th Marines finally reached Hagaru-ri two days ago. There they are now holding off further Chinese attacks as four thousand Marine and army wounded are lifted out by an air shuttle and the dead are readied for mass graves. A news reporter who saw the survivors described men with exhausted and red-rimmed eyes, filthy stubble on filthy faces, clothes stiff with ice, some with blood frozen over wounds, some using rifles as crutches, limping along on frostbitten feet.

Aboard fresh truck convoys, the Marines soon pass through the Hamhung-Hungnam defense perimeter manned by Isham's 17th Infantry and other U.S. and South Korean troops.

Facing this huge new entrant in the war, MacArthur and his generals and admirals are quickly organizing a sealift for evacuating all U.S. and South Korean forces from Hungnam and other east coast ports, while Eighth Army retreats overland in the west.[9]

Meanwhile, the defensive loop north of Hamhung must hold.

Uneventful days pass as the evacuations begin. The Chinese are believed regrouping after taking severe losses in the fighting around the reservoir. Finally, the attacks come, always at night. Over one two-day period, wave after wave of Chinese try to storm the hilltop positions of Isham's and other companies. Under the glow of flares, amid exploding mines, the dug-in Americans unleash machine-gun and rifle fire as well as mortar and howitzer rounds on the massed Chinese, leaving hillsides littered with dead.

With scarce artillery support and no air or armor backup, the attackers never break through, and Easy Company suffers few casualties. But during a lull, amid small talk about high school days, better days, a GI sitting on the edge of their foxhole is struck by a sniper's bullet and Isham sees his neighbor keel over backward, dead, shot in the head.

The eighteen-year-old rifleman is growing hardened to war's cruel randomness. "You didn't want to make real close friends because it would hurt worse."

Back home in Milwaukee, the *Sentinel* newspaper announces in a banner headline, "GIs Quitting Korea at Northeast Port, Men Boarding Yank Fleet at Hungnam." It reports the 17th Infantry is among units that have "eluded Chinese traps" and made it to the coast.[10] Homer and Frances Isham can at least have more hope their soldier son Gilbert is safe.

In the Chiri-san mountains of Korea's far south, news of the American setbacks appears in blurry purple ink on the mimeographed pages of a communist guerrilla "newspaper." The editor is Ri In-mo.

Local Workers' Party leaders asked the party propagandist from the North to produce a weekly bulletin after they accepted him into their guerrilla ranks in early October, as a member of the "armed propaganda teams."

It was a difficult assignment in their remote, thinly populated surroundings. But Ri and local comrades managed to track down a mimeograph machine, two thousand Japanese-made stencils, and a stock of paper and ink.

He runs off a small number of the bulletins each week, for delivery across the forested valleys and mountainsides, to be shared hand to hand among the southern leftist insurgents and left-behind KPA soldiers who joined them. He relies on guerrilla radio operators for news from North Korean broadcasts and from their own Chiri-san fighting units.

Enemy pressure is building on the guerrilla havens. A newly formed ROK Army division, the 11th, has spread across three provinces in an eradication campaign, at times engaging in pitched battles with large insurgent formations, killing hundreds and forcing the guerrillas to operate in smaller groups.[11]

The rear-area fighters are especially effective in hit-run raids on rail traffic and motor convoys. The guerrilla networks maintain good communications and coordination. They scavenge food from farmers. Armed with an odd mix of Soviet and Chinese weapons, captured American M-1 rifles, even old Japanese rifles, the insurgents replenish their arsenals with attacks on police posts and weapons depots.[12]

The antiguerrilla offensive invites new atrocities. The South Korean military is employing a "safe hamlets" strategy of evacuating and destroying villages suspected of guerrilla support. In some cases, they simply kill the villagers rather than relocate them to guarded hamlets. In Hampyong County, South Cholla Province, ROK Army troops have killed 249 civilians in a single operation.[13]

The retreating KPA and leftist guerrillas commit their own atrocities. In the South Cholla county of Muan, local leftists have killed at least 100 people, including women and children from families considered right-wing, some children being thrown into deep wells.[14]

As the South Korean hunt for the Chiri-san guerrillas steps up, Ri In-mo himself has had narrow escapes.

In one costly episode, as Ri's guerrilla command shifted its base deeper into the Chiri-san range, police surprised a headquarters group of

50 on the move. One party officer led a handful of guerrillas in a counter-attack. All were killed, but it allowed the others to escape, including Ri.

In the face of such ever-present dangers, and of the hardships of an approaching mountain winter, rank-and-file fighters take heart from the brief reports in Ri's news sheets of battlefield success in North Korea. The veteran party loyalist, the boy revolutionary of the 1930s, does his best to rally the troops to the communist cause, extolling guerrilla sacrifices, even writing and publishing in his pages a poem urging them to "hoist higher the ever-victorious banner of reunification."

The lines of verse also betray Ri's yearning for a more personal re-union, with Sun-im, the wife he feels he neglected in favor of the party's needs. "Our wives wished us a triumphal return," he writes. "When may we see their smiling faces again?"

Ri finally gets word about Sun-im from a relative of hers he encounters in the Chiri-san, who tells him she fled north from fighting around Hungnam. He hopes she is safe, with their little girl and his mother, in their home area of Phungsan in the far north.

Chung Eun-yong, returning home from Seoul to their cramped room in Chugok-ri, finds his wife weeping over a photograph of Koo-pil, their dead four-year-old.

It's the portrait of the boy at his first birthday party, buried with other keepsakes in a leather box when U.S. troops ordered the family and other villagers to evacuate Chugok-ri in July. Other items in the box were badly damaged from the heat of the Americans' "scorched-earth" fires, but this photo somehow survived, with only singed edges. It's one of the few remaining mementos of a child of whom his parents once expected so much.

For Park Sun-yong, Nogun-ri seems to haunt every waking moment and disturb her sleep. Her plump face has grown paler, thinner, her cheekbones now evident. She'll awaken in the night, shake Eun-yong awake, and ask whether he, too, hears their dead son's voice. She tells him the faces of Koo-pil and Koo-hee, his two-year-old slain sister, sometimes appear in the darkness.

Eun-yong traveled to Seoul to determine when Chung Ang College, where he was studying law, might reopen. What he learned was not encouraging, nor was the war news from the North. He hurriedly took a train back the hundred miles to Yongdong, to return to the safety of nearby Chugok-ri.

The young husband was facing a decision. The government was rounding up conscripts for the army or for police units tracking guerrillas in the southern mountains. He finally acted, rejoining the provincial police headquarters in Taejon, a relatively safe haven. He and Sun-yong move in with his brother, the Taejon prison guard, who lost his wife and two of their four children to the 7th Cavalry's guns. It's a grieving household, living under a dark cloud of the memory of Nogun-ri.

SATURDAY, DECEMBER 9, 1950

As frantic refugees drown, evacuee Chung Dong-kyu steams away from North Korea

At Songjin, a large sheltered harbor on North Korea's east coast two hundred miles north of the 38th Parallel, a wintry wind whips over the quay in the early afternoon this day, as a small task force of U.S. Navy vessels and merchant ships begins to pull away with full loads of evacuees, part of one of the greatest seaborne rescues in modern military history.

Aboard are thousands of soldiers of South Korea's Capital and 3rd Infantry Divisions and forty-three hundred North Korean civilians, many of them young men, some unsure of what lies ahead, some expecting to be drafted into the southern army.

The eighteen-hundred-foot pier is still jammed with civilians who streamed down to the seafront in hopes of fleeing south—men, women, and children wrapped in heavy quilted coats and blankets, bearing whatever possessions and clothing they can carry in hand luggage or on their backs.[15]

They include people fearful of retaliation from the communists because of their backgrounds or their brief cooperation with the southern invaders, others frantic to get away from a new foreign invader, the Chinese, some hoping to reunite with family in the South, still others driven simply by hunger and privation.

As the crew of the last transport raises the gangplank, the desperation turns tragic. Amid anguished cries and shouts, the huge crowd of those left behind surges forward. Those closest to the pier's edge begin to tumble, pushed, into the icy sea. As the ship edges away, evacuees at the ship's railing look on in disbelief, the screams of the doomed following them. Hundreds are plunging into the dark waters and drowning.

One unlikely passenger is spared the terrible sight, having gone belowdecks. By fortune, good or ill, eighteen-year-old Chung Dong-kyu is bound for South Korea, one of millions touched by the sudden reversal of the war. In just two weeks' time, weeks of heartache and horror, Chung has been transformed from a hospital aide hopeful for a reunified Korea to a refugee.

In late November, after South Korean troops passed through his hometown of Chu Ul, headed north, Chung left his grandmother's barn, where he hid from the North Korean draft, to go back to work at the local hospital. On his very first day, he and others were summoned to a spot in the mountains where a mass killing had been discovered. The scene was ghastly: several dozen local women, naked and bound, half frozen in a snowy ditch, brutally killed not by gunshot, but with multiple stabs from pointed sticks. A stunned Chung saw that some had sticks still protruding from their vaginas.

They had been murdered by the retreating North Koreans for allegedly giving food and other support to an anticommunist guerrilla group that had formed in the mountains in recent weeks, mostly draft evaders from the women's own families. Chung found an aunt, his father's sister-in-law, among the dead. He wasn't surprised. She had been taken away by the security police in mid-November.

Most who went to the site with him were searching for a wife or mother or sister, and most found their bodies. Through the grim, tearful afternoon, they loaded the victims onto a truck for return to their families.

The unrelenting cruelties of this war weighed heavily on the young man's spirit. He learned that local Chu Ul women were being raped by ROK soldiers. This brought back a boyhood memory of a horrible night in Harbin, when drunken soldiers from the Russian occupation force in Manchuria invaded the Chung family home and raped his older sister.

War is insanity, he told himself over and over. But at least this one will end soon, as triumphant ROK troops advanced up the east coast.

Then a week ago, returning from a medical mission in the hills, Chung found endless columns of ROK troops and vehicles reversing course, heading south down the road through Chu Ul. Civilians trudged south with them, in parallel columns through the fields.

In the snowy twilight, he asked a military policeman why they were retreating. "Young man, this is only a three-day tactical withdrawal," the soldier said.

Even so, Chung knew the North Koreans would fill the vacuum, bringing with them the dreaded security police, who this time might track down and seize this draft evader.

He rushed home and told Mother what was happening and that he, too, must head south. She knew he was right. She packed some rice and dried cuttlefish and clean socks for him. She hung his Chongjin Medical College identification booklet around his neck. She gave him her white silk scarf, a personal treasure. In the final moments, however, the abrupt departure of her only son left her in uncontrollable tears.

Outside, in the blowing wet snow, Chung joined the long south-bound lines of soldiers and refugees. The farther south they walked through the night, the more the refugee throngs swelled.

Over the next three days, Chung pushed on, finding shelter and snatches of sleep where he could. He had eaten the last of his rice and cuttlefish when his column arrived in the town of Kilchu.

In search of food, he spotted a dozen mostly young men sitting in a schoolyard, each wearing an armband reading "Local Volunteer Youth Group." Assuming they were somehow attached to the ROK Army, Chung quietly moved in, sat behind them, and followed when they rose and left.

They ended up at the leader's house nearby, where they were fed a good, filling dinner. Chung introduced himself to the others, mostly college students or graduates, and they accepted him into their ranks, awarding him an armband. Their ultimate role remained vague to all, but they felt more secure as an organized group.

On Thursday—finally a warmer day—word came that ROK Army officers wanted them to head as quickly as possible to Songjin, a difficult twenty-mile trek to the south over the mountains. Picking up other "volunteer youths" along the way, they arrived at Songjin late last night, to collapse into sleep in an empty warehouse.

Awakened before dawn this morning, the group, now numbering some two hundred, was shepherded aboard the evacuation ship. Chung realized then that young men, likely army conscripts, were being favored for evacuation.

Now he is in the southbound ship's overcrowded hold, sinking into a deep melancholy, not knowing where he is headed, sorrowful over what he has left behind. He told his mother when they parted that he'd return in three days, eager to believe what the military policeman said.

That was seven days ago, and mother and son had both sensed that wasn't true. His eleven-year-old sister clung to him as he headed for the door last Saturday. "Please don't leave us!" she begged him. "You're the only brother I have. Don't leave me!"

At the open door, weeping, Mother clutched his sleeve. "My son! My only son!" cried the woman who was his lifelong anchor. "Don't leave me. You have been my whole life!"

Up and down the east coast of North Korea, countless such agonizing partings are taking place. In Songjin, meanwhile, the tragedy of the quayside is compounded when the U.S. Air Force returns overhead, to drop tons of bombs on the people left behind.[16]

A MID-DECEMBER AFTERNOON, 1950

After seeing too much death, "boy soldier"
Shin Hyung-kyu faces his own

The stream of retreating Americans is thinning, mostly 2nd Infantry Division troops. The last should soon pass through the checkpoint Shin Hyung-kyu mans with a handful of other South Korean military policemen, at a mountain pass flanked by steep, snow-covered slopes south of Pyongyang.

In the days since the pullout from that burning city, as they deployed as part of a rear guard, Shin has seen war's carnage anew in many small battlefields, in the mangled, frozen, incinerated bodies of friendly and enemy soldiers. He has witnessed the death of comrades. He'll never forget the sight of a severed arm, with wristwatch still ticking, of a soldier blown to pieces by an artillery shell.

At the same time, war's absurdities intrude.

In the first town where they halted in their withdrawal south, seventeen-year-old Corporal Shin, filthy from weeks without bathing, found a bathtub in the ruins of an isolated house, filled it with snow, lit firewood beneath, and enjoyed a warm soak in the chill night, humming old songs to a distant chorus of howitzers and tank engines. He'd feel clean for the next day's inspection, itself an absurdity in the midst of a humiliating retreat.

The young MPs have grown disdainful of the combination in the Korean officer corps of ludicrous discipline, military incompetence, and everyday corruption. Shin has seen officers commandeer military trucks to ship looted goods and produce south to business partners across the 38th Parallel.

In part to escape the officers, some MPs volunteer for checkpoints, temporary posts leapfrogging southward on the "MSR," main supply route, just ahead of withdrawing rearguard troops. It's dangerous duty. On their first night at the post at the mountain pass, Shin and his squad had to fight off a Chinese patrol. On this afternoon, they hope their platoon sergeant will come to retrieve them before sunset at 5:15 p.m., to shut down the operation.

In midafternoon, four trucks of 2nd Division troops stop at the checkpoint to get their bearings, men who have survived their division's rout at Kunu-ri and the murderous gauntlet of Chinese ambushes that pursued them in the long, wintry retreat south. Now they're just a few miles from a safe zone, to reorganize to fight another day.

Suddenly, gunfire erupts from the slopes above. Shin quickly realizes they're nearly surrounded by Chinese, who have quietly infiltrated over the mountains and apparently waited for a large target to assemble.

American GIs leaping from the first two trucks manage to flee down into a ravine leading south. But the second two trucks are trapped. The battle-weary men aboard, slow to react, are being cut down in the truck beds or the roadside. Shin can hear Chinese firing hundred-round-a-minute "burp gun" submachine guns, deadly at such a close range. He and the other MPs fire back with their lightweight M-1 carbines, but targets are hard to pinpoint among the trees and boulders of the mountainsides.

The din of the firefight goes on for long minutes, punctuated by cries from the wounded. Shin hears an American nearby, shouting to watch out for oncoming Chinese, being silenced in midsentence. The American soldiers, outnumbered and helpless in the rain of bullets, fall one by one into the snow.

The rattle of burp guns and crack of rifle fire gradually die down. No one is firing back, and the Chinese begin to descend to the body-littered roadway.

Shin, still alive, unhurt, senses instantly his only hope is to play dead. He wedges himself, facedown, between two dead Americans. He hears wounded men some distance away crying in pain, or fear, and being shot. He hears the attackers, muttering to each other in Chinese, approaching, kicking bodies along the way, hunting those feigning death.

One stops over Shin, evidently suspicious. He fires. The poorly aimed bullet pierces the calf of Shin's left leg. He feels "a shock as if I had touched a live electrical wire." He somehow remains perfectly still. The enemy soldier kicks his head. Again, he lies motionless. Still, the soldier lingers, standing over him—"the most excruciating moment of my life." Finally, he walks away.

Shouts from the mountain seem to be a commander's call to pull back. The withdrawing Chinese set the trucks ablaze, and the air fills with the putrid smell of burning flesh.

Shin drags himself up, pulls a belt from a soldier's body, and tightens it as a tourniquet around his bleeding, painful leg. He sees he was lying next to a dead American whose blood, flowing from a shattered face, a young face of blankly staring eyes, had smeared Shin's own face. That's why the Chinese thought he was dead. "This American saved my life," he tells himself. "He came many thousands of miles away from his home and family and now lies dead in the snow in North Korea." Will anyone tell his family? he wonders.

A Korean MP who escaped has summoned help, and eventually reinforcements arrive, to collect the dead and the few survivors, including the young corporal from Kochang, the "boy soldier" who is now a hardened, wounded war veteran.

TUESDAY, DECEMBER 12, 1950

Peng Teh-huai is pained by chants of "March south!"

Kim Il-sung is speaking from the balcony of Pyongyang's city hall, assuring a shivering crowd gathered from among the capital's shrunken population that final victory is at hand. Mere weeks ago from that same spot, South Korea's Syngman Rhee proclaimed Korea would never be divided again. Today the North's Great Leader concludes with a new slogan, "March south!"[17]

At a reception last evening, a victory celebration with Kim as guest of honor, Peng Teh-huai heard chants of "March south!" The North

Korean leader and his deputies, impressive looking in their medal-bedecked, Soviet-style military dress, sounded upbeat. But the newly arrived Peng, in his worn, wrinkled uniform, was pained to hear talk of moving on. The Chinese general is too aware of his army's logistical shortcomings.

For his current "Second Campaign," food supplies were so short he had to drop two divisions from his original plan of attack in the west. He can count on only three hundred trucks for three hundred thousand troops. As Kim celebrates in Pyongyang, Chinese soldiers sent into battle in the east without winter clothing are succumbing to the killing cold by the hundreds. Newly arriving reinforcements are unnerved by the sight of "snowmen," bodies of soldiers or porters frozen erect or kneeling, covered in snow.[18]

Peng messaged Mao Tse-tung in Peking requesting a rest and rebuilding period of a few months before resuming the attack. Mao has now replied that a delay is undesirable. "Our army must cross the 38th Parallel," his telegram reads. Mao has told Kim the goal is to drive the foreign forces completely from the South.[19] In fact, General MacArthur has laid out contingency plans to the Pentagon for complete evacuation of U.S. troops from Korea.[20]

In the coming days, in an exchange of messages, Peng bargains with China's supreme leader, eventually winning agreement on a compromise, a delay of major new offensive operations until early January and flexibility for him as field commander to stop when he feels necessary.[21]

As if in reminder of the power of Peng's enemy, B-29 bombers appear over Pyongyang two days after Kim's rousing speech and drop 175 tons of bombs. It is the beginning of months of catastrophic U.S. Air Force attacks on the centuries-old city.[22] In Washington, Harry Truman summons two dozen congressional and cabinet leaders to an urgent White House meeting, where they're told events in Korea mean Moscow is bent on "world domination."[23] The U.S. military buildup must be greatly accelerated. On Friday night, the president addresses the nation on radio and proclaims a national emergency, which allows him to rapidly expand the armed forces and arms production.[24] In mere months, the military budget quadruples over pre-Korea levels. The American armed forces are to grow to 3.5 million men.[25] Almost overnight, the Cold War has become a global military confrontation.

A MID-DECEMBER MORNING, 1950

Clarence Adams reaches the end of a death march,
lame, despairing, but alive

Bent, limping figures shuffle through the Yalu River town of Pyoktong, ragged men leaning weakly on each other, bloody bandages around arms or legs.

Clarence Adams hobbles along painfully, trying to keep up, dragging a right foot wrapped in filthy rags.

They're near the end of a ten-day nightmare, a death march of battlefield prisoners that began after the U.S. Eighth Army's disastrous rout and retreat from the Chongchon River and Kunu-ri. This march and others like it meant death for unknown numbers of American soldiers, too crippled with wounds or illness, shot by North Korean guards when they fell out of the grim processions.

Not all laggards were murdered. Corporal Adams, suffering from frostbite in his right foot and falling ever behind during the hundred-mile march, believes he was spared because of his color, because communist soldiers seem taught to feel solidarity with black Americans.

After he and another black GI were captured, a Chinese army interpreter approached them. "You are not the exploiters," he told them. "You are the exploited!"

The two initially were taken to a spot where hundreds of new prisoners were being gathered. On the way, Adams saw U.S. F-86 jets on a bombing run drop napalm on a Korean hut. A woman with a baby on her back came running out, on fire, fell to the ground, and burned to death as the shocked GIs looked on. Adams could see the imprint of the charred baby on her back.

Appalled, he thought that if their guard shot them then and there, they deserved it as Americans. "We should not be here in Korea," he told himself.

Later, at the collection point, the Chinese turned the prisoners over to North Korean home guard militiamen in smaller groups for the agonizing journey north to prison camp, through the deep freeze of the North Korean winter, over rough roads and trails, stumbling over rocks, slipping on ice.

By the second day, Adams kept falling behind, dragging his right leg, the foot crippled with frostbite, the leg swollen from possible infection.

A guard pulled him to the roadside. Adams thought these were his final moments. He had seen the weaker, slower men removed by the Koreans and then, after some minutes, had heard shots.

But this guard left him standing there and hurried back to the column, which was soon out of sight. Adams had no choice but to follow, struggling on alone for hours into the late night. Finally, a Korean stepped out of the darkness to find him on the road and lead him down to a village where the others had settled earlier for the night.

He was fed a rice ball with bean paste and a cup of hot water. Then a guard made clear to him he must start out again alone into the night, to gain some distance before the others left at dawn.

The next day the group passed him, and he again walked on into the night, eventually catching up and joining them for the daily rice ball at a rest stop.

This went on for days. The pain in his foot and the exhaustion were so great he would sometimes crawl, sometimes slide down inclines, on the ice or mud. Because of unbearable pain from the combat boot chafing on his right foot, he wrapped the foot in rags and carried the boot over his shoulder.

As he sought to keep up, Adams's hunger deepened and his mental state declined.

Crossing a bridge over a frozen river, he stopped. He was hallucinating. He saw a vision of his mother in a beautiful dress dancing on the ice. He felt an urge to jump, to join her, but pulled himself back at the last minute. It was then he realized how badly he wanted to live.

At times he was helped by the rudimentary Korean he picked up on his tour as a military policeman in the South two years ago. "*Mul ju seh yo,*" he would ask villagers. "Water, please." But late in his ordeal Adams feared it would be local Koreans who would kill him.

Turning a bend in the road, he saw a dozen teenagers waiting. They grabbed the helpless American and shoved him back and forth between them, playing with him, making him stagger through their gauntlet over and over. He tried to lighten the mood by weakly singing a Korean song he knew, but they simply grew more violent. Just then, an old man with a wispy white beard appeared, waved his stick, and shouted at the gang, and the youths filtered away. Just as quickly, the old man vanished.

Clarence Adams survived, and now he has caught up with his fellow prisoners in Pyoktong, some five hundred or so. They're told their internment camp lies just ahead on the edge of the North Korean town, sixty-five miles up the Yalu from the river's mouth at Sinuiju. There they'll find hot food, warm shelter, and medical care, these weak and desperate Americans are led to believe.

SATURDAY, DECEMBER 16, 1950

Too late, Corporal Shin Hyung-kyu finds the orphan Hy-sun

Corporal Shin Hyung-kyu was sent back to his MP company after two days in a field hospital, but his leg wound from the Chinese ambush still has not fully healed. His company commander has assigned him to light duty, as a traffic policeman directing the retreating army through a central intersection in Kaesong, astride Route 1 headed south forty-five miles to Seoul.

Shin has finally reached the last stop of the train that carried nine-year-old Lee Hy-sun from Pyongyang eleven days ago. Going off duty this afternoon, he decides to look for the orphan girl and the Pyongyang couple who helped her. A cold wind is whipping the fallen snow into swirls of flakes as a motor-pool driver, doing Shin a favor, takes him to Kaesong station.

The waiting room is packed with refugees, some apparently from that last train of December 5. Shin, limping with his injury, makes his way through the crowds, scanning the huddled groups. Again and again, he asks whether anyone has seen a little girl in an oversize army jacket, with a bad, chronic cough. No one can help.

He goes out into the railyard, where dozens of boxcars sit abandoned on the tracks. Here and there, he sees frozen bodies, now a common sight to the seventeen-year-old battle veteran. He leans over the smaller ones, praying he won't find Hy-sun's face. He goes from car to car, checking. At the last boxcar in one line, he sees a small body inside, on the snow-covered floor.

He climbs up and walks over toward it. He has to wipe snow and hair from the child's face. He sees the frightened-looking eyes, wide open, seemingly looking at him. It's Hy-sun.

He feels her hand—cold, frozen. She has been dead for some time. He lifts her stiff body and holds it close, combing the white flakes from her black hair with his fingers. He tries to close her eyes. They won't close.

Carrying the dead child in his arms, he wanders from the railyard, to the bank of a small creek nearby. He finds a spot beneath a poplar tree, gently puts the body down, and draws out his bayonet to begin digging.

The earth's frozen crust isn't very deep. He digs on, finally getting down two feet, and places the dead girl inside. He still can't close her eyes.

He pulls a sheet of paper from his pocket and places it over her face and then scrapes the dirt back in, patting it down, forming a small mound on top.

He cuts a branch from the tree, splits it in two, and carves into the flat surface the Korean words "Lee Hy-sun. Died: December 16, 1950," a humble marker on a grave no one will visit.

The girl he tried to save is now just one among the countless many beyond saving in the madness consuming the Korean nation. As he leaves the train station, the pointlessness of all the death stops him for a moment. Should I simply hitchhike a ride to the south and home? he asks himself. Should I desert? It would be easy. This is hell.

But the moment passes. His sense of duty returns—even more, a desire to stop retreating, to turn and fight for his country and for his own future. The pale schoolboy of June has become the committed soldier of December.

In the swirling snow, Shin limps out to the main road to hitchhike a ride back to the MP headquarters in Kaesong, to return to hell.

MONDAY, DECEMBER 18, 1950

Bill Shinn reports South Korea will accelerate executions

The advance of the Chinese from the north, sending vast waves of refugees before them, confronts the South Korean government with urgent new problems. Even Seoul's executioners are feeling the pressure.

Bill Shinn and other Korean reporters are told by President Rhee that trials and executions of communist collaborators will be speeded up "in view of the military situation and lack of prison facilities."[26]

The mass executions were already stirring outrage internationally. Shinn has reported that, as of late November, 877 people were condemned to death by civil and military courts for aiding the North Koreans during the three-month occupation. Perhaps 300 have been killed, trucked off to be shot in groups by firing squads on Seoul's outskirts and other isolated locations.[27]

But beyond these court-ordained executions, supposedly carried out through due process, uncounted hundreds or thousands of other alleged collaborators are being summarily killed across South Korea, on simple orders from police or military commanders, or in explosive bloodbaths carried out by self-appointed militias.

Just sixteen miles northeast of Seoul, at Namyangju, police and a local militia have begun the slaughter of more than 460 people, including at least 23 children under the age of ten, children of alleged collaborators.[28] And in the far south, in North and South Cholla Provinces, every week brings mass killings in villages suspected of aiding communist guerrillas.[29]

South Korean Workers' Party activists, operating underground since September's Inchon landing, are tracking the killings and ultimately, in a secret report to Pyongyang, claim 29,000 executions in Seoul alone.[30]

The British, fighting and dying for the South Koreans, are among the most alarmed at their actions. A company of British troops has seized "Execution Hill," outside Seoul, to block further mass killings there.[31] Shinn's report last month on the execution of 20 prisoners at the site alerted the outside world to what was happening in one location.

Now, within hours of his Associated Press report on Rhee's "speedup" of executions, the State Department in Washington cables the U.S. Embassy in Seoul to say the move is "creating exceedingly bad reaction here and abroad." It suggests the embassy "urge all possible moderation" on the South Koreans.[32]

A response from William J. Sebald, the State Department's Tokyo-based liaison to General MacArthur, says MacArthur's command regards the atrocity reports, which include accounts of inhumane conditions and torture in the prisons, as an "internal matter" for South Korea and has "refrained from taking any action."[33]

WEDNESDAY, DECEMBER 20, 1950

Gil Isham is among thousands escaping by sea
from the Chinese trap

In mere days, Hungnam Harbor has become one of the world's busiest ports, as an epic seaborne evacuation unfolds over its cold, dark waters.

The three-mile-wide anchorage on North Korea's east coast is crowded with Liberty and Victory ships of the U.S. Merchant Marine, U.S. Navy landing craft and big troop and cargo transports, chartered merchantmen from Japan, and a small fleet of lighters shuttling from shore to ship. Five thousand local men recruited as stevedores labor day and night at dockside.

The job General MacArthur's army handed his navy is daunting: to pull 105,000 U.S. and South Korean troops, more than 18,000 vehicles, and 350,000 tons of cargo out from the path of Chinese armies pouring into North Korea.

Unlike the retreat in the west, X Corps' overland roads south are blocked by the enemy. The sea is the only escape route, and the early northern winter makes the hurried evacuation doubly demanding. Some boatmasters must be helped back aboard their mother ships after hours exposed to the icy spray and wind while ferrying cargo and men.

The job also has grown much bigger than planned. From the nearby city of Hamhung, from as far off as mountain villages destroyed in the U.S.-Chinese fighting at the Changjin Reservoir, tens of thousands of North Korean refugees have converged on the seaport, desperate to be taken aboard and away.

Last Friday the Marine regiments crippled in the reservoir fighting were the first to sail for South Korea. Then the more battle-worn units of the 7th Infantry Division and remaining South Korean troops were evacuated.[34]

Now it's the turn of Private Gil Isham and the other infantrymen of the 7th Division's 17th Regiment. Regiment rosters count 3,260 men, and its casualty charts show 20 killed in action and 95 wounded since they came ashore at Iwon on October 29.[35]

The 17th has seen less combat in this doomed campaign than some other units, but they're still a ragged formation as they shuffle aboard the giant troopship USS *Breckenridge*.[36] Their grim, unshaven faces and grime-coated fatigues, some with holes in their knees, tell of grueling weeks in a harsh climate, pushing north to the Yalu and then withdrawing south two hundred miles and finally manning Hungnam's outlying defenses.

Preparing for the overnight journey to Pusan, Isham has his first shower in months, in heated seawater whose salt stings his cracked, wind-burned face. "Boy, did that ship feel good, and even that hot shower, 'cause we had been so cold."

The Hungnam perimeter has contracted in stages since early December, beginning as a looping defensive line twelve to fifteen miles distant from the port and ending in positions just a mile away. Earlier this day, men of the 3rd Infantry Division, the last U.S. unit to join X Corps, relieved the 17th Infantry on the perimeter. The 3rd Division troops now fall back to tighter defense lines. The enemy, seeing he'll soon control the area without a fight, has shown no interest in mounting a major assault.[37]

Throngs of civilian refugees, meanwhile, have squeezed into the port area, hoping for rescue—women with bulging bundles on their heads, old men sheltering small grandchildren in their overcoats, mothers with babies on their backs, all standing stoically, silently, in freezing temperatures. Their reasons for fleeing range from fear of retribution for association with the Americans and South Koreans to a simple belief that life must be better in the South.

The U.S. command first planned to evacuate only four thousand or so North Koreans who worked closely with the brief occupation. But Dr. Bong Hak-hyun, a northern-born physician from South Korea who joined X Corps as a top adviser, pleaded with corps commander General Almond on behalf of the desperate tens of thousands, many of them Christians, like Bong. Almond relented and agreed to evacuate as many as possible.[38]

Some refugees, after security checks for enemy infiltrators, are loaded onto South Korean LSTs. Designed to transport tanks and two hundred troops, one of the landing craft carries seven thousand people southward. Others are evacuated in smaller groups among departing cargo vessels.[39]

The last to leave is the Merchant Marine's *Meredith Victory*, a 455-foot freighter with berths for sixty crew and passengers. Hour by hour on Friday, some five thousand refugees are taken aboard, lifted atop pallets by wharf-side booms and lowered into the ship's holds, where they have no heat or light, food or water. Around midnight, the ship's captain, Leonard LaRue, orders still more taken aboard. By late Saturday morning, fourteen thousand refugees are packed into the *Meredith Victory*'s holds and atop its deck as it sets sail for South Korea. Five healthy babies are born during the trip.[40]

In all, the evacuation fleet rescues more than eighty-six thousand refugees from Hungnam. Together with thousands evacuated from Songjin to the north and Wonsan to the south, the U.S.–South Korean operations transport more than ninety-eight thousand to South Korea. At least as many seeking rescue are left behind.

On Sunday, as U.S. warship guns lay down a barrage across Hungnam's outskirts, the last 3rd Division troops, platoons holding beachhead positions, are evacuated. Then navy and army demolition teams head for getaway boats while setting off explosives, including two hundred tons of left-behind ammunition, that demolish the Hungnam Harbor front and its facilities in huge explosions.[41]

By then, Christmas Eve, the 17th Infantry is being rested, resupplied and issued fresh, clean uniforms in bivouac at Yongchon, South Korea. "It is considered that the morale of the command is excellent," says a 7th Division personnel report.[42]

Gil Isham, for one, after three months at war, might question that. Passing through nearby Taegu, the eighteen-year-old private sees a new military cemetery, with its neat white rows of wooden grave markers. "Most of them were guys that fought in the first summer, August and September, in the perimeter. It made us think about what we were in for now, to see all those crosses and to know what we were headed for."

<hr />

An older woman on crutches was among those thousands of refugees sailing away from Hungnam, a local widow who required help from friends to make her way aboard one of the last ships to depart the harbor.

No Kum-sok's mother, who suffered a broken leg in an accident, at first didn't want to leave. She told those friends that her son, her only child, is in the North Korean navy, at the Naval Academy. She needed to be in Hungnam when he eventually came home.

But they warned her that vengeful returning communists might target her as a Christian and widow of a "Japanese collaborator," a rail executive under Japan's old colonial regime. She must stay alive if she's ever to meet her son again, they said. She finally relented.

His mother may be southbound to Pusan through the Sea of Japan, but No Kum-sok, the former naval cadet, is much farther from the sea and the navy at the moment, undergoing flight training at a Chinese air base at Yenchi in Manchuria, near the North Korean border.

The training began in early autumn and has been intense, keeping the student pilots occupied from 4:30 a.m. to bedtime, seven days a week. In just weeks, they have had to absorb courses in aerodynamics, aircraft engines, navigation, instrumentation, weaponry, and other subjects. They finally took to the air with instructors in Yak-18 trainers, Soviet-made two-seater propeller planes.

Those instructors are a mix of Koreans and Russians. As early as August, American intelligence detected a buildup of Soviet air force elements in Manchuria and the Soviet Far East. Mysterious new swept-wing aircraft were spotted at Chinese airfields. Then, in November's first days, these new jets rose into the skies over the Yalu River to meet incoming American bombers and their F-82 Twin Mustang and F-84 Thunderjet escorts. The communists quickly claimed several "kills" of B-29s and fighters.[43]

The appearance of this new weapon, the MiG-15 interceptor, alarmed the U.S. air command after months of American domination of Korean skies. "[Aircraft] can apparently turn very sharply and have very steep angle of climb. Also very, very fast," MacArthur's air force chief, Lieutenant General George E. Stratemeyer, reported back to Washington.[44]

The Soviet-built jet flies one hundred miles an hour faster than the American F-80, climbs higher, and dives and turns faster.[45] The U.S. Air Force remained outmatched until it sent its newest jet fighter, the F-86 Sabre, into action in early December.

The Americans assume the MiG-15 pilots are Chinese, but most are Russians flying in Chinese uniforms and with either Chinese or North Korean markings on their planes. These pilots are restricted to flying in the northern half of North Korea. They also have instructions, implausibly, to speak only Chinese or Korean over the radio in flight. Josef Stalin doesn't want to provoke the Americans openly into a world war.

The U.S. leadership in Washington, also wary, has denied a request from General MacArthur and his air force deputies for authority for "hot pursuit," to chase the MiGs back to their safe-haven bases in China to destroy them there.[46] "The Americans will never bomb Manchuria," a Russian instructor tells No, whose middle school Russian helps him in training. "They're afraid it will start World War III."

Soviet leader Stalin, dispatching more and more MiGs to Manchuria, also agreed to send the instructors to help rebuild the North Korean air force.[47]

At the Yenchi airfield, No Kum-sok finds these Russians to be skillful but at times "crazy" fliers. On one training mission, his Russian instructor, showing off, went into a sudden dive to about thirty feet above ground and streaked along above Chinese farm fields, terrifying the farmers and their chickens.

No Kum-sok, soon to turn nineteen, is among the better students, one of the first to fly solo in the Yak-18. They next graduate to the heavier, faster Yak-11 trainer. And North Korean planners, desperate to defend against the Americans' airborne devastation, have something still bigger and faster in mind for their best novice pilots.

THURSDAY, DECEMBER 21, 1950

Yu Song-chol joins an angry Kim Il-sung as he purges "disloyal" generals

The small city of Kanggye, among the copper-zinc mines of far northern Korea, one of the coldest spots on the peninsula, is where Kim Il-sung's government temporarily resettled after fleeing Pyongyang as U.N. forces plunged into the North.

With a Chinese ally now in the fight, Pyongyang Radio, relocated to Kanggye, has again taken on the triumphant tone that accompanied last summer's unstoppable northern offensive. The radio says the socialist forces will push below the 38th Parallel and retake Seoul. Final victory is said to be certain.[48]

It's in Kanggye, too, on this frigid December day, that Kim Il-sung has convened a plenary session of the Central Committee of his Korean Workers' Party. Premier Kim has a new confidence, but he also is agitated and vengeful, as Yu Song-chol witnesses firsthand.

Angry that his regime was almost obliterated, requiring rescue by China, Kim opens the session with a long, bitter speech denouncing supposed mistakes by his generals. He declares the need for a purge. "Loyal party members and those who are not loyal have been exposed in the course of the war," he says. "We need to strictly prohibit such disloyal members from the party, regardless of the position they hold."

Kim has Lieutenant General Yu, KPA operations chief, sit beside him as he summons his first victim, a general named Kim Il, head of the army's cultural training bureau. Kim Il-sung demands to know if it's true that the general said in the midst of the war that it was difficult to mount combat operations without air support. The general admits having said this. The Great Leader proceeds to excoriate him for such defeatism and

strips him then and there of his positions. One after another, in front
of the entire plenum, other generals are hauled up for questioning and
relieved of their positions.

Yu Song-chol knows this is farce. First of all, the denunciatory speech
was written by a Central Committee vice chairman with no knowledge
of the conduct of the war and without consulting the general staff. Second, it was plain to everyone that engaging the U.S. military without
one's own airpower was a daunting task. Finally, the greatest blunder
of this war was Premier Kim's own dismissal of the possibility of U.S.
intervention. Yu knows these things, but can say nothing. Since their
days together in the 88th Separate Rifle Brigade, in the Soviet Far East
toward World War II's end, Yu has seen the intolerant, ruthless side of
Kim emerge repeatedly.

On this day, as Kim purges the "disloyal" in the leadership's bomb-
proof shelter, American B-29 SuperFortresses are nearby, bombing the
main rail line leading from Kanggye south to the battlefront.[49] Beyond
that front, relatively quiet today, the American commander General
Walker is preparing his troops for the Chinese onslaught he knows is
about to come. The people of Seoul are fleeing the capital in huge numbers. They're sure their city will fall again to the enemy, this time to
foreigners, a Chinese army.

FRIDAY, DECEMBER 22, 1950

*Pete McCloskey and fellow graduates ponder their future
in a wounded Marine Corps*

Snow flurries fly over the Potomac River on a gray day.

After eleven weeks of training in the riverside marshes and the classrooms of the Marines' base at Quantico, Virginia, Pete McCloskey and
359 other lieutenants of the first Special Basic Class have reached their
graduation day.

Beyond Quantico's gates, the civilian world is busy with Christmas
shopping. The radio airwaves are filled with cowboy singer Gene Autry's
holiday hit about a red-nosed reindeer. But for these newly activated reserve officers and for the entire Marine Corps, it's a cheerless, anxious
season.

In the early weeks after Stanford graduate McCloskey and his platoon
mates began their accelerated course on September 29, as Marines and

army troops in Korea were retaking Seoul, the officers in training were a confident, relaxed group. Mostly college men, they took their instructions seriously, in platoon and company tactics, weapons deployment, small-unit paperwork. But they found diversions where they could, driving thirty miles upriver to Washington for nights on the town.

That mood changed after Thanksgiving, after the massed might of Chinese armies was thrown against the U.S. Eighth Army and allied forces in the west of northern Korea and against the U.S. 1st Marine and 7th Infantry Divisions in the east. The news reports of the Marines' disaster at the Changjin Reservoir left these young new officers more somber by the day.

Those shattered Marine regiments, evacuated by sealift from Hungnam, are now regrouping at Masan in Korea's far south, assessing their losses and needs. One company alone, Charlie Company of the 5th Marines, which numbered 230 men and officers when it disembarked at Wonsan in October for the northeastern campaign, lost 181 killed and wounded in the fatal encounter at the reservoir. The Marines are woefully short of lieutenants, the platoon leaders often among the first casualties in such a "war of platoons," fought by small units in the tight confines of a mountainous terrain.

At Quantico, as they pose for their graduating class photos this day, McCloskey and the other trainees know many of them must fill those gaps in the war zone. The need is great. "Threat to Seoul Grows," reads the *Washington Post* headline.[50]

Of 45 graduates smiling wanly for the camera in McCloskey's section, 20 are to be shipped to Korea immediately. And the avid reader from California, the boy who once imagined himself a Marine at Belleau Wood, awaits the next call.

Near midnight on this evening, not far upriver from Quantico, Lieutenant General Matt Ridgway is enjoying an after-dinner highball at the house of an army friend at Fort Myer. The holiday party is a bit of relaxation after another long day at the wartime Pentagon.

Amid the banter of departing guests, his host tells him he's wanted on the telephone. It's General Joe Collins, army chief of staff. He tells Ridgway that Johnny Walker—Eighth Army commander Walton H. Walker—is dead. After five months of peril, triumph, and now new setbacks in Korea, the tough sixty-one-year-old general is suddenly dead in a jeep accident north of Seoul.

Collins adds to the stunning news an even bigger headline for his right-hand man: Ridgway is to replace Walker in Korea. Unknown to him, his standby selection as successor had been made long ago, by Douglas MacArthur, with Collins's approval.

After hanging up the phone, Ridgway sees his young wife, Penny, across the room. She is looking at him with questioning eyes. He smiles and shrugs and shakes his head. He won't tell her until morning.

Matt Ridgway is surprised but not unprepared. Two weeks ago, amid the grim news from Korea, something impelled him to climb to his attic, out of Penny's view, and to find and ready his boots and battle dress, the combat gear that in 1945 he hoped he had put away forever.

Now, within twenty-four hours, he is flying west, leaving behind a Christmas he'd so anticipated spending with twenty-month-old Matt Jr., and instead heading toward another war and the greatest challenge of a long military career.

MONDAY, DECEMBER 25, 1950

Chung Dong-kyu, newcomer to the South, awakens
to Christmas carolers

The ROK Army "volunteers" lie huddled together against the winter cold, asleep in a vacant thatch-roofed farmhouse outside Hongchon, on the central war front.

It's after midnight. An older man among these young northern refugees shakes Chung Dong-kyu awake. "Listen," he tells him. "The Christians are out singing."

Chung raises and turns his head. He hears a slow, sweet melody sung by mixed male and female voices. His comrade tells him it's a song called "*Goyohan Bam*," "Silent Night." It's the morning of December 25, he says. "Baby Jesus of Nazareth was born 1,950 years ago today."

Chung knows little about Christianity. But he recalls how Christian students in the North were discriminated against and prevented from attending holiday services at this time of year. It's yet another difference between North and South, he reflects. He drifts off back to sleep.

Since boarding the evacuation ship at Songjin two weeks ago, the eighteen-year-old medical student has embarked on yet another new chapter in his life.

With the two hundred other members of the so-called Local Volunteer Youth Group, he arrived on December 12 at a small southern port up the coast from Pusan. They were weak from hunger, dehydration, and seasickness.

Disembarked onto a beach, they were fed by southern soldiers. Then a tough-looking sergeant addressed them, telling them it was time to show their gratitude to the Republic of Korea for rescuing them from the North. They were handed army enlistment forms to sign. They all did. Stranded in an unfamiliar land, they saw little alternative.

They were told they would form a reconnaissance company attached to the 23rd Infantry Regiment of the ROK 3rd Division, the division whose troops they accompanied on the three-day journey south. They then were marched inland to board boxcars for a long train ride north into the unknown. Along the way over the past two weeks, desertions reduced their number to some 150.

They're now in reserve, awaiting outfitting with uniforms and weapons and some scant training. The 3rd Division is establishing a main line of resistance against the expected renewed offensive by the Chinese and North Koreans.

Chung is pained by the irony of having fled his home to avoid military service, only to end up in the other side's military, "in the care of my southern cousins," as he thinks of it.

It matters little to him who wins this war, which he blames on America and Russia, the great powers that divided the Korean people and then set them against each other. We'll fight, he tells himself, because if all of us fight hard we might help end this madness that much sooner. And then we can return home.

The 7th Cavalry has dug in along the ragged defense line stretching eastward from Seoul, on alert, like everyone else, for a Chinese offensive.

It's a bleak Christmas for young men who expected by now to have left Korea as a victorious army. But at least the army cooks have managed to serve up a hot holiday dinner, and from somewhere in the rear they've brought along radios. The troopers tune in to the armed forces network, hear snatches of Christmas melodies, long still more for home.

When Private Buddy Wenzel is unexpectedly summoned to the G Company command tent, he's mystified. Bad news from home? A promotion?

Strangely, it's about James Hodges.

Wenzel finally wrote to James's sister Dorothy, his old pen pal, to tell her how sorry he was about her brother's death. Now his captain, confused, tells Wenzel the distraught Hodges family wrote to the army for an explanation.

How do you know Hodges was killed? he asks Wenzel, who then recounts the events of last September 18, when he discovered his friend's body.

The surprised officer tells him Hodges was somehow listed as missing in action, and the family was so informed. Wenzel now is to sign an affidavit attesting to James's death, and the family at least can rest assured about the fate of their nineteen-year-old son and brother. But the remains of the Florida sharecropper's boy still lie somewhere unknown in the turmoil of the war, misplaced or misidentified.

WEDNESDAY, DECEMBER 27, 1950

Matt Ridgway takes command of a dispirited army

The terrain rolling by far below at 180 miles an hour is new to him—rumpled mountain country, veined with winding valleys, its ridges and peaks rising to six thousand feet. Needing to quickly learn more about this land called Korea, the three-star general has buckled himself into the bombardier's seat in the all-seeing Plexiglas nose bubble of a B-17 bomber, as the Flying Fortress ferries him north toward his war.

It's the kind of thoroughness and drive that Matt Ridgway, the new Eighth Army commander, has shown throughout his military career, from the 1920s and his days as a company captain with the 15th Infantry Regiment in northeast China; to the 1930s and staff positions under the man destined to head the U.S. Army, General George C. Marshall; and on to his pioneering role as a paratroop commander in World War II. The cliché label sticks to him, "a soldier's soldier."

He certainly looks the part: the aquiline profile of a Roman legionnaire, the hard, fit body, five-foot-ten and 175 pounds, that graces a uniform. But it's his performance as a leader of men that wins him the respect of all ranks.

He's the general who stood in the front lines with his troops at the Bulge, who got to know individual soldiers and what they faced, who wants to see things for himself.

There's no substitute for personal reconnaissance, he believes, including from his perch on the B-17, where he checks the landscape passing below against his topographical map, a landscape where his new army, a retreating army, may have to take a stand.

The air force is flying Ridgway from Taegu, Eighth Army headquarters, two hundred miles to Seoul and the army's advance command post. It's his first full day in Korea, just three days after he took off from Washington following a rushed early "Christmas Eve" celebration late Saturday with Penny and baby Matty. They've been exhausting days filled with crucial meetings, especially Tuesday's with General MacArthur in Tokyo.

The supreme commander confided to Ridgway that he had recommended widening the war, having Chiang Kai-shek's Nationalist troops strike against southern China. But Washington rejected the idea. Now, he told him, the objective is simply to beat back the enemy and restore South Korea to its prewar state. Ridgway should hold Seoul as long as possible and otherwise take a stand "in the most advanced positions in which you can maintain yourself"—if necessary, falling back to the old Pusan Perimeter.

Taking his leave, Ridgway had a final question, asking whether MacArthur would object if he went on the attack in Korea. "The Eighth Army is yours, Matt," MacArthur replied. "Do what you think best." The Far East chief clearly was giving his new subordinate more latitude than he ever gave Ridgway's predecessor, the late Johnny Walker.

Despite his misgivings about MacArthur's recent strategic moves, Ridgway remained impressed by the older general's command of detail, his frankness, his professionalism. They are both army men through and through, masters of military science, keepers of tradition, reared on army posts across America as the sons of officers. Ridgway likes to recall that his earliest memories are of marching men, and of "Reveille" at dawn and of "Taps" when being put to bed.

From Tokyo, he flew on to Taegu and more memories—this time of war, suddenly finding himself among the jeeps and growling trucks, the tents, the stacked supplies and ammunition, the men in battle dress, the trappings of war, whatever the decade and place.

He spent the night at Eighth Army headquarters reviewing the latest on the war situation with top staff, some of them old friends. The latest was not good: slow moving though it is, the oncoming Chinese army has finally crossed the 38th Parallel.

Now, this morning, his B-17 has landed at Kimpo Airport, and he is driven to the army command post in snowy Seoul. The first thing he finds is an undermanned advance headquarters. In his view, too many staff colonels and majors are in Taegu, far from the war front. In a busy next four days, he finds much more to trouble him, in general a sense of gloom, of fatigue, and of a lack of initiative, from the lower ranks he quizzes in the field to the upper ranks who brief him on operations. He finds more specific problems as well. At the soldier level, there's a shortage of gloves and other winter clothing, poor food, even a lack of stationery for writing home that has troops griping. Ridgway quickly tends to such demoralizing failings.

Perhaps most crucially, he is beginning to identify weak links in the U.S. command chain, generals and colonels to be eased out of their positions. Meantime, he orders commanding generals to move their posts from the rear closer to the action.

He sets an example, riding into forward areas in an open jeep, with a grenade and a first-aid kit fixed to the shoulder straps of his paratrooper's harness, a practice he picked up in the last war. The grenade is his personal defense in a tight spot. But it also burnishes his image among the troops as a true soldier.

On this, his first day in Seoul, Ridgway also meets with Syngman Rhee.

Ridgway and MacArthur had discussed the potential for ROK Army defections to the northerners if it appeared the U.S. military might abandon South Korea. Ridgway is determined to reassure the president he has not come to evacuate Eighth Army to Japan.

As they shake hands, the new American commander tells the elderly Korean, "I'm glad to see you, Mr. President, glad to be here, and I mean to stay." Rhee is visibly relieved.

By evening, Matt Ridgway, feeling sufficiently briefed and in command, is convinced the Chinese will launch a major attack within days, probably at New Year's, when they would calculate the defenders might relax their guard. Their chief objective will be Seoul, but he is also worried about a possible flanking attack looping around from the east, through Wonju, to cut off the capital's routes to the south.

By day's end he has ordered the 2nd Infantry Division, in reserve and still reorganizing after the battering it took in late November, to accelerate a planned move up from the south and to take a blocking position at Wonju.

PART 2
1951

Carrying their faith in a bundle

They disappeared to faraway corners of this land. . . .

I bury my poor song in this dark earth

Before leaving Seoul for the second time.

—**Cho Chi-hun**, "At Chongro," from *Brother Enemy*

As 1950 fades into 1951, the scale of General MacArthur's miscalculation becomes clear. By aggressively pushing U.S. and South Korean forces far beyond the 38th Parallel, he presented the Peking leadership with little choice but to counter what they saw as an existential threat from an anticommunist America. MacArthur's blunder was compounded by U.S. intelligence reports vastly underestimating the size of the huge Chinese army pouring into Korea. The sight of the mighty American military in full retreat has shocked the world.

In a January 1 broadcast address, Kim Il-sung congratulates his communist ally, "firmly convinced that you will win a greater victory." In Washington, a nervous Joint Chiefs of Staff messages MacArthur that if an unstoppable Chinese force advances deep into the South, "it then would be necessary, under those conditions, to direct you to commence a withdrawal to Japan." Within the space of a few weeks, the whole mood of the war has changed. The prospect of a swift end to the fighting has disappeared. Instead of a Korea reunified on U.S. and South Korean terms, the Americans are on the verge of ceding all recently gained ground, and more.

Fear returns to Seoul. Tens of thousands of the war-shattered city's population take to the roads south. Families are again separated in the turmoil. American firepower once more is turned on refugee columns and villages seen as potential cover for the enemy.

The southern capital, abandoned by its defenders, falls again under communist control as U.N. forces withdraw to the 37th Parallel. Months of thrust and parry by two giant armies follow, culminating in the war's greatest battle, at the end of which the two sides, gaining little with their blood, reach a late-spring standoff. Meanwhile, a belligerent, insubordinate MacArthur has been fired by President Truman.

In Washington and at the United Nations in New York, U.S. strategists and international diplomats envision a possible truce where the armies stand, roughly at the original 38th Parallel dividing line. In late June the Americans offer negotiations, and the communists accept.

The two sides dig in deeper, reinforcing their defensive positions for a new kind of conflict, of trench warfare, of fearful patrols into no-man's-land, of sudden attacks in the night against isolated hilltop positions, and of life-and-death aerial duels miles high over the North Korean countryside between MiG pilots and their American Sabre jet foes.

The truce talks turn bitter, sporadic, and slow, as prospects for a prolonged war grow. The North Koreans call 1951 "the year of unbearable trials"; in truth it's a description that applies to both sides equally.

JANUARY

MONDAY, JANUARY 1, 1951

Chung Dong-kyu narrowly escapes in a first enemy encounter

Just as General Ridgway foresaw, the Chinese and North Koreans opened their new offensive on New Year's Eve, aiming their sharpest blows at South Korean divisions. The attacks began in late afternoon on Sunday, with artillery barrages along the Imjin River, the front line twenty-five miles north of Seoul. After dark, the assault forces crossed the frozen Imjin and, bugles blaring, gongs clanging, stormed the dug-in positions of the ROK 1st Division. Then, over the midnight hours and toward dawn, the Chinese and North Koreans pushed south along a broader forty-four-mile front, sweeping over snowy hills and rice paddies. Companies, battalions, whole regiments reeled before them. With daylight, American air attacks and artillery have slowed but not stopped the offensive.[1]

Now it is midafternoon at Hongchon on the central front, and troops of the ROK 3rd Division are withdrawing south along the main road. But Chung Dong-kyu and his comrades of the 23rd Infantry's reconnaissance company are marching north against the tide, for reasons unknown to them, but apparently to help form a rear guard.

After sunset, as the temperatures drop into the teens Fahrenheit, the 150 or so men, still in their summer uniforms, halt at a small village for the night. Sentries are posted, and the soldiers disperse to local houses for shelter and sleep.

Chung, short, slight, and at eighteen one of the youngest in this unit of northern conscripts, has become a kind of informal orderly for the company commander, a Lieutenant Kim. He, Kim, and four other soldiers settle into a house where an old woman lives alone, the village's one remaining occupant. She seems glad to have company, making them a dinner of rice and kimchi before they bed down for the night.

Their sleep is disturbed only by the woman's coughing fits until, around midnight, they hear sporadic gunfire in the distance. It grows closer.

"What's going on? I don't like it," someone whispers to Chung.

Suddenly, automatic fire explodes in the village lanes outside. Men running past are shouting "*Namu jige!*" (wooden A-frame), the night's password, and "Come on! We're moving out!"

Lieutenant Kim seems confused, frozen. Chung looks through a crack in a wall and sees company soldiers with their hands up, surrounded by men in KPA uniforms. The North Koreans somehow learned the password and penetrated past sentries and into the village.

When he turns, he finds Kim has slipped out a back door with two men. Chung and two others now also head out the back. He stops to plead with the woman, calmly smoking her clay pipe, not to inform on them.

They creep through the darkness into the family barn and lie down. A foul smell quickly tells them they've chosen a pile of decomposing ox dung for a hiding place, but they can't move. By the light of the woman's kerosene lamp, shining from her back room, they see two North Korean soldiers walk into the barnyard, burp guns at the ready.

Spotting the woman inside, one shouts, "Any ROK soldiers here?"

She's silent. Chung is terrified. He slowly points his old bolt-action Japanese rifle toward the North Koreans. The soldier shouts at her again.

"I told you before," she replies. "I haven't seen any." The two move on.

Chung and his companions must get away or eventually be found. He feels along the barn's back wall and finds a tiny opening at the floor, perhaps for the family dog. They squeeze through with their rifles pushed ahead, but must leave behind their helmets and packs.

In the pitch-black night, they head away from the village, dashing over snow-covered fields in what they sense is a southerly direction. After some minutes, breathless, exhausted, they see a column of what must be KPA soldiers about to cross their path ahead. They drop into a shallow irrigation ditch between two paddies.

As the line of enemy passes, Chung can hear them hissing and cursing at their prisoners, his former comrades captured in the village, pushing them along.

When all is quiet, they climb from the ditch and jog to the base of a nearby hill, circling it to regain their southerly direction. They walk and trot through the early-morning hours, as an icy fog descends on the countryside. Finally, somehow, they blindly stumble upon a ROK Army unit.

Soldiers there throw blankets over their violently shivering bodies, and they're taken to a battalion commander, a grim-faced lieutenant colonel whose demeanor alarms Chung. Will they be shot as deserters?

Instead, taking them to a wall map, he questions them for details about the night's events and locations. Armed with this new information, he picks up a field telephone and orders a fire mission by his artillery battery.

The trio is next taken to a bivouac area where others of the reconnaissance company are gathered, including company commander Kim. Still more trickle in during the day, including a group who escaped their captors during the South Korean artillery barrage. A muster eventually finds a dozen of their number have been killed or captured.

In the coming days, Chung's company and the rest of the 3rd Division are withdrawn some forty miles south to a line through Wonju, Chechon, and Yongwol.[2] It's a time of retreat and discouragement, in the depths of a winter of unusually arctic temperatures, but also a time when Chung's unit of dragooned northern refugees is finally given warmer uniforms, boots and gloves, and modern M-1 rifles.

Back in Seoul, Matt Ridgway orders a withdrawal of all forces north of the capital, into a "Seoul bridgehead," a line he has mapped out since taking command just five days ago. It's an umbrella perimeter looping ten to fifteen miles west, north, and east of the capital, far enough to keep enemy artillery from striking pontoon bridges that are the main escape route south from Seoul across the Han River.

Off to the east, the newly arrived general's foresight in prepositioning the U.S. 2nd Infantry Division around Wonju is slowing the enemy advance. But hard-pressed American troops cannot hold forever, and the enemy might soon sweep westward to cut off the escape route south. Time is running out.

On government radio, President Rhee has insisted "the defense of Seoul is secure" and urged people to remain calm.[3] But news of the Chinese advances has spread rapidly.

In the house in Sindang-dong, among the extended Kim family, the debate went on for weeks, as eleven-year-old Chang Sang listened in. Should they leave Seoul for the south? But how, and where will they go? Will they never return home to the far north, to North Pyongan?

Finally, the decision was made for them. In-laws arranged for a truck south to Taegu and invited everyone in the Kim house aboard. They will be joining one of the greatest spontaneous exoduses of the twentieth century.

For weeks they have streamed into Seoul, hundreds of thousands of northern and southern Koreans fleeing ahead of the Chinese, flowing down roads, down railroad track beds and riverbeds, in lumbering columns of families wrapped in layers of quilted clothing, carrying children, pulling crude carts bearing what's left of a household, sometimes leading an ox, fording icy streams in bare feet, choking on dust kicked up by truckloads of retreating troops, and seldom with any real notion of where they're headed, only of what they're escaping from. Four out of five people in the path of the Chinese have joined the exodus, U.N. officials estimate.

Back in June, the invaders were fellow Koreans. Many southerners stayed in their homes. Now, after the experience of that occupation and of the war that visited them daily from the skies, and with word it's an alien army sweeping toward them this time, they are taking to the frozen roads.

The influx from the north is matched by the flood of people heading south out of Seoul, a city where the early winter—ten-degree-Fahrenheit days by late December—has made wartime survival even more difficult, especially for the homeless refugees from elsewhere, for city residents made homeless by the devastation of war, and for the growing numbers of new orphans, of newly created street beggars, of new amputees and cripples.

If lucky, they have found refuge in government or aid-agency shelters. But South Korean officials complained that essentials—clothing and blankets—were slow in coming from U.N. and other international sources.[4]

It's estimated that eighty thousand a day are abandoning the city,[5] and now the sprawling Kim family is joining them.

First they load the open truck with their baggage, tied around with ropes, and then they climb atop the bags, in their cocoons of white quilted coats, hats, padded socks.

Aboard the bulging truck are Sang; her forty-six-year-old mother, Bong-hyun; her mother's parents; her sister and brother-in-law; her aunt Cho Myung-suk and Myung-suk's half-dozen children; plus the Cho in-laws and a family friend, Professor Samuel Shin, and his wife. The driver rings this human cargo with another rope and tells them to hang on tight to each other as they set off to cross the Han River by pontoon bridge and on to the road south.

Tragic scenes unfold along the wretched refugee route, as the lucky ones like the Kims, aboard cars and trucks, make their way down the jolting road between lines of family groups walking wearily through the blowing snow.

Motionless bodies lie by the roadside, perhaps sleeping, perhaps lifeless. On Christmas night, three infants were found to have died of exposure while their exhausted parents slept. On the parallel railroad, half-frozen people tumbling from the jammed roofs of railcars are left behind to die.

United Nations relief teams try to help, distributing bags of rice along the road, setting up vaccination tents to inoculate against typhus and other diseases spread by war's disruptions. But the refugee numbers are overwhelming. In makeshift off-road encampments, many succumb—to the cold, to pneumonia, to despair.[6]

The truck driver is determined to get his passengers to Taegu non-stop, some two hundred road miles. As they push on through the icy air, Professor Shin sees Chang Sang shivering.

"Sang-*iyah*, come, sit on my lap." Sang edges over and does what he says.

"Yes, *Umma*, I'm all right," she tells her mother. "I'm warm."

Moving steadily south, they begin to weary and doze. Then, when the driver takes an abrupt turn, Bong-hyun drops from atop the pile of luggage and falls down to the road. She's hurt, but they cannot stop for long. Sang watches as the others pull her mother back atop the truck, and they drive on. The broken rib is to pain her for years.

After many hours, they hold on tight for the steep climb and winding curves of the seven-hundred-foot-high Autumn Wind Pass, the landmark Chupungnyong, gateway to the south, and then drive on through Kimchon, a city of ashes, burned to the ground by the 1st Cavalry Division early in the war. The relieved Kims and Chos finally cross the Naktong River and the last thirty miles to Taegu.

They have escaped Seoul, soon to be consumed again by war. But Bong-hyun cannot forget the last words of one they have left behind.

When she knew they had a means to flee the city, Sang's mother rushed across town to the house of her mother-in-law, Sang's paternal grandmother, the widowed matriarch who eventually made her way to Seoul after being chased from the family estate in the North.

You must come with us, Bong-hyun told her. No, the mother-in-law replied; I won't go. Bong-hyun insisted. The family must stay together.

But the pious old woman, the pioneering Christian convert of their Yongchon hometown, sent her daughter-in-law on her way with an enigmatic reassurance: "I want to go to heaven, and it's much closer from here than any other place."

WEDNESDAY, JANUARY 3, 1951

Hurh Won-moo flees with his mother across the frozen Han

The only sound they hear is the crunch of snow beneath the feet of hundreds and thousands of silent people and the wind stinging their ruddy cheeks. Every step forward is terrifying. Just below the dark green ice, the frigid waters of the Han River still rush toward the sea. How thick is the ice? Will it hold?

Hurh Won-moo and his mother shuffle across the frozen Han, more than a half-mile wide, within an endless column of fearful people fleeing Seoul. The Americans' makeshift bridges are filled with military traffic and will shortly be closed completely to civilians. All that's left is the "ice road" of the river itself.

The Hurhs are among the last to leave in the unparalleled refugee exodus that began in mid-December. Word has spread that President Rhee and his cabinet abandoned the city this morning. At three in the morning, the Chinese attacked American rearguard positions just ten miles to the northwest.[7]

The sad, strung-out multitudes push slowly over the ice, wrapped in layers of coats, in scarves and fur hats. Women balance bundles on their heads. Men lean forward with bags on their shoulders or with children on their back A-frames. Heavily laden oxen and oxcarts test the ice most dangerously, but it holds.

The eighteen-year-old Hurh, hefting a bulging duffel bag on his back, and his mother, carrying bundles of clothing, were not supposed to be leaving Seoul this way, on foot, uncertain of how they'll get to their destination, Chonan, fifty miles to the south.

The ever-resourceful businesswoman had arranged for a man with a truck to transport the family and possessions last Friday to Chonan, where this miller's daughter owns a disused rice mill she hopes to reopen someday. The family would sit out this latest phase of the war in the old mill workers' quarters.

They waited all day Friday, and the trucker never appeared. In despair and furious—she had paid him a good sum in advance—they had to quickly find an alternative.

The next morning, cold and gray, the entire family went to Seoul Station, where civilians could mount the roofs of southbound freight trains evacuating military matériel. Hurh and his mother would stay behind, in hopes of finding the trucker and moving more belongings to Chonan. But his four siblings—three sisters aged six to nineteen and his nine-year-old brother—would be sent south with their maternal grandfather.

The scene at the station was chaotic, as families struggled to stay together and find space atop a train. The Hurhs saw a clear spot atop one car, and Mother quickly paid two young men to help lift all her charges aboard. With ropes, they tied their suitcases to an air vent, forming a square of luggage within which they hunkered down.

When the whistle blew and the train pulled away, Hurh and his mother could only watch and pray they would arrive safely at Chonan.

Back home, they did what they could to further close up the household and secure the family farm-machinery shop. They never located the truck driver.

Now, this morning, they finally reach the southern shore of the frozen Han, after what seemed to Hurh an eternity. Behind them, silent throngs still stream down from the city onto the icy white path toward the unknown. More than 2 million people, many from North Korea, have crossed the frozen river to safety.[8]

Mother and son make their way through the snowy afternoon to Yongdongpo rail station, find a place atop a twenty-car military train, and hours later arrive in Chonan.

In the dying light of the blustery afternoon, the American general stands above the Han River's northern bank and watches the masses of refugees flow sorrowfully over the ice toward the far shore. Nearby, his army rolls south in retreat, endless columns of tanks and heavy guns, and of troops in trucks and on foot, filing over the pontoon bridges. Behind him, under the gray clouds, uncontrolled fires burn across Seoul.[9]

Matt Ridgway is determined to make this retreat different from the rout Eighth Army experienced in December, when the Chinese struck in force. The army's new commander has decided this time they will not run but will withdraw methodically, from defense line to defense line, keeping contact with the enemy, striking him, counterattacking and then pulling back, inflicting heavy casualties day by day, until Eighth Army is ready to strike back full scale.[10]

He must husband his resources. After he ordered the withdrawal Monday to the initial "bridgehead" defense line north of Seoul, one of his corps commanders, Major General Frank Milburn, instructed his units to hold Seoul "at all costs." Learning this, Ridgway countermanded the order, telling his old friend Milburn that such a stand-or-die command was demoralizing to the troops and a potential waste of manpower that will be needed later. Only he, the army commander, will ever make such a drastic demand on his soldiers, Ridgway said.[11]

He has ordered today's latest move south, leaving Seoul to the enemy once more, both because of the overwhelming power shown by the Chinese in their three-day-old offensive and because he fears they'll soon be able to outflank him from the east, even advancing down the frozen river, cutting off the escape routes from Seoul.[12]

Ridgway ordered the three pontoon bridges that were built by his engineers, replacing the Han's single roadway-pedestrian bridge destroyed in June, to be closed to any but the military after 3:00 p.m. His orders are harsh: if fleeing civilians try to cross the floating bridges after that, the American MPs guarding the spans are to fire warning shots and then to fire into the crowds if necessary.

In buttoned-up field jacket and flap-eared pile cap, the Eighth Army commander has now stationed himself above the riverbank to observe the withdrawal over the main pontoon span, the trucks bumper to bumper, the armor and big guns widely spaced to not overburden the sagging bridge sections. He sees army engineers in rubber boats, armed with pike poles, grappling with the river ice to keep it from crushing or upending the floating roadway.

Well past twilight, satisfied the bulk of his exposed army is across the river, Ridgway returns to his room at the Seoul command post and packs his few things in a musette bag. Before departing in his jeep for the south riverbank, he and his orderly take a useless, worn-out pair of the general's pajama bottoms, tack it to his office wall, and scrawl above it in large block letters: "To THE COMMANDING GENERAL CHINESE COMMUNIST FORCES—WITH THE COMPLIMENTS OF THE COMMANDING GENERAL EIGHTH ARMY." Barely a week into his new command, Ridgway is already retreating, but he doesn't feel defeated.

In a devastating parting shot, he has asked the U.S. Air Force to deliver a blow to Pyongyang, the northern capital, as he surrenders the southern capital. Sixty-three American B-29 bombers rain incendiary bombs on the city. Sixty more attack on Friday. "The entire city burned like a furnace for two whole days," the North Korean radio reports.[13]

THURSDAY, JANUARY 4, 1951
As Seoul burns, Bill Shinn commandeers a switchboard to send final dispatches

The fires are most intense in central Seoul, where thick smoke fills the streets. Shadowy figures flit in and out of the glare of the spreading fires. Looters? Arsonists? The crackle of gunfire, unexplained, is heard now and then above the dull roar of the flames.

Near city hall, the Chosun Hotel stands untouched, silhouetted against buildings ablaze to its front and rear. Inside, Bill Shinn, who once helped oversee the Chosun as assistant manager, is manning the telephone switchboard, last link to the outside world for him and his fellow correspondents. The hotel's Korean staff has fled. The reporters must get out the news of Seoul's impending fall.

Shinn traveled to the front himself last week, to the ROK Army's 1st Division, when he reported the defiant words of its general, Paik Sun-yup. He reported President Rhee's dismissal of talk he was headed south. The situation "is quite secure," the president said. Now, a week later, the bravado is gone.

Shinn has filed a brief, rueful article to the Associated Press in Tokyo about his adopted city's fate at the center of a devastating war, a city about to change hands for the third time in just six months, and whose panicked residents still trudge southward across the frozen Han River in these final hours. "The deserted streets, the abandoned homes, the emptied office buildings—survivors of the first communist occupation—make observers feel the whole pathetic situation more acutely," he writes.[14]

Via the hotel switchboard, his AP colleagues report the Chinese offensive reached the outskirts of Seoul in the predawn hours this morning. Only small rear guards of U.S., British, and Australian troops remain in the city, steadily pulling back. The U.N. forces' front line across the entire Korean peninsula is withdrawing southward. It's time for the journalists to go.

Days ago, Shinn sent wife Sally and their two boys south to Taegu. Now his connections get him a seat in the official sedan of Seoul's mayor, Kim Tae-sun. The others drive off in their assigned jeeps, rumbling over one of the pontoon bridges stretching across the Han.

From the opposite riverbank, correspondents witness wrenching scenes of desperation among the civilians fleeing the city and crossing the river ice.

Stumbling at times on the difficult footing, families struggle to stay together. Heavy loads are discarded. Oxen being led across, some pulling carts, are slipping and crashing to the ice, unable to get up, bellowing, likely with broken legs.

Then word comes down from somewhere, and American military police move out onto the ice, leveling their guns at the refugees, signaling for them to go back. They shoot the fallen oxen. They push the stunned people backward, step by step. Some cry out in disbelief and fear. But the soldiers' menacing gestures finally force them to turn around, back to the northern shore.

This is soon followed by the *whump, whump* of mortars, lobbing shells onto the midriver ice, breaking it up. The U.S. military's fear of infiltrators, its primal fear from the war's first days, has taken hold again.[15]

An instruction goes out from the U.S. Eighth Army command authorizing units to "stop all civilian traffic in any direction." The means for doing it can be deadly. "Responsibility to place fire on them to include bombing rests with you," the classified message says.[16]

In the 1st Cavalry Division, whose rearguard troops are among the last leaving Seoul, an order reads, "Effective immediately no refugees or other traffic, human or beast, will be permitted to cross Han River."[17] Tragically, U.S. warplanes strafe and kill some thirty refugees on the ice, people turning back toward Seoul.[18]

Bill Shinn and other correspondents face long hours of slow progress southward down roads jammed with military traffic and refugees, through Suwon and Taejon and finally to Taegu, where they again establish reporters' bases.

Behind them, the last rear units pull back across the Han, military engineers blow up the remaining pontoon bridges linking Seoul to the rest of South Korea, and Chinese troops filter warily into the city. The war is entering a new chapter.

THURSDAY, JANUARY 11, 1951

Peng Teh-huai halts his exhausted army and faces down Kim Il-sung

Always quick to anger, Peng Teh-huai is aiming his wrath this evening at someone not accustomed to rebuke.

Kim Il-sung has traveled sixty miles by nighttime convoy to Peng's general headquarters at Kumhwa, in the rear of the central front. The North Korean leader is pushing for a quick resumption of the New Year's offensive, Peng's "Third Campaign," building on the success in driving U.N. forces from Seoul. But the Chinese commander in chief knows his troops need weeks of rest and rebuilding. Raising his voice, he chastises the younger man, "You are gambling with the fate of the people, and that's only going to lead this war to disaster."[19]

Beginning with their jump-off at twilight on December 31, the more than two hundred thousand Chinese and North Korean troops striking southward took just eight days to cross the 38th Parallel, recapture Seoul and drive the U.S. and South Korean divisions 80 miles down to the 37th Parallel. Pyongyang Radio now proclaims 1951 "the year of victory." The Chinese government has organized fireworks in Peking in celebration. An editorial in China's *People's Daily* newspaper calls for "driving the American invading forces into the sea."[20]

But three days ago Peng called a halt. He had been reluctant even to mount this Third Campaign so early. The fighting in November and

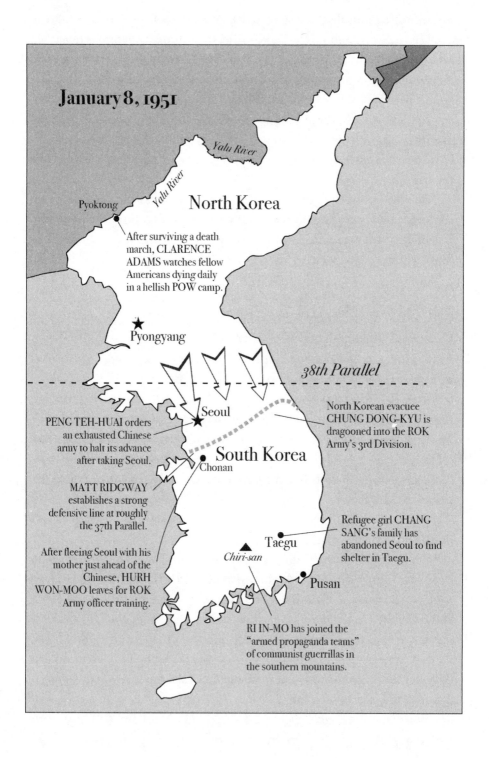

January 8, 1951

Yalu River

Pyoktong

North Korea

Yalu River

After surviving a death march, CLARENCE ADAMS watches fellow Americans dying daily in a hellish POW camp.

★ Pyongyang

38th Parallel

Seoul

PENG TEH-HUAI orders an exhausted Chinese army to halt its advance after taking Seoul.

North Korean evacuee CHUNG DONG-KYU is dragooned into the ROK Army's 3rd Division.

South Korea

Chonan

MATT RIDGWAY establishes a strong defensive line at roughly the 37th Parallel.

Refugee girl CHANG SANG's family has abandoned Seoul to find shelter in Taegu.

Taegu

Chiri-san

After fleeing Seoul with his mother just ahead of the Chinese, HURH WON-MOO leaves for ROK Army officer training.

Pusan

RI IN-MO has joined the "armed propaganda teams" of communist guerrillas in the southern mountains.

December took a heavy toll among his troops, not just from American bombs and bullets, but also from the below-zero temperatures that killed or crippled thousands of ill-clothed Chinese soldiers. They're exhausted from the long-distance nighttime marches. Chinese supply lines and depots have been bombed on a daily basis, leaving the ranks short on ammunition, food, even shoes. When they finally entered Seoul, Chinese soldiers scavenged widely for American rations left behind.[21]

The swift victory surprised the Chinese, but Peng understands the Americans deliberately evacuated Seoul to take up more defensible positions. His marching army was unable to pursue and inflict heavier casualties on the more mobile, motorized enemy in retreat. He believes the Americans now want to lure him farther south and then to land an amphibious force behind him—as at Inchon—to trap him, cutting off supplies and reinforcements.

Kim Il-sung and his vice premier and foreign minister, Pak Hon-yong, with him at Kumhwa, have a different view.

Kim tells Peng the two communist allies must occupy more southern territory to be in a stronger position in any eventual negotiation over reunification. Pak says recent intelligence reports from Moscow indicate the Americans are ready to withdraw from Korea. All they need is a push.

Peng loses his patience. He tells them they're dreaming. "In the past you said that the United States would never send troops," he says. "You never thought about what you would do if they did send troops. Now you say that the American army will definitely withdraw from Korea, but you are not considering what to do if the American army doesn't withdraw."

He repeats that his forces are in no condition to mount a new offensive. He then challenges Kim, telling him to take his own well-rested IV Corps of the North Korean People's Army and go on the attack. "If the American army really does withdraw from Korea as you think," he says, "I will happily exclaim, 'Long live the liberation of Korea!'" If they don't withdraw, he says, the Chinese People's Volunteer Force will have had time to rest and resupply and will go on the offensive again.

Kim can only admit his army, too, has not recovered sufficiently. He relents. The talk turns to a two-month rebuilding period.[22]

MONDAY, JANUARY 22, 1951

Hurh Won-moo heads to officer candidate school and war

On their last-minute flight from Seoul, over the Han River's ice and on to his mother's mill outside Chonan, Hurh Won-moo, a draft-eligible eighteen-year-old, was able to pass through ROK Army checkpoints by showing a precious piece of paper. It's his orders to report to artillery officers' school, news of which he broke belatedly to his mother.

The war made a normal path to higher education impossible for the talented high school senior. He managed to hide from North Korean conscription last summer, crouched beneath their living-room floorboards. But when it became inevitable he'd be drafted by the South Koreans, he applied for and was accepted into officers' training. This will be safer, he told his mother. The artillery is not in the front line.

He took leave of the mill and his family on a frigid Thursday in early January. Because trains had stopped running, he hiked 110 miles through the winter countryside, sheltering at night in abandoned homes, eating dried food his mother packed, following the tracks through Taejon and on to Taegu.

Now he is there, soon to report for duty, and feelings of helplessness overcome him. For the first time in his young life, he wonders, "What will become of me?" Once he is commissioned as an artillery lieutenant, a forward observer sent back north to the war zone, will his fate be to die for his country?

WEDNESDAY, JANUARY 24, 1951

Matt Ridgway attacks; "methodical destruction"
kills hundreds of civilians

The time has arrived for retaking the offensive. Matt Ridgway has set dawn tomorrow as H-hour for the start of Operation Thunderbolt, the biggest "reconnaissance in force" he has ordered since the withdrawal from Seoul three weeks ago.

American troops will jump off from a line Eighth Army established after abandoning the capital, defenses that run from the west coast forty miles south of Seoul eastward along a ridge system General Ridgway himself picked out on his first flight north, when he surveyed the Korean landscape from his B-17 bombardier's seat. The general's notion was turned into reality by thousands of Korean laborers, digging and building a fortified line of gun emplacements, log barriers, and bunkers.

More hard work followed through January, as its new commander sought to rebuild the strength, confidence, and morale of his army, adding more tanks and artillery battalions, supplying improved rations and medical services. Ridgway also has been replacing cautious, often older officers with more aggressive younger men.

An expected Chinese attack never came. Ridgway instead sent out reconnaissance patrols to find the enemy, forays that expanded from platoon-size missions to entire regiments probing forward, making sporadic contact.

Meanwhile, Ridgway and his army took other, defensive steps, deadly steps, declaring Korean refugees, still trickling south in the depth of winter, to be an ever-present danger, potentially harboring enemy infiltrators. The 1st Cavalry Division's Major General Gay ordered signs posted saying anyone trying to pass through American lines would be shot.[23]

Civilians staying in their homes are threatened as well. At a staff conference, Ridgway suggested U.S. fighter-bombers destroy villages in the path of the Chinese, reprising the "scorched-earth" policies of 1950, denying any source of shelter or support to the enemy.[24] His X Corps commander, General Almond, ordered "without delay the methodical destruction of dwellings and other buildings forward of the front lines."[25]

Five days after Almond's order, waves of U.S. Navy and Air Force planes descended on the village of Sansong-dong, in an upland valley one hundred miles southeast of Seoul. At the sound of the low-flying aircraft, people came out of their houses or looked up from their apple orchards, only to be cut down by strafing. At least fifty-one villagers were killed, and more than half the homes were destroyed. No enemy were in the village.

The next day, twenty miles away, eleven U.S. warplanes repeatedly attacked a cave sheltering hundreds of South Korean refugees, dropping napalm bombs at the cave's mouth and strafing those trying to flee. These people had crowded into the narrow, eighty-five-yard cave in fear that their villages would be bombed. Many tried days earlier to flee south, but were turned back at gunpoint at a U.S. Army roadblock. At least two hundred were killed at the Yongchun cave—suffocated, burned, or shot.

"People screamed in the darkness," Cho Byung-woo, a boy who escaped the inferno, later recalls. "It was hell. How could they not tell civilians from North Korean troops? They wouldn't have died like that if they had allowed the refugees to pass through their lines."

A U.S. infantry patrol reaching the cave in late January confirms the dead were refugees, not enemy troops.

Unusually, the Sansong-dong village attack is investigated by army and air force inspectors-general, at the request of South Korean authorities. They confirm no enemy were among the dead, but General Ridgway closes the matter by finding the attack "amply justified."[26]

Across a broad swath of northern South Korea, in such places as Yong-in, Sung-ri, Chinpyong-ri, the blood of innocent civilians is staining the January snows. Columns of refugees trekking down southbound roads, to get out of war's way, are suddenly struck from the air, their bodies left to freeze by the roadsides, just as South Korean refugees were strafed and left to rot in last summer's sun. Few such attacks make their way into the U.S. military record. It's left to survivors to attest to what is happening. But the record holds clear markers. Eighth Army's new Civil Assistance Command, which views refugees as a "problem" more than a group to be protected, notes in its monthly report for January, "Any persons or columns moving toward the United Nations forces will be fired upon."[27]

Now Thursday is dawning, and the 25th Infantry Division in the west and 1st Cavalry Division in the east launch General Ridgway's Operation Thunderbolt. Infantry and tanks move behind furious artillery barrages and air attacks on possible Chinese strongpoints. Offshore in the nearby Yellow Sea, U.S. Navy gunners join in the bombardment.

Mile by mile, the Americans encounter only light Chinese resistance, rear guards left behind to harass the attack force. The general broadens the operation to include two more U.S. divisions and two South Korean regiments. The "reconnaissance" turns into a full-fledged offensive to retake and hold ground. In a move both tactical and morale boosting, he orders all units to fix bayonets when on the attack. Men at the front are seen sharpening their bayonets and practicing thrusts. Ridgway can sense a new aggressiveness in his army.[28] "A damned good part of our army is on the offensive," he tells a correspondent.[29]

As January nears its end, Eighth Army has reached a line fourteen miles south of the Han River and Seoul.

On their way north, Ridgway's troops see more than dead Chinese. On Thunderbolt's second day, American journalists with the 25th Division come upon the frozen bodies of at least 200 Koreans in civilian clothes strewn along a roadside. They're told the refugee column was strafed by U.S. planes more than a week earlier because Chinese soldiers hid among them. But the reporters see no weapons or other signs of soldiers. "Old men, women, children, frozen stiff. I was quite overwhelmed by it," Associated Press correspondent Jim Becker later remembers. "You could see on their faces, the fright, looks of terror frozen on the faces of these bodies."[30]

In another instance of indiscriminate air attack, American bombs kill 108 children at an orphanage established by an American church group at Anyang, south of Seoul. A *New York Times* correspondent reaches Anyang afterward and reports possibly 150 other civilians also have been killed, caught in the instant death of a U.S. napalm attack, a horrible sight he calls "a macabre tribute to the totality of modern war."[31]

In the days before going on the offensive, Matt Ridgway knew his troops were questioning the very idea of this war, after seven months of advance, retreat, and wholesale death. "What the hell are we doing here, in this God-forsaken spot?" was how he summarized the questions he was hearing. In reply, his command distributed a "Letter to the Men of the 8th Army" that Ridgway wrote, describing "the things for which we fight."

Their general told them the real issues "are whether the power of Western civilization, as God has permitted it to flower in our own beloved lands, shall defy and defeat Communism."

FEBRUARY

TUESDAY, FEBRUARY 6, 1951

Chung Dong-kyu marks a bleak birthday at war

Winter among the two-thousand-foot mountains of the central front
is hard on Private Chung Dong-kyu and the others in his ROK Army
scouting unit.

Temperatures often dip below zero. Chung's fingers are frostbitten,
leaving him barely able to pull the trigger on his M-1. Others among
these North Korean refugee conscripts have frostbitten feet. In the hop-
scotching back-and-forth of advances and withdrawals in this section of
the line, the North Korean and Chinese enemy might be found behind
them just as easily as to their front.

Their reconnaissance company usually takes the lead for the ROK
23rd Infantry Regiment, scouting ahead for enemy positions when the
order comes down for the regiment to take a certain hill, occupy a village,
pull back down a valley. These scouts must be self-sufficient as they scale
the snowy hilltops and range out a mile or more ahead of the rest of the
regiment, sometimes for days at a time. They carry their own provisions
on farmers' wooden back frames. When cut off from regular rations, they
forage for dried corn or frozen potatoes in abandoned farmhouses. Most
carry a small bag of dried biscuits as last-resort sustenance.

They long ago recognized their utility to the ROK Army as men with
northern accents. They're sometimes given North Korean uniforms on
missions to penetrate enemy lines. At times they disguise themselves in
white peasant garb to reconnoiter new ground. Men sometimes don't
return from such missions, being killed or captured, or deserting. The
company's numbers are slowly dwindling.

On a winter's day early in their deployment, as regimental units moved north, Chung and a comrade were sent out ahead of the company's main body. Rifle pointed forward, eyes scanning left, right, and up the road, Chung at one point stopped and ducked behind a boulder, signaling rearward for everyone to halt.

He had seen a "bump" on a hilltop ahead that somehow seemed out of place. The two soldiers stared at it for long minutes. They thought they saw it move. Then, suddenly, other bumps appeared, then many more, soldiers, and rifle fire poured down from the hill. One round struck Chung's steel helmet. The pair tumbled down a roadside slope to a stream and ran south through the shallow water.

Once back in friendly ranks, Chung found he'd suffered a slight graze wound on his left shoulder and realized he'd left his helmet and rifle behind. But he felt elated, a proven veteran. He had saved his company from an ambush. When the main body moved forward to seize the hill, the enemy had fled.

Along with such minutes of terror, the war means long hours of idleness for the scouts. They fill them with endless games of blackjack, wagering with cigarettes. They haven't been paid since they were pressed into joining the southern army in December, but they do receive a ration of two packs of cigarettes a day. Chung is an enthusiastic card player and a nonsmoker, but he soon begins smoking his winnings. He develops a two-pack-a-day habit.

On this midwinter Tuesday, as U.S. forces in the west inch toward Seoul, the medical student from Chu Ul turns nineteen, on a birthday far from any family who would care. It is now sixty-six days since he told his mother in North Korea he would return home in three. When will he see her again?

EARLY FEBRUARY, 1951

In the hell of the Pyoktong camp, Clarence Adams survives while many don't

In the frigid midwinter in the Yalu River valley, the Americans began dying almost immediately on arrival at the Pyoktong prison camp. Even men on burial detail are dropping and dying at the edge of a mass grave, to join those who came before.

The promise of decent food, shelter, and medical care that Clarence Adams and the others heard from their guards on the death march north proved to be a cruel lie.

Those who didn't die or weren't shot on that horrible hundred-mile trek in December found only cold and crowded huts at Pyoktong, a starvation diet, and a lone Korean doctor whose prescription for ill prisoners was "fresh air," a sentence to death by hypothermia or pneumonia.

The first to die among the captive American soldiers were the wounded, whose wounds went untreated, became infected, and killed them.

Now men die from starvation, in some cases because they simply can't stomach the paltry daily ration, a quarter cup of raw corn, beans, or sorghum. Some refuse to eat and let themselves fade away.

In their inhumanly crammed hovels—twenty-five prisoners in rooms of perhaps eighty square feet—the men sometimes prop the dead against the wall, as though alive, so their rations can be shared by the living.

They're also dying from disease, from frostbite-related gangrene infections, from deficient-diet killers such as beriberi and pellagra, but especially from untreated dysentery and cholera from contaminated water, so common that prisoners can hardly avoid walking on human feces everywhere.[1] The blood-sucking lice that crawl over every man weaken them further. Some die from exposure simply from going outside to relieve themselves.

The North Korean civilians running the camp, overseen by two army officers, show little sympathy in a country where food and medical supplies have been badly disrupted by the U.S.–South Korean invasion of the North and continuing air bombardment.

Corporal Adams, the cocky would-be prizefighter, is a survivor. At twenty-two he is older than the teenaged recruits who find themselves in this unimagined hell just months from a soft life in the States, the ones who vomit up their ration, the prisoners dying fastest.

Adams finds that the black soldiers, often from impoverished backgrounds, generally cope better with the harsh deprivation. He himself, fed chicken feet as a boy in Memphis, slowly chews every grain of millet or sorghum, grateful for the distasteful nutrition.

At times the men's desperation turns them against each other, as they fight for scraps of food, steal grain from each other's stashes, strip the dead of clothing and boots. The Koreans have thrown white and black

Americans together indiscriminately in the fetid huts, and racial tensions are mounting.

Adams did feel a tie to one young white soldier, known to him only as "Peach," who tried to help him during the December ordeal on the road, until a guard chased him away. Finding Peach in another hut, Adams saw he was slowly dying from an untreated wound. He returned every day, holding and comforting Peach, squeezing pus from the wound, until he died.

The daily burial detail is their only real activity. They build stretchers from tree limbs and rope, and four weakened prisoners then carry a corpse up to the shallow mass graves on a camp hillside. They toss the body in, then cover it with snow or rocks. It happens at times that a stretcher bearer himself will collapse and die right there.

Adams otherwise spends his waking hours lying on his hut's cold earthen floor, pondering his fate, wondering whether his stricken foot, his frostbitten right foot, will deteriorate as he has seen others' do.

THURSDAY, FEBRUARY 15, 1951

Matt Ridgway savors a first setback for the Chinese

Among frozen rice paddies and low hills east of Seoul, the U.S. 2nd Division's 23rd Infantry Regiment and French troops of the U.N. command have beaten back repeated massive Chinese attacks on their positions at the village of Chipyong-ri. Supported by tanks and air strikes, an American relief force finally breaks through to the surrounded defenders this day, ending the siege and sending the Chinese into retreat.

From his forward command post in Wonju, twenty miles to the southeast, Matt Ridgway flies in by helicopter to congratulate the bloodied but victorious troops. He finds hundreds of Chinese corpses lying unburied, covered by a lightly falling snow. For the Eighth Army commander, Chipyong-ri is a turning point, the first major tactical defeat for the Chinese. It sets the stage for the large offensive he has long contemplated.[2]

He dubs it Operation Killer and schedules the jump-off for next Wednesday. The coldblooded code name troubles some in Washington, who suggest softening it. But Ridgway sticks with his choice, later reflecting, "I am by nature opposed to any effort to 'sell' war to people as an only mildly unpleasant business that requires very little in the way of blood."

WEDNESDAY, FEBRUARY 21, 1951

At the start of "Killer," Pete McCloskey sees war's reality

The stark winter of earlier this week has given way to today's rainy, muddy early spring. The runoff of melting snow ripples over the packed-dirt roads, turning fields into slushy mires. Rivers and streams overflow, filled with floating ice. Some low bridges have been washed out.

Corporal Phil Elson, a big machine gunner with the 5th Marine Regiment, is keeping a diary. "When we got up this morning our clothes were still wet," he writes. "Everyone is sure in a bitter mood." Someone remarked that General Washington's men had it worse at Valley Forge. "We figured Washington maybe had one edge on us though," Elson notes. "He KNEW for sure what he was fighting for, and where he was going."

This war's American commander, General Ridgway, knows where he's going, but his Operation Killer is getting off to a slow start across a seventy-five-mile front.

Supply convoys are bogged down. Reserve units are slow coming up from the south to their backup positions. Elson and other men of the 5th Marine Regiment had to double-time march this morning to get to the jump-off point at Wonju in time for the opening assault.

Despite the problems, the 5th Marines' advance began as scheduled at ten, with Charlie Company in the lead, under Captain Jack Jones, who walked out of the Changjin Reservoir trap with just a handful of his men still standing. Scores of fresh replacements have refilled the ranks.

The Marine company has pushed northward up the dirt road dubbed Route 29, paralleling the churning Som River, leading from Wonju to the town of Hoengsong, twelve miles north, their objective in enemy territory.[3]

For the first couple of hours, they saw nothing but abandoned villages. Chinese troops are pulling back. Now Jones has reached a low rise with his newest junior officer at his side, Second Lieutenant Pete McCloskey.

Too inexperienced to lead a full rifle platoon, McCloskey has been assigned to take over the nineteen-man 60-millimeter mortar section.

Standing there with his company commander, they see a village a thousand yards to their front. And they hear a hissing sound new to McCloskey, but not to Jones—snipers' bullets, from riflemen left behind in the village to slow the Americans' advance. The veteran captain hastily retreats with his new lieutenant to the back slope.

Marines take cover behind a tank as it fires on the enemy near Hongchon on May 22, 1951. The next day, Second Lieutenant Pete McCloskey and his Marines are ordered northward at the start of fateful days confronting a new Chinese–North Korean offensive. The conflict soon settles into a war of trenchworks and patrols, of "active defense," as truce talks begin. (U.S. Marine Corps)

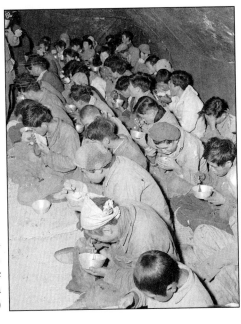

Captured guerrillas are fed at a stockade in the far south after being caught in a sweep through the Chiri-san mountains by two South Korean divisions in December 1951. As the enemy nears, Ri In-mo must leave behind a guerrilla comrade to die, a hometown friend whose frostbitten feet have been amputated. (U.S. Army)

Prisoners are assembled at a POW camp in Pusan, where both North Korean and Chinese are held. Truce talks stall in 1952 over whether prisoners can refuse repatriation to their communist homelands. At the negotiating table one day, interpreter Chi Chao-chu must sit frozen in his chair while the two sides angrily face off in total silence for a half hour. (U.S. State Department)

At a train station, a South Korean mother bids goodbye to her son, heading for the war front. As Hurh Won-moo begins his 110-mile trek to officer training in Taegu, his mother tells him, "Don't look back. Go on, and we shall meet again, if God wills." (Republic of Korea Armed Forces)

American troops thread their way over snowy ridges east of Seoul on March 1, 1951, as Operation Killer, General Ridgway's first major counter-offensive, pushes the Chinese back mile by mile. Fighting with the 17th Infantry, Gil Isham breaks down crying on killing his first enemy and finding a family photo in his pocket. "All the killing got to me." (U.S. Army)

In early 1951, in North Korea's eastern port city of Wonsan, a huge blast set off by a U.S. Air Force parachute bomb destroys a church the Americans determined housed munitions. Traveling to the Panmunjom talks, Chi Chao-chu sees devastation everywhere in North Korea and tells himself the Americans haven't dropped the atom bomb, but they might as well have. (U.S. Air Force)

A seemingly endless column of South Korean refugees clogs a road headed south in the biting cold of early January 1951. It is estimated that four out of five people in the path of the Chinese join the mass flight, one of the greatest spontaneous exoduses of the twentieth century. Eleven-year-old Chang Sang and her family are among them. (United Nations)

On January 8, 1951, a refugee column winds through deep snow near South Korea's northeast coast, south of Kangnung. Many refugees end up in Pusan, in the far south. Arriving there to open a clinic, Sister Mary Mercy sees homeless people blanketing the sidewalks and alleyways. "There is so much to be done here." (U.S. Army)

The early winter of 1950–1951 makes survival even more difficult in devastated Seoul. Here an elderly woman scavenges for salvageable material among the ruins, and a young homeless brother and sister search empty cans in a railyard for bits of food. The girl Chang Sang's family debates whether to flee Seoul as U.N. forces retreat from the north. (U.S. Army)

On December 3, 1950, civilians clamber dangerously over a bomb-wrecked bridge across the Taedong River, fleeing Pyongyang as Chinese armies approach. Before retreating, Shin Hyung-kyu, teenaged military policeman, gathers up nine-year-old orphan girl he rescued from a destroyed village and puts her aboard a southbound train, with a promise to find her later. (U.S. Army)

On December 8, 1950, the frozen corpses of Marines killed in the surprise Chinese offensive are unloaded to be buried in a mass grave. At Quantico, Virginia, Pete McCloskey and other Marine officer trainees follow the disheartening news with apprehension as they prepare for Korea. (U.S. Marine Corps)

Refugees crowd aboard small craft during the evacuation from Hungnam, North Korea, in late December 1950. Some 86,000 civilians are rescued by U.S. Navy and other vessels, along with U.S. and South Korean troops. At Songjin, farther north, as Chung Dong-kyu is evacuated aboard a navy transport, panic among those left behind pushes countless people into the icy sea to drown. (U.S. Navy)

U.S. demolition teams blow up port facilities and abandoned ordnance at Hungnam, North Korea, on December 24, 1950, after the evacuation of retreating U.S. and South Korean troops. The mother of North Korean pilot trainee No Kum-sok is among the last civilians evacuated, fearing communist retribution as the widow of a Japanese colonial-era "collaborator."

Chinese troops under General Peng Teh-huai cross the Yalu River into North Korea, intervening to "fight the American devils," as 16-year-old soldier Chen Hsing-chiu puts it in a letter home. It's "the poor beating the rich, and the weak beating the strong," the teenaged medic writes in his diary. (Foreign Languages Publishing House, Pyongyang)

By late November 1950, General Peng Teh-huai has amassed 450,000 Chinese "volunteer" troops in North Korea and launches overwhelming attacks in both the east and west. Here a unit of his 40th Army assaults a hilltop position near the eastern Changjin Reservoir. "Lure the enemy," and then annihilate him, Mao Tse-tung told Peng. (Chinese Military Science Academy)

U.S. Marines retreating from a Chinese trap at the Changjin Reservoir observe U.S. aircraft dropping napalm bombs to help clear the way on December 6, 1950. At the Pentagon, Matt Ridgway, army deputy chief of staff, watched uneasily from afar as General MacArthur's plunge into North Korea left the Marines vulnerable to Chinese attack. (U.S. Marine Corps)

The U.S. battleship *Missouri* fires on Chongjin in North Korea's northeast as U.S. and South Korean divisions drive into North Korea in October 1950. After an earlier attack on the city by B-29 bombers, medical student Chung Dong-kyu was pressed into service as a medic. He and his classmates found hundreds of civilians dead or grievously wounded among the ruins. (U.S. Navy)

Outside Hamhung, North Korea, family members search for loved ones among the bodies of three hundred political prisoners slain by retreating northerners, who forced them into caves that were then sealed off, suffocating them. Advancing north with his military police unit, 17-year-old Shin Hyun-kyu sees evidence of atrocities by both sides. "Have we gone insane?" he wonders. (U.S. Army)

Troops of the U.S. 2nd Infantry Division take up position along the Pusan Perimeter defense lines in September 1950. The late September "breakout" from the perimeter sends North Korean divisions reeling. Yu Song-chol, the young North Korean acting chief of staff, must hide his tears from subordinates as he orders the northward retreat. (U.S. Army)

A woman discovers her husband among bodies found at a mass grave at Chonju, South Korea, on September 29, 1950. Thousands of southern "reactionaries" have been slain by the retreating North Koreans and local leftists in the occupation's last days. The girl Chang Sang is told to stay away from their local church in Seoul. It is filled with bodies. (U.S. Army)

In Taegu in October 1950, young women identified as North Koreans, captured in the south during the U.N. forces' advance from the Pusan Perimeter, are herded toward a train and prisoner-of-war camp. Just days after she was impressed into the North Korean army, South Korean refugee Ahn Kyung-hee is ensnared in such a roundup. (Associated Press)

U.S. Marines storm ashore at Inchon on September 15, 1950, to drive the North Koreans from nearby Seoul. Bill Shinn is the first to report to the world on this historic turning point in the war, beating other journalists by hours in confirming that General MacArthur's bold amphibious assault is under way. (U.S. Marine Corps)

In Seoul street fighting in late September 1950, U.S. Marines check on fallen enemy. As the Americans push into the South Korean capital, teenager Hurh Won-moo watches from a window, transfixed. (U.S. Navy)

U.S. Marines march a line of captives off in Seoul on September 26, 1950. The day before, Gil Isham first experiences combat after landing with the army's 7th Infantry Division at Inchon, and he is sickened to see a Marine officer summarily execute a wounded North Korean prisoner. (U.S. Marine Corps)

A U.S. Air Force photograph shows the "carpet bombing" of 27 square miles of North Korean–held territory across the Naktong River from U.N. defense lines in August 1950. Countless South Korean civilians are killed in such indiscriminate attacks. Chang Sang and her mother are caught in one, when the ten-year-old sees two peasants killed. (U.S. Air Force)

The caption on this U.S. Army photograph says these civilians, at Yongsan, near the Pusan Perimeter defenses, were "caught in the line of fire during night attack by guerrilla forces." But U.S. commanders also have ordered civilians fired on indiscriminately for fear of North Korean infiltrators. At No Gun Ri, Park Sun-yong's two children are shot dead in a U.S. massacre of many refugees, mostly women and children. (U.S. Army)

All-black units of the U.S. Army move up to the war front after arriving in Korea in July 1950. Clarence Adams is shocked by what he sees, including civilians crushed under American tanks. "What kind of war is this where such things happen?" he wonders. (U.S. Army)

American troops are seen on the move near the southern end of the last-ditch defense line behind the Naktong River. Along this so-called Pusan Perimeter, Buddy Wenzel sees platoon mates killed and maimed through the summer of 1950. "What the hell are we here for?" he thinks. (Associated Press)

A U.S. Army officer's declassified photographs show one in a series of mass killings of political prisoners by South Korean military and national policemen outside Taejon in July 1950. When Alan Winnington finds the mass graves and reports the slaughter, his *Daily Worker* article is denounced as an "atrocity fabrication" by the U.S. Embassy in London. Investigations decades later conclude at least 100,000 were executed. (U.S. National Archives)

"The North Korean army will suffer defeat very soon," Korean journalist Bill Shinn assures American readers as the first U.S. troops land in South Korea. Organized as Task Force Smith, the "stopping force" is seen here disembarking at Taejon, on their way to a calamitous encounter with the invaders. (U.S. Army)

Captured American soldiers are marched off northward through Seoul to North Korean prisoner-of-war camps. In Tokyo in August 1950, General MacArthur tells Matt Ridgway the North Koreans have fielded as tough an army as he has ever faced. (Korean Central News Agency via Associated Press)

North Korean troops enter Seoul in late June 1950, in this unique photo from Pyongyang's Korean Central News Agency. "It's war, at last," thinks young North Korean revolutionary Ri In-mo. (Korean News Service via Associated Press)

South Korean troops retreat from Suwon, south of Seoul, in early July 1950, their army shattered by the lightning North Korean invasion. The northern general Yu Song-chol sees an imminent end to the war. (U.S. Information Agency)

The northern invasion sends streams of South Koreans fleeing farther south. Ahn Kyong-hee, privileged daughter of a Seoul editor, reaches a refuge in the southwest with her mother and siblings. But North Korean troops soon occupy the area, and she fears her family will be condemned as "reactionaries." (Associated Press)

Two 155mm howitzers fire support for 25th Infantry Division troops on the central front in November 1951. American firepower inflicts massive casualties on the Chinese, swamping Chen Hsing-chiu's aid station with wounded, including soldiers driven mad in the carnage. "Heaven, why are you so unfair?" the young medic asks in his diary. (U.S. Army)

A photo from Pyongyang's Korean Central News Agency shows the devastation wrought by U.S. bombing of the North Korean capital. Meeting with Josef Stalin in Moscow, Peng Teh-huai boasts of his Chinese army's successes in the war, but North Korea's Kim Il-sung grimly tells the Soviet leader he wants an early armistice "in view of the serious situation in which the Korean people have found themselves." (Korean News Service via Associated Press)

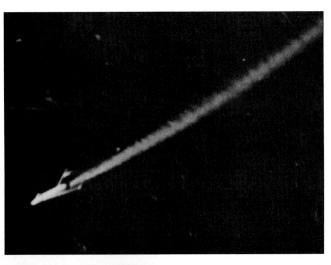

A Soviet-built MiG-15 jet fighter is shot down over Korea in late 1952. Young MiG pilot No Kum-sok, who hoped the war would end before his flight training did, feels he is "wagering my life against mere chance" as he watches North Korean wing mates fall from the skies on their daily missions against the Americans. (U.S. Navy)

In August 1952, American troops man a tunnel and trench position near much-contested Heartbreak Ridge. Shin Hyung-kyu, military police corporal, often escorts U.S. units forward to such posts. The Korean hears them spew hate toward "this goddamned country" and "goddamned gooks," but he nonetheless feels grateful toward these Americans. (U.S. Army)

Chief U.S. and North Korean negotiators sign the armistice agreement ending the fighting in Korea on July 27, 1953. Chi Chao-chu, exhausted after days of painstakingly typing the document, sits nearby, observing. Three years after he left behind studies in America to help his homeland, the Chinese interpreter feels relief the "fruitless bloodbath" is over. But the truce only puts the war on hold, with no lasting peace. (U.S. Navy)

Jones wants to call in help from Marine fighter aircraft, Corsairs, flying cover overhead.

"Put a marking round into that village," he orders McCloskey. Suddenly, the twenty-three-year-old mortar officer feels lost. He has forgotten how to order a mortar crew to fire. There was only a brief two-hour class on 60mm mortars at Quantico.

It was at that Virginia base that McCloskey received his orders for Korea, after graduating on December 22 from the accelerated officers' course, at a time when a humiliated U.S. military was reorganizing in South Korea after being routed from the north by the Chinese.

Five days ago, McCloskey and forty-three other Quantico lieutenants arrived in Pohang by sea from San Diego via Japan. He and eight others reported to the 1st Battalion, 5th Marines, whose eleven hundred men then immediately drove north to Wonju to join Operation Killer.

Four days later, on this D-Day morning, they headed out of Wonju on foot, past a clutch of officers, including an old man in army greatcoat and gold-braided cap who saluted the weary Marines. It wasn't until he was yards past the group that McCloskey realized they were being seen off into action by General MacArthur himself.

The new Charlie Company lieutenant was preoccupied with his own problem, a bout of dysentery he blamed on a poorly washed mess kit. He was quickly learning lessons.

Now, a few hours later, McCloskey is facing his first enemy, and he's about to fail, to confess to Captain Jones he's unsure how to order a marking round fired, when the company's veteran mortar sergeant, Emory Naboni, quickly shouts out range and direction, and off goes the round. The company's air liaison radios the Corsairs to strike where they see smoke.

Four of the gull-winged propeller planes roar in, each dropping a five-hundred-pound bomb, then tanks of napalm that engulf the village in flame. They make further runs strafing with their .50-caliber machine guns. Captain Jones's riflemen soon set out across a slushy field to the village, a burning, smoldering place, and find scenes of horror inside and outside the hundred or so huts.

They eventually count eighty-five villagers—old men, women, and children—killed or wounded, many burned to death, others burned horribly but still alive. Those not in silent shock are screaming. Terrified children wail. Corpsmen are ordered in to try to help the wounded.

Walking into this little hell, McCloskey is stunned. "Holy Christ," the boyhood reader of war stories says to himself. "So this is what Marine firepower can do to a bunch of people."

What the Marines don't find are the Chinese. They apparently withdrew before the Marines devastated a village to silence their sniping.

Three days later, after witnessing this scene of mothers and children slaughtered in their own homes, and as the 5th Marines press on northward, McCloskey receives a telegram from home: "Congratulations. Daughter born February 16, 8½ pounds. Mother fine. Grandmother." On the day the young lieutenant entered Korea, his first child entered the world.

Operation Killer's troops advance steadily, sometimes slowly because of lagging supply lines. The 1st Marine Division eventually clears the town of Hoengsong with little opposition, and units move forward three miles to a new defensive line, dubbed Line Arizona. But the key objective, to trap and kill large numbers of enemy, the goal for which Ridgway named the operation, has not been achieved. The Chinese and North Koreans have carried out a strategic withdrawal, denying the American commander the crucial battle he desired.[4]

MONDAY, FEBRUARY 26, 1951

Gil Isham kills his first Korean and breaks down in tears

He saw the big corporal carried down past him on a litter. Now, as Gil Isham's 2nd Platoon reaches the crest of the hill, he sees the ten dead Chinese, the carnage wrought by this one soldier. A war-weary Private Isham feels a peculiar kind of envy.

Word spread quickly through Easy Company about the heroics of earlier in the day, when the 3rd Platoon corporal mounted a one-man assault on two machine guns, hurling grenades, firing his M-1, single-handedly overwhelming two enemy positions despite his own shrapnel and bullet wounds.

Now, surveying the bloody scene in disbelief, having seen the day's hero carried off to be evacuated, eventually back to the States, Gil Isham thinks thoughts only a desperate soldier could have. "I think myself—if I would have been able to do something like that and get it over with and go home and get out of the mess, instead of having to go back all the time, I would have given up a leg or a foot. I would have given up anything to just get the hell out." Still, he couldn't do what others have done—shoot himself in the foot or hand, inflict his own "million-dollar wound" to win a trip home, to escape the madness.

The 17th Infantry Regiment has been under almost daily pressure since arriving on the central front in early January with the rest of the 7th Division, with barely two weeks' rest and refitting after their evacuation by sea from Hungnam.

Reaching front-line positions fifty miles south of the 38th Parallel, they were attacked almost immediately by resurgent North Korean units. Together with the 2nd Infantry Division, the 7th Division fought off that blow and began to push slowly northward, hill by hill, as the U.S. command clawed back territory theater-wide. Then, on February 11, a Chinese–North Korean counterattack on the central front drove the South Koreans and Americans back. The vanguard South Korean divisions suffered thousands of casualties.[5]

Now the 17th Infantry has joined in General Ridgway's Operation Killer, which has carried them forward again to the area of the corporal's heroics this day, near the Maltari Pass, forty miles south of the 38th Parallel.

Through the weeks of killing and seeing comrades killed, one death haunts Isham more than others, the first enemy soldier he killed up close.

Easy Company had taken a ridgeline when Isham spotted a "souvenir" rifle by a foxhole. As he approached it, a North Korean soldier jumped up, and Isham reacted instantly, firing an M-1 round into the back of his head. Searching the dead man's pockets, he found a photograph. It was of the soldier with his wife and two small children. Eighteen-year-old Gil Isham burst into tears. "It got to me. I figured I blew away a whole family. All the killing got to me."

The killing goes on. The men tell each other it's true, that it's official: Ridgway calls it Killer because he wants no prisoners. "A lot of guys took General Ridgway at his word," Isham will recall.

The hard winter is harder on no one more than the guerrillas in the Chiri-san mountains.

In straw huts or the open air, Ri In-mo and his comrades sleep on beds of dried leaves on the frozen ground, wrapping themselves in their quilts as best they can, often awakening covered in snow. During the day the bare limbs of the forest make it easier for the hunters, South Korean troops, to spot them against the wintry white backdrop. At night they dare not light warming fires, lest they give away their position.

They avoid encounters with the military as much as possible, using their knowledge of the terrain to shelter in hidden hollows and caves at times of danger. In these winter months, they fight hunger more than the enemy, raiding food stores or soliciting barley from friendly farmers, or simply taking it with vague promises of repayment after victory.

From their current base in a well-concealed upland valley, Ri In-mo and a few comrades have been instructed to head south to Hadong, where Ri is to collect news of fighting in the area for his mimeo bulletins, and the others are to pick up provisions.

Making their way along a southbound trail, they happen on the body of a white-clad farmer, his chest covered with congealed blood from gunshot wounds. One of the men speculates the peasant may have tried to flee what he hears was a massacre some days ago of villagers outside nearby Kochang.

Word of the massacre is spreading across the south. The guerrilla-hunting ROK 11th Division rounded up and shot more than seven hundred peasants in Kochang-area villages, including women and children, accusing residents of having helped guerrillas with food and clothing.

Similar massacres of villagers are being carried out by the military in counties across the region where the insurgents roam, in such places as Namwon, Sunchang, and Hampyong. The great majority of victims are women, children, and old men, since the younger men have either been conscripted into the ROK Army or joined the insurgents. The methods can be particularly cruel, the soldiers often telling villagers they're rounding them up to protect them and then shooting them.[6]

Now the fate of this nameless, solitary victim, frozen in death, touches Ri and his fellow guerrillas. They want to bury him, but the ground is too hard. Instead, they collect stones to cover the body, stand over him in silence for some moments, and then move on.

LATE FEBRUARY, 1951

Peng Teh-huai meets with Mao, bereaved father

The journey from the war front to Peking is a demanding one—traveling the bomb-cratered North Korean roads at night, crossing the frozen

Yalu River, continuing on by train or plane from Manchuria to the Chinese capital.

Peng Teh-huai has finally arrived at the end of a three-day journey and sits behind the high walls of the Chung Nan Hai, face-to-face with Mao Tse-tung, on a mission to brief China's supreme leader on the realities of their war in Korea.

It's their first meeting since Peng led the Chinese army into Korea in October. It's also their first encounter since Mao's eldest son died in Peng's own headquarters cabin, burned to death by American napalm, to be buried in a battlefield grave.

In this difficult moment, Peng offers condolences to his old comrade, his "Elder Brother," and speaks of his shame at not having better protected twenty-eight-year-old An-ying.

Mao crumples in his chair. They both then sit silently for minutes. Mao tries to light a cigarette, but cannot, his hand trembling. Finally, he lifts his bowed head and describes An-ying—who was assigned to Peng's staff by Mao himself—as "one of thousands" dying in Korea. "You shouldn't take it as something special just because he was my son," he tells Peng.[7]

The long moment passes. They move on to the business at hand, the enormous challenges in waging war against the Americans.

Chinese supplies of food, ammunition, fuel, weapons, winter clothing have fallen far short of what is needed, Peng tells Mao. The Americans have learned that if they keep a unit engaged in battle for a week, the Chinese must withdraw, exhausted, hungry, and without supplies. Too few antiaircraft units and the lack of their own air cover open Chinese troops to slaughter from the air. Peng is also losing huge numbers of men to illness, to frostbite. Hundreds are deserting, trickling north, looting and causing havoc on both sides of the Chinese–North Korean border. The replacements coming down from Manchuria are insufficiently trained.[8]

Peng tells Mao this war is not like their civil war, and "the Korean War cannot be a quick victory." The chairman seems finally to accept that.

"Win a quick victory if you can. If you can't, win a slow one," he tells Peng.[9]

The newly chastened Mao sends off a telegram to Moscow and Josef Stalin, China's main war supplier. "The Korean War may possibly become a prolonged war, and we should be prepared for at least two more years," he tells the Kremlin chief. He informs Stalin 30–40 percent of supplies for Peng's army are being destroyed in transit by American bombing. He asks for more Soviet air force help, protective flights deeper into North Korea.[10]

Leaving Peking, Peng arrives back at his Korea headquarters in Kumhwa on March 5. He finds his army in a defensive stance, as he had instructed before leaving for China. The surprise U.N. offensive of late January forced him, prematurely, to wage his "Fourth Campaign," not a broad offensive, as before, but instead a series of smaller back-and-forth battles into mid-February, when the failure of some twenty-five thousand Chinese troops to overcome six thousand Americans and French at Chipyong-ri signaled a new phase. It was the final attack of the Fourth Campaign.[11]

After that, Peng's forces slowly withdrew northward in the face of the Americans' "Killer" operation. Now, at his command post across the Han River, Peng's opposing commander, Matt Ridgway, signs orders to launch a new, more ambitious operation, dubbed "Ripper."[12] In Moscow, meanwhile, Stalin orders his Soviet MiG fighters to widen their air umbrella over northern Korea.[13]

MARCH

WEDNESDAY, MARCH 14, 1951

Matt Ridgway's army recaptures Seoul

Word comes in to General Ridgway's Eighth Army operations staff: a patrol from the ROK 1st Division has raised the South Korean flag over the capitol dome in Seoul. The city has been recaptured once again, this time with no opposition, in contrast to the bloody, smoke-filled days of block-to-block firefights of last September.

The South Koreans and the U.S. 3rd Infantry Division began sending patrols across the Han River on Monday. They found more and more defensive positions abandoned by the North Koreans and Chinese. Probes east and west of the city also are advancing without seeing enemy. Air observers report spotting enemy defenses being built several miles north of Seoul. Ridgway will order his own troops to establish a defense line just north of the city.[1]

The Seoul now returning to South Korean hands is a smoldering shell of its former self. One American journalist likens the conquest to "capturing a tomb." Barely 200,000 people remain in a city that had a prewar population of 1.5 million.[2] Vast stretches of the capital are rubble, the devastation of last summer's U.S. air attacks now compounded by weeks of new strikes by air and artillery. United Nations reconstruction officials are to find the war has destroyed 85 percent of Seoul's industrial capacity, 75 percent of its office space, and 50 to 60 percent of its housing. In the freezing late-winter nights, in a city without power and short on food, desperate people survive in hollowed-out buildings, on the streets, or in shelters, burning scrap wood from the rubble for heat.[3]

"Ripper," the latest U.S.–South Korean offensive, opened just before daylight a week ago when elements of the 25th Infantry Division crossed the Han River a dozen miles east of Seoul, with Ridgway looking on. As the division pushed north day by day against fading resistance, it threatened the left flank of Seoul's defenders, prompting their withdrawal.

Meanwhile, as Ridgway methodically advances north, a gulf is opening between him and General MacArthur.

The Far East commander flew to Korea just hours after the launch of Ripper, visited combat units, and then read a statement to reporters that could only anger the Truman administration. The old general's long-winded prose subtly challenged Washington for imposing "abnormal military inhibitions" on his Far East Command that would produce, at best, a stalemate in Korea. He was indirectly reviving his idea to go to all-out war against and in China.[4]

Five days later, this Monday, Ridgway held his own press conference and declared that regaining the 38th Parallel, restoring the Republic of Korea to its prewar borders, would be a "tremendous victory" for Eighth Army. "We didn't set out to conquer China," he added.[5]

Ridgway fears that such talk from MacArthur—that men are dying, in effect, for a useless "tie"—will undermine the morale of his forces, at a time when their performance is improving and their self-confidence growing. His own confidence in his army is growing, too, especially in the "terrifying" firepower of artillery he is amassing. This artillery colonel's son is putting new emphasis on the killing power of concentrated howitzer fire, in the face of human-wave attacks by the Chinese.

Almost three months into his command, Matt Ridgway's personal morale is improving as well. In his early weeks he felt, professionally, a bit alone. As a young general in World War II Europe, he always had superiors to his rear he could turn to—for reinforcements, for a helping hand from another division, for tactical counsel. Now he has only himself. But he is feeling ever more sure-handed in the role.

His new forward command post helps, atop a twenty-five-foot bluff overlooking the Han River near centrally located Yoju. Two interconnected eight-by-twelve-foot tents offer him a back "room" with cot, table, washbasin, and gasoline heater stove, as well as a front "office" where he works with aides for hours over a giant tabletop relief map of the battle area.

As an unsurpassed student of terrain and tactics, Ridgway is in his element, planning troop movements in great detail. The roads and ridges, valleys and peaks of central Korea have become second nature to him. He spends still more hours being flown out to units, his L-19 taking off from a gravel airstrip on the river bottomland below his CP. Then, at night, after issuing orders for men to go out and kill other men, he can retire to his "bedroom," glimpse at his photograph of Penny and Matty, and get a few hours' sleep. The fifty-six-year-old lieutenant general is feeling more at home in his war, but he's regularly reminded, too, there's more to life than war.

SUNDAY, MARCH 18, 1951

Teenaged soldier Chen Hsing-chiu heads south to fight the "Yankee bandits"

For a sixteen-year-old People's Volunteer far from home, about to step foot in a foreign land for the first time, the wide Yalu River stretching before him is an inspiring sight. Looking downriver in the late afternoon, "all I see is a beautiful sunset reflecting on the water. It's like 10,000 gold pieces shining on the river surface."

The young Chinese soldier, Chen Hsing-chiu, is keeping a diary. Perhaps he'll be a writer someday. But for the moment he and his comrades are focused on the job at hand, joining the war against the Americans. They know they're on the winning side, having heard reports of victory after victory on Chinese government radio. "The poor beating the rich, and the weak beating the strong" is how he thinks of it.

The Chinese radio is slow to acknowledge communist setbacks, such as the retreat from Seoul last Wednesday. Only later this week will Peking report its troops have "temporarily" left the southern capital.[6]

Soldier Chen is one of a five-man team of medics assigned to an antiaircraft artillery battalion of the PLA's 12th Army, whose three 10,000-man infantry divisions, with attached units, traveled sixteen hundred miles by train from southeast China to reach their Manchurian riverside staging area at Hokou, fifty miles upstream from the Yellow Sea.

They're part of commander in chief Peng Teh-huai's "second wave" of forces entering the conflict, nine armies that began crossing the Yalu a month ago to more than double Peng's strength in Korea, to 950,000 men. Chen's is among the first antiaircraft units joining Peng's forces, badly hurt by U.S. air attacks on their positions and supply routes.[7]

"After all nine armies of the second wave arrive, we will launch a new and stronger campaign," Mao Tse-tung confides in a telegram to

Josef Stalin in Moscow. It will be a campaign mounted in many cases by untested troops, units needing further training once they've reached the combat zone—if there's time.[8]

Chen, for one, is spirited, if inexperienced. He wrote his widowed mother in their hometown of Taiyuan, in northern China's coal country, to report "the good news that your son has been enlisted in the Volunteers to fight the American devils." He recalled for her his last visit home, when he chatted with their landlady about his new role and China's recent history, and how the landlady's family members were killed by both the Japanese and the Chinese Nationalists in their country's wars.

"Go fight those Yankee bandits, so we can live in peace!" the woman told him. He ended the letter saying he's sure his mother also is encouraging him, "to defend our beloved motherland and to defend all mothers."

Undereducated but intelligent and sensitive, Chen Hsing-chiu was just fourteen when he managed to sign up with the People's Liberation Army in May 1949, as Mao's armies liberated vast swaths of China and revolutionary enthusiasm swept the population. A month earlier the communists had marched into Taiyuan.

The civil war was in its waning days and the boy in the small PLA uniform saw no combat. Now his older, more experienced teammates have put him under their tutelage, especially Li Wen-hai, twenty-six, like Chen a Shanhsi Province native.

Li is a veteran PLA medic of both the anti-Japanese guerrilla campaign and the civil war, and he took part in the battle liberating Taiyuan. To Chen, he is the model soldier.

It was Li who organized a little send-off party Friday for the five of them, after the day's training at their temporary base in Hokou. They bought some peanuts, tofu, and rice wine and grew mellower as the evening wore on and the *michiu* dwindled in the bottles.

"We're like brothers," Li told them. "We'll take care of each other. If there are problems, talk to me or talk to each other." They cheered and toasted the sentiment. Then he turned to Chen Hsing-chiu. "Hsing-chiu is the youngest of the five of us. He's our little brother. Take care of him. Help him." They saw their teenaged comrade grow moist-eyed as Li spoke.

Earlier, battalion officers gathered the troops for a briefing on the discipline and order of march as they move into North Korea. The officers also sought to rally spirits for the coming campaign.

The Americans threaten our homeland, their chief trainer told them, and have violated our sovereignty by bombing and strafing our border. In three campaigns, your fellow soldiers have wiped out "hundreds of thousands" of the enemy, he said. The task ahead is daunting, but "we must do everything we can to overcome the difficulties and succeed in our mission. Carry on, comrades! Can you do it?"

"Yes, we can!" they shouted back in unison.

Now the time has come to cross the Yalu.

During the day, the battalion arrayed its antiaircraft guns along the riverbank, to guard against air attack. None materialized. The American warplanes did their damage weeks ago, destroying the Hokou bridge.[9] Meantime, an unusually warm late winter did its work as well, melting the "ice bridge" across a frozen Yalu.

Army engineers have now pieced together temporary bridges for the nighttime crossings, bridges that must be dismantled by the time U.S. fighter-bombers prowl the borderland looking for targets after dawn.

Standing on the stony riverbank as the light fades, Chen sees dark specks floating downriver toward him. They're thirty-foot boats, soon to be aligned and swarming with engineer troops hammering planks into place connecting one hull to the next, creating a roadway.

The infantry units go first, marching in columns of sixes over the pontoon bridge, above the Yalu's cold waters. Chen's battalion eventually follows in trucks hauling their wheeled guns. Each span dips and rises with the passing weight.

On the far shore, in blacked-out North Korea, Chen stands in the truck bed and turns for a last look north, across the Yalu to China. Gazing up into the clear night sky, he sees the *Peitou Chi Hsing*, the seven stars of the Big Dipper. The boy soldier feels the pull of home.

"Goodbye, dear motherland," he mutters to himself. His convoy plunges south into the shadowy hills, headlights off, guided by soldiers afoot, trotting ahead, bright white cloths tied to their arms showing the way.

MONDAY, MARCH 19, 1951

Sister Mary Mercy lands in a Pusan crushed by refugees

It's a cold late-winter evening in Pusan. A brisk breeze blows in off the sea, from a harbor teeming with ships of many flags.

In the darkness, through the filthy windows of an old bus, the three nuns can make out the silhouettes of a wartime city—fields stacked with crates of military supplies, lines of newly landed jeeps and army trucks, arrays of tents and Quonset huts.

Less visible, in the nighttime gloom of a city starved for electricity, is the vast new population of refugees. The bus headlights occasionally illuminate ragged family groups slowly making their way along the road. Nearing the city center, the Maryknoll sisters can see it more clearly—homeless refugees settling in for the night, blanketing the sidewalks and alleyways.

Sister Mary Mercy and her two companions have flown in from Japan after the forty-eight-year-old physician nun finally won permission from MacArthur's Far East Command to reopen the Maryknoll clinic in Pusan.

It was Sister Rose of Lima and Sister Augusta, her companions, who began to set up the clinic last year, only to be evacuated when war broke out. Sister Rose, a pharmacist, worked with Mary Mercy in far northern Korea in the 1930s. Sister Augusta, a nurse, is a veteran of the Maryknolls' China mission.

Reaching the city center, escorted by a local mission priest who met them at Pusan airport, the nuns are greeted with shouts of joy and tears by a small knot of Korean clinic staff, led by Patricia, the cook who helped run Mary Mercy's mission in Sinuiju long ago. In a refugee story so common in riven Korea, this woman from the far north found her way to the far south over the years. She has a special dinner prepared for the new arrivals—a "chicken banquet," Mary Mercy calls it.

The Pusan clinic fills a compound of several hillside acres abandoned by a wealthy Japanese after World War II. Two roomy houses with many wings and outbuildings surround a derelict garden. Korean refugee nuns of various orders occupy some rooms, and dozens of Korean laypeople occupy others, awaiting the arrival of the Maryknolls and employment.

Four other Maryknoll nuns are to arrive soon by sea and air, bringing with them medicines, equipment, and various medical skills.

The need is enormous. The number of people crowding into hilly Pusan has probably tripled the prewar population of 250,000. They include not only families who made the arduous trek from elsewhere in South Korea, but also tens of thousands evacuated by sea from Hungnam and other North Korean ports in December and delivered to this southern seaport.

Along with makeshift shelters and the homes of relatives or friends, the refugees fill 122 camps in the Pusan area established by the U.N. command and the South Koreans. They subsist on government rice rations amounting to only fourteen hundred calories a day, hundreds short of the minimum required. Pusan in the daytime swarms with refugees seeking odd jobs, unloading cargo at the docks, selling or bartering their belongings or black-market items.[10]

Sanitation is abysmal and disease endemic. Existing medical facilities fall far short of what's needed to deal with the typhoid, typhus, smallpox, and tuberculosis spreading through the refugee population. An inoculation program has barely begun.[11]

"We are so happy to be back," Mary Mercy writes in first letters home. "I guess we are the only Americans thrilled about being in Korea. . . . There is so much to be done here."

TUESDAY, MARCH 20, 1951

Chen Hsing-chiu witnesses an "unforgettable" scene of war's carnage

For Chen Hsing-chiu and his antiaircraft battalion, it's their third overnight on the road south toward Korea's battlegrounds. Their trucks make slow progress, feeling their way through the darkness without lights, along mountain roads, downshifting to stay abreast of the slower marching infantry and horse-drawn artillery.

Yesterday and again today, before dawn, the entire 12th Army left the roads and filtered into the surrounding woods, hiding among the pines, beneath camouflaged tents and nets, out of sight of the American fighter-bombers crisscrossing northern Korea during daylight.

Soon after the army fell in again tonight, forming columns and moving south, a line of infantrymen coming alongside greeted Chen and his four medic teammates aboard their truck, towing a battalion gun. "Artillery brothers!" one big, muscular soldier shouted up to them. "You're working hard!" A medic hollered back, "Infantry brothers, you, too! I can see the sweat on your faces."

For these peasant soldiers, their feet have been their main transport all their lives, feet now shod in a kind of padded sneaker. Their uniforms are cotton quilted khaki, padded with cotton wool. Each man shoulders a personal weapon—a mix of Soviet-made rifles and American or Japanese rifles seized in the communists' wars—and is issued a grenade, eighty rounds or so of ammunition, a haversack packed with washing kit, a small enameled eating bowl, a metal spoon and chopsticks, a water bottle, and a week's worth of rations, of tea, rice, and, if one is lucky, small tins of fish or meat. Machine gunners and mortarmen must carry their heavy weapons on their backs. The biggest weapons are borne by pack animals or porters, who tote loads from both ends of flexible poles across their shoulders.[12]

Despite the bumpy road, Chen is sleeping in the truck bed when he suddenly awakens to explosions. Off to the south he sees flames in the night sky. Their truck reaches a crossroads where sentries tell them they're about to pass through a town newly bombed by the Americans and to watch for craters in the road and unexploded bombs.

Entering the town, they see devastation everywhere, homes ablaze. The smoke burns their eyes. Then they hear the desperate voices of trapped women and children crying for help, under collapsed walls and roofs. Korean rescue teams rush here and there.

Moving on, the convoy halts at a bomb crater that has obliterated the roadway. The damage to surrounding houses seems total. The pleas Chen now hears from the trapped and wounded are the most pitiful yet. His instinct is to try to help, but he knows he cannot. They hear planes in the area. They must go. In the light of the fires, dozens of soldiers work quickly to clear brush from around the crater, for a makeshift roadway. Soon they're rolling south again into the safety of the darkness, away from a heartbreaking scene that, sixteen-year-old Chen notes in his diary, "left me with an unforgettable memory."

The U.S. Air Force is engaged in a "peak level" of bombing, from the Yalu River in the northwest to the port cities of North Korea's southeast. American pilots flew a record 850 sorties yesterday alone. Meanwhile, U.S. Navy warships, including the battleship *Missouri*, standing off the southeast coast, have pounded Wonsan port with thousands of shells. The navy claims to have killed or wounded more than three thousand enemy troops there since last Thursday. Its report says nothing about the number of civilians killed.[13] "Wonsan is a dead city," reports Rear Admiral Allen E. Smith, the navy task force commander.[14]

Chen's 12th Army takes many more days to reach its base area around Ichon, twenty miles north of the central front lines, seventy miles southeast of Pyongyang. By then, "brother" infantrymen and artillerymen alike are exhausted, short on rations, infested with lice, afflicted with dysentery and other illnesses, and demoralized by the tension of living and hiding like hunted animals, in constant fear of attack from the sky.[15]

—∞∞∞—

Back north in southern Manchuria, safe from American bombing, former naval cadet No Kum-sok enjoys a lavish banquet at his training base, arranged by base commanders for No's graduating class of student pilots.

Lieutenant No downs glasses of vodka from the stocks of their Russian flight instructors. It's the first liquor this nineteen-year-old from Hungnam has ever tasted. He finds the feeling pleasurable, and the mood among the young North Koreans turns noisier and more cheerful as the evening wears on. After all, they're now an elite group, chosen for training as MiG-15 pilots, the first class of North Koreans destined to fly the world's most advanced warplane.

FRIDAY, MARCH 23, 1951

Paratrooper Matt Ridgway lands amid airborne action

It's a clear, chill morning, with the promise of a warm early spring day. Matt Ridgway's pilot is circling at three thousand feet in their L-19 Cub, looking for a safe place to put down. The general wants to see what's happening on the ground.

Nine days after retaking Seoul, the Eighth Army commander has ordered a parachute assault by the 187th Airborne Regimental Combat Team around the town of Munsan, twenty-three miles northwest of the capital. The drop, dubbed Operation Tomahawk, is part of the continuing Operation Ripper, the push north along the entire Korean war front. The paratroopers are to hold a salient just below the Imjin River while a U.S. armored column drives up Route 1 from the Seoul area. Between them they hope to trap troops of the North Korean I Corps before they can withdraw across the Imjin.

Ridgway, the World War II airborne general, has looked on from the two-seater plane as the 3,447 men of the 187th and attached Ranger companies began jumping at nine this morning from scores of C-46 and C-119 transports.

Now the L-19 descends to a likely "landing strip," a straight road among the assembling paratroopers. Stepping from the plane, the general hears the crack of an M-1 rifle and then the sound of a North Korean soldier's body thrashing through the bushes, rolling down a roadside slope to a halt on the bank just above Ridgway. The old soldier again feels the immediacy of battle, the rush of adrenaline, as gunfire echoes around him.

After consulting with the paratrooper commanders, he and his pilot fly back south. By evening, the armored column links up with the paratroopers, securing a new piece of territory, up to the Imjin River, for the U.N. command. But Tomahawk's goal of trapping the North Korean I Corps has not been met. Most pulled back across the Imjin before the paratroopers fell upon them.

Along much of the front, the enemy has been withdrawing, and Operation Ripper is fast recovering more of South Korea. Ridgway's battlefield successes are getting international attention, putting him on the cover of *Time* magazine.

His grinding offensives since mid-January have killed tens of thousands of enemy troops. But the news reaching the home front barely hints at the countless deaths of others, Korean civilians, villagers caught in air and howitzer bombardments as they seek shelter, refugees shot by nervous troops as they try to flee battle zones. The orders to fire indiscriminately on refugees, out of fear of enemy infiltrators, date back to last summer. But they date, too, to Ridgway's own commands of early January, during the retreat from Seoul, and have spread across the current war front, where some officers carry them out, some question them.

When further instructions come down from Eighth Army to shoot refugees trying to cross front lines, one intelligence officer objects. Captain Rizalito Abanto of the 38th Infantry Regiment, a Filipino American and Silver Star winner for gallantry, reports to his commander that the directive is difficult to carry out because of "the hesitancy on the part of younger soldiers to fire directly upon groups of old men, women and children." He recommends refugees be let through the lines. Nothing in the record indicates his words are heeded.[16]

Matt Ridgway senses a long war lies ahead, that his enemy is pulling back to regroup and rebuild for a spring counteroffensive.

Although reaching the 38th Parallel, restoring the prewar status quo, is the American goal, General MacArthur in Tokyo continues to frustrate Washington's plans, which include eventually offering negotiations to the

Chinese and North Koreans. MacArthur's headquarters has now issued a communiqué dismissing the Chinese as "weak," threatening a U.N.-sanctioned invasion of China, and all but demanding that the communists capitulate in Korea.

Truman administration officials, infuriated, meet into the weekend in Washington to discuss what should be done with the Far East commander, who has repeatedly been insubordinate to a U.S. leadership that wants no wider war. It's agreed he must be relieved of duty, but not in haste.[17]

FRIDAY, MARCH 30, 1951

Pete McCloskey lays an ambush and is ambushed in turn

On the central front, the pullback has taken the Chinese northward toward the Soyang River, a natural defense line. Facing them, Pete McCloskey's 5th Marine Regiment has had only sporadic contact as it advanced twenty-five miles from Hoengsong, its objective in late February's Operation Killer, to positions sixty miles northeast of Seoul.

It's a terrain of crisscrossing ridgelines and mist-draped peaks in which the Marines send out daily patrols to their front and flanks and fend off nighttime probes by Chinese rearguard troops. Rain, sleet, and snow make life more wretched for the drenched and filthy Americans in their rudimentary two-man tents. The weather has washed out roads, slowing resupply. Even food is growing short.

"It's part of my job to try to make my men see that we must endure," Phil Elson, machine-gun squad leader, writes in his diary. "It isn't easy. I can't answer their question 'Why?'"

At each halt, Charlie Company's veteran commander, Captain Jones, takes advantage of the relative quiet to educate his growing number of "green" lieutenants, including McCloskey, in the finer points of this kind of war. The twenty-three-year-old Californian has been upgraded from the mortar section and given his own rifle platoon, Charlie's 1st Platoon.

The young officers have been shown how to position their riflemen and machine guns defensively, where to dig foxholes and how to camouflage them, how to arrange the best nighttime security and guard schedule. One morning Jones singles out McCloskey for a special tutorial on terrain appreciation, how to view the ground from the angle of a foxhole, how to determine likely avenues of enemy attack.

On this night, Jones deems McCloskey and his platoon ready for a daring mission, to grab a Chinese prisoner or two, a prize for Marine interrogators to learn more about the enemy's location and movements.

In intermittent rain after midnight, leaving their packs behind to quicken their pace, McCloskey and thirty of his men set out from the company's base on a hill designated "663" and trek five miles northward along the main north-south ridgeline, reaching their destination, a spot outside the village of Anhyon-ri, before dawn.

Marine intelligence says rearguard Chinese units based in this area south of the Soyang River are confiscating rice from local villages. The Marines plan to surprise Chinese emerging from Anhyon-ri and take prisoners. McCloskey places his men in a hillside ambush position, hidden behind low brush west of the village.

Just after dawn, a column of Chinese leaves Anhyon-ri, bags of rice on their backs. At the right moment, McCloskey orders his men to open fire with their M-1s and Browning automatic rifles. A few Chinese are hit and fall, and others scatter, dropping their loads on the trail. Still others, out of range, scurry with their bags toward an opposite ridgeline, the last of them soon clearing the hilltop.

The platoon now receives return fire from the village and—unexpectedly—from above, from the ridge they've just traversed. Far from taking prisoners, McCloskey realizes his mission is abruptly changing to saving his men from a trap, miles from their own lines.

They can't retreat the way they came. Their only way out would be across four hundred yards of open rice paddies, to the cover of a low rise. But McCloskey can't be sure more Chinese aren't waiting there. Exchanging occasional fire, he and his men cling to their position as the hours pass, on the first sunny day in a week. They left Hill 663 in predawn temperatures just above freezing, but the winter-clad men are now sweltering in the warmth of early spring.

Suddenly, in midafternoon, a platoon-size patrol of U.S. Army troops appears from the south and is chased back by Chinese fire. The young Marine officer now knows that route is safe and organizes his men for a withdrawal, one squad at a time sprinting across the fields. Luckily, they've heard only rifle and burp-gun fire from the Chinese, no machine guns that could devastate the exposed Marines.

One after another, the squads make it cleanly across, as Chinese rifle rounds whistle by, and then over the rise with a final exhausting climb.

Hours later, just before sundown, McCloskey approaches Hill 663 with his weary platoon, prepared for a dressing-down and some new lessons in leadership from Captain Jones.

⸻

The makeshift knife is finally sharp enough for the job to be done.

As the weather warmed around the Pyoktong prison camp, Clarence Adams saw that the gangrene in the frostbitten toes of his right foot was worsening, growing green. The flesh was rotting, bones poking through. Something had to be done, or he might lose the entire foot to infection, or even his leg. Now he has the tool.

He fashioned it from a steel arch support pulled from one of his combat boots. He patiently sharpened the edge until he was satisfied it would do the job quickly.

First he scrapes away dead flesh from the right foot's two smallest toes, the afflicted toes, to see the joints more clearly. Then he places the blade atop the toes, and counts to ten. Again and again he counts, freezing at the last moment, until finally, at "ten," he looks away and slams the blade down, cutting them off.

In a place without the simplest medical care from the North Koreans, let alone anesthesia, where prisoners have died by the dozens every day, it can take unimaginable mental toughness to survive.

Adams goes on to help other men amputate their own toes to save themselves.

APRIL

THURSDAY, APRIL 5, 1951

Sister Mary Mercy's clinic opens; the needs
"are so very great"

The sick line up early outside the Maryknoll sisters' hillside clinic in Pusan—malnourished children in their mothers' arms, feverish women,
tubercular men. Only a hundred or so appear on opening day, but the
nuns know the number will grow once word spreads among the tens of
thousands of war refugees.

The medicines and equipment arrived by sea last Saturday with Sister
Andre, an old Korea mission hand, and Sister Agnus Therese, a young
newcomer to overseas work and the clinic's second doctor, with Mary
Mercy.

In their gray habits and dark coats, the two M.D.s have been making
morning "house calls" in the shantytown uphill from the clinic, on Nam-
san, Pusan's South Mountain, where people live in cave-like holes they've
dug into the slope, or in flimsy hovels made of cardboard, straw matting,
and struts of driftwood.

In this filthy, vermin-infested setting, they've brought a girl back
from the brink of death from pneumonia, treated skin ailments, and begun a campaign to vaccinate children against smallpox. In the gangs of
kids who follow them around, they sometimes see half are infected with
smallpox, their faces showing the rashes or pustules of the disfiguring,
sometimes deadly disease.

TUESDAY, APRIL 10, 1951

In a futile assault, a Chinese bullet fells Buddy Wenzel

After more than two months of costly, stop-and-go advances, the 1st Cavalry Division has helped drive the enemy from South Korea. The division has reached a point on the central front five miles north of the 38th Parallel. It's time for the battle-worn "Cav" to go into temporary reserve. But higher command has held back one regiment, Buddy Wenzel's 7th Cavalry, for an urgent mission at the giant Hwachon Dam.

The twenty-year-old Private Wenzel has taken on his own special mission, meanwhile, volunteering as a G Company sniper, his M-1 equipped with a telescopic scope, his job to pick off Chinese foolish enough to show too much of themselves. He believes he's improving G Company's odds, one dead enemy soldier at a time. But he has another motive as well. His personal odds are stacking up against him. He's been at war too long. He has been wounded twice. Sniping keeps him out of the first wave of attack, out of "getting my ass shot off."

George Company rises at five to a cold morning fog. It has been tapped to lead the 2nd Battalion on the attack to capture the towering, 826-foot-wide Hwachon Dam, which in peacetime supplies electricity to Seoul, sixty miles to the southwest, but in this war poses a threat to the advancing Americans. The Chinese have begun to open the dam's gates, and the U.S. command fears they plan to flood American positions farther down the Pukhan River.

The 7th Cavalrymen move up a half-mile-wide tongue of land, with the Hwachon Reservoir on their right, the dam at its north end, and on their left a loop of the meandering river. The terrain is too difficult to bring up 105mm howitzers for artillery support, and the murky weather rules out air support. "George" must take a Chinese-held ridge guarding the dam with nothing more than mortars, machine guns, and M-1s.

They soon run into strong resistance. Chinese mortars and well-placed machine guns stop them, pinning them down through midday. It's hopeless, and finally an order comes to pull back.[1]

Buddy Wenzel is on high ground behind the forward elements. As trapped GIs run back past him, Chinese machine-gun fire follows. Wenzel rises up to shout, to show the way. A machine-gun round rips into his right hand. He goes down. His trigger hand, his letter-writing hand, is in crippling pain.

As he is evacuated, soon all the way to Japan and then the States, a friend tells him, "You're the last one." The young soldiers of G Company who landed at Pohang nine months ago, whose introduction to war was the refugee slaughter at Nogun-ri, are now mostly dead or maimed or broken men.

In a diary he keeps when he can, Wenzel's platoon sergeant, Bob Spiroff, laments the steady loss of "good soldiers." "I firmly believe Korea is as close to hell as anyone can get!" the decorated World War II veteran writes in despair.[2]

In the morning, the 7th Cavalry tries again, this time with an attached company of army Rangers paddling across the reservoir for a flanking attack. Once ashore, they are mauled by the defenders and must withdraw. Higher command suspends the operation and sends the 7th Cavalry to the rear, to the division reserve.

After several more days, U.S. Marines finally end enemy control of the threatening dam. The Chinese recede farther north. More and more, however, field intelligence hints at an imminent Chinese offensive.[3]

———

It's only twenty-three names, but the short list lifts a heavy burden on twenty-three American families in towns from Alabama to California.

In an article in the U.S. Communist Party's *Daily Worker* newspaper, Alan Winnington cites a Peking Radio announcement that twenty-three American prisoners of war will record statements to be broadcast by the Chinese radio over the next week—"messages to their families and the American public."[4] The list of names is the first confirmation of the identities of Americans in enemy hands, men previously listed as missing in action.

Winnington, who left Korea on the eve of September's Inchon landing, has since closely followed developments at the war front from his base in the Chinese capital.

The well-connected reporter feels he understands what Mao and Peng Teh-huai are trying to do: not to drive the Americans and their allies into the sea and to seize the entire peninsula for the Korean communists, but to bring the enemy to a standstill and force them to negotiate a cease-fire, thereby keeping the war from spreading and engulfing all East Asia, possibly accompanied by American atomic bombs.

During his time in the Chinese capital, the forty-one-year-old *Daily Worker* correspondent has been occupied with more than the news. He has grown close to a young journalist at the government news agency Hsinhua, a young woman half his age named Esther Cheo Ying.

Of mixed Chinese and British heritage, she is depressed over a broken love affair and the oppressive atmosphere of revolutionary Peking. In the sophisticated Londoner, she sees an independent mind, someone to confide in. Over cups of tea, Winnington draws her out about her unhappiness as a racial misfit, a bourgeois in proletarian China, a rebel against ideological office politics. He offers himself to her as a "Dutch uncle."[5]

WEDNESDAY, APRIL 11, 1951

General MacArthur is relieved of duty; Matt Ridgway takes command

A hailstorm has Matt Ridgway and his visitor, Army Secretary Frank Pace, sheltering in a command post of the 5th Regimental Combat Team, one of the units launching a new operation, called Dauntless, on the central front. Ridgway's VIP visitor is on an inspection tour. A journalist reporting on the visit approaches the Eighth Army commander with hand extended. "Well, General," he says, "I guess congratulations are in order." Puzzled, Ridgway replies, "What for?" Surprised the general hasn't heard, the abashed reporter backs away without a word.

Later in the afternoon, Pace receives a message from Washington via Eighth Army headquarters. He shares it with Ridgway: General MacArthur has been relieved of duty by President Truman, and Ridgway has been named Far East commander to replace him.

The firing of Douglas MacArthur has been predictable for some time, as he repeatedly ignored directives from Washington to refrain from pronouncing publicly on foreign policy and promoting his ideas of a wider war against China. The "final straw" seemed to come six days ago, when Joe Martin, the Republican minority leader in the U.S. House of Representatives, read a letter from MacArthur on the House floor endorsing anew the idea of having Chinese Nationalist troops from Taiwan open a second front by invading the Chinese mainland.

The context is more complex, however. Intelligence indicators suggest the Soviet Union might be preparing for greater involvement in Korea, perhaps air strikes, perhaps the entry of "volunteer" Soviet Asian troops. In view of that, Truman has ordered atomic weapons sent to Guam, bombs that might be dropped on enemy air bases. With tensions heightening, the Joint Chiefs and the White House want a steadier, less unpredictable hand at the helm in the Far East.[6]

Ridgway himself has strong mixed feelings about Douglas Mac-Arthur. He is "truly one of the great captains of warfare," he later writes. But MacArthur's overbearing ego, his stubbornness, the "aura of infallibility" in which he wraps himself inevitably led to a clash with his superiors.

"There is no substitute for victory," MacArthur wrote in his explosive letter to Congressman Martin. Ridgway knows the victory MacArthur has in mind is a global military defeat of communism. The younger general also knows the American people would never accept such an impossible crusade, "endless war in the bottomless pit of the Asian mainland." He knows, instead, his rejuvenated Eighth Army can fight to an acceptable finish in Korea.

The hail gives way to an unseasonable snow in the Taebaek Mountains. Ridgway and Pace, having seen Operation Dauntless off to a good start, return to the Yoju command post on the Han River. In the morning they fly south to Pusan and from there to Tokyo and Ridgway's final conference with his "great captain."

MID-APRIL 1951

At the Soyang River, Gil Isham is left with a mystery

From the snow and slush of January at Chechon, to the springtime rains in the mountains near Inje, the 17th Infantry Regiment has advanced seventy-five miles on the central front, in fits and starts, taking a hill, losing it back, regaining it, and moving on northward to the next one, as ground campaigns dubbed Killer, Ripper, Rugged, Dauntless followed one on the other. Over three months, the regiment has lost 137 men killed and many more wounded.

Gil Isham and the rest of the regiment's battle-hardened troops have now crossed the Soyang River, a major tributary of the Han, flowing northeast to southwest, on their way to the invisible line of the 38th Parallel. Just beyond that lies another mapmaker's notion called Line Kansas, a wavy thread stretching across the peninsula whose terrain makes for what Eighth Army tacticians deem a strong, defensible front. The U.N. command's lead divisions are moving steadily toward it.

The North Koreans and their Chinese allies continue to withdraw methodically, but not without putting up rearguard fights, to slow the Americans and South Koreans.[7]

Easy Company's 3rd Platoon, holding a hill on the north side of the Soyang, is under artillery fire and taking casualties. Isham and three others from the 2nd Platoon, in reserve on the south riverbank, are told to take a rubber raft across the river to retrieve two wounded.

The four paddle to the far bank and carry two litters up the hill, first finding a soldier with a leg wound. They bandage him and help him onto a litter.

Then they find a second man, remarkably still conscious despite what appears to be a severe head wound. Isham unpacks the gauze compress from his first-aid pouch and tells him to hold it to his head and get onto the second litter. "I don't need a litter no more," the soldier says. He starts to walk downhill by himself.

Amazed—he's sure he saw brain through the man's shattered skull—Isham can only help his three buddies lift the first casualty and carry him gingerly down the slope, as the second soldier somehow comes along, making it to the boat, climbing in.

Isham, still dumbfounded, looks at him again. The soldier gazes back.

"Hey, guys," he says. "I'm going home."

"Yeah," Isham replies. "You got a million-dollar wound. You're going Stateside."

What the soldier says next, as they paddle away from shore, confuses them: "My home ain't in the States no more."

What could he mean? each man wonders, distracted for once from the infernal din of artillery.

Pulling the boat up on the south riverbank, they turn to tend to the pair and discover the soldier with the head wound is motionless, dead, having expired sometime in the final minutes on the river.

"No, it's true," one boatmate later tells Isham. "He knew he was dying. He knew he was going to heaven."

Isham isn't religious, despite his mother's efforts to bring up young Gilbert as a churchgoer. He does read his tiny army-issued New Testament over and over, only because it's the sole reading material available. And now he does write the Methodist minister at home in Milwaukee about this mysterious episode, hoping for some kind of answer. But in the end Gil Isham simply accepts that along with unimaginable cruelties and inhumanity, war has its mysteries that may never be explained.

———

Shin Hyung-kyu grows more nervous as he walks the streets of Kochang, headed for the home and family he left as a frightened sixteen-year-old refugee last summer. Are they still here? Are they still alive? And Father? Was he executed? Where is he buried?

The roadsides leading to Kochang were strewn with ashen ruins and wreckage. On just one day last September, the U.S. Air Force sent twenty-five B-29s to rain 863 quarter-ton bombs on targets in the Kochang-Chinju-Kimchon area, as American and South Korean divisions drove the northern army from their positions in southernmost Korea.[8] Kochang and nearby towns now anchor the southern end of a landscape of unparalleled destruction wrought up and down the Korean peninsula in less than a year of war.

The military police corporal drew a lucky assignment in early April, to escort North Korean prisoners from the war front to a POW camp in Pusan. He seized the opportunity to hitchhike from Pusan eighty miles west to Kochang, in hopes of reuniting with his family, or what was left of it.

There's no mail service to the front, and so he has heard nothing of them since his mother watched him disappear around a bend in the road that August day, after which she gathered up his five younger brothers and sisters to find shelter from the war in an abandoned mine.

Approaching, he can see from a distance the house is undamaged. He pushes open the gate and crosses the *madang*. His mother looks up to see the slight figure silhouetted in the doorway, in oversize green fatigues, a rifle hanging from his shoulder, and then she sees Shin's boyish face and erupts in joy, embraces, and tears. She never knew whether he was alive or dead.

He learns they have all survived, including Father. But they have heard nothing of *Hyongnim*, Older Brother, who was studying in Seoul when war broke out.

Shin cannot linger. He mustn't return late to his unit. He rushes over to the local government office where his father still works, to surprise him and to learn about his miraculous reprieve from execution as a "leftist," while thousands of others were being summarily shot by their own government in last year's summer of terror.

In the end, it was money, Father tells him. A wealthy friend's family bribed the police to spare both the friend and Father. The police guards then vanished at the North Koreans' approach. By the time he found his wife and children hiding in the derelict mine, she had delivered herself of a baby girl, their tenth child.

Back at the house, Shin's brothers and sisters tell him of the traumatizing weeks of war last summer while they hid in the hills—of the terrifying sounds of the U.S. warplanes, of civilians and North Korean soldiers alike coming under strafing fire, of bodies rotting in the rice paddies.

Mother tells him of the bloodiest incident of all: their own ROK Army's massacre in February of more than seven hundred peasants, including women and children, from villages outside Kochang, villagers accused of having helped guerrillas with food and clothing. The slaughter has gained national attention only because a relative of the Shins, Shin Jung-mok, the National Assembly member representing the area, has demanded an investigation.

The news of atrocities doesn't surprise Shin, who has seen and heard of many in the process of growing from sixteen-year-old boy to seventeen-year-old soldier. With more tears and embraces, he leaves to return north, to rejoin his company in the unending war on the central front.

SUNDAY, APRIL 22, 1951

Peng Teh-huai wins an argument, and the war's greatest battle is joined

It's a cool, crisp day. Springtime, the war's first, is spreading north. Azalea and forsythia bloom in the thaw and the April rains, and here and there on Korea's ravaged slopes a glint of white shows among the pink and yellow, the skeletons of unclaimed dead from ten months of conflict.

Smoke drifts over much of the front lines. The Chinese have set brushfires to obscure their movements from the air. At dusk, their artillery opens fire along the line north of Seoul, barrages that grow more widespread by the minute. Then, under a full moon rising after eight o'clock, its glow dimmed by smoky haze, tens of thousands of Chinese troops in the west and North Koreans in the east advance in wave after wave against U.N. forces along a ninety-mile front. A major blow in the west is aimed at retaking Seoul. The eastern offensive is more diversionary.

The Americans, advancing north in small steps through April, detected signs of a Chinese buildup in recent days. Expecting a counteroffensive, they took a more defensive stance.[9] Tonight, within hours, word is flashed across the Pacific. The heavy attack "indicates that the long anticipated Communist 'Spring' offensive has begun," the CIA advises the White House.[10]

General Peng Teh-huai says the fate of the Korean War hangs on this battle. It begins on this night because he won an argument.

For months the Chinese commander has feared an Inchon-like amphibious landing behind his lines in North Korea, cutting his army off from supplies and reinforcement. He proposed an all-out new offensive southward, to throw the Americans off such plans. But at a tense meeting at his headquarters, now housed in caves at Kongseok-dong, seventy miles southeast of Pyongyang, Hong Hsue-chi and Peng's other deputies objected, favoring instead a strategy of biding their time, drawing the Americans and their allies farther north and trapping them above the 38th Parallel, after which the Chinese would strike. Newly arriving Chinese reinforcements are too raw to immediately go on the attack, they argued.

Finding little support for his idea, a stubborn Peng angrily asserted rank. "Do you want to fight this battle or not?" he demanded of his deputies. Resigned, accustomed to his willfulness, they relented. "You're the commander in chief," Hong said.

The "second wave" of Chinese reinforcements has been arriving from Manchuria since March. Twenty-seven infantry divisions, 10,000 men each, along with artillery and antiaircraft units, have doubled the size of the Chinese force. With the North Koreans, the communist army numbers well over 1 million. Plans envisioned a month's in-theater training before a major offensive in mid-May. But Peng's fears of an amphibious envelopment led him to recommend and win Mao Tse-tung's approval for an earlier attack.

When it comes on this evening, it is massive, the war's greatest battle, some 700,000 troops in forward and reserve units assaulting U.N. positions from Munsan on the Imjin River in the west, near the Yellow Sea, to positions in the east just twenty miles from the Sea of Japan.

The most devastating strike is aimed at the South Korean 6th Division in the center, forty miles northeast of Seoul. Last June that division stood its ground the longest, bravely, against the North Korean invasion. But now it is too lightly armed—no heavy machine guns, too little artillery—to stand against the dense ranks of attacking Chinese. Within hours the division is broken, its survivors stumbling south, exposing U.S. units on each side to Chinese flanking movements.[11]

But not everything is going well for Peng's "Fifth Campaign." Trying to wade across the normally shallow Imjin around midnight, several hundred Chinese troops drown in the river, as it swiftly rises to more than twenty feet deep. Their commanders were unfamiliar with the sudden violent tides that rush up from the Imjin estuary. East of there, Chinese troops, reinforcements just reaching the war zone, are late to the attack, having to run for up to an hour to get into position. Farther east, China's 60th Division captures scores of American howitzers in routing the ROK 6th Division, but its peasant soldiers don't know how to drive captured vehicles to tow them.[12]

Hong was right: the offensive has been mounted too early, utilizing "green" divisions untested at the Korea front.[13] And Peng was wrong: the Americans never planned an amphibious landing.

In a deep sleep, Second Lieutenant Hurh Won-moo is dreaming, wrapped in two blankets on the unheated floor of an abandoned house.

His subconscious summons a vision of his mother, standing outside the mill near Chonan, waving good-bye. A heavy snow falls. "Don't look back," she tells him, as she did in January after they fled Seoul and he departed for artillery officer training. "Go on, and we shall meet again, if God wills."

A shout—"Enemy attack!"—shatters his reverie, shocks him back to the waking world. It's a company officer. He orders the new lieutenant to get to his forward observation post (OP) immediately.

Hurh arrived at the front line and his assigned artillery company only earlier this evening, after graduation and a weeklong hitchhiking journey from the officers' school in Taegu. He reported for duty, was fed a meal, and bedded down just in time for the long-expected Chinese spring offensive.

But the new Lieutenant Hurh is confused. He was trained as a targeter for 105mm howitzers, but this company—the 102nd Independent Artillery Company, of the ROK 11th Division, holding the line near the east coast—is equipped only with 4.2-inch heavy mortars. Little difference, he's told. Also, Hurh points out, he doesn't know where his observation post is. See Corporal Lee, he's told.

The corporal first helps his new lieutenant get outfitted with a map, compass, flashlight, and binoculars as well as with a .30-caliber carbine—again, a weapon he hasn't trained on. Hurh is fast learning about the absurdities of military life.

Finally, under the full moon, he sets out for the OP two miles to the north, with Lee, a radio operator and a field telephone operator. There, atop a steep hill, the four-man team settles in and waits.

Hurh, eighteen-year-old newcomer to war, is nervous. They've been seeing and hearing the flashes and thunder of artillery fire to the north. They're isolated and may be attacked at any time. But as the anxious hours pass slowly in the dark, there's no sign of enemy.

The sun rises, and Hurh puts his men to work digging a defensive trench. He works with his company's fire direction center to preset coordinates for later mortar-fire missions. But still no enemy appears.

Although the alarm was sounded across the entire front when the Chinese attacked massively on Sunday night, the big blow came sixty miles west of Hurh's position, where the ROK 6th Division disintegrated.

MONDAY, APRIL 23, 1951

With truckloads of wounded, Chen Hsing-chiu falls into U.S. gunsights

The little two-truck convoy, lights out, navigating in the clear moonlight, slowly makes its way along North Korean back roads toward a Chinese field hospital far to the rear. In the open bed of the second truck, Chen Hsing-chiu tends to three men, stretcher cases, badly wounded in the first hours of the new Chinese–North Korean offensive.

One suddenly screams in pain. The truck has hit a bad bump. Chen bangs on the front cab. The frightened driver turns and shouts, "Airplane?!" Chen reassures him there's no airplane, that he simply wants him to slow down.

The young medic was unhappy at first when assigned the escort duty to the rear. He wanted to go to the front line with his antiaircraft battalion, shielding a regiment of Chinese howitzers, when they moved out on Saturday to join General Peng's Fifth Campaign. Their 12th Army was designated to lead the main thrust, the attack on U.S. and Turkish units on the western front.[14] (Thai, Turkish, Dutch, and Canadian troops by now have joined the U.N. force.) But a furious air-to-ground duel with American pilots earlier Saturday changed things for Chen.

About nine that morning, four F-80 jet fighter-bombers, unaware of the camouflaged antiaircraft guns nearby, swept in and bombed a village adjoining the Chinese positions. The gunners took to their weapons, firing a wall of flak that caught the Americans when they wheeled around for a second run on the village. One jet was hit, burst into flame, and crashed. The others flew off. "Enemy dogs!" the gun crews shouted.

As expected, the Americans returned later, this time a dozen or so jets screeching in at low altitude looking to destroy the antiaircraft guns, dropping bombs and strafing wildly over a wide area, catching some soldiers in the open as they lugged ammunition. The air–ground firefight raged for two hours, on and off, and the battalion reported downing or damaging several planes. On their side, the Chinese suffered one platoon leader killed and eleven men wounded.

The deputy battalion commander summoned medic Chen Hsing-chiu and an officer named Ma and gave them the job of getting the wounded to the distant field hospital. Seeing the disappointment in the teenager's eyes, the deputy commander told him he had shown he was skillful enough to handle the wounded on his own, without diverting a second medic. With that, Chen looked on the assignment differently.

During their day, when they're off the road, Chen has been busy with all eleven patients, changing bandages and administering antibiotics and morphine injections. Now, on their third night driving, he's watching over the three stretcher cases, two with shattered legs heavily bandaged and in splints. The soldier who cried out in pain is now shivering in the night chill. Chen removes his own coat and wraps it around him.

As the two trucks slowly climb a hill, they hear a sudden roar. A pair of American "night intruder" warplanes seem to have caught a glimpse of them in the moon's glow. The planes dive in, firing their guns and dropping a bomb, but too far behind the trucks to do damage. The drivers quickly veer off into the cover of the surrounding woods as the planes return, strafing the road, their bullets sending sparks flying off the surface. One of Chen's charges leaps to his feet in reflexive terror, despite the broken legs. The medic helps him back down to his stretcher and tries to calm the three men. Just then a ricocheted bullet slams into Chen's torso. The pain is searing, but it doesn't penetrate. He doesn't bleed.

Then, in disbelief, he watches as Officer Ma directs his truck back onto the road, with its headlights turned on. After a few moments, the lights go off and the truck turns back. A loitering American pilot takes the bait, dropping bombs up the road where the truck would have been. As the duped pilot veers off to circle for another run, Ma shouts, "Let's go!" They speed down the road, past smoking, burning trees, and on to safety.

TUESDAY, APRIL 24, 1951

Pete McCloskey spends a fearsome night under Chinese attack

Not confidence, but fear. For the past two days of pullback, in the face of General Peng's new offensive, Lieutenant Pete McCloskey and his Marine platoon have felt something much different from the self-assurance of their weeks of advancing north into the Hwachon Reservoir area, facing no serious resistance.

In their hurried withdrawal southward, sometimes in an exhausted slog, sometimes atop rubber-wheeled amphibious vehicles, the men of Charlie Company, 5th Marines, have felt instead the dread of soldiers who sense the enemy is closing in on them from behind, or from the flanks, or is even lying ahead in ambush as they retreat.

Units of the 1st Marine Division are leapfrogging down the Pukhan River valley to escape a potential Chinese trap made possible by the collapse of the ROK Army 6th Division on the Marines' western flank. The Chinese drove ten miles south after routing the South Koreans two nights ago, threatening to loop around the Marines and cut off their supply link to Chunchon. The Marine division's reserve regiment, the 1st, rushed westward to block the Chinese, while the 5th and 7th Marines moved toward new defenses farther south.[15]

On Sunday, when they were still advancing northward, McCloskey and his men, point platoon for the 1st Battalion, had seen signs the Chinese were unusually close, not at a distance moving north, as they had been. Dug in on their ridgetop position, under a bright full moon,[16] the company suddenly came under the heaviest artillery barrage of McCloskey's two months in Korea. The heaviest shelling was directed at a

Marine position a mile to McCloskey's right and the South Koreans a mile to his left. Flashes of shellfire on the left steadily moved south, driving panicked Korean troops before them. The great Chinese offensive had begun.

Then yesterday his battalion was ordered to retreat down the Pukhan Valley. As they headed south, they could detect Chinese troops advancing through the hills behind them. Digging in for another night, as temperatures dipped toward freezing and men found it hard to sleep, McCloskey feared the worst. The battalion organized cooks, bakers, and drivers into reserve platoons to fight if things turned dire. But the enemy held off, and this morning the 1st Battalion, 5th Marines, pulled up stakes and was on the move again, though now ordered to veer westward, to an east-west ridgeline where it would join units of the 1st Marines taking a stand against the oncoming Chinese.

McCloskey's platoon had to double-time up the slopes, and he lost men to simple exhaustion. Reaching the thousand-foot crest, he found a 1st Marines platoon taking positions at his side. In the dying afternoon light, they beheld the unnerving sight of Chinese pouring over the low hills beyond and the valleys below. Swinging their entrenching tools feverishly, Marines dug in.

It's now around midnight, after several quiet hours, and McCloskey's men are in their foxholes atop the forward slope when an explosion and flare draw all eyes to a spur running north off their crest. Chinese soldiers dragging a two-wheeled machine-gun cart up the slope have tripped a booby trap and illumination grenade and stand frozen in the glare. The platoon opens fire with its two machine guns, its M-1s and BARs. Immediately, the cymbals, bugles, and shouts of a Chinese attack erupt.

"Hello, hello, Marine!" the Chinese yell up the slopes in clear English. "You must die!" One of McCloskey's men, adrenaline and imagination flowing, hears a Billboard hit tune in the bugle charge. "They're playing 'Open the Door, Richard'!" the veteran machine gunner shouts.

As they hold off the attacks, McCloskey's well-positioned 1st Platoon gets a big, unexpected assist from American airpower, transports that fly back and forth through the night over the scene, dropping parachute flares exposing the Chinese to McCloskey's gunners for minutes at a time. Chinese casualties mount and the attack fades. Off to his left, however, McCloskey can see that his neighboring platoon's line appears overrun in spots, where flashes of gunfire appear on the rear slope. He repositions one machine-gun crew to face leftward along the crest, in case he's attacked from that flank. But with first light he sees that battalion's lines have been restored. The valley and lower slopes are strewn with Chinese bodies.

Twenty miles east of McCloskey's Marines, Gil Isham's 17th Infantry Regiment is holding off an attack by a North Korean division and slowly pulling back two miles to the Line Kansas defenses.[17]

But Private Isham isn't with them. After seven months unscathed in combat, the eighteen-year-old infantryman has been wounded, not by enemy fire, but by shrapnel from his own American artillery.

An airborne spotter somehow failed to see the colored panels Easy Company laid on the ground, as all U.S. units do to identify themselves as friendlies to attacking aircraft. The confused observer called in an artillery barrage that struck the dug-in Americans squarely. Four were killed and three wounded, including Isham, hit in the right leg just above the knee. By day's end he was on a medical evacuation plane headed for Japan.

AN EVENING IN LATE APRIL 1951

Peng Teh-huai informs Mao his costly spring offensive is stalling

From the nighttime shadows outside, Hong Hsue-chi steps into the cave and the glow of candlelight.

Peng Teh-huai spots him. "Old Hong!" he shouts with relief. General Peng has urgently summoned his deputy and logistics chief to his sheltered command post in Kongseok-dong. "You must make a trip back to China immediately," the commander says.

"Go back now?" a surprised Hong asks.[18]

The Chinese spring offensive is faltering. Peng has sent a coded telegram to Mao Tse-tung and the Central Military Commission in Peking reporting the difficulties: insufficiently trained reinforcements, exhausted veteran troops, lagging food and ammunition supplies, artillery and tank units unable to reach the front on time.[19]

The Chinese casualties have been enormous: as many as sixty thousand dead, wounded, or captured in a week of nonstop fighting, compared with four thousand casualties on the U.N. side.[20]

Despite their overwhelming strength—with their North Korean allies they outnumber the defenders two to one—the Chinese are a premodern army hurling itself ineffectively against a modern one.

American air attacks are destroying whole shipments in an already failing supply system. Before the offensive was launched, one bombing run on a northern train station destroyed 1,440 tons of cooked food and grain and hundreds of thousands of uniforms and shoes. An inexperienced Chinese transport unit lost seventy-three trucks, with cargo, in a single U.S. air attack because it entered Korea with its convoy too tightly bunched.[21] Five days into the offensive, two of Peng's thirty-thousand-man armies, the 20th and 27th, ran out of food and ammunition as they were on the verge of overwhelming units of the U.S. 24th Infantry Division. They had to suspend the attack.[22]

Meanwhile, the Americans have learned how to better fight this huge army and inflict the heaviest casualties. The new Eighth Army commander, Lieutenant General James A. Van Fleet, has ordered his forces to withdraw only a short distance each night, the distance the Chinese, on foot, can advance overnight. This way, the defenders hold the Chinese in place for air and artillery firepower to reduce their ranks during the day.[23]

The Chinese have regained some previously lost territory, but they haven't penetrated deeply enough to encircle and destroy any American units, General Peng's stated objective. In some cases, defenders have held out courageously, stalling what Peng hoped would be a swift, overwhelming attack seizing Seoul.

The Gloucester Battalion of the British 29th Brigade stood its ground through the first three nights and days of massed Chinese assaults against their hilltop positions, astride the route to the South Korean capital. While taking steady losses themselves, the British exacted much-heavier casualties among the Chinese. Surrounded, considered beyond rescue by the U.S. higher command, the "Glosters" finally tried to break out southward, but relatively few made it. Of 773 men, 662 were either killed, wounded, or, mostly, captured and marched off to prison camps.[24]

In his message to Peking, Peng credited his enemy's superior weaponry and shrewd tactics. "We have been unable to break open gaps for penetration deep into the enemy rear without engaging in bloody, costly battles," he wrote. In reply, Mao and the military commission approved his plan to order a pause in the offensive.[25]

Now a worried Peng Teh-huai has his thirty-eight-year-old deputy, "Old" Hong, before him in the flickering light and quiet of Kongseok-dong's command cave, fifty miles north of the din of the battlefields. Neither man brings up the obvious: that Hong warned against a premature offensive. Instead, they discuss the business at hand, making Peking more aware, in detail, of the dire supply problems.

The first step to protect their vulnerable supply lines is clear: greatly expanding Chinese antiaircraft batteries in Korea. And a second, vital, step would be getting more jet fighters into the air to intercept the U.S. warplanes.

Taking his leave of Peng, Hong returns to his cave quarters, packs a few things, and departs immediately on the long journey to Peking.[26] Meanwhile, Peng orders a halt to the "first step" in the spring offensive, effective Sunday, April 29, cutting this phase of his all-important campaign short by one week.[27]

By that day, Pete McCloskey, his platoon, and the rest of the 1st Battalion, 5th Marines, are holding a line near Chunchon, an area they struck north from a month ago. Charlie Company machine gunner Phil Elson, a World War II veteran growing cynical in this seesaw war, notes in his diary, "All this hard fighting and good men's lives lost . . . and it's all been in vain."

By the last day of April, Elson, promoted to sergeant, and the rest of Charlie Company have moved ten miles still farther south. American and allied forces are settling into a strong defense line north of Seoul and the Han River and stretching northeast through the steep ridges and dangerous valleys of what is to be the central cockpit of still more hard fighting, and of many more lives lost.[28]

Though not under direct North Korean attack, Hurh Won-moo's 11th Division is withdrawing fifteen miles to the south, taking its place along the continuous defense line with units driven back on their heels by the powerful communist offensive.

His mortar company reaches a fishing port called Daepo-ri, where they are put in reserve, bivouacking near the tree-lined shoreline of a dark blue Sea of Japan. Killing and dying may be going on farther inland, Hurh thinks, but this is like a holiday.

The newly minted lieutenant, yet to face his first combat, is taking a nap when he's awakened by an announcement: a group of girls has arrived to entertain the troops. Puzzled, he envisions singers and dancers. He quickly discovers he's wrong.

Each officer is given a ticket to see a girl in a specified room at a nearby farmhouse. He now understands and is surprised and shocked. A traveling army-sponsored brothel has come to Daepo-ri.

The company's master sergeant approaches the teenaged lieutenant. "Sir, we may all die tomorrow. Please enjoy. It will boost your morale!"

Unsure what to do, Hurh goes to the farmhouse and enters his assigned room. He finds a girl about age seventeen waiting there for customers. To him she looks like his sixteen-year-old sister.

Flustered, he tells her he doesn't want anything from her. He gives her his ticket, so she can redeem it for money, and leaves. Outside he meets a friend who good-naturedly asks, "How was it?" Told what happened, the disbelieving lieutenant erupts: "What a waste! You should have given me the ticket so I could have a second round."

This is his country's army, Hurh thinks, using poor peasant girls this way, fellow Koreans, desperate refugees perhaps. "Death at the front. Sex at the rear. So this is war."

The Chinese offensive in Korea's midsection has brought both relief and new opportunities for the bands of communist guerrillas clinging to mountainsides and remote valleys in the far south.

The ROK 8th Division, which took over the guerrilla-hunting mission from the 11th Division in February, has been rushed north to help hold the line against the Chinese and North Koreans. That leaves weaker national police forces in the rear to counter the guerrilla threat.[29]

Guerrilla numbers have dwindled, as the relentless army sweeps killed hundreds, both fighters and hapless civilians. After months of struggling to survive in the inhospitable terrain, others have deserted, especially southerners who simply head home.

But springtime brings advantages to the insurgents in the Chiri-san mountains, where the melting of knee-deep winter snows and the greening of vegetation allow more mobility and cover. They're stepping up attacks, as in the past when they've coordinated actions with communist offensives in the north.

The small market town of Sichon lies in a valley at the base of six-thousand-foot Mount Chiri. It's a vital crossroads, one held by police manning a solid, strategically placed pillbox. Ri In-mo's guerrilla commanders—the Workers' Party cadre of South Kyongsang Province—have planned an operation to neutralize the police presence, at least temporarily. Ri's armed propaganda team takes part in the attack, which is led by the "whistle unit," a squad that maneuvers via whistle signals.

As always, the insurgents wait for darkness, then open the late-night assault with a barrage of light mortar shells on the pillbox. As the lead attackers crawl toward the objective, the aroused defenders rake the approaches with machine-gun fire. Wounded guerrillas cry out. Over the gunfire, a whistle is heard in the night. Ri sees a small shadow rise up at almost point-blank range from the pillbox and toss a grenade. It lands inside with a flash and powerful bang, and the outgoing fire stops. Survivors flee out the rear, and the attackers move in. Guerrilla dead and wounded are carried off, including the attack leader, the man with the whistle, who has been killed.

Ri and his propaganda team order Sichon villagers from their homes, where they've been cowering through the fight, and gather them in groups. The village center still smells of gun smoke as Ri and the others deliver their standard revolutionary speech. "We are guerrillas fighting to crush the U.S. imperialist aggressors and their stooges, the Syngman Rhee clique," the villagers are told. "We're fighting for the Democratic People's Republic of Korea, a people's society like the one in northern Korea, where all the people are well off."

As they go on, Ri In-mo and his comrades cannot know how many of their listeners sympathize, and who may help them, or join them, and who might turn against them. For that reason, the guerrillas linger only long enough to solicit—or take—food, clothing, or other helpful items from the villagers, before withdrawing back toward their base in a hidden valley.

Ri learns the grenade-tossing hero of the attack is a young woman, Choe Jong-ok, a Russian-language student from North Korea's Wonsan teachers' training college and now another model fighter for him to glorify in the mimeo bulletins he distributes across the Chiri-san guerrillas' shrinking territory.

MAY

A DAY IN EARLY MAY 1951

In smoldering Pyongyang, Yu Song-chol spots a face from the past

The Pyongyang newspaper *Nodong Sinmun* describes this as "the year of unbearable trials."[1] For Yu Song-chol, the thirty-four-year-old general, it is also the year that changes his life.

The trials for the people of North Korea stem, first and foremost, from the incessant American bombing that is turning their cities into vast fields of rubble, smoking plains in which people dig through the nights to pull out the bodies of the latest victims or to scavenge for what remains of their clothes, their food, their family keepsakes. They're digging, too, to build underground shelters amid the ruins. "Half-naked people and naked, haggard children are nesting in caves in the hills," reports a Polish diplomat.

Although some factories and workshops have been disassembled and rebuilt underground, the production of essentials—from railroad cars to clothing—has collapsed. The bombing of the rail network, of bridges and tunnels, has strangled distribution of what can be produced. The shortage of labor for planting and harvesting—with much of the male population at the war front—has slashed rice production. The government must send its office workers into the fields to help sow and weed the paddies. Women are being drafted to work in the coal mines. They're also the indispensable wartime stretcher bearers. With few ambulances or other vehicles available, the wounded must often be carried northward at night on stretchers, stopping in villages during daylight, until reaching a hospital far to the rear.[2]

With all the trials, and all the death dealt daily from the skies, North Koreans still manage to carry on. Schools operate, often underground.

Black markets spring up to meet people's needs. And government meetings are convened in relatively safe places. It's at one of those meetings that Lieutenant General Yu has his fateful encounter. The war front has entered a lull after the end of the communists' Fifth Campaign, and the army operations director is invited to a symposium discussing the role of North Korean women in the war.

There he sees a face he hasn't seen in six years.

Now a young army nurse, she was a sixteen-year-old Pyongyang office worker when he grew infatuated with her and she with him, a handsome twenty-eight-year-old Soviet soldier newly arrived in his Korean ancestral homeland. Her name is Kim Yong-ok.

Back then, in late 1945, he made excuses to visit her office, a government movie-distribution center, as often as possible. They took walks together along the Taedong River. They fell in love, and Yu Song-chol told the girl, twelve years his junior, he wanted to marry her. But her family stepped in.

Devout Christians, they tolerated this communist soldier's attentions to Yong-ok, but marriage was out of the question. Two older brothers called on Yu and told him she was too young. She would have to finish her studies before thinking about marriage. Song-chol and Yong-ok stopped seeing each other.

Now here she is before him again. The colorful *hanbok* gown of 1945 has been replaced by a severe Soviet-style uniform. The bright, smiling teenager's face is more mature, more serious. They sit together and talk, filling in the missing years, and Yu learns what she has been through.

After graduating from an American missionary school in Pyongyang, Yong-ok entered the city's medical college and emerged at the top of her class in 1949. In the new North Korea, it was decreed that the number-one graduate should enter the Korean People's Army as a field nurse. With the outbreak of war, she was commissioned a junior lieutenant and followed the invading army south, eventually to the Naktong River line, to a field hospital in Chinju. After the U.S.–South Korean breakout of last September, her unit was disbanded and small groups began the grueling trek north in retreat.

Yong-ok had undergone rigorous military training before the war and found she was able to keep up with the regular soldiers in her group. But the ordeal nearly finished them.

They first followed the mountain ranges from the southwest to the northeast and then north. They huddled in the woods during the day out of sight of American pilots and walked overland via mountain trails at night. They would beg or pilfer food from villagers along the way, but often had to resort to eating wild berries, arrowroot, or grass to survive. After weeks of suffering, and more than two hundred miles, she finally crossed into North Korean territory.

Over the past six years, Yu Song-chol never stopped thinking about Yong-ok. His heart now goes out to this young nurse who endured so much, probably at times last year not far from where he was overseeing KPA operations. As she finishes her account, he tells her he has been with other women since 1945, but never married. He once more asks Kim Yong-ok to be his wife. She rebuffs him, claiming she has a fiancé. But the young general won't be deterred.

MID-MAY, 1951

For Clarence Adams, a starvation diet improves to merely meager

The Chinese have taken over operation of the Pyoktong POW camp from the North Koreans. The American prisoners who survive are slowly emerging from a life in hell to a life of simple misery.

It began when the ice broke up on the Yalu and a small boat pulled into the riverbank below Pyoktong's piney hillsides to unload a shipment of rice and millet from China. The new camp overseers built a kitchen, and the prisoners got their first hot meals since their capture last year. The improved diet is still meager, however, and the emaciated internees have a long struggle ahead to recover their strength. Clarence Adams's weight has dropped to below 100 pounds from 140.

With the warmer weather, he and other hungry prisoners dig for roots in the surrounding hills, finding edible varieties to supplement their meals of barley and turnips, sometimes rice, and, lately, occasional bits of pork.[3]

While foraging they've also discovered clumps of wild marijuana. They bring the leaves back to their shacks to dry, to roll in scavenged bits of paper, and to smoke, its sweet scent drifting through the camp. The mellow mood is a welcome evening's distraction from their grim existence.

In his many empty hours, Corporal Adams nurses a growing resentment over his capture, a belief that army commanders chose to sacrifice his all-black artillery battalion last November, to allow white soldiers to retreat first from the Chinese trap at Kunu-ri.

Segregated into black and white units while fighting the war, the two American races now find themselves mixed together in Pyoktong's crowded mud huts, and tensions sometimes burst into the open.

At one point a white prisoner, taking a dislike to Adams, sneered at him, "Nigger, if I had you back home, you wouldn't talk to me like this."

"Yeah, but you ain't home. You're a stinking prisoner just like me," Adams shot back, then delivered a punch to the head of his tormentor. After that, the man left the former army boxer alone.

A deadlier incident began when a white soldier erupted in anger at the stench from the badly infected leg wounds of a young black lying beside him, a soldier who was caught in an American strafing of a marching column of prisoners.

The white GI kicked him in the legs, shouting, "Filthy nigger!" Outraged blacks shouted back at him to leave the dying soldier alone. Then, in the night, Adams awoke to someone climbing over him and attacking the white man. In the morning, both the white soldier and the young black were found dead.

Under the Chinese, prisoner deaths are declining in Camp 5, as they now designate the compound. But the toll already has been tremendous, possibly fifteen hundred men—more than half their number—since most were captured last November and December.[4]

The Chinese finally bulldoze over the half-open mass graves on a nearby hillside, where the prisoners carried and left the dead through the winter and early spring.

THURSDAY, MAY 17, 1951

A lightning offensive traps Chung Dong-kyu and thousands of other ROK troops

The sounds of battle are moving closer to Hyun-ri—explosions, the whistle of mortar rounds, staccato bursts of machine-gun fire.

Thousands of men from two South Korean divisions, including Chung Dong-kyu's 3rd Division, sit in a long, bumper-to-bumper line of trucks in the small town or are sprawled exhausted on the ground, waiting for word that a task force has cleared an enemy roadblock that keeps them from retreating down the lone southbound route from Hyun-ri.

Close to midnight, shells begin to fall on the town itself. The Chinese to the south and the North Koreans to the north are closing a trap. Orders are shouted up and down the line: abandon the convoy, set it afire, scatter into the hills, the mountains of Gangwon province on the east-central front.

Chung drops from his truck and heads for a steep forested slope to the east, joining in the panicky rout. Two whole infantry divisions are disintegrating around him.

Eight days ago the 3rd and 9th Divisions, comprising the ROK II Corps, were pulled back to the Hyun-ri area, along what the U.S. command dubbed the "No-Name Line," to better defend against an expected renewed Chinese offensive.

Then, yesterday afternoon, eleven Chinese and North Korean divisions jumped off on General Peng's "Sixth Campaign," along a twenty-mile frontage deemed the weakest link in the U.N. line. Peng chose his target well. The PLA's 81st Division attacked down the seam between the ROK 5th and 7th Divisions, west of Hyun-ri, and scattered both. By this morning, having advanced more than fifteen miles, Chinese units swinging in from the west cut off the road south from Hyun-ri. At the same time, two North Korean divisions pressured the town from the north.[5]

The ROK II Corps was bottled up. Unable to break the Chinese hold on the road, commanders have now taken the humiliating step of ordering a disorganized overland flight, through mountains rising to two and three thousand feet.

Now, looking back down at Hyun-ri, the northern ROK Army conscript Chung sees the whole town ablaze—trucks, houses, supply stores. Ammunition dumps explode in thunderous blasts.

He turns back to climbing upward in the light of the inferno below, along with hundreds of other soldiers on all sides. The higher he goes, however, the darker the night he must penetrate and the less sure he is of his surroundings. Feeling alone in the gloom, over the next hours he skirts mountainsides, traverses ridges, fords streams as he does his best to estimate a southerly direction. When he hears voices or the snapping of underbrush, he can only hope he hasn't stumbled onto the enemy. He pushes on toward dawn.

At first light from the east, he finds he has, indeed, been heading south. He also begins to make out others scrambling southward, usually without weapons, some having ripped insignia of rank from their uniforms. They gradually form a group that grows as the morning lengthens and the nighttime chill warms toward the fifties Fahrenheit.

They stop at a stream to quench their parched throats. Chung sees a neighbor from Chu Ul, his home village in North Korea, a young man who was a student at the Chongjin teachers college while he studied at the medical school there. Just as Chung was about to shout a greeting, a gunshot rings out, then fusillades of fire rain down, bullets kicking up dirt all around them. An enemy patrol crossing the mountainside above has spotted them.

Chung sprints away from the stream, downhill, his friend right beside him. The other young man suddenly falls onto his face, shot in the ankle. Chung turns to help, but just then another bullet strikes and the soldier's head explodes in a shower of blood, bone, and brain. Chung is stunned. He retches at the paralyzing sight. But in an instant he's off again with others, running for his own life.

Hundreds of yards along, a single ROK soldier stands and shouts at them, "Stop! We can hold here!" But Chung, one of the few who still clings to his M-1, knows this is madness. He dashes past.

The desperate men soon regroup and resume their trek. It takes five more grueling days of climbing and descending the rocky terrain, scouting out and evading enemy positions, foraging for wild mountain greens to eat or rice or potatoes found in vacant farmhouses. Finally, they reach the new ROK defensive line at Hajinbu-ri, twenty-five miles south of Hyun-ri. Only one-third of Chung's 3rd Division has reassembled there. The North Koreans claim to have taken twelve hundred South Korean prisoners around Hyun-ri.[6]

<hr />

Twenty miles to the northeast, along the coast road, Hurh Won-moo's 11th Division is in hasty retreat, converging on Kangnung, a historic old city on the Sea of Japan. They've covered fifty miles over two days in the face of the new enemy offensive.

The eighteen-year-old artillery lieutenant's baptism of fire has come in a harrowing two weeks of on-the-job training as forward observer for his heavy-mortar battery.

It began with a counterattack May 7 by six ROK divisions on the eastern front, including the 11th, a thrust that in ten days recaptured most territory lost to the huge Chinese–North Korean offensive in April.[7] Resistance was light, and the South Koreans had powerful support from U.S. Navy guns offshore and U.S. Air Force fighter-bombers overhead.[8] But this, his first campaign, left Hurh exhausted.

Every morning he and his team of three enlisted soldiers had to pack up their gear, advance with the infantry another few miles, and then climb another hillside—often past the charred bodies of unknown soldiers from earlier combat—to dig yet another hilltop observation post as their battery's target-spotting eyes.

Along the way, he began to question the prudence of their aggressive company commander, Captain Lee, who was placing their 4.2-inch mortars closer to the infantry front line than is standard, running a greater risk of being overrun in an enemy attack.

On the night the enemy launched the new offensive, Lieutenant Hurh and his men were dug in at a new OP, with an infantry platoon among one-thousand-foot hills near Kansong, twenty-five miles above the 38th Parallel, when they faced the first North Korean salvo. It was the most intense fire the green lieutenant had come under, streams of machine-gun tracer bullets all seemingly aimed at him. But the infantry defenders and the mortar fire he directed blunted the North Korean ground attack.

The next night the KPA struck again, behind walls of machine-gun fire and showers of mortar rounds. Hurh again called in his battery's fire, but this time the enemy infantry steadily pushed closer, across the valley to their front, and he had to repeatedly reduce the firing range by fifty yards at a time.

When it dropped to a mere seven hundred yards, indicating the enemy was closing in, an agitated Captain Lee shouted back on the radio, "What's going on? The range is getting too short. We can't stay here any longer. Is the infantry retreating?"

Hurh pleaded with him to keep the battery firing, but the radio went silent and the big mortars stopped firing. An infantry lieutenant rushed over, enraged, demanding to know what happened to their artillery support. Hurh told him he was helpless.

The North Koreans attacked in a new wave. The defenses began to disintegrate. The infantry officer signaled they were withdrawing down the back slope. The young artillery lieutenant and his men followed, stumbling blindly down the hillside in the predawn, over rocks, shrubs, the remnants of trees. Hurh felt defeated and frustrated—that the ROK Army doesn't have bigger artillery, that his captain took a foolish risk with his placement of the mortars.

Finally reaching a roadway at the bottom as the sun rose, they were stunned to find Captain Lee and his jeep waiting. Lieutenant Hurh thanked his company commander for seeking them out.

"I'm glad we found you alive," Lee replied. He told Hurh the ROK Army units to their west had collapsed under a huge Chinese attack, and their 11th Division had to quickly move south to avoid being outflanked from the west.

Retreating past the pine forests and sandy beaches of the Gangwon Province coast, the division's troops have now reached Kangnung, a onetime royal seaside resort, a town of pavilions, gazebos, and gardens. Hurh Won-moo, the Seoul city teenager, is taken with the place—and depressed at the thought of leaving, of climbing more hills, digging more OPs. "Why this stupid war?" he asks himself. "Brothers are killing each other and destroying everything. For what purpose?"

In three days, as the Chinese–North Korean attacks falter, their divisions having suffered heavy casualties, the U.S. command orders a new counteroffensive on the far eastern front.[9]

SATURDAY, MAY 26, 1951

Gil Isham watches fellow GIs torture dying enemy soldiers

The 17th Infantry Regiment in the east and other American forces in the west are closing a giant loop trapping thousands of Chinese troops on the south side of the Hwachon Reservoir.

It's part of the Korea-wide counterpunch by the U.N. command, surprising the enemy just as General Peng was positioning his armies for a disciplined withdrawal after their offensive of mid-May stalled. Once more, the casualty toll and failing supply lines had killed the Chinese–North Korean momentum.

Rapid U.S. and South Korean advances are throwing Chinese units into a panic. In one battalion, out of ammunition, officers used their last grenades to kill themselves and their attackers. Survivors of a devastated Chinese division, trying a daylight crossing of the Pukhan River, lost six hundred officers and men to the rapid currents and U.S. air attacks.[10] Without food for days, some starving men are surrendering.[11]

Private Gil Isham missed the grim days of late April and early May, when the great Chinese offensive knocked his 17th Infantry and the rest of the 7th Division back twenty-five miles. The day before that attack began, he was wounded by errant U.S. artillery fire. Now he has returned from hospitalization in Japan to a regiment in its final days of retaking the lost territory. He is promoted to corporal, moved from a rifle squad to his 2nd Platoon's weapons squad, given a bazooka.

But eight months after landing in Korea, Gil Isham is a troubled young man—"not old in years but old at war." After seventeen years of an ordinary life in Wisconsin, when his greatest adventures were going fishing and hunting with his half-Chippewa father, and after a few months of peacetime in Japan, he has in Korea seen too much death and depravity.

Depravity goes on in the American ranks, despite such steps as an order from a "shocked" General Ridgway that officers do more to demand "a decent respect for the lives and persons of other people."[12]

Isham is disgusted by an older sergeant in his Easy Company who organizes patrols into villages solely to rape the women. He once watched the man pistol-whip a village elder for not leading him to young women and then rape the man's wife in front of him.

He is disgusted by the memory of fellow GIs torturing fallen enemy, by the sight of men poking the exposed brain of a wounded, dying North Korean, laughing as they made his muscles twitch, his tongue stick out; by the vision of another dying soldier whose legs were tied to a tree and to a bent sapling that the Americans then released, pulling the moaning, crying Korean's legs apart, lifting him upside-down into the air.

"I don't know why some of our people did things like that. Maybe they were just like that inside, sadistic. . . . Maybe they're sick, sick of all the fighting, sick of Korea, sick of everything."

He is troubled as well by the memory of the day they found fifty dead American soldiers, 2nd Infantry Division men captured by the North Koreans, hands bound with their own field telephone wire and shot in the back of the head. "It really got to some of the guys. We were ready to kill anything."

Gil Isham himself has dealt out too much death. He no longer cries when he kills.

He seeks relief from the madness in small things, an occasional hot meal shared with a buddy, hometown stories traded over cigarettes, the sight of trout needing a fishing pole in the Hwachon Reservoir, of pheasants ripe for hunting in the rice paddies. One morning he stands watch as the sun rises over the ridges and shines on a glowing green Korean valley. "I was thinking, man, this is beautiful. What are we over here tearing it up for?"

MONDAY, MAY 28, 1951

Pete McCloskey shoots a man for the first time

The Marines are up against it. On the ninth day of the U.N. command's counterstrike against the latest Chinese offensive, the advancing 2nd Battalion, 7th Marine Regiment, has been stopped by North Koreans dug in on a hill dubbed "659," near the source of the Soyang River in the thickly wooded Taebaek Mountains of central Korea.

From bunkers atop a cliff on the left and a steep finger ridge on the right, North Korean machine guns have cut down attacking Marines since yesterday. The Americans are stalled on an opposing ridge, trading long-distance fire with this enemy rear guard. Pete McCloskey's Charlie Company, 5th Marine Regiment, has been ordered to help break the standoff.

It has been a grim few days for "Charlie," now under the command of First Lieutenant Richard (Spike) Schening, a decorated World War II veteran like Captain Jones, who has been promoted to the battalion staff.

The regiment was ordered north five days ago to back up the 2nd Infantry Division, hit hard by the renewed Chinese and North Korean offensive on the Soyang. On that first day, McCloskey's men discovered a grisly scene, the aftermath of a bloodbath, 187 dead and wounded 2nd Division soldiers. "God, what a sight!" Sergeant Elson wrote in his diary. "The wounded were suffering horribly . . . A lot of them cracked up with despair that they wouldn't be found! And the dead! It was apparent they were taken by surprise. . . . The look of horror and shock still on their faces. They were half in fox holes . . . some in sleeping bags. . . . The smell of death is everywhere. We are sleeping among them tonight."

Now, facing the determined North Koreans on Hill 659, Schening has sent his 2nd Platoon splashing through the terraced rice paddies on his right to begin pushing up the enemy-held ridge. But the platoon leader has radioed back that they're under fire and cannot move. An angry Schening turns to the 1st Platoon's McCloskey and orders him to head there, take over his fellow lieutenant's men, and resume the attack.

Overhearing this, 2nd Platoon corpsman Don Dickson asks to join McCloskey. Dickson was left behind by his platoon to help tend to the 7th Marines' badly wounded. The two set off at a run, as the sun begins to drop behind the western hills. McCloskey soon outpaces the stocky Dickson in the late-afternoon heat. The medic is yards behind, off to McCloskey's side, as the lieutenant hikes up a steep ridgeline trail, among the trees, scanning for signs in the twilight of the pinned-down platoon.

McCloskey stops at the edge of a small clearing. He has gone dangerously far up the ridge. The panting Dickson is catching up, struggling along the overgrown slope below. McCloskey suddenly senses movement ahead, yards uphill across the clearing. Then he sees a bayonet, a rifle rising from the brush, a helmet camouflaged with leaves. The gun barrel is swinging around toward the sound of the approaching Dickson. Facing his first close-quarters enemy, "scared stiff," as he is to recall, McCloskey shakily raises his carbine, aims, and pulls the trigger. Nothing happens. He has left the safety on. He pushes the lever and, holding his breath, steadying the weapon, squeezes off three quick rounds. The soldier falls.

McCloskey turns, running down the darkening hill, dashing past Dickson with a shout, "Let's get the hell out of here!" The California law student who pined to go to war has killed his first man.

LATE MAY 1951

Casualties swamp Chen Hsing-chiu's medical team, including "disgusting" Americans

In the attacks and counterattacks of late May, the battalion aid station has been busy around the clock. Chen Hsing-chiu and the other medics get little sleep as the casualties are brought in by fellow soldiers or Chinese civilian stretcher bearers or limp in on their own. Heavy rains and mud make the work all the more miserable.

The numbers have swelled since General Peng's army was caught by the surprise U.N. counteroffensive. The "walls of fire" from American artillery and air attack have left hilltops, slopes, and valleys strewn with Chinese and North Korean dead and with bloody, broken wounded waiting to be rescued, legs or arms blown off, bones splintered, blinded, or in agony from napalm burns. The U.S. Air Force announced in mid-May it had dropped its 3-millionth gallon of the frightening gasoline-gel weapon.[13]

The Third Army Group, parent unit to Chen's 12th Army and two other armies, is in chaotic withdrawal. A single air attack on May 24 destroyed the vehicles carrying the army group's communications equipment, leaving it unable for days to organize a coordinated pullback of its eighty thousand troops, a proper withdrawal in which units would protect each other's flanks against attack. It has lost fifteen thousand men killed, wounded, or captured. An estimated eight thousand wounded Chinese are being left behind in the field.[14]

In the back-and-forth melee of fighting, the Chinese also have taken hundreds of American, South Korean, and other prisoners, and Chen and his team have had to treat wounded captives. One afternoon he goes to look over a fresh group of prisoners held in a nearby house.

All are filthy, their faces caked with dirt. "Some looked like dead dogs lying on the floor." Their Chinese guards ticked off the nationalities for Chen: British, Turkish, American. One pointed to a "big-nosed guy," American, standing beside a window, eating a noodle dish they'd been given, and told Chen about his capture. "When our guns were pointed at his head, he cried and offered up his gun with both hands while kneeling down begging for mercy," Chen records in his diary.

The sixteen-year-old medic, unfamiliar with foreigners, writes of his "disgust" for Americans. It began earlier in May, on a rare peaceful morning, when he took a walk outside their temporary cave shelter to smoke a cigarette and stumbled across a U.S. Army helmet. Stashed inside was a packet of photographs. They sickened him.

First, he saw pictures of "big-nosed women with blonde hair and red lipstick on their mouths." They looked like "evil spirits" that "have just eaten a child." Then he found photos of naked women, including pictures of Korean women who seem to have been raped. "These Americans have still kept these disgusting photos," he notes. "The American government says they are civilized. Ah, sure, they're civilized!"

In the army of the "new" China, endless sessions of political education shape the thinking of the young, poorly educated men filling the ranks. Like all recruits, Chen has learned the American soldiers are simply tools of Wall Street millionaires. And he knows well Mao Tse-tung's "Eight Points for the Attention of the Chinese People's Liberation Army," including the final two: "Do not take liberties with women" and "Do not mistreat captives." In time, Koreans both North and South comment on how well-disciplined Chinese soldiers generally are in the war zone, compared with other armies.

As for treatment of prisoners, Chen tells of a recent encounter on nighttime duty as an air-raid watchman. Spotting a glowing cigarette in a stopped, blacked-out convoy, he instructed the driver to douse it. The man ignored him, and Chen raised his voice. A convoy leader then explained to Chen that the driver, obscured in the darkness, was an American prisoner who didn't understand his Chinese.

"Something new," Chen writes. "Using prisoners to work for us. It shows how well we treat them."

JUNE

SATURDAY, JUNE 2, 1951

Pete McCloskey's "Charlie" faces its toughest test

Charlie Company's Marines, shivering in their hilltop foxholes, are sorry they exchanged their sleeping bags for light blankets. Early June is warming up, but the nights remain chilly in the Taebaek Mountains. Along with avoiding enemy bullets and shrapnel, staying warm at night is a priority for a Marine in Korea.

Awaking on this cloudless morning, Pete McCloskey's C Company, 5th Marines, has a daunting job ahead, to take a hill designated "610," a two-thousand-foot bunker-rimmed summit protected by two lower ridgelines on the approaches, well defended by the North Koreans.

The failure of General Peng's May offensive has put the war in Korea in a new, indecisive phase. On Friday in Washington, appearing before a U.S. Senate committee investigating General MacArthur's dismissal and the conduct of the war, Secretary of State Acheson said a cease-fire at or near the 38th Parallel would "accomplish the military purposes in Korea." General Ridgway said the same earlier: restoring South Korea's territory to the original 38th Parallel would amount to a U.N. victory.[1]

To McCloskey and his 1st Platoon, an invisible line of latitude has less concrete meaning than the next hill. On this day, in fact, they already sit ten miles "north of 38," as a result of the hard-driving success of the counterattack against Peng's faltering offensives. The plan now calls for the 1st Marine Division and the fourteen other U.S. and South Korean divisions to push north to Line Kansas, the defensible line first established in March's U.N. campaigns. For the Marines, that means advancing ten miles to positions overlooking a huge ancient volcanic crater, the "Punchbowl."[2]

The 5th Marine Regiment is starting by throwing Charlie Company against the obstacle of Hill 610, and "Charlie" will start with McCloskey's platoon in the lead, assigned to take the first of two rises guarding the approach to the summit. The company's two other platoons are then to leapfrog over McCloskey's, assaulting the second ridge and then the summit itself.

In bright sunshine, the young 1st Platoon leader jumps off at 9:15 a.m. Recent fighting has taken a toll: his forty-five-man platoon is reduced to thirty-five. The target ridgelines have been softened up by the usual Marine artillery barrages and air attack. But the challenge is a steep one, beginning with a forty-five-degree slope to a plateau leading to that first fortified rise.

McCloskey moves to the front. With his two squad leaders and radioman, Private First Class Henry (Rocky) Bruder, he scrambles to the top of the slope and then charges at a dead run across a level one hundred yards toward an unmanned machine-gun position at the base of the hill. They spot the machine gunner coming over the hill to his weapon. Seeing them, the Korean pulls a grenade from his belt. McCloskey raises his carbine, squeezes the trigger. Nothing. Once more he's left the safety on, as he did five days earlier at Hill 659.

The grenade rolls toward them. They dive away, McCloskey finally firing and killing the North Korean at point-blank range. The grenade just lies there, unexploded. In his nervousness, the young soldier failed to arm it.

He and Bruder run to the hilltop and to a startling sight: some thirty North Koreans on the back slope emerging from bunkers to join the fight. For a fatal moment, surprised, they stare back up at the Americans. Bruder opens fire with a .45-caliber pistol, and McCloskey empties his thirty-round rifle clip. Those not hit run down the back slope. McCloskey's Marines catch up with their lieutenant and join in firing on the fleeing Koreans.

The platoon hunkers down into abandoned foxholes, and McCloskey radios for a 105mm howitzer barrage on the next ridgeline. But the Marine shells fall instead on his own position, wounding several of his helpless men as he screams into the radio and the shellfire finally ends. In three months at war, the former boy student of military history has learned one's friends can be as dangerous as one's enemies.

By now North Korean mortar shells are also zeroing in on the captured hilltop, and the Marines pile into the strongest bunkers they can find. McCloskey and his platoon sergeant are the last to jam into one, sitting facing each other in the opening as deafening blasts shake the earth around them. They hear an especially loud incoming round, then a huge thud. Sitting back up as the dust settles, they see the tail of an embedded 122mm mortar round sticking up from the ground between them. A dud. They can only stare in momentary shock. It's a second reprieve in the space of an hour for McCloskey.

By noon, the leapfrogging 2nd Platoon takes the intermediate ridge, but even there the 1st Platoon leader suffers a loss. Word comes back that McCloskey's radioman Bruder, lent to the sister platoon for the assault, is dead. At age nineteen, he was killed instantly when a bullet severed his jugular vein.

The toughest job now falls to the 3rd Platoon, the final attack on the strongly defended Hill 610 itself. Its Marines are soon pinned down by heavy enemy mortar and machine-gun fire, and its lieutenant is disabled by a concussion grenade. Around four McCloskey is ordered to take his platoon through the 3rd Platoon position and storm the hill. But when he and his men reach the 3rd Platoon, in a wooded ravine at the base of 610, the sergeants who have taken over angrily tell McCloskey to back off, to provide covering fire as the 3rd Platoon does the storming.

They charge up the right side of the slope with a yell, under the overhead fire of McCloskey's machine guns. Despite enemy grenades skipping down the hillside, they quickly make the top and close with the defenders, foxhole by foxhole, in vicious hand-to-hand combat. The sergeants report by radio they've cleared that area but are running out of ammunition and need reinforcement. McCloskey tells his men to fix bayonets, and they now push up the left-hand slope, to be stopped near the summit by showers of Korean grenades.

At one point, a Marine machine gunner firing next to the prone McCloskey catches a grenade fragment in his throat, blocking his breathing. First Platoon corpsman Tom Burchick rushes in, pulls out his sheath knife, and punctures a hole in the man's throat, prying it open with a twig—a battlefield tracheotomy, under exploding grenades, that saves the man's life.

The grenade shower begins to ease, the Koreans apparently running low, perhaps withdrawing. McCloskey leads his men up the final few yards, over the top, and, bunker by bunker, they kill the remaining defenders. At the final bunker, McCloskey drops in a white phosphorous grenade, completing the bloody job.

Charlie Company has taken its day's objective on the route north to Line Kansas, but the cost has been heavy. McCloskey's own platoon is down to sixteen men and four stretcher cases waiting to be evacuated. To his relief, he sees Marines of a sister company moving up the hill to take over the forward positions. His men now divide into fours, at the corners of four makeshift stretchers, and wend their way through a hilltop strewn with Korean bodies, smoking bunkers, and the splintered trees and shell holes of the latest "next hill" in a war soon to be a year old.

"One of the hardest things for a man to take," Sergeant Elson writes in his diary, "is the pitiful sight of the poncho wrapped bodies of the dead, on litters, waiting their turn to be evacuated." When you find a buddy under a poncho, he writes, "it takes everything you have to hang on. . . . You look and look and look . . . for you know you'll never see him again!"

A MID-JUNE DAY, 1951

Hurh Won-moo learns of his sister's encounter with the Americans

The lieutenant strides toward a woman washing clothes outside a small thatched-roof house. She looks up, puzzled by the young man in army fatigues, then rushes up and grabs his hands. "Is that you?" she asks through tears. "Won-moo, my son!"

Lieutenant Hurh Won-moo has managed a brief surprise reunion with his family, five months after he and his mother fled from Seoul across the frozen Han River.

In late May's U.N. counteroffensive, his 11th Division, part of the ROK I Corps holding the line on the east coast, made dramatic gains as enemy units steadily withdrew northward. By June 4, the ROK troops stood at Kojin-ri, more than fifty miles up the coast from their jump-off point at Kangnung.[3]

Lieutenant Hurh's work as a forward observer for his heavy-mortar company impressed his commander, Captain Lee, who promoted him to leader of the 2nd Platoon, in charge of forty-five men and four 4.2-inch mortars. When the eastern front settled into days of unusual quiet, Lee learned of his star lieutenant's concern about the family he left behind at his mother's mill south of Seoul in January and issued him a three-day pass.

Riding the company truck on a supply run, Hurh was told by relatives in Seoul he could find his family in Onyang, not far from the Chonan mill.

Now his three sisters and younger brother have joined him and their overjoyed mother in the front yard. They retreat inside for a celebratory dinner and hours of talk as well as a hot bath and long restful sleep for Hurh—luxuries for a frontline soldier.

Meanwhile, in their catching up on the past five months, he has heard a disturbing tale from his older sister, twenty-year-old In-moo, explaining why they moved to Onyang.

She tells him that not long after he left for officer training last winter, a U.S. artillery battery moved into the Chonan mill compound. This was when the Americans were planning their late January operations against the Chinese.

The twenty members of the extended Hurh and Eum families sheltering there kept their distance, staying inside the mill building as much as possible. But at one point several unruly soldiers barged in, shouting, "Sexee! Sexee!"—their version of a Korean word for "young woman."

One grabbed pretty In-moo by the arms. Mother reacted instantly, picking up a heavy stone, lifting it over her head, and shouting in Korean, "You damned American bastard! Leave my daughter alone or I'll kill you!"

The startled soldier got the message, whatever the language, let go of In-moo, and the soldiers left.

That evening, worried about their young women, Mother called everyone together and suggested they disperse elsewhere in smaller groups. She moved with her four children to this rented two-room house in Onyang. Finishing, In-moo tells Won-moo their mother prayed to Buddha every day for his safety.

As the appointed hour approaches for the company truck driver to pick up Lieutenant Hurh, Mother insists he first have his photograph taken at a studio in town.

Looking younger than his nineteen years, Hurh poses in uniform and helmet, with two grenades taped to his harness—standard for such a road trip—before a tranquil painted backdrop of rooftops and church steeples. Deep down, he knows why Mother was so insistent on a portrait. She fears she may never see her first-born son again.

Meanwhile, soldiers like those who tried to assault In-moo worry General Van Fleet, Eighth Army commander. On June 24, lamenting the "prevalence of criminal offenses against civilian personnel," he instructs officers to crack down or risk losing support of the South Korean people.[4]

The Chinese metropolis of Tientsin, seaport to Peking, is a revelation to No Kum-sok and his fellow student pilots from North Korea. After arriving by train from their Manchurian training base last month, the young trainees took a tour of the sprawling city and were amazed at the commercial bustle and the Western people and consumer goods everywhere in this "communist" country, unlike anything they've seen at home. The capitalist urge is hard to suppress, No realizes.

They're in China, at an air base north of Tientsin, to continue their training for flying the MiG-15 in the air war with the Americans. They've had months of classroom instruction in the technology of this advanced Soviet jet interceptor, in flying techniques, and in the Russian language, to work more closely with their Soviet instructors.

The seven-day-a-week schedule has been grueling, but No, a top student, has succeeded in flying solo in a Yak-17, a slower, less advanced jet. He looks forward, with some nervousness, to flying the 500-mph MiG, the interceptor that, with Russian pilots, has evened the odds in the battle for the skies over North Korea.

After one year of war, the U.S. military says the airborne toll is, indeed, even—about five hundred aircraft destroyed or damaged on each side.[5] The MiG's prowess as a predator has led the Americans to all but end daylight bombing by its greatest prey, the B-29.[6]

American intelligence, meanwhile, has a sense that something like No Kum-sok's class of eighty Korean MiG pilots is in the pipeline. The CIA reports that efforts to upgrade air facilities in North Korea "indicate Communist intentions to utilize his air force in the near future."[7]

WEDNESDAY, JUNE 13, 1951

Pete McCloskey is ordered to lead a suicidal charge

Charlie Company is on the move again on a clear, cool morning, and Lieutenant Pete McCloskey is agitated. He spent yesterday at the battalion aid station, having a leg wound from shrapnel tended to and sleeping for many hours, the deep sleep of an exhausted soldier. Now he's climbing up a narrow forested ridgeline, passing through the ranks of Charlie Company's Marines as he looks to rejoin his 1st Platoon.

Since the battle to capture Hill 610 on June 2, the 5th Marine Regiment has pushed north, up and down ridges and hilltops, driving North Koreans before them as they advance toward their final objective, the ridges forming the southern rim of the Punchbowl. The retreating Koreans have taken a heavy toll of Marines with their deadly mortar and machine-gun fire. The three platoons of "Charlie" are being filled out by replacements, including green officers. McCloskey passes by one lieutenant he doesn't even know, commanding a sister platoon.

The company has been ordered to take yet another "next hill," this one dubbed "808." As he heads up the slope McCloskey suddenly realizes, with a shock, that his 1st Platoon has been sent into the lead for the attack without him, its lone officer. A mere corporal, named Eck, has taken over McCloskey's thirty men.

Quickening his pace, he finally catches up with familiar faces, his Marines. And just then the clatter of machine guns sends them all diving for cover.

The platoon's point man, in the lead for the entire company, has climbed over a slight grassy rise directly into the machine-gun fire of North Koreans lying in wait in bunkers on the summit. He is now dead, others behind him are wounded, and the platoon can only hug the ground, each man helpless and shaking, as fusillades of bullets streak overhead, shearing the bark and branches off trees.

McCloskey crawls to a dip in the ground offering more cover, where much of the platoon is huddled. "Boy, are we glad to see you, Lieutenant," says Corporal Eck.

The ridge is just twenty yards wide, falling off in cliffs on each side. As the enemy fire eases, McCloskey peers through a bush, seeing a slight slope leading up two hundred yards to four log-built bunkers. Trying to rush the Koreans over this open ground would be suicidal. The Marines are so pinned down they can't even set up their own machine guns. Only artillery or an air strike can help.

Instead, word comes by radio: "The colonel wants you to take the hill by noon."

The colonel, the battalion commander, considered an incompetent by junior officers, is demanding the impossible. McCloskey replies that the colonel should come forward to see the situation himself or send another battalion company to assault the hill from another direction.

Nothing happens. Meanwhile, the slightest movement by the Americans draws fire from the machine gunners. McCloskey is told the battalion is lining up artillery support and he should attack at 1:00 p.m. But no artillery backup materializes. The 1st Platoon holds fast.

The company commander, a newcomer who took over two weeks ago when Spike Schening was badly wounded, again radios: "McCloskey, either get moving or you'll be court-martialed. Regiment wants that hill taken by two o'clock." Next a 3:00 p.m. deadline is set and passes, and the angry McCloskey's radioed replies grow more profane.

Finally, an artillery forward observer and his radioman—from a different regiment, the 11th Marines—make their way up the ridge and tell McCloskey they're arranging for a "time on target" barrage by three dozen of their regiment's howitzers, a storm of shells set for precisely 4:00 p.m.

The barrage comes in three steps, "walking" up to the bunkers. Bayonets fixed, McCloskey leads his men right behind, in a charge toward the smoke, dust, and flashes of the artillery shells, expecting any moment to be hit by enemy fire. But they emerge unscathed through the smoke and, clearing the summit, see North Korean soldiers hundreds of yards away downhill, disappearing into the woods. They retreated, by chance, just before the artillery hit.

Two have stayed behind, with hands up to surrender, but still carrying burp guns. As McCloskey approaches, one turns and runs, and Marines open fire, killing both.

Reaching the bodies, the lieutenant searches them and finds a family photograph on one. It shows a large group, old and young, grandparents and children, lined up stiffly outside a humble thatched-roof home. The formality reminds him of daguerreotypes he saw in the Civil War histories he read as a boy. He wonders about this dead youth, about what right he has, an American from ten thousand miles away, to come here and kill him, maybe just a hundred miles from the home he's defending.

What right do we all have, Pete McCloskey wonders, to do this to these peasant families?

Phil Elson, the platoon's machine-gun sergeant, notes in his diary that during this terrible long afternoon he saw one Marine sitting under a tree muttering gibberish to himself. "He'd cracked up from shock," Elson writes. "He, too, had had his belly full of war!"

In fact, during the most intense fighting in Korea, army doctors have reported a stunningly high rate of psychiatric casualties among American troops, as many as one in four men calculated on an annual basis. Combat veterans tell doctors they find the fighting in this war tougher than in World War II.[8]

It takes another four days, but the 1st Battalion reaches the approaches to the final objective, the Punchbowl, at Hill 907.

Baker Company tries but fails to take the seemingly invulnerable heights. "Charlie" gets the job the next morning, with the 1st Platoon again in the lead. McCloskey fears his luck may finally have run out. Five hundred yards from the top, unexpectedly, he sees another battalion's Marines charging up a ridge from the left flank and overrunning the defenses. The North Koreans have again retreated.

SATURDAY, JUNE 30, 1951

Matt Ridgway speaks to his enemy and offers negotiations

At precisely 8:00 in the morning, General Matthew B. Ridgway's imposing voice is heard on radios across Japan and beyond.

"Message to the commander-in-chief, Communist forces in Korea," he begins. "As commander-in-chief of the United Nations command, I've been instructed to communicate to you the following . . ."[9]

This day, this announcement, an offer to open armistice talks, has been in prospect for weeks, but it began looking more likely last Saturday, when the Soviet U.N. ambassador, Jakob A. Malik, envoy of the vital ally of North Korea and China, went on a routine U.N. radio program in New York and said "the Soviet peoples" believe cease-fire talks should begin.

Secretary of State Acheson immediately issued a statement welcoming the overture. On Monday, first anniversary of the North Korean invasion, President Truman also offered an olive branch in a speech in Tennessee. "We are ready to join in a peaceful settlement in Korea now, just as we have always been," Truman declared.

By Friday morning, Ridgway and his staff were in a telex conference with Pentagon and State Department officials as they reviewed a draft statement Washington had prepared. The final version, approved by the president, landed at Ridgway's headquarters in the early hours today. He arrived at 7:30 a.m. to make the announcement over Japanese government radio and Voice of America.[10]

"I am informed that you may wish a meeting to discuss an armistice," he continues. He says that if the communist side confirms this, he will name his representative and recommend a date for meeting their representative. He suggests the meeting place be the harbor in Wonsan—the bomb-devastated North Korean port—aboard the *Jutlandia*, a Danish hospital ship based at Pusan.[11]

Across Korea and Japan, American troops listening to their commander's words break into cheers. "This is it!" is the common refrain among soldiers who want to believe that peace—and going home—is at hand.[12]

The announcement is repeated through the day, in English, Korean, Chinese, and Japanese, on all available radio stations. The communist side is known to monitor the various radio frequencies. But no reply is heard. Ridgway is unperturbed. Urgent discussions must be under way among leaders in Pyongyang, Peking, and Moscow. Besides, he has a social engagement.

As the new post–World War II "SCAP," Supreme Commander of Allied Powers, Ridgway is the preeminent figure in occupied Tokyo, with duties ranging from the military to the diplomatic and ceremonial. In that second category, on this day he and wife Penny host a grand garden party at their residence, with some five hundred guests from among the Japanese elite, the various allied militaries, and the diplomatic corps.[13]

The pretty, vivacious young Mrs. Ridgway is a center of attention, as she has been since arriving in the Japanese capital in mid-May with their two-year-old Matty. In her first public appearance, on a military parade reviewing stand with her husband, the press reported she "stole the show" in a dramatic black shantung dress and wide-brimmed black hat. She has represented the general at the funeral of Japan's Dowager Empress, while he was away in Korea, and is to take on such duties as throwing out the first pitch in a U.S.–Japan exhibition baseball game.[14]

She also brings a softer, human touch to a wartime general's life after five months of round-the-clock intensity in the mud and grit of a combat zone. Matt Ridgway can finally retreat daily to two or three dinnertime hours in something better than a canvas command post on the Han.

While the Ridgways' party guests mingle and speculate about cease-fire chances, at General Headquarters the day's dispatches from the war tell of only light clashes among small-unit patrols.

Ridgway, who flew to Korea on Tuesday to confer with his successor, General Van Fleet, is satisfied that the current U.N.-held line is where they should stand while exploring a possible cease-fire. Trying to advance, to take more territory, would merely cost American lives for land that might be given back in an armistice.

The human cost of this war clearly is driving both sides toward negotiations.

Army statisticians calculate total battle casualties on all sides in twelve months of war at just short of 2 million. That includes 78,800 American dead, wounded, captured, or missing, 21,300 of them men killed in action. Total casualties in the South Korean military top 212,000. The South Korean civilian toll is put at 469,000, including 170,000 dead, almost certainly an underestimate. The communist side is not announcing casualties, and U.S. estimates of those—more than 1.2 million North Korean and Chinese military casualties combined—are considered much inflated. But clearly hundreds of thousands have been killed and wounded.[15] The number of dead and wounded among North Korean civilians, the targets of ceaseless U.S. Air Force bombing for almost a year, can only be guessed at by outsiders. But it must be enormous.

Among those casualties are 58 killed or wounded in Pete McCloskey's 1st Platoon, C Company, 5th Marine Regiment.

Few of the Marines who jumped off with McCloskey from Wonju back in February, in the slush and mud, under the gaze of a saluting General MacArthur at the start of Operation Killer, have made it to June with Charlie Company and their twenty-three-year-old second lieutenant. Now it's his turn to go.

Unlike U.S. troops in World War II—and Chinese and Korean soldiers, North and South, in the current conflict—individual Americans fighting in Korea in 1951 are not committed "for the duration," but for a deployment of one year or less. For Marine lieutenants serving as infantry platoon leaders, one of the deadliest jobs in Korea, the Marine Corps rotates them to the rear if they survive four months. Pete McCloskey has now drawn that reprieve, being assigned to the 5th Marine Regiment's rear-echelon support unit at Masan, two hundred miles south of the front lines. He'll work as an assistant personnel officer.

"Boy, did we all hate to see him go," Sergeant Elson writes in his diary. "No one can ever take Mr. Mac's place with us."

JULY

SUNDAY, JULY 1, 1951

Peng Teh-huai and Kim Il-sung declare, "We agree to meet"

The broadcast monitors in Tokyo this evening hear a Peking Radio announcer break into normal programming to say an important statement is upcoming. Then it is read, first in Chinese and English, later in Korean.

"We agree to meet your representative for conducting talks concerning cessation of military action and establishment of peace," says the terse reply from Peng Teh-huai and Kim Il-sung to General Ridgway's offer of armistice negotiations.

Rather than the American's proposed shipboard meeting place off Wonsan, in eastern North Korea, they favor meeting in Kaesong, on the 38th Parallel in the west. They propose starting by mid-July.[1]

In this stalemated war, each side thinks it will have the stronger hand in the talks.

North Korean broadcasts claim Ridgway's offer has come because "the armed aggression of the United Nations forces has ended in failure."[2] It's clear the U.S. goal of reunifying Korea—under the southern regime or with a U.N. occupation authority in the North—is no longer attainable at a cost acceptable to Washington.[3] But, similarly, the Chinese goal of driving the Americans from the peninsula and uniting the two Koreas under Kim is also beyond reach.[4]

As word of tonight's announcement spreads to men on both sides of the fighting fronts, and to people in bombed-out cities and refugee camps across Korea, hopes rise for a quick end to their ordeal.

Two days later, in the wartime capital of Pusan, an agitated Syngman Rhee paces up and down the driveway of his temporary residence, trailed by Bill Shinn and other Korean reporters. He repeatedly utters the word "appeasement." They hurriedly write in their notebooks.

The South Korean president sees the looming truce negotiations as an obstacle to his ambition to unite all Korea under his leadership.

The U.N. secretary-general, Trygve Lie, says a cease-fire maintaining the 38th Parallel dividing line would meet the goals of the United Nations in authorizing last year's defense of South Korea. The U.S. secretary of state, Dean Acheson, has said the same.

But the seventy-six-year-old Rhee, who spent his life campaigning for the independence of all Korea, tells the journalists this would merely appease the North Korean aggressor. "Our people have died, been killed, their homes destroyed and cities ruined. Boys of friendly nations have sacrificed their lives," Rhee says. "We didn't do it all without purpose."

In sometimes confusing statements, his government indicates some flexibility, but also has laid down such "minimum requirements" for an agreement as complete disarmament of the North Korean communists and denial of any foreign assistance to the North.

After a year of war, and of observing the diplomatic and political dance among all sides, Bill Shinn knows these impossible demands bode ill for a united U.S.–South Korean front to negotiate an end to the conflict.[5]

At their camouflaged base behind the central front, news of the truce talks has Chen Hsing-chiu and his fellow medics thinking of home, of returning soon to China. They gather for a "political discussion," the kind their army's commissars encourage.

"I think the American people are demanding a halt to the Korean War. Antiwar sentiment is rising," young Chen tells the others.

Li Wen-hai agrees: "Every four years they have a presidential election. President Truman needs the voters' support."

EARLY JULY 1951

*Yu Song-chol takes over as chief, facing a quick truce
or a long standoff*

The Great Leader, his commander from the 88th Brigade's World War II
days, has called upon Yu Song-chol once again.

Premier Kim Il-sung has designated Lieutenant General Nam Il,
Korean People's Army chief of staff, as lead negotiator for the truce talks.
To replace him temporarily, Kim has again named KPA operations di-
rector Yu as acting chief of staff, just as Yu filled in for the fallen Kang
Kon last summer.

Lieutenant General Yu and his staff now play only a subsidiary role to
General Peng and his Chinese strategists. The KPA divisions hold down
the far eastern and far western flanks of the cross-peninsula war front,
away from the central action of the Chinese-held middle.

The two communist allies muster 569,000 troops at the front. Facing
them are 554,000 U.S., South Korean, and allied troops.[6] In the ninety-
degree heat and on-off rains of early July, the two sides are digging deeper
and reinforcing their defensive positions for what could be either a relatively quick truce agreement or a drawn-out standoff after a year of the
violent ebb and flow of offensive and counteroffensive.

Both sides seem confident they can hold their own. Concludes the
American CIA, "Unless . . . the Communists commit substantial numbers of heavily equipped troops with strong air support, we believe that
they will continue to be unsuccessful in their efforts to defeat UN forces."[7]

THURSDAY, JULY 19, 1951

Sudden death strikes on the slopes above Mary Mercy's clinic

The pounding rains of last night have eased. The nuns at the Pusan clinic
are left to wonder how the poor people above them have fared in the
storm, in the shantytown on the lower slopes of South Mountain.

As the sisters prepare for the day's hundreds of patients, two men
rush in, each carrying a small child. A little girl follows behind. All are
coated with mud, and the two children, limp in the men's arms, look
lifeless.

A landslide, the men blurt out. It crushed some of the crude huts in
the shantytown. The wife of one of the men was found dead when they

dug into their buried hut. The two injured children were pulled from the debris of another shack, the second man's, their father.

Sister Mary Mercy sees that the smaller child, a two-year-old girl, has terrible head and torso injuries and is dying. She quickly baptizes her as she breathes her last. The other, a four-year-old boy, seems to have been dazed and is coming around.

The father's name is Myong-dok. Sorrowful stories like his have become everyday tragedies in Korea.

When the fighting came too close to their farm in upper South Korea, the family of six set out southward on a weeks-long trek to Pusan, despite Myong-dok's wife's serious illness. First, they awoke one morning on the roadside to find their newborn baby, with no milk from the weakened mother, had died. Then, a week later, she herself succumbed.

Myong-dok managed to reach Pusan with the three remaining children and to find a spot to build a shelter beneath a cliff overhang among the South Mountain squatters. Protection from the wind, he told himself. He was lucky to land work as a laborer for the U.S. Army.

Last night, in the torrential storm, he set out containers to catch rainwater. Several times through the night he rose from his sleeping mat to empty full containers into a big crock inside. Then, stepping out into the downpour close to dawn, he saw it: a sudden waterfall tumbling over from above. He sensed it could weaken the entire overhang.

He awoke his neighbors, and they climbed the slope with a shovel to try to divert the flow of water. Then, as they stood atop the cliff, the earth gave way, and Myong-dok and other men were swept downhill in a wave of mud and water. Stunned but not seriously hurt, they climbed back up to find one hut vanished under the mud and Myong-dok's half-buried.

He saw his six-year-old daughter, Pok-ja, pulling her little brother from the shack. He then crawled inside, brought out the fatally injured two-year-old, and hurried down to the clinic.

Now he can only climb back uphill with her broken body, to bury her and find shelter with neighbors until he can build a new shack for his dwindling family. He worries now about Pok-ja. She has a bad cough and fever—probably tuberculosis, her father fears. He tells himself he'll take her back to the sisters for treatment later.

"The night's drizzling rain turned into a wind-blown downpour in the early morning hours," Sister Agnus Therese writes her mother. "Nonetheless, two hundred patients slept outside in the lines last night."

FRIDAY, JULY 20, 1951

Luckier than many, Chang Sang's family still endures tragedy

United Nations officials estimate 5 million Koreans, from North and South, are now refugees in South Korea. After months of a U.S. military strategy of "scorched earth," as its forces advanced and retreated over the landscape, four hundred thousand homes have been destroyed in South Korea alone, according to Korean government figures.[8]

The hundreds of thousands of "lucky" refugees in camps run by the U.N. command or the South Korean government are often living in misery, underfed, victims of disease run rampant.

On this summer Friday, as a tropical storm's winds and torrential rains batter South Korea, a *New York Times* correspondent cables home a report on a camp near Seoul holding thirty-seven thousand refugees, almost all North Koreans, people living in leaking tents or mud huts, "forced to live worse than any animal kept by an American farmer."[9]

The International Committee of the Red Cross has complained to the U.S. government that the American military is blocking access to the camps by Red Cross inspectors, inspections authorized under the Geneva Conventions. The U.S. Army secretary, Frank Pace, will inform the new defense secretary, Robert A. Lovett, that any international inspections would expose deplorable conditions in the camps.[10]

The United States contributes the most to the relief programs, but often only grudgingly. Last December, the Congress cut in half the army's proposal for $100 million in aid. One Republican senator was quoted as saying, "We ought to be more concerned now with shooting the communists instead of feeding them."[11]

The eleven-year-old refugee Chang Sang and her family have been relatively fortunate. After fleeing south and spending some months in Taegu, they have moved to the central city of Taejon, seventy miles closer to their adopted home of Seoul. They have a little money and a single rented room for the four of them—mother Bong-hyun, daughter Sang, and Sang's sister, Ran, and her husband, Kang Ki-suk. They have also added a fifth, a son born to Ran and Ki-suk, their first child.

The young couple's joy quickly turns to distress when the infant falls very ill, with a high fever. It's meningitis.

Young Sang, helping care for her baby nephew as his condition worsens, is holding him in her arms one day when he suddenly stops breathing. She cries out, and Ran and Ki-suk rush over, but there's nothing to be done.

Across Korea, North and South, the destruction of hospitals and clinics and the death of health professionals, the malnutrition and near starvation, the crowding of camps and unsanitary conditions spreading contagions, the exposure to the elements, the disruption of medical supply systems—all contribute to wartime deaths as surely as the bombs and bullets of the contending armies.

A Danish physician visiting a refugee camp in the far south reports the "inconceivable sight" of a "hospital" that was more like an open shed, with six to seven hundred patients, victims of smallpox, typhoid fever, typhus, tetanus, leprosy, and other diseases, lying or sitting on the bare earth or on grass mats soaked with urine and feces. "I shall never forget the hopelessness I see in the eyes of a mother who is sitting with her little dying child at her flabby, hollow breast," Dr. Mogens Winge writes.[12]

After the death of Sang's newborn nephew, mother Bong-hyun finds a place for them among fellow Christian refugees from the North, in a Presbyterian church–sponsored settlement of small houses on the outskirts of Taejon. Life is spartan. Rice supplies are short, and boiled barley, a mark of poverty, is the daily meal offering. But they find moral support in the church community, and the enterprising Bong-hyun, as before, earns *won* working here and there, laundering, sewing, cleaning house.

Sang is enrolled in a nearby school for refugee girls, in a hastily built, flimsy wooden building where she flourishes, clearly a gifted child.

Once when she, as usual, knows the answer during a lesson and raises her hand, the teacher remarks, "Sang! You're five seconds faster than the other students."

She thought, "I'm five seconds faster. I know what that means."

Her mother, the unschooled farmer's daughter, encourages her. War's upheavals fail to dim the Korean people's Confucian devotion to education. "You can miss a meal, but you cannot miss a class," she tells Sang.

THURSDAY, JULY 26, 1951

"White Commie" Alan Winnington covers the truce talks

The two sides in this stalemated, costly war first met July 10 to negotiate an armistice. Across a long table covered in green baize, they promptly

began arguing over preliminary details, ranging from the absence of journalists and the presence of armed North Koreans, to just what it was they
wanted to talk about.

Now at least they have agreed on an agenda.[13]

"The first phase of the talks has ended successfully," Alan Winnington
reports from Kaesong, the town in North Korean–held territory where
the negotiations are taking place.[14]

But already the time lost makes a quick armistice look less likely.

After the two sides in early July agreed on negotiations, the Americans rejected a Chinese–North Korean proposal that military action cease
during the talks. General Ridgway wanted to keep up pressure, especially
continued air bombardment of the North.[15] Winnington, witness to the
vast destruction of the U.S. air campaign, takes note of this. "All day
long while the negotiations are proceeding, American warplanes pass in-
solently overhead," his *Daily Worker* dispatch observes.[16]

The British communist was among the last correspondents to reach
Kaesong, arriving from Peking with Wilfred Burchett, a leftist Australian
reporting for France's *Ce Soir* newspaper. Their appearance on the other
side intrigues the American reporters at the talks, who crowd around the
"two white Commies" asking where they came from, how they got there.
Winnington likens it to "South Sea islanders meeting Captain Cook,
almost feeling our clothes."

The antique walled city of Kaesong, capital of the Koryo dynasty a
millennium ago, lay in South Korean territory just below the 38th Parallel, thirty-five miles northwest of Seoul, until June 25 last year, when
the northern army seized it in the war's first hours. As the venue for the
talks, the North Koreans have chosen an old teahouse, a former restaurant whose tile roof corners turn upward, pagoda style.

The communist side is led by the young, chain-smoking North
Korean chief of staff, Nam Il, buttoned up in dress uniform and high
leather boots in the midsummer heat. The delegation includes two other
North Korean officers and two Chinese. By contrast, the Americans,
led by Vice Admiral C. Turner Joy, Far East naval commander, dress in
comfortable, open-necked summer tans. Their U.N. delegation includes
three other Americans and Major General Paik Sun-yup, commander of
South Korea's I Corps.[17]

The talks got off to a difficult start July 10 when Joy's convoy was
stopped by North Korean guards on the twelve-mile road to Kaesong

from a base camp near Munsan, in a U.S.-held area south of the Imjin River. The delegates were told the twenty journalists in the convoy could go no farther.

That led to days of debate between the delegations and an agreement allowing reporters from the U.N. side to travel to the talks site and clearing the road and a half-mile-radius area around the teahouse of armed North Koreans. A wider "neutral area," five miles in radius, now holds only lightly armed northern military police.

Then began the back-and-forth over the talks agenda. The communist side objected in particular to a U.S. proposal to discuss Red Cross visits to prisoner-of-war camps in the North. The Americans balked at a communist proposal to make the 38th Parallel the eventual armistice demarcation line, saying the line should be negotiated.

Both have now accepted a more vaguely worded agenda leaving to negotiation the fixing of the armistice line and the arrangements for overseeing the cease-fire and for dealing with prisoners.[18]

These tensions in the conference's early days dismay Winnington. His dispatch is headlined "Shadow Hangs over Cease-Fire Talks." But under questioning by curious Western reporters, he's upbeat. "I can assure you there is a sincere desire for peace in China," he says.

He's also asked how he feels covering a war in which his fellow Britons are fighting on the other side. "I am a war correspondent," Winnington replies. "I have to go where the war takes me."[19]

MONDAY, JULY 30, 1951

A camp library introduces Clarence Adams to "revolutionary society"

To fight the boredom of captivity, high school dropout Clarence Adams devours one book after another in the new library at his POW camp. In fact, Adams is the librarian, having volunteered to work with the Chinese commanders of Camp 5.

Although life improves slowly for the prisoners, it remains a wretched existence. Dysentery, fevers, night blindness, and other ills from infections and deficient diets afflict many. Winter's plagues of lice are followed by summer's arrival of bedbugs, rats, fleas, and flies. Air raid alerts in the Yalu River valley fray their nerves.

But compared with the malign neglect of North Korean overseers last winter, when hundreds of American POWs died of starvation, disease, and untreated wounds, summer's survivors now have reason to hope they'll outlast this war.

Soon after taking control of the Pyoktong camp, the Chinese became aware of racial tensions among the prisoners and separated Adams and the other American blacks from white prisoners. Adams also suspects their new overseers believe that isolating this oppressed American minority would make it easier to "educate" them to communism's virtues.

The Chinese told the prisoners each hut must select a representative to work with the command. Adams's all-black group chose a popular older man, a corporal, but he refused, saying he feared being court-martialed later for collaborating with the enemy. The twenty-two-year-old Corporal Adams then volunteered, telling the others that in their situation, beyond any U.S. help, they must do what's necessary to help themselves survive.

Meeting with the Chinese, Adams laid out an ambitious list of requests for the entire camp: sports equipment, a place for Sunday services, the ability to cook their own food, reading material.

It took some weeks, but things began changing. They were given bats and baseballs, footballs, a basketball court. They set up their own small kitchens. Medicines were distributed to medics among the prisoners. An abandoned building became a recreational center where they played cards, table tennis, checkers, and chess. The men began to exercise regularly.

Hundreds of English-language books were delivered for a library, from Dickens and Twain to Marx and Engels, and Adams was put in charge. The prisoners also can read old issues of the London and New York *Daily Worker*, as well as a weekly propaganda sheet the North Koreans produce for the POW camps.[20] Adams, his mind increasingly preoccupied with the racial injustices of America, is impressed with what he reads about the "new societies" being built in China and the Soviet Union.

The Chinese also have organized political lectures that all prisoners must attend, given by English-speaking professors and other Chinese civilians. They repeatedly drive home the point that the American intervention in Korea is the work of Wall Street profiteers, that it's "a rich man's war but a poor man's fight."

Adams at first dismisses the talk as propaganda, but when the lecturers turn to American racism, he sees the truth in what they're saying, recalling the humiliations he and other blacks suffer in America. He joins others in voluntary study groups led by the Chinese.

Most of the American POWs dismiss the lectures and reject the study groups. Those who show an interest are labeled "progressives" by the Chinese, "pros" to the POWs. Those who show contempt for the lessons—and for the pros—are called "reactionaries." The most defiant and disrespectful are sometimes put in solitary confinement for days, in a cramped hilltop mud hut.[21]

Meanwhile, the prisoners find another new pastime in the skies, craning their necks and watching American Sabre jets and communist MiGs engage in almost daily dogfights over the Yalu.[22]

Pyoktong itself is not a major target for bombardment, but the devastating U.S. air war goes on elsewhere. On this day, 110 miles to the south, more than four hundred planes attack Pyongyang in a massive raid unpublicized by a U.S. command worried about world opinion as truce talks begin. The North Koreans say ten thousand people are killed or wounded in the capital.

"There are very few houses left in Pyongyang," a Polish diplomat reports to Warsaw. "We saw scenes of despair . . . children who were pushing aside the rubble with their little hands in search of their mothers."[23]

AUGUST

WEDNESDAY, AUGUST 1, 1951

Chi Chao-chu joins the multitudes cheering Mao
in Tien An Men Square

A sea of blue and green cotton fills Tien An Men Square, tens of thousands of citizens in Mao suits and huge formations of uniformed soldiers, assembled in the vast Peking plaza to mark People's Liberation Army Day.

On the far back edge of the crowd, a tall, bespectacled student strains to hear the speeches over the echoing loudspeakers, in a language he is still working to recover from his childhood in China, before his family moved to America. Chi Chao-chu has bicycled ten miles from Tsinghua University for the celebration, marking the twenty-fourth anniversary of the founding of the communist-led army that has fought the mighty U.S. military to a standstill in Korea.

From his great distance, Chi cannot make out the faces, but four leaders share center stage on the balcony of the towering, pagoda-like Tien An Men Gate: Mao Tse-tung himself, Premier Chou En-lai, PLA overall commander Chu Teh, and General Peng Teh-huai, fresh from Korea, where the armistice talks have gotten off to a plodding start.

In his address, full of pride for the PLA's accomplishments, Peng warns the Americans against breaking off those negotiations. "World public opinion will see more clearly who is insisting on war and does not want peace," the famous general declares.[1]

When Mao speaks, he is met with a roar, with waving red flags and banners. The twenty-two-year-old chemistry student Chi, seeing and hearing the revolutionary hero for the first time, is swept up in the emotion, in the feeling of the Chinese people as one, and of Mao as the father of the nation.

Earlier this year, despite his father's advice, Chi felt obliged as a patriot to apply to join the Chinese People's Volunteers in Korea, although his submission thus far seems to have been ignored. He also aspires to join the Communist Party, and in the coming days he immerses himself in Mao's writings, which supplement his language studies as he compares the original Chinese with English translations.

Chi finds that conflict and struggle—"endless revolution"—are central to Mao's thinking.

Students in the capital like Chi are insulated, unaware of what is happening in the Chinese countryside, how that endless revolution is playing out as the communists, in bloody fashion, impose their land redistribution scheme, seizing upon China's involvement in a foreign war to justify the crushing of political opposition, real or potential, at home.

Two days after Mao ordered Peng to enter Korea with his army last October, the Communist Party Central Committee issued a directive instructing party members to take "ruthless" action to destroy "all reactionaries and reactionary activities." This was necessary "for guaranteeing the smooth progress of land reform and economic reconstruction, as well as for the consolidation and further development of the Chinese people's revolution."[2]

It is eventually revealed that in months of terror, millions of "reactionaries"—landlords, businesspeople, "profiteers," suspect intellectuals, Nationalist sympathizers—have been arrested. At least 1 million and perhaps 2 million people have been executed after summary trials or been beaten or hacked to death by peasant mobs for what Mao calls "heinous crimes" that have "incurred the bitter hatred of one and all."[3]

WEDNESDAY, AUGUST 15, 1951

In a drenched South Korea, Mary Mercy's medics work
long hours to keep up

At noon, church bells peal and sirens sound across Pusan, on the anniversary of Korea's liberation from Japan in 1945 and the founding of the Republic of Korea in 1948. The bells and sirens could just as well be warning of dangers over the horizon.

Two typhoons are bearing down on the peninsula, on the west and east, storms that will add a devastating final note to weeks of torrential downpours that have flooded roads, washed out bridges, and threatened to drown the all-important rice harvest.[4] The deluge also complicates the work of Sister Mary Mercy's medical mission, where the sick line up outside in the hundreds and are soaked to the skin.

The Maryknoll nun's fellow physician Sister Agnus Therese writes home to her mother that they're now dealing with a thousand patients a day, sometimes twelve hundred. And the young nun laments, "So many terminal tuberculosis cases! . . . These poor, poor people!"

In the mud and heat, the stench and mosquitoes of camps and shantytowns across South Korea, workers from many government and private aid agencies are struggling to help the estimated 5 million refugees, people from both North Korea and the embattled upper provinces of South Korea. The armistice talks thus far offer little hope for an early cease-fire and a return to their homes.

"A task of monumental proportions lies ahead," Joseph P. Lehman, head of the private American Relief for Korea, reports at the end of a two-week inspection tour.[5]

The Catholic sisters vaccinate scores every day, mostly children inoculated against whooping cough, which is spreading widely in Pusan and is particularly fatal to the young in the refugee hovels.

In their summer white habits, the nuns circulate through the shantytown above their hillside mission, slipping and sliding on the yellow clay underfooting, often crawling on hands and knees into the flimsy huts, visiting those too sick to make it to the clinic.

They're dying of tuberculosis, meningitis, beriberi, malaria. The sisters—"*Su Nyo*," "practicing virtue ladies," as the Koreans address them—try to help with antibiotics, injections of vitamin B, and food.

"There seem to be no minor complaints," Mary Mercy writes. "Everything is serious."

Up at 5:15 a.m. each day, they find a queue of patients who waited through the long overnight hours, on straw sleeping mats stretching out along Taechong-dong Road. The clinic staff has grown to help meet the growing demand. The original five Maryknolls have been joined by two others—lab technician and old Korea hand Sister Herman Joseph and a young nun and pharmacy aide, Alberta Marie, who has studied Korean at Yale University.

A male Korean doctor and Korean nuns of other orders, war refugees themselves, support the Maryknoll medics. And since word spread of the clinic's opening in April, American doctors and nurses from the Pusan military hospital volunteer their time. One army doctor comes on off-duty mornings to apply casts to children with crippling spinal tuberculosis.

The clinic relies chiefly on the National Catholic Welfare Council back home in the States for medicines and other supplies. But the nuns supplement those shipments with appeals to family and friends, supporters who air-express packages to meet urgent needs. Mary Mercy, at the end of one of her long, exhausting days, writes her brother John Hirschboeck, dean of Marquette University's medical school, to ask for chloromycetin, penicillin, and other antibiotics.

"The children are so sick and pathetic!" she writes in the mission's daily diary. "We see real starvation."

THURSDAY, AUGUST 23, 1951

Alan Winnington tells of a nighttime intrusion blowing up the talks

The armistice negotiations are off.

The communist side announced it was suspending the talks early today, after the quiet of the Kaesong site was shattered by the sound of a low-flying plane followed by explosions, in what the Chinese and North Koreans say was a bombing attack on their delegation. The Americans deny responsibility.

In reports to the *Daily Worker* in London, Alan Winnington says he and other journalists on the communist side heard the plane approaching at 10:20 p.m. last night, quickly doused the lights of their press camp, and threw themselves to the ground. "I personally heard bombs fall and detonate," he reports, "and, later, I heard strafing in the direction of this delegation."[6]

No one was injured in the incident, but it comes just three days after the communist delegation sharply protested the mysterious ambush killing of a Chinese military policeman and wounding of another as they patrolled the ten-mile-wide "neutral zone" around Kaesong, which lies in North Korean–held territory. The protest blamed infiltrating U.N. forces for that attack. Witnesses, however, said the killers wore civilian clothes, and the U.S. military suggested they were either North Korean or South Korean partisans trying to sabotage the truce talks.[7]

After six weeks, the negotiations were deadlocked over the first agenda item, fixing the location of an armistice line between North and South across the Korean peninsula. The Americans reject the communist proposal to place the buffer zone at the 38th Parallel, but vague U.S. military briefings left Western reporters uninformed about the American counterproposal, until Winnington informed them.

The *Daily Worker* correspondent, regularly briefed by the Chinese, told American reporters chief U.S. negotiator Admiral Joy is demanding a demarcation line well above the 38th Parallel and in some cases north of the current battle lines, "real estate"—in Joy's words—totaling some forty-six hundred square miles. To the northerners, this would be an outrageous surrender of land.

The American journalists approach Winnington with a mixture of curiosity, camaraderie, and anticommunist disdain. Some view the pipe-smoking Englishman as haughty, others as a clever, genial man to share a drink with. Journalistically, however, all find him useful.

Being based in Kaesong, he inevitably is privy to more news than are the U.S. correspondents, housed twelve miles to the south in a parked "press train" at U.S.-held Munsan. He willingly shares his information and even escorted a handful of the Americans to a memorial service for the slain Chinese soldier.[8]

After last night's incident, he was on the spot as U.S. liaison officers arrived to investigate the reported bombing. "They refused to examine the evidence closely and refused to complete the investigation," he writes.[9]

The Americans insist their flight logs show no such intrusion by U.N. aircraft, but their radar picked up an unidentified plane flying over Kaesong at that time. They claim the "attack" must have been "100 percent staged" by the communists as a pretext to break off the talks.[10]

But Winnington, in a follow-up report, writes that his daylight inspection of the area "proves American guilt to the hilt," citing what he says are U.S.-made bomb casings he found. He suggests it was the Americans who sought to "wreck the truce talks on an issue other than their demand for a huge slice of North Korea."[11]

Whatever the case, General Ridgway in Tokyo sends a message to Kim Il-sung and Peng Teh-huai saying the Americans are prepared to resume negotiations when the other side is ready. Peking Radio, meantime, reads a statement from Peng and Kim expressing "our hope that the armistice negotiations will proceed smoothly."[12]

SEPTEMBER

SATURDAY, SEPTEMBER 15, 1951

Chen Hsing-chiu views the harvest moon and yearns for home

The starry sky is clear as crystal, ideal for gazing at the full moon on this unusually cool night of *Chungchiu Chieh*, the Moon Festival. But what is a Moon Festival without mooncakes?

As men at war have always done, men in this war think constantly of food, especially Chinese soldiers, chronically short of it. On this night it's the vision of mooncakes that obsesses Chen Hsing-chiu.

Those round bean paste–filled pastries are the centerpiece of holiday reunions across China, as families savor the sweets while viewing the harvest moon, remarking on its brightness, making out the shape of the Moon Rabbit on its surface, reflecting on the season past and the winter to come.

It has been six months since Chen and his comrades left China, and the young medic, soon to turn seventeen, feels pangs of homesickness on a night like this.

He thinks about a bakery in Taiyuan, his hometown, especially popular for its mooncakes. He sees his mother in his mind's eye and remembers childhood holidays, happier times. He reflects again, sadly, on the fact he hasn't heard from her since entering Korea. He remembers the ending of a famous Tang Dynasty poem, "I raise my head to view the bright moon, then lower it, thinking of my home village."

Upbeat by nature, the teenager tells himself at least the people back home will enjoy their mooncakes. Thanks to the revolution, "their lives are getting better every day." He even finds positives in his food situation, devoting a lengthy entry in his diary to the wonders of "compressed crackers," *yaso ping*, a Chinese army staple that was vital to the Fifth Campaign last spring. "Especially when you're in the trenches, standing by for action, they're the best source of food," he writes.

He describes how they're made from flour, yellow beans, corn meal, and spices and then compressed into hard, three-by-two-inch crackers, nutritious little meals. "So let me praise the compressed cracker, easy to carry, filling, delicious."

The quiet of this Moon Festival Saturday proves to be only a brief respite from Operation Strangle, the U.S. bombing campaign authorized by "Li Chi Wei" (their pronunciation of "Ridgway") designed to interdict Chinese supply lines immediately behind the war front.

On Sunday night, they're shaken awake by explosions and see a mountainside ablaze from napalm bombs. Chen knows of no target in that area. The Americans must be randomly bombing and strafing.

His battalion's antiaircraft gunners are frustrated, unable to spot the speeding targets in the darkness. "You're all cowards!" one shouts into the night. "Wait until daylight. I'll shoot you bastards down!"

General Ridgway himself has noted that Chinese antiaircraft artillery have become more numerous and more successful in downing U.S. B-29 daylight bombers in particular.[1]

The Americans are trying new approaches in the air war, showering the roads with four-pointed metal spikes, to blow the tires of nighttime Chinese truckers, and dropping more time-delay bombs.[2]

Riding in a truck one night, Chen is stopped by a sentry and sees teams of North Korean women up ahead hauling bombs away from the road and placing them in a trench. He's amazed at the risk-taking and courage. "How many Korean women are clearing bombs in how many places along the railroads and highways?" he wonders. A short time later, riding on, he hears a huge explosion. The bombs have been detonated.

The U.N. command now holds more than 163,000 prisoners of war. Beginning last spring, it shipped most to a huge camp on the island of Koje, a winding fifty-mile sea journey southwest of Pusan and an isolated location with more room for a growing POW population—of North Koreans, Chinese, and South Koreans who were forced into or volunteered for the northern army. Although these groups are segregated from each other, vicious antagonisms have developed within each, between committed "Reds" and the anticommunists and noncommittal.[3]

Back on the mainland, at the women's POW camp outside Pusan where KPA conscript and improbable prisoner Ahn Kyong-hee is held, the hundreds of detainees have also separated into opposing camps, just as in the men's compounds on Koje-do.

The U.S. and South Korean authorities ordain that the female "communists"—the nurses, other northern women soldiers, and southern sympathizers—wear a *W*, for prisoner of war, on the backs of their U.S.-issue olive-drab uniforms. Most southern conscripts are deemed civilian internees and wear *C.I.* on their backs.

Inevitably, the two sides erupt in rounds of chanted slogans and shouted insults aimed at each other. Occasionally, the antagonisms grow violent. The young women also band together to fend off another kind of violence, rapists among the guards. Their defense is not always successful.[4]

All undergo repeated interrogations, aimed in the case of the northerners at gaining intelligence about their army, and in the case of the C.I.'s at establishing their background and the nature of their collaboration with the invaders.

Kyong-hee at first believed this would quickly lead to her release. But despite repeated questioning by fellow South Koreans, and convincing explanations that they were forced into KPA service, neither she nor any other civilian internees have been freed.

It's easy to slip into despair. When will she ever see her family again? Are they all well? When will this infernal war end?

At the sound of a train whistle headed off somewhere, at the sight of a beautiful sunset beyond the barbed-wire fence, the young woman can grow philosophical. "How can people even think of killing one another when such sunsets are there laid out before them?" she wonders. "Isn't peace more precious than anything the war is being fought over?"

In her wartime limbo, she knows it's best to keep occupied. From early in her captivity, now lasted one year, she has helped organize C.I.'s for common goals, in one case as a leader of a hunger strike—one that included the W's. The protest won better food and real beds for both the camp's eastern, W, half and the western C.I.'s.[5] Soon afterward, the civilian internees held formal elections, and Kyong-hee, the city sophisticate from Ewha University, was chosen overall leader to represent them to camp authorities. It's a job requiring the twenty-one-year-old Prisoner 2518 to act at times as adviser and morale officer.

One day she's tapped on the shoulder by Kim Sang-im, a teenaged barracks mate she recruited as an aide. Turning around, Kyong-hee sees the girl in a new dress, from one of the regular gift distributions made by Christian missionaries, who conduct services for the faithful and often distribute lipstick, sweets, and other gifts, both to proselytize and to try to wean northerners away from communist sympathies.[6]

Showing off her new acquisition, Sang-im sighs. "Oh, how I wish I were in the streets of Pusan, all dressed up."

Kyong-hee chides the girl, reminding her that if they were not in this camp, they would be on the bloody front lines with the KPA. "It's literally the difference between life and death." Then, softening, she tells her young friend, "I'm sure it's only a matter of time before we'll be released."

Despite the antagonisms, Kyong-hee also sometimes finds herself sympathizing with the W's as well, so far from home. "What are they thinking of, these communist women?" she wonders. "Do they also think of home and loved ones before falling asleep? Do they also feel homesick? Of course they do."

TUESDAY, SEPTEMBER 18, 1951

Matt Ridgway lunches with the emperor as "Heartbreak"
bloodies his troops

Matt and Penny Ridgway have crossed the moat for the first time.

Within the gleaming, fifteen-foot-thick stone walls of Tokyo's Imperial Palace compound, the Far East commander and the Japanese emperor and their wives are having lunch. The regal hosts and American guests are celebrating the recent signing of a U.S.–Japan peace treaty formally ending World War II.[7]

As they sit down to a meal prepared by the palace's French chef, in Korea on this day men of the 23rd Infantry Regiment are pinned down on the eastern slopes of what war correspondents are dubbing "Heartbreak Ridge," a miles-long, north-south range of hills reaching to a height of three thousand feet.

General Ridgway authorized Eighth Army five days ago to send the 2nd Infantry Division on the attack to drive North Korean defenders from this steep, rocky redoubt, which overlooks and threatens U.S. and South Korean positions and movements in the Punchbowl area, twenty-five miles west of Korea's east coast.

Day after day, the 23rd Infantry's companies barely inched upward toward an enemy deeply dug into tunnel complexes and gun positions. American casualties mounted, into the hundreds. Behind them, South Korean civilian bearers zigzagged up the slopes, lugging ammunition and food on their back A-frames, and then headed back down with American dead and wounded on litters.

Late on this wet, windy day in Korea, after General Ridgway returns to his official Tokyo residence for the night, the 23rd's L Company, deploying flamethrowers along with small arms, mounts a nighttime attack on Hill 931, the highest Heartbreak promontory, and pushes the North Koreans back along the ridge. But an immediate counterattack drives the Americans off the hilltop, with heavy casualties. Four more times in the coming days, U.S. troops take Hill 931 and then lose it.

By then, the 23rd Infantry and other 2nd Division units have suffered more than 1,650 dead and wounded, as they strike first one objective and then another, looking for weak spots. Higher command finally throws all three 2nd Division regiments, reinforced by its attached French battalion, against major objectives in a single operation. It takes more than a week, after days of preparatory air attacks and artillery barrages, but all of Heartbreak Ridge falls into American hands. Untold thousands of North Koreans are killed.[8]

Matt Ridgway, having contended with them now for nine months, reflects on the fearsome terrain and untiring enemy in Korea. "Always just one more hill to seize, to keep the current position secure," he later writes.

WEDNESDAY, SEPTEMBER 26, 1951

*No Kum-sok learns how to combat the Americans
at twenty thousand feet*

By afternoon, in an awesome display of air warfare, some 250 jet fighters streak and circle through the clear blue skies over northwestern Korea, crisscrossing and climbing, diving at each other, firing bursts of machine-gun or cannon rounds, then pulling away toward new targets. It's the war's greatest dogfight thus far.

The furious battle—between 150-plus MiG-15s and 100 American and Australian jets—ends after thirty-five minutes, with both sides claiming "kills."

The Manchuria-based MiG-15s, piloted by Soviets and some Chinese, have been growing in number and stepping up efforts to counter the U.S. bombers striking North Korea's rail and road supply lines from China.[9] On many days they're succeeding, evading the Americans' F-86 Sabre jet escorts and closing in on the bombers, downing them with their four-hundred-round-per-minute cannon or forcing them to jettison their bombs and flee south.[10]

The MiG buildup also raises a new fear among U.S. commanders: that the enemy will send the jets into action in the ground war, the first such close air support for frontline communist troops. Just yesterday, a reconnaissance pilot spotted airfield construction deep inside North Korea, a sign the North Koreans plan to deploy a newborn air force of their own.

One of those newly minted pilots, nineteen-year-old No Kum-sok, is completing his MiG-15 training at an air base at Anshan, Manchuria, one hundred miles from the North Korean border.

The training has been arduous, culminating this summer with his first solo flight on the MiG. Unlike his earlier trainer planes, the MiG has only one seat, no room for an instructor. All he learned about flying the jet came on the ground, in lessons interspersed with useless ideological lectures by Korean Workers' Party political officers.

When his turn to fly solo arrived, No, strapped into the cockpit, eased the throttle forward, felt the four-ton machine roar down the runway and lift off the ground, retracted his landing gear, and pulled back on the control stick to climb. It shot up like a rocket, astounding him with the power of the gas-turbine engine. Trying to level off, but diving instead, he realized he had to throttle back to take better control and return safely to the airstrip, which suddenly looked "like a one-inch-long white thread."

His landing was less than perfect, but he went on to learn better-controlled flying and landing. His new trainer, a good-natured Ukrainian captain named Pisanenko, flew his jet alongside Lieutenant No's own MiG, designated "008," teaching him formation flying and tactics in daily simulated dogfights.

The experienced Pisanenko told No he must always fly near top speed—at 620 miles an hour—to elude the Americans' agile F-86 Sabres. Another MiG-15 pilot fresh from the flight line lectured No's entire class on airborne dueling: never fly level with the Sabres because they have the advantage of a tighter turn radius. Always maintain a higher altitude. Always attack from above and then regain altitude.

This first graduating class of Korean MiG-15 pilots is ready, and the high command has decided to deploy them into North Korea, away from the protection of a Chinese sanctuary. For No Kum-sok, former naval cadet, youngest MiG pilot in the war, it means his stratagem of a year ago—to take the spin test, go into pilot training and wait for the war to end—has backfired. "It's now safer to be in a foxhole than in a cockpit," he reflects with regret.

OCTOBER

THURSDAY, OCTOBER 25, 1951

Alan Winnington reports resumed talks make progress

The desolate village called Panmunjom, "Inn of the Wooden Door," is a place of just three crumbling mud huts, a dirt road, and a few large, hastily erected tents. But as the new site for resumed armistice negotiations, it seems to have brought a new attitude to the talks. "Very amicable" is how Admiral Joy, chief U.S. negotiator, describes this day's session, the first in more than two months.[1]

The communist side has surprised the Americans by dropping their demand that the armistice line be drawn at the 38th Parallel. They now accept the U.S. view that it should generally follow the line of contact, where the armies face each other.

The hard-fought capture of Heartbreak Ridge has added to the large swath of North Korean territory the Americans and their South Korean allies hold in the east. At the front's western end, the communist armies hold a smaller slice of South Korean territory below the parallel.

As a subcommittee of the two sides debates maps in the coming days, it becomes clear that the Americans' main objective is to bring the nearby city of Kaesong, the previous site of the talks just below the parallel, back under South Korean control, as it was before the war. "Kaesong remains the crucial issue," the *Daily Worker*'s Alan Winnington writes.

In fact, U.S. commanders have launched offensive moves in the area, trying to edge closer to Kaesong. As the subcommittee talks go on, the nearby war intrudes.

"American shells have screamed across the sky most of the morning and afternoon," Winnington reports one day from Panmunjom.[2] "Nobody could say the atmosphere is being helped by the constant pounding of American guns trying to alter the map at this stage."

When General Ridgway made overtures to the Chinese and North Korean leaders for renewed talks, he proposed abandoning the Kaesong venue, whose location in communist-held territory led to incidents and tensions between the two sides, and moving the negotiations to the no-man's-land between battle lines, near the tiny village six miles east of Kaesong and thirty miles north of Seoul.

At Panmunjom, four barrage balloons, floating at one-thousand-foot altitude,[3] mark the perimeter of the neutral zone to warn away aircraft, a job done at night by two powerful searchlights.[4] The area is guarded equally north and south by military police of the two sides.

Besides the new attitude, Panmunjom's Western journalists note the new clothes on their opposite numbers Winnington and the Australian Wilfred Burchett. The pair have donned green "Mao" uniforms. Burchett explains their personal wardrobes proved inadequate: "We only planned on being here three weeks when we came last July."[5]

The reporters, north and south, now greet each other like old friends on opening day of the resumed talks. The "U.N." press men have learned to draw on Winnington's knowledge, with his Chinese connections, of what's going on in the closed sessions. They frequent the communists' press tent, sharing news and drinks—"anti-freeze," they call it.[6]

LATE OCTOBER, 1951

Peng Teh-huai plans a war of "small bites" and an underground "Great Wall"

After a cool September, Korea has experienced an unusually warm, dry October. Across the peninsula's midsection, in the lull when the howitzers go silent, the sound that can be heard is of digging, of men chipping away at sandstone, of tens of thousands of Chinese soldiers and laborers hauling baskets of earth, pushing makeshift wagons loaded with it, driving oxcarts and pony carts full of broken stone.

Peng Teh-huai's army has been building an "underground Great Wall" since late summer, after a pivotal meeting in Peking of the Communist Party Central Committee to plot war strategy. China's leaders took a stance similar to that of the Americans: we've accomplished our mission.

Just as General Ridgway declared the U.N. goal was to push the North Korean invaders out of South Korea, and that had been done, the view in Peking was that "we had already achieved our political goal, that is, that the enemy should be driven out of northern Korea," acting chief of staff Nieh Tung-chen later explains. Now both sides look to the newly resumed truce talks to end the struggle.

Since the failure of General Peng's spring offensive, and except for an occasional larger-scale battle such as the one for Heartbreak Ridge, a stalemate has taken hold along the front. But it is to be a bloody one, a war fought over bits of ground, reminiscent of the trench warfare of World War I.[7]

The U.N. lines also have strengthened, as U.S. commanders mount localized attacks to take and hold better defensive positions. There are no gaps between units of the kind the Chinese exploited earlier in the year.[8]

Peng tells his Chinese and North Korean generals they will plan no major offensives through the rest of 1951, "unless unexpected circumstances require us to do so." Instead, they are adopting a strategy Mao calls "small bites," tactics of attrition—ambushes, overwhelming but narrow attacks to inflict heavy casualties on an enemy company or platoon, constant sniper fire to kill enemy soldiers one by one. To do so, they must be able to withdraw to a strong, secure base—their new "Great Wall."[9]

Lacking the mechanized technology of U.S. Army engineers, the Chinese do the work by hand, men wielding shovels and swinging pickaxes. They put makeshift wheels on ammunition boxes to haul away the earth. To illuminate work sites at night or deep in the lightless underground, they burn pine resin or fabricate oil lamps from shell casings or tin cans.

Underground honeycombs are taking shape. Surface trench works crisscross hilltops, covered in spots by earth-covered roofs, with walls indented every twenty feet as one-man air-raid shelters. Far below ground, long tunnels penetrate the earth, connecting hollowed-out sleeping quarters, kitchens, communications and command centers, latrines, even "club" caverns where troops can relax. Entire units can live underground, leaving only observers above.

The tunnels are usually five or six feet high and four feet wide and laid out in zigzags, to limit the enemy's field of fire from the entrance. They begin on the rear slopes and often end opening on the front slopes, in firing positions for riflemen, machine gunners, or larger weapons. This defense is built in depth, with fortifications sometimes extending miles behind the forward line. They are placed in patterns, often ladderlike ("fish-scale," the Chinese call it), which allow rear positions to fire in the gaps between forward positions.

American engineers are impressed with captured defense works. The Chinese–North Korean coast-to-coast defense has assumed "a positional character of remarkable strength," one specialist writes. Yang Teh-chi, a Peng deputy, eventually reports almost eight hundred miles of tunnels constructed and almost four thousand miles of trenches dug.[10]

But underground "positional" warfare is also punishing for the Chinese soldier, who sometimes spends most of his hours and days in the dark, dank depths, under near-constant air bombardment or artillery shelling, often among the bodies of dead or dying comrades, human excrement and garbage, rats and insects.

The bombing causes cave-ins, burying men alive. Smoke from rudimentary oil lamps sickens them. And, as ever, China's troops, whether above- or belowground, are plagued by shortages of supplies, including proper food and even potable water.[11] More reinforcements have streamed in from Manchuria, this month raising the strength of Peng Teh-huai's army to more than 1.1 million. The logistics system never catches up.[12]

NOVEMBER

LATE FALL, 1951

Ri In-mo buries the ashen remains of a young woman comrade

The well-planned guerrilla attack on a police post in the village of Agyang, along Mount Chiri's southern approaches, is collapsing in confusion.

The attackers, Ri In-mo's comrades from the South Kyongsang insurgent detachment, quickly surrounded the target, a pillbox ringed by two bamboo palisades. But the defending machine gunners kept them at bay. Then one of the sapper mines, meant to blow a hole in the fences, exploded prematurely, setting surrounding homes ablaze.

The sudden nighttime illumination has made the guerrillas easier targets. They hear enemy reinforcements arriving. Their leaders pull them back, as they try to extinguish the fires, a disaster inflicted on the very people they claim to be helping. Having done what they can, they withdraw toward their base, in a protective highland valley to the north.

Agyang, twenty miles from Korea's south coast, sits along the Seomjin River in a lowland that's relatively broad for this mountainous territory. The guerrillas hoped to tap its farms for provisions for the upcoming winter, likely to be even more challenging to their survival than the last. The stalemate at the northern war front may allow South Korea's generals to divert more troops to crushing the guerrilla nuisance in their rear. It's already a diminished threat, guerrilla numbers having dwindled to about half—some seventy-five hundred by U.S. intelligence estimates—of what they were last year.[1]

In the days following the Agyang failure, the guerrillas learn that a follow-up police sweep is about to close in on them. They must quickly move deeper and higher into the Chiri-san maze of remote peaks and valleys. But one stricken fighter will be left behind.

Choe Jong-ok was the eighteen-year-old woman whose well-aimed grenade led to the capture of the Sichon police strongpoint last spring. A later engagement left her wounded and with a broken leg. Hobbled, the Wonsan college student was taken out of combat and put to work on propaganda with Ri and his weekly mimeo news sheets.

The young woman came to confide in the older guerrilla, telling him of her widowed father's pride when she began training as a teacher, but also of her despair over her boyfriend back home, a fellow student now in the KPA. She feared he would reject her as a wife because of her deformed leg.

Ri reassured her the boy would love her even more, or otherwise wouldn't be worthy of her. Her face brightened. "You're right. I also think so," she said.

Now Jong-ok has come down with the recurrent fever long afflicting the guerrilla ranks. She's in and out of a coma, unable to walk, and must be left behind in their urgent daylight shift of base. Her comrades first conceal her in a thick bamboo grove, telling her to lie still and that they'll return later.

Around midnight, the police having passed through, Ri and others climb back down to the old base and, horrified, find that the enemy has burned the bamboo to the ground. Jong-ok was trapped and killed, burned to death. All that is left is ashes and bones.

Burying her remains, the grieving Ri In-mo regrets he never asked her for her lover's name. But he resolves that once peace returns, he'll travel to Wonsan, find the young man, and tell him about Jong-ok's devotion to him and about how courageously she fought in the Chiri-san.

A NOVEMBER NIGHT, 1951

A Chinese bayonet takes down Gil Isham

Floodlights turn night into slices of day in the valley below. The men of Easy Company see them coming, a wave of Chinese looking to take one of Mao Tse-tung's "small bites."

Since mid-October the 17th Infantry Regiment and the rest of the U.S. 7th Division have been dug into hilltop positions along Heartbreak Ridge and the northern Punchbowl, having relieved a depleted

2nd Division. They're key to a strong new defense line on the central front, dubbed "Jamestown," a dozen miles north of the old Line Kansas and twenty miles north of the 38th Parallel. The 2nd Division's capture of Heartbreak Ridge put the U.N. command in a solid strategic position and helped bring the North Koreans and Chinese back to the truce negotiations.[2]

Gil Isham was wounded for a second time in June, a Chinese bullet in the same right thigh where he was hit before. Battalion doctors found him also suffering from "combat exhaustion." He was reassigned to the division graves registration unit. But processing the dead, especially Easy Company friends, proved harder to take than combat. He requested and was reassigned back to Easy, where he is now the machine-gun sergeant for the 2nd Platoon.

This late night Isham and his gunners are prepared for the attack. He has placed his two .30-caliber machine-guns in widely spaced positions with intersecting fields of fire. Riflemen are dug in on their flanks and in between. Isham himself takes up his M-1, pistol, and bayonet.

The Chinese rush uphill behind the sounds of gongs and bugles. American artillery and mortar fire pours down on them. In the flash of explosions, attackers are seen falling everywhere. The machine gunners cut down still more. But through the darkness, Easy's defenders see some attackers have broken through.

Isham and others climb out of their holes to close around the machine guns, to shield the vital weapons. Just then an enemy soldier appears out of the night. He jabs his bayonet into Isham's midsection. Driven backward, Isham fires his M-1 from his hip, point blank, a fatal shot, spinning his assailant around, and then he collapses in searing pain.

The surviving Chinese, their attack blunted, pull back down the hill.

Treated first at the battalion aid station, Isham is evacuated to Japan, where doctors find the wound hasn't caused serious damage. The thin Russian-style bayonet did not penetrate deeply enough. They send him back to Korea and into the line.

Death along Line Jamestown is dealt out not just to enemy soldiers.

Isham learns that a friend who manned a roadblock below Easy Company's hill opened fire one day, with devastating "Quad 20" automatic cannon, on a group of civilians moving south down the road—children, women with babies, old men. He hated doing it, the friend tells him, but he had orders from commanders fearful of infiltrators. The fatal policies of 1950 and early 1951, authorizing the shooting of approaching refugees, live on in the second year of war.

The November nights soon turn freezing cold along the soaring ridgelines and in the valleys of the Taebaek range. Early winter snows follow. At Panmunjom, meanwhile, the delegations give final approval to an armistice buffer zone based on the battle line at the time a truce takes effect.[3]

THURSDAY, NOVEMBER 15, 1951

High above Korea, No Kum-sok faces his first American Sabres

A few scattered clouds drift through the clear skies north of Pyongyang as No Kum-sok's MiG fighter and seven others in his formation speed southward at forty thousand feet. They're on an early-morning mission to hunt American bombers and their fighter escorts.

Lieutenant No, novice pilot, hopes this mission will prove as uneventful as the others since his first flight in the war zone, after his 2nd Air Regiment, 1st Air Division, North Korea's first MiG unit, was moved a week ago from the safety of Chinese Manchuria to a newly built airbase at Uiju, just across the Yalu River in northernmost Korea. The move signaled growing confidence on the communist side that their deadly MiG interceptors, flown mostly by Russian and Chinese pilots and vastly outnumbering the best U.S. jet, the F-86 Sabre, were establishing air superiority over northwestern Korea, an area the Americans have dubbed "MiG Alley."[4]

One recent engagement showed the shifting balance in skies where the Americans once flew unchallenged. On October 23, some 150 MiGs pounced on 9 U.S. B-29 bombers and their 55 fighter escorts headed for a bombing run on a new North Korean airfield at Namsi, north of Pyongyang. Within minutes, brushing aside the U.S. fighters, the MiGs destroyed 4 of the bombers and badly damaged 4 others. That put a final end to daytime missions for the vulnerable B-29s.[5]

The growing confidence was evident when North Korean leader Kim Il-sung visited the new Uiju air base. Standing at attention in the pilot ranks, Lieutenant No was just thirty feet away when the Great Leader inspected the cannon of a MiG-15. "With a plane with a weapon like this, we could kill even the granddaddies of the Americans," Kim quipped. He turned to the ten-year-old boy beside him, dressed like Kim in a

Mao-style uniform, complete with puffy cap. He asked the boy if he would like to fly the plane.

"Yes," son Kim Jong-il replied.

"You will have to study very hard," his father told him.

The 2nd Air Regiment's political officers also seem to take the enemy lightly. "The cowardly Americans will flee and desert their comrades to certain death," one assured the new pilots. For once, No told himself, I hope these people are telling the truth.

Now Lieutenant No and his wingmates are on the lookout for those Americans. In the usual way, they took off this morning heading north into Manchuria, where they gained their forty-thousand-foot altitude before turning south into the combat zone.

Approaching Pyongyang, they suddenly spot Sabres, spread out behind them. They must have flown out of the blinding sun and to their rear. Just as suddenly, four American jets are diving from above, firing their machine guns, scattering the MiGs in every direction. Those four peel away, without scoring a hit, and the MiGs begin to climb. Four other Sabres are now following, but steadily falling behind, losing to the MiGs' superior climbing power. They give up, and No and his comrades turn north, homeward to Uiju.

After many months of training, No Kum-sok tells himself one new lesson has been learned: the Americans are no cowards.

Three days later, he is standing on the tarmac at Uiju when two of those daring Americans streak in without warning in their Sabres, flying low over the air base, terrifying the ground crews, strafing the flight line. After they roar off and No gets up off the deck, unhurt, he learns a fellow pilot, a good friend, has been killed sitting in his cockpit and a MiG has been destroyed.

A DAY IN LATE 1951

Yu Song-chol has two questions answered; one wins him a wife

Since the front stabilized into a kind of trench warfare, with no large-scale troop movements requiring long-range planning and his minute-to-minute attention, KPA operations chief Yu Song-chol has had time to reflect on questions he put aside in the daily upheaval of war. How and when, for example, did Kim Il-sung decide to plunge the Korean peninsula into this ruinous conflict?

Now an old friend has given him an answer.

Mun Il has been one of Yu's closest confidants since the early 1940s, when the two Soviet-born Koreans trained with other Korean and Chinese partisans in the 88th Brigade.

Under Soviet Red Army tutelage in snowy pine forests on the Amur River, thirty miles downstream from the Russian Far Eastern border city of Khabarovsk, the young men were taught intelligence-gathering and guerrilla tactics and were sent on reconnaissance and sabotage missions across the border into Japanese-occupied Manchuria. The Soviets were preparing for the day they might enter the war against Japan, the day that eventually came on August 9, 1945. They were also preparing these young Korean communists, led by Kim Il-sung, for possible leadership roles in a liberated Korea.

Yu Song-chol went on, at barely thirty years of age, to become a founding officer of the Korean People's Army. And Mun Il, former communications platoon leader in the 88th Brigade, was taken into Kim Il-sung's inner circle as secretary during Kim's rise to power in Pyongyang. The bilingual Mun Il also served as a Russian translator for the Great Leader, who never mastered the language of his Soviet sponsors.

Yu and Mun Il stayed in touch, and it's Mun Il who has now entrusted to his old comrade the story of the war's origins, a story Mun Il knows well since he was there, translating the fateful words.

It began in March 1949, during the first visit to Moscow of an official delegation from the new Democratic People's Republic of Korea. Premier Kim sought Josef Stalin's approval for a military operation to force reunification of the Koreas under the northern communists. Stalin rejected the idea, not on principle, but for practical reasons, chiefly that the U.S. occupation army remained in South Korea and the northern army was not yet strong enough.

Besides, Stalin said, Syngman Rhee's South Korea seems bent on invading the North. "Sooner or later it will start the aggression," he told Kim. "In response to the attack, you will have a good opportunity to launch a counterattack. Then your move will be understood and supported by everyone."

The Soviet leader remained cautious for months, advising Kim to keep the matter from discussion even among the Pyongyang leadership. But by early 1950 he signaled the Korean that he thought circumstances had changed. The U.S. Army was gone from the South, leaving behind a handful of military advisers. The Chinese communists had won a final victory in their civil war. The Soviets had matched the Americans with their own atomic bombs.

Kim and his vice premier and foreign minister, Pak Hon-yong, returned to Moscow in early April last year, with Mun Il again by their side. This time Stalin approved the invasion.

The Soviet Union would supply weapons and other support, but would not participate directly. Kim told Stalin that "the attack will be swift and the war will be won in three days." But Stalin also told Kim the North Korean leader must first consult with China's Mao Tse-tung. That Kim did, traveling to Peking in mid-May, winning Mao over by telling him Stalin, upon whom both depended economically and otherwise, was solidly behind an invasion.[6]

It wasn't until Mun Il filled in the background for him that Yu understood Stalin's critical personal role in the decision to go to war. At the same time, the U.S. leadership in Washington has been attributing too much to Stalin, describing the war as a move in a Stalinist master plan of world conquest, when it actually was a homegrown Korean idea that a wary Stalin warmed to slowly.

Lieutenant General Yu can have only mixed feelings regarding Stalin, Soviet premier and Communist Party general secretary. Song-chol was born in a farming area near Vladivostok in the year of the Bolshevik Revolution, 1917. He grew up in an atmosphere of Stalinist propaganda and hope for poorer people in the new Soviet Union, but also of bigotry against ethnic Koreans in the Soviet Far East.

In 1937, Stalin's forced migration policy gave Yu's family and other Koreans just forty-eight hours to pack up and move thousands of miles away to Soviet central Asia. The Kremlin dictator suspected Koreans of pro-Japanese leanings, at a time when he envisioned likely war with Japan.

For most uprooted Koreans, the mass displacement led to years of hardship. But for Yu Song-chol, life was transformed by the wartime Soviet military draft, which led to his training in intelligence gathering, his assignment back to the Far East, and his role now in his ancestral homeland, being reshaped in the Soviet image.

The stalemate at the war front has given General Yu time to ponder other things, as well, including his personal life and future.

After his chance reunion with lost love Kim Yong-ok last spring, when the army nurse gently rebuffed his marriage proposal, pretending she was engaged, he couldn't get her out of his mind. He finally yielded to the temptations of power. He had the pretty young KPA lieutenant transferred to his Operations Bureau. There he energetically courted her, and she finally succumbed to his entreaties, wedding him this fall.

LATE NOVEMBER 1951

Leaving Korea, Pete McCloskey cannot leave the war behind

In the freezing temperatures, the offshore sea spray has made the cargo net slippery with ice. But if he wants to leave Korea, Pete McCloskey must climb the ropey rungs up the side of the navy transport anchored off Pusan.

After several months of rear-echelon duty, the Marine lieutenant finally received his orders to depart the war zone. He's bound for a training assignment at Camp Pendleton, California. In charge of a group of 5th Marine Regiment men with their own transfer orders, he led them this morning to the Pusan waterfront, where they boarded the small Higgins boats now bobbing in the Sea of Japan's waves as they struggle, one by one, to reach their outbound ship's deck.

McCloskey, the ranking Marine, is the last up the net, wondering with each step of the climb whether he'll make it, as he and the hull rise and fall in the swells. He finally swings over the top and rolls onto the deck, thinking, "The war's over."

Lying there for a long minute, he reaches into his pocket. It's gone. His Silver Star—"for conspicuous gallantry and intrepidity as a Platoon Leader of Company C, First Battalion, Fifth Marines . . . on 11 June 1951"—has fallen into the sea. He smiles at the irony, telling himself once more he should have been court-martialed, not given a medal.

June 11 was one of his final days in the front lines. The 1st Marine Division was fighting to move the last few miles to Line Kansas and the southern rim of the Punchbowl. Once U.S. and South Korean forces established that defense line across the peninsula, north of the 38th Parallel, Ridgway and the Washington leadership believed they would be in a good position to call for armistice talks.

On that late-spring morning five months ago, Charlie Company and the rest of the 5th Marines' 1st Battalion had been brought forward after a few days' rest in reserve, following their capture of the Hill 610 area.

McCloskey's infantry platoon was assigned to escort a Marine tank platoon—four M-46 medium tanks—on a scouting mission three miles north up the Soyang River valley. But steady mortar fire from hidden North Korean crews slowed and finally stopped the patrol, which turned around to make it back to battalion lines by nightfall.

The Marines piled onto the tanks as they crossed a ford of the river. McCloskey was riding on the last M-46 when a deafening blast lifted the tank up, flung the platoon leader into the river, and wounded other Marines. The tank had hit a buried mine and was wrecked.

The light was fading as the platoon's two corpsmen bandaged up the casualties. McCloskey ordered his men to dig in for the night around a riverside rice paddy, creating a perimeter for a new tank platoon that arrived to replace the first and take up this forward position. But the Marines had just begun digging when they were fired on, apparently by a North Korean antitank gun hidden on a nearby knoll.

The tank gunners couldn't locate the enemy crew to return fire, and the platoon could do little but hug the ground as shells exploded around them. When the North Korean fire ceased, McCloskey ordered the platoon up and digging again. Then a sudden final round exploded in their midst, its shrapnel severely wounding four men, including the two medics.

McCloskey, himself hit by shrapnel in the right leg, now crawled from one casualty to the next, administering morphine, bandaging wounds as best he could. He then hopped up on the newly arrived lead tank, banged on the hatch, and when the tank platoon lieutenant appeared told him to take his casualties back to the battalion aid station or they would die.

"I'll get court-martialed if I leave this post," the tanker replied.

McCloskey trained his carbine on his fellow lieutenant and said he'd shoot him if he didn't comply. The men were taken back.

McCloskey would later be cited, with his Silver Star, for having "directly aided in saving the lives of four critically wounded Marines."

That medal now lies at the bottom of the sea, but the fear and pain of that day remain embedded in the memory of the young Californian, finally sailing for Japan and then home, his war receding into the past.

DECEMBER

SUNDAY, DECEMBER 2, 1951

"Ratkiller" closes in, and Ri In-mo's old friend
endures the unendurable

Tens of thousands of South Korean troops have thrown a ring around the snowy, densely forested peaks of the Chiri-san in southernmost Korea. It's the biggest antiguerrilla operation of the war. General Van Fleet calls it "Ratkiller."

Remnants of the communist guerrillas struck out from their Chiri-san havens in November in an upsurge of hit-run attacks, especially against the Pusan-to-Seoul rail line, vital to war-front supplies.[1] Mysterious explosions and fires in Pusan—destroying an arsenal and a building in the American Embassy compound—further alarmed the U.S. command.[2] Van Fleet decided it was time for a decisive blow against the insurgents. The relative lull along the northern front enabled planners to move two ROK divisions south.

The operation began yesterday. Around a 163-mile perimeter, the ROK Capital Division is tightening the noose from the south, from the direction of Hadong and Chinju, and the 8th Division from the direction of Hamyang to the north, the troops pushing in and up toward central Mount Chiri, at times flushing out guerrilla bands, driving others higher and deeper into the mountain range.[3] Insurgents and pursuers both are slowed by sometimes thigh-deep snows.

Fifteen miles north of Hadong, Ri In-mo, and his core guerrilla group, the Workers' Party cadre of South Kyongsang Province, are staying ahead of the dragnet, traversing the midslopes, mountain to mountain. At one point they see smoke rising from their former base, set ablaze by the army. Ri knows his stencils and paper stock, tools for the mimeo news bulletins he has produced for more than a year, have been destroyed. Now his only weapon is his rifle.

Climbing through the night in a snowstorm, they make their way up the two-thousand-foot Ssari peak, lying across a valley from the foothills of Mount Chiri. At dawn, exhausted and hungry, they rest below the summit, awaiting a meal of rice gruel cooked with melted snow, when someone shouts, "Enemy!" and rifle fire rings out from below. Leaping to their feet, the guerrillas scramble toward a ridge that leads away from Ssari peak.

Once they're over the ridge, the shooting stops. They're not being pursued. Taking stock, the leaders discover some of their number are missing, caught by the army or lost earlier in the predawn climb through the storm. One is Song Jung-myong, an old friend of Ri, a party colleague from their hometown in Korea's far north.

The southerners among the guerrillas have come to know Song as a quiet but reliable comrade, a northerner as notably short as his friend Ri is tall. Now he needs rescue, but in the face of the approaching army they must move on.

After some days, newly based in a relatively safe elevated valley, they learn that Operation Ratkiller has shifted elsewhere. Three men are sent back to the Ssari peak area to search for stragglers. One returns saying they found Song, heard moaning from behind rocks where he hid from the soldiers for days. He is crippled with badly frostbitten feet. Two men are dispatched with a strong *jige* wooden A-frame, and they bring him back to the unit.

His comrades remove his sneakers and see that his feet are black, or a horrible flesh-red where the skin pulls away with the footwear. Despite the clearly excruciating pain, he only grits his teeth and breaks into a cold sweat.

When a guerrilla medical team eventually arrives, the doctor says the feet should be amputated or he'll die of gangrene and infection. But they have no anesthetics and no way to obtain them, with the towns teeming with troops.

Apprised of the situation, Song quietly tells his amazed comrades to go ahead with the amputations anyway, without anesthetic. "I can stand the pain," he says. The doctor consents.

When the table is prepared, Ri and a half-dozen others hold Song down tightly as the doctor wields a saw to amputate the feet. "Like a wooden block," Ri thinks. The man's heart-wrenching screams resound through the snowy pines.

A DECEMBER NIGHT, 1951

Asleep amid snowdrifts, Gil Isham hears the enemy approach

A heavy snow is falling, whipped by wind through the bleak nighttime hours. The Korean winter, the second of this war, is taking hold in the steep-sided granite mountains on the central front.

Along a road at the foot of Easy Company's fortified hill, two men lie buttoned up in their sleeping bags beneath an abandoned truck. Snow-drifts build around them.

It was a year ago, in that first brutal winter, that Private Gil Isham and his Easy Company comrades were dug in, in the path of the Chinese deep in North Korea, awaiting their turn to join the seaborne retreat from Hungnam.

Now Sergeant Isham and his partner, a greenhorn private new to the 17th Infantry, are waiting out this snowstorm until morning. They were on a routine afternoon mission to the 2nd Battalion command post when caught on their return by the weather and the darkness, and they found shelter between the rear wheels of the wrecked vehicle.

The eighteen-month-old war is in its quietest phase yet. All across the 150-mile-wide peninsula, the Chinese and North Koreans are burrowed into their underground redoubts, facing the Americans, South Koreans, and their allies holding their own strong, interconnected defense line of bunkers and trenches.

While the Panmunjom talks go on, no one is attempting major offensive action. The communists generally mount only platoon- or company-size assaults on outposts. The Americans stress patrolling into no-man's-lands, laying ambushes and capturing prisoners.

Casualty tolls tell the story: from eighty thousand a month in the early fall, amid battles over Heartbreak Ridge and other objectives, communist casualties are now estimated to be falling to twenty thousand a month, while the U.N. command figure is dropping to three thousand from twenty thousand.[4]

Lower or higher, Gil Isham doesn't want to be in any casualty count. The nineteen-year-old combat veteran, three times wounded, is now "short." He'll be rotated out soon. He doesn't know when, and that's fine with him. "Don't think about it too much," he tells himself. "You don't want to do something different and get hurt or killed."

As the night deepens, so do the drifts around the two sleeping Americans. Then, suddenly, they're startled awake. They hear men talking. It's indecipherable, in a strange language. They're either Chinese or North Koreans, a patrol probing the valley floor below Easy Company.

The two in their sleeping bags are paralyzed with fear. Should I crawl out and start shooting? Isham wonders. Instead, he and the private just lie there, perfectly still, hidden in the snow drifts. After more tense moments, the enemy patrol moves on.

At daylight, after carefully surveying their surroundings, the two GIs climb back up the snow-covered hill and into Easy's defenses.

Before many more days pass, returning from a patrol, Gil Isham and others who landed at Inchon with him in September 1950 are told they're being rotated out of Korea. He ships out from that same Inchon Harbor and in Japan boards a transport ship back to the States for reassignment.

The young soldier diagnosed with "combat exhaustion" six months ago carries with him a heavy burden of memory, of what he has seen and done, of men he killed, of friends he watched die, of his own brushes with death, and of the inhumanity of men at war. Sergeant Isham also carries with him an unwanted extra twelve months in the U.S. Army, thanks to the "Truman year," the president's extension of all enlistments in the Korea emergency. Instead of June 1952, he now must serve until June 1953.

In Korea's deep south, the ROK Capital Division has launched an aggressive new phase of Operation Ratkiller in the central Chiri-san. Ri In-mo's party command group must again hurriedly move its guerrilla base. Green helmets seem to be scaling every ridge.

Before evacuating, Ri rushes to the tent serving as their field hospital. There's no time to take wounded and sick with them. It's a sacrifice every wounded fighter knows can befall him. The little that can be done is to try to camouflage the site.

Ri must bid farewell to Comrade Song Jung-myong. He finds the double foot amputee lying on his rough bed, leg stumps in bandages. Ri holds out a hand grenade, telling him it's to use on himself if the enemy approaches. "It's the only 'gift' I can give him," Ri tells himself.

Song smiles and pulls out his own grenade from beneath the bed. Give that one to someone else, he suggests. Then he makes a final request of his hometown friend: "Tell my wife I died a worthy death."

Taking his leave, brushing away tears, Ri joins the others in striking out higher up the mountain slope. Sometime later they hear shots and a grenade explosion down below. Flames and smoke rise from the direction of the hospital tent. The green helmets were closer than they knew. They push on, higher and farther away.

MONDAY, DECEMBER 24, 1951

A lost nun's spirit hovers over Christmas at Mary Mercy's clinic

The government in Pusan has compiled a list of 117,361 South Korean civilians it says are missing or known to have been abducted by the North Koreans in the war's early months, when the invaders impressed young southerners into their army and forced skilled workers and professionals to retreat north with them.

Speaking in Paris, where the U.N. General Assembly is meeting, South Korea's premier, John Chang, says these kidnapped citizens must be freed under any negotiated truce. They are "in precisely the same category as other United Nations prisoners of war," he says.[5]

Chang has a special tie to one of the missing, a Maryknoll nun, Agneta Chang, his younger sister, born Chang Chung-eun.

The Maryknolls at Sister Mary Mercy's Pusan clinic have heard the story of Sister Agneta from refugee nuns from the North. One of those Korean nuns, Sister Peter, has written a detailed account for the Maryknoll motherhouse in New York.

Agneta, forty-three, was the last Maryknoll in North Korea when the war broke out eighteen months ago. She was an overseer, a "novice mistress," for forty young Korean nuns of a newly established community of Sisters of Our Lady of Perpetual Help.

A month before the June 1950 invasion, and after two years of harassment by the communists, their Pyongyang convent was seized by the government, forcing the community to disperse and the frightened young women to don inconspicuous street clothes.

On the day of the invasion, the last priests in Pyongyang were arrested. The novice nuns now worried in particular for Agneta because of her American connections and her prominent politician brother in the South. They shuttled her from safe house to safe house, while a chronic back problem worsened, leaving their "saintly mother" unable to walk.

Finally, on October 4, 1950, her whereabouts somehow betrayed, an army officer and plainclothes security man pounded on the door of a village house where Agneta was bedridden in pain. They made neighbors load her, on her bed, onto an oxcart and took her away, claiming she was needed because of her knowledge of nursing. As the cart pulled away, she was heard repeating in English, "My Jesus, mercy! My Jesus, mercy!"

No one knew her fate, Sister Peter wrote, but rumors arose that a number of women in the area were shot at that time and buried in a mass grave.

On this Christmas Eve, as the Maryknolls of Pusan gather for midnight Mass in the clinic chapel, Sister Agneta is on many minds.

As the service begins, Pusan's feeble electricity grid dies, but they continue by candlelight, the priest praying, the congregants responding, on to the Christmas Gospel of Luke 2:1–14, to "her firstborn," to the swaddling clothes and the manger, the angel and the shepherds, and to the prayer on many lips, Christian and non-Christian, in Korea this season, ". . . and on earth peace to men of good will."

"It was a beautiful service in that plain little chapel," Army nurse Frances Register, a regular clinic volunteer, writes home afterward.

To the north, freezing rain falls across the war front. Only a few small clashes are reported this day, while B-29 bombers hammer targets in far northern Sinanju.[6] At the Panmunjom talks, the two sides agree to allow POWs to send letters home to their families.[7]

PART 3

1952

In the spring sky overhead
A leisurely cloud
Drifts toward the North.
I burst into tears
Before this grave of dear enemies
At the sound of cannon in the distance.

—**Ku Sang**, "Poetry on Burnt Ground," from *Brother Enemy*

THE WAR IN KOREA IS INCREASINGLY FOUGHT ON TWO fronts in 1952, on the battle line in bloody little forays to seize this hilltop or that ridgeline and in the truce tent at Panmunjom, where the clash of angry words now centers on a single issue: the fate of prisoners of war.

The Americans propose allowing their North Korean and Chinese prisoners to choose not to return to their homelands under an armistice, a notion rejected out of hand by the communist side. In South Korea's POW camps, the possibility of such "nonrepatriation" incites violence between pro- and anti-communists, climaxing with the kidnapping of an American camp commander. The U.S. Army's response to the unrest leaves scores of North Korean and Chinese prisoners dead. At the same time, the ROK Army largely suppresses communist guerrilla activity in the deep south.

The war is waged ever more viciously on a third front as well, in the northern skies, as the two sides introduce more lethal models of their dueling jet fighters, the MiGs and Sabres. Ground antiaircraft batteries inflict major damage on the U.S. Air Force, but the massive bombing of North Korean cities never stops, including the most devastating of the war against Pyongyang. The Americans' strategy, pressuring the enemy into concessions at Panmunjom, seems to be working. In Moscow, Kim Il-sung tells Josef Stalin the bombing is damaging his people's morale, and "we are interested in the quickest possible conclusion of an armistice."

Morale is low not only in the North. Seeing his vision fade of a reunified Korea, President Syngman Rhee rallies the South Korean people in opposition to the truce talks. Across the Pacific, polls show Americans are weary of the war and of President Truman, who decides not to seek reelection. By year's end, a newly elected president, a celebrated general, comes to Korea, vowing to end the fighting.

WINTER

AN EARLY MORNING IN 1952

*Another morning at war, and Chang Sang relives
a terror from a time of peace*

Caught! The girl and her mother are headed for the 38th Parallel fence, walking down a mountain path, trying to get to the South, when they are spotted by North Korean guards. Three soldiers surround them and demand to know what they're doing. The mother tells the truth. The soldiers raise their rifles and . . . *Crack, crack* . . .

Terrified, Chang Sang startles awake, looking around in the darkness. All is fine. It is 1952, she's in Taejon, and she and mother Bong-hyun are safe.

The nightmare has haunted the girl for five years, surging up from her subconscious repeatedly since that frightening spring day in 1947 when something—a miracle?—saved them from death.

Life has been hard in the South—shuttling here and there, eating poorly, relying on their church, the government, and *Umma's* scant earnings from lowly work, uncertain of their future after two years of war. But twelve-year-old Sang knows—her mother has told her—life would be worse if Bong-hyun had not decided to flee their northern home after the communists seized the family land and began arresting friends and neighbors.

By 1947, the desperate trek south—up to 4 million northerners did the same by 1948—had become risky. Northern border guards were known to beat and imprison those caught trying to cross, or simply to shoot them on the spot.

Mother and daughter traveled by train from North Pyongan as far south as they could and then covered the final miles over mountain trails, carrying just a small bag with a bit of clothing, Bible, hymnal, and money (the same *won* still circulated North and South).

Bong-hyun found a woman whom she paid to guide them to the border. If stopped, the woman told them, their story would be that they were doing laundry at a nearby stream.

But before long the guide vanished, and three North Korean soldiers appeared. They seized Bong-hyun and Sang and took them to their post. They asked Sang's mother what they were doing.

She could not bring herself to lie. Going to the South, she replied. Why? they asked. Because we are Christian.

Even at age seven, having seen the upheaval at home in Yongchon, little Sang knew these were dangerous words, that *Umma* was supposed to say they were doing laundry, but she was too honest. The soldiers looked surprised. All the girl could think of was to pray, but not in front of the guards. She asked for the toilet and was directed to a filthy place nearby.

"Oh, God, help me," she prayed over and over. As she left, she saw something frightening, a dead body lying in the brush. She rushed back. And just then a local village woman emerged from the woods, bringing lunch to the soldiers.

Seeing the mother and child, sensing their likely fate, the villager summoned an old Korean proverb, telling the soldiers that if they harmed the two, the lunch would leave a bad taste in their mouths. Three times she appealed for their freedom, but the soldiers were silent.

Finally, she added an enticement, an extra lunch later that afternoon. In an ill-fed North Korean army, the offer was irresistible.

Not only did the soldiers release them, but they showed Bong-hyun how to avoid soldiers of the Soviet northern occupation army, at a post farther ahead, and where to find a hole in the 38th Parallel fence.

Bong-hyun and Sang set off and once through the fence walked to a nearby refugee camp, their first stop on the way to Seoul.

The experience so terrified a seven-year-old girl that for years in the alternate world of her dreams, mother and daughter didn't survive. The soldiers shot them. The child's growing subconscious came to accept another thing as well: the power of prayer.

WEDNESDAY, JANUARY 2, 1952

Clarence Adams learns his army is desegregated;
his mother learns he's alive

Only a trickle of new prisoners arrives these days at Camp 5, but each group brings news from the outside world. To Clarence Adams and the other black American POWs, the most surprising is word that the U.S. Army is no longer segregated.

At General Ridgway's recommendation, the Pentagon has ordered the army's all-black units inactivated and their soldiers sent to previously white regiments and battalions.

The 24th Infantry Regiment, for eighty-five years an army symbol of segregated black soldiering, was disbanded, and its 3,000 or so troops were transferred to other infantry divisions. The men and equipment of Adams's old 503rd Field Artillery were distributed to other 155mm howitzer battalions.

At the same time, the outside world is learning more about the POWs. The two sides at the Panmunjom talks finally exchanged the first expansive lists of the names of prisoners they hold, including 3,198 Americans held by the communists.[1]

At home in Tennessee, Clarence Adams's mother learned earlier that her son is a prisoner, after being listed as missing in action for more than a year. Newspapers told of a Peking Radio report about the "humane treatment" of POWs, including a Thanksgiving Day party at which an "Adams of Memphis" danced.[2]

Their treatment continues to improve. Because of the prospect of an armistice and prisoner release, the Chinese may want healthier-looking captives. They're getting more rice, soybeans, and pork. The camp supplies pigs that the men themselves butcher and dole out.

Just as important, at the start of Adams's second winter in captivity, the Chinese had the prisoners burn their old lice-infested U.S. uniforms and provided them with blue cotton padded jacket and trousers, as well as winter caps, gloves, and padded shoes.[3] Adams's right foot, with its amputated toes, has slowly healed.

Most American prisoners still chafe under blasts of communist propaganda, at times delivered over a loudspeaker by Larance Sullivan, a deep-voiced black GI who, like Adams, finds the Chinese message of egalitarianism and racial equality appealing.

Their communist overseers have asked the Camp 5 prisoners to sign the Stockholm Peace Petition, a two-year-old global appeal to abolish nuclear weapons, lately expanded to call for an end to outside interference in Korea.

Adams signs the petition, denounced in Washington as a communist propaganda device.[4] He tells himself he's helping the cause of peace, not betraying his country. But among the prisoner huts, the white "reactionaries" and even some of the blacks think otherwise.

Meanwhile, on this day at Panmunjom, an obstacle arises in the talks on an eventual prisoner exchange. The American negotiators demand their North Korean and Chinese POWs be allowed to decline repatriation, to refuse to return to their communist homelands at war's end. The communist side dismisses the notion as "absurd."[5]

SATURDAY, JANUARY 19, 1952

In a valley of ancient temples, "Ratkiller" traps Ri In-mo

Weak from fever and hunger, Ri In-mo struggles uphill in the darkness before dawn, through the deep snow, with the help of his comrade Jo Yong-rae. Once more the Chiri-san guerrillas are fleeing encroaching troops.

The South Koreans opened "Phase III" of their Operation Ratkiller on January 6, in what planners hope will be a fatal blow.

One Capital Division regiment has spread out in a blocking position on the northern edge of the innermost peaks. The division's two other regiments have moved in from the south, in consecutive waves, and are engaged in dozens of small firefights across the wintry landscape. In the central Taesong Valley, troops report they have trapped what they believe to be the core Chiri-san guerrilla group, caught between their advancing formations and the blocking regiment.[6]

The Taesong Valley, broad and deep, runs north-south between three-thousand-foot peaks, five miles west of Chiri-san's six-thousand-foot summit. It's a place of venerable temples, in centuries past a remote, quiet retreat for reclusive Buddhist and Confucian scholars.

On instructions from the provincial Workers' Party, various guerrilla units converged there under Ri Hyon-sang, an overall commander, to better resist the developing offensive. Some questioned the wisdom of concentrating so many in one place.

The fever-stricken Ri In-mo was resting after trekking into the valley with the command group of the South Kyongsang guerrillas. He was being given medicine by his friend Jo, like Ri a dedicated party member from North Korea, a young man who impresses the older Ri with stories of having met the Great Leader, Kim Il-sung.

Suddenly, the sounds of explosions and gunfire erupted everywhere, filling the valley. Smoke rose from several directions. They sensed they were surrounded.

Ri and Jo managed to take shelter among some rocks as firefights flared up and down the valley. Now that night has fallen, having fortified themselves with rations of rice balls, they and others are climbing toward a ridgeline that should lead them away from danger. In the shadows, against the background of white, they spot a man crawling downhill toward them. They see he's a member of their unit, from a group that went ahead, and he's leaving a trail of blood in the snow.

Grievously wounded in the stomach, he warns, "Don't go up there!" A ROK machine-gun team is dug in on the crest, he says. Ri's group then disperses into the cover of the forest, to wait out the approaching day.

After sunset, they move out again uphill, the only possible escape route. For hours they make halting progress through the darkness, through snow growing deeper the higher they climb. Then, toward dawn, they hear army gunfire again, this time close by.

Something suddenly strikes Ri in the knee. He collapses into the snow. Looking up ahead, he sees others have been felled by the gunfire as well. His friend Jo rushes to him, rips a strip of fabric from his own clothing, and binds Ri's wound. As gunfire crackles around them, Jo then helps the limping Ri to a hiding place in the woods.

The loss of blood leaves Ri drifting in and out of consciousness, unaware of the time passing as he lies there. Finally, he is startled awake by someone shouting, "Don't move!" A South Korean soldier stands over him, rifle muzzle in Ri's chest. For Ri In-mo, who bid good-bye to his wife and mother in Honam-dong eighteen months ago sure he would help reunify Korea, the war is over.

At U.S. Eighth Army headquarters, briefing officers announce the operation has broken the guerrilla enemy's back. They claim eight thousand have been killed over seven weeks and seven thousand others captured.[7] The numbers provoke immediate skepticism, since intelligence reports beforehand estimated many fewer thousand active guerrillas in the Chiri-san. If true, the fatalities figure suggests hundreds or thousands of local villagers were also slain in the all-out offensive called Ratkiller.[8]

Eighth Army commander Van Fleet, celebrating the operation's success, declares that the Korean War has been "a blessing" for having awakened the world to fight the communists.[9]

The operation failed in one respect, however. The U.S. Army announcement says it's believed top commander Ri Hyon-sang was wounded, but escaped.[10]

Of the captured guerrillas, like Ri In-mo, Van Fleet says many will be "re-educated to make them good citizens." After that, he claims, they will be released.[11]

Of Jo Yong-rae and the others in Ri's group, almost all have been killed.

THURSDAY, JANUARY 24, 1952

Far from the front, a wartime death grieves
Mary Mercy's family of nuns

Alberta Marie, youngest of the Maryknolls at the Pusan clinic, has felt fatigued for days. This evening she appears in the doorway of their common room, where the other sisters relax at the end of a demanding day, and announces she has a problem: "speckles" on her arms and all over her body, small hemorrhages under the skin.

Mary Mercy and Agnus Therese rush to examine her. She's had a nosebleed all day, she says. Even her gums are bleeding. The two doctors confer and quietly speculate it's thrombocytopenia—a serious condition of reduced platelets in the blood, brought on by any of many causes.

They take a blood sample, and Sister Herman Joseph hurries it to the lab. It seems to confirm their preliminary diagnosis. Alberta is taken immediately to the army's 21st Evacuation Hospital.

It has been a trying month for the clinic nuns, and even more so for the thousands of war refugees they serve. Sharp winds off the Sea of Japan have blown down many of their tents and makeshift shacks. Others catch fire from their primitive stoves, leaving families even more exposed to temperatures well below freezing.

"We came across two young mothers who expect their babies in a matter of days," Sister Agnus writes home. "One lives in a cardboard box at present. The other is simply on the street since her tent was blown down." The sisters give them warm clothing, along with comforters made by the mission's refugee nuns from North Korea.

Even as a stalemate persists on the fighting front, the refugee situation in Pusan has neither improved nor stabilized. The longer the war drags on, the more people drift southward in hopes of finding work or assistance. It's believed Pusan's population is now well over 1 million, three or four times its prewar size.

By the weekend, Sister Alberta improves slightly, but then day by day she deteriorates again. A priest administers last rites. On Thursday, January 31, Sister Mary Mercy can see the end is near.

She spends the night with Alberta, placing a comforting crucifix in her grasp. The young nun slips into a coma, as Mary Mercy and Army nurse Frances Register, a Maryknoll friend, kneel and pray at her bedside. At eleven o'clock she breathes her last.

They bury her uphill from the clinic, next to an empty mausoleum built for the property's Japanese owner before he fled in 1945. Her soldier's coffin is borne to the grave by eight young American servicemen. In a way, Sister Alberta Marie is a war casualty as much as any.

In far-off New York, the Maryknoll mother house reports the death of the twenty-six-year-old missioner, "a beautiful religious," in a statement that envisions her interceding in heaven on behalf of "the poor, harassed people of Korea for whom she labored so happily."[12]

FRIDAY, JANUARY 25, 1952
A command blunder costs No Kum-sok's MiG battalion in blood

Amid all the death and dread, men at war fall back on dark humor to ease the tension, if only for a moment. So it was this morning, before taking off on their daily combat mission, that the MiG battalion commander joked that if he met an American pilot as inexperienced as his young Lieutenant No Kum-sok, "I would eat him alive."

Now Major Pak, Lieutenant No, and the rest of their formation of 24 North Korean jet interceptors are flying into the combat zone on the lookout for enemy Sabre jets. They're at twenty-six thousand feet, an unusually low altitude for entering North Korea and MiG Alley from Manchuria.

For months, the American F-86 Sabres and the MiG-15s, flown mostly by Russian and Chinese pilots, have dueled to a standoff over this corner of North Korea. From September to December, the Americans and their allies lost 423 aircraft of all kinds over North Korea, mostly to antiaircraft gunners on the ground, while the communists lost 336.[13]

The Sabres and other fighters have been shielding the broader American bombing strategy, Operation Strangle, which has zeroed in on North Korea's rail network. That operation is sputtering toward an end, largely because the North Koreans, fielding tens of thousands of laborers, are adept at speedily repairing damage. It's not worth the sacrifice of U.S. aircraft and pilots.[14]

American bombers have, however, managed to chase No's 2nd Air Regiment from North Korea. In mid-December, after only six weeks there, they abandoned their bomb-battered base at Uiju, just across the Yalu River in Korea, and returned to their Manchurian sanctuary and an airfield they share with Russian and Chinese MiG units southwest of Antung, where the Yalu empties into the Yellow Sea.

The MiG Alley duels may be entering a new phase. The MiG pilots—and the Americans—are growing more aware of the Soviet-built fighter's drawbacks. Although it can climb faster than the Sabre, the U.S. jet can dive faster. The MiG's cannon, slower firing and harder to sight, are inferior to the Sabre's machine guns in a dogfight. Because low-grade Soviet fuel leaves a long, telltale contrail, the MiG can be spotted from a hundred miles away. And MiG pilots have poorer visibility to their rear.

On this morning the Americans clearly have spotted their enemy before he spotted them. No Kum-sok's twenty-four-plane mission has strayed blindly into the midst of a swirling Sabre formation.

The mission commander immediately orders his jets to climb, but it's too late. In his headphones, No can hear the rattle of Sabre machine guns. Two of the Americans, lurking above and behind them, are diving at subsonic speed through the Koreans' formation, guns blazing.

No sees three MiGs plummeting to fiery deaths. Only one parachute opens. Among the fallen is Major Pak, the popular, joking battalion commander. No and the others, scattered and disorganized, turn hurriedly for home.

No now realizes the higher command's controllers should have instructed the mission to gain much higher altitude before entering MiG

Alley. The ineptitude of their superiors has cost them three MiGs and two pilots' lives.

Such dueling plays out daily in the thin icy air, miles above northwestern Korea. No Kum-sok, just turned twenty, is at the flight line every morning at 5:45, awaiting the signal to run to his plane, to take off and climb toward the stratosphere in his freezing cockpit, fearful that this may be the day he doesn't return. And as the Americans introduce faster, deadlier F-86Es and F-86Fs, and Soviet pilots field a new, improved MiG-15*bis*, more than ever it becomes a duel of technological advance and production capacity, as much as a test of pilot skills.

SATURDAY, FEBRUARY 2, 1952
Chen Hsing-chiu sees a saboteur caught in the ranks

It's a quiet morning. A bright winter sun shines outside the dark dugout shelter where the off-duty Chen Hsing-chiu sleeps. Someone nudges the teenaged medic awake. It's San-lin, the battalion runner. "There are traitors in our ranks!" he says in an agitated whisper. Chen is confused. "San-lin, what are you talking about?" The messenger explains as the worried Chen hurriedly dresses.

When the crews of the 2nd Battery went to their four antiaircraft guns this morning, they found the lenses on the gunsight scopes had been smashed, rendering the weapons useless. The saboteur had to be from their own ranks, since the guns are under guard overnight.

The battalion commander has summoned all eighteen guards from last night's shifts. Three men are on duty for each two-hour shift from 7:00 p.m. to 7:00 a.m., two in a makeshift guard tower and one patrolling the area. As each guard is questioned, Chen and others crowd around the command bunker. The commander reaches the guards of the fifth shift—3:00 a.m. to 5:00 a.m.—and Chen sees that one of them, a soldier named Tu, is trembling, his face dripping sweat. "Did you break the scopes, Soldier Tu?" the officer demands.

Tu stands mute. Another guard from that shift speaks up, saying he remembers hearing noises from the 2nd Battery area, but thought it must be the wind knocking things over.

"Soldier Tu!" the commander repeats. "Tell me, did you break the scopes? Did you do it? Say it, say it now!" The crowd of shaven-headed young soldiers, shivering, pounding hands together in the chill, are all now shouting for Tu to talk.

Finally, he collapses to his knees and admits he did it. The shouts grow louder. The commander assembles the battalion's Communist Party members, who organize a handful of older veterans as an interrogation team.

"Everyone is angry," Chen notes in his diary. "It's difficult to defend against inside enemies like this." These weapons have contended with American jets in a dozen encounters without suffering damage, he writes, but now one of their own has disabled them. "I despise him."

Soldier Tu is held and questioned over several days, a time of relative inactivity for the battalion. Finally, the interrogators gather other battalion soldiers in the cookhouse bunker to brief them.

They've learned that Tu carried out two other acts of sabotage, damaging an antiaircraft gun in the 4th Battery last September, and tampering with ammunition in December, causing it to fail when gunners opened fire on warplanes overhead.

They also learned what motivated Tu. Back home in China, before the unit departed for Korea, an uncle gave his family forty silver coins and told Soldier Tu to sabotage the battalion's mission at the war front as best he could. Now Chen understands. "A counterrevolutionary!"

The battalion sounds merciless. "We should cut him into pieces!" one gunner shouts. Soldiers begin chanting loudly, "Down with the traitor Tu!"

A battalion political commissar calms them. "The traitor will be brought to a military court," he announces. Four of the interrogators hustle the bound Tu up into a truck, and he's driven off to division headquarters.

The antiaircraft guns, on which medic Chen Hsing-chiu is training as a potential backup crewman, have become critical for the Chinese. In Tokyo on this day, the U.S. Far East Air Forces reports the loss of fifty-two American planes in January, forty-four of them to antiaircraft gunners. Chen's battalion claims some of the "kills." It's the biggest one-month loss of the war. Over nineteen months the American air losses now exceed one thousand planes.[15]

SATURDAY, FEBRUARY 9, 1952

Ridgway tries to bar "fraternizing" with Alan Winnington

Within earshot of U.S. officers, *Time* magazine's Dwight Martin steps out from a gaggle of American reporters and loudly invites Alan Winnington for a stroll along the Panmunjom road. He ostentatiously pulls out a flask, Winnington takes a swig of whiskey, and then the American does the same.

"That's to us, and fuck the military!" Martin shouts.

It's a toast defying the wishes of the supreme commander himself, General Ridgway, who put out word in Tokyo yesterday that Western reporters covering the truce talks should not engage in "fraternization and trafficking with the enemy" by meeting with Winnington and other journalists from the communist side.

A memorandum from Ridgway's chief information officer accused correspondents of "excessive social consorting, including drinking of alcoholic beverages with communist" journalists.

Martin's gesture spoke for the entire Panmunjom press corps, rejecting this bid by the U.S. military to gag Winnington in particular, as a way of asserting more American control over the flow of news from Panmunjom.

An Associated Press dispatch explains that at one point the U.S. delegation announced an end to briefings until further notice, but the communist journalists continued being briefed by their side. They, in turn, "briefed" the Western reporters. "For days that was the only armistice news the newspapers of the free world got," the AP said.

The Tokyo command seems especially upset about the "Pappy Noel affair" of late January.

The AP team at Panmunjom arranged with Winnington and his colleague Wilfred Burchett to get a camera, film, and flashbulbs—surreptitiously handed over at Panmunjom—to an AP photographer, Frank (Pappy) Noel, languishing in a POW camp in North Korea since his capture in late 1950 with the Marines at the Changjin Reservoir.

Eleven of Noel's photos made it back to Panmunjom and on to U.S. newspapers on January 24, giving the world a first glimpse of how American POWs are faring. Almost a year after the worst of the starvation, disease, and death in the camps, then under North Korean control, the surviving prisoners, now under the Chinese, look generally healthy.

Ridgway's office complained about that collaboration with the communist journalists, but the photos drew great interest and gave some comfort to POWs' families back home.[16]

In his *Daily Worker* dispatch today, reporting on his fellow journalists' defiance of Ridgway, Winnington writes that the U.S. military "has tried to keep all possible facts from the Press—driving Pressmen to come to us for the simplest information. Now Ridgway has told the public that freedom of the Press is dangerous to his aims."[17]

Those aims, the Englishman is convinced, include stalling the talks to allow more time for military gains. Winnington contends the Americans are making "impossible demands," such as voluntary repatriation, their position that their North Korean and Chinese prisoners be allowed to refuse to return to their homelands under a truce, contrary to the Geneva Conventions' stipulation that all POWs be repatriated.

As it happens, minor progress in the talks soon leads Ridgway to veto plans to attack and seize more territory.[18]

SUNDAY, FEBRUARY 10, 1952
Chung Dong-kyu's comrades are sacrificed to a
failed experiment of war

Shivering under the icy light of the stars, lying in a gully in some no-man's-land in useless ambushes, Chung Dong-kyu often broods over the waste of war, especially this war of Korean brother against brother, cousin against cousin.

The onetime teenaged medical student, now a twenty-year-old veteran of war, thinks back to the days after the panicky rout of the 3rd Division in the enemy offensive of last May, when the remnants of his 23rd Infantry reconnaissance company were sent to the rear to be refitted and rested.

That was when these North Korean refugees, the Local Volunteer Youth Group pressed into service after evacuation from the north in late 1950, were told they had passed their "probationary" period and now would be entered officially into the ROK Army rolls. This was news to Chung and the others, and they were outraged.

It explained why they had never been paid. It meant they had been fighting—and dying and being maimed—as "ghost soldiers," meeting anonymous deaths on forgotten hillsides, with no formal recognition as the heroes they knew they were. They had willingly joined in the defense of South Korea in hopes of helping achieve reunification. But the Republic of Korea, for its part, dishonored them. At that point, in mid-1951, Chung calculated that one-quarter of his unit's original 156 men were either dead, wounded, or missing in action.

But in those silent moments on ambush he mostly thinks about home, and grows despondent. He pictures his mother in Chu Ul. He mourns his interrupted ambition to become a doctor. He worries that the stalemates at the war front and in the truce talks mean he may never return to Chu Ul. But even dwindling hopes of home are what keep him doing his part day by day, now as an assistant squad leader with the rank of sergeant.

The unsuccessful ambushes became a pointless routine over the winter months.

Because intelligence officers wanted prisoners for interrogation about enemy deployments, small groups from Chung's company of scouts would venture out in the night to set up silent positions near enemy lines, to try to capture Chinese or North Koreans on nighttime patrols. They never did.

On this February morning, the company has a more elaborate assignment, to take prisoners by luring the enemy to a supposedly abandoned position. It's part of "Operation Clam-up," a decoy operation devised by U.S. commanders.

At four in the morning, the reconnaissance company moves to the 3rd Division's northernmost outpost, Hill 662. The troops holding this twenty-one-hundred-foot strongpoint then make an open show of withdrawing in the dawn's light. The hope is to deceive the Chinese, on a hill a half-mile to the north, into believing this hilltop of bunkers and pillboxes is theirs for the taking. But for Chung and his comrades, the wait proves miserable and the operation a debacle.

To maintain the subterfuge, Chung's squad in their crowded pillbox is ordered to maintain silence and not move about. In the freezing temperatures, there can be no fires, no lights. For food, they subsist on cold rice balls brought up overnight by regimental porters. Because they're forbidden during the day to exit to relieve themselves outside, the stench in the pillbox quickly becomes appalling.

As day follows empty day, the Chinese don't take the bait. But finally, in the early morning Thursday, four days after they moved into Hill 662, a sentry reports by hand signal he sees an enemy patrol approaching. His platoon leader, an inexperienced second lieutenant, then commits a fatal blunder. Rather than allow the Chinese to advance up the slope and into their trap to be taken prisoner, the nervous lieutenant sets off a line of command-detonated land mines in their path. The Korean defenders react instinctively, opening fire all along the hilltop. The Chinese flee, leaving behind three dead.

Their ruse exposed, Chung and his comrades now prepare for a full-scale attack, which comes just before two on Friday morning. Their positions are pounded with heavy mortar and artillery fire and raked with machine-gun fire from the Chinese-held hill. Then, around three, he hears on his walkie-talkie the Chinese have launched a massed infantry attack up Hill 662.

From his pillbox's firing port, through the smoke of the bombardment, Chung can see only shadowy figures running here and there. The breathless chatter on the radio tells him there's hand-to-hand combat in the compound. His squad opens fire blindly on any moving figures. Somehow in this melee his position isn't directly threatened. Finally, an order comes to withdraw across a saddle ridge to a neighboring hill. "Every man for himself!" he hears.

In the darkness—the moon has set—he and his squad dash from the pillbox. They reach the hill, designated "748," just before sunrise, with the last of the company's survivors. They're led rearward to the regimental command post, where their officers report on the operation's failure.

Stragglers come in through the day, but Chung, surveying the scene, realizes his reconnaissance company's losses have been substantial, all for nothing in the madness of war. A battalion-size force retakes Hill 662 before dark on Friday. Chung Dong-kyu hears that in places the hilltop snow was a carpet of bright red.

Across the front, Operation Clam-up's decoy tactic is a failure. The six-day experiment is ended a day early, with few prisoners taken.[19]

WEDNESDAY, FEBRUARY 13, 1952

Chen Hsing-chiu proves loyal to Mao's crackdown on "terrible capitalists"

"To the Medical Clinic and Chief Surgeon Li: I have a very important issue to report to you. . . ."

Chen Hsing-chiu is writing to division-level authorities about a discovery he fears may harm his fellow soldiers. He's sure it's the work of "sinister profiteers."

"Soldier Hu Chung-hua was injured recently in a truck rollover," he writes. "After a bandage from our Shanghai Pharmaceuticals first-aid kits was applied, his small lacerations developed into a big infected wound."

The young Chinese medic explains this happened with another soldier as well, and his experience is that such infections in the cold of winter are rare. "I immediately examined other Shanghai Pharmaceuticals kits, and pulled apart the gauze and cotton wadding, and found black, hairy mold and a foul smell."

One after another proved to be contaminated, Chen says. He urges the medical staff to check emergency kits across the division. He points out that if there's a sudden upsurge in wounded from a major battle, there's a risk of many dying from infections.

Chen is convinced that expired, rotting bandages were knowingly sold to the army. In his diary, he lashes out at the "damned profiteers, mercenaries who are causing so much suffering to our wounded Volunteers, for them to reap huge profits." These "terrible capitalists" should be put to death, the angry teenager writes.

In his report to the clinic, Chen also cites Mao Tse-tung's "Five-Anti Campaign" against corruption, announced last month in Peking. The "anti" identified by Chen in this case is No. 4, "cheating on government contracts."

The seventeen-year-old medic, who like millions of other young Chinese aspires to Communist Party membership, has his eye out for other signs of corruption as well.

Earlier this month, during political sessions in which they were told to "self-examine" and to look at others for signs of "capitalist thinking," Chen and some comrades all focused on two battalion drivers who seemed always to be smoking and drinking, getting red-faced drunk at times.

"They get the same pay we get," Chen wrote in his diary. "Where do they get so much money?"

As talk about the drivers spread around the battalion base, commanders had the two confined and questioned. They confessed to selling spare truck tires and other army items on supply runs back to China, and buying their little luxuries with the proceeds.

Chen learned one was asked why he would throw away the money on tobacco and wine. "This is war," he replied. "You don't know when you'll die. You might as well enjoy things while you can."

The two were sent back north to be imprisoned and reeducated according to Mao's dicta.

In China, meanwhile, groups of "anticapitalist activists" are parading through the streets of cities, going door to door, calling on business leaders to confess to violations of the chairman's campaigns against the "Three Evils" (corruption, waste, and bureaucracy) and the "Five Anti," the other four crimes—along with cheating the government—being bribery, theft of state property, tax evasion, and stealing state economic information. Many oblige with "confessions" in hopes of fending off worse, but grow to regret their statements as the persecution spreads.[20]

SUNDAY, FEBRUARY 24, 1952

"Soldiers are dying of starvation," Peng Teh-huai tells Peking

A weary Peng Teh-huai has sat and listened patiently as one Chinese official after another explains to the Central Military Commission why his factories or farms or railroad have failed to produce and deliver the food, clothing, ammunition, and other goods the general's troops need in their war against a rich Western power. Peng's notoriously short fuse is near its end.

Chou En-lai summoned him to Peking from Korea for the special meeting with government representatives in the hope that face-to-face dialogue might produce solutions to the worsening logistical problems. But the premier underestimated Peng's frustration with what he sees as Peking's lack of understanding of the reality of his war.

Tiring of the litany of excuses he's hearing, the plainspoken general bursts out, "You have this and that problem! . . . You should go to the front and see with your own eyes what food and clothing the soldiers have!"

He complains he has no air force protection. Supply trucks are easy targets for the American warplanes. "More and more soldiers are dying of starvation," he tells them.[21]

In fact, at times Chinese units have run out of food and have had to scavenge the countryside, "borrowing" food from local Koreans, digging up wild herbs or roots, at times surrendering to the enemy in order not to starve.[22]

General Peng Teh-huai, who as a boy begged in village streets to survive, is angry for another reason as well: he believes much of the hardship at the end of the line among his soldiers can be traced to corruption and waste along the way.[23]

Peng's outburst so startles the participants that Chou, commission chairman, adjourns the meeting.

But Peng, returning to Korea, has had his desired effect. Chou convenes further meetings and manages to get more supplies to the Korean front in the coming months.[24] The enemy notices. For one thing, in some locations, Chinese artillery units double or triple their daily rate of fire into American and South Korean lines.[25]

SATURDAY, MARCH 15, 1952

Chen Hsing-chiu learns of Soldier Tu's execution

Word spreads quickly through the battalion base camp: soldier Tu has been executed.

Several soldiers traveled to division headquarters yesterday for the court martial of the confessed saboteur. Returning today, they tell their comrades the military judges came to a verdict and sentence quickly, and Tu was taken out immediately and shot by firing squad.

"That's what he deserved," says Wang Chih-jung, one of the anti-aircraft gunners. "He 'blinded' our 2nd Battery, so we can't do our job. He deserved to die."

Seventeen-year-old medic Chen Hsing-chiu is learning that not all his countrymen are as enthusiastic as he is about the communist revolution transforming China. He notes in his diary, "I've come to understand why the Communist Party and Chairman Mao have launched a crackdown on anti-government activities. The traitor Soldier Tu has made me understand the importance of suppressing counter-revolutionaries."

But Chen, like many Chinese, cannot know the true scope, the full human cost, of that crackdown, which has targeted millions of landlords, businessmen, and other "reactionaries," and killed hundreds of thousands.

Perhaps Tu's uncle is among them—the man whose money induced the soldier to betray his comrades and smash their gunsights. "So bad, so evil," writes Chen.

The urgent summons comes as Chi Chao-chu is working on his chemistry thesis for graduation from Peking's Tsinghua University. As directed, he reports to the department's Communist Party secretary.

"Your request to join the Chinese People's Volunteers has been accepted," he's told.

Chi is stunned. That application was made more than a year ago. This timing is inopportune. Then the party representative tells him he'll be reporting not to an army base, but to the Foreign Ministry.

Bicycling to that ornate old building, Chi decides his language skills must be saving him from carrying a rifle in Korea. At the ministry he's led to an office where he finds a familiar face, a newspaper colleague of his father's from New York's Chinese community, Fang Ti-huai.

Swearing Chi to secrecy, Fang tells him they and others are being assigned as a new Chinese–English translation team for the Panmunjom talks. Security demands he not disclose this to anyone, even family. Pack your things and report back immediately for orientation, Fang tells him.

Chi returns to the university, gathers up his belongings, and then pedals to his parents' house near the Forbidden City, where his mother and little sister have finally returned from New York to join his father.

He wakes his confused parents from their afternoon nap, telling them he "just came by on a little visit. And then I must go"—his somber tone suggesting a long separation.

His father, the law school dean and political veteran, quickly grasps that Chao-chu cannot tell him everything.

"I see," he says. "It's a pile of eggs," a Chinese expression for a sensitive situation.

Tea and small talk follow, and then Chao-chu takes his leave, a son saddened by the fact he must hide from his father news of a mission that would make the old man proud.

A LATE WINTER DAY, 1952

A Sabre on his tail, No Kum-sok scrambles and survives

At forty thousand feet, far above the jagged mountains east of Pyongyang, a radioed alert comes in from their controllers: Sabres are in the area.

Lieutenant No Kum-sok and fellow pilots on the twenty-four-plane mission scan the skies. They see only other MiG-15s. Suddenly, tracer bullets streak past. They're under attack from behind, by four F-86 Sabres.

No banks his jet sharply to the right, pointing his nose north, to home. But a stream of bright red tracers follows him, flashing over his canopy. He twists his head around. A Sabre is tailing him, at his altitude and a half-mile behind.

He throttles forward and pulls back on his stick, summoning the MiG's five thousand pounds of thrust to climb. In a cold panic, he swings the stick back and forth, pounds on the rudder pedals, swerving his sleek, silvery jet to the left and right, dodging the machine-gun fire as he ascends. The glowing tracers follow—above, to the side, but not hitting him. Long minutes pass until No finally looks back, sees the Sabre growing smaller in the distance, no longer firing, unable to match his climb.

A sense of relief overwhelms the terrified No Kum-sok. He has survived his closest call.

For months, every day, sometimes twice a day, No and his comrades have taken off into Manchurian skies and turned south into North Korea to hunt F-86s, as the Sabres hunt them. Most days one hundred MiGs rise into their miles-high combat zone, and No estimates, on average, one is shot down per day. Usually it's a Russian pilot, since they're the most daring. On some days, it's many more, on both sides.

No has grown to admire the skill and courage of the Soviet flyers, many of them World War II veterans who switched smoothly to jet warfare. With his steadily improving Russian, he has enjoyed sharing meals with them in their mess hall at the joint Antung base, downing vodka rations, learning to savor thickly buttered black bread with caviar.

By late winter, however, as the initial contingent of Soviet MiG pilots is rotated home, the steady toll on their ranks has left them demoralized, questioning the purpose of such sacrifice. About one in five have been killed. The night before their departure, No hears them singing drunkenly in their barracks—in gratitude for having survived, one tells him.

The costly air war leaves Americans demoralized as well. In February, the Sabre pilot George A. Davis Jr., the Americans' greatest ace, having downed fourteen enemy planes in the war, was shot down and killed by a Chinese MiG. That dispiriting news was compounded by word from the air force major's wife in Texas about his misgivings about the air war.

"Things can't go on like they are," he wrote her shortly before his last mission. He lamented the loss of so many men and pilots, saying the MiGs "are so much better than the Sabres." She said she wished he'd died "for some good reason," but "this is a war without a reason."[26]

With or without reason, it goes on. The North Koreans, determined to rebuild their air force, have added a 2nd Air Division of MiG-15s to No Kum-sok's 1st Air Division. They have plans for a 3rd Division.[27]

In fact, that prospect of a northern air arm capable of attacking South Korea has become a roadblock in the Panmunjom truce talks. The Americans insist that any armistice agreement forbid rebuilding of airfields in Korea, an idea the communists reject.[28]

Meanwhile, without warning in early spring, the communist flyers lose the sanctuary of their Manchurian airfields. As No Kum-sok watches from the ground at Antung, a dozen Sabre jets scream in from across the Yalu River, chasing Soviet-piloted MiGs returning to the base. Five MiGs are shot down. The Americans don't attack aircraft on the ground, but begin to appear regularly in Manchurian skies in "hot pursuit," and life for No Kum-sok and the other hunters and hunted grows more dangerous.

MONDAY, MARCH 17, 1952

For Mary Mercy and her medical team, the challenges mount

The line along Taechong-dong Road, outside Pusan's Maryknoll clinic, only gets longer.

Distraught mothers and tubercular children, emaciated babies and feeble grandmothers, amputees and cripples—they all wait patiently, sometimes into the next day, for their precious turn under the knowing eye and stethoscope of Sister Mary Mercy and the other doctors.

The tragic scenes play out hour by hour through each long day, far from any war front. Some are briefly noted in the mission's daily diary.

This morning, a poor, frantic woman rushes in with a tiny, very ill baby, begging Mary Mercy, "Grandmother Doctor," to save her. She has already lost five children. Another small child seems to be breathing its last when an injection of a heart stimulant suddenly brings it back to life. Turning away from that patient, the nun physician finds an eight-year-old boy in convulsions. She ministers to him, leaving him lying peacefully on the examination table, and then comforts the exhausted mother, who has come a great distance in the frigid late winter and had to press her way through the crowds outside.

The clinic is now staffed with seven doctors—Mary Mercy, Sister Agnus Therese, a Swede, and four Koreans—and eight nurses, both American nuns and Koreans. More American military doctors and nurses are volunteering to help part-time. More than two thousand patients are treated each day, given examinations, prescriptions, injections, clean dressings, replenished medicines.

But still the Maryknoll clinic and other medical facilities in Pusan cannot keep up.

It's estimated the endless flow of refugees from the war-depressed countryside has swollen this overwhelmed city's population to 1.65 million people, many times its prewar number. Although this week's toll of combat deaths among the U.S. military—123—will be the lowest of the war thus far, among Pusan's civilians the disease and starvation seem only to worsen. More and more people are dying in the streets.

The radio news from the Panmunjom talks offers little encouragement that the fighting might end anytime soon. In the so-called Iron Triangle area, along the static central front, the two sides clash in small, indecisive, platoon-size firefights.[29]

Back in the United States, the war grows increasingly unpopular, as casualties mount and people see it's not a war to be "won," like the great conflict that ended seven years ago. Opinion polls show President Harry Truman's popularity has sunk—to about 30 percent—along with that of the conflict he drew his country into in June 1950. As winter gives way to spring, he announces he will not run for reelection in November.[30]

But Mary Mercy, just turned forty-nine, and her medical team are in it for the duration, as the daily drama of life and death goes on. In Saturday's diary she noted that the gate man "came to tell us a dead baby was out at the gate, but we were so glad to hear a tiny cry as we unfolded the blankets, so we baptized him Joseph right away. The poor mother had no milk to give him and the little baby practically starved to death."

SPRING

AN APRIL DAY, 1952

*Shin Hyung-kyu treats prisoners well, but a black
memory still clings*

In the daytime, in the sun, they feel the warmth of the early Korean
spring on their faces. But in their tents at night, in the mountains north
of the Hwachon Reservoir, the lingering chill of the hard winter keeps
Shin Hyung-kyu and his comrades in its grip.

Their B Company, 3rd Military Police Battalion, is assigned to the
central front and the ROK Army's new II Corps, under the command
of Paik Sun-yup, a fast-rising young general who distinguished himself
in the Naktong defense of summer 1950. Comprising the ROK Capital,
3rd and 6th Divisions, II Corps is designed as the most powerful South
Korean army organization yet, bolstered by battalions of new 155mm
artillery.

For now the fighting has entered a lull across the new corps' eighteen-
mile-wide front, and Lieutenant General Paik has ordered infantry probes
out to ambush patrolling enemy, to take prisoners for the intelligence
they might provide.[1]

On this day, a patrol has returned with several North Koreans and
handed them over to the MPs, who are feeding and organizing them for
a trip to a camp in the rear.

One prisoner's leg is badly wounded. The eighteen-year-old Corporal Shin sees it's infected, covered with maggots, and takes pity, trying
to help, washing it with some alcohol-rich Korean corn whiskey, and
bandaging it. He tells the suffering young northerner he'll soon be in a
hospital where he'll be cared for.

362

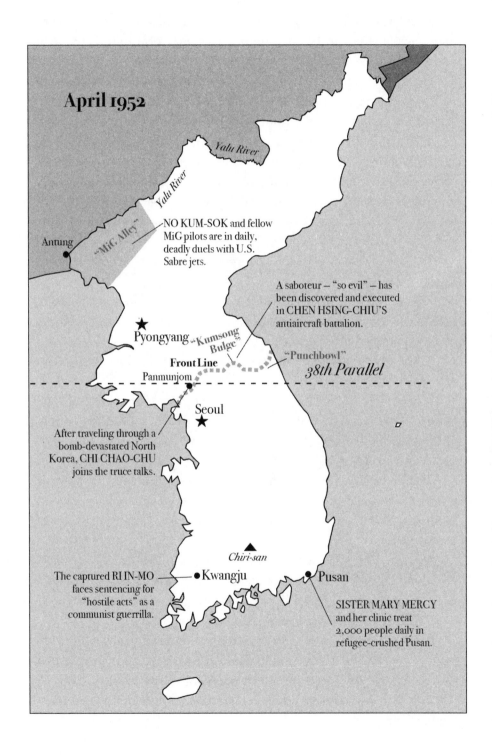

April 1952

Yalu River

Yalu River

"MiG Alley"

Antung

NO KUM-SOK and fellow MiG pilots are in daily, deadly duels with U.S. Sabre jets.

A saboteur – "so evil" – has been discovered and executed in CHEN HSING-CHIU'S antiaircraft battalion.

Pyongyang ⭐ *"Kumsong Bulge"*

Front Line *"Punchbowl"*

Panmunjom *38th Parallel*

Seoul ⭐

After traveling through a bomb-devastated North Korea, CHI CHAO-CHU joins the truce talks.

▲ *Chiri-san*

The captured RI IN-MO faces sentencing for "hostile acts" as a communist guerrilla.

● Kwangju ● Pusan

SISTER MARY MERCY and her clinic treat 2,000 people daily in refugee-crushed Pusan.

Shin has seen South Korean troops badly abuse captured enemy soldiers. But for himself, he's determined to cling to his humanity in the midst of war's brutality.

He remembers the time, during the December 1950 retreat from the North, when he was assigned to escort a North Korean prisoner to a camp thirty miles from the front line. Hitchhiking south, Shin cadged a cigarette from a fellow soldier aboard one truck they rode and lit it for the POW, loosening his rope ties so he could smoke. At a roadside food stand, the MP corporal, without any money, cajoled a woman vendor into offering his prisoner sausage and rice soup, while Shin himself went without. When he delivered him to the camp, the prisoner thanked him and Shin turned and saluted.

"We are all soldiers," he told a dumbfounded camp sergeant witnessing the exchange.

He'd learned the prisoner had a wife and two children in the North and, like Shin and hundreds of thousands of other Koreans in uniform, he simply wanted the war to end, to return home.

At the same time, a terrible, blacker vision also clings to Shin's memory, of helpless prisoners dying at his own hands.

It happened during a fire at the Pyongyang prison in the fall of 1950, when a cell overcrowded with northern POWs, a room still holding cotton-padding clothing material from prewar days, erupted in flames, apparently ignited by inmates trying to create a disturbance, possibly to escape.

The fire spread quickly, engulfing trapped inmates. As burning prisoners screamed in agony, one of the prison's U.S. military advisers shouted at Shin, "Corporal, shoot! Shoot!" The American wanted to end their suffering.

Shocked, the teenaged MP froze. "Shoot!" The American finally pulled out his own pistol and fired into the prisoners. At that point, Shin raised his carbine and began shooting point-blank at the doomed young men. He'll never know how many he killed.

Prisoners remain central to the armistice talks at Panmunjom. On April 19, the U.S. delegation tells the North Koreans and Chinese that two weeks of POW screening at the southern prison camps has found that only half the prisoners want to return home to North Korea or communist China.[2]

⎯⎯∞⎯⎯

The communist delegates stand outside the north entrance to the Panmunjom tent, awaiting the signal to enter when the Americans do, for another frustrating session of the truce talks. On this day a gangly, bespectacled new translator has joined them.

It has been nineteen months since Chi Chao-chu abandoned Harvard and America to return to the China he left as a child, to help his homeland in the conflict he foresaw in Korea. Now the twenty-two-year-old student has landed in the midst of that war, to contribute in his small way to ending it.

His journey to Panmunjom was a frightening introduction.

At Antung, on the Yalu, Chi and the rest of his translator team, in their winter army uniforms, fur caps, and heavy boots, climbed with their luggage atop the cargo on an open supply truck. They clung to the cargo ties to keep from falling as the truck lurched through a city filled with Chinese troops and with dozens of antiaircraft gun emplacements, manned by Soviet crews.

After crossing the Yalu at dusk, their convoy entered the dead moonscape of North Korea. Chi saw devastation at every turn, flattened towns and villages with only chimneys standing, burned-out shells of brick buildings, bomb craters, distant flashes of light from another town under attack. Chi told himself the Americans haven't dropped the atom bomb, but they might as well have.

After driving south for some time with dimmed headlights, they suddenly heard a rifle shot—a sentry's warning.

"*Ping chi! Ping chi!*" a shout went up. "Planes! Planes!"

They heard machine-gun fire, bits of earth ricocheting off their truck, and then the strafing fighter roaring past overhead. Terrified, they tumbled off the truck and into a roadside ditch for cover. Pressing himself facedown to the cold, damp ground, Chi's mind flashed back to the time as a nine-year-old, during the Sino-Japanese war, when he cowered among burial mounds as enemy bombers flew over Fenyang, his hometown.

No other planes appeared and the convoy resumed its journey, arriving the next morning in Pyongyang, where Chi and his companions found the Chinese Embassy reduced to operating in a bunker, with earthen floors, bare lightbulbs, and candlelight. They spent a night and day there, feeling the shudder of bombs falling near and far, before continuing on to their truce negotiations base at Kaesong.

Now, in the truce tent, the newcomer Chi has taken his place as a translator, notepad at the ready, behind the delegates at the green baize-covered table. His initiation doesn't last long.

The North Korean Nam Il, chief communist delegate, pulls out a prepared statement and denounces "barbaric" air attacks on civilians and other American actions in the war. Nam is followed by a Chinese delegate who echoes the Korean's points.

Chi watches in amazement as, across the table, Lieutenant General William K. Harrison, a deputy chief American delegate, ostentatiously rolls his eyes at his communist counterparts, in a show of disrespect.

Harrison then looks at his watch, throws up his hands in seeming exasperation, stands up, and stalks out, as the other Americans follow.

It lasted three minutes. Without having to take a note in English, Chi Chao-chu has been introduced to the theatrics and antagonisms of the Panmunjom talks and to the stern, Bible-toting General Harrison, whose attitude grates on the other side's representatives, as he whistles, sighs loudly, or drums his fingers on the table during sessions.

As it happens, however, Chi is joining a process on the verge of some progress.

The talks lately have been stalemated over three issues: which "neutral" nations should sit on an armistice oversight commission, the U.S. demand for a freeze on building or rehabilitating airfields in Korea under a truce, and the U.S. proposal to allow prisoners of war to refuse repatriation to their homelands.

In the coming days, the two sides trade concessions on the first two issues. The communists withdraw their insistence on placing the Soviet Union on the oversight commission. The Americans withdraw their demand on the airfields.

The fate of the prisoners remains the last obstacle. The communists dismiss the American claim that only half the North Korean and Chinese prisoners want to return home and reject entirely the notion of "voluntary repatriation." On this matter, the two sides seem far from agreement.[3]

In the vast POW camps on Koje Island, meanwhile, the American screening of prisoners, the demand they make a fateful choice on repatriation, continues to stoke tensions between committed communists and anticommunists.

A MID-APRIL DAY, 1952

Ri In-mo faces sentencing for his "hostile acts" as a guerrilla

The prisoner is transported back years in his mind as he confronts his interrogator.

He sees himself in 1933, a sixteen-year-old "boy revolutionary," sitting across from a Japanese colonial prosecutor in Korea's northeast. The face of the man shouting at him now suddenly looks like that angry face of long ago. The word "Red" drops from this South Korean's lips as easily as it did from the Japanese interrogator's.

Nothing has changed, the prisoner tells himself.

It has been three months since Ri In-mo was wounded and captured in the ROK Army's massive Ratkiller trap in the Chiri-san mountains. He was recently transferred from a prison camp in Kwangju to the nearby South Cholla provincial police jail. His leg wound has yet to heal, but he has been subjected to almost daily interrogations, being pressed, unsuccessfully, to identify guerrilla comrades, intentions, locations. Beatings from his guards have been just as regular.

South Korean and U.S. commanders claimed in January the Ratkiller operation was a fatal blow to the Chiri-san guerrillas. But ROK Army spokesmen now say two to three thousand insurgents remain in their mountain havens and are expected to step up attacks this summer.[4]

Ri and his fellow prisoners take courage from each other in resisting their interrogators' demands. They're newly inspired, in particular, by the example of Ko Chin-hui, a young woman insurgent who has taken her own life in the South Cholla jail.

A veteran of the Cheju island uprising of 1948, Ko joined the Workers' Party underground after war broke out. In recent weeks, the small, slight female guerrilla volunteered for a dangerous mission, to reconnoiter the Kwangju camp for a planned guerrilla assault to free their comrades. But she was caught in Kwangju, and the operation was canceled.

Ri and his cellmates were cheered by news that the surviving guerrilla force had not forgotten them. They learned that Ko was resisting severe torture by her captors. Then they heard she committed suicide in the night, throwing herself down the jail's very deep toilet pit, first covering her head with her skirt. It was said that before plunging into that dark hole, she shouted, "Long live the Democratic People's Republic of Korea!"

Hers was not the only death. At the Kwangju camp, the army regularly took ex-guerrillas sentenced to death to execution grounds at Kwangju's Mudung-san mountain, or sometimes shot them against a camp wall, in front of all, to intimidate other prisoners.

Ri has protested repeatedly that he is a regular member of the Korean People's Army and should be sent to the big Koje island POW camp. At best he is ignored. But at times the guards pull this troublesome prisoner from his cell and flog him.

Now, after his latest futile interrogation, he has been brought before a judge and peremptorily sentenced to seven years' imprisonment for "hostile acts" he committed as a guerrilla.

In a courtroom where the death penalty is routine, it is a light sentence. The judge explains he views the defendant leniently, as a war correspondent, a noncombatant. But it means Ri In-mo will languish in prison as a criminal, not as a prisoner of war eligible at war's end for repatriation to North Korea, to his home and family.

MONDAY, MAY 5, 1952
Mary Mercy's patient rolls grow as the Red Cross
sees refugees "slowly dying"

The six-week-old baby girl is just one of hundreds of sick children and adults in the tide of humanity that washes up to the front gate of the Pusan clinic every day.

The baby's father explains to Sister Mary Mercy she was born by the roadside as the family slowly made its way south, escaping the stark deprivation of Seoul, looking for work, food, and shelter. Then his wife, her mother, died of starvation. Now he has come with their six other children to ask the Maryknoll nuns to take the baby, to find it a home.

He's told the sisters will supply milk and clothing, that he can keep the child while she gains strength and he and the older children find work. The man is relieved. He's a shoemaker, he says. He'll keep her next to him while he works.

It's the start of another day, a new week tending to the needs of a refugee population that only grows, as the disruption of war drags on. Analyzing one day's work for an official survey, the sisters count 2,219 patients treated, 401 of whom are tuberculosis cases, the greatest killer in the refugee multitudes that populate the squatter settlements across Pusan.

"Such desperately sick people that it would take a book to tell about them all," Mary Mercy writes in their daily diaries.

Well into its second year, the Maryknolls' mission is expanding. A two-story children's clinic is nearing completion. They've opened a special eye clinic, whose most serious cases are sent on to a surgeon at the U.S. military hospital. They receive crates of clothing for distribution from the U.S. military's Civil Assistance Command, and even directly from soldiers and sailors, one shipment coming from the aircraft carrier USS Bataan offshore. As word of their work spreads, the nuns' motherhouse in New York receives more cash contributions, large and small.

But they can barely meet the demand. So many half-starved babies come through their gate that they have resorted to using Coca-Cola bottles for milk, with rubber nipples attached.

The typical lineup of cases one day this week brings them a woman reduced to skin and bone by tuberculosis, who walked a great distance to the clinic despite badly swollen feet; an extremely malnourished, emaciated two-year-old boy who cannot even sit up, brought from a village seventy miles away; a ten-year-old girl so swollen from beriberi that she cannot even open her eyelids; and then a case of leprosy in a little boy, and probably in his mother.

Sister Mary Mercy is struck daily with pity and awe for the mothers. "The anxiety . . . their love for their sick children . . . the length they will go in self-sacrifice, make us more eager than ever to do all we can to help them," she writes.

The international Red Cross sees a worsening situation because long-term starvation and malnutrition invite disease. Millions of displaced people in South Korea are "slowly dying," it warns in a confidential report.[5]

The starving are not only in the South. The continuous U.S. bombing in North Korea, the diversion of manpower to the military, and other factors have contributed to a shortfall in harvests, a breakdown in transportation, and a resulting shortage of available food.

The Soviets now promise to ship fifty thousand tons of food aid to North Korea. A humbled Kim Il-sung sends a letter of gratitude to Josef Stalin, telling him, "The government of the DPRK is moved by your fatherly concern about the urgent needs of the Korean people."[6]

FRIDAY, MAY 9, 1952

Bill Shinn learns of an "astonishing coup" on the U.S. prison island

It's just a chance encounter for Bill Shinn.

Walking past Pusan's rail station, the journalist crosses paths with an American acquaintance, a U.S. Army civilian employee. Aware of the Korean's good connections, the man asks Shinn what he knows about "this incredible incident at Koje-do."

Caught off guard, but feigning knowledge, Shinn draws out of the American the basic news: An important U.S. hostage has been seized by the prisoners at the giant Koje island POW encampment.

It's a huge story the U.S. command has kept secret, clearly fearing embarrassment. But Shinn needs more authoritative information.

First he goes to a U.S. Army press officer, who nervously declines to comment. Next he rushes to the office of South Korea's defense minister, Shin Tae-yong. As he did with General Chung to confirm the Inchon landing in 1950, the reporter plays on the defense minister's Korean pride, suggesting the Americans might be negotiating secret concessions to the North Koreans at Panmunjom to win their hostage's release, concessions detrimental to South Korea's interests.

The minister seems persuaded. He fills in the details of the story for Shinn, stressing he must remain anonymous as the source. Shinn then hurries to South Korean government spokesman Clarence Ryee, who also confirms the account. The correspondent has his story.

"Red prisoners of war on Koje island seized the American general commanding the prison Wednesday and are still holding him inside the stockade," he leads off his dispatch to the Associated Press in Tokyo.[7]

But U.S. military censors prevent the AP from distributing the story on its news wires. Confusion ensues. Learning of Shinn's "scoop," other news organizations pursue and write their own stories for the censors. Finally, the U.S. command, facing an open secret, announces to the world what has happened.

On Wednesday afternoon, Brigadier General Francis T. Dodd, the Koje-do commander, was asked by representatives of the six thousand North Korean prisoners in the complex's Compound 76 to meet them at the compound gate for talks. They indicated they would finally cooperate in a prisoner census, for compiling accurate POW lists. After Dodd arrived outside the gate, with the prisoner leaders on the inside, the discussion also ranged over food, clothing, and other grievances.

Suddenly, when the gate was opened to allow a POW work detail to leave, prisoners lunged outside, grabbed Dodd, and dragged him inside, locking the gate behind them. It happened so quickly that his guards, yards away, couldn't react in time.

Shinn's article notes that "the sensational capture of the camp commandant was the third major outbreak on the prison island in three months."

In the earlier episodes, eighty-nine Korean prisoners were killed in clashes with U.S. and South Korean troops. Encouraged by hard-line communist organizers, prisoners were resisting continuing efforts to screen them, to identify southerners forced into North Korean service, and North Koreans and Chinese unwilling to be repatriated to their homelands in an eventual prisoner exchange negotiated at Panmunjom.

General Ridgway is on a farewell visit to Korea before leaving his Far East command to head NATO in Paris. He instructs Eighth Army to "take whatever action . . . use whatever force" needed to free Dodd. Eighth Army commander General Van Fleet sends word to Koje-do to "wait them out." Meanwhile, U.S. troops and tanks are mobilized to head for the island. Bill Shinn and other correspondents are barred from traveling there to get a firsthand look themselves.

The North Koreans holding Dodd demand their POW association be recognized and given a telephone connection and vehicles. To meet another demand, some thirty communist leaders from other Koje-do compounds are brought to Compound 76, and Dodd is put on "trial."[8]

Through interpreters, he hears stories from prisoners about brutality among the guards, violent coercion of prisoners to refuse repatriation, theft of food and other supplies by guards, and rapes of female prisoners. At first Dodd refuses to believe such things have been happening under his command, but the weight of the testimony eventually convinces him.[9]

On Saturday morning, almost three days after he was seized, Dodd signs a statement acknowledging responsibility for prisoner abuse. Meanwhile, through a telephone link, he and Brigadier General Charles F. Colson, sent from Seoul to take temporary command at Koje-do, negotiate with the POW representatives over a broader statement. The haggling, translation, and rewriting takes many hours, but the two American generals finally sign the four-point document.

They commit to "humane treatment" of prisoners in the future, to "no more forcible screening," and to recognition of the POW association. On the prisoners' fourth point, demanding an end to voluntary repatriation, the Americans stipulate that this is subject to negotiation at Panmunjom.[10]

Dodd is released Saturday night, after two days of sensational headlines and recriminations in Washington political circles over the national humiliation of what Bill Shinn describes as "an astonishing coup"—of an American general becoming the prisoner of his own prisoners.

The episode also heightens tensions at the Panmunjom talks, where the communist side, pointing to the U.S. troop movements, accused the Americans of plotting "another massacre" of prisoners to free Dodd.[11]

Five days after Dodd's release, General Mark W. Clark, the new Far East commander, repudiates the Koje-do agreement as having "no validity whatsoever," having been made "under great duress."[12]

THURSDAY, MAY 15, 1952

A broken, haunted Buddy Wenzel is discharged from the army

The Defense Department has reported its latest numbers on American casualties in Korea: 19,096 dead and 77,025 wounded.[13]

One of those thousands of wounded, Buddy Wenzel, is finally being discharged from the Army today at Camp Kilmer, New Jersey, down the road from the family home he sought to escape when his mother approved the seventeen-year-old's enlistment four years ago.

The Chinese bullet that shattered Wenzel's right hand at the Hwachon Dam did serious damage, requiring months of rehabilitation at Murphy Army Hospital, outside Boston. The young man who devoted so much Tokyo barracks time to his female pen pals now has difficulty writing. And his wounds aren't only physical.

From Camp Kilmer, Wenzel returns home to South River to live with his mother and sisters and to take up where he left off with Dot, his hometown girlfriend. His mother soon finds her son is haunted by frightening dreams that disturb their nights, and even daytime visions.

He sees faces he identifies as refugees killed at Nogun-ri, especially a little girl he remembers spotting in his M-1 sights, the girl he believes he killed. He is convinced she is trying to speak with him.

"I was hallucinating, scaring the hell out of my mother."

His girlfriend, too, is frightened, as Wenzel slips repeatedly into angry, inexplicable outbursts. She breaks off the relationship.

Meanwhile, in Florida, James Hodges's sisters write periodically to young Wenzel, witness to their brother's death in Korea. They inform him that almost two years after James was killed in the breakout from the Pusan Perimeter, the army still has not located his body in what they imagine must be a chaotic collection of unidentified soldiers' remains.

James Hodges is one of 1,080 7th Cavalrymen killed or listed as missing in action in seventeen months of combat for the regiment, which has been rotated back to Japan.[14]

Ahn Kyong-hee is stunned and puzzled at what she's reading.

She has now languished twenty months at the women's POW camp outside Pusan. She and other "C.I.'s," civilian internees, many like her captured after being coerced into joining the KPA's southern "volunteer" auxiliary, have come to think of their release date as some distant, never attainable point on the calendar. Snatches of news about the stalled truce talks deepen their hopelessness.

But now she has a letter in her hand telling her otherwise.

The guard who delivered the anonymous note to Kyong-hee, the well-known leader of the C.I.'s, finally reaches out to retrieve it. He was told not to leave it in her hands. But she cannot let go. She must reread it one more time before handing it back.

"Please, please, do not give up," it says. ". . . Freedom is dawning for you. I am not exaggerating."

Tomorrow, the writer tells her, "there will be another—the last—interrogation of the prisoners," last in a long-running series that has done nothing for Kyong-hee and the others, despite their highly credible accounts of how they ended up in KPA uniforms.

"Do take a little more heart this time. You shall see," the note concludes.

It's signed, enigmatically, "Your Guardian."

One thing stuns Kyong-hee even more than the message itself. It addresses her as "Rosa." Only one person has ever called her that. But that couldn't be.

Chen Hsing-chiu is friendly with a soldier working for the rear-area People's Volunteers radio station. From him he has learned about General Ridgway's departure from the war zone. The seventeen-year-old medic and Chinese patriot has some ready thoughts about American commanders.

Writing in his diary, Chen notes that Douglas MacArthur predicted the war would end by December 25, 1950. "He underestimated the Chinese military," he writes. "And he made mistakes. As a result, after a couple of battles, they were defeated by the Chinese and North Korean armies. He completely lost the trust of the American government. Because of this, MacArthur was relieved of duty by U.S. President Harry Truman."

As for "Li Chi Wei," Ridgway, "even when he took over the position, they still lost battles and he had to take on a more defensive strategy. . . . All their attacks failed. He was moved to another position."

The new man is named Mark Wayne Clark, Chen has learned. "He probably won't end up well either, maybe even worse off than Ridgway and MacArthur," he predicts.

News from outside reaches the Chinese troops only sporadically—in Chen's case, especially news from home. But after more than thirteen months in Korea, with no response to three letters he wrote to her, Chen has finally received a letter from his widowed mother. Upon first seeing the envelope, the unfamiliar return address mystified him. Not until he opened it did he understand.

Writing on April 12, his mother told him she had received his letter of March 20, which he mailed to an aunt in hopes she could pass it on. "It made me really happy!" she added, because she hadn't heard from him since he entered Korea. "Some people said you died in North Korea. Some said the Americans captured you. If not, why haven't you written?" Hearing news of huge battles, she had lost all hope until receiving his latest letter.

Then she informed her son that last July she married again, this time to his uncle Po Lien, her late husband's older brother, and moved from Taiyuan to his home in Antse, a mountain town one hundred miles to the south. That explained Chen's lost letters: they were not forwarded by the postal service.

"We are doing well," his mother wrote. "My life has been settled. I hope you continue to fight hard in North Korea, learn and listen to the orders of your leaders." She closed with an order of her own: "Reply to this letter as soon as you get it."

He did, telling her of the lost letters, reassuring her that he is well, and telling her he feels better now knowing she has someone to care for her. He finished by announcing he has "made up my mind." After the war, he hopes to become a Communist Party member and join the new Chinese government. "This is my ambition and my dream."

Chen, his fellow medics and the rest of their antiaircraft artillery battalion have moved into a new, well-camouflaged position, on a plateau giving them a broader view of the skies to better carry out their mission of protecting the howitzers of the 28th Artillery Regiment. Their 12th Army is now holding the very center of the peninsula-crossing front line, north of the Heartbreak Ridge area.

They and the rest of General Peng's expanded antiaircraft arm continue to inflict losses on U.S. airpower. Together with the growing communist MiG force over northern Korea, they have finally forced the Far East Air Forces to suspend all daytime bombing by the vulnerable B-29s and B-26s, leaving daylight raids to the fighter-bombers, faster but capable of only lighter bombloads.[15]

WEDNESDAY, MAY 21, 1952

Ahn Kyong-hee reports for interrogation

The day has dawned clear and cool. It has been an unusually dry May across Korea's far south.

Under close guard, almost five hundred prisoners have been trucked this morning from the women's POW camp north of Pusan to an interrogation center in a nearby compound, a place they know well.

When her turn comes, Ahn Kyong-hee steps before a U.S. Army officer sitting at a desk with a Korean interpreter.

"Are you prisoner Number 2518?" she is asked. "Yes," she replies.

"What is your name?"

"My name is Ahn Kyong-hee."

"Which side are you on?"

"I am on the side of the Republic of Korea."

"Do you mean that you are anticommunist?"

"Yes, I do," she says.

The interpreter tells her she now must go see the "repatriation officer." He smiles. Kyong-hee, already confused by yesterday's anonymous letter, is further mystified. A smile from the interrogators? What does it mean?

She's directed down a corridor to a door on which is stenciled "Commander—Repatriation Office." Opening it, stepping inside, she sees a uniformed ROK Army officer behind a desk. He stands up and smiles.

Strangely, he seems familiar. Accustomed to lowering her eyes before camp authorities, she now dares to stare at this man for a long moment.

Finally, shocked, she blurts out, "Han Muk! Is it you?"

She bursts into tears. He comes forward with arms open and embraces her. She can only weep, in her confusion and joy at seeing this man she was so close to in the terrible summer days of 1950. She knew that only Han Muk would call her "Rosa," as in yesterday's unsigned letter, a pet name he gave her back in 1950, saying Rosa was a character in a favorite novel. But she was sure Han Muk was dead, last seen by her in Chung Paui Kol led away by three KPA soldiers as an accused spy.

They sit on the office's small sofa as the questions pour out of her: What happened? How is it he is here? Who is he, really?

They talk for almost an hour as he explains he was, indeed, a spy, a ROK Army intelligence officer sent into KPA-held territory with authentic-looking credentials as a member of the northern security police. One of his missions was firing off those nighttime rockets as signals to U.S. planes.

When he was detained that day, Han explains, he warned the three soldiers they'd be severely punished for mistreating a member of the secret police. He showed them his papers and told them this was a clear case of mistaken identity. The soldiers, uneducated peasants, grew worried enough to unbind his hands. He instantly seized one's rifle and, in a furious few seconds, bayoneted all three. Fleeing Chung Paui Kol, he eventually crossed back over to the southern side.

"Don't you think it's a miracle that we should now be face-to-face like this?" he asks the still-dazed Kyong-hee.

He located her father in Pusan, he tells her, and learned some sad news: her younger brother, the junior ROK Army officer, was killed in action.

It's a sudden blow to the young woman.

"Are you sure, are you positive?" she finally asks. He assures her it's confirmed and says her brother was very brave, much admired by his men. The emotions tearing through her are almost overwhelming—first confusion, then happiness, now yielding to sudden grief.

It's time to go. The women POWs are boarding trucks outside. Han tells her that she and the other civilian internees will be released in a few days, after first being transferred to a center at Masan, farther south. The few days of detention Ahn Kyong-hee was promised when she was seized by ROK troops almost two years ago are finally at hand.

WEDNESDAY, MAY 28, 1952

Pete McCloskey is presented with the Navy Cross and troubling memories

In Paris this day, riotous protesters led by French communists pour through the streets, denouncing the arrival of "the killer" General Ridgway to lead NATO. In Korea, poor weather keeps much of the U.S. Air Force grounded.[16] But the day is balmy and peaceful at southern California's Camp Pendleton, and Pete McCloskey, his Korea days months behind him, finds the only foe he faces is an opposing team of officers in an afternoon game of volleyball.

An enlisted Marine rushes up. "Lieutenant McCloskey!" He's wanted immediately at the base theater. Puzzled, he begs off the game, hurries down to the theater and is directed to a back door. Onstage, he discovers the Marines are hosting a live national radio show extolling their accomplishments in that far-off war, and he's a featured guest, to be presented with the Navy Cross, second only to the Medal of Honor as an award for heroism.

A narrator recounts the action of May 29, 1951, at Hill 659. Someone supplies sound effects, crumpling paper to simulate machine-gun fire. A band plays. The senior officers present, Marine regulars in dress uniform, look askance at the sweatsuit-clad reservist McCloskey. Did no one tell him? No worry. It's radio.

On that foggy May 29 morning—could it be only a year ago?— Charlie Company's new commander, First Lieutenant Spike Schening, aroused his troops for a bloody day with his usual "Up and roll your gear!"

McCloskey's 1st Platoon was to lead an assault. In the predawn gloom, he took his men back up the ridgeline where the evening before he and corpsman Dickson had strayed and encountered a North Korean sentry, who was then shot by McCloskey. Now they passed by that soldier's corpse as they crossed the final uphill stretch, shrouded in fog, toward the first North Korean trench line. McCloskey was at the point with two of his squad leaders, their squads trailing behind.

The rising sun began to lift the fog and McCloskey saw the dim figure up ahead of an enemy soldier sitting behind his machine gun, eating rice from a silvery bowl. The former Stanford University outfielder pulled the pin on a grenade and flung it with all his might, like a throw to home plate. The machine gunner barely got off a round before the explosion killed him.

Alarmed heads popped up from the trench above and enemy grenades followed, rolling down the hill, exploding, doing damage in the trailing platoon.

"Fix bayonets!" McCloskey ordered. Leading the charge over the final yards, he was the first to crest the top of the trench and found a dozen North Koreans below preparing more grenades. He opened up with his carbine, sweeping back and forth, emptying the thirty-round clip. Marine bayonets killed the survivors.

"We've got 'em by the balls!" McCloskey was heard to shout. "Let's squeeze 'em!"

He led his Marines farther up the ridge, where he surprised more North Koreans gathering on the reverse slope for the fight. He emptied his second thirty-round clip into them as survivors fled. The attacking squads rooted out and killed other enemy from the bunkers and foxholes as the 5th Marines' Charlie Company completed the capture of Hill 659, an objective that had held off troops of the sister 7th Marine Regiment for two days. The record showed forty North Koreans killed and twenty-two captured.

On the Camp Pendleton stage, before four hundred assembled Marines, the citation is read, "The President of the United States of America takes pleasure in presenting the Navy Cross to Second Lieutenant Paul Norton McCloskey Jr., United States Marine Corps Reserve, for extraordinary heroism. . . ."

Scenes from that May day crowd the twenty-four-year-old Californian's memory: of the platoon's navy corpsman Tom Burchick, toting a fallen Marine's unwieldy Browning automatic rifle, and screaming, "Look out, Lieutenant!" as he opened fire, blasting four North Koreans about to shoot McCloskey from behind; of the platoon locked in a grenade duel with dug-in enemy on the next hill, and Private First Class Whitt Moreland rolling over onto an exploding grenade, sacrificing himself to save McCloskey and others, an act honored by a posthumous Congressional Medal of Honor; of another platoon in Charlie Company overrunning a regimental headquarters, coldly executing at least one wounded enemy soldier, and watching as their platoon leader, McCloskey's friend, shoved a captured North Korean major off a thousand-foot cliff.

The radio ceremony over, Pete McCloskey returns in the morning to his Camp Pendleton training job, preparing other lieutenants, future platoon leaders, for what they'll face in Korea. He can never prepare them for all of it. Nor can he ever describe the look on the young faces of the Koreans in that first trench that May morning, their short lives about to be snuffed out by a big American with an automatic weapon, faces that are to haunt their killer's memory for the rest of his days.

WEDNESDAY, JUNE 4, 1952

Bill Shinn follows a political crisis on the home front

While trench warfare grinds on in the hills up north, and the truce talks bog down, President Syngman Rhee has mounted an all-out offensive against fellow South Koreans in the tense provisional capital of Pusan.

With little justification, the autocratic leader has reimposed martial law on the city and surrounding southern provinces. He has had eleven opposition members of the National Assembly arrested on baseless charges of plotting with communists and driven more than thirty others into hiding.[17]

The intimidation campaign stems from the seventy-seven-year-old Rhee's determination to change South Korea's 1948 constitution before his four-year presidential term expires this summer. The constitution stipulates that the National Assembly elects the president, but the high-handed Rhee has so alienated fellow politicians he knows he would not be reelected. He demands instead a constitutional amendment providing for direct, popular election of the chief executive. That would require a two-thirds parliamentary vote.

Day by day, Bill Shinn follows the developments, filing dispatches informing the world that South Korea's government, defended by U.S. and other troops in the name of "freedom and democracy," may fall to pieces and fall under military rule.

Pro-Rhee rallies, the only kind allowed, rock the city center. Taxis equipped with loudspeakers crisscross Pusan blaring slogans. In one demonstration, an estimated ten thousand gather to shout their allegiance to the president, who issues a statement describing them as "delegates of the people."

Shinn circulates among his well-developed government sources and learns that Rhee has received an urgent message from the American president. "Korean government informants said Truman wrote that he was 'shocked' by the political crisis," the journalist reports. This may stay Rhee's hand in his plan to dissolve the parliament, Shinn writes.

The standoff simmers on as the assembly's anti-Rhee and centrist members refuse to muster a quorum and consider Rhee's amendment, until finally a mob of six hundred people—pro-Rhee politicians from the provinces—besieges the National Assembly, demanding approval of the amendment. They catch one assemblyman and beat him badly, before police end the violence.[18]

The crisis reaches a point at which top Korean generals secretly approach the U.S. Embassy's number two, E. Allan Lightner, to seek U.S. approval for putting Rhee under house arrest and having the National Assembly elect a new president. The plan is debated but rejected at the State Department, because it's believed the Pentagon would oppose a change in South Korean leadership in the midst of war.[19]

Seeing no way out, the National Assembly relents and adopts Rhee's amendment, after police force some members to attend.[20] As the only figure with his national standing, the old independence campaigner and unification champion will win 70 percent of the vote against token opposition in the August 5 election.

FRIDAY, JUNE 6, 1952

Shin Hyung-kyu sees the "war of the outposts" claim its victims

Like moles burrowed into tens of thousands of holes in the Korean earth, a half-million armed men face each other across the front line of a war turning two years old, a line winding from the Yellow Sea east 150 miles to the Sea of Japan.

The June nights explode with the sights and sounds of conflict—the echoing thunder of big guns, the streak of machine-gun tracers over a shadowy landscape, the bursts of light from illumination rounds and flares, the sudden eruption of flaming pillars of napalm.

But it's a conflict of little gain or loss, other than of men's lives.

A year ago General Van Fleet observed that the fluid war of pursuing the enemy and pursuing victory had ended, and a new defensive war had begun. On "Line Kansas," the U.N. forces' core defense line built by tens of thousands of men of the Korean National Guard, a network of log-and-sandbag bunkers, linked by trenches, now stretches from the mouth of the Imjin River, northeastward paralleling the river's south bank, then east to the huge Hwachon Reservoir and the Taebaek Mountains and on to the east coast, generally running a few miles north of the 38th Parallel.

The bunkers, on forward slopes, are manned by machine-gun crews. Revetments atop the trenches are cut through with firing bays for rifle-men. Mortar crews are dug in on the reverse slopes. Engineers even cut roads up the back slopes, for tanks to move up and fire from protected ridgeline positions.[21] By some measures, the fortifications and firepower eclipse those of the western front in World War I.

Fifteen divisions hold that line—nine South Korean, five American, and a British-led Commonwealth Division, in all some 248,000 men. Opposing them are eight frontline Chinese armies and three North Ko-rean corps, 290,000 men. Hundreds of thousands more back up the two sides as reserve and support troops.[22] Young Corporal Shin Hyung-kyu is one of them.

As a military policeman, Shin's two main duties are escorting Chinese and North Korean prisoners south, and U.S. and South Korean troop convoys north, to face the enemy guns.

On the central front, where his MP battalion supports the U.S. IX Corps and ROK II Corps, the mountain roads are dangerous, both be-cause they're rough and narrow and because enemy patrols at times stage ambushes. In the lead jeep, Shin shows the way, guiding U.S. Army truckers whose confusing maps and ignorance of Korean place-names might otherwise lead them straight into enemy strongholds.

In the swelter of a late spring heat wave, Shin and fellow MPs have drawn the assignment of escorting troops of the U.S. 45th Infantry Di-vision northward in Operation Counter, one of those limited tactical advances that now define a seesawing war. The relatively inexperienced Americans, most from the Oklahoma National Guard, have been given the mission to drive the Chinese from eleven hilltop positions the generals have decided give the enemy too good a view of U.S. Army movements.

The "Okies" jump off on this early June night and easily rout the few Chinese defenders from most of the observation posts. But two eight-hundred-foot-high objectives prove tougher, Hill 255, to become known as Pork Chop Hill, and Hill 266, Old Baldy.

The 45th Division riflemen pushing up the slopes are cut down one by one by heavy automatic fire and a rain of grenades. Others hug the ground for cover. Regrouped, they take Pork Chop Hill after an hour's firefight, but the defenders a mile away on Old Baldy hold out.

The assault platoons call in artillery support, and five hundred howitzer rounds pound a summit already stripped "bald" by months of shelling. Drifting smoke drapes the hillsides. The Americans shift to the rear slopes and, shortly after midnight, manage to seize the crest, littered with dead Chinese.[23]

Over four weeks, in taking and then defending the hilltops against almost daily Chinese counterattacks, the 45th Infantry Division suffers 275 men killed.[24] Shin saw the "deuce-and-a-half" trucks taking the young Americans forward. Now he sees the ambulances coming back down those same bruising roads.

A hardened veteran at age eighteen, the "boy soldier" remembers the desperate days of retreat in late 1950, when he was recovering from his own wound after his checkpoint was ambushed, and rumors spread through the hospital that the Americans would soon abandon South Korea. But they stayed and are still dying, in this "goddamned country" that he hears them cursing, helping "goddamned gooks" that they seem to hate.

"I don't care what they say," Shin thinks. He can't help but feel grateful.

Operation Counter is typical of a "war of outposts" along the front line, as both sides maneuver for small advantages while the Panmunjom meetings drag on.

Shin Hyung-kyu, student turned refugee turned soldier, listens for the latest scraps of information about the truce talks, and meanwhile steals away in any free time to read, study, and reread his little footlocker library of science books, and to dream of a return to school and of a future, once this war ends.

A DAY IN MID-JUNE 1952

Ahn Kyong-hee walks out a prison camp's gates, a free woman

Anticipation turned yesterday into a holiday for the women prisoners at the transient center beside Masan Bay, on the south coast twenty miles from Pusan. Gathering in circles after dinner, they broke out in song, delivered impromptu farewell speeches, quietly wept with joy and with the melancholy of parting from friendships forged in the stress and privation of POW life.

The morning dawns crisp and bright. Ahn Kyong-hee and the other civilian internees pack up their few belongings and exchange final goodbyes. Most are too nervous even to eat breakfast.

When each group is called by the guards, they file toward the main gate and into the outside world, some met by relatives, some boarding trucks taking them closer to their hometowns.

Kyong-hee spots them beyond the barbed wire—her father, mother, younger sister, and brother. They've driven over from Pusan. Han Muk, her "guardian," is with them. She passes through the gate and rushes to them, embracing each one by one, tears streaming down her face.

The twenty-two-year-old woman is to forever reflect on this horrible war that took two years from her life and all the remaining years from her young brother's life, separated her from her family, left her fearful every day for their well-being, and made her a murderer, with an indelible blot on her conscience. The vision of a drugged, helpless man plunging to his death can never leave her.

President Truman on June 10 approved General Clark's plan to release Ahn Kyong-hee and the other thirty-seven thousand civilian internees, those judged to be southerners forced into North Korean service.[25] On that same day, the U.S. military took bloody action against North Korean prisoners judged to be dangerous.

After the humiliation of the General Dodd kidnapping last month, the command was determined to end the northern loyalists' domination of large Koje-do compounds, by dispersing the North Koreans to smaller, controlled compounds on Koje-do, on Cheju Island farther south, and in the Pusan area.

Because the inmates in hard-line Compound 76 on Koje-do, site of the Dodd episode, refused to be moved, the new camp commander, Brigadier General Haydon L. Boatner, sent in troops of the 187th Airborne Regimental Combat Team, backed up by tanks. The prisoners were waiting in trenches with homemade knives, spears, and pikes.

The paratroopers attacked with tear gas, concussion grenades, bayonets, and gunfire, in a two-and-a-half-hour battle that left 31 POWs and 1 American dead as well as 139 North Koreans and 14 Americans wounded. The U.S. command reported some dead prisoners were killed by the loyalists.

Clearing out compounds through June, the U.S. troops free scores of "anti-Reds" held prisoner by the loyalists. In one compound, No. 77, they find the bodies of 16 murdered prisoners.[26]

SUMMER

THURSDAY, JULY 10, 1952
Chi Chao-chu scours the dictionary for incendiary words
to hurl at Panmunjom

At the desolate tent village of Panmunjom, the armistice negotiations are now a year old, lasting longer than anyone anticipated when first convened. The two sides remain deadlocked over a single issue, the question of prisoner repatriation.

The Americans say their position—that under a truce North Korean and Chinese POWs be given a choice of not returning to their homelands—is "solid, final and unchangeable." The communists counter that voluntary repatriation would flout the Geneva Conventions and amounts to "forceful retention."[1]

To Chi Chao-chu, the Chinese translator, the process has degenerated into a charade.

The sessions grow shorter and the recesses longer. Some of the most heated arguments are over the schedule, not substance. Loud, vituperative voices fill the truce tent. And yet one day Chi had to sit frozen in his chair as the delegates faced each other stonily across the negotiating table in total silence for a half hour.

Because General Harrison, now the chief U.S. negotiator, speaks so rapidly when angry, Chi has had problems keeping up in his note taking. He and translation partner and good friend Kuo Chia-ting—they're "Little Kuo" and "Little Chi" to each other—then sent for Gregg shorthand manuals from Peking. In their spare time, they mastered the skill.

Weary of the tedium, Chi and other interpreters decided one day to spice up the language of vituperation. "'Liar' and 'lying' have lost their punch," they told each other.

Poring through an American dictionary, they hit on the word "perfidy," explaining to Chinese delegates it means "treachery" or "bad faith."

A delegate tried it out, in English, in one tense session. The American across the table flew into a rage, demanding the word be withdrawn. The Chinese stood his ground. "You are perfidious," he added. The red-faced American shot back, "You are just a bunch of common criminals!" and stormed out of the tent.

In their boredom, the goading can sink to schoolboy pranks. Speculating one evening that Harrison would walk out of the next session, the translators came up with a scheme. The next day the general took offense over some minor point and did, indeed, stalk out. On cue, as soon as he left, the Chinese burst into loud laughter, suggesting to reporters and others outside that the American had said something foolish and lost face.

In their off hours, in the ninety-degree heat and monsoon rains of July, the interpreters contend with other challenges at their barracks-like housing five miles away in Kaesong. Mosquito nets help fend off one pest, but ravenous fleas get through and torment them. Chi has taken to sleeping in buttoned-up shirt and long underwear, with stockings pulled over his hands and feet, even in the steamy July nights. Still he awakens with welts all over face and neck.

Through it all, Chi, soon to turn twenty-three, keeps alive his hope the war will end soon, he can return to university studies in chemistry, and someday he can help build China's atom bomb. The daily backdrop of artillery fire beyond the talks' neutral zone reminds him of his good fortune in not being at the front, and of the death and destruction wrought by every day's continued failure at Panmunjom.

Meanwhile on this summer Thursday, at bases throughout the Far East, the U.S. Air Force is preparing a massive bombing attack on Pyongyang. They call it "Operation Pressure Pump," a bid to use American airpower to pressure the communists into concessions in the stalemated talks.[2]

SUNDAY, JULY 20, 1952

Alan Winnington witnesses "the horror of Pyongyang"

Hundreds of American planes flying more than twelve hundred sorties over most of a day have bombed, napalmed, and strafed Pyongyang in the biggest air attack of the war, described by U.S. commanders as a blow against military targets in the North Korean capital.[3]

Alan Winnington is now there and finds something different. "Hundreds of people could be seen in the dawn light searching, turning over rubble, looking for their little possessions or their dead," he reports in a dispatch to London's *Daily Worker*.

At one hospital, he reviews a daily report showing eighty casualties treated—thirty-one women, twenty-one children under age sixteen, twenty-two adult male civilians, and only six soldiers. "If the Americans had been less concerned with terror against civilians, they could have tried a little harder to hit some military targets," he writes.[4]

Pyongyang Radio reports fifteen hundred buildings destroyed and seven thousand people killed, wounded, or missing in the July 11 air strikes.[5] Winnington cites almost four thousand dead or missing in the debris.[6]

Operation Pressure Pump dropped fourteen hundred tons of bombs and twenty-three thousand gallons of napalm. It extended beyond the capital to seventy-eight North Korean towns and villages considered part of the military supply line from China.[7]

"For ten miles or more around the city, nearly every village had two or three bombs flung at it in passing," reports Winnington.[8]

The British communist correspondent has come to Pyongyang from Kaesong, where he is covering the stalled truce talks at nearby Panmunjom. The savage pounding of the capital is aimed at forcing the communist side to yield more at those talks. The Far East Air Forces operations chief, Brigadier General Jacob E. Smart, has made clear the Tokyo command views civilians as an auxiliary to the military, and a target of that pressure.

Smart directed that his staff find military targets "so situated that their destruction will have a deleterious effect upon the morale of the civilian population actively engaged in the logistic support of the enemy forces."[9]

Winnington tells readers about the horrors in particular of napalm, "the jellied petrol atrocity" that sticks to and burns through the skin. "Many people die horribly from the burns and shock, and still more survive as walking monstrosities sickened by their own images," he writes.

He tells of Cho Chong-suk, "a beautiful girl in her late teens," whose face is so badly burned that "the doctors could not at first discover the line of juncture of the eyelids." When she finally saw herself in a mirror, she screamed and ran from the hospital, looking for a way to kill herself.

For those who survive, the healing of napalm wounds means "the hands become drawn backward like claws of birds, the eyelids are pulled up and down, leaving bulbous eyeballs staring, apparently terrified, from wide red frames of the out-turned eyeball itself." People must try to sleep with eyes open since the lids will not close, he reports. "Burned little children become petulant, sleepless, impossible to soothe."

Winnington suggests napalm is designed not so much to kill, but to disfigure, to produce "living corpses whose appearance will strike terror into others, and to break morale."[10]

In the aftermath of the devastating attack, Kim Il-sung has sent an "extremely urgent" telegram to Josef Stalin in Moscow, appealing for more antiaircraft weapons, interceptor jets, and trained Korean pilots. He tells the Soviet leader, "The enemy, making use of this situation, makes demands in the negotiations that are unacceptable to us."[11]

For his part, Winnington writes that it's time "to debunk the American pretence that such madness can bring peace nearer. It can only make any settlement more difficult."[12]

A MIDSUMMER AFTERNOON, 1952

Misery breeds dangerous talk among Chung Dong-kyu's comrades

In the hills above the Pukhan River, on the central front seventy miles northeast of Seoul, the temperatures climb regularly into the nineties. The malarial mosquitoes and the flies, the rats and snakes, the mud from monsoon rains, and the smell of an army at war all help make life dismal for the men of the 23rd Infantry's reconnaissance company, now dug in like regular infantry troops on a hilltop of stumps, splintered wood, and shell craters.

Worst of all is the shortage of food. Most mornings Chung Dong-kyu and the rest of the company's rank and file are each given a day's ration of less than a cup of rice, to be cooked in their canteen cups, and some pickled vegetables. Too often they must forage for edible greens or scavenge for abandoned crops and food stores at vacant farms.

The men know why they're so hungry: the top-down corruption in the ROK Army is siphoning off rations at every level, for sale in towns in the rear.

On this stifling afternoon, a half-dozen soldiers gather in Chung's trench to trade war stories and complaints. The talk eventually turns to a riskier topic: desertion.

Such talk goes back months. One night in early spring, three of the company's men, members of Chung's original group of North Korean refugees, talked their way past a forward listening post, saying they were hunting for food, and never returned. Chung and others had heard the trio discuss defecting.

The discontent is unsurprising. The stalemate in the war, the infrequent need for the company's scouting skills, the weeks and months of being cooped up in trench lines and bunkers leave them with idle time for grumbling about empty stomachs and mistreatment by the ROK Army. Such grievances first grew out of the discovery last year that, as North Koreans, they hadn't been accorded full status—or any pay—as ROK soldiers in their first months in combat.

A few weeks after the three men deserted, several soldiers gathered one day in Chung's trench to pass the time with talk about the latest rumors and problems.

One, an older man who had been a supply truck driver, surprised them with a scheme: to steal a truck and drive to the far south and the great mountain Chiri-san, where they'd heard northerners were fighting a guerrilla war. They'd be welcomed by the insurgents, he assured them.

Chung listened, but said little.

Now several of the same group have returned, and the subject of desertion arises again. But this time Chung is distracted, hardly hearing them. He has developed a severe headache. His body aches. Soon he feels chills, his teeth chattering. He climbs up to sit in the sun. He's covered in sweat. Finally, he collapses, toppling over. Pulling himself up, he staggers off to report to his platoon leader, who sends him to the regiment's dispensary.

Chung has malaria, the scourge of Korea. The medics inject his arm with the antimicrobial drug Salvarsan and tell him he must stay overnight. Because of swelling and pain from the injection, he cannot sleep. He has waking dreams and visions. He sees himself as a thirteen-year-old in Manchuria, lying in the hospital after his emergency appendectomy, his mother sitting at his bedside. It has been many months since he told her he would return to Chu Ul in three days. Through the night in this frontline dispensary, he longs to sense her dozing beside him, holding his hand.

In the morning, his symptoms have abated. The talk of desertion among his transplanted northern comrades also subsides, as all wait for some word, some sign of hope for an end to the fighting.

MIDSUMMER, 1952

Asleep or awake, Korea memories possess Gil Isham

In Korea the contest for the hilltops goes on interminably.

Americans and Chinese, North Koreans and South Koreans, fight and die, win and then lose back objectives given such names as Bunker Hill, Siberia, Finger Ridge. They look important on the map to a tactician, but seem absurd to soldiers on the ground who must carry dead comrades off a promontory that will be given back to the enemy the next day.

In far-off Fort Ord, California, where he has been assigned as a drill instructor for basic trainees, Sergeant First Class Gil Isham climbs those hills and fights the war in his subconscious, in nightmares so disturbing he has begun trying to fend off sleep. He is always a prey, always on the run from an enemy giving chase.

Even during waking hours, he has flashbacks to his fifteen months in Korea. One day he sees children quibbling over food in a restaurant, and his subconscious recalls a time when he saw Korean boys fighting over food scraps in army garbage and one boy grabbing a big rock and bashing the skull of another.

After returning from Korea last January, he tried to tell people what it was like over there, "and they looked at me like I was crazy." He stopped talking about it. And he began drinking heavily.

THURSDAY, SEPTEMBER 4, 1952

Peng Teh-huai, in Moscow, gets an earful from Josef Stalin

The gruff and domineering Peng Teh-huai, a fighting soldier since his teenaged years, sits quietly by as a stout old man with a drooping mustache lectures him on how to wage war.

Your front lines are too close to the enemy's, Josef Stalin scolds, and you're using too few land mines. Your Chinese pilots need better training. And as for the supposed absence of ranks in the egalitarian Chinese military, the Soviet leader is dismissive. "They think that all this is against communism," he says. On the contrary, "ranks . . . insignia . . . awards" have "great importance."

Stalin is holding forth before an illustrious audience at the Kremlin: from the Far East, Chinese Premier Chou En-lai, North Korean leader Kim Il-sung, Korean War commander Peng, and several other Chinese generals, and on the Soviet side such leading communists as Vyacheslav Molotov and Georgy Malenkov.

Chou has been in Moscow for two weeks, with a delegation of dozens of specialists, for detailed negotiations over long-range Soviet economic aid to the young People's Republic of China. He now has been joined by Kim and Peng to meet with Stalin to discuss the war, more arms for the Chinese–North Korean forces, and approaches to the Panmunjom armistice talks.

Kim, in particular, seems deeply concerned. Asked by Stalin about the "mood" of his people and military, the North Korean says it is "good . . . if the bombing is not considered." He goes on, "In view of the serious situation in which the Korean people have found themselves, we are interested in the quickest possible conclusion of an armistice."[13]

It was two and a half years ago that a thirty-seven-year-old Kim Il-sung traveled to Moscow to win Stalin's approval for invading South Korea, assuring the Soviet general secretary the war would be over in three days.[14] As their ultimate sponsor and military supplier, the North Koreans and Chinese want Stalin's acquiescence in an armistice. But before the truce talks started more than a year ago, the Kremlin chief told Mao Tse-tung he favored a "drawn-out war," one that would keep the Russians' American adversary bogged down in Korea for a very long time.[15] He still shows no enthusiasm for a speedy peace.

On the issue of "voluntary repatriation" and the communists' opposition to this U.S. plan to allow war prisoners to refuse to return to their communist homelands, Chou has floated a compromise idea to Stalin: having a neutral nation, such as India, screen those prisoners.[16] But Stalin rejects the entire notion that captured North Korean and Chinese soldiers would decline repatriation. "It ought to be declared that we do not believe this," he says.

Instead, he favors another idea: if the Americans retain 20 percent of the POWs they hold, China and North Korea should retain 20 percent of the American POWs, to bargain over them after a cease-fire. The Chinese and Koreans listening to him know the U.S. negotiators would never let that happen.

Stalin closes the subject by telling them to stall. "Nothing new ought to be offered" in the talks, he says, and then turns to questioning Peng about the state of the war. "Are the Americans fighting well?" he asks.

It's a chance for the Chinese commander in chief to boast—and to exaggerate. He tells Stalin his forces are "80–90 percent successful" in their attacks, while the Americans succeed in only one of one hundred attacks, that communist pilots and antiaircraft crews have shot down 5,800 American aircraft, and that his army has taken more war prisoners than his enemy has.

All these statements are untrue, but Stalin is a receptive audience.[17] In his separate meetings with Chou, he has disparaged the U.S. military. "It's been already two years, and the USA has still not subdued little Korea. . . . America's primary weapons are stockings, cigarettes and other merchandise," he joked to the Chinese premier. "They want to subjugate the world, yet they cannot subdue little Korea. No, Americans don't know how to fight."[18]

Chou stays on in Moscow for three more weeks, but Peng and Kim quickly return to the war, with no useful direction from the Soviets on the armistice talks. At least the military aid will continue. Stalin promises more jet fighters for North Korean pilots and many more antiaircraft guns. "Send us a list of materials you need," he tells them.[19]

FALL

SUNDAY, OCTOBER 5, 1952

An air attack claims the life of Chen Hsing-chiu's "Elder Brother"

The sun is just lifting above the horizon on a clear morning when a terrifying whine and roar shatter the calm. Four F-80 fighter-bombers streak in from over a mountaintop to the south, dive toward the battalion's camouflaged camp, drop four bombs, and fire off a hail of machine-gun bullets, in a swift attack that's over before the antiaircraft crews can reach their guns. The Americans plainly detected the Chinese air defense base previously and waited for a vulnerable moment to strike.

Chen Hsing-chiu, awake for only a few minutes, grabs his medic's kit and dashes toward the area of the attack. As the smoke clears with no calls for help, he believes no one has been hurt. Then, from another direction, he hears the screams, "Medic! Medic!"

He rushes over to the clinic area and finds fellow medics bending over their comrade Li Wen-hai, leader of the team, Chen's mentor and teacher during a year and a half at the war front.

Li has been wounded grievously in the chest and abdomen by shrapnel or bullets, his ribs crushed, the ground beneath him coated with his blood. Chen sees his face go white. He knows there's nothing they can do. But one of them shouts, "We've got to get him to the field hospital!"

They gently place the unconscious Li onto a stretcher. A stunned and weeping Chen and three others lift the four corners and begin a slow trot toward the hospital, more than a mile away. A dozen other men follow. Halfway there, Chen realizes he must return to the base. It's his duty shift, and others may need help. A fellow soldier takes over on the stretcher.

On Monday morning, word spreads that team leader Li Wen-hai has died. Seven grieving comrades organize to dig a grave. They find an auspicious spot according to *feng shui* principles, facing China and a large wood, and dig a perfectly proportioned resting place. Young Chen is given the honor of inscribing an epitaph for his "Elder Brother"—name, army unit, date of death—on two wooden planks, one to go into the grave, one as a marker above.

The battalion commander presides over the burial of his chief medic—"Comrade Li Wen-hai, Shanhsi Lan County man, twenty-eight years old, poor peasant origin." He pays tribute to Li's courage in the anti-Japanese war and the communist revolution, listing the battles in which he took part.

"He repeatedly braved enemy fire to rescue wounded comrades," he says. He ends with a call for the battalion to strike back in Li's memory. "Revenge!"

It comes the next day. The gunners now man their weapons before dawn, watchful. In early afternoon, a dozen B-26 bombers and F-80s approach. All the battalion's guns open fire in unison, filling the sky with white puffs of exploding shells and sending an F-80 into a fiery spiral, to crash into a hillside. Li Wen-hai's vengeful comrades let out a cheer.

WEDNESDAY, OCTOBER 8, 1952

Alan Winnington sees a U.S. bid to "wreck" negotiations

At Panmunjom, the communist negotiators last Thursday delivered a damning protest to the U.S. side over the latest shocking news from the prisoner-of-war camps in the far south. American troops killed fifty-six Chinese prisoners during a riot at a compound on Cheju Island. The communist note denounced it as a "barbarous yet cowardly massacre."[1]

On this day, however, a wet and unusually warm one for October, it's the Americans who break off the stalled truce talks.

The two delegations are returning from a ten-day recess during which General Harrison, the lead American negotiator, urged the communists to consider and accept his side's latest proposals on the deadlocked POW issue.

The proposals amount to a tinkering with details of the long-held U.S. position: that North Korean and Chinese prisoners be allowed to choose not to return to their homelands under an armistice, a position consistently rejected by the other side, citing the Geneva Conventions' stipulation that all POWs must be repatriated.

These days they meet in a wooden conference building built after a summer typhoon blew down the original tent. Speaking first, the communists surprise the Americans, saying all Chinese prisoners must be sent back to China, but indicating agreement to some "nonrepatriates" among North Koreans.[2]

Harrison, hearing only partial acceptance of the U.S. demand, launches into a prepared statement in which he unilaterally calls an indefinite recess in the negotiations, until the other side accepts the American position or "makes a constructive proposal of your own." The army general lectures the communists on what he views as their credo "that the individual is the property of the state." He accuses them of "completely ignoring their rights as men" by denying prisoners a choice.[3]

Briefed by the Chinese after the sixty-three-minute session,[4] Alan Winnington reports to *Daily Worker* readers that it's the "most serious of all efforts to wreck the talks completely."

After a year of covering the on-off negotiations, the British communist correspondent remains convinced the Americans prefer continued war to an early truce.[5] General Clark, in Tokyo, sees it differently. "I can only conclude that they do not sincerely desire an armistice," the Far East commander says of the communists in a statement to journalists.[6]

As the negotiations bog down, the turmoil in the southern POW camps only worsens. In the weeks to come, American and South Korean guards at a compound on the island of Pongam kill eighty-four North Korean and southern communist prisoners in what the U.S. military says was an attempted mass breakout.[7]

At the war front, the death toll mounts daily in the heaviest fighting in more than a year, as the Chinese attack repeatedly along the central front to gain better positions before winter sets in. Thirty-five miles northeast of Panmunjom, they are in the third day of furious assaults to drive the South Korean 9th Division off strategically placed Hill 395, White Horse Hill, in a battle taking on the look of a classic determined defense by an improved South Korean army.[8]

MID-AUTUMN, 1952

No Kum-sok feels he's "wagering my life against mere chance"

The young MiG pilot, risking death with every takeoff, is troubled by unsettling dreams. Among them is a vision of New York's Empire State

Building, a scene from a long-ago schoolbook. It rises like a spire, above the clouds, and he's flying toward it.

No Kum-sok, the boy with the blonde pinup in his childhood bedroom, inherited his fascination with America from his late father, the railroad official and baseball fan. He also inherited his father's dislike of communism, something No buries deep inside. Self-preservation is his number-one mission, both in the air and in North Korea's communist system.

That's why, at the Naval Academy, he made sure he won top grades from his political instructors. That's why he joined North Korea's communist Workers' Party at his MiG base in Manchuria, making such a show of dedication that he now has been named party deputy for his battalion and is called on at assemblies to read, with great fervor, statements from Kim Il-sung.

Inside, however, No despises the priggishness and backstabbing of party members. He is appalled by the ruthlessness of one-party rule, by the expulsion of one comrade from the air force because his brother fled to South Korea, for example, and by worse. He learns that a colonel in another air division was executed without trial after being accused of planning to defect to the south. The twenty-year-old lieutenant is also resentful at having been passed over for promotion.

His anger at his predicament grows daily. He and other North Korean MiG-15 pilots have finally been equipped with the advanced, faster MiG-15*bis*, which the Russians have been flying in Manchuria. But the Americans' improvements to the F-86 Sabre give them a clear edge in air combat. More and more MiGs are shot down, and No feels he is "wagering my life against mere chance."

One day, with his good Russian, he's chatting with an older Soviet mechanic he has befriended at their Antung base. The Russian, who helped train North Korean pilots before the war, tells No about a Korean pilot who flew south, defecting, with his Ilyushin propeller fighter plane in early 1950.

No hasn't heard the story before. He hasn't known that a flying defection has ever been done.

WEDNESDAY, NOVEMBER 5, 1952

Chi Chao-chu is a "war hero" in combat-free Panmunjom

In a landslide vote, General Dwight D. Eisenhower has been elected president of the United States, defeating Democrat Adlai Stevenson. The news leaves Chi Chao-chu and his fellow Chinese interpreters at Panmunjom perplexed and worried.

They know that during a bitter election campaign centered on the Korean stalemate, Eisenhower vowed no "appeasement" by his administration, railed against "godless communism," and spoke of "cracking the communist front."

His bunkmates in the translators' barracks turn to Chi, the longtime U.S. resident and Harvard dropout, to explain "your Americans" and the bellicosity.

"Pure reactionary rhetoric," he tells them. But he himself is at a loss. Anyone looking at a map can see that China was merely defending its borders by entering the Korea conflict. China isn't trying to conquer the world. And the only real "front" he sees are the U.S. bases confronting East Asia, from the Philippines to Japan, far from America. Some bases clearly hold atomic weapons. "They could easily do to us what they did to Hiroshima and Nagasaki," he tells himself.

His comrades look to Chi not only because of his American experience, but also because they're quietly aware of his connections, through the prominent Peking communist Chi Chao-ting, his elder half-brother. In addition, Chao-chu has unintentionally won some status as a truce-talks "hero."

It happened when a stray artillery shell landed in the Panmunjom neutral zone. No one was hurt, but the U.S. delegates rejected the communist assumption it was an American shell. A joint inspection was ordered and Chi went along, notebook in hand.

Above the impact crater, the two sides continued to bicker over who was to blame. Chi was the first to notice a second round half-buried in the earth. "There's an unexploded shell in there," he said in his booming voice. The others all shrank back, but the tall, rangy Chi, without a second thought, jumped into the crater. "Little Chi!" his friends shouted.

Peering through his thick glasses, Chi took notes on the shell's markings, clearly American. A flustered American officer, shown the findings, could only blurt out, "Well . . . accidents happen!" The daring young translator, meanwhile, was the recipient of much backslapping on returning to the barracks.

The advancing Korean winter has rid those barracks of summer's fleas and mosquitoes, but introduced new miseries.

The building is unheated. As temperatures plummet, the men take to sleeping fully clothed, their padded cotton hats pulled down over their ears. Some still awaken in the morning with white spots of frostbite on the tips of their noses. Meanwhile, the stream where they bathed freezes over, leaving them waiting for spring to fully wash.

The daily work routine, a month after the Americans suspended the full-scale truce talks, has settled into debates over truce-zone violations, treatment of POWs, and updates of prisoner lists. In mid-November, however, at the United Nations in New York, India introduces a General Assembly resolution to try to break the crucial impasse over prisoners.

To deal with the question of POW repatriation, the resolution calls for establishment under a truce of a commission of neutral nations to take control of those prisoners said to refuse return to their communist homelands and to verify their choices. The proposal offers a potential basis for resumed negotiations.[9]

SUNDAY, NOVEMBER 16, 1952

A dutiful Chen Hsing-chiu slips away to visit a snowy grave

In the hills of late autumn along the central front, temperatures are dipping below freezing. Chen Hsing-chiu, with a fallen pine branch, brushes away the windblown snow from atop the grave.

The thick overcast means the Americans aren't flying and the anti-aircraft battalion is standing down. It's a good morning to visit Li Wen-hai's burial place. More important, it's the start of the seventh and final week of the traditional mourning period after his comrade's death.

Chen gathered steamed bread, buns, and vegetables to take as an offering. As he approached the wooded site, tramping over the soft carpet of snow, he suddenly, spontaneously, burst into tears, surprising himself. "How much I have missed him!"

With the snow swept away, he can read the marker, his own writing in seven characters: "Comrade Li Wen-hai's grave." He quietly sobs. "He taught me, took care of me and set a great example for me . . . like a true brother," the eighteen-year-old medic has written in his diary. "This kind of camaraderie and brotherly relationship is a much stronger bond than a father-son relationship!"

He thinks back to his father and his death, when the boy Hsing-chiu didn't even cry, until Mother slapped him, drawing a little tear. In these many months of war, Chen Hsing-chiu grew closer to Medic Li than he had to anyone else in life, other than Mother.

Chen places the offerings on a small wooden altar they set atop the grave after Li's burial. He stands there lost in thought. Scenes of working together on wounded soldiers, of joking and eating together, of talking about life after the war, play out in Chen's mind.

There are no flowers to be had, so he burns slips of paper, "ghost money," in the ancient Chinese way of providing for the dead in the afterlife. Twenty minutes go by. He bows three times, turns, and heads back to camp. He feels strangely elated. He has fulfilled his duty to his friend.

The war's third winter is approaching. Just to the south, the opposing forces, including a division of Chen's 12th Army, are in the final throes of a battle that has grown from an expected few days into six weeks, one of the biggest of the war.

General Clark had authorized a limited offensive thrust—by the U.S. 7th and the ROK 2nd Divisions—to seize heights north of Kumhwa, to better defend the central U.N. lines. The Chinese, in their formidable warrens of tunnels and strongpoints, refused to give the hills up.

During the day, the attackers would seize a summit, but at night the Chinese would counterattack and take it back, often emerging from hidden tunnel entrances.[10] On this day, South Korean defenders repulse a Chinese assault on a rocky knob known as Pinpoint Hill, which has been taken and retaken fifteen times over the past month.[11]

Chinese artillery, steadily reinforced over the past two years, have fired 350,000 rounds in this battle, on a par with American firepower. Thousands of men have been killed. Over one twelve-day period early in the battle, the Americans' 7th Division lost 2,000 men killed, wounded, or captured. A single division of the Chinese 15th Army has lost 8,752 out of 10,000 men.[12] By the end of it, little is changed by this Battle of Triangle Hill, as the Americans call it. To the Chinese, it's Shang Kan Ling and it's acclaimed as a great victory. Victory, loss, or draw, it confirms both sides in a determination to hold fast and hope for a truce.

Official Chinese radio cautions the new American president to adhere to that policy. In an English-language broadcast on Monday, it claims President-elect Eisenhower's military advisers are urging him to advance again to the Yalu River, as General MacArthur tried to do in 1950. "Eisenhower will get an even sounder thrashing if he is not prepared to accept the lessons of MacArthur's defeat," the radio declares.[13]

But Eisenhower seems resigned to something well short of triumph, in a war now deeply unpopular among the American people. In early

December, the president-elect spends three days in Korea, conferring with commanders, meeting briefly with President Rhee, never hinting at an interest in military victory, saying he came with "no panaceas" for ending the conflict.[14]

A LATE FALL DAY, 1952

Megaphone in hand, thirteen-year-old Chang Sang
speaks for many

Ranks of schoolgirls are parading through the heart of Taejon, demonstrating in favor of a future for Korea very different from the one being negotiated by the Americans and communists at Panmunjom.

"Unification!" the students chant, answering the call from a tall, skinny girl with a megaphone at the head of the march.

"We'll never accept division!" thirteen-year-old Chang Sang shouts, and scores of her schoolmates echo her refrain.

Sang is even taller and more confident than on that Sunday morning two years ago when she dashed out into Seoul's streets to learn that war had begun. She's only a first-year middle school student—class representative, in fact—but the seniors at her school for refugee girls have asked this northerner with the straight black hair, top grades, and strong voice to lead their marches, and have taught her the slogans.

Sang is pleased with the prestige—and fun—of heading up the protests in support of Syngman Rhee's stance against the Panmunjom talks. The white-haired president's antidemocratic ways are an embarrassment to his American allies, but many South Koreans admire him nonetheless, as a symbol of what they are fighting for: unification.

The loudest voices of protest in Taejon are those of disabled veterans, who have gravitated to South Korea's cities in the thousands. They can be disruptive, bullying passersby into buying items they're peddling, barging into government offices demanding financial help, drinking and brawling. Although they get little official aid, they support Rhee in his opposition to an armistice and for continued war. Otherwise, they feel, they sacrificed arms and legs at the war front for nothing.[15]

The president's organized campaign—"Unification or Death!"—has even reached down to schools across South Korea, where teachers suspend classes for a day and order the children into the streets.

Again and again, Chang Sang will lead her refugee schoolmates as they join up with students from other schools and march along Taejon's broad avenues, past the ruins of 1950, to rally at city hall.

They first form up at the Taejon railroad station, where the doomed troops of Task Force Smith debarked two years ago to plunge into the first American military disaster in Korea. Now the Americans and other powers are trying at least to end the killing. But South Koreans feel betrayed, on down to thirteen-year-old Sang. "We'll never accept the agreement!" she shouts through her megaphone.

TUESDAY, DECEMBER 16, 1952

A bereft mother, Park Sun-yong, can smile once again

The daily commotion in Taejon's streets is little noticed by one young woman in a rented house in the Mokdong district. On this day, the childless mother Park Sun-yong gives birth to a baby girl, two and a half years after losing her two small children to American bullets at Nogun-ri.

The infant, to be named Koo-suk, brings comfort and joy to a grieving household. Life grows no easier for the young couple, however, as millions up and down the peninsula have also found.

Husband Eun-yong's salary as a policeman is so paltry that Sun-yong's family, back in Shimchon village after sheltering in Pusan during the worst of the war, must regularly send them bags of rice for their Taejon larder. And Eun-yong's future prospects remain uncertain.

He will shortly earn a degree from a nearby branch of Chung Ang College, but his hopes for advanced studies have vanished. Sun-yong's parents underwrote his college costs and said they would pay for later studies abroad. But last year her father was suddenly dead at age forty-nine, killed in an automobile accident, and the family's means abruptly shrank.

Despite the truce protests, many in Taejon and elsewhere long for an end to the fighting, and the rebuilding and economic revival they hope it will bring, along with an end to the fears and tensions of a nation at war. The front lines may lie many miles north of Taejon, but the conflict can hit closer to home as well. Just three weeks ago, guerrillas derailed an eighteen-car U.S. military supply train outside the city.[16] Though diminished by the South Koreans' antiguerrilla campaigns, small bands still stage hit-run raids across the south.

At the house in Mokdong, meanwhile, where Sun-yong busies herself with the tasks of caring for a newborn, sorrowful memories still cling. She will suddenly see their faces in the middle of the day. She'll muse with Eun-yong about them. Koo-pil would be six years old now, she'll point out, and Koo-hee would be four. And then she will quietly sob.

For the second straight Christmas season, New York's Francis Cardinal Spellman visits the Maryknolls' Pusan clinic and delivers a check, a donation from U.S. Catholics, to Sister Mary Mercy.

Later, at a Christmas Eve midnight Mass, the man considered the dean of American cardinals tells a congregation of U.S. troops that "should this enemy win, then civilization's clock spins backwards into the periods of barbarism."[17]

Another celebrated American clergyman, the Protestant evangelist Billy Graham, touring Korea earlier in December, unleashed his own fiery denunciation of the "diabolical religion" of communism.

"Communism is like an evil octopus stretching out its tentacles to seize its victims all over the world," Graham declared to American soldiers gathered in a Taegu theater.[18]

The communist side likewise portrays its enemies in Korea as "bestial" and "diabolical." In an end-of-year speech, North Korea's Kim Il-sung tells his generals to prepare for a new American offensive, especially an Inchon-like amphibious landing in North Korea. And troop training must focus on "intensifying the hatred of the enemy."[19]

PART 4
1953

The sky and the earth
Are both gloomy.
Would a white horse of peace come
To this cursed bit of land?
Will it really come?

— **Mun Sang-myong**, "White Horse Hill," from *Brother Enemy*

As 1953 BEGINS, THE TRUCE TALKS REMAIN PARALYZED over the prisoner-of-war issue. The Panmunjom delegations bicker over other minor matters while the war, the killing, goes on. Then suddenly, unexpectedly, at his dacha outside Moscow, Josef Stalin dies, and a major obstacle to progress is removed. Quickly, the Kremlin's post-Stalin leadership instructs the Chinese and North Koreans to accept an American proposal to exchange sick and wounded prisoners.

It's a prelude to more progress, but meanwhile the opposing armies struggle over bits of territory to improve their final positions. At Pork Chop Hill, the slopes are strewn with dead as each side wins, loses, retakes the summit through months of back-and-forth fighting, typical of the seesawing battles flaring up along the peninsula-wide front line.

In June the two sides near a final agreement, under a compromise plan for handling North Korean prisoners refusing repatriation to their communist homeland. An angry President Syngman Rhee, favoring a decisive war, not negotiation, tries to sabotage the talks by unilaterally releasing those prisoners into South Korea. The Chinese retaliate with their biggest attack in two years, aimed at South Korean divisions. Tens of thousands are killed or wounded on both sides before it's over.

Finally, on July 27 at Panmunjom, the armistice is signed, to end the "great toil of suffering and bloodshed on both sides." Kim Il-sung, whose government has survived only because of the Chinese intervention, celebrates "a great victory." But no one has won this war. With millions dead and the two halves of a divided nation in ruins, it remains a war on hold, suspended, under a truce, not a peace.

WINTER

TUESDAY, JANUARY 27, 1953

Corporal Shin Hyung-kyu puts on a show,
then returns to the real war

General Joe Collins, U.S. Army chief of staff, likes much of what he sees on his seventh inspection visit to the Korean front from Washington.[1] The man at his side, General Mark W. Clark, Far East commander, isn't so happy.

Three months ago, Clark dispatched three staff officers to Washington to brief Collins on a plan to pressure the other side in the truce talks by launching an all-out offensive toward Pyongyang, compelling the communists to accept an immediate armistice. Clark proposed strengthening the U.N. forces for the operation with seven new divisions, including two from the Chinese Nationalist army on Taiwan. He also envisioned air attacks on targets in China.

The idea of widening the war to China and with anticommunist Chinese recalled General MacArthur's aggressive proposals of 1950–1951. As before, it found little support at the top. And now President Eisenhower, inaugurated a week ago, is committed with the Joint Chiefs of Staff to a strategy of holding firm, holding down casualties, and negotiating their way to a Panmunjom truce.[2]

On this day, on the Imjin River line in the western front's I Corps sector, Collins is inspecting the ROK Army's well-regarded 1st Division, entrusted with guarding the road to Seoul, thirty-five miles to the south. In July 1950, on his first visit to a new war, army chief Collins saw the South Korean forces in demoralized defeat and disarray. Now he tells accompanying journalists he is impressed with the improvements he finds.[3]

In the background at 1st Division headquarters, one of those impressive soldiers stands by, a tough little military policeman.

Corporal Shin Hyung-kyu's MP battalion was transferred from the central front to support the 1st Division in the west on New Year's Eve day. One of their roles is escorting such VIP visitors. Before the generals arrived, Shin and the other escorts pressed their khakis, spit-polished their shoes, and fluffed up white mufflers at their necks, to put on a dressy, unreal show in the grime and grit of war.

In between the petty pomp of VIP visits, Shin and his fellow MPs return to that real war and to escorting much lowlier ranks—some of the tens of thousands of older Korean men drafted into the Service Corps, frontline laborers who carry food, ammunition, and fuel to dug-in troops and support combat units in many other ways.

Shin's B Company is assigned to lead Service Corps porters wading across the 150-yard-wide Imjin River at fording spots, and up the back slopes of 1st Division hilltop positions on the other side, in the Imjin's "Double Horseshoe," a much-contested part of the river marked by broad S-shaped bends.

The job is dangerous. The porters, bending under wooden back frames loaded with supplies, sometimes stumble onto "friendly" land mines. The Chinese dug in on opposing hills regularly call in artillery or mortar barrages, or send raiding parties to harass the South Korean posts, particularly at night, when searchlights scan the valleys and hillsides, and battle cries and bugles blare over Chinese loudspeakers.

For "boy soldier" Shin Hyung-kyu, who played dead to survive a Chinese ambush south of Pyongyang two years ago, and who witnessed the wholesale waste of young soldiers' lives in the "war of the outposts" on the central front, this time on the Imjin, day after day of unpredictable and sometimes fierce combat is becoming the most terrifying episode of a war gone on too long. Like hundreds of thousands crouching in bunkers and trenches across Korea's midsection, on both sides of the line, Shin looks toward Panmunjom and listens for word of when it will finally end.

FRIDAY, JANUARY 30, 1953

A giant fire threatens Mary Mercy's clinic and all of Pusan

The first shouts and alarms are heard around eight, as Sister Mary Mercy and her nuns are settling in for an evening of rest and reading. Looking outside, they see an orange glow in Pusan's night sky, then frightened refugee families streaming down the icy slope from their shantytown above, away from the flames.

The fire began down the street, a block away from the Maryknoll clinic. It seems to have been fed by stored fuel and is quickly spreading on fifteen-mile-an-hour wind gusts. It's moving away from the mission, reaching up and around nearby slopes and through the tumbledown houses and shops of the city's black-market district.

Taking no chances, the mission's Korean workers form bucket lines and climb to the clinic roof to wet it down against stray sparks. Mary Mercy immediately orders the staff to begin consolidating equipment and supplies, to prepare for evacuation. This pious mother superior also seeks divine help, sending a relay of sisters to recite the rosary, one in the chapel, one before their statue of St. Joseph, Catholics' patron saint for Korea.

People have begun crowding into the Maryknolls' garden and clinic. Some are injured, a few with burns but many with cuts, contusions, broken bones suffered in the panic and trampling of hundreds fleeing the fire. The sisters go to work treating them.

Slowly, the city's fire brigades gain ground on the conflagration, knocking down buildings to create fire breaks, helped by U.S. Army engineers' bulldozers. Water pumped up from the harbor beats down the flames. The U.S. Embassy and other nearby buildings are saved, and after midnight the fire, the worst in Pusan's recent memory, is contained. A citywide inferno has been averted, but an area of one square mile has been consumed.[4]

Fires are an ever-present danger in this numbingly cold winter. Nineteen were reported in Pusan over one two-day period in mid-January. Crowded into their tiny huts of cardboard, burlap, and scrap wood, the refugees are desperate for warmth from open coal stoves, for light from kerosene lamps. Accidents are inevitable.

Along with their primitive shelter, what they can lose in a flash is meager but essential—their family quilts, their rice pot, kimchi jar, perhaps a little stand from which they sell apples or castoff clothing or pencils.

The nuns work on toward morning, tending the injured. After sunrise, the huddled families at the compound are given breakfasts of rice balls from supplies that were, fortunately, newly replenished.

Daylight shows that the uphill shanties were not widely damaged, the fire having burned hottest through the dilapidated city blocks below, destroying some fifteen hundred buildings. An estimated nine thousand people are left homeless.[5] The American command sends trucks to take them to military warehouses for temporary shelter.

Daylight also brings the usual line of hundreds of sick refugees to the Maryknolls' front gate. Smallpox has reappeared in Pusan, and the nuns have again made special trips through the squatter settlements to vaccinate the children.

They also have seen their first child in more than a year with diphtheria, a killer if untreated. "We hope there will not be any more among the poor people," Mary Mercy writes in the diaries.

SUNDAY, FEBRUARY 22, 1953

Clarence Adams and other POWs appeal to the United Nations

Clarence Adams has been given the title of "monitor," bestowed on their most favored POWs by the Chinese running Camp 5. Not only does the black American corporal act as a liaison between prisoners and the command, but he's considered sufficiently trained in the camp's study groups to lecture on his own to curious prisoners, on such subjects as slavery, capitalism, and imperialism.

He and Larance Sullivan, his like-minded POW friend, also regularly write political articles for *Toward Truth and Peace*, a propaganda sheet distributed among the prison camps in North Korea.[6]

By now, Adams recognizes, he falls very much into the "progressive" ranks among the internees.

On this Sunday, he and other "pros" send a letter to the U.N. General Assembly in New York supporting the communist position at Panmunjom on a prisoner exchange, rejecting the U.S. proposal that POWs be allowed to refuse to return to their homelands.

Only by resolving this issue "can our hopes and desires of returning home be fulfilled," they write.

But Adams at times sounds less than convinced on this point. In quiet conversations deep in the night, he tells a younger black buddy named Robert Fletcher that he'll never return to the oppressive segregated life of Memphis.

He observes that at Camp 5 the Chinese treat whites and blacks with "equal indifference." He has never before in his life felt like an equal, rather than an inferior.

The miseries of POW life, meanwhile, continue to ease.

The men now sleep four to a room in their three-room shacks, compared with two dozen sick and dying men jammed into each unheated room in the winter of 1950–1951. They have sports, reading, and other diversions, including an "Olympics," when POWs from various camps competed in football, basketball, and other sports, and the army welterweight Clarence Adams boxed.

The daily diet also improves—potatoes replacing turnips, more rice, bread as a daily staple.[7] The food can still be meager, however, and when Adams defends the Chinese to other black prisoners, blaming the food shortages on U.S. Air Force bombing of supply lines, he further infuriates the "reactionaries."

The twenty-four-year-old Adams has drawn particular hatred from some whites, who fling the "nigger" slur at him and at times threaten to "get" him when they all return to the States. He has taken to sleeping in the camp library, where two black friends sometimes stand guard. The friends are not particularly political, but feel a Memphis hometown allegiance. The three call themselves "The Boys from the Big M."

The daily prison diet also includes rumors, primarily talk of an imminent armistice. At Panmunjom, however, the deadlock persists. On this day, General Clark sends a letter from Tokyo to Kim Il-sung and General Peng repeating an earlier request for an exchange of sick and wounded prisoners, with little hope of acceptance.[8]

EARLY MARCH, 1953

Chi Chao-chu hears threats of wider war, then history intervenes

The new American president has sounded a bellicose note.

In his first State of the Union address, Dwight Eisenhower said he would remove the U.S. Navy shield separating the Chinese Nationalists on the island of Taiwan from the mainland communists. The world sees this as an invitation for the Nationalists to attack, to divert Chinese resources from the Korean war front.[9]

At Panmunjom, in a stern note to General Harrison, chief communist delegate Nam Il denounces this threat of "using Asians to fight Asians" and the "planned design of your side to overthrow the armistice negotiations, extend the Korean War, and further violate peace in the Far East."[10]

But Chi Chao-chu's fellow interpreters at the truce talks laugh off Eisenhower's threat as empty. What can "a few thousand lazy and corrupt reactionaries" on Taiwan do against the might of China? his friend "Little Kuo" asks Chi. "Even the mighty American paper tiger couldn't defeat us. Your Americans are either stupid or crazy or both!"

The senselessness of continuing this war, after almost three years, has Chi wondering about the America he loved as a "second homeland." He has treasured memories of growing up—of the dockside immigration officer who pinched the nine-year-old's cheek when the family arrived in New York, of the kind Americans who schooled him and helped pay for that education, of his father's *China Daily News* and its work promoting the U.S.–China alliance against Japan.

Now, in his year at Panmunjom, he has seen a different America, in the belligerence of the U.S. negotiators, in the destruction of North Korean cities and villages. This "dichotomy," as he thinks of it, is never far from Chi's mind.

Air attacks have stepped up around Pyongyang, including on a village where 300 of 340 inhabitants are killed. The radio warns of an impending American offensive, likely via amphibious landings. Kim Il-sung exhorts his military to make coastal fortifications "defenses of steel."[11] Indeed, General Clark's plan to greatly reinforce U.S.–South Korean divisions and attack toward Pyongyang, to force a capitulation at the truce talks, remains in reserve.

Then, on Thursday, March 5, everything changes. At his dacha outside Moscow, Josef Stalin dies of a cerebral hemorrhage.[12]

The Soviet leader, sponsor and quartermaster for the two communist armies, long strove to draw the war out, to keep his American adversaries tied down. That obstacle has now been cleared away. In the coming days, things move quickly.

On March 19, the Soviet Council of Ministers instructs Mao and Kim Il-sung to reply favorably to General Clark's proposal for an exchange of sick and wounded prisoners of war and to indicate that this is a step toward resolving the entire POW issue.[13] On March 28, the two communist leaders write to accept the exchange, which comes to be known as "Little Switch," in contrast to the "Big Switch" of a final exchange.

On March 30–31, the Chinese and North Koreans signal approval of November's Indian proposal at the United Nations, for a commission of neutral nations to deal with POWs who don't wish to return to their countries. The communists suggest lower-level discussions resume soon at Panmunjom.[14]

After six months of dealing with technical trivia and bombast, as they look forward to thawed streams, long-deferred baths, and the Korean spring, Chi Chao-chu and his comrades can also look forward to translating matters of substance, on ending the war, going home. But a now-departed Soviet dictator wasn't the only obstacle.

SPRING

The refugee girl Chang Sang returns to Seoul and painful news

Chang Sang has returned with her mother to Seoul from Taejon, more than two years after fleeing in the great winter exodus of 1951. They find a city half dead.

Ruins stretch in every direction, buildings gutted by bombs, artillery shells, fire. Fallen bricks litter the streets and shabbily dressed people pick their way through the rubble. Hundreds of street children roam the city, scavenging, begging, tagging alongside American GIs, selling them pencils, razors, their "sisters."

Half the capital's homes have been destroyed, but thirteen-year-old Sang is lucky.[1] They're able to move into the empty house of relatives of her late father, people who remain refugees in the far south. It relieves the crowding in the Kim household in Sindang-dong. Sang also has won a place at a good middle school, Sookmyung Girls' School.

With their fortune, however, comes heartbreaking news. Mother finds that Grandmother Cha, Sang's paternal grandmother, the widow who stayed behind two years ago because "heaven is much closer from here," is missing from her home.

Neighbors say that after the communists retook Seoul in January 1951, North Korean soldiers barged into the house and found Grandmother Cha reading her Bible. They took her away. Mother fears the worst for the old woman, the devout Christian refugee from the North.

She also learns that Grandmother Cha's youngest daughter and her husband, Sang's highly educated aunt and uncle, both college professors, departed for the North on their own in early 1951, apparently in sympathy with the communists, possibly in fear of retribution as collaborators.

It's just one of countless family tragedies unfolding across the Koreas, as parents and children, brothers and sisters, remain separated, unaccounted for, inexplicably gone.

At least Chang Sang, for one, is back in the city she most thinks of as home. And the girl who led marches against the truce talks now puts such things aside and devotes herself to her studies. She impresses the Sookmyung teachers so much she is awarded a full tuition scholarship.

Hurh Won-moo is another returnee to Seoul, this time as a first lieutenant and operations officer for a newly formed ROK Army unit, the 76th Field Artillery Battalion. He asked for a return to combat duty. Now he will get it.

The bookish high school senior who vowed he'd join no one's army as he hid beneath the floorboards in 1950 has experienced a lot since his officer training and months of action in the heavy fighting of 1951.

He was selected, one of an elite one hundred officers, for six months of advanced artillery training at the U.S. Army's Fort Sill, Oklahoma. There he marveled at American life—the automobiles and the movies, the hot dogs and cheap beer, the friendly people. He also rode in the "For Colored" section on a municipal bus, and thereby learned about a grimmer side of America.

Back in Korea, he was assigned as an instructor at the ROK Army's artillery officer school. But after too many months there of an overly heavy workload and daily tedium, he felt burned out. He was only twenty years old, he told himself, "but I feel like an old man."

Finally, he asked for and was granted a transfer back to the line.

Now he has helped assemble the new battalion at a Seoul supply depot, to be equipped with U.S.-made 155mm howitzers before heading for the front. It's part of a huge buildup of the ROK Army's weak artillery arm, a quadrupling of South Korean big guns since mid-1952.[2]

In Seoul, he also can visit his widowed mother and siblings, now back in the old house where he once hid from the North Korean draft. She has been busy, reinventing the family's farm-equipment store, looted after they all fled in January 1951. It will be an ice-cream parlor in the warmer months and a noodle shop in winter. Seven years after his father's death, Hurh is still amazed at his forty-two-year-old mother's energy and enterprise amid all the dislocations of war.

TUESDAY, APRIL 21, 1953

Alan Winnington accompanies sick and wounded
prisoners to freedom

As usual, Alan Winnington has outmaneuvered his fellow journalists at Panmunjom, this time on the "Little Switch" story.

The London *Daily Worker* correspondent, on the northern side in the war, traveled last week to POW Camp 5 at Pyoktong, on the Yalu River, to join an ambulance-and-truck convoy bringing dozens of sick and wounded prisoners the two hundred miles to Panmunjom for the newly arranged prisoner exchange. His dispatches along the way tell an upbeat tale of their confinement.

"'The Very Best of Treatment,'" today's *Daily Worker* headline assures readers, quoting a POW interviewed by Winnington.

"A bare handful are stretcher cases," Winnington wrote in one of his first articles. "Most are suffering from ailments resulting from wounds or frostbite, which occurred at the time of their capture."

He quotes British and American prisoners, still in communist custody pending the exchange later in the day, as praising the medical care received from the Chinese at Pyoktong.

Although U.S. news reports later this week focus on accounts from released prisoners of the 1950 death marches and of the hundreds of deaths from disease and hunger at Camp 5 two years ago, there is no mention of such brutality and neglect in Winnington's reports.

He writes that the "repatriates" want the Panmunjom negotiators to clear away the obstacles to peace, for the sake of prisoners left behind. "The boys back there are waiting for the day when the British public will get this war ended," he quotes one Briton as saying.

He closes the article by writing of the "grim contrast" he sees in the sick and wounded released at Panmunjom from the U.S.-run POW camps in the south. "Half a mile away, from the American ambulances, ghosts of men tottered, straight from the horrors of Koje island," he reports. Their faces are "stamped with suffering," and they included "an extraordinary number of men with missing limbs."[3]

Winnington views his journalism as a tool for advocacy. A member of the British Communist Party for two decades, he has told Panmunjom colleague Wilfred Burchett, the leftist Australian correspondent, that they're in a "propaganda fight" in Korea.

On earlier visits to POW camps, he delivered a lecture to prisoners on class struggle and sat in on the Chinese-led "political study groups." He told Burchett they should encourage POWs to "write, agitate and make news" on behalf of peace.[4]

At the same time, he also took photographs of every British prisoner for their families, facilitated mail exchanges and arranged for recreational equipment for the camps.[5] But his activities have steadily aroused resentment back home, especially among British conservatives.

The anger extends back to his 1950 reporting on the mass executions by the South Koreans, with U.S. assistance, of thousands of political prisoners outside Taejon, reporting denounced at the time as fabricated and even treasonous. The slaughter is entering official U.S. military history as the North Koreans' work, "one of the greatest mass killings of the entire Korean War."[6] The truthfulness of Winnington's reporting is proven by U.S. military photographs and documents, but those are secreted away at the Pentagon.

The anti-Winnington vitriol was fed more recently by his articles endorsing North Korean and Chinese claims that the U.S. military waged biological warfare, by dropping disease-infected insects on enemy territory, claims vehemently rejected by the Americans.[7]

In this way his Korea reporting has planted the seeds of potential future trouble for Alan Winnington. And that future now embraces more than this single Englishman.

In his periodic shuttling back to Peking from Korea, the forty-three-year-old Winnington has deepened his relationship with the twenty-one-year-old half-British Esther Cheo Ying, who turns to him for comfort and reassurance amid the frustrations of her work at the Hsinhua news agency.

Finally, one day, she blurted it out: "Marry me, Alan." She told herself she wasn't serious. But then, a day before he left again for Korea, chatting over lunch at a food stall, they found themselves talking as though marriage was inevitable, at some indefinite date. Now she is pregnant, awaiting his return.[8]

For the moment, he remains in Panmunjom, where the Little Switch process goes on for two weeks, in the end exchanging 6,670 North Korean and Chinese sick and wounded for 684 American and other U.N. prisoners.

Meanwhile, this Sunday, April 26, plenary sessions resume in the truce talks for the first time since the Americans broke them off last October. The negotiators face the same single issue: whether North Korean and Chinese POWs can choose not to return to their homelands.[9]

The war and the bloodshed sputter on. Forty-five miles northeast of the negotiations site, the Chinese have been thrown back, at a grim cost in lives, in another attempt to take Hill 255, Pork Chop Hill, from its American defenders.[10]

A DAY IN LATE APRIL, 1953

A reprieve from the hell of the front dangles before
Chung Dong-kyu

It has become a joke at company headquarters. Every day for weeks, Chung Dong-kyu has stopped by, asking whether his transfer has come through.

On this day, it's no longer a joke. A surprised first sergeant tells Chung his name appears on a set of orders from their 3rd Division headquarters. He is being transferred to the headquarters of the ROK 8th Division. Finally, he'll get the reprieve he has long sought.

For more than two years, Chung has fought in the vanguard of a grinding, filthy war, in misery, facing danger every day, going hungry on short rations, with a shrinking brotherly band of conscripted North Korean refugees. Their reconnaissance company seems to draw the most difficult missions. They are convinced they're viewed by the ROK command as expendables, cannon fodder.

"Now I'll be able to stop watching my friends die, one by one," he tells himself.

Months back, he learned that a cousin from the North who fled to South Korea in 1947 was the senior intelligence officer for the 8th Division, on the line immediately to the west. Visiting this Colonel Chung Mong-ho, the twenty-one-year-old sergeant got right to the point: His time in combat has more than repaid his obligation as a refugee to South Korea. He is pressing his luck and might not survive to see his mother again. Could Mong-ho get him a job on his headquarters staff?

Now the order has come to report for duty there. But he immediately worries that his company's longtime commander, Lieutenant Kim, will resist losing an experienced sergeant. He decides to skip the protocol of reporting to Kim seeking release from his command.

After nightfall, he packs his gear and finds a ride west to the 8th Division, reporting for duty at the intelligence staff in the morning. But by noon word comes to report back to his old company and Lieutenant Kim immediately.

Chung was always on good terms with Kim, under whom he served bravely through many campaigns. But now, back facing him later in the day, the lieutenant's look frightens him. Chung has seen how brutal he can be.

"Stand at attention!" Kim barks, and then walks up to the shorter, younger man and slaps him across the face with his full strength. Chung reels.

The lieutenant warns him to "absolutely never" try to transfer from his company again and sends him back to his platoon.

In the evening, a depressed Chung is once more summoned to the company command. This time he's again stunned. Kim simply tells him he's approving his transfer.

Feeling tears coming on, Chung pulls himself up to his full five-foot-four, smartly salutes, and is saluted in return. He can never know whether Kim has had a change of heart, recognizing his honorable service, or was reprimanded by Lieutenant Colonel Chung Mong-ho or other superior officers.

Returning to his tent, Chung this time can openly bid proper farewells to the fellow refugees he has fought beside since December 1950, after they came together in Kilchu, North Korea, as the Local Volunteer Youth Group.

Chung, the aspiring doctor and interrupted medical student, is soon to be assigned to the 8th Division's medical battalion, helping treat casualties in the combat of spring and summer, but facing a much smaller chance of becoming one himself, and a better chance of someday returning to Chu Ul, where twenty-nine months ago he reassured his mother he would be gone for just three days.

On this final evening with old comrades, Chung Dong-kyu makes another of his grim periodic estimates of war's wages. Of the 156 who initially made up his company of refugee scouts, only about 40 remain. The rest have been killed, been disabled, or gone missing in this war without end.

MONDAY, MAY 18, 1953
Matt Ridgway deflects "wider war" talk as the U.S. escalates, bombing dams

The Cold War in Europe is the topic. But the questioning turns inevitably to the real and confounding war in Korea, and General Matthew B. Ridgway is caught in Washington's partisan crossfire.

The onetime Pentagon deputy who rose to international fame rescuing America from defeat in Korea has been named by President Eisenhower as the new army chief of staff, pending Senate confirmation. But he has been summoned to Washington in his current role, supreme commander of NATO in the Western alliance's confrontation with the Soviets.

He is testifying before the House Foreign Affairs Committee on Soviet military strength and U.S. military aid to the Europeans. The talk of armored divisions and Pentagon budgets drones on until one conservative congressman shifts the focus to Korea. Representative Laurie C. Battle, an Alabama Democrat, asks Ridgway whether a U.S. military victory is essential to establishing peace in Korea. It's an invitation to endorse a wider war.

Many Washington hard-liners still support the MacArthur view that restraints on the U.S. military should be lifted and the war escalated, to include attacking targets in China. Almost two years into the difficult Korean armistice negotiations, and as opinion polls show the war to be deeply unpopular among Americans, these conservatives complain of the "sit-down policy" in Korea.

The ever-careful Ridgway dodges Congressman Battle's question.[11] Privately, however, the four-star general still applauds the Truman approach. The American people "would not sanction a war that might spread over much of continental Asia and require the expenditure of hundreds of thousands of lives," he later writes.

Few in Washington know, however, that U.S. military planners are already envisioning that wider war. The Joint Chiefs of Staff are preparing to send the White House a plan to escalate the Korea conflict sharply if the Panmunjom talks break down. It even foresees use of atomic bombs in northern China. Later this week, John Foster Dulles, visiting India as the new U.S. secretary of state, tells Prime Minister Jawaharlal Nehru that U.S. forces will attack bases in China if the stalemate persists—a threatening message intended to be relayed to Peking.

Meanwhile, with little notice outside North Korea, the U.S. Air Force is already escalating the conflict. In March, the Far East Air Forces' target committee began studying the possibility of bombing irrigation dams in North Korea's "rice bowl," the western provinces of South Pyongan and Hwanghae, dismissing any humanitarian concerns and effectively targeting the survival of the northern population, by washing away thousands of acres of rice.

Those attacks began last week.

On Wednesday, waves of F-84 fighter-bombers struck the Toksan dam, holding back waters of the Potong River in a three-square-mile lake twenty miles north of Pyongyang. The twenty-three-hundred-foot earth-and-stone dam was hit repeatedly with thousand-pound bombs. Air reconnaissance the next morning found the water had broken through overnight, sweeping down twenty-seven miles of river valley. It devastated the main north-south railroad and highway, destroyed seven hundred buildings, and washed away five square miles of newly transplanted rice.

On Friday and Saturday, the Thunderjets struck the Chasan dam, ten miles farther northeast. It finally gave way, sending walls of water southward over roads, another rail line, and field after field of young rice. Both floods reached the streets of bomb-wrecked Pyongyang.

The North Koreans denounced these "barbarous raids on peaceful agricultural installations." Emergency food aid from China, the Soviet Union, and other communist nations is needed to stave off widespread famine.[12]

⸻

In the coming days, the Panmunjom talks are suddenly moving ahead.

Bill Shinn, citing "reliable South Korean officials," reports the Americans have dropped their demand regarding the thirty-five thousand North Koreans who don't want to return north. They had insisted these POWs be released immediately in South Korea under a truce. Instead, under instruction from Washington, the U.S. negotiators now accept the position that these northerners, like the twenty-two thousand Chinese "nonrepatriates," should first be handed over to a commission of neutral nations for a ninety-day period, during which North Korean and Chinese representatives would try to persuade them to return home. This follows the outline of an Indian proposal adopted by the U.N. General Assembly last December and accepted by the communist side at Panmunjom.[13]

Things then continue to move quickly. On June 8 the two sides sign the "terms of reference" of the POW agreement, paving the way to a final armistice document.[14]

WEDNESDAY, JUNE 10, 1953

Hurh Won-moo learns about "public welfare projects"

As darkness spreads over the hills of the central front, Chinese artillery fire steps up. The unnerving noise of bugles and gongs follows. At the center of the "Kumsong Bulge," a twenty-five-mile loop of front line jutting north into enemy territory, elements of two armies attack the positions of the ROK 5th Division.

Progress at the armistice talks is pressuring the two sides to take more territory before a truce freezes them in place. The new operation to eliminate the Kumsong salient is the biggest by the Chinese since spring 1951. As usual, they target a South Korean division.[15]

Miles to the west, at the left flank of the Kumsong Bulge, First Lieutenant Hurh Won-moo's ROK 6th Division holds the line facing the Chinese 67th Army, in an area that remains relatively calm for now.

Hurh's newly organized battalion of 155mm howitzers took up its fire-support positions just two weeks ago, and has been occupied with continued training and sporadic exchanges of fire with Chinese mortars. Hurh, meanwhile, has learned about the more questionable activities of fellow officers.

They call it *hooseng sa-op*, "public welfare projects," a euphemism for the wholesale corruption happening all around him, particularly among senior officers, men who often suddenly vanish from their duty stations. They've gone to nearby towns to sell food rations or stolen U.S. equipment to the civilian market, or to "lease out" military trucks for civilian purposes. Seoul's black market offers an astonishing array of weapons and military gear.

It verges on accepted practice because, as the new ROK Army chief of staff, Lieutenant General Paik Sun-yup, has written to President Rhee, "The terrible salary we pay our officers fosters graft and corruption."[16]

Young Lieutenant Hurh has had to deal with the problem already, as the officer in charge of the battalion's fire direction center.

His master sergeant reported one day that a battalion telephone switchboard had been stolen. At a loss at first, Hurh finally ordered him, "Get the damn thing back right away, whatever it takes!" Days later, the sergeant returned with a switchboard, likely after doing a "public welfare project" of his own.

The new Chinese offensive takes hill after hill, pushing the 5th Division back, and it then broadens, striking ROK units on the right and left. The Koreans withdraw an average of two miles. Only massive air strikes—a record 2,143 sorties by U.S. and South Korean aircraft on one day—stop the Chinese advance.

For a war in apparent stalemate, the casualty tolls are enormous: an estimated seventy-three hundred South Korean dead and wounded over the nine-day offensive and thirteen thousand Chinese casualties, including six thousand dead. And the Chinese are regrouping, preparing for more.[17]

THURSDAY, JUNE 11, 1953

Raucous antitruce protests keep Mary Mercy's nuns indoors

They parade in the rain through the streets of Pusan at all hours of day and night, thousands chanting "Unification or Death!"—slogan of die-hard South Koreans. Huge demonstrations continue to rock Seoul and other major cities as well.

The U.S. military command in Pusan is urging caution on Sister Mary Mercy's Maryknoll nuns, potential targets of anti-American anger over the truce talks.

"We were advised not to go out without necessity," she writes in today's clinic diary. In their telltale gray or white habits, they stop calling at the army post office for mail and teaching classes at a small Pusan library. "All ages and stations in life have been represented in the streets: university students, women, wounded ROK soldiers, particularly amputees, and still others," she writes.

On Tuesday in Pusan, still the country's temporary capital, the National Assembly voted unanimously to denounce the proposed armistice.

It demanded that any agreement include the dismantling of the North Korean military, the ouster of Chinese troops from the peninsula, and the immediate release of North Korean POWs who don't wish to return to the North.[18]

The government is posting police guards at all U.S. installations in Pusan and elsewhere to ward off possible attacks.[19] Outside the U.S. Embassy in Pusan, the old Bank of Japan building, amputee ROK veterans are staging a sit-in.[20] Elsewhere in the crowded city, American GIs aboard a truck open fire with a warning volley of rifle shots to clear their way through a rock-throwing crowd.[21] In Seoul on Tuesday, a wave of protesters surged against a roadblock outside U.S. Eighth Army headquarters, and many were injured when military policemen turned fire-hoses on them.[22]

The political turmoil, the most intense since the Maryknolls opened their clinic here more than two years ago, has their mother superior worried.

"Some think these loud demonstrations are Communist-inspired," Mary Mercy writes—an unlikely scenario, since the communist side is eager for an armistice, a reprieve from the unending hostilities.

Most South Korean people apparently also feel the war has gone on too long.

Although President Rhee's partisans can fill the streets with marchers from universities, schools, and other institutions controlled by the government, opinion surveys find a weary South Korean populace wants peace, on whatever terms.[23]

His generals tell Rhee his threat to fight on alone against the communists is empty, hopeless. On Saturday, after another day of rock-throwing violence in Seoul, the president calls on the marchers to go home. The amputees abandon their sit-in at the Pusan embassy.[24]

Day in, day out, meanwhile, the clinic's work among the long war's displaced people goes on. The sisters are grappling with new epidemics of smallpox and measles, a potential killer of children in an impoverished setting like Korea. And soon they're also facing a sudden spread of typhoid and paratyphoid fever among the refugees, brought on by heavy rains that contaminate Pusan's water supplies.

The routine of war goes on as well. The nuns stage their monthly air raid drill and Mary Mercy notes that "most of the city remained lit during black-out for some reason, probably failure to enforce regulations."

More and more, people sense an end is near.

SUNDAY, JUNE 14, 1953

On this graduation day, Pete McCloskey cannot escape the past

The newspapers this morning tell of heavy fighting in the Korean central front's Kumsong Bulge, even as the belligerents put final touches on an armistice.[25] But on this perfect spring Sunday in Palo Alto, among the palms and pathways of Stanford University, Pete McCloskey isn't thinking about Korea, but about the future. It's Stanford Law School's graduation day, and, like his fellow graduates, McCloskey is focused on next month's announcement of the results of the California bar exam. He's also preoccupied with a growing family.

Last Christmas, Caroline delivered a baby boy to join the daughter born the day their father, the Marine reserve lieutenant, landed in Korea more than two years ago, at the beginning of an experience whose anxious days and moments of horror have taken root in his subconscious. Those freeze frames of war are to emerge over the years, in nightmares, in daytime flashbacks when a glance at a calendar reminds him of an indelible date from 1951.

The man who once thrilled to war stories as a boy is to someday write that "as one ages, the killing and maiming of other human beings seems to become pointless," and the "idea that we should make love not war, is better, I think, than my dreams as a youth to be nothing more than a good Marine."

On this day, as twenty-five-year-old Pete McCloskey accepts his J.D. degree and the Korea conflict nears its final act, the newspapers tell of trouble elsewhere, reporting that Western powers are increasingly concerned about the communist-led insurrection in Indochina, in a place little known to American readers called Vietnam.[26]

THURSDAY, JUNE 18, 1953

Syngman Rhee frees prisoners; "We want to fight for South Korea," one tells Bill Shinn

At precisely 2:00 a.m. on this rainy morning, ROK Army guards at prisoner-of-war camps across South Korea begin waking their prisoners and telling them they're free to go. The gates are open.

Under orders from President Rhee, a secret plan is being carried out to release thousands of "nonrepatriates," captive North Korean soldiers who don't want to return north but who won't be freed for months after an armistice under the plan the Americans have accepted at Panmunjom.

This is Rhee's way of undoing the U.S. concession.

"The anti-communist Korean prisoners have been released," government radio announces later in the day. "The entire population of the Republic of Korea is asked to protect and help these patriotic youths."

By day's end, some twenty-five thousand POWs are freed from four camps, melting into the cities and countryside. Two thousand more are to be freed on Friday.

Seizing on this startling turn of events, Bill Shinn quickly tracks down seven of the men freed from Pusan's Prison Camp No. 9. The journalist climbs a Pusan hillside to find them lying low in the small home of a local shopkeeper, told by police to harbor any northerners sent his way.

Tired and dirty, they tell Shinn of their surprise at what happened, getting just three minutes' notice to escape into the predawn darkness. "We're grateful to President Rhee for ordering our release," says one, a KPA sergeant named Nam who believes his family fled to South Korea at some point. "We want to fight for South Korea now," he tells Shinn.

They have already changed from their POW fatigues into civilian clothes their host has collected from neighbors. Nam says they're told they'll be issued official South Korean identification cards shortly. "Once we have our cards, we can walk the streets like truly free men."[27]

Rhee's bold stroke provokes immediate fury on the communist side at Panmunjom, where they suspend the talks.[28] The Americans are outraged as well, concerned the South Korean's action might derail the armistice at the last moment.

In Washington, within hours of the prisoner release, President Eisenhower convenes a National Security Council meeting at which he and Cabinet officials discuss a blunt warning to be sent to Rhee. Eisenhower raises the possibility, if things get worse, of sponsoring a South Korean military overthrow of Rhee.

But first Eisenhower dispatches a team to Seoul led by Walter Robertson, assistant secretary of state, to meet with Rhee and rein him in.[29]

After days of those meetings, on a foggy Sunday morning, the everpresent Bill Shinn catches Rhee emerging from services at Seoul's redbrick Chungdong First Methodist Church.

Asked about the discussions, a subdued seventy-eight-year-old president tells Shinn, "I am trying to clear up misunderstandings."[30]

Before the week's end, Rhee and Robertson issue a joint statement declaring their "close collaboration for common objectives." The Americans have given Rhee informal assurances of U.S. Senate passage of a mutual defense treaty, and of substantial economic and military aid in years to come. Rhee has given them assurances he will no longer seek to sabotage the armistice.

The Americans make one other commitment as well: they will withdraw from an envisioned postarmistice political conference, talks on Korean reunification, if that conference makes no substantial progress within ninety days of convening. In effect, that effort to reach a permanent peace has been stamped with an expiration date.[31]

SUMMER

FRIDAY, JULY 3, 1953

"Heaven, why are you so unfair?" Chen Hsing-chiu asks

The two Chinese soldiers have lost their minds. Chen Hsing-chiu is shocked. He has seen men trembling in fear, screaming in pain, struck dumb by what they've seen and done in battle. But the young medic has never seen anything like this.

The two 12th Army infantrymen are being held in a house adjoining the battalion camp, awaiting nighttime movement north. They're being escorted back to China for treatment. Their guard tells Chen that after a dozen intense battles, in the mad chaos of killing young enemy soldiers, watching their friends blown to bloody pieces, living in constant terror for their own lives, something snapped in these soldiers and they lost touch with reality.

Chen looks in through a window. The taller of the two has his left arm in a sling. His uniform is flecked with cigarette ash. The shorter one is pale, and his forehead bears black bruises. Chen suddenly sees why, as the soldier runs to a wall and bashes his head against it. The taller soldier follows suit. They rush around the room, jumping, wailing, taking up shooting positions, or hurling phantom grenades. They shout out epithets and warnings.

"Let me out of here and I'll kill them all!" the shorter one yells, a strange, blank look in his eyes. "We must hold!"

"We must hold until 7 tonight!" the taller one joins in. "Stay down, comrades!"

A feeling of helplessness overcomes Chen. His instinct is to help, but treating mental illness wasn't a subject at the army medics school. He turns back to the escort.

"Maybe they should be tied up with ropes, so they can sleep," Chen suggests. The soldier tells him no, it would only worsen their illness, and they'd break free anyway.

For the rest of the day, Chen is troubled by what he's witnessed. He envisions battle scenes that might drive men to such depths. He feels a pang of guilt, at not having to live in such a front-line slaughterhouse, day in and day out. It's difficult to write about it in his diary, but he does. "These two guys are so tortured," he notes. "Heaven, why are you so unfair?"

SATURDAY, JULY 11, 1953

A troubled Gil Isham faces court-martial

Endless rain has drenched the central front for days, and mist fills the valleys.

At Pork Chop Hill, fifty miles northeast of Seoul, armored personnel carriers clank down the rear slopes carrying the remnants of its defenders, including Easy Company, Gil Isham's old 17th Infantry outfit.

The Americans are giving up the eight-hundred-foot hill after months of fighting in which it changed hands multiple times. Tens of thousands of shells from both sides fell on Pork Chop and its honeycomb of bunkers, in an artillery display unprecedented for such a small area—a hill the size of a twenty-acre farm.

After suffering hundreds of casualties, and inflicting thousands on the Chinese, the American generals have decided the small elevated piece of land isn't worth the continued price as an armistice approaches and have ordered the withdrawal of the 7th Infantry Division units.

Pork Chop Hill has come to symbolize the near futility of the seesawing hill fighting of the past two years—the "small bites," as Mao Tse-tung once called it, of making minimal territorial gains at what proves to be maximal cost.[1]

In thirty-four months at war, the 7th Division has suffered more than fifteen thousand casualties, including almost four thousand dead, more dead than it suffered in both world wars combined.[2]

Gil Isham himself, eighteen months after leaving Korea, has his own view of his war. "After I was there for a while, there would be a dead GI and a couple of dead Chinese or dead North Koreans, and it got to me where, what the hell is going on? They're all human, you know. This is wrong. To me it got so a lot of things over there were wrong. And a lot of the things I did over there, all the killing, that was wrong." All that he did and saw have left the young soldier deeply troubled.

Soon to turn twenty-one, he was supposed to have been discharged from the army this June, but he spent much of the past year AWOL, away without leave from his assigned units. He has been brawling, disobeying orders, and has twice done time in the stockade at Fort Sheridan, outside Chicago. He now faces a second court-martial for continued AWOL violations. He has been "busted" from sergeant first class to private, and his enlistment has been extended to June 1954 because of his absences.

He often paces barracks floors in the middle of the night or roams an army base's streets, afraid of sleep, fearful of the nightmares from Korea that seem never to leave him.

In Korea, meanwhile, as a new troop of young Easy Company soldiers carry their own memories away from Pork Chop, the Panmunjom truce talks resume.

MONDAY, JULY 13, 1953
Chen Hsing-chiu is wounded on a day ending with
"happy music" of Chinese guns

The enemy shelling along the central front has been intense since early morning.

Chen Hsing-chiu and most of the antiaircraft battalion are hunkered down in their large cave shelter. The heat and summer downpours have been especially oppressive. Some men play poker or *hsiang chi*, Chinese chess. Some try to sleep despite the explosions, the shuddering earth, the dust shaken from the cavern's ceiling.

As the day drags on, only a few officers, plane spotters, and radiomen remain exposed outside. Then, around two in the afternoon, enemy artillery crews seem to zero in on the battalion position. A half-dozen rounds crash down simultaneously. Smoke spreads across the camp.

It must be revenge, Chen decides, payback for the battalion's shootdown yesterday of an F-84, downed by a crew the medic Chen joined as a temporary gunner. The Americans seem to have pinpointed the coordinates of the battalion's well-camouflaged position. Yesterday, there was cheering, today retaliation.

Expecting casualties, Chen instinctively grabs his medic's kit and turns to the company executive officer. "Should I go out there?" he asks. "Be careful," the officer replies.

He hurries outside, then slows to a walk, trying to judge where he might be needed.

Suddenly, four more artillery rounds land in quick succession. Rocks and sand blow into his face. Stopped in his tracks, crouching, he feels a numbness in his left arm. He looks and sees a slender piece of shrapnel dug into the flesh above his wrist. He reaches for it, and the searing metal burns his fingers. "Fuck!"

Calming down, taking cover, all he can do is apply antiseptic and bandage the arm. More rounds are landing, every seven or eight seconds. Timing the intervals, Chen dashes from trench to bomb crater to trench. One blast blows his cap away. Finally, he reaches a trench serving as a temporary command post, where he finds that his company commander also has caught shrapnel in an arm. Chen patches him up, and then a fellow medic tends to Chen's wound.

Four gun crews are on alert. In late afternoon, as sporadic shellfire continues, they swing into action. Four American P-51s, propeller-driven Mustangs, are spotted flying in at low altitude, perhaps looking for the antiaircraft unit or for the field artillery emplacements it protects. With rapid-fire orders, the commander has them put up a wall of flak. The surprised Americans turn away.

The enemy barrages taper off as darkness falls. The rain picks up. Then, at nine, the nearby howitzers of the 28th Artillery Regiment and Chinese guns all across the central front open fire. "It must have been a thousand cannons," Chen writes in his diary. "Very happy music . . . like New Year's firecrackers when you're a child."

The company commander tells them it's the start of a great Chinese offensive.

—⟶∞⟵—

General Peng has returned to Korea after his latest shuttle to Peking, where he has been named to head the party's Central Military Commission.

In consultation with Mao by cable, and with his local commanders in Korea, Peng decided that Syngman Rhee must be "taught another lesson" after his defiant release of 27,000 North Korean prisoners, "nonrepatriates."

He and Mao speak of a need to inflict 10,000 to 15,000 more casualties on the South Koreans as punishment.[3]

As the new offensive jumps off, 150,000 troops from five Chinese armies, supported by hundreds of big guns, advance along the central front's twenty-five-mile Kumsong sector, held by South Korean divisions. Peng aims finally to flatten the Kumsong Bulge jutting north into communist lines.[4]

TUESDAY, JULY 14, 1953

In the giant enemy offensive, Hurh Won-moo saves his battalion

A fog-dimmed sun floats above the ridges to the east. The deafening overnight artillery exchanges slacken. But a rattled First Lieutenant Hurh Won-moo has an urgent problem this morning: His battalion commander is nowhere to be found, in the midst of the Chinese attack.

The first big blows of General Peng's new offensive came last night against three ROK divisions, the Capital defending the left flank of the Kumsong Bulge and the 3rd and 5th at the right flank. But masses of Chinese troops also were thrown at the Koreans in the center, including Hurh's 6th Division.[5]

Eighteen 155mm howitzers of his 76th Field Artillery Battalion joined with other batteries in the ceaseless fire and counterfire through the night. Thousands of crisscrossing rounds filled the valleys with smoke, the smell of phosphorous, and a continuous roar. The lightning and thunder of a monsoon added to the hellish scene.

As the lieutenant in charge of the fire direction center, Hurh was firing blind. His forward observers couldn't spot targets through the fog, rain, and smoke. Instead, he ordered howitzer salvos placed on likely targets, preset coordinates. It was a losing battle.

At one 6th Division outpost, at the twenty-five-hundred-foot mountain Kyoam-san, an infantry company locked in hand-to-hand combat repeatedly called in artillery fire on its own positions. Only ten of the two-hundred-man company escaped with their lives.[6] Across the Kumsong sector, the Korean infantry was pulling back.

It wasn't until midnight last night that Hurh learned his battalion commander wasn't in his bunker. He was told the major had gone in the morning to Chunchon to check on a "public welfare project," officers' euphemism for their illicit black-market activities. Hurh was enraged. The battalion's executive officer also was gone.

Now the morning is lengthening, neither has returned, and the 6th Division's situation is growing dire. By midafternoon, the incoming fire intensifies. The Chinese draw closer. Hurh tries to call the battalion's artillery group command, but the telephone line is dead.

Just then one of his men shouts, "Sir, the 96th Battalion is pulling out! Look!" Through his bunker's viewing slot, Hurh can see the neighboring battalion's guns being towed rearward. Who gave them an evacuation order?

Months of advanced training at Fort Sill never prepared him for such a situation. He knows he can be court-martialed for leading an unauthorized retreat. But the lives of six hundred men and the protection of their guns and equipment now depend on him. Hurh decides he has no choice.

He alerts the three battery commanders to prepare to pull out, to convoy ten miles south to a prearranged location for regrouping. But they have disturbing news: they don't have enough two-and-a-half-ton trucks to tow all their 155s. Senior officers sent two of the trucks to Chunchon for a "public welfare project," probably to rent to local businessmen.

Hurh seethes with anger, but forces himself to stay focused. He tells them to test whether their three-quarter-ton trucks can pull the loads. If not, he says, they must destroy the two howitzers. Tense minutes follow until finally he's told the lighter trucks might do the job. He orders the entire battalion to move out.

In a drenching late-afternoon rain, the 76th Field Artillery, under the control of lieutenants, all under age twenty-one, joins a retreat on Route 17, the only road down the Kumsong River valley, pointing thirty miles south to Chunchon. The packed-dirt road is clogged with hundreds of other vehicles, artillery pieces, and tanks. Endless columns of rain-soaked infantrymen, miserable and exhausted, trudge down both sides of the muddy road.

Riding in the battalion's last jeep, Hurh sees disabled trucks pushed to the side. All the 76th's vehicles, including the howitzer-towing light trucks, roll on without incident. But Hurh's mind keeps looking back in anger at how they were abandoned by their commanders.

As the twilight fades around eight, the battalion finally steers off to its regrouping area, a roadside clearing. Hurh is relieved. He sees that all are accounted for. Then he sees something that stuns him: the battalion commander is already there, standing before his jeep.

Hurh dismounts and walks over, controlling his rage. But the major speaks first.

"What took you so long to get here?" he asks.

Something explodes inside the lieutenant.

"You bastard," he thinks and he reaches for his pistol. His angry impulse is to shoot his commander. But he stops. In his mind he hears his mother's voice, "Don't do it, son." Just then another lieutenant shouts to the major that communications broke down, no evacuation order came, and "Lieutenant Hurh saved our battalion."

Hurh now takes charge.

"Where were you when we needed you most?" the twenty-year-old Hurh asks the absentee major, quietly but sharply. "Sir! What were you doing while we were under enemy attack?"

The major mumbles inaudibly. Hurh stalks away.

The Chinese final offensive eliminates the Kumsong Bulge, seizing some two hundred square miles of territory. But it halts for the usual reasons: meager resupplies of ammunition, food, and other essentials, and heavy casualties.

In the coming days, American reinforcements help launch a counterattack that regains half the ground lost, to the south bank of the Kumsong River. South Korean generals want to push beyond the Kumsong, but the Americans refuse, wary of still more bloodshed so close to an armistice.

Over ten days of fighting, the South Koreans have suffered casualties of 14,373 killed, wounded, or missing. The Chinese casualties total an estimated 33,000.[7]

SUNDAY, JULY 19, 1953

Chi Chao-chu is tasked with delivering an armistice

The communist side at Panmunjom has agreed to proceed immediately with "preparations prior to the signing of an armistice."[8]

The Chinese turn to their fastest, most accurate typist, Chi Chao-chu, to produce their final English version of the seventy-eight-hundred-word document, the summation of two years and nine days of exhausting and bitter negotiation.

Twenty-three-year-old Chi, Peking chemistry student, Harvard University dropout, has mastered his delegation's old manual typewriters in seventeen months of transcribing his translations of truce-talks dialogue, typing up messages, and handling other documents.

He sets to work as July's downpours and sweltering heat settle over the compound in Kaesong, five miles from the negotiations site.

"The undersigned," he begins, ". . . in the interest of stopping the Korean conflict, with its great toil of suffering and bloodshed on both sides . . ."

As the tall Chinese interpreter leans over the typewriter keys, squinting through his thick eyeglasses and pounding away, he swats at mosquitoes, has his meals brought to him, and fends off sleepiness, night after night. The draft has to be perfect, without a single typographical error or eraser mark. When he errs—more and more as he grows wearier—the entire page must be torn up, and he must start over.

The document also is being edited as he goes along. The two sides are still working out last-minute details for transfer of repatriated prisoners and handling of those refusing repatriation. Marked-up pages come back to Chi, to be retyped. The fighting, meanwhile, continues across the peninsula, for bits of territorial advantage. Officers of the two sides hurry back and forth with rolled-up maps, making new adjustments to the final line of demarcation.

Through it all, sleep or no sleep, Chi Chao-chu is motivated. Home beckons. The new China beckons.

The negotiators initially set Friday, July 24, for the signing. But inevitable delays push it back to Monday, July 27.

———

At Pyoktong, Camp 5, POW Clarence Adams seeks out a trusted instructor among the Chinese who lead the study groups. He has something important to discuss.

As the armistice and prisoner release near, after more than thirty-one months as a captive who follows orders, who merely survives, the U.S. Army corporal has been thinking deeply about what to do when he is finally a free man.

All of his reading in the camp library, all of what he has heard in the political lectures, has left him more than curious about communism.

Maybe it's as good and fair a system as they say it is, he thinks. He can't be sure, not having been to China, but he is sure about the system he'd go home to as a black man in Memphis—segregation, degradation, lack of opportunity.

He tells the instructor about his dilemma. He's told that under the truce agreement prisoners can choose not to return to their homeland.

But can he go to China?

The instructor consults with the camp command, returns, and tells Adams that China is an option.

But what would he do there? Adams wonders. What do you want to do? the instructor asks.

Adams, the twenty-four-year-old high school dropout, says he wants an education and a job. He's told he could go to university and certainly would get a job. Adams says he also wants a wife. The instructor laughs.

"We have a lot of women in China," he tells him. "But it's up to you to find your own wife."

FRIDAY, JULY 24, 1953

After three hundred missions, No Kum-sok survives

No one wants to be the last man to die in a war.

At their MiG-15 base at Antung, Manchuria, near the Yalu River, No Kum-sok and his fellow 2nd Air Regiment pilots spot a half-dozen Sabre jets crisscrossing the bleak gray skies above them, looking for a fight. Everyone knows the armistice is just days away. The Americans want to destroy as many MiGs as possible before the truce. The Koreans want to stay alive.

To their disgust, sixteen of them are ordered to scramble, to confront the F-86s.

Lieutenant No takes his MiG up as a wingman to a battalion captain's jet. Soon after they take off in tandem, the captain shouts into his radio, "My landing gear won't retract!" No, following standard procedure, radios that they should return to base. "Land at once!"

They land and taxi to their protective revetments, where mechanics are waiting.

Climbing down from his cockpit, No hears and then sees a MiG-15 roar in over the airfield at low altitude, pursued by a Sabre. The American opens fire, his machine-gun tracers tearing into the MiG's fuselage. His jet crippled, the Korean pilot tries to crash-land on the runway, but he overshoots and slams into the ground beyond, exploding into a fireball, as the victorious Sabre flies off. Far from the impact, No can feel a pulse of heat from the flames.

The doomed lieutenant is an old friend. Su Chul-ha was a schoolmate in Hungnam and had ridden together with No to the Naval Academy in 1949. They had gone off together for flight training in Manchuria in 1950. Now his friend is the last MiG pilot to die in this senseless war, but No Kum-sok, after three hundred missions, survives.

The opposing air forces' claimed "kills" have been questioned throughout the war, since jet pilots flashing by at high-subsonic speeds often have only glimpses of stricken enemy. But it seems more than a hundred of the North Korean MiGs have been destroyed in air-to-air combat, and probably more than six hundred Soviet and Chinese MiGs. The Americans reject communist claims of similar numbers of Sabres downed, but acknowledge at least two hundred lost, plus hundreds more of other aircraft types, including B-29 bombers, most of them victims of ground antiaircraft fire.[9]

MONDAY, JULY 27, 1953

An armistice is signed, ending years of blood and ruin,
as Chi Chao-chu looks on

Weeklong rains have left Panmunjom soggy with mud. As the appointed hour of 10:00 a.m. approaches, the sun is struggling to break through the clouds.

Somewhere in the distance, beyond the low hills ringing the neutral zone, the thud of artillery resounds. Minutes later the delegates enter the hastily built "Armistice Hall" to sign the agreement that will halt hostilities at 10:00 p.m. tonight, after three years, four weeks, and four days of war in Korea and more than two years of bitter negotiation.

The *T*-shaped hall, more like a shed, was erected in a week's time by the North Koreans. Wall panels of thatch are tacked to wooden frames under a roof of upturned eaves, pagoda-like. The North Koreans sought to adorn the entrance with "doves of peace"—a Pablo Picasso creation—but the Americans refused to enter under such a "communist symbol."

Translator Chi Chao-chu and other Chinese and North Korean staff have taken their places on metal folding chairs at one end of the large empty room, and the American staff at the other. In the center stand three tables. No South Korean officer is present, because of President Rhee's opposition to the agreement.

At 10:01 a.m. the chief delegates sit at two of the tables, the young Lieutenant General Nam Il of North Korea, in his gray, bemedaled dress uniform jacket, and the older American lieutenant general, William K. Harrison, in open-necked summer tans. A small red-star North Korean flag hangs limply from a tabletop stand before Nam, and the blue United Nations flag before Harrison. It is hot, temperatures rising toward the nineties.

The two men begin signing nine copies of the armistice document placed before each of them. The middle table is used for aides to transfer one side's signed documents to the other side for signing.

The silence is total, except for the whirring of newsreel cameras and the clicking of photographers' shutters. Neither general looks at the other. In ten minutes, the work is done. Eighteen signed copies, in blue and maroon binders, are stacked at the center table.

Harrison, who smiled faintly as he finished, now casts a long, searching look at Nam. The Korean barely notices. They rise and leave. The tension, the animosity, has held to the last.[10]

Chi Chao-chu, still drained from sleepless nights typing the final draft in English, feels enormous relief that the "fruitless bloodbath" is ending, three years after he left behind his studies in America to return to his homeland, to declare himself a patriot. His future now lies in the new China.

Besides the cease-fire, the final agreement provides for a two-and-a-half-mile demilitarized buffer zone along the final line of contact between the two sides, stretching across the peninsula; a Military Armistice Commission of five officers from each side to oversee the truce and the zone; and the freeing of war prisoners, beginning as early as later this week.[11]

The communists report holding 12,763 POWs, including 8,186 South Koreans, 3,313 Americans, and 1,264 Britons and other U.S.-allied soldiers. The Americans say 69,000 North Koreans and 5,000 Chinese will be returned to their countries, but 14,500 Chinese and 7,800 North Koreans refuse repatriation—those left after Syngman Rhee unilaterally freed 27,000 into his country in June.[12]

The "nonrepatriates" will be turned over to a commission of neutral nations for ninety days, during which representatives from their countries will try to persuade them to change their minds. Any still refusing repatriation will be sent to a neutral nation's territory and from there to wherever they wish, presumably Taiwan or South Korea.

The armistice also recommends that the warring governments convene a political conference within three months "to settle through negotiation the questions of the withdrawal of all foreign forces from Korea, the peaceful settlement of the Korean question, etc."[13]

Left untouched in the document are two explosive matters: the status of tens of thousands of southerners said to have been abducted to North Korea, and the question of justice for victims of war crimes, on all sides.

As the delegations depart Panmunjom, another artillery barrage echoes from afar.[14] The Korean War has hours yet to run.

Bill Shinn is in the streets of Seoul this armistice day, streets damp with rain as on that June Sunday three years ago when war first engulfed Korea. The journalist is sampling the feelings of ordinary people in the half-flattened city, the adopted hometown he twice fled and twice regained through the months of uncertain conflict.

What he finds are "mixed emotions of relief and fear," he writes.

The relief is over the end of the fighting, however tenuous, the end of the exhaustion of struggling to survive, of living uprooted lives.

The fear stems from the possibility—likelihood?—of renewed war. Shinn reports the Home Ministry is warning people communist guerrillas even now may be infiltrating the South. He cites refugees returning to Seoul who hesitate to rebuild their homes, afraid the enemy may come again.[15]

For the thirty-four-year-old Shinn, the correspondent who "broke" the Inchon landing story, the war has supplied countless moments of watching history unfold. But it has left him with disturbing memories, too—of his frightening last-minute dash across the Han River bridge with his little family, of his narrow escape from capture by the North Koreans, of the cries of the doomed on Execution Hill.

On this final day, his mind also turns northward, to his mother, father, and three sisters at their home near bombed-out Hamhung, above the 38th Parallel. Bill Shinn is now one of 10 million Koreans separated from their loved ones by the truce line. Will he ever see them again?

Typhoid. Dysentery. Typhus. Smallpox. Tuberculosis.

Disease is heedless of any truce. At the Maryknoll clinic in Pusan, in the midsummer's wilting heat, the stricken still line up in the hundreds.

In her pragmatic way, Sister Mary Mercy makes no mention in today's diary entry of what's happening at Panmunjom, but does record the good news that a donor installed a ceiling fan in the children's clinic and it "makes a noticeable difference in the hot building."

The diary also records the news from Sisters Augusta and Agnus Therese after a recent trip north, of "the utter and indescribable destruction" in the Seoul area.

Korea can lay claim to a "sad superlative," the mother superior writes. "It is the most devastated country of modern times. War's surge and ebb have left ruined rice paddies, gutted factories and hospitals, charred villages, broken churches and schools, 3,500,000 refugees and 100,000 homeless orphans."

Four out of every five South Korean hospitals have been destroyed in the war. In Pusan, only forty hospital beds are available to the public.[16] That's now the overriding goal for Doctor Elizabeth Hirschboeck, otherwise known as Sister Mary Mercy: a new hospital for this needy city.

Twice in recent weeks, she and her nuns held special days of prayer "to beg God's mercy and care of Korea." Afterward, they retreated to the wisteria arbor higher in the compound, to catch the breezes off the Sea of Japan, and the fragrance of the roses that adorn the grave of Alberta Marie, these Maryknoll sisters' own casualty of war.

At Camp 5 on the Yalu, the American and other POWs are ordered to fall in on the rain-soaked parade ground. They sense something big is about to happen.

A murmur slowly builds to a loud rumble among the excited prisoners. A Chinese camp instructor has to bellow out the news over the noise: the armistice has been signed.

A shout goes up over the muddy field as men laugh, cry, hug each other, slap backs, collapse with joy.

Clarence Adams is as happy as any. This young man who should have been discharged from the U.S. Army three years ago has instead spent thirty-two bleak months in enemy captivity, during which he had to amputate his own toes, lost nearly a third of his weight, watched friends die of starvation and disease.

Along with happiness, however, Adams harbors a secret from fellow prisoners: he won't be going home with them.

In the squalid cellar of an old Japanese house on Taegu's northern edge, the armistice offers some hope to men who have none.

This "special cell" of the Taegu military prison, once the storeroom for apples from the property's orchard, is where Ri In-mo has been serving out a seven-year sentence since his summary trial fifteen months ago for "hostile acts" as a communist guerrilla.

To the thirty-five-year-old North Korean party loyalist, this life underground, with fifty other prisoners jammed into an impossibly small space, is one of "unspeakable sufferings."

Almost all political prisoners, with a few common criminals, they receive a small ball of rice twice a day as rations, and have withered to gaunt, skeletal figures. They must sit on the floor most of the day in orderly rows, forbidden to speak unless spoken to, under the watchful eye of a brutal cell chief, a criminal trusty appointed by the guards. Men are beaten regularly. Men die.

Sometimes a body is not reported and removed for a day or two, so the cell chief can claim his rations. When the body grows cold, lice crawl out of it and swarm over the dead man's neighbors.

Unlike the men and women held in POW camps, these prisoners aren't covered by Panmunjom's repatriation process. But recently, unexpectedly, more sun has shone on their pale, sickly faces.

Instead of a daily ten minutes outdoors to exercise, they have been allowed into a yard for hours at a time. Someone decided their deathly appearance could prove an embarrassment if they are repatriated later under a settlement reached in the political talks envisioned in the armistice.

That is the hope held out to Ri In-mo on this day: to reunite with Sun-im, their daughter, and his mother in a peaceful Korea.

In the misty valleys of the central front, where some of the war's deadliest fighting has occurred, the big guns fall silent. It is 10:00 p.m., and First Lieutenant Hurh Won-moo, chief of the 76th Field Artillery's fire direction center, has his 155mm howitzers cease fire.

Word came down in early afternoon. The rumors were confirmed. Papers were signed at Panmunjom.

"So the war will be over tonight!" one of Hurh's men shouted.

But until then it went on. Around 8:00 p.m. the battalion's forward observers reported the Chinese were attacking, seemingly eager to take every possible new inch of territory before the curtain came down. Howitzers fired in support of the ROK 11th Division defenders. Chinese guns responded.

Now it has ended. On this seventh straight night of rain and fog, an unfamiliar quiet takes hold.

"So this is the solution?" Hurh asks himself. "And for what? Millions of people killed, but nothing has changed except for the destruction of human lives and their dreams."

The dreams destroyed include this star student's vision of university and law school, of a normal, peaceful life in Seoul, not years spent at war. Looking back, Hurh Won-moo feels miserable at having had a role in the killing. Looking ahead, he feels lost.

As the appointed hour passes, and white, red, and green flares burst in the black sky, his fire direction team doesn't celebrate in their bunker.[17] Instead, all are silent, alone with their thoughts. They have survived, when others haven't. But what lies ahead?

The nighttime streets of Kaesong blaze with lights for the first time in three years, reports Alan Winnington, who has based himself in that ancient city since the negotiations began there in July 1951. Before the war, Kaesong lay in South Korea. Now it will belong to the North.

In those earlier days, the London *Daily Worker* correspondent expected peace within three weeks. But he has long insisted to readers that the Americans sabotaged the negotiations, and "the war lasted almost two years longer than necessary." In the process, much was lost. "No country was ever so utterly destroyed as North Korea."

Now, he writes, "the armistice here has to be an uneasy one, full of hope and full of danger."[18]

As long ago as the war's first months, in those days when he discovered the vast mass graves of Taejon, the British communist journalist wrote of his fear that this Asian conflict would replicate what happened "after Spain and Czechoslovakia" in the 1930s. "After Korea?" he asked back then.[19]

As though in reply, a recent joint U.S.–British–French communiqué declared that "the struggle in defense of the independence of (Indochina) against aggressive communism is essential to the free world."[20] At a time when lights are coming on across Korea, shadows are falling over another corner of Asia.

As for Alan Winnington, after Korea, it's back to Peking, to his fiancée, Esther, and their newborn son and to vilification in the West for the unique window he offered on the horrors of war.

<hr />

A late-night haze clings to the broad, black Yalu as the truce hour passes.

Aboard a barge being towed across the river, Lieutenant No Kum-sok and four other pilots accompany five disassembled and crated-up MiG-15 jets, bound from Manchuria to Uiju airfield on the North Korean side, to beat the Panmunjom agreement's ban on transporting weapons into the Koreas post-truce.

The pilots are exhausted from days of hard work preparing the aircraft, but elated at having survived the vicious air war over Korea. The twenty-one-year-old No is more reserved, grateful to be among the living, when so many of his comrades are dead, but troubled at the prospect of returning to a society and system he cannot abide.

He'll also be returning to a land gutted to its core by war.

The Americans have dropped a total of 635,000 tons of bombs on Korea, almost all in the north, including some 33,000 tons of napalm, more total bomb tonnage than in the entire Pacific theater of World War II. Eighteen of the north's twenty-two major cities have been at least half destroyed. No's hometown of Hungnam is 85 percent gone, Pyongyang 75 percent.

The North Koreans count six hundred thousand homes demolished, along with eighty-seven hundred factories, five thousand schools, and one thousand hospitals. People emerging from underground shelters find that fishing boats, livestock, irrigation dams, agricultural equipment have been destroyed, portending great hunger. And where is the manpower to rebuild? How many have died? One million? Two million?[21]

No believes his mother is among them. He was told by an uncle, an air force major, that she died in the Hungnam bombings. The uncle, a loyal communist, didn't want the truth spread, that his sister-in-law had betrayed the nation and fled south.

To No Kum-sok, then, there's nothing left to go home to.

Now, midway across the river, the barge becomes stuck on a sandbar. They'll have to wait for the morning tide, coming in from the Yalu estuary, to lift them up to complete the crossing. They'll be violating the truce terms, but no matter. The North Koreans plan more secret shipments of MiGs across the Yalu in the coming days.

When the "2200" hour arrives to cease all fire in Korea, it's Monday morning in Washington, early on an oppressively hot day along the Potomac, much like the Sunday when the war began.

Fourteen months after leaving the Far East, General Matthew B. Ridgway takes satisfaction in how things are turning out in Korea.

Just yesterday, an article in the Sunday *New York Times Magazine* admiringly profiled the new army chief as "every inch the military man," who made his reputation "by deeds in the field—particularly when he helped to rejuvenate the beaten Eighth Army in Korea."[22]

His satisfaction stems, too, from having helped stave off pressure from some in America's political and military elite to widen the peninsular war into something bigger and more dangerous. He agreed with Truman, Acheson, and Marshall that the United States should not pursue a "vaguely defined 'victory'" over global communism. "We couldn't devastate the world," Ridgway later writes, "and go down the road of international immorality and pass the point of no return."

Matt Ridgway accepts congratulations from colleagues and friends for his role in helping restore peace in Korea, even a tentative one. On this armistice day, he can recall the backdrop of the past three years, of torn-up terrain "that looked like a landscape from Dante's Inferno" and "villages so blasted by heavy bombardment that hardly a roof remained," of the smell of human manure in the rice paddies, and the stench of human remains in the valleys and hills.

"War is the worst thing in the world," he will reflect. And, like every soldier, he has his own worst memories.

During his year as NATO commander, Matt Ridgway addressed the high commissioners overseeing the occupation of West Germany on a subject troubling leaders of the Western allies: whether to lighten the sentences of German generals convicted of committing war crimes during World War II. Prominent Germans were seeking such commutations, to better prepare for rebuilding a German army to join NATO in the midst of the Cold War.

Fifteen were sentenced to death for such crimes as the murder of Jews, of political prisoners, and of captured enemy soldiers.[23] In their defense, German pressure groups pointed to Korea and reports of mass political executions by U.S. ally South Korea, and to the U.S. carpet bombing of North Korean cities. The German generals were no worse, they suggested.[24]

Ridgway told the American, British, and French commissioners that he favored pardons. In a remarkably forthright statement, the former Eighth Army commander said he himself had given orders in Korea of the kind for which the German generals were sitting in prison.[25]

Ridgway didn't specify which orders from Korea he had in mind. Was it the January 1951 command to shoot refugees trying to cross the Han River in desperate flight from Seoul? The recommendations around the same time for the U.S. Air Force to destroy by firebombs all villages in the path of the Chinese advance, and to level Pyongyang in retribution for the loss of Seoul? Or the Eighth Army order to shoot all approaching civilians during the offensives and counteroffensives of spring 1951, an order that a lone Captain Abanto objected to? Might his statement also have related to Operation Killer in February 1951? Army veterans of "Killer" in later years will speak of instructions to "kill everything in front of us, including women and children."[26]

Ridgway did specify one thing in his stunning admission to the commissioners: that leniency should be shown only to those who fought for Hitler's Germany on the eastern front, against the Soviet communists.[27]

TUESDAY, JULY 28, 1953

On a morning of silent guns, the sight of the enemy
stuns Shin Hyung-kyu

The sun rises at 5:31 a.m. beneath gathering monsoon clouds, on this
first full day of peace and quiet after 1,129 days of the clamor and cries
of war, of the "insane world of kill or be killed," as Shin Hyung-kyu
thinks of it.

Across the Imjin River from the trenches of his ROK 1st Division,
the MP corporal watches as hundreds, even thousands, of Chinese troops
emerge from their holes, no longer in terror of artillery and napalm. He
is in awe, never imagining they faced an enemy of such numbers.

Elsewhere up and down the war front, now the armistice line, other
unimagined scenes play out.

In the Heartbreak Ridge area a North Korean shouts across, "Hey,
GI! No more shoot, shoot. We both go home!" Over barbed wire, American and Chinese troops exchange greetings, cigarettes, sweets. Soldiers
south of the line can hear the gongs and horns that once signaled attack
now accompanying *yangko*, Chinese peasant dancing.

Units on both sides are withdrawing to form the two-and-a-half-
mile-deep armistice buffer zone. First, they gather their fresh dead from
no-man's-land, victims of the final days' combat. Some of the missing
from years of war are never to be found, lost in a mountainous land, sun-
bleached skeletons.[28]

As the day simmers toward ninety-five degrees, Shin Hyung-kyu and
comrades retreat to the cooler confines of bunkers.

It always seemed their war would never end. Now that it has, they're
numb, silent like the guns. Shin thinks about all he has been through
since hunger drove him to sign up three Augusts ago, a sixteen-year-old
"boy soldier." In his mind's eye he sees the faces, of Mother, of fellow
MPs, of Americans, of Korean porters on the Imjin, men who went forward and didn't return. And he sees the frozen staring eyes of a little girl
he buried beside a Kaesong creek, so long ago now.

⸭

In the dark cave that has served as their latest battalion quarters on the
central front, Chen Hsing-chiu stirs from sleep well past dawn. He re-

tired earlier than the others last night, yet, as he looks around, he sees they're all gone. He's also the last of the medics to rise.

Was it unusually quiet overnight? He seems to have slept straight through, undisturbed by the usual thunder and vibration of enemy harassment shelling and bombing. But then, not all is quiet. In recent weeks, after twenty-eight months at the war front, Chen Hsing-chiu the weary soldier has begun hearing faint echoes of bombardment in his head, phantom sounds. Now that he's awake, they begin again. The eighteen-year-old medic has prescribed sedatives for himself, but they do no good.

He hurriedly dresses, picks up his aid kit, and walks out into the daylight toward the battalion clinic. He sees a large truck headed south on the base's rough road. It's a shocking sight, a Chinese army vehicle exposed in daytime. He runs toward it, waving it down. He shouts up to the driver.

"Comrade, be careful! Enemy planes!"

The baffled driver stares at the oblivious young medic.

"The war has ended!" he shouts back.

Chen is confused. "The war has ended?" he repeats quietly to himself.

As the truck rolls past, he sees it's loaded with wooden planks marked, "Demarcation Line." Another truck follows with more markers.

What? It must be true, Chen realizes. He knew the Panmunjom talks had made progress, but his simple act of heading off to sleep early meant he missed last night's message that guns would go silent at 10:00 p.m.

The war Chen Hsing-chiu entered at age sixteen—the days and months and years of dread and boredom, of terror and blood, of friends made and friends martyred—had become life itself. And now it's over.

"War is evil," he writes in his diary. "It destroys forests, homes, villages. It kills and maims human beings. It is a threat to the survival of mankind on Earth."

But this one, at least, has ended, he has survived, and he can go home a hero, one who helped humiliate the mighty U.S. imperialists.

"The entire Chinese people are proud. How can we not be, being victorious in this war? Rejoice! We are proud because we are Chinese."

⸺⁂⸺

Peng Teh-huai has spent the night at the compound of the truce delegation in Kaesong.

Last evening, this hero general of China's revolution, the Politburo member who encouraged Mao in his Korean gamble, the strategist who fought the enemy to a standstill and saved North Korea, celebrated what Peking Radio is calling a "glorious victory" at a grand banquet with the delegates and staff.

But as he prepared to sign the armistice as supreme Chinese commander in Korea, the tough old soldier was feeling some regret, not because of the huge human losses his army suffered in almost three years of war, but because he didn't inflict more on the Americans. "We had just become so well organized for combat. We had not fully used our might to deliver bigger blows to the enemy."

Now, at 9:30 this morning, he sits down in a Kaesong meeting room and puts his signature to copies of the armistice, signed last night by Kim Il-sung at his official mansion in Pyongyang, and earlier yesterday by General Mark Clark in Munsan, South Korea.

Supreme U.N. commander Clark also felt some disappointment, deeming himself the first American general to agree to an armistice without victory. "I cannot find it in me to exult at this hour," he said at Munsan.[29]

In their borrowed house in Donam-dong, on Seoul's hilly northeastern edge, Chang Sang and her mother greet the news with relief. Their odyssey through the Koreas may finally be ending. The privation, the fear of three years seem over.

But sadness shadows the happiness. Grandfather Kim is sinking into despair. The uprooted farmer who awakened ten-year-old Sang to news of war that Sunday long ago senses that his time will run out before he ever returns to his home country, the Yalu River bottomlands of North Pyongan Province.

They worry, too, about the fate of those left behind in the north: four brothers and two sisters of Sang's late father, offspring of wealth and land, and four of Mother's sisters, fervent Christians in a society that no longer tolerates them.

For Sang, meanwhile, star student at Sookmyung Girls' School, life has barely begun, and war's hardship, in its way, has prepared her for it.

"You have no brother, no father, a mother who is uneducated," she tells herself. "You're alone and you'd better fight. And you know what you have. You have only a mind."

⎯⎯∞⎯⎯

In Taejon, Park Sun-yong and husband Chung Eun-yong hope seven-month-old Koo-suk now can grow into girlhood in a land at peace in their brand-new home. With money borrowed from his father, Eun-yong has bought land and built a three-room house, a grand one by Korean standards, with a tile roof, pine-board floors, and a vegetable garden.

But the young couple remains weighed down with *han*, the crushing feeling of a wrong needing to be made right, of a need for justice, for the truth about Nogun-ri.

"Necks broken, legs broken, bullets in children's hearts. How can death be so tragic?" Sun-yong asks herself. "I will wonder for the rest of my life: Why did they kill my children? . . . Didn't the Americans come to help us? Why did they kill innocent people?"

Korea's innocent dead lie moldering, in uncounted numbers, in mass graves and trenches, on mountainsides and hilltops and in rice paddies, at the bottom of the Naktong River and the Songjin Harbor, in the rubble of Wonsan and the thick forests of the Chiri-san, on the slopes above POW Camp 5, in the lonely graveyards of the refugee camps.

Hon bul flicker and dance over the killing fields of Korea. *Han* grips the hearts of its long-suffering people. Three years of agony are ending. Decades more of division and danger have only just begun.

AFTER THE WAR

Chang Sang was graduated from Seoul's Ewha University, earned a master's degree at Yale Divinity School and a Ph.D. at Princeton Theological Seminary, was ordained as a Presbyterian minister, and as Rev. Dr. Sang Chang became president of Ewha University and Asia president of the World Council of Churches. In 2002, she served briefly as acting prime minister of South Korea.

Ri In-Mo was held as a prisoner in South Korea for forty-one years, until his release in 1993, when he was repatriated to a hero's welcome in North Korea and was reunited with his wife and daughter. His mother, who always believed she would see him again, died years earlier.

Park Sun-Yong reared a daughter and four sons in a busy Taejon household but remained haunted by the loss of her two children at Nogun-ri. Husband Chung Eun-yong's campaign to establish responsibility for the massacre culminated in 1999 when the Associated Press confirmed 7th Cavalry Regiment responsibility. In 2001, a U.S. Army investigation reaffirmed those findings, but the United States refused to apologize or grant compensation.

Yu Song-Chol, after returning to Pyongyang in 1958 from two years of study in the Soviet Union, was subjected to interrogations and an eventual purge from his position in the Korean People's Army, apparently because of old grudges held by Kim Il-sung and suspicions about the Siberia-born Yu's relations with the Soviets. He and wife Kim Yong-ok resettled in Soviet Kazakhstan.

Matthew B. Ridgway, as army chief of staff, successfully persuaded President Eisenhower against involving the U.S. military in another Asian land conflict, this time in Indochina. In the 1960s, after U.S. troops did enter the war in Vietnam, he was an early public advocate for a negotiated settlement and phased withdrawal.

No Kum-Sok defected to South Korea on September 21, 1953, by flying to Seoul's Kimpo Airport with a MiG-15, a prize for U.S. military intelligence. There he was reunited with his mother. He later worked in the United States as an aeronautical engineer with defense manufacturers and as an engineering professor.

Clarence C. Adams, after refusing repatriation and opting to go to China, was graduated from Wuhan University in Chinese literature, worked as an English translator in Peking, and married a Chinese woman. In 1966, amid the turmoil of China's Cultural Revolution, the couple left for the United States with their two small children. They eventually opened a chain of Chinese restaurants in his hometown of Memphis.

Sister Mary Mercy, Elizabeth Hirschboeck, M.D., oversaw the start of construction of a U.S. Army–supported, 160-bed Maryknoll Hospital in Pusan, as she envisioned. She then became administrator of Queen of the World Hospital, the first racially integrated general hospital in Kansas City, Missouri. She left that position in 1958 when elected vicaress general of the Maryknoll Sisters Congregation.

Chung Dong-Kyu remained in the ROK Army until 1956, then obtained a medical degree from Seoul's Soo-Doo Medical College, and later emigrated to the United States, where he became a prominent cardiologist in Long Beach, California, under the name Donald Chung. He was finally able to travel back to North Korea in 1983, but his mother, to whom he promised only a three-day absence in 1950, had died years earlier.

Buddy Wenzel accepted an invitation from James Hodges's family to work on their Florida farm. He was there in 1954 when Hodges's remains, finally identified by the army, came home from Korea for burial. He married a Hodges sister, Decar. He remained deeply troubled by what he did at Nogun-ri and by other war experiences, and received extensive treatment for post-traumatic stress disorder.

Bill Shinn served as a correspondent for the Associated Press in Seoul until 1957 and then worked for several other news organizations in Seoul and Tokyo. He and his wife, Sally Kim, later emigrated to the United States, settling in Los Angeles with their family. He never reunited with his family in North Korea.

Alan Winnington was refused renewal of his British passport in 1954, after being vaguely accused of treason in the British Parliament for his activities in North Korea's POW camps. Stranded in exile, he later relocated to East Germany, where he remarried, continued his *Daily Worker* reporting, and wrote thriller novels and children's books. His passport was restored in 1968. Declassified U.S. military materials eventually confirmed his 1950 reports on the Taejon political massacres.

Hurh Won-Moo remained an artillery officer in the ROK Army until 1958, when he won a scholarship to Monmouth College in Illinois. He later earned a Ph.D. at the University of Heidelberg, Germany, and taught sociology at Western Illinois University. Wartime nightmares never left him.

Shin Hyung-Kyu, discharged from the ROK Army in 1955, pursued his scientific interests in the United States, graduating from the University of Utah and doing doctoral and post-doctoral studies in chemistry at Utah and Cornell University. He taught at the University of Nevada–Reno and published scores of scientific papers on molecular chemistry. He dreamed often of being under attack in Korea's killing fields. His family never learned the fate of Older Brother in Seoul.

Ahn Kyong-Hee married her "guardian" Han Muk, the South Korean security agent who persuaded her to join him in killing her North Korean tormentor. The two reared two children in postwar South Korea.

Chi Chao-Chu went on to a distinguished career in China's Foreign Ministry, as English interpreter for Chou En-lai, Mao Tse-tung, and Deng Hsiao-ping; as the official who established the first Chinese diplomatic office in Washington; as ambassador to Britain; and as a United Nations under-secretary-general.

Pete McCloskey became a prominent California trial attorney and served sixteen years in the U.S. House of Representatives. In 1972 he ran unsuccessfully for the Republican presidential nomination on an anti–Vietnam War platform. Disturbed by war memories and at a counselor's suggestion, he once wrote a "letter" to the young North Koreans he surprised and killed in a trench on Hill 659, asking forgiveness.

Gil Isham, after his discharge in 1954, worked for twenty-five years at the Veterans Administration Hospital in Milwaukee. He underwent years of VA mental health counseling and eventually was declared 100 percent disabled with post-traumatic stress disorder. "I dream and fight the war over and over," he would say. "I did things I can't tell about."

Peng Teh-Huai worked to modernize the Chinese military as defense minister in the 1950s. In 1959, after criticizing aspects of Mao Tse-tung's "Great Leap Forward" economic program, he was removed from all official positions. In 1966, at the start of the Cultural Revolution, he was arrested, harshly interrogated, denounced as an "antiparty element," and brutalized. He died in detention.

Chen Hsing-Chiu returned to China in October 1953, became a Communist Party member, and spent several more years in the People's Liberation Army before assuming a civilian post as an administrator of a suburb of his hometown of Taiyuan. He also published several novels.

EPILOGUE

As recommended in the armistice agreement, the warring parties in April 1954 convened a political conference in Geneva, Switzerland, to try to establish a framework for elections and peaceful unification of the two Koreas. After sixteen sessions, the conference ended in failure in mid-June 1954. The communist side, deeming the United Nations a belligerent in the war, rejected its authority to oversee elections. It proposed instead oversight by a commission of neutral nations, an idea rejected by the United States and its allies, who declared the conference deadlocked and walked out.

Through the more than six decades that followed, no serious new effort at reunification was ever mounted. North Korea continued under the authoritarian rule of Kim Il-sung, his Workers' Party, and his family, down through the leadership of his son Kim Jong-il and then grandson Kim Jong-un. In the South, Syngman Rhee's repressive regime collapsed in 1960. South Korea then was ruled by military dictators from 1961 to 1988, when a democratic constitution was introduced.

During a brief democratic interlude in the South in 1960–1961, aggrieved survivors sought justice for atrocities committed by their own military and police against South Korean civilians during the war. That movement was quickly quashed. In 2005–2010, investigations by the government's Truth and Reconciliation Commission confirmed for the historical record many of the mass political executions of 1950–1951, but the National Assembly ignored the commission's recommendation for compensation to victims' survivors. Similarly, the commission confirmed a representative handful of cases of more than two hundred alleged massacres of South Korean civilians by the U.S. military, mostly air attacks, but the government did not take up a recommendation to seek U.S. reparations.

Final casualty figures from the war remain imprecise, except for the number of American dead, 36,574, and missing in action, 7,649 as of July 2019. Estimates of South Korean and North Korean military dead and missing vary widely—from 200,000 to 400,000 for each side, or even higher. Estimates of Chinese dead and unaccounted for range from 400,000 to 600,000.

It is generally accepted that at least 1 million civilians in the South and 1 million civilians in the North died.

ENVOI

My Fatherland! Country of resentful ghosts!
Your only constant companion
Has been calamity.
Once again your trusting and threadbare children
Are shaking their fists at Panmunjom
With desperate fury and anxiety.
But we hear no song to console the dead souls.

—**Ku Sang**, "Poetry on Burnt Ground," from *Brother Enemy*

ACKNOWLEDGMENTS

Bringing to life the experience of war seventy years ago in Korea would have been impossible without the willingness of twenty individuals to lay bare that chapter of their lives, through memoirs and other personal papers or directly in conversation with the author.

In that latter category, I am deeply grateful to Rev. Dr. Sang Chang, Park Sun-yong, Dr. H. K. Shin, Pete McCloskey, and the late Buddy Wenzel for the gift of their time in reliving those terrible days with me. Surviving spouses and other family members were also helpful, particularly Dr. Chung Koo-do on the story of his mother, Park Sun-yong, as well as Gloria Hurh, Della Adams, Esther (Cheo Ying) Samson, Ardith Isham, Decar Wenzel, and the late Juanita Royal.

Many others contributed to this work in many different ways over the years.

Simon Chiew and Ben Huang were admirably patient and astute in translating the story of young medic Chen Hsing-chiu for me. Stephanie Conning of the Maryknoll Mission Archives and Katie Blank at the Marquette University library helped flesh out the story of Sister Mary Mercy, Valerie Komor of Associated Press Corporate Archives the story of Bill Shinn, and Sonya Lee of the Library of Congress the story of Yu Song-chol.

I am indebted to Dr. Kim Maeng-ki of Kongju National University for historical Korean weather information, to *Busan Ilbo*'s Kim Ki-jin for his pioneering archival work on the war, and to Peter Englund for an inspiration, his World War I epic *The Beauty and the Sorrow*.

The resources of the U.S. National Archives, the New York Public Library, the Truman Library, the Wilson Center, and Hal and Ted Barker's online Korean War Project were vital to my research.

I was two years old when the Korean War broke out. It would be another forty-eight years before I took a serious interest in the subject, when I was teamed up with three remarkable younger Associated Press journalists—Choe Sang-hun, Martha Mendoza, and Randy Herschaft—to investigate and confirm the 1950 massacre at Nogun-ri. Those headlines were shocking to many Americans. Such a U.S. atrocity didn't fit the script of history. But our reporting barely scratched the surface of a dark underside of the war. The Nogun-ri story of 1999 opened the floodgates of suppressed memory and grief in South Korea, as accounts poured in of scores of other mass killings in 1950–1953. Through the years I reported on those events with colleagues from AP's Seoul bureau, especially Kim Hyung-jin and Chang Jae-soon, assisted by the investigators of South Korea's Truth and Reconciliation Commission under the leadership of Dr. Kim Dong-choon. That journalism, the product of many hands, underpins much of this current work.

It's a work enhanced by the illustrations of Jenni Sohn. More than a mapmaker, however, Sohn Jung-hee was also an invaluable guide and counselor on many things Korean as the book took final shape.

I am thankful to my agent, Peter Bernstein, for his perseverance in ensuring that the story of this hidden war would be told in depth, and to my editor, Clive Priddle, for ensuring that it would be told well. I also thank Kelly Lenkevich for shepherding the manuscript through to production so smoothly and professionally and Annette Wenda for her deft, sensitive copy editing.

Finally, as ever, I remain grateful to my beloved wife, Pamela, a source of encouragement, of "ghost editing," and of strength through many miles and many years of global travel and professional challenges.

A NOTE ON SOURCES

The individual narratives in *Ghost Flames* are drawn from memoirs, diaries, letters, personal interviews, and other primary sources, as well as from biographies written by others. The story of the broader war is based on numerous secondary sources, along with archival documents.

PRIMARY SOURCES

Chang Sang—In-person interviews, Seoul, September 22, 2014, and December 10, 2018; telephone interviews January 20, 2015, January 10, 28, and September 4, 2016. Also, "The President as Refugee," in Allan R. Millett, *Their War for Korea* (Washington, DC: Brassey's, 2002).

Ri In-mo—*Memoirs: My Life and Faith* (Pyongyang: Foreign Languages Publishing House, 1997); *Incarnation of Faith and Will: Notes of Ri In Mo, Former War Correspondent of the Korean People's Army* (Pyongyang: Foreign Languages Publishing House, 1993).

Park Sun-yong—In-person interview, Yongdong County, South Korea, September 19, 2014; interviews with son Chung Koo-do, 2018–2019; interviews with Park Sun-yong and husband Chung Eun-yong, 1998–2000, by Sang-hun Choe (Associated Press). Also, Park Kun-woong and Chung Eun-yong, *Massacre au Pont de No Gun Ri*, translation from Korean (Paris: Verso Graphic & Coconino Press, 2007).

Yu Song-chol—"Yu Song-chol's Testimony," nineteen-part memoir published in 1990 in the Seoul newspaper *Hanguk Ilbo*, translated and published in Sydney A. Seiler, *Kim Il-song, 1941–1948: The Creation of a Legend, the Building of a Regime* (Lanham, MD: University Press of America, 1994); Yu Song-chol memoir, "The Untold Story," *Koryo Ilbo* newspaper, Kazakhstan, 1991 (in Korean).

Matthew B. Ridgway—*Soldier: The Memoirs of Matthew B. Ridgway, U.S.A., Ret.* (New York: Harper & Brothers, 1956); Matthew B. Ridgway, *The Korean War* (New York: Doubleday, 1967). Also, George C. Mitchell, *Matthew*

B. Ridgway: Soldier, Statesman, Scholar, Citizen (Mechanicsburg, PA: Stackpole Books, 2002.)

No Kum-sok—*A MiG-15 to Freedom: Memoir of the Wartime North Korean Defector Who First Delivered the Secret Fighter Jet to the Americans in 1953* (Jefferson, NC: McFarland, 1996).

Clarence C. Adams—*An American Dream: The Life of an African American Soldier and POW Who Spent Twelve Years in Communist China*, ed. Della Adams and Lewis H. Carlson (Amherst: University of Massachusetts Press, 2007).

Sister Mary Mercy (Elizabeth Hirschboeck, M.D.)—Maryknoll Sisters Diaries, Pusan, Korea, 1951–1953, Maryknoll Mission Archives, Maryknoll, NY; Letters, Hirschboeck—Mary Mercy Papers, Raynor Memorial Libraries, Marquette University, Milwaukee, WI. Also, Sister Maria del Rey of Maryknoll, *Her Name Is Mercy* (New York: Charles Scribner's Sons, 1957).

Chung Dong-kyu—Donald K. Chung, M.D., *The Three-Day Promise: A Korean Soldier's Memoir* (Tallahassee: Father and Son, 1989).

Leonard (Buddy) Wenzel—In-person interviews, Lithia, Florida, March 28, September 12, and December 6, 2000; telephone interviews, July 7, 14, 20, 1999, and December 17, 2000. James Hodges's letters courtesy of Juanita Royal.

Bill Shinn—*The Forgotten War Remembered, Korea 1950–1953: A War Correspondent's Notebook and Today's Danger in Korea* (Elizabeth, NJ: Hollym International, 1996); Associated Press articles, 1950–1953, AP Corporate Archives.

Alan Winnington—*Breakfast with Mao: Memoirs of a Foreign Correspondent* (London: Lawrence and Wishart, 1986); *Daily Worker* articles, 1950–1953, Milstein Microform Reading Room, New York Public Library.

Hurh Won-moo—*"I Will Shoot Them from My Loving Heart": Memoir of a South Korean Officer in the Korean War* (Jefferson, NC: McFarland, 2012).

Shin Hyung-kyu—*Remembering Korea, 1950: A Boy Soldier's Story* (Reno: University of Nevada Press, 2001); telephone interviews, September 9, 2014, and March 21, 2016; correspondence, December 2016.

Ahn Kyong-hee—"Story of a POW Girl," in *6 Insides from the Korean War*, ed. Henry Chang (Seoul: Dae-Song Moon Hwa Sa, 1958).

Chi Chao-chu—*The Man on Mao's Right: From Harvard Yard to Tiananmen Square, My Life Inside China's Foreign Ministry* (New York: Random House, 2008).

Paul N. (Pete) McCloskey—Helen Hooper McCloskey, ed., *The Taking of Hill 610, and Other Essays on Friendship* (Woodside, CA: Eaglet Books, 1992); Pete McCloskey, ed., *A Year in a Marine Rifle Company, Korea, 1950–51* (Sunnyvale, CA: Patsons Press, 2013); telephone interviews, March 12, 2014, and January 10, 2015.

Gil Isham—John A. Sullivan, *Wounded in Action* (Catskill, NY: Press-Tige, 1996).

Peng Teh-huai—*Memoirs of a Chinese Marshal: The Autobiographical Notes of Peng Dehuai (1898–1974)*, trans. Zheng Longpu (Beijing: Foreign Languages Press, 1984). Also, Zhang Xi, "Peng Dehuai and China's Entry into the Korea War," trans. Chen Jian, *Chinese Historians* 6, no. 1 (1993); Juergen Domes, *Peng Te-Huai: The Man and the Image* (London: C. Hurst, 1985).

Chen Hsing-chiu—*A Thousand Days in the Korean Battlefield: A Diary of a Volunteer Soldier* (Beijing: Military Science Press, 2003; in Chinese).

SECONDARY SOURCES

Official histories of the Korean War were an essential resource, beginning with the three-volume U.S. Army series: Roy E. Appleman, *South to the Naktong, North to the Yalu: United States Army in the Korean War (June–November 1950)* (1960); Billy C. Mossman, *Ebb and Flow: November 1950–July 1951* (1990); Walter G. Hermes, *Truce Tent and Fighting Front* (1992), all published by the Office of the Chief of Military History, Department of the Army, Washington, DC.

Other official histories:

Charles R. Smith, ed., *U.S. Marines in the Korean War* (Washington, DC: History Division, United States Marine Corps, 2007).

Robert F. Futrell, *The United States Air Force in Korea, 1950–1953* (Washington, DC: Office of Air Force History, 1983).

The Sea Services in the Korean War (Annapolis, MD: Naval Institute Press, 2000).

Korea Institute of Military History, *The Korean War*, 3 vols. (Lincoln: University of Nebraska Press, 1997).

Research Institute of History, Academy of Sciences of the Democratic People's Republic of Korea, *History of the Just Fatherland Liberation War of the Korean People* (Pyongyang: Foreign Languages Publishing House, 1961).

The reports of the Truth and Reconciliation Commission of the Republic of Korea were invaluable in exploring long-hidden episodes of the war, as were declassified U.S. military documents unearthed at the National Archives by Associated Press investigative researcher Randy Herschaft, available at the Wikimedia site https://commons.wikimedia.org/wiki/Category:No_Gun_Ri_Massacre.

The book also draws on the digital archives of the Woodrow Wilson International Center for Scholars, Washington, DC; of the Harry S. Truman

Presidential Library, Independence, MO, particularly the joint 2010 Truman Library–CIA publication and DVD *Baptism by Fire: CIA Analysis of the Korean War*; and of the Associated Press and the *New York Times*.

More than 150 other books and journal articles illuminating aspects of the Korean War were consulted. Among the most important:

Xiaobing Li, Allan R. Millett, and Bin Yu, trans. and eds., *Mao's Generals Remember Korea* (Lawrence: University Press of Kansas, 2001).

Xiaobing Li, *China's Battle for Korea: The 1951 Spring Offensive* (Bloomington: Indiana University Press, 2014).

Chen Jian, *China's Road to the Korean War: The Making of the Sino-American Confrontation* (New York: Columbia University Press, 1994).

Kim Ki-jin, *The Korean War and Massacres* (Seoul: Blue History, 2006, in Korean, with 260 pages of English-language declassified and other archival documents).

Kim Dong-choon, *The Unending Korean War* (Larkspur, CA: Tamal Vista, 2009).

Taewoo Kim, "War Against an Ambiguous Enemy," *Critical Asian Studies* 44, no. 2 (2012).

Taewoo Kim, "Limited War, Unlimited Targets: U.S. Air Force Bombing of North Korea During the Korean War, 1950–1953," *Critical Asian Studies* 44, no. 3 (2012).

Sahr Conway-Lanz, *Collateral Damage: Americans, Noncombatant Immunity, and Atrocity After World War II* (New York: Routledge, 2006).

Su-kyoung Hwang, *Korea's Grievous War* (Philadelphia: University of Pennsylvania Press, 2016).

Stanley Sandler, ed., *The Korean War: An Encyclopedia* (New York: Garland, 1995).

Paul M. Edwards, *Korean War Almanac* (New York: Facts on File, 2006).

John W. Riley Jr. and Wilbur Schramm, *The Reds Take a City: The Communist Occupation of Seoul, with Eyewitness Accounts* (New Brunswick, NJ: Rutgers University Press, 1951).

William H. Vatcher Jr., *Panmunjom: The Story of the Korean Military Armistice Negotiations* (New York: Frederick A. Praeger, 1958).

Clay Blair, *The Forgotten War: America in Korea, 1950–1953* (New York: Times Books, 1987).

Sheila Miyoshi Jager, *Brothers at War: The Unending Conflict in Korea* (New York: W. W. Norton, 2013).

Allan R. Millett, *The War for Korea, 1950–1951: They Came from the North* (Lawrence: University Press of Kansas, 2010).

Conrad C. Crane, *American Airpower Strategy in Korea, 1950–1953* (Lawrence: University Press of Kansas, 2000).

Bruce Cumings, *The Korean War: A History* (New York: Random House, 2010).

Bruce Cumings, *The Origins of the Korean War*, vol. 2, *The Roaring of the Cataract, 1947–1950* (Princeton, NJ: Princeton University Press, 1990).

Russell Spurr, *Enter the Dragon: China's Undeclared War Against the U.S. in Korea, 1950–51* (New York: Newmarket Press, 1988).

Max Hastings, *The Korean War* (New York: Simon and Schuster, 1987).

John Toland, *In Mortal Combat: Korea, 1950–1953* (New York: William Morrow, 1991).

Lewis H. Carlson, *Remembered Prisoners of a Forgotten War: An Oral History of Korean War POWs* (New York: St. Martin's Press, 2013).

Richard M. Bassett, *And the Wind Blew Cold* (Kent, OH: Kent State University Press, 2002).

Virginia Pasley, *22 Stayed: The Story of 21 American GIs and One Briton Who Chose Communist China—Who They Were and the Reason for Their Choice* (London: W. H. Allen, 1955).

NOTES

PART 1
1950

June

1. Korea Institute of Military History (KIMH), *The Korean War* (Lincoln: University of Nebraska Press, 1997), 1:158.

2. KIMH, 1:237; George M. McCune, *Korea Today* (Cambridge, MA: Harvard University Press, 1950), 169.

3. Sheila Miyoshi Jager, *Brothers at War: The Unending Conflict in Korea* (New York: W. W. Norton, 2013), 38–51.

4. Bruce Cumings, *The Korean War: A History* (New York: Random House, 2010), 121–131.

5. Bill Shinn, *The Forgotten War Remembered: Korea, 1950–1953* (Elizabeth, NJ: Hollym International, 1996), 61.

6. KIMH, 1:157.

7. Roy E. Appleman, *South to the Naktong, North to the Yalu: United States Army in the Korean War (June–November 1950)* (Washington, DC: Office of the Chief of Military History, Department of the Army), Chapter 3.

8. KIMH, 1:187.

9. Appleman, 9.

10. Appleman, 10.

11. KIMH, 1:167.

12. Allan R. Millett, *The War for Korea, 1950–1951: They Came from the North* (Lawrence: University Press of Kansas, 2010), 94–95.

13. Report of the Ministry of Internal Affairs, Democratic People's Republic of Korea (DPRK), June 25, 1950, in the Digital Archive, History and Public Policy Program, Woodrow Wilson International Center for Scholars (Wilson Center).

14. Max Hastings, *The Korean War* (New York: Simon and Schuster, 1987), 73.

15. Department of the Army, Classified Teletype Conference DA TT 3415, June 25, 1950, Truman Library.

16. Jager, 66.

17. Raymond B. Maurstad, *SOS Korea, 1950* (Edina, MN: Beaver's Pond Press, 2003), 219.

18. Jager, 69.

19. KIMH, 1:160.

20. Associated Press (AP), June 26, 1950.

21. Maurstad, 236.

22. Maurstad, 236.

23. John Toland, *In Mortal Combat: Korea, 1950–1953* (New York: William Morrow, 1991), 35.

24. Dean Acheson, *Present at the Creation: My Years in the State Department* (New York: New American Library, 1970), 402.

25. AP, June 25, 1950.

26. Maurstad, 95.

27. Cumings, 56–57.

28. KIMH, 1:161.

29. KIMH, 1:166, 169.

30. Appleman, 29–30.

31. KIMH, 1:186.

32. William T. Bowers, William M. Hammond, and George L. MacGarrigle, *Black Soldier, White Army: The 24th Infantry Regiment in Korea* (Washington, DC: Center of Military History, United States Army, 1996), 37.

33. AP, June 26, 1950.

34. AP, June 26, 1950.

35. KIMH, 1:180.

36. KIMH, 1:185.

37. KIMH, 1:181–183.

38. Millett, 101.

39. John W. Riley Jr. and Wilbur Schramm, *The Reds Take a City: The Communist Occupation of Seoul, with Eyewitness Accounts* (New Brunswick, NJ; Rutgers University Press, 1951), 8.

40. Maurstad, 181.

41. Jager, 66–67.

42. Cumings, 14.

43. 7th Cavalry Regiment War Diary, June 25–July 1, 1950.

44. Research Institute of History, Academy of Sciences of the DPRK, *History of the Just Fatherland Liberation War of the Korean People* (Pyongyang, North Korea: Foreign Languages Publishing House, 1961), 28–29.

45. Suzy Kim, *Everyday Life in the North Korean Revolution, 1945–1950* (Ithaca, NY: Cornell University Press, 2013), 82–83.

46. Cornelius Osgood, *The Koreans and Their Culture* (New York: Ronald Press, 1951), 254.

47. Suzy Kim, 76–77, 37–38.

48. Department of the Army, Classified Teletype Conference DA TT 3426, June 27, 1950, Truman Library.

49. KIMH, 1:221; Millett, 102.

50. KIMH, 1:221.

51. Toland, 44.

52. O. H. P. King, *Tail of the Paper Tiger* (Caldwell, ID: Caxton Printers, 1962), 106–112.

53. Department of the Army, Classified Teletype Conference DA TT 3426, June 27, 1950, Truman Library.

54. Maurstad, 176, 226.

55. Maurstad, 176, 202.

56. KIMH, 1:228.

57. Riley and Schramm, 18; KIMH, 1:223; Toland, 46.

58. Robert F. Futrell, *The United States Air Force in Korea 1950–1953* (Washington, DC: Office of Air Force History, 1983), 12–13, 27–29.

59. Suh Ji-moon, ed. and trans., *Brother Enemy: Poems of the Korean War* (Buffalo, NY: White Pine Press, 2002), 43.

60. KIMH, 1:235–237; Maurstad, 228.

61. Harrison E. Salisbury, *The New Emperors: China in the Era of Mao and Deng* (New York: Avon Books, 1992), 106.

62. Xiaobing Li, *China's Battle for Korea: The 1951 Spring Offensive* (Bloomington: Indiana University Press, 2014), 11.

63. Li, 9.

64. Chen Jian, *China's Road to the Korean War: The Making of the Sino-American Confrontation* (New York: Columbia University Press, 1994), 126–127.

65. Statement by the President on the Situation in Korea—June 27, 1950, Timeline, CIA DVD *Baptism by Fire*, Truman Library.

66. Chen, 127–131.

67. Appleman, 38.

68. Chen, 131–132.

69. CIA Weekly Intelligence Report, June 27, 1950, DVD *Baptism by Fire*, Truman Library.

70. Research Institute of History, Academy of Sciences of the DPRK, *Just Fatherland Liberation War*, 34.

71. Appleman, 34–35.

72. Hastings, 73–75; Riley and Schramm, 49, 130.

73. KIMH, 1:287.

74. Futrell, 29–30.

75. AP, June 30, 1950.

76. Foreign Broadcast Information Service (FBIS), CIA, Weekly Survey, June 29, 1950, DVD *Baptism by Fire*, Truman Library.

77. KIMH, 1:287–288.

78. Appleman, 9, 27; Millett, 96.

79. KIMH, 1:290, 292; Appleman, 103.

80. Ciphered telegram, Shtykov to Stalin, July 1, 1950, Wilson Center.

81. Appleman, 46–48; Clay Blair, *The Forgotten War: America in Korea, 1950–1953* (New York: Times Books, 1987), 81–86.

82. CINCFE to COMGENARMYEIGHT, CX56978, June 30, 1950, Elsey Papers, Truman Library.

83. Blair, 84.

84. Blair, 78–79, 85.

85. CIA, "The Korean Situation," June 30, 1950, DVD *Baptism by Fire*, Truman Library.

86. Blair, 78.

87. Appleman, 55–58.

88. AP, July 2, 1950; King, 112–113.

89. Donald Nichols, *How Many Times Can I Die?* (Brooksville, FL: Brooksville Printing, 1981), 128.

90. AP, May 19, 2008.

July

1. KIMH, *The Korean War*, 1:287–291.

2. Kim Dong-choon, *The Unending Korean War* (Larkspur, CA: Tamal Vista, 2009), 110–111.

3. Appleman, *South to the Naktong*, 61–65.

4. AP, July 4, 1950.

5. *New York Times*, July 6, 1950.

6. U.N. Security Council Resolution S/1588 of July 7, 1950; Hastings, *The Korean War*, 346.

7. Bruce Cumings, *The Origins of the Korean War*, vol. 2, *The Roaring of the Cataract, 1947–1950* (Princeton, NJ: Princeton University Press, 1990), 316.

8. Cumings, *Origins*, 2:323.

9. Cumings, *The Korean War*, 116–139.

10. AP, May 19, 2008.

11. Appleman, 97.

12. Futrell, *The United States Air Force in Korea*, 93–103.

13. Riley and Schramm, *The Reds Take a City*, 124.

14. Riley and Schramm, 70.

15. Riley and Schramm, 49, 76; Kim Dong-choon, 116.

16. Riley and Schramm, 34–39; AP, June 29, 1950.

17. Riley and Schramm, 103–106.

18. Riley and Schramm, 72.

19. Kim Dong-choon, 51.

20. Riley and Schramm, 62.

21. DPRK Military Committee, Decree No. 18, "The Food Situation in Seoul," July 17, 1950, Wilson Center.

22. Riley and Schramm, 54–56.

23. Appleman, 210–211.

24. Appleman, 192.

25. Appleman, 197–198.

26. Futrell, 73.

27. *Daily Worker*, July 27, 1950; *I Saw the Truth in Korea*, pamphlet, September 1950.

28. Sahr Conway-Lanz, *Collateral Damage: Americans, Noncombatant Immunity, and Atrocity After World War II* (New York: Routledge, 2006), 87.

29. Futrell, 98; *The Sea Services in the Korean War* (Annapolis, MD: Naval Institute Press, 2000), Chapter 5.4.

30. Appleman, 198.

31. Appleman, 200.

32. Charles J. Hanley, "No Gun Ri: Official Narrative and Inconvenient Truths," *Critical Asian Studies* 42, no. 4 (2010): 598–599.

33. Eighth U.S. Army, Office of the Assistant Chief of Staff, G-2, Interrogation Report: "North Korean Methods of Operation," July 23, 1950; Hanley, 596.

34. Appleman, 200.

35. Conway-Lanz, 98–99.

36. Committee for the Review and Restoration of Honor for the No Gun Ri Victims, *No Gun Ri Incident Victim Review Report* (Seoul: Government of the Republic of Korea, 2009).

37. Charles J. Hanley, Sang-Hun Choe, and Martha Mendoza, *The Bridge at No Gun Ri* (New York: Henry Holt, 2001), 75.

38. Journal, 8th Cavalry Regiment, July 24, 1950.

39. G-1 Journal, 25th Infantry Division, July 26, 1950.

40. *New York Times*, July 26, 1950.

41. Major General Hobart R. Gay, directive to staff, 1st Cavalry Division, July 27, 1950.

42. Harold Joyce Noble, *Embassy at War* (Seattle: University of Washington Press, 1975), 152.

43. AP, July 26, 1950.

44. Appleman, 121–181.

45. CIA Daily Summary, July 25, 1950, DVD *Baptism by Fire*, Truman Library.

46. CIA Daily Summary, July 26, 1950.

47. Radio and Television Address to the American People on the Situation in Korea, July 19, 1950, DVD *Baptism by Fire*, Truman Library.

48. Appleman, 251.

49. *Times* (London), July 24, 1950.

50. FBIS, Weekly Survey, August 10, 1950, DVD *Baptism by Fire*, Truman Library.

51. Hanley, Choe, and Mendoza, 86.

52. *Cho Sun In Min Bo*, August 19, 1950.

53. AP, July 30, 1950.

54. AP, July 30, 1950.

55. Millett, *The War for Korea, 1950–1951*, 215.

56. Hanley, Choe, and Mendoza, 185.

57. Outgoing Classified Message JCS 87522 to CINCFE Tokyo, July 31, 1950, Truman Library.

58. Conrad C. Crane, *American Airpower Strategy in Korea, 1950–1953* (Lawrence: University Press of Kansas, 2000), 168.

59. Outgoing Classified Message JCS 87570 to CINCFE Tokyo, July 31, 1950, Truman Library.

60. Millett, 169.

61. Appleman, 210–211; Research Institute of History, Academy of Sciences of the DPRK, *Just Fatherland Liberation War*, 54.

62. *Daily Worker*, August 9, 1950.

63. Jon Halliday and Bruce Cumings, *Korea: The Unknown War* (New York: Pantheon Books, 1988), 92; AP, May 19, 2008.

64. Su-kyoung Hwang, *Korea's Grievous War* (Philadelphia: University of Pennsylvania Press, 2016), 121.

65. AP, May 19, 2008; "Korean Situation," CIA, July 3, 1950, Truman Library; G-2 Interrogation, Item 2, Headquarters 1st Cavalry Division, August 17, 1950.

66. Cumings, *The Korean War*, 202; AP, July 11, 2010; Kim Dong-choon, "Forgotten War, Forgotten Massacres: The Korean War (1950–1953) as Licensed Mass Killings," *Journal of Genocide Research* 6 no. 4 (2004): 523–544.

August

1. Hanley, Choe, and Mendoza, *The Bridge at No Gun Ri*, 75.

2. 35th Fighter-Bomber Squadron, mission reports, July 20 and July 31, 1950.

3. Truth and Reconciliation Commission, Republic of Korea (TRCK), Comprehensive Report III, Incidents of Large-Scale Civilians Deaths, 2010, 188; Cable, US Embassy–Seoul to State Department, "ROK Press Reporting on Incidents said to be similar to Nogun-ri," October 20, 1999.

4. Appleman, *South to the Naktong*, 225–226.

5. Hanley, Choe, and Mendoza, 150–156.

6. Log, 1st Battalion, 8th U.S. Cavalry Regiment, August 9, 1950.

7. Command Report, 2nd Infantry Division, July 8–August 31, 1950.

8. Blair, *The Forgotten War*, 172.

9. *Daily Worker*, August 7, 1950.

10. *Daily Worker*, August 11, 1950.

11. Appleman, 11, 263–264.

12. Kim Dong-choon, *The Unending Korean War*, 104–106, 97.

13. Shtykov to Foreign Ministry, Moscow, August 11, 1950, Wilson Center.

14. Taewoo Kim, "War Against an Ambiguous Enemy," *Critical Asian Studies* 44, no. 2 (2012): 216.

15. Appleman, 271–272; Charles R. Smith, ed., *U.S. Marines in the Korean War* (Washington, DC: History Division, United States Marine Corps, 2007), 24–30.

16. George C. Mitchell, *Matthew B. Ridgway: Soldier, Statesman, Scholar, Citizen* (Mechanicsburg, PA: Stackpole Books, 2002), 67.

17. Blair, 184–185.

18. Dai-Ichi Life Insurance Co. website.

19. Blair, 185–186; James F. Schnabel, *Policy and Direction: The First Year* (Washington, DC: Center of Military History, United States Army, 1972), 131; Appleman, 289–291; Jager, *Brothers at War*, 81.

20. Millett, *The War for Korea*, 202–204; Blair, 187; Jager, 81.

21. AP, April 20, 2000.

22. Kim Dong-choon, *The Unending Korean War*, 97.

23. TRCK, newsletter, March 2010.

24. TRCK, Report on the Activities of the Past Three Years, January 2009.

25. Kim Dong-choon, *The Unending Korean War*, 108–109.

26. Futrell, *The United States Air Force in Korea*, 131.

27. Hanley, Choe, and Mendoza, 157–158; Melbourne C. Chandler, *Of Garry Owen in Glory: The History of the Seventh United States Cavalry Regiment* (Annandale, VA: Turnpike Press, 1960), 251–257.

28. Appleman, 347–350.

29. Journal, 1st Cavalry Division Artillery Command, August 29, 1950.

30. Hanley, Choe, and Mendoza, 200; AP, July 7, 1951.

31. Appleman, 376–392.

32. Clifford memo to Truman, June 29, 1950, Truman Library.

33. AP, July 11, 2010.

34. AP, August 4, 2008.

35. AP, July 11, 2010.

36. TRCK, newsletter, June 19, 2009; Cable, US Embassy–Seoul to State Department, "ROK Press Reporting on Incidents Said to Be Similar to Nogun-ri," October 20, 1999.

37. AP, July 11, 2010; TRCK, Report of Civilian Sacrifice Subcommittee, March 2008; Hwang, *Korea's Grievous War*, 175.

38. Futrell, 138–139.

39. Incoming Message, W88697, General Headquarters, Far East Command, Adjutant General's Office, August 15, 1950.

40. Unit Journal, Headquarters, 61st Field Artillery Battalion, August 29, 1950.

September

1. *Harvard Crimson*, September 1, 1950.

2. Stanley Sandler, ed., *The Korean War: An Encyclopedia* (New York: Garland, 1995), 215.

3. *Harvard Crimson*, September 1, 1950.

4. *Daily Worker*, September 1, 4, 1950.

5. Futrell, *The United States Air Force in Korea*, 148–149.

6. Esther Cheo Ying, *Black Country to Red China* (London: Vintage Digital, 2009), 211–214.

7. Jon Halliday, "Anti-Communism and the Korean War (1950–1953)," *Socialist Register* 21 (1984): 146.

8. Appleman, *South to the Naktong*, 412.

9. Sandler, 282–283.

10. James L. Stokesbury, *A Short History of the Korean War* (New York: William Morrow, 1988), 55–56.

11. Stokesbury, 58–61; KIMH, *The Korean War*, 1:511.

12. Blair, *The Forgotten War*, 242–264; Stokesbury, 61–62.

13. *New York Times*, September 13, 1950.

14. Hastings, *The Korean War*, 346.

15. Smith, *U.S. Marines in the Korean War*, 7.

16. Smith, 70.

17. Kim Dong-choon, *The Unending Korean War*, 126–127.

18. *International Herald Tribune*, July 21, 2008.

19. Robert J. Dvorchak, *Battle for Korea: The Associated Press History of the Korean Conflict* (Conshohocken, PA: Combined Books, 1993), 59.

20. Appleman, 503–509.

21. Sandler, 144.

22. Phillip Knightley, *The First Casualty* (New York: Harcourt, Brace, Jovanovich, 1975), 341.

23. Sandler, 284–286.

24. Chandler, *Of Garry Owen*, 269–271.

25. *New China News Agency* (Pyongyang), September 18, 1950.

26. KIMH, 1:656.

27. Appleman, 546.

28. KIMH, 1:656.

29. Research Institute of History, Academy of Sciences of the DPRK, *Just Fatherland Liberation War*, 67.

30. Appleman, 575.

31. Appleman, 9, 23, 287, 365.

32. Appleman, 603; David A. Mason, "Jirisan: Sacred Aspects and Assets," *Transactions of the Royal Asiatic Society—Korea Branch* 82 (2007): 89–107.

33. KIMH, 1:169–176.

34. Smith, 143, 163.

35. Appleman, 520–523.

36. Appleman, 527–536.

37. History of the 7th Infantry Division, 7th Infantry Division Association, https://7ida.us/documents/History_of_the_7th_Infantry_Division.pdf.

38. Summary of Information, Headquarters, 7th Div Team, October 4, 1950.

39. Walter G. Hermes, *Truce Tent and Fighting Front* (Washington, DC: Center of Military History, United States Army, 1992), 233.

40. Command Report, 2nd Infantry Division, September 1–October 31, 1950.

41. Appleman, 530–536.

42. Appleman, 541.

43. *U.S. News and World Report*, November 3, 2003.

44. Sandler, 316.

45. Telegram from Shtykov to Gromyko and Stalin, September 29, 1950, Wilson Center; Telegram from Kim and Pak Heon-yeong to Stalin, September 29, 1950, Wilson Center.

46. Futrell, 101–102.

47. Telegram from Kim and Pak Heon-yeong to Stalin, September 29, 1950, Wilson Center.

48. *The Sea Services in the Korean War*, Chapter 2.3.

49. Chen, *China's Road*, 172.

October

1. AP, October 3, 1950; Appleman, *South to the Naktong*, 587–588.

2. Riley and Schramm, *The Reds Take a City*, 121, 149.

3. AP, October 5 and October 4, 1950.

4. Taewoo Kim, "Limited War, Unlimited Targets: U.S. Air Force Bombing of North Korea during the Korean War, 1950–1953," *Critical Asian Studies* 44, no. 3 (2012): 477.

5. Reginald Thompson, *Cry Korea* (London: MacDonald, 1951), 94.

6. Joseph C. Goulden, *Korea, the Untold Story of the War* (New York: McGraw-Hill, 1983), 230.

7. *New York Times*, September 30, October 8, 1950.

8. *New York Times*, September 30, 1950.

9. Wolfgang Bartke, *Who Was Who in the People's Republic of China* (Munich: K. G. Saur, 1997), 2:361; Alfred K. Ho, *China's Reforms and Reformers* (Westport, CT: Praeger, 2004), 33.

10. Sergei N. Goncharov, John W. Lewis, and Que Litai, *Uncertain Partners: Stalin, Mao, and the Korean War* (Stanford, CA: Stanford University Press, 1995), 185.

11. Futrell, *The United States Air Force in Korea*, 221.

12. Appleman, *South to the Naktong*, 615, 622–625.

13. Blair, *The Forgotten War*, 328–336; Jager, *Brothers at War*, 113–114.

14. Jager, 117–118; Blair, 346–349.

15. Chen, *China's Road*, 169; Clayton Laurie, "The Korean War and the Central Intelligence Agency," in DVD *Baptism by Fire*, Truman Library, 13.

16. Li, *China's Battle*, 30–36; Anthony Farrar-Hockley, "A Reminiscence of the Chinese People's Volunteers in the Korean War," *China Quarterly*, no. 98 (June 1984): 293.

17. Xu Yan, "The Chinese Forces and Their Casualties in the Korean War: Facts and Statistics," trans. Li Xiaobing, *Chinese Historians: The Journal of Chinese Historians* 6 (Fall 1993): 48.

18. Zhang Xi, "Peng Dehuai and China's Entry into the Korean War," *Chinese Historians: The Journal of Chinese Historians* 6 (Spring 1993): 23–24; Chen, *China's Road*, 196–200.

19. Chen, 206–208.

20. Li, 35–36.

21. Farrar-Hockley, 294; Salisbury, *The New Emperors*, 116; Li, 30, 38.

22. *New York Times*, October 21, 1950.

23. Zhang, 27.

24. Thompson, 143.

25. Hanley, Choe, and Mendoza, *The Bridge at No Gun Ri*, 172.

26. Blair, 357–358; Toland, *In Mortal Combat*, 248; Thompson, 181.

27. Hanley, Choe, and Mendoza, 171.

28. James Wright, "What We Learned from the Korean War," www.theatlantic.com/international/archive/2013/07/what-we-learned-from-the-korean-war/278016/.

29. Chandler, *Of Garry Owen*, 285–286.

30. United Press, October 29, 1950.

31. AP, October 25, 1950.

32. KIMH, *The Korean War*, 1:861.

33. Blair, 365–366.

34. Blair, 363–364.

35. *New York Times*, October 31, 1950; AP, October 30, 1950.

36. Roy E. Appleman, *Disaster in Korea: The Chinese Confront MacArthur* (College Station: Texas A&M University Press, 2009), 316.

37. Appleman, *South to the Naktong*, 62.

38. *New York Times*, October 31, 1950; Cumings, *The Korean War*, 106, 191.

39. Osgood, *The Koreans and Their Culture*, 44.

40. Sunghoon Han, "The Ongoing Korean War at the Sinchon Museum in North Korea," *Cross-Currents: East Asia History and Culture Review*, e-journal, no. 14 (March 2015); Kim Dong-choon, "Forgotten War, Forgotten Massacres," 523–544.

41. Letter, Colonel Francis Hill, Civil Assistance Section, Headquarters, U.S. Eighth Army, to U.S. Embassy, Seoul, November 16, 1950, in Kim Ki-jin, *The Korean War and Massacres* (Seoul: Blue History, 2006; in Korean), 397.

November

1. Li, *China's Battle*, 35–43.

2. Appleman, *South to the Naktong*, 689.

3. Richard A. Peters and Xiaobing Li, *Voices from the Korean War: Personal Stories of American, Korean, and Chinese Soldiers* (Lexington: University Press of Kentucky, 2005), 89–92.

4. Appleman, 689–708.

5. Li, 46–47.

6. Memorandum for the President, CIA, November 1, 1950, DVD *Baptism by Fire*, Truman Library.

7. AP, October 30, 1950.

8. Office of the Chief, U.S. Military Advisory Group to the Republic of Korea, Memorandum to Commanding General, Eighth U.S. Army Korea, August 15, 1950.

9. BL/695, To the ICRC Geneva, October 23, 1950, in Kim Ki-jin, *The Korean War and Massacres*, 444.

10. AP, July 7, 2008.

11. *New York Times*, November 9, 1950; Glenn D. Kittler, *The Maryknoll Fathers* (Cleveland: World, 1961), 268–276.

12. Appleman, 736.

13. Blair, *The Forgotten War*, 417.

14. Appleman, 733.

15. AP, November 21, 1950.

16. Blair, 418; AP, November 20, 1950.

17. Appleman, 735–736.

18. Blair, 390; AP, November 21, 1950.

19. Appleman, 762.

20. Li, 30; Juergen Domes, *Peng Te-Huai: The Man and the Image* (London: C. Hurst, 1985), 61.

21. Chandler, *Of Garry Owen*, 288.

22. Billy C. Mossman, *Ebb and Flow: November 1950–July 1951* (Washington, DC: Center of Military History, United States Army, 1990), 49; Thompson, *Cry Korea*, 236.

23. Command Report, 2nd Infantry Division, November 1950.

24. Xiaobing Li, Allan R. Millett, and Bin Yu, trans. and eds., *Mao's Generals Remember Korea* (Lawrence: University Press of Kansas, 2001), 85–86, 118–121; Alan Winnington, *Breakfast with Mao: Memoirs of a Foreign Correspondent* (London: Lawrence and Wishart, 1986), 124; Salisbury, *The New Emperors*, 118.

25. Zhang, "Peng Dehuai and China's Entry," 15.

26. Sahr Conway-Lanz, *Collateral Damage*, 109.

27. Futrell, *The United States Air Force in Korea*, 221, 223; Taewoo Kim, "Limited War," 480.

28. Sahr Conway-Lanz, 151.

29. Taewoo Kim, 484.

30. Li, *China's Battle*, 49–50.

31. Mossman, 61–83; Li, *China's Battle*, 34, 49.

32. Command Report, 38th Infantry Regiment, 2nd Infantry Division, November 1950.

33. Mossman, 126.

34. David Halberstam, *The Coldest Winter* (New York: Hyperion, 2007), 467.

December

1. President's News Conference, November 30, 1950, Truman Library.

2. AP, November 30, 1950.

3. Hanley, Choe, and Mendoza, *The Bridge at No Gun Ri*, 173–175.

4. Journal, 2nd Battalion, 7th Cavalry Regiment, December 2, 1950.

5. Hanley, Choe, and Mendoza, 174–175.

6. Mossman, *Ebb and Flow*, 131; Command Report, 7th Infantry Division, 1 December–30 December 1950.

7. Shinn, *The Forgotten War Remembered*, 159.

8. Smith, *U.S. Marines in the Korean War*, 234–241, 251, 261–265, 287–295; Pete McCloskey, ed., *A Year in a Marine Rifle Company, Korea, 1950–51* (Sunnyvale, CA: Patsons Press, 2013), 43–81.

9. Mossman, 103–104, 128–130.

10. *Milwaukee Sentinel*, December 13, 1950.

11. KIMH, *The Korean War*, 2:177.

12. Colonel John F. Greco (IX Corps assistant chief of staff, G-2), "Enemy Tactics, Techniques and Doctrine," September 14, 1951, 46–47; Paik Sun-yup, *From Pusan to Panmunjom* (Washington, DC: Potomac Books, 1992), 187.

13. TRCK, Report on the Activities of the Past Three Years, January 2009, 92.

14. TRCK, Report on the Activities of the Past Three Years, January 2009, 107.

15. *The Sea Services in the Korean War*, Chapter 9.2; Mossman, 165.

16. AP, December 24, 1950.

17. Russell Spurr, *Enter the Dragon: China's Undeclared War Against the U.S. in Korea, 1950–51* (New York: Newmarket Press, 1988), 224–233.

18. Spurr, 224–233, 265–267; Li, Millett, and Yu, *Mao's Generals Remember Korea*, 17, 52.

19. Li, Millett, and Yu, 17–18, 45; Li, *China's Battle*, 53–55.

20. Blair, *The Forgotten War*, 528–529.

21. Li, Millett, and Yu, 17–18, 45; Li, 53–55.

22. Sandler, *The Korean War: An Encyclopedia*, 286–288.

23. Meeting of the President with Congressional Leaders in the Cabinet Room, Wednesday, December 13, 1950, President's Secretary's Files, Truman Library.

24. Schnabel, *Policy and Direction*, 299–300.

25. Spencer C. Tucker, ed., *Encyclopedia of the Korean War* (Santa Barbara, CA: ABC-CLIO, 2000), 1:5.

26. AP, December 18, 1950.

27. AP, December 17, 1950.

28. TRCK, News Letter, Issue 4, September 19, 2008.

29. TRCK, Report on the Activities of the Past Three Years, January 2009.

30. Cumings, *Origins*, 2:702.

31. United Press, December 18, 1950.

32. Outgoing Telegram, Department of State, AMEMBASSY, Seoul, December 18, 1950, U.S. National Archives.

33. *New York Times*, October 27, 1950; Incoming Telegram, Department of State, From: Tokyo, To: Secretary of State, Unnumbered, December 19, 1950, U.S. National Archives.

34. Mossman, 165–175; *The Sea Services in the Korean War*, Chapter 9.4.

35. Strength Report, Adjutant General, 7th Infantry Division, December 20, 1950; Personnel Daily Summary, 7th Infantry Division, December 20, 1950.

36. G-3 Journal, 7th Infantry Division, 20 December 1950.

37. Mossman, 165–175; *The Sea Services in the Korean War*, Chapter 9.4.

38. Kim Hyung-chan, *Distinguished Asian Americans: A Biographical Dictionary* (Westport, CT: Greenwood Press, 1999), 127–129.

39. AP, December 22, 1950.

40. Korea Society, *Last Ship in the Harbor*, video documentary, 2010; *The Sea Services in the Korean War*, Chapter 9.4.

41. Mossman, 165–175; *The Sea Services in the Korean War*, Chapter 9.4.

42. Personnel Periodic Report, 7th Infantry Division, December 24, 1950.

43. Millett, *The War for Korea*, 306; Crane, *American Airpower*, 48; Kathryn Weathersby, "New Russian Documents on the Korean War," *Cold War International History Project Bulletin* (Winter 1995–1996): 48.

44. George E. Stratemeyer, *The Three Wars of Lt. Gen. George E. Stratemeyer: His Korean War Diary*, ed. William T. Y'Blood (Washington, DC: Air Force History and Museums Program, 1999), 252.

45. Crane, 49.

46. Crane, 49.

47. Telegram from Stalin to Kim Il-sung, November 20, 1950, Wilson Center.

48. FBIS, Far East Survey, December 21, 1950, DVD *Baptism by Fire*, Truman Library.

49. *New York Times*, December 23, 1950.

50. *Washington Post*, December 25, 1950.

PART 2
1951

January

1. Mossman, *Ebb and Flow*, 192–195.

2. KIMH, *The Korean War*, 2:350 (map).

3. FBIS, Far East Survey, December 21, 1950, January 5, 1951, DVD *Baptism by Fire*, Truman Library.

4. AP, December 11, 1950.

5. *New York Times*, December 28, 1950.

6. *New York Times*, December 26–28, 1950; Millett, *The War for Korea*, 386; Blair, *The Forgotten War*, 598.

7. Mossman, 198.

8. Hurh Won-moo, *"I Will Shoot Them from My Loving Heart": Memoir of a South Korean Officer in the Korean War* (Jefferson, NC: McFarland, 2012), 46.

9. AP, January 3, 1951.

10. Blair, 594.

11. Blair, 597.

12. KIMH, 2:368.

13. Blair, 603; Futrell, *The United States Air Force in Korea*, 378.

14. AP, January 3, 1950.

15. Rene Cutforth, *Korean Reporter* (London: Allan Wingate, 1952), 116–117.

16. Incoming Message, Office of the Adjutant General, Eighth U.S. Army Korea, January 3, 1951.

17. S-1 Journal, Headquarters 2nd Battalion, 8th Cavalry Regiment, January 3, 1951.

18. CIA, Information Report, "Conditions in Seoul During the Second Communist Occupation," August 24, 1951, www.cia.gov/library/readingroom /docs/CIA-RDP82-00457R008100530006-2.pdf.

19. Jager, *Brothers at War*, 162–163; Shen Zhihua, "Sino-North Korean Conflict and Its Resolution During the Korean War," *Cold War International History Project Bulletin* (Wilson Center), nos. 14–15 (2002): 15.

20. Li, *China's Battle*, 57–58; FBIS, Weekly Survey, January 5, 1951, DVD *Baptism by Fire*, Truman Library.

21. Li, Millett, and Yu, *Mao's Generals Remember Korea*, 19, 90.

22. Jager, 162–163; Shen, 15.

23. Journal, 2nd Battalion, 8th Cavalry Regiment, January 20, 1951; Command Report, 1st Cavalry Division, January 19, 1951.

24. Memorandum for General Ridgway, Headquarters, Eighth United States Army, January 5, 1951.

25. Kim Dong-choon, "The Long Road Toward Truth and Reconciliation," *Critical Asian Studies* 42, no. 4 (2010): 578.

26. AP, August 4, 2008.

27. Steven Lee, "The United States, the United Nations, and the Second Occupation of Korea, 1950–1951," *Japan Focus/Asia-Pacific Journal* (March 16, 2009).

28. Mossman, 240–247; Blair, 655–663.

29. *New York Times*, January 29, 1951.

30. AP, December 28, 1999; AP interview with Jim Becker, December 1, 1999.

31. *New York Times*, March 29, 1951; letter, Christian Children's Fund, March 19, 1951, at Korean War Children's Memorial website, www.koreanchildren.org; *New York Times*, February 9, 1951.

February

1. Lewis H. Carlson, *Remembered Prisoners of a Forgotten War: An Oral History of Korean War POWs* (New York: St. Martin's Press, 2013), 153–154.

2. Mossman, *Ebb and Flow*, 295–300; Shinn, *The Forgotten War Remembered*, 173–174.

3. 1st Battalion, 5th Marines, War Diary, February 1951; Smith, *U.S. Marines in the Korean War*, 365–366; Mossman, 308.

4. Mossman, 310.

5. Mossman, 615, 689–690.

6. Kim Dong-choon, *The Unending Korean War*, 159–170, 174; TRCK News Letter, December 19, 2008; Kim Dong-choon, "Forgotten War, Forgotten Massacres," 523–544.

7. Philip Short, *Mao: The Man Who Made China* (London: I. B. Tauris, 2017), 427–428.

8. Li, Millett, and Yu, *Mao's Generals Remember Korea*, 99.

9. Li, Millett, and Yu, 21.

10. Li, *China's Battle*, 61, 69.

11. Li, 60.

12. Mossman, 313.

13. Li, 69.

March

1. Mossman, *Ebb and Flow*, 328–330.

2. Sandler, *The Korean War: An Encyclopedia*, 315.

3. Conway-Lanz, *Collateral Damage*, 150–151.

4. Mossman, 319; Blair, *The Forgotten War*, 743.

5. Mossman, 320.

6. CIA, Daily Intelligence Digest, March 21, 1951, DVD *Baptism by Fire*, Truman Library.

7. Futrell, *The United States Air Force in Korea*, 338.

8. Li, *China's Battle*, 63–69.

9. Li, Millett, and Yu, *Mao's Generals Remember Korea*, 131.

10. AP, July 7, 1951.

11. Penny Lernoux, *Hearts on Fire: The Story of the Maryknoll Sisters* (Maryknoll, NY: Orbis Books, 2012), 230.

12. Farrar-Hockley, "A Reminiscence," 294–295.

13. AP, March 19–20, 1951.

14. Conway-Lanz, 110.

15. Li, 68; Futrell, 339.

16. Headquarters, 38th Infantry, S-2 Evaluation, May 1951 (June 29, 1951).

17. Jager, *Brothers at War*, 173–175; Blair, 766–770.

April

1. Mossman, *Ebb and Flow*, 356–361; Command Report, Headquarters, 7th Cavalry Regiment, April 10–11, 1951.

2. Boris R. Spiroff, *Korea: Frozen Hell on Earth* (New York: Vantage Press, 1995), 46.

3. Matthew B. Ridgway, *The Korean War* (Garden City, NY: Doubleday, 1967), 117.

4. *Daily Worker*, April 11, 1951.

5. Ying, *Black Country*, 156, 201–206.

6. Jager, *Brothers at War*, 175–176; Cumings, *The Korean War*, 156–157.

7. Mossman, 353–367; Blair, *The Forgotten War*, 894–896.

8. Futrell, *The United States Air Force in Korea*, 143–144.

9. Blair, 821–822; Jager, 183–189.

10. CIA, Daily Digest, April 23, 1951, DVD *Baptism by Fire*, Truman Library.

11. Li, *China's Battle*, xviii, 73–91, 100; Li, Millett, and Yu, *Mao's Generals Remember Korea*, 22.

12. Li, 103, 108–109, 119.

13. Li, 73–74.

14. Li, 115.

15. Smith, *U.S. Marines in the Korean War*, 384–393.

16. 1st Battalion, 5th Marines, War Diary, April 23, 1951.

17. Mossman, 390.

18. Li, Millett, and Yu, 122.

19. Li, 146.

20. Li, 124.

21. Li, 117.

22. Li, 121.

23. Li, 134; Farrar-Hockley, "A Reminiscence," 300.

24. Mossman, 421–429.

25. Li, 133.

26. Li, Millett, and Yu, 122–129.

27. Li, 101, 118.

28. Mossman, 380.

29. KIMH, *The Korean War*, 2:581.

May

1. Charles Armstrong, "The Destruction and Reconstruction of North Korea, 1950–1960," *Asia-Pacific Journal* 8, issue 51, no. 2 (2010).

2. Polish Foreign Ministry Archive, Report from the Embassy of the Polish Republic in Korea, June 30, 1951, and Report from the Embassy of the Polish Republic in Korea for the Period of July through August 1951, September 1, 1951, Wilson Center.

3. Richard M. Bassett, *And the Wind Blew Cold* (Kent, OH: Kent State University Press, 2002), 47.

4. Carlson, *Remembered Prisoners*, 122.

5. Mossman, *Ebb and Flow*, 447–462.

6. Mossman, 460n59.

7. Mossman, 439.

8. Blair, *The Forgotten War*, 867.

9. Mossman, 469, 482.

10. Mossman, 470–479.

11. Li, *China's Battle*, 203.

12. AG 250.1, "Criminal Offenses," Office of the Commanding General, Eighth United States Army, April 7, 1951.

13. Release No. 818, May 12, 1951, in Kim Ki-jin, *The Korean War and Massacres*, 421.

14. Li, 197–198.

June

1. Mossman, *Ebb and Flow*, 495.

2. Smith, *U.S. Marines in the Korean War*, 440.

3. Mossman, 484–486.

4. AG250.1, "Criminal Offenses," Office of the Commanding General, Eighth U.S. Army Korea, June 24, 1951.

5. *New York Times*, June 24, 1951.

6. Paul M. Edwards, *Korean War Almanac* (New York: Facts on File, 2006), 212.

7. CIA, Current Intelligence Bulletin, April 26, 1951, DVD *Baptism by Fire*, Truman Library.

8. Hanley, Choe, and Mendoza, *The Bridge at No Gun Ri*, 161.

9. *New York Times*, June 30, 1951; Shinn, *Forgotten War Remembered*, 185.

10. Blair, *The Forgotten War*, 924–925.

11. *New York Times*, June 30, 1951; Shinn, 185.

12. AP, June 30, 1951.

13. *New York Times*, July 1, 1951.

14. AP, October 21, 1951; AP, May 14, 1951; Robert C. Alberts, "Profile of a Soldier: Matthew B. Ridgway," *American Heritage* (February 1976).

15. Blair, 924–925.

July

1. *New York Times*, July 2, 1951.

2. *New York Times*, July 2, 1951.

3. Allan R. Millett, *Their War for Korea: American, Asian, and European Combatants and Civilians, 1945–1953* (Washington, DC: Brassey's, 2002), 109.

4. Li, *China's Battle*, 214.

5. AP, June 30 and July 3, 1951.

6. Mossman, *Ebb and Flow*, 502.

7. CIA, Special Estimate, "Possible Communist Objectives in Proposing a Cease Fire in Korea," July 6, 1951, DVD *Baptism by Fire*, Truman Library.

8. Conway-Lanz, *Collateral Damage*, 150–151.

9. *New York Times*, July 21, 1951.

10. Conway-Lanz, 168–170.

11. *New York Times*, December 13, 1950, and August 9, 1951.

12. Conway-Lanz, 169.

13. William H. Vatcher Jr., *Panmunjom: The Story of the Korean Military Armistice Negotiations* (New York: Frederick A. Praeger, 1958), 35–43.

14. *Daily Worker*, July 28, 1951.

15. Mossman, 504–505.

16. *Daily Worker*, July 28, 1951.

17. Hermes, *Truce Tent*, 17, 22–23.

18. Vatcher, 35–43.

19. Reuters, July 26, 1951.

20. Carlson, *Remembered Prisoners*, 142.

21. Carlson, 44.

22. Bassett, *And the Wind Blew Cold*, 70.

23. Futrell, *The United States Air Force in Korea*, 433; Polish Foreign Ministry Archive, Report from the Embassy of the Polish Republic in Korea for the Period of July through August 1951, September 1, 1951, Wilson Center.

August

1. AP, August 1, 1951.

2. Chen, *China's Road*, 193–194.

3. Denis Twitchett and John K. Fairbank, *The Cambridge History of China* (Cambridge: Cambridge University Press, 1987), vol. 14, pt. 1, 87; Maoist Documentation Project, www.marxists.org/reference/archive/mao/selected-works /volume-5/mswv5_14.htm.

4. *New York Times*, August 13, 18, 20, 1951; Polish Foreign Ministry Archive, Report from the Embassy of the Polish Republic in Korea for the Period of July through August 1951, September 1, 1951, Wilson Center.

5. *New York Times*, August 12, 1951.

6. *Daily Worker*, August 24–25, 1951.

7. AP, August 20, 1951.

8. AP, August 20, 1951.

9. *Daily Worker*, August 24, 1951.

10. Vatcher, *Panmunjom*, 64–65.

11. *Daily Worker*, August 27, 1951.

12. Vatcher, 64; AP, August 24, 1951.

September

1. Ridgway, *Korean War*, 186.

2. John C. Fredriksen, *The United States Air Force: A Chronology* (Santa Barbara, CA: ABC-CLIO, 2011), 189.

3. Mossman, *Ebb and Flow*, 502.

4. Alan Winnington and Wilfred Burchett, *Plain Perfidy* (London: Britain-China Friendship Association, 1954), 88.

5. Winnington and Burchett, 88.

6. Winnington and Burchett, 88.

7. Hermes, *Truce Tent*, 220.

8. Hermes, 83–97; Stokesbury, *A Short History*, 160–164; Sandler, *The Korean War: An Encyclopedia*, 127–128.

9. *New York Times*, September 27, 1951.

10. Futrell, *The United States Air Force in Korea*, 404–406.

October

1. *New York Times*, October 26, 1951.

2. *Daily Worker*, October 30, 1951.

3. Vatcher, *Panmunjom*, 75.

4. AP, October 25, 1951.

5. AP, October 25, 1951.

6. Hugh Deane, *The Korean War: 1945–1953* (San Francisco: China Books & Periodicals, 1999), 27–28.

7. Li, *China's Battle*, 216–219.

8. Scott R. McMichael, "A Historical Perspective on Light Infantry," Research Survey No. 6, 1987, Combat Studies Institute, U.S. Army Command, Fort Leavenworth, KS, 78.

9. Li, 216–217.

10. Li, Millett, and Yu, *Mao's Generals Remember Korea*, 152–155; Hermes, *Truce Tent*, 180–181; McMichael, 71.

11. Jager, *Brothers at War*, 241.

12. Li, 222.

November

1. Hermes, *Truce Tent*, 76.

2. Brian Catchpole, *The Korean War, 1950–53* (New York: Carroll & Graf, 2001), 146; History of the 7th Infantry Division, https://7ida.us/documents/History_of_the_7th_Infantry_Division.pdf.

3. Vatcher, *Panmunjom*, 239.

4. Futrell, *The United States Air Force in Korea*, 401–405.

5. Stanley Sandler, *The Korean War: No Victors, No Vanquished* (London: UCL Press, 1999), 182; Futrell, 410.

6. Kathryn Weathersby, "'Should We Fear This?': Stalin and the Danger of War with America," Working Paper No. 39, Wilson Center, July 2002; James I. Matray, "Revisiting Korea: Exposing Myths of the Forgotten War," *Prologue* (National Archives and Records Administration) 34, no. 2 (2002).

December

1. Hermes, *Truce Tent*, 182–183.

2. AP, November 26 and 30, 1951.

3. Hermes, 182–183.

4. Hermes, 181, 199.

5. AP, December 24, 1951; *New York Times*, December 24, 1951.

6. Edwards, *Almanac*, 265.

7. *New York Times*, December 24, 1951.

PART 3
1952

Winter

1. *New York Times*, December 18, 1951.

2. AP, December 11, 1951.

3. Carlson, *Remembered Prisoners*, 126; Bassett, *And the Wind Blew Cold*, 48–49.

4. William Stueck, *The Korean War: An International History* (Princeton, NJ: Princeton University Press, 1995), 59.

5. Hermes, *Truce Tent*, 144.

6. Hermes, 183; AP, January 19 and 25, 1952.

7. AP, January 25, 1952.

8. Hermes, 183n31.

9. United Press, January 20, 1952.

10. AP, January 25, 1952.

11. United Press, January 20, 1952.

12. "Sister Alberta Marie Hanley," Biographies, Maryknoll Mission Archives.

13. *New York Times*, January 20, 1952.

14. Stokesbury, *A Short History*, 181.

15. AP, February 2, 1952.

16. Associated Press, *Breaking News: How the Associated Press Has Covered War, Peace, and Everything Else* (New York: Princeton Architectural Press, 2007), 323–325; Dvorchak, *Battle for Korea*, 127.

17. *Daily Worker*, February 9, 1952.

18. Hermes, *Truce Tent*, 187.

19. Hermes, 184.

20. Jonathan D. Spence, *The Search for Modern China* (New York: W. W. Norton, 1991), 536–540.

21. Barbara Barnouin and Changgeng Yu, *Zhou Enlai: A Political Life* (Hong Kong: Chinese University Press, 2006), 148–149.

22. Li, *China's Battle*, 175, 203.

23. Zhang Shu-guang, *Mao's Military Romanticism: China and the Korean War, 1950–1953* (Lawrence: University Press of Kansas, 1995), 213.

24. Barnouin and Yu, 148–149.

25. Hermes, 285.

26. AP, February 14, 1952.

27. Gordon L. Rottman, *Korean War Order of Battle: United States, United Nations, and Communist Ground, Naval, and Air Forces, 1950–1953* (Westport, CT: Praeger, 2002), 170.

28. Hermes, 163.

29. *New York Times*, March 18, 1952.

30. Blair, *The Forgotten War*, 968; *New York Times*, March 30, 1952.

Spring

1. Paik, *From Pusan to Panmunjom*, 194–200.

2. Hastings, *The Korean War*, 349.

3. Vatcher, *Panmunjom*, 111–113.

4. AP, April 12, 1952.

5. Conway-Lanz, *Collateral Damage*, 170.

6. Russian Archives, Telegram from Mao Zedong to Stalin, conveying 22 January 1952 telegram from Peng Dehuai to Mao and 4 February 1952 reply from Mao to Peng Dehuai, February 8, 1952, Wilson Center; Telegram from Babkin to Shtemenko, conveying letter from Kim Il Sung to Stalin, April 16, 1952, Wilson Center.

7. AP, May 9, 1952.

8. Hermes, *Truce Tent*, 243–249; AP, May 9, 1952.

9. Peters and Li, *Voices from the Korean War*, 252–258.

10. Hermes, 250–253.

11. AP, May 11 and 9, 1952.

12. AP, May 15, 1952.

13. United Press, May 15, 1952.

14. Hanley, Choe, and Mendoza, *The Bridge at No Gun Ri*, 180.

15. Zhang Xiaoming, *Red Wings over the Yalu: China, the Soviet Union, and the Air War in Korea* (College Station: Texas A&M University Press, 2003), 132.

16. *New York Times*, May 29, 1952.

17. AP, May 25 and June 4, 1952.

18. AP, June 6, 8, 9, 12, 14, and 28, 1952.

19. E. Allan Lightner Jr., Oral History Interview, October 26, 1973, Truman Library; John J. Muccio, Oral History Interview, February 10, 1971, Truman Library.

20. AP, July 4, 1952.

21. Hermes, 73–75.

22. Hermes, 283–284.

23. Hermes, 285–287.

24. Website "koreanwaronline," "Korean War Weapons and History," www.koreanwaronline.com/history/TruceTent/Frames/295.htm.

25. Hermes, 141.

26. Hermes, 257–260, 269.

Summer

1. Li, Millett, and Yu, *Mao's Generals Remember Korea*, 223; Vatcher, *Panmunjom*, 151.

2. Futrell, *The United States Air Force in Korea*, 515–517.

3. Futrell, 517.

4. *Daily Worker*, July 21, 1952.

5. Futrell, 517.

6. *Daily Worker*, July 21, 1952.

7. Futrell, 515, 517.

8. *Daily Worker*, July 21, 1952.

9. Futrell, 516.

10. *Daily Worker*, July 26, 1952.

11. Russian Archives, Ciphered Telegram, Kim Il Sung to Stalin via Razuvaev, July 16, 1952, Wilson Center.

12. *Daily Worker*, July 21, 1952.

13. Russian Archives, Record of a Conversation Between Stalin, Kim Il Sung, Pak Hon-yong, Zhou Enlai, and Peng Dehuai, September 4, 1952, Wilson Center.

14. Weathersby, "'Should We Fear This?'"

15. Jager, *Brothers at War*, 193.

16. Vojtech Mastny, *The Cold War and Soviet Insecurity: The Stalin Years* (Oxford: Oxford University Press, 2010), 147–148.

17. Russian Archives, Record of a Conversation, September 4, 1952.

18. Robert Gellately, *Stalin's Curse: Battling for Communism in War and Cold War* (New York: Alfred A. Knopf, 2013), 341.

19. Russian Archives, Record of a Conversation, September 4, 1952.

Fall

1. *New York Times*, October 3, 1952.

2. Vatcher, *Panmunjom*, 164–167.

3. *New York Times*, October 8, 1952.

4. AP, October 8, 1952.

5. *Daily Worker*, October 9, 1952.

6. *New York Times*, October 8, 1952.

7. *New York Times*, December 16, 1952.

8. Hermes, *Truce Tent*, 303–306; AP, October 8, 1952.

9. Vatcher, 174–175; Li, Millett, and Yu, *Mao's Generals Remember Korea*, 265.

10. Hermes, *Truce Tent*, 310–318; Li, *China's Battle*, 219–221.

11. *New York Times*, November 17, 1952.

12. Li, 219–221; Hermes, 317.

13. FBIS, Far East Survey, November 20, 1952, DVD *Baptism by Fire*, Truman Library.

14. Hermes, 367.

15. Sandler, *The Korean War: An Encyclopedia*, 296.

16. *New York Times*, November 23, 1952.

17. AP, December 30 and 25, 1952.

18. AP, December 19, 1952.

19. Research Institute of History, Academy of Sciences of the DPRK, *Just Fatherland Liberation War*, 182–183.

PART 4
1953

Winter

1. *New York Times*, January 28, 1953.

2. Hermes, *Truce Tent*, 366–367.

3. *New York Times*, January 28, 1953.

4. *New York Times*, January 31, 1953.

5. AP, February 2, 1953.

6. Virginia Pasley, *22 Stayed: The Story of 21 American GIs and One Briton Who Chose Communist China—Who They Were and the Reason for Their Choice* (London: W. H. Allen, 1955), 54.

7. Bassett, *And the Wind Blew Cold*, 67–69.

8. Hermes, 411.

9. *New York Times*, February 3, 1953.

10. Vatcher, *Panmunjom*, 179.

11. Polish Foreign Ministry Archive, Note from Polish Embassy, Pyongyang, February 11, 1953, Wilson Center; FBIS, Far East Survey, February 12, 1953, DVD *Baptism by Fire*, Truman Library.

12. Nikita Sergeevich Khrushchev, *Khrushchev Remembers* (Boston: Little, Brown, 1970), 340–345.

13. Russian Archives, Resolution, USSR Council of Ministers, with draft letters, March 19, 1953, Wilson Center.

14. Vatcher, 180–182; Li, Millett, and Yu, *Mao's Generals Remember Korea*, 265.

Spring

1. AP, December 1, 1952; Conway-Lanz, *Collateral Damage*, 150–151.

2. KIMH, *The Korean War*, 3:404–405.

3. *Daily Worker*, April 17, 18, 20, and 21, 1953; AP, April 18, 1953.

4. Tom Buchanan, *East Wind: China and the British Left, 1925–1976* (Oxford: Oxford University Press, 2012), 132–133.

5. S. P. Mackenzie, *British Prisoners of the Korean War* (Oxford: Oxford University Press, 2012), 52–53.

6. Appleman, *South to the Naktong*, 587.

7. *Daily Worker*, February 23, 1953.

8. Ying, *Black Country*, 156, 201–206.

9. Vatcher, *Panmunjom*, 265–266.

10. Edwards, *Almanac*, 392.

11. AP, May 18, 1953.

12. Crane, *American Airpower*, 158–163; Futrell, *The United States Air Force in Korea*, 666–669; Hermes, *Truce Tent*, 461; Armstrong, "Destruction and Reconstruction of North Korea."

13. AP, May 27, 1953.

14. Hermes, 431.

15. Hermes, 465–468; KIMH, 3:616–629.

16. Paik, *From Pusan to Panmunjom*, 212.

17. Hermes, 465–468; KIMH, 3:616–629.

18. *New York Times*, June 10, 1953.

19. *New York Times*, June 9, 1953.

20. *New York Times*, June 12, 1953.

21. AP, June 14, 1953.

22. *New York Times*, June 9, 1953.

23. *New York Times*, June 12, 1953.

24. *New York Times*, June 14, 1953.

25. *New York Times*, June 14, 1953.

26. *New York Times*, June 14, 1953.

27. AP, June 19, 1953.

28. Hermes, 451–453.

29. Memorandum, "Discussion at the 150th Meeting of the National Security Council," Thursday, June 18, 1953, Truman Library.

30. AP, July 5, 1953.

31. Vatcher, 197–198; Hermes, 457.

Summer

1. Hermes, *Truce Tent*, 473–474; Hastings, *The Korean War*, 370–371; AP, July 12, 1953.

2. Bruce Gardner and Barbara Stahura, 7th Infantry Division Association, *Seventh Infantry Division: World War I, World War II, Korea and Panamanian Invasion, 1917–1992, Serving America for 75 Years* (Paducah, KY: Turner, 1997), 77.

3. Li, Millett, and Yu, *Mao's Generals Remember Korea*, 229–230.

4. Hermes, 474–475; KIMH, *The Korean War*, 3:641–660.

5. Hermes, 474–475; KIMH, 3:641–660.

6. KIMH, 3:661.

7. Hermes, 475; KIMH, 3:679–680.

8. AP, July 20, 1953.

9. Li, *China's Battle*, 227–230; Crane, *American Airpower*, 167; Futrell, *The United States Air Force in Korea*, 691–692; Leonid Krylov and Yuriy Tepsurkaev, *Soviet MiG-15 Aces of the Korean War* (New York: Osprey, 2008), 86.

10. AP, July 27, 1953.

11. AP, July 27, 1953.

12. *New York Times*, July 28, 1953.

13. Vatcher, *Panmunjom*, 303.

14. AP, July 27, 1953.

15. AP, July 27, 1953.

16. *New York Times*, March 22, 1953.

17. *New York Times*, July 28, 1953.

18. *Daily Worker*, July 27, 29, 1953.

19. *Daily Worker, I Saw the Truth in Korea* (pamphlet), September 1950.

20. *New York Times*, July 15, 1953.

21. Crane, 168; Armstrong, "Destruction and Reconstruction of North Korea."

22. *New York Times Magazine*, July 26, 1953.

23. David Clay Large, *Germans to the Front: West German Rearmament in the Adenauer Era* (Chapel Hill: University of North Carolina Press, 1996), 114–117.

24. *New York Times*, February 24, 1952.

25. Large, 117.

26. CBS News, "More Korean War Massacres?," October 8, 1999, www .cbsnews.com/news/more-korean-war-massacres/; Marilyn B. Young, "Remembering to Forget," in *Truth Claims: Representation and Human Rights*, ed. Mark Philip Bradley and Patrice Petro (New Brunswick, NJ: Rutgers University Press, 2002), 17.

27. Large, 117.

28. AP, July 29, 1953; Winnington and Burchett, *Plain Perfidy*, 68–69.

29. Sandler, *The Korean War: An Encyclopedia*, 85.

CHARACTER
PHOTO CREDITS

Chang Sang—Courtesy of Rev. Dr. Sang Chang.
Ri In-mo—Foreign Languages Publishing House, Pyongyang.
Park Sun-yong—Courtesy of Dr. Chung Koo-do.
Yu Song-chol—Copyright, *Hanguk Ilbo*.
Matthew B. Ridgway—U.S. Army.
No Kum-sok—U.S. Air Force.
Clarence C. Adams—Courtesy of Della Adams.
Sister Mary Mercy—Maryknoll Mission Archives.
Chung Dong-kyu—Courtesy of Father and Son Publishing.
Leonard (Buddy) Wenzel—Charles J. Hanley.
Bill Shinn—Used by permission of Hollym International Corporation.
   All rights reserved. Copyright 2019.
Alan Winnington—Courtesy of Esther Samson.
Hurh Won-moo—Courtesy of Mrs. Gloria Hurh.
Ahn Kyong-hee—Dae-Dong Moon Hwa Sa, Seoul.
Chi Chao-chu—White House photo.
Paul N. (Pete) McCloskey—Courtesy of Pete McCloskey.
Gil Isham—Courtesy of Mrs. Ardith Isham.
Peng Teh-huai—Foreign Languages Press, Beijing.
Chen Hsing-chiu—Military Science Press, Beijing.

INDEX

Charles J. Hanley reported from some one hundred countries in his four-decade career at the Associated Press, including coverage of a half-dozen wars. Reporting on the U.S. military's massacre of South Korean refugees at Nogun-ri won him and his colleagues a Pulitzer Prize and Polk Award, among other honors, and yielded the 2001 book *The Bridge at No Gun Ri*. He regularly lectures on the Korean War and investigative journalism and contributes scholarship on the conflict to academic journals. He lives in New York City.